MAX WEBER

REINHARD BENDIX is professor of political science at the University of California in Berkeley, where he has been teaching since 1947. Born in Berlin in 1916, Bendix fled the Hitler regime when he was twenty-two, and came to the United States, where he entered the University of Chicago. There he studied sociology and obtained a B.A. in 1941, an M.A. in 1943, and his Ph.D. four years later. In 1970 he was president of the American Sociological Association.

Among his numerous books are *Work and Authority* (1956; reissued by the University of California Press in 1974), for which he received the American Sociological Association's McIver Award in 1958; *Nation-Building and Citizenship* (1964); *Embattled Reason* (1970), and *Kings or People* (1980, published by the University of California Press).

This was the man, who always does return
as time draws to a close once more
and consummates its value.
Then one man lifts the burden of his age
and hurls it down the chasm of his heart.

All those before him had but joy and grief;
yet he can only feel the weight of life
and that his mind grasp things as all in one,—
still there is God above beyond his will:
and he does love Him with high enmity
for that transcendence.
      Rainer Maria Rilke, *Das Stundenbuch*
      Part I, "Das waren Tage Michelangelos . . ."

Selections from *From Max Weber*, translated and edited by H. H. Gerth and C. Wright Mills. A Galaxy Book. Copyright 1946 by Oxford University Press, Inc. Reprinted by permission.

Selections from *The Theory of Social and Economic Organization*, by Max Weber, translated by A. M. Henderson and Talcott Parsons. Copyright 1947 by Oxford University Press, Inc. Reprinted by permission.

Selections from *Max Weber on Law in Economy and Society*, edited by Max Rheinstein. Translated by Max Rheinstein and Edward Shils. Copyright 1954 by The President and Fellows of Harvard College. Reprinted by permission of the publishers.

Selections from *The Protestant Ethic and the Spirit of Capitalism*, by Max Weber, copyright 1958 by Charles Scribner's Sons, are reprinted by permission of the publisher.

Selections from the following books are reprinted by permission of the publisher, The Free Press of Glencoe, Illinois: *Ancient Judaism* (1952); *The City* (1958); *General Economic History* (1950); *Max Weber on the Methodology of the Social Sciences* (1949); *The Religion of China: Confucianism and Taoism* (1951); *The Religion of India: The Sociology of Hinduism and Buddhism* (1958).

Two stanzas from *Stundenbuch*, by Rainer Maria Rilke. Translated into English by Reinhard Bendix. By permission of Insel-Verlag, Wiesbaden, Germany.

Max Weber was originally published by
Doubleday & Company, Inc. in 1960.
Anchor Books edition: 1962

University of California Press
Berkeley and Los Angeles, California
University of California Press, Ltd.
London, England

California Paperback Edition, 1977
ISBN: 0-520-03194-6

6 7 8 9 0

The paper used in this publication meets the minimum requirements of American National Standard for Information Sciences—Permanence of Paper for Printed Library Materials, ANSI Z39.48–1984. ⊗

MAX WEBER
An Intellectual Portrait

REINHARD BENDIX

*With an Introduction to
the new edition by
Guenther Roth*

University of California Press
Berkeley, Los Angeles, London

To my wife

CONTENTS

INTRODUCTION
TO THE NEW EDITION

by Guenther Roth

Much scholarship and partisanship continue to revolve around the works and impact of Max Weber and Karl Marx. Though there is a steady stream of studies on other individual writers and on various isms in the history of modern social thought, nothing compares to the sheer magnitude of the concern with Marx and Weber. This is not at all surprising in Marx's case, since political ideologies linked with his name legitimate the governments of a large part of the globe, and since in many other countries variants of Marxism are kept alive by radicalism—by the ineradicable revolutionary sentiments of alienated intellectuals—in the face of persistent inequalities and inequities. Weber, however, never created an ism in politics or scholarship, not even the political decisionism or the methodological individualism that have sometimes been attributed to him.

What, then, maintains so much interest in Weber's work? Primarily its intrinsic scholarly superiority, as a comparative approach to macrosociological investigation, over reductionist Marxism and ahistorical structural functionalism. However, there are also political and epistemological reasons for Weber's continued importance. As a researcher probing into the relations between ideologies and social structures, and as a methodologist concerned with the relations of values and facts, Weber must remain controversial in the battles, inside and outside the academy, about the purpose and consequences of social knowledge for polity and society—empirical study is never an innocent or neutral undertaking. Moreover, in the face of his own denials that he was concerned with philosophy, Weber took a distinctive

A portion of this introduction is based on a survey review published in *Contemporary Sociology* 4, no. 4 (July 1975), pp. 366–73, and used with the permission of the American Sociological Association.

personal stance that made Karl Jaspers choose him as the heroic figure of his existentialist philosophy. This stance of stoic existentialism may survive the results of his scholarship, just as the Promethean and messianic spirit of Marx has survived his scientific accomplishments. The hoped-for progress of scholarship cannot resolve the need for making existential choices for which Marx and Weber remain exemplary.

Reinhard Bendix's intellectual portrait of Max Weber appeared in 1960, before the politicization of the American academic scene. At the time the execution of its purpose, to provide a dispassionate exposition of the broad range of Weber's empirical work, was widely acclaimed in the United States and abroad. As the German sociologist Friedrich Tenbruck recently put it in a spirited critique of the Weber reception (which has been no less fragmented in Germany than in the United States, albeit for other reasons): "For decades we were faced with attempts at grasping this or that aspect of Weber's writings. His work as a whole became visible for the first time when Reinhard Bendix presented us with his intellectual portrait, in which he sketched the main ideas that permeate Weber's work."[1] In a recent book a young German sociologist distinguished his own purposes from Bendix's by noting: "Bendix's book is quite different from my own, although it deals in its own way with something equally important. His work is concerned not with a systematic clarification of Weber's conception of.sociology [as is mine] but with making more accessible the tremendous wealth and density of Weber's theoretical and historical analyses. Undoubtedly Bendix succeeded in an outstanding fashion in this very difficult enterprise."[2]

[1] Friedrich H. Tenbruck, "Das Werk Max Webers," *Kölner Zeitschrift für Soziologie*, Vol. XXVII (1975), pp. 663–702. For overviews and expositions of Weber's work as a whole since 1960, see Raymond Aron, *Main Currents in Sociological Thought* (New York: Doubleday, 1967; French edition also 1967), Lewis A. Coser, *Masters of Sociological Thought* (New York: Harcourt, Brace, Jovanovich, 1971); Julian Freund, *The Sociology of Max Weber* (New York: Vintage Books, 1969; first published in French in 1966).

There are two readers on Weber: Dennis Wrong, ed., *Max Weber* (Englewood Cliffs: Prentice-Hall, 1970); Dirk Käsler, *Max Weber* (Munich: Nymphenburger Verlagshandlung, 1972).

[2] Johannes Weiss, *Max Webers Grundlegung der Soziologie* (Munich: Verlag Dokumentation, 1975), p. 12.

As these two comments indicate, more than a decade and a half after its publication Bendix's study continues to be appreciated for the purpose that underlay its conception—to provide a comprehensive exposition of Weber's empirical studies. Deliberately, he neglected Weber's critical methodological essays and their context in the methodological controversies of his day (*Methodenstreit* and *Werturteilsstreit*) as well as the dimensions of political and intellectual history.[3]

By the late 1950s a situation had arisen that made a broad overview of Weber's empirical writings most desirable. In fact, Bendix's study became part of what I perceive as the second stage of Weber reception in the United States. During the first stage *The Protestant Ethic and the Spirit of Capitalism* (1904–5), in Talcott Parsons' translation of 1930, had become a widely assigned reading on American campuses, but without reference to Weber's comparative studies of the world religions. With the growing interest in large-scale organization and stratification in the wake of the Second World War, Weber's notions of bureaucracy and of class and status were widely diffused, but without their systematic location in his typologies. Bendix himself contributed to this first stage with his study of *The Higher Civil Servants in American Society* (1949), several articles on bureaucracy and stratification, and the first comprehensive and historically oriented reader in stratification, *Class, Status and Power* (1953).[4] Gerth and Mills' 1946 selections from Weber, contrasting bureaucracy and charisma, became very influential in shaping an image of Weber's work, and Parsons' translation of the difficult-to-read categories of Part I of *Economy and Society* (published in 1947 under the misleading title *The Theory of Social and Economic Organization*) made

[3] On the *Methodenstreit* (between Gustav Schmoller and Karl Menger), see Werner Cahnmann, "Max Weber and the Methodological Controversy in the Social Sciences, in Cahnmann and A. Boskoff, eds., *Sociology and History* (New York: Free Press, 1964), pp. 103–27. On the *Werturteilsstreit*, see Christian von Ferber, "Der Werturteilsstreit 1909/1959," *Kölner Zeitschrift für Soziologie*, Vol. XI (1959), pp. 21–37; for a comprehensive account of the methodological and political conflicts in which Weber was involved, see Dieter Lindenlaub, *Richtungskämpfe im Verein für Sozialpolitik*, 2 vols. (Wiesbaden: Steiner, 1967).

[4] Bendix, *Higher Civil Servants in American Society* (Boulder: University of Colorado Press, 1949). Bendix and S. M. Lipset, eds., *Class, Status, and Power* (Glencoe: Free Press, 1953; second revised edition, 1966).

available that segment in splendid isolation from the main body. Moreover, Parsons' "creative misinterpretation" of Weber in *The Structure of Social Action* (1937) and subsequent writings—implying that Weber was one of his intellectual forebears and a systems theorist manqué—received much attention after 1950 with the ascendancy of Parsons' structural functionalism.[5]

Bendix resolved to counter this Parsonian interpretation by putting before the reader the historical substance of Weber's comparative sociology of politics, law, and religion on the level of its own intentions. Parsons had at first treated Weber as one among several predecessors of his own theory of voluntarist social action; later, with regard to social systems analysis, Parsons believed that he had achieved a more definite departure from Weber. Now he could offer a framework for studying the relations of social actors irrespective of time and place. From his systems perspective Weber's definitions of various kinds of social action and his historical typologies appeared atomistic. Yet Weber too presented, in the first chapter of *Economy and Society*, a general, "ahistorical" sociology of the social group, which moved logically from individual social action through various forms of social relationships to the concerted actions in the organization (*Verband*) with its legitimate domination. For Weber these definitions provided the basis for an historical typology within which the dis-

[5] See H. H. Gerth and C. Wright Mills, eds., *From Max Weber* (New York: Oxford University Press, 1946); Talcott Parsons, ed. and trans. (with A. M. Henderson), *Max Weber: The Theory of Social and Economic Organization* (New York: Oxford University Press, 1947). Parsons, *The Structure of Social Action* (New York: McGraw-Hill, 1937). On Parsons' Weber interpretation, see also Jere Cohen, Lawrence Hazelrigg, and Whitney Pope, "De-Parsonizing Weber: A Critique of Parsons' Interpretation of Weber's Sociology," *American Sociological Review* 40, no. 2 (1975), pp. 229–41, and the subsequent exchange, 40, no. 5 (1975), pp. 666–74. On the first stage of the Weber reception, see Roth and Bendix, "Max Webers Einfluss auf die amerikanische Soziologie," *Kölner Zeitschrift für Soziologie*, Vol. XI (1959), pp. 38–53. On the notion of "creative misinterpretation," see my essay on "Value-Neutrality in Germany and the United States," in Bendix and Roth, *Scholarship and Partisanship* (Berkeley: University of California Press, 1971), p. 35, and on its effect in the context of the gradual Weber reception, see H. Stuart Hughes, *The Sea Change: The Migration of Social Thought, 1930–1965* (New York: Harper & Row, 1975), pp. 31 ff.

tinctive and historically unique course of western rationalism could be studied. By contrast, Parsons came to relate his systems approach to a neo-evolutionism that perceived the "progress" from tradition to modernity as a process of almost unilinear structural differentiation and value transformation—in sharp distinction from Weber's acute sense for the ambiguities and paradoxes of western rationalism.

Both Bendix and Parsons shared prominently in the second stage of the Weber reception, which was reached reciprocally with the revival of comparative studies in the fifties. Whereas many development studies followed a "Weberian-Parsonian" approach emphasizing the predominance of values in social systems old and new, Bendix's intellectual portrait showed the reader the intricate ways in which Weber related ideas and material and ideal interests. Moreover, Bendix facilitated the study of development issues by clearly relating *The Protestant Ethic* to Weber's studies on the world religions, and by embedding bureaucracy and charisma in their proper typological matrix within the Sociology of Domination in *Economy and Society*. Again, Bendix contributed his share to the revival of the great tradition of comparative studies through his own investigations, *Work and Authority* (1956), the first comparative study of ideologies of management in the course of industrialization, and *Nation-Building and Citizenship* (1964), its theme encompassing western and eastern Europe as well as Japan and India. Apart from methodological and substantive essays, he also edited, with a group of students, the first reader in comparative political sociology, *State and Society* (1968), which was based on a Weberian conception of historical sociology in contrast to the functionalist approach with its evolutionary overtones.[6]

The third stage of dealing with Weber began with the centen-

[6] Bendix, *Work and Authority* (New York: Wiley, 1956; reprinted by University of California Press, 1974); *Nation-Building and Citizenship* (New York: Wiley, 1964; reprinted by University of California Press, 1977); Bendix et al., eds., *State and Society* (Boston: Little, Brown, 1968; reprinted by University of California Press, 1973). For the contrast between Weberian historical sociology and structural functionalism see Randall Collins, "A Comparative Approach to Political Sociology," *State and Society*, pp. 42–69.

ary commemoration of his birth at the Heidelberg meetings of the German Sociological Association in 1964.[7] The event turned out to be the beginning of the great onslaught on Weber as arch representative of liberal or bourgeois social science, an onslaught carried forth by a new political generation without any memories of the Second World War and hence without any personal yardsticks for comparing the present with the past. At Heidelberg in 1964 Bendix raised his voice against Herbert Marcuse's opening salvo aimed at Weber. In 1970 he presented the quintessence of his own position in his presidential address before the annual meetings of the American Sociological Association, when the rebellion inside and outside the university community crested. Bendix published two volumes of essays that endeavored to combine critical observation with dispassionate scholarly inquiry, *Embattled Reason* (1970) and *Scholarship and Partisanship* (1971)[8]—both indicative of his continued involvement in the third stage of the Weber controversy.

It is important to understand that the three stages are not exclusive sequences: *The Protestant Ethic* is still frequently interpreted in isolation; the selections from the very popular Gerth and Mills edition continue to be widely used as the major reading assignment on Weber; the definitions from Part I of *Economy and Society* are ritually quoted out of theoretical and historical context even today. However, the comparative approach is now well established, although funding for foreign area studies has declined severely. Bendix himself was not deterred by the politicization of American social science from concentrating on the writing of a large-scale comparative study of the formation and transforma-

[7] Otto Stammer, ed., *Max Weber and Sociology Today*, Transactions of the Fifteenth German Sociological Congress (New York : Harper & Row, 1971).

[8] See Herbert Marcuse, "Industrialization and Capitalism," in Stammer, *Max Weber*, pp. 133–151; see also Bendix's comment, *ibid.*, pp. 154–161. For Bendix's presidential address, see "Sociology and the Distrust of Reason," *American Sociological Reivew* 35, no. 5 (October 1970), pp. 831–43, reprinted in Bendix and Roth, *Scholarship and Partisanship: Essays on Max Weber* (Berkeley: University of California Press, 1971), pp. 84–105; see also Bendix, *Embattled Reason: Essays on Social Knowledge* (New York: Oxford University Press, 1970).

tion of political authority in Japan, Russia, Germany, England and France.[9] Finally, political critiques of Weber's work from the Right and Left date back to the 1930s, quite apart from the heated scholarly controversies about *The Protestant Ethic* and issues of *Wertfreiheit* in which Weber was embroiled for many years.[10]

What has been the progress of Weber scholarship since 1960? Bendix's intellectual portrait of Weber was written in a situation in which "as a comprehensive whole his work remains relatively unknown" (see p. xlv below). Therefore much of this book is a careful exposition of Weber's comparative studies, especially in *Economy and Society*. It was not until 1968 that the complete text of Weber's magnum opus was available in English, and then only in an expensive hardcover edition that effectively reduced student access and precluded classroom use.[11] (Eight years later about half of all scholarly citations refer to the various fragmentary selections rather than to the complete edition.) My introduction to *Economy and Society* was written with a view toward supplementing Bendix's book by giving particular attention to those studies omitted there, especially the early inquiries into ancient and medieval capitalism, and by reconstructing chronologically the long gestation of Weber's conceptualization of *Economy and*

[9] Bendix, *Kings or People; Power and the Mandate to Rule* (Berkeley: University of California Press, 1978).

[10] Cf. Chapter III, "Political Critiques," and Chapter II, "Value-Neutrality in Germany and the United States," in Bendix, *Scholarship and Partisanship*.

[11] G. Roth and Claus Wittich, eds., *Max Weber, Economy and Society*, 3 vols. (New York: Bedminster Press, 1968). This edition is based on the fourth German edition edited by Johannes Winckelmann. *Wirtschaft und Gesellschaft* (Tübingen: J. C. B. Mohr, 1956). The fifth edition, with almost 300 pages of annotations by Winckelmann, was published in 1976. A new critical edition of all of Weber's work, similar to the Marx/Engels edition, is called for. However the situation is complicated by the fact that because of the Nazi regime and the Second World War the greater part of Weber's original manuscripts and much of his voluminous correspondence with many scholars and political men seem to have been lost or widely scattered. The absence of the original manuscripts is particularly irksome because much of Weber's work, especially the bulk of *Economy and Society* was published posthumously in a rather inadequate fashion in spite of Marianne Weber's valiant efforts. A German editorial group is presently planning a complete edition of Weber's works.

Society.[12] Weber's comparative studies on the world religions have been available in English since the 1950s, but they are in need of critical editions both in the original and in translation.[13] Bendix's overview of Weber's sociology of religion in the present volume remains basic reading on the intricate relationship among its various parts.

In spite of the political polemics which have surrounded Weber in the controversies about the nature and course of contemporary social science since the mid-sixties, and partly in response to them, many valuable studies have been done since, and there is no sign of any letup. The literature in which Weber is a major reference has grown so large that the individual reader can no longer keep track of it.[14] Since most of Bendix's references are more than two decades old, it seems appropriate to present an overview of some major publications—some essays, some books—which are supplements or antitheses to his portrait in that they address themselves to epistemological, sociological, political and biographical aspects that transcend the purpose of his book.

There tends to be a broad split in the Weber literature between his historical sociology and his methodological and programmatic writings, even among the political critics. This dichotomy has created two Weber images, but much of the literature is highly specialized within and outside this distinction. Given the broad scope of Weber's work, it is inevitable that many publications stress one aspect to the exclusion of another; given the realities of the scholarly division of labor, of which Weber was extremely conscious, it takes different kinds of expertise to be competent in

[12] See Roth and Wittich, eds. *Economy and Society*, Introduction, pp. xxvii–civ.

[13] The three volumes on the sociology of religion, *Gesammelte Aufsätze zur Religionssoziologie* (Tübingen: J. C. B. Mohr, 1920), have been republished unchanged several times. Only *The Protestant Ethic and the Spirit of Capitalism* has been edited, by Johannes Winckelmann, together with the critiques and anti-critiques. See J. Winckelmann, ed., *Max Weber: Die protestantische Ethik I und II* (Hamburg: Siebenstern Verlag, 1972/3).

[14] Cf. C. Seyfarth and G. Schmidt, *Max Weber—Bibliographie: Eine Dokumentation der Sekundärliteratur* (Stuttgart: Enke, 1977); for the outdated Gerth bibliography, see p. xlviii of Bendix's introduction below. For the latest bibliography of Weber's own writings, see Dirk Käsler, *Kölner Zeitschrift für Soziologie*, Vol. XXVII (1975), pp. 703–30.

one area or another. As a rough classification, I would like to distinguish, and take up in turn, six dimensions in the literature: (1) the comparative studies and historical typologies; (2) basic methodological and epistemological contributions, including the availability of Weber's own writings in English; (3) his place among theorists of "the bureaucratic age"; (4) his general and his academic politics; (5) the Marxist struggle against Weber, but also scholarly comparisons of Weber and Marx; and finally (6) Weber's biography in the context of the intellectual history of his and our time.

1. Compared to 1960, there is today, with the benefit of Bendix's writings and the publication of *Economy and Society*, a much greater awareness of the whole of Weber's sociology of domination, law and religion. In the literature on state- and nation-building and on economic and social development, there has been an increasing realization that the applicability of models of western modernization and bureaucratization is analytically and practically very limited. Here it has been helpful that to the dichotomy or dialectic of bureaucracy and charisma, which is only one part of Weber's vision of rationalization, have been added his notions of patrimonial forms of government. S. N. Eisenstadt, for instance, observed in 1973 that "perhaps one of the most important—albeit somewhat recent—developments in this context was the growth of the 'patrimonialism' concept to describe the political regimes of several new states."[15] In the realm of religion an exemplary Weberian approach, without undue literal depen-

[15] S. N. Eisenstadt and Stein Rokkan, eds., *Building States and Nations: Models, Analyses and Data across Three Worlds* (Beverly Hills: Sage Publications, 1973), Vol. I, p. 4; in Vol. II the notion of patrimonialism is given explicit treatment in the essays by Simon Schwartzmann on regional contrasts in Brazil and by Stuart Gellar on West Africa. For an application of the concept of patrimonialism to Nepal, past and present, see Ernest Gellner, "The Kathmandu Option: Patrimony and Bureaucracy," *Encounter* (October, 1975), pp. 56–68; for a detailed analysis of Weber's views on patrimonialism in the Arab context, see Bryan S. Turner, *Weber and Islam* (London: Routledge and Kegan Paul, 1974); for a reformulation of patrimonial rulership in the context of Weber's typology, see my essay on "Personal Rulership, Patrimonialism and Empire-Building," chapter VIII of Bendix and Roth, *Scholarship and Partisanship*.

dency, was taken in the brilliant study by Clifford Geertz, *Islam
Observed*, comparing Indonesia and Morocco; and notable critiques of some of the difficulties of Weber's sociology of religion
have been presented by Bryan S. Turner, again in the Islamic
context, and by Terry Lovell in his comparison of Weber and
Lucien Goldmann.[16]

However, while Weber's political and religious typological
analyses are now better understood, the practiced methodology
embodied in his comparative studies still requires more attention
than it has received, especially compared to his critical methodological writings. Only a few writers, notably John Rex and Stephen
Warner, have dealt with Weber's actual research strategy, which
involves the elaboration of socio-historical models ("ideal types")
and of historical theories proper.[17] Failure to look closely at
Weber's research strategy has led and misled much of the development literature of the past twenty-five years to search in a
one-sided fashion for functional equivalents to the Protestant
ethic. Yet neither in *The Protestant Ethic and the Spirit of Capitalism* nor in the comparative studies did Weber consider any one
religious factor as crucial or decisive for the rise or absence of

[16] See Clifford Geertz, *Islam Observed* (Chicago: University of Chicago
Press, 1968); T. Lovell, "Weber, Goldmann and the Sociology of Beliefs,"
Archives of European Sociology Vol. XIV (1973), pp. 304–23; Turner,
Weber and Islam. For a follow-up on *The Protestant Ethic*, see Constans
Seyfarth and Walter M. Sprondel, eds., *Seminar: Religion und gesell-
schaftliche Entwicklung: Studien zur Protestantismusthese Max Webers*
(Frankfurt: Suhrkamp, 1973). Insufficient attention is still paid to Weber's
study of ancient Judaism; exceptions are Freddy Raphaël, "Max Weber et
le judaïsme antique," *Archives of European Sociology*, Vol. XI (1970), pp.
297–336, and Peter L. Berger, "Charisma and Religious Innovation: The
Social Location of Israelite Prophecy," *American Sociological Review* 28,
no. 6 (1963), pp. 940–50.

[17] See John Rex, "Typology and Objectivity," in Arun Sahay, ed., *Max
Weber and Modern Sociology* (London: Routledge and Kegan Paul, 1971),
pp. 17–36; R. Stephen Warner, "The Methodology of Max Weber's Com-
parative Studies" (Ph.D. diss., University of California, Berkeley, 1972).
See also my essays "Socio-Historical Model and Developmental Theory,"
American Sociological Review 40, no. 2 (1975), pp. 148–57; "Religion and
Revolutionary Beliefs: Sociological and Historical Dimensions in Max
Weber's Work," *Social Forces* 55, no. 2 (1976); "History and Sociology,"
British Journal of Sociology 27, no. 3 (1976), pp. 306–18.

various forms of capitalism; instead, in his comparative studies he tried to lay the basis for establishing the mix of "material" and "ideal" factors accounting for the uniqueness of occidental history.

2. What Bendix did for Weber's empirical studies, Hans Henrik Bruun has done in the meantime for his methodological statements—a lucid and cohesive exposition and analysis rather than intellectual history or political critique. Bruun once more makes it clèar—and it still seems to be worth repeating—that the principle of freedom from value judgment (which may be a better translation than the customary "value neutrality") was rooted not in a relativistic or nihilist attitude but in the logical consideration that values are undemonstrable by scientific methods and in the conviction that "values and science are two closed spheres containing the key to each other."[18]

Two other epistemological and methodological investigations in English are noteworthy: W. G. Runciman's interpretation of Weber as a philosopher of science (1972) and John Torrance's lengthy essay on "Methods and the Man" (1974), which in part is a rejoinder to Runciman. The massive but subtle study by Gerhard Hufnagel, *Critique as Vocation: The Critical Content in Max Weber's Work* (1971) and the concise study by Fritz Loos, *On Max Weber's Doctrine of Values and Law* (1970) are German contributions. An older German critique, from a phenomenological viewpoint, is Alfred Schutz's *The Phenomenology of the Social World* (1932), which since its translation in 1967 has received considerable attention among a new breed of phenomenologically oriented sociologists and philosophers of science. This is a prime example of a very narrow focus on Weber's definitions of social action, subjective meaning, ideal type, and interpretive sociology to the exclusion of everything else. Schutz and his latter-day followers endeavor to provide a phenomenological grounding to Weber's basic categories and to supplement them with an epistemological buttressing in which he was not interested, since he merely wanted to construct baseline concepts this side of episte-

[18] Hans Henrik Bruun, *Science, Values and Politics in Max Weber's Methodology* (Copenhagen: Munksgaard, 1972), p. 290.

mology and philosophy of science from which to get on with his empirical inquiries.[19]

Weber's methodological and programmatic writings were posthumously published under the misleading and well-nigh untranslatable title *Wissenschaftslehre*, a term which he did not employ—literally "the theory of science," substantively "the logic of historical analysis." They comprise the critical essays on Wilhelm Roscher, Karl Knies, Eduard Meyer, Rudolf Stammler, Lujo Brentano and Wilhelm Ostwald, the programmatic essays on objectivity and "value neutrality" (aimed in part at Gustav Schmoller and his reigning dispensation), and the basic definitions of social action and the social group (perhaps written in part against Durkheim), with the familiar "Science as a Vocation" tagged on. Although these essays and fragments were mostly written in a specific polemical context and address themselves to targets no longer recognized by most of today's readers, they still make worthwhile reading because of their continued pertinency to present interests and their programmatic aspects.

In 1949 Shils and Finch rendered their translations of "The Meaning of 'Ethical Neutrality' in Sociology and Economics," "Objectivity in Social Science and Social Policy," and the critique of Eduard Meyer together with the essay on objective possibility and adequate causation in historical explanation. For many years these essays, important though they are, were the only ones accessible to the English reader. Now the situation has improved

---

[19] W. G. Runciman, *A Critique of Max Weber's Philosophy of Social Science* (Cambridge: At the University Press, 1972); John Torrance, "Max Weber: Methods and the Man," *Archives of European Sociology*, Vol. XV (1974), pp. 127–65; Gerhard Hufnagel, *Kritik als Beruf: Der kritische Gehalt im Werk Max Webers* (Frankfurt: Propyläen, 1971); Fritz Loos, *Zur Wert-und Rechtslehre Max Webers* (Tübingen: J. C. B. Mohr, 1970): Alfred Schutz, *The Phenomenology of the Social World*, trans. G. Walsh and F. Lehnert (Chicago: Northwestern University Press, 1967); for a critical appraisal of the claims of Schutz and of those of Peter Winch, from the perspective of ordinary language analysis, see Susan Hekman, "Max Weber's Philosophy of Science: A Modern Critique" (Ph.D. diss., University of Washington, 1975). For the latest contribution, see Thomas Burger, *Max Weber's Theory of Concept Formation: History, Laws, Ideal Types* (Durham: Duke University Press, 1976).

considerably and most of the other parts of the *Wissenschaftslehre* have become available: the 1913 fragment "On Some Categories of Interpretive Sociology," a first version of the introductory terminology of *Economy and Society*; Weber's earliest methodological, book-length treatise *Roscher and Knies: The Logical Problems of Historical Economics*; and the critique of Lujo Brentano, "Marginal Utility Theory and the So-Called Fundamental Law of Psychophysics," in which Weber argues that economics, as an analytical enterprise concerned with economic rationality, is not dependent on basic psychological theories, thus defending the rationale of marginal utility theory against critics from ranks of institutional and historical economics. (Joseph Schumpeter once noted that among his peers Weber was remarkably free from any animus against formal economic theory, although he never worked in that competing medium.[20] Finally, the two critiques of Rudolf Stammler are now available. This leaves only the shorter attack on Wilhelm Ostwald, " 'Energetic' Theories of Culture," untranslated.[21]

3. Before the relevancy of Weber's historical typologies for the comparative study of social and political change or "development" was fully realized, his ideal type of bureaucracy received much attention in the literature of the forties and fifties on large-scale and formal organization, but the ideal type was usually separated from his historical theory of bureaucratization and democratization. In recent years, however, the level of Weber interpretation in the literature on formal organization has improved—witness

[20] Edward Shils and Henry Finch, trans. and eds., *Max Weber: The Methodology of the Social Sciences* (New York: The Free Press, 1949); Edith E. Graber, trans. and ed., "On Some Categories of Interpretive Sociology," M.A. thesis, University of Oklahoma, 1970); Guy Oakes, trans. and ed., *Roscher and Knies: The Logical Problems of Historical Economics* (New York: The Free Press, 1975; Louis Schneider, trans. and ed., "Marginal Utility Theory and the So-Called Fundamental Law of Psychophysics," *Social Science Quarterly* 56, no. 1 (1975), pp. 21–36.

[21] Guy Oakes, trans. and ed., *Critique of Stammler* (New York: Free Press, 1977); also Martin Albrow, trans., "Rudolf Stammler's 'Surmounting' of the Materialist Conception of History," *British Journal of Law and Society*, Vol. II, 1975, pp. 129–52; Vol. III, 1976, pp. 17–43.

Charles Perrow's treatment of the Weberian approach in his critical essay, *Complex Organization*.[22] Moreover, and quite properly, there has been increasing recognition that for many purposes of formal organization or systems theory Weber's utility is rather limited. Yet it is probably fair to say that Weber received most attention in both Europe and the United States as theorist of "the bureaucratic age." Wolfgang Schluchter's *Aspects of Bureaucratic Domination* (1972) is the most judicious and comprehensive account we presently have of Weber's place in the literature on bureaucratization and democratization.[23] The book draws together 150 years of intellectual history and most of the American and European discussion of bureaucratization and democratization. In both historical and contemporary perspective it compares Weber's vision with its two alternatives, the Saint-Simonian and the Marxian. Schluchter deflates the Saint-Simonian hope shared by so many American organization theorists that politics can ever be reduced to efficient administration and that replacing office authority with functional authority (expertise) can ever bring about the vaunted change from "the domination of men to the administration of things." Far from being uncritical toward Weber, Schluchter identifies the theoretical ambiguities and empirical lacunae of Weber's thought, yet he concludes that Weber's perception of the ineluctable dialectic of formal and substantive rationality intensified by "progress" provides us with the best basic model for understanding the nature of modern society; and similar to Bruun he makes it plain that Weber's postulate of value neu-

[22] Charles Perrow, *Complex Organizations: A Critical Essay* (Glenview: Scott, Foresman, 1972), chapter 4. In the literature on professionalization there has also been a more sophisticated understanding of Weber. Jeffrey Berlant's study of the American and English medical associations as monopolistic professions and status groups benefited from the availability, in *Economy and Society*, of Weber's treatment of monopolist and expansionist tendencies within various kinds of groups. See J. Berlant, *Profession and Monopoly* (Berkeley: University of California Press, 1975).

[23] Wolfgang Schluchter, *Aspekte bürokratischer Herrschaft: Studien zur Interpretation der fortschreitenden Industriegesellschaft* (Munich: List, 1972). Previously, Schluchter wrote a tightly-reasoned essay on the relation between science and politics, value freedom and the ethic of responsibility in Weber's thought: *Wertfreiheit und Verantwortungsethik* (Tübingen: J. C. B. Mohr, 1971).

trality is the dialectical precondition of political rationality and of the defense of Reason against its perversions. We owe to David Beetham the best extant treatment of Weber as theorist of modern politics.[24] Beetham synthesizes Weber's perception of the preconditions of liberal democracy mainly from his political writings on Imperial Germany and Imperial Russia. He shows that Weber's scholarly and political writings differ in approach, not just in content. His political analysis is concerned with the assessment of a given distribution of power with a view toward changing it; it explicitly addresses questions of how to bring about change—parallel to Marx's interests. In essence, Weber practices situational class analysis. By contrast, the scholarly writings focus on long-range transformations and historical comparisons. Beetham correctly points out that in the latter the emphasis is on types of legitimation and on bureaucracy as a superior technical instrument, whereas in the political essays bureaucrats are treated as a status group with vested interests. In turn, capitalism appears as part of occidental rationalization in the scholarly writings, whereas in the political ones capitalism's capacity for creating class conflicts is stressed. Weber fully recognized that the introduction of advanced capitalism into "underdeveloped" countries such as Germany and Russia militated against the opportunities for liberal democracy by reenforcing both traditionalism and radicalism. Beetham's account of Weber's untranslated writings on Russia cannot be found elsewhere in such clarity and completeness.

[24] David Beetham *Max Weber and the Theory of Modern Politics* (London: Allen & Unwin, 1974). The following observations draw on my elaboration of Beetham's analysis and of Weber's views on the preconditions of liberal democracy in my essay "History and Sociology." On Weber's political thought see also Ilse Dronberger, *The Political Thought of Max Weber* (New York: Appleton-Century Crofts, 1971; Christian von Ferber, *Die Gewalt in der Politik* (Stuttgart: Kohlhammer, 1970); Karl Loewenstein, *Max Weber's Political Ideas in the Perspective of Our Time* (Amherst: University of Massachusetts Press, 1966); Daniel Rossides; "The Legacy of Max Weber: A Non-Metaphysical Politics," in A. Effrat, ed., *Perspectives in Political Sociology* (Indianapolis: Bobbs-Merrill, 1972), pp. 183–210; Lawrence A. Scaff, "Max Weber's Politics and Political Education," *American Political Science Review*, Vol. LXVII, no. 1 (1973), pp. 128–41.

4. If much of Weber's sociological vision, both in his scholarly and political writings, remains viable, the same cannot be claimed for his politics, which had to be time-bound, as Wolfgang Mommsen shows in his comprehensive account of Weber's place in German politics. The first edition appeared in 1959, almost at the same time as Bendix's intellectual portrait. The second edition (1974) incorporates all the new source materials and the secondary literature since accumulated, and contains a lengthy reply to numerous critics, including Bendix and myself. In 1959 the book was representative of the youngest scholarly generation's attempt to come to terms with "the German catastrophe" (as the octogenarian Friedrich Meinecke had titled his last work) and with the web of intellectual guilt for the rise of Nazism. It was written partly under the impact of Anglo-American re-education, with its appeals to the ghosts of the natural law tradition, and partly in response to the attempt by parliamentary survivors of Weimar Germany to install Weber as patron saint of the fledgling Federal Republic—a role for which he was not well suited. His advocacy of a democratized form of national integration that would permit Germany to take a more responsible part in the politics of the great powers makes Weber the politician a man of his time and not ours. However, Mommsen does not rest his case there. He also posits a fateful intellectual link via Carl Schmitt, the theoretician of the authoritarian state, to Hitler's appearance as the "charismatic leader with a political machine." This construction, coupled with a tendency to view Weber's sociological writings as indicative of his political views, led to a sometimes acrimonious clash with mostly older scholars and political men. Bendix, Paul Honigsheim, Karl Loewenstein, Benjamin Nelson, and Parsons became prominent participants in a controversy that eventually broadened into the political warfare that engulfed American and European universities from 1964 on.

In *The Age of Bureaucracy* Mommsen put his views in his own English words, but the slim volume of five essays on Weber's politics and sociology cannot substitute for the author's main opus. This English volume is paralleled by a partly overlapping collection of previously published essays in German, which also contains a discussion of the United States in Weber's political thought and a new contribution on "Verstehen und Idealtypus." In both volumes Mommsen goes beyond his political biography in that he now tries to demonstrate explicitly an underlying intellectual unity of Weber's political and sociological vision.[25] Partly in reaction to Mommsen, Marcuse, and Lukacs, Anthony Giddens has offered his own interpretation in *Politics and Sociology in the Thought of Max Weber*, a small volume that is an addendum to his comprehensive treatment of Marx, Durkheim, and Weber in *Capitalism and Modern Social Theory*.[26] Giddens rightly considers "one of the most urgent tasks confronting modern social theory . . . that of re-examining the social and political environments which generated the main parameters of social thought which exist today. In the case of Weber, this means making something of a return to the sort of discussion which his works stimulated in Germany during his own lifetime."[27]

If Weber's politics come from a much different time and place, his views on the role of the university and a specifically academic "freedom from value judgments" have remained ideal and target in contemporary American academic politics. Edward Shils has edited, translated, and for the first time collected Weber's editorials, articles, speeches, and memoranda, which at several occasions precipitated a public éclat involving government officials, professors, and parliamentarians.[28] The collection is intended as a "classic" contribution to the present-day discourse. It is also useful because it shows the concrete political incidents and

[25] Wolfgang Mommsen, *Max Weber und die deutsche Politik, 1890–1920* (Tübingen: J. C. B. Mohr, 1959; second revised edition, 1974); *The Age of Bureaucracy: Perspectives on the Political Sociology of Max Weber* (New York: Harper & Row, 1974); *Max Weber: Gesellschaft, Politik und Geschichte* (Frankfurt: Suhrkamp, 1974); on some of the exchanges between Mommsen and his critics, see Bendix and Roth *Scholarship and Partisanship*, p. 66; on one of Bendix's comments, see p. 471 below.

[26] Anthony Giddens, *Politics and Sociology in the Thought of Max Weber* (London: Macmillan, 1972); *Capitalism and Modern Social Theory* (Cambridge: At the University Press, 1971).

[27] Giddens, *Politics and Sociology*, p. 8.

[28] Edward Shils, trans. and ed., *Max Weber on Universities: The Power of the State and the Dignity of the Academic Calling in Imperial Germany* (Chicago: University of Chicago Press, 1974). Quotations are from pp. 6 and 22.

issues which finally made Weber state his position more systematically in "The Meaning of 'Ethical Neutrality' in Sociology and Economics" (1913) and in "Science as a Vocation" (1919). Weber wished to preserve "the proud tradition of academic solidarity" against interference from the governments, the churches, and various interest groups and therefore advocated, *inter alia*, a national organization or union of professors in opposition to the cartel of the ministries of education against the universities. He denied that there was meaningful academic freedom as long as political and religious criteria determined appointments; he feared that the increasing manipulation of younger scholars by the ministries through often secret preferment would breed academic place-hunters and operators, at the same time that he castigated the growing tendency of bourgeois students to look upon academic patents and fraternity membership as qualifications for joining the "feudal" establishment.

As civil servants, German professors were under even greater restrictions than American government employees are under the Hatch Act, restraints to which American academics are unaccustomed, although, as Weber pointed out at the time, American university administrations tend to take the place of the German ministries of education. Weber condemned authoritarian indoctrination and patronage of students not only for pedagogical reasons, but also because he desired the universities to have a moral justification for rejecting interference on the part of "religious, economic, social and political parties [which otherwise] would then all possess the right to have separate universities or professorships provided for them, in which instruction in accordance with their own ideals would be given." Anybody opposed to such a state of affairs must also for himself forego "instruction in ultimate values and beliefs." We must not forget, however, that this political stand was not directly related to the epistemological distinction between value and fact on which Weber founded the logical possibility of scholarship and science.

5. Both this epistemological distinction and the advocacy of a liberal university as an elite of scholars committed foremost to the intergenerational continuity of academic competence are totally

unacceptable to the long line of Weber's Marxist critics, recently
joined by Lefèvre and Therborn. Lefèvre, one of the leaders of the
student rebellion at the Free University of Berlin in the late sixties,
wrote a highly controversial dissertation on which the examiners
split, *On the Historical Character and Historical Function of the
Method of Bourgeois Sociology*.[29] It was part of the theoretical
justification for the attack on one of the outposts of "American-
ized" social science, which subsequently was largely displaced by
the Marxist "science of society." The book is a narrow case study
limited to Weber's methodology and *The Protestant Ethic*, but
since it proceeds from a total theory of cognition and society it can
claim to demolish all of contemporary social science by proving
Weber's "insufficiency of method" (the title of the first chapter).
The method is "insufficient" because it separates the Ought from
the Is, takes the epistemological possibility of a purely empirical
science as unproblematical, and studies only limited causal connections—all of which adds up to veiling the "truth" about capitalist exploitation. Weber's personal recognition of capitalism's
inherent inhumanity thus would appear irrelevant to his method
of inquiry, as indeed it was, in contrast to his substantive concerns.
For Lefèvre, Weber's work, and hence all of social science today,
rests on a "naive and optimistic research liberalism," which parallels the free enterprise model with its glorification of the anarchy
of production. Here there are satirical possibilities, but Lefèvre
cannot afford to be anything but deadly serious in his insistence on
a unity of theory and practice that will totally transcend the
prevailing mode of production and domination. Mommsen correctly views this stance as "naive Hegelianism with a Marxist
twist."[30] After all, the alternative to the imperfect liberal university can only be central political control or a universal consensus
on a philosophy of history—and the former is much more likely
than the latter.

Goeran Therborn's *Science, Class and Society* is intended
as a contribution to the formation of sociology and historical

[29] Wolfgang Lefèvre, *Zum historischen Charakter und zur historischen
Funktion der Methode bürgerlicher Soziologie* (Frankfurt: Suhrkamp, 1971).
Quotation is from p. 17.
[30] Mommsen, *Max Weber*, p. 446.

materialsm.[31] He offers his study as an exercise in the sociology of
knowledge, even more, as a "historical materialism of historical
materialism, or, in other words, a social scientific study of the
development of [Marxist] social science" that reduces sociological
theorizing to "underlying" relations of production and class
struggle. With Althusser, he believes that Marxism became a
science by turning to working-class politics. The equation of philosophy and class struggle in Althusser—"philosophy is, in the last
analysis, class struggle in theory"—appears to Therborn "a philosophical practice of the greatest significance." In this view the
whole history of sociology and contemporary American social
science, which Therborn reviews extensively if superficially, must
look like apology. Since class commitment is crucial, it is revealing
to Therborn that, in contrast to Marx, Engels, and Lenin, those
"proletarian" intellectuals, "there is not a single prominent sociologist of the capitalist world who, as a sociologist, has been
formed by being part of a militant labor movement." Therborn's
treatment of Weber does not differ much from Lefèvre's. Just like
him, he makes only fleeting references to the bulk of Weber's
historical studies and stresses the individualist perspective of social action at the expense of the practiced methodology and the
substantive historical explanations. If Therborn would admit the
closeness of Marx and Weber as historical analysts, as Turner has
demonstrated, he would have to explain how a self-professed
"class-conscious bourgeois" could hold views similar to those of a
"proletarian" thinker.

These two examples are representative of other Marxist or
neo-Marxist endeavors.[32] They have been balanced by com-

[31] Göran Therborn, *Science, Class and Society* (Göteborg: Tryck Revo
Press, 1974). Quotations are from pp. 49, 46, 47 and 255.

[32] For some other recent Marxist or neo-Marxist comparisons, see Rich-
ard Ashcraft, "Marx and Weber on Liberalism as Bourgeois Ideology,"
Comparative Studies in History and Society 14, no. 2 (1972), pp. 130–168;
Jean Cohen, "Max Weber and the Dynamics of Rationalized Domination,"
Telos 14 (Winter 1972), pp. 63–86; John Lewis, "Max Weber and Karl
Marx," *Marxism Today* (November 1974), pp. 328–339; Joachim Streisand,
"Max Weber: Politik, Soziologie und Geschichtsschreibung," idem, ed.,
Die bürgerliche deutsche Geschichtsschreibung (East Berlin: Akademie-
Verlag, 1965), pp. 178–89. Cf. also the older account by Norman Birnbaum,
"Conflicting Interpretations of the Rise of Capitalism: Marx and

parisons made by Bendix, Giddens, Mayer, and Runciman.[33] In general, Marx-Weber comparisons, political and nonpolitical, have almost become a specialty. The genre was initiated in 1932 by Karl Loewith (cf. p. 66 below) with a famed philosophical inquiry, the Weberian part of which is now available in English.[34]

6. Apart from uncompromising Marxists for whom personal qualities must recede behind class membership, most of the writers considered so far seem sympathetic to Weber, and some even engage in intellectual hero worship. However, while few sociologists would dismiss Weber's achievements out of hand, a quite substantial number are ambivalent about the work and unsympathtic to the person. The man who was known to his contemporaries for his easy laughter is almost invariably pictured in that formal portrait that graces so many books—including Donald MacRae's—confirming the cultural stereotype of the grim-faced German professor. MacRae's sketch in the Modern Masters series is the first overall account that is a frank exercise in debunking.[35] Beginning with Weber's reputation and depicting the life, the man, the country, and his academic surrounding, MacRae conjures up an image that probably will leave "the curious" to whom it is addressed with little curiosity and will not encourage many readers to take seriously much of Weber's sub-

Weber," *British Journal of Sociology* 55 (1963), pp. 125–41. For an attempt at synthesizing Marx and Weber, see Irving Zeitlin, *Rethinking Sociology* (New York: Appleton-Century Crofts, 1973), pp. 123–38.

[33] Bendix, "Inequality and Social Structure: A Comparison of Marx and Weber," *American Sociological Review* 39, no. 2 (1973), pp. 149–61; Anthony Giddens, "Marx, Weber and the Development of Capitalism," *Sociology* 4 (1970), pp. 289–310; see also his *Capitalism and Modern Social Theory*; Carl Mayer, "Max Weber's Interpretation of Karl Marx," *Social Research* 42, no. 4 (1975), pp. 701–19;, W. G. Runciman, "Karl Marx and Max Weber," idem, *Social Science and Political Theory* (Cambridge: At the University Press, 1963), pp. 43–63. For more references, see my essay on Weber's relationship to Marx in Bendix and Roth, eds., *Scholarship and Partisanship*, chapter XII.

[34] Karl Loewith, "Weber's Interpretation of the Bourgeois-Capitalistic World in Terms of the Guiding Principle of 'Rationalization,' " in Wrong ed., *Max Weber*, pp. 101–120.

[35] Donald G. MacRae, *Max Weber* (New York: Viking Press, 1974). Quotation is from p. 103.

stantive work, which is treated in the later chapters. MacRae appears to be irked by the observation, that "practically all that is written on Weber is written in awe," although he concedes that "it is remarkable that despite this awe so much written about Weber is so good, even if so incomplete."

MacRae takes a clear position: he identifies himself with the evolutionary and positivist tradition from Spencer and Durkheim to Hobhouse; he prefers "successful" sociologists like them and Pareto to "unsuccessful" ones like Weber and Marx, and he likes his heroes dead and done with in the name, presumably, of scientific progress. Put another way, he does not care for historical sociology, for which clear-cut explanations, his apparent criterion of success, are not feasible. MacRae seems to belong to those who are troubled by the Germanness of Marx and Weber and by their persistent importance in the Anglo-Saxon realm, where they continue to be living presences instead of dead saints (as Erich Fromm and Anthony Giddens have put it). His ultimate explanation is in line with the cultural stereotypes: Weber and Marx, about whom he wrote earlier,[36] succeed by obfuscation rather than Gallic clarity or English common sense. Weber must be a magus, at heart an irrationalist exerting an irrational appeal far beyond what is tolerable to the positivist view of the world.

This image contrasts with Martin Green's mythological universe in which Weber incarnates the Apollonian spirit as a nemesis of Demetrian and Aphroditean irrationalism.[37] In Green's mythology almost the whole twentieth century, as a cultural configuration, is the creation of two diametrically opposed spiritual attitudes: those of D. H. Lawrence and of Weber. There is too much heavy-handed symbolism in Green's reconstruction, and a preoccupation with establishing point-by-point parallels and oppositions between persons and ideas. But his work makes fascinating reading and has a lesson for sociologists and intellectual historians; it provides a wealth of scattered and jumbled materials

[36] Donald G. MacRae, "Karl Marx," in Timothy Raison, ed., *The Founding Fathers of Social Science* (Baltimore: Penguin, 1969), pp. 59–67.

[37] Martin Green, *The von Richthofen Sisters: The Triumphant and the Tragic Modes of Love* (New York: Basic Books, 1974). Quotation is from pp. 66 ff.

for the study of intellectual circles as originators of new ideas and for some of the major transmissions of ideas from central Europe to the Anglo-Saxon realm, a topic previously dealt with by Parsons and H. S. Hughes. Foremost, Green succeeds in sketching one important story relatively unknown to Americans—the rise of Schwabing, the bohemian suburb of Munich, around 1900 as the locus of the new movement of aesthetic and libidinal liberation and as the vanguard of much that is familiar to us today in the American counterculture. The central figure was the calamitous, drug-addicted Otto Gross, who in his rebellion against an authoritarian father, a famous criminologist, radicalized Freudian ideas in the direction of an intensely-lived way of life that was politically and erotically anarchic. Frieda von Richthofen, a distant relative of the Red Baron, converted D. H. Lawrence to the anti-paternalistic creed of Gross, her erstwhile lover, and thus changed the English literary climate. Frieda's older sister Else, one of the first women Ph.D.s at the University of Heidelberg, taught Weber the moral value of eroticism, which may have found a reflection in successive changes in his sociology of religion. After Else gave birth to one of Gross's illegitimate children in 1907, Weber began to read Freud and Gross, and he wrote to her a scathing attack on the tenets of total libidinal freedom (reprinted under camouflage in Baumgarten, 1964).[38] But regardless of his opposition to Otto Gross's anarchism, he became the legal adviser and helper-in-need to members of Gross's circle in matters of divorce, child custody, draft dodging and criminal prosecution. Green casts Weber in the role of the "greatest, though most self-divided, representative . . . of the patriarchal mode," as "the Brutus of Patriarchy, the virtuous rebel," while Lawrence plays the part of the worshipper of Demetrian matriarchy and Gross that of Aphroditean enthusiast. As the tortured defender of moral responsibility Weber appears ultimately as the embodiment of patriarchalism's enlightened Apollonian side. Green seems to be quite right in perceiving Weber's promotion of his wife Marianne, as a leader of Women's Liberation and a scholar, as a form of liberal patriarchalism intended to bring women into the Apol-

[38] Eduard Baumgarten, ed., *Max Weber: Werk und Person* Tübingen: J. C. B. Mohr, 1964), pp. 644–58.

Ionian world or work, which Frieda, the Demetrian spokeswoman of total feminine liberation, hated so passionately.

After Mitzman's psychohistory[39] and Green's mythologizing enterprise, it is only fair that Marianne Weber's own account, with its sometimes vexing mixture of unabashed glorification and overly discreet cover-up, should finally be available to English readers.[40] The biographies of these men and women by Green, Mitzman and Marianne Weber and the story of Heidelberg and Schwabing as intellectual constitutents of the twentieth century are important for cultural, social and political history, especially for understanding some of the antecedents of our own intellectual and professional environment. Beyond that, they can make a contribution, as case studies, to the sociology of the intelligentsia.

However, the utility of Weber's comparative sociology remains independent of the question of its origins. Here intellectual development, rather than social or psychological reductionism, is called for. Yet this development is not possible without bringing about and preserving a thorough grasp of the complexity and breadth of Weber's work. Each generation neglects at its own peril the accomplishments of its predecessors, and if it does so, it is condemned to suffer the consequences of the resulting scholarly discontinuities. The mere passage of time and the discovery of new statistical techniques are insufficient to guarantee scholarly progress.

On this score Bendix's intellectual portrait continues to be important as the major integrated introduction to most of Weber's empirical works. The book summarizes not only *Economy and Society* and the three volumes on the sociology of religion, but its first part also familiarizes the reader with Weber's early writings on German industrialization, including his studies of the capitalist transformation of the land-owning Prussian aristocracy (the *Junkers*), the individualist transformation of the traditionalist rural workforce in eastern Prussia, and his explanation of the stock

[39] Arthur Mitzman, *The Iron Cage: An Historical Interpretation of Max Weber* (New York: Alfred A. Knopf, 1970).

[40] Marianne Weber, *Max Weber: A Biography*, trans. and ed., Harry Zohn (New York: Wiley, 1975).

exchange as both an impersonal market mechanism and a capitalist status group with internalized standards of probity.

In its sociological emphasis Bendix's treatment of Weber's writings remains independent of the political interpretations by Wolfgang Mommsen and David Beetham and of Arthur Mitzman's attempt at psychological analysis. In a significant sense, then, the book is outdated as little as is Alexander von Schelting's 1934 study of Weber's *Wissenschaftslehre*, which remains a classic introduction to his critical and programmatic statements on methodology.[41]

Bendix's work need no longer substitute for the lack of a complete edition of *Economy and Society*, but it will remain a lucid introduction to a most complex work. It is not true that Weber is an opaque writer in the proverbial sense of the "deep" German thinker—he himself hated that tradition and wanted to be a researcher rather than a philosopher. (However, his precise but complex syntax requires careful reading. Most of his magnum opus remained a first draft—as did so many of Marx's writings—and his essays on religion are longish working papers, unrevised with the exception of the first volume. He never intended to appeal to a broad readership.) When Bendix's intellectual portrait first appeared, Parsons expressed the hope that it would not become a trot for students enabling them to escape the primary reading. This would indeed amount to taking the easy way out, although many students may have to add only a few samples of primary reading to get a sense for Weber's accomplishment. However, for those with genuine macrosociological and comparative interests Bendix's book will remain a stepping stone on the long and arduous road toward the kind of comprehension without which creative scholarly research is impossible.

[41] Alexander von Schelting, *Max Webers Wissenschaftslehre* (Tübingen: J. C. B. Mohr (Siebeck), 1934).

Bibliographical Note on the Writings of Max Weber

Below I list the German works of Max Weber for which abbreviations have been used in this volume:

WuG *Wirtschaft und Gesellschaft* (2nd ed.; Tübingen: J. C. B. Mohr, 1925), 2 vols.

GAzRS *Gesammelte Aufsätze zur Religionssoziologie* (Tübingen: J. C. B. Mohr, 1920–21), 3 vols.

GAzSuW *Gesammelte Aufsätze zur Sozial- und Wirtsschaftsgeschichte* (Tübingen: J. C. B. Mohr, 1924).

GAzSuS *Gesammelte Aufsätze zur Soziologie und Sozialpolitik* (Tübingen: J. C. B. Mohr, 1924).

GPS *Gesammelte Politische Schriften* (München: Drei Masken Verlag, 1921).

In addition there are the following German works to which reference is made without abbreviation, or not at all:

Zur Geschichte der Handelsgesellschaften im Mittelalter (Stuttgart: F. Enke, 1889).

Die Römische Agrargeschichte in ihrer Bedeutung für das Staats- und Privatrecht (Stuttgart: F. Enke, 1891).

Die Verhältnisse der Landarbeiter im ostelbischen Deutschland, Schriften des Vereins für Sozialpolitik, Vol. LV (Berlin; Duncker & Humblot, 1892).

Gesammelte Aufsätze zur Wissenschaftslehre (Tübingen: J. C. B. Mohr, 1922).

Wirtschaftsgeschichte, ed. S. Hellmann and M. Palyi (München: Duncker & Humblot, 1924).

Staatssoziologie (Berlin: Duncker & Humblot, 1956).

Several of these writings have been reissued in critically revised

editions by Dr. Johannes Winckelmann. Since these new editions
contain a page-by-page comparison with the old editions, I have
used the latter for reasons of convenience.

The English translations of Weber's works have been used with
the following abbreviations:

Protestant Ethic	*The Protestant Ethic and the Spirit of Capitalism* (London: George Allen & Unwin, 1930; New York: Charles Scribner's Sons, 1958).
Essays	*From Max Weber: Essays in Sociology* (New York: Oxford University Press, 1946).
Methodology	*Max Weber on the Methodology of the Social Sciences* (Glencoe: The Free Press, 1949).
Theory	*The Theory of Social and Economic Organization* (New York: Oxford University Press, 1947).
Religion of China	*The Religion of China: Confucianism and Taoism* (Glencoe: The Free Press, 1951).
Religion of India	*The Religion of India: The Sociology of Hinduism and Buddhism* (Glencoe: The Free Press, 1958).
AJ	*Ancient Judaism* (Glencoe: The Free Press, 1952).
Law	*Max Weber on Law in Economy and Society* (Cambridge: Harvard University Press, 1954).
Economy and Society	*Economy and Society: An Outline of Interpretive Sociology*, 3 Volumes (New York: Bedminster Press, 1968).

At the time five further translations were available, to which
reference is made without abbreviation, or not at all:

General Economic History (Glencoe: The Free Press, 1950).

"The Social Causes of the Decay of Ancient Civilization," *Journal
of General Education*, Vol. V (1950), pp. 75–88.

The City (Glencoe: The Free Press, 1958).

Rational and Social Foundations of Music (Carbondale: Southern
Illinois University Press, 1958).

"The Three Types of Legitimate Rule," *Berkeley Publications in
Society and Institutions*, Vol. IV (1958), pp. 1–11.

In using these various publications I have cited the translations of Weber's works wherever these are available. In some instances I have retranslated the original for reasons of fluency and accuracy; this has been noted in each case. An English quotation is my own translation wherever a German source is cited.

For the reader's convenience the chapters of *Economy and Society* (in the sequence of the 1956 and 1964 German editions) and the previous translations partially used in the complete edition are listed below:

Economy and Society	Partial Previous Translations
Part I	
I. Basic Sociological Terms	
II. Sociological Categories of Economic Action	*Theory*,
III. The Types of Legitimate Domination	87–429
IV. Status Groups and Classes	
Part II	
I. The Economy and Social Norms	*Law*, ch. II
II. The Economic Relationships of Organized Groups	Previously untranslated
III. Household, Neighborhood and Kin Group	Partially in T. Parsons et al. eds., *Theories of*
IV. Household, Enterprise and Oikos	*Society* (Glencoe: Free Press, 1961), pp. 296–
V. Ethnic Groups	98, 302–09
VI. Religious Groups (The Sociology of Religion)	E. Fischoff, trans., *The Sociology of Religion* (Boston: Beacon Press, 1963)
VII. The Market	*Law*, pp. 191–97
VIII. Economy and Law (The Sociology of Law)	*Law*, chs. III–XI
IX. Political Communities	*Law*, ch. XIII *Essays*, pp. 159–95

Economy and Society	Partial Previous Translations
X. Domination and Legitimacy	*Law*, ch. XII
XI. Bureaucracy	*Essays*, pp. 196–244
XII. Patriarchalism and Patrimonialism	Previously untr.
XIII. Feudalism, *Ständestaat* and Patrimonialism	Previously untr.
XIV. Charisma and Its Transformation	*Essays*, pp. 245–66
XV. Political and Hierocratic Domination	Previously untr.
XVI. The City	*The City*
1925 German appendix: not included	*Rational and Social Foundations of Music*

English appendix:
*Parliament and Government
in a Reconstructed Germany*
(from *GPS*)

The following references to the 1925 edition of *Wirtschaft und Gesellschaft* and to *GSP* are found in *Economy and Society* and its appendix:

	Economy and Society
p. 3, n 2	pp. 1168–70
57, n 15	477–80
72, n 44	1244 f.
73, n 45	365–69
74, n 47	1247
88, n 13	424 ff.
89, n 16	405
89, n 18	439
90, n 19	439–51
92, n 22	512
93, n 23	399 f.

		Economy and Society
p.	93, n 24	pp. 468–86, 1177–81
	94, n 25	472
	96, n 26	481 ff.
	n 27	500 ff.
	102, n 9	1047 ff.
	137, n 58	447 f.
	201, n 3	541–55
	270, n 22	448 ff.
	279, n 34	431 552–56
	292, n 16	212 943 ff.
	296, n 23	14 26 f.
	298, n 1	1111–1157
	306, n 7	1123–25
	308, n 9	1158–1211
	309, n 11	1135
	312, n 13	1140 f.
	327, n 28	1133 f.
	330, n 2	1006 f. 356–84
	334, n 7	1006–1110
	335, n 10	1090 ff.
	339, n 14	1046
	348, n 21	1009
	353, n 24	1048
	354, n 25	1048 f.
	359, n 29	omitted (also in later German editions)
	368, n 39	1088
	370, n 42	1071 f.
	371, n 44	1075
	372, n 45	1075 f.
	376, n 46	1059–64 1276–80

INTRODUCTION
TO THE ORIGINAL EDITION

Max Weber is a name to conjure with in modern social thought. His work is used as a source of authoritative knowledge and insight, and even those who have criticized him severely do not question the value of his contributions. Appreciation of his work, especially among American social scientists, is reflected in the large number of translations that have appeared in recent years, and others are in prospect. There is also a large and growing literature about his work. Yet despite this widespread familiarity with some of his ideas, and despite the general esteem in which he is held, there is considerable evidence that, as a comprehensive whole, his work remains relatively unknown.

My purpose in writing this book has been to make Weber's sociological work more accessible and more thematically coherent than it is either in the original or in translation. Weber's writings comprise some thirteen volumes of complex texts that in many cases remained fragmentary. Toward the end of his life, he was working on his most systematic treatise, *Wirtschaft und Gesellschaft*, which has been published posthumously in two different editions. But since the original remained incomplete, Weber's attempt to integrate his work demands an interpretation. For the English reader, this task of interpretation is made still more difficult by the scattering and incompleteness of many translations. The available translations of Weber's work are, of course, a great help and, given the special difficulties of the original, we should be grateful to the scholars who have undertaken this laborious assignment. It does not disparage their effort, however, to observe that the English reader can hardly be expected to master the work of a man whose most systematic, if uncompleted, book is available in five separate volumes, while more than a third of that book remains untranslated. (For details, see pp. xiii–xiv above.) Moreover, even if all of it were available in translation, a com-

prehensive interpretation of Weber's work would still be
needed. My hope is that this volume will be used as an introduction to the study of the original, and while the objectives
I have set myself are also limited, the book attempts to give
the reader a systematic presentation of Weber's sociological
studies. Other intellectual portraits have been written of
Weber the theorist and methodologist, or Weber the politician.
Still other intellectual portraits are possible and would be wel-
come; as yet we have no comprehensive psychological study
of Weber the man nor an examination of his place in the history of ideas. Here is a book on Max Weber the sociologist.

In the United States Weber became known in several
stages.[1] In the 1930's, his essay *The Protestant Ethic and the
Spirit of Capitalism* was published in translation and discussed
widely. After World War II, two selections of essays were published, and among these Weber's concepts of the "ideal type"
and of "bureaucracy" received special attention. Subsequently,
three volumes of his sociology of religion, the first part of
Wirtschaft und Gesellschaft, his sociology of law and of the
city became available in translation. Nevertheless, it is still very
difficult to get a comprehensive view of Weber's work, as the
comments and citations in our learned publications all too
plainly reveal. For example, the vast critical literature on
Weber's thesis on the influence of Puritanism pays next to no
attention to either his related study of *Ancient Judaism* or his
investigation of urban communities in western Europe, though
without these other studies that thesis cannot be properly understood. Again, Weber's study of bureaucracy has been criticized for being too rationalistic, while his study of authority
has been censured for not being rationalistic enough. Yet the
first criticism ignores Weber's detailed discussion of bureaucratic maneuvering under autocratic rule, while the second
overlooks a whole volume (the sociology of law) dealing with
the development of formal reasoning in the growth of the modern state. Even the titles of some translations are a source of
confusion, and in a recent article we were told of Weber's two
concepts of bureaucracy by an author who was apparently

---

[1] For details see Guenther Roth and Reinhard Bendix, "Max Webers Einfluss auf die amerikanische Soziologie," *Kölner Zeitschrift
für Soziologie,* Vol. XI (1959), pp. 38–53.

unaware of the fact that Weber developed at least three such concepts and a number of variants of these as well.

Not all misinterpretations are due to a reliance on translations, however. The plain fact is that Weber's work is difficult to understand. Whatever may be said in justification of long sentences and scholarly qualifications is not enough to explain the characteristic "style" of Weber's sociological writings, which tends to bury the main points of the argument in a jungle of statements that require detailed analysis, or in long analyses of special topics that are not clearly related to either the preceding or the ensuing materials. Weber undertook several interdependent lines of investigation simultaneously and put all his research notes into the final text without making their relative importance explicit. A comment in Marianne Weber's biography of her husband points to the root of this difficulty:

> He was entirely unconcerned with the form in which he presented his wealth of ideas. So many things came to him out of that storehouse of his mind, once the mass [of ideas] was in motion, that many times they could not be readily forced into a lucid sentence structure. And he wants to be done with it quickly and be brief about it on top of that, because ever new problems of reality crowd in upon him. What a limitation of discursive thought that it does not permit the simultaneous expression of several lines of thought which belong together! Therefore, much must be pressed hurriedly into long involved periods and what cannot be accommodated there has to be put into the footnotes. After all, let the reader take as much trouble with these matters as he had done himself.[2]

[2] Marianne Weber, *Max Weber* (Heidelberg: Lambert Schneider, 1950), p. 350. Similar sentiments were voiced by other great scholars of the second half of the nineteenth century, though not with the same consequences for style as in Weber's case. There is, for example, the famous epigram of Pollock and Maitland: "Such is the unity of all history that any one who endeavors to tell a piece of it must feel that his first sentence tears a seamless web. . . ." See F. Pollock and F. W. Maitland, *The History of English Law before the Time of Edward I.* (2nd ed.; Cambridge: At the University Press, 1898), Vol. I, p. 1. This attitude towards history was probably a part of the preoccupation with the irrational forces

In addition, Weber indicated reservations of every kind by the ample use of quotation marks, conditional phrases, and other linguistic symbols of scholarly caution. He also used italics, differently numbered paragraphs, different type faces and other devices to structure his material and distribute his emphases. Therefore no simplification of sentence structure, terminology and paragraphing in an English translation can remedy the defects of exposition from which the original suffers.[3]

In the secondary literature on Weber much attention has been devoted to his methodological and theoretical writings or to only one or another aspect of his empirical work. Inadvertently perhaps, this approach reverses the original distribution of emphasis, and as a result the reader cannot easily get a view of Weber's sociological work as a whole. For all their inherent interest, Weber's methodological writings do not provide an adequate guide to that work because it contains important theoretical contributions that do not appear anywhere else. Nor is it sufficient to rely on Weber's elaborate definitions of sociological concepts for an understanding of his empirical studies. Weber sought to give a comprehensive set of definitions rather than merely to specify the meaning of terms most relevant for his own studies. This explains in part the large amount of space that he devoted to concepts like action, social relationship, etc., and the small amount devoted to "class" and "status-group," although in his substantive work this emphasis is reversed. Consequently, many of Weber's concepts do not

underlying human institutions which characterized this generation of intellectuals. Cf. the analysis by H. Stuart Hughes, *Consciousness and Society* (New York: Alfred A. Knopf, 1959), *passim*.

[3] In addition to the translations, several over-all accounts of Weber's work are available in English. Among the most notable recent contributions are Talcott Parsons, *The Structure of Social Action* (New York: McGraw-Hill Book Co., 1937), which was republished by The Free Press in 1949, and his introduction to *Theory* (1947); the introduction by Gerth and Mills in *Essays* (1946); the recently published translation of an older book by Raymond Aron, *German Sociology* (London: Heinemann, 1957); and H. Stuart Hughes, *Consciousness and Society*, Chapter 8. A comprehensive bibliography of writings on Weber is available in H. H. Gerth and H. I. Gerth, "Bibliography on Max Weber," *Social Research*, Vol. XVI (March, 1949), pp. 70–89.

throw much light on what he did when he analyzed specific materials, and those concepts that do are often not as fully developed as one would wish.[4]

On the basis of these considerations the present study approaches Weber's work with a major emphasis on his empirical rather than his methodological writings.[5] His early studies of farm laborers in eastern Germany and of the stock exchange, with which I begin, contain in rudimentary form the basic concepts and central problems which occupied him for the rest of his life. These studies are particularly useful for an understanding of *The Protestant Ethic*. In Part Two, I take up the three-volume work on the sociology of religion, discussing in turn Weber's studies of China, India, and ancient Judaism. This was a pioneering work in the comparative study of civilizations; the passage of some forty years since its first publication has not notably diminished its value. Today the concern with economic development outside the Western world gives renewed significance to Weber's study of cultural variations in the development of civilizations. In Part Three, I examine Weber's typology of domination together with his sociology of law and his political writings. Weber himself seems to have felt that this part of his work contained his most original con-

---

[4] It is awkward, therefore, to have the concepts available in translation, while the empirical materials to which they refer are either not translated at all, or are available in many different places. It may be added that Weber's two short chapters on classes, status groups and parties (*Theory*, pp. 424–49; *Essays*, pp. 180–95) were merely a beginning and there are several indications of how he intended to develop these ideas. These unfinished plans have been collated by Johannes Winckelmann, "Max Weber's Opus Posthumum," *Zeitschrift für die gesamte Staatswissenschaft*, Vol. CV (1949), pp. 374–75.

[5] Some omissions were necessary aside from the intentional omission of Weber's methodological writings. Most notable among them are his early studies of Roman agriculture and of the medieval trading companies as well as his later treatise "Agrarverhältnisse im Altertum," *GAzSuW*, pp. 1–288, and his "Zur Psychophysik der industriellen Arbeit," *GAzSuS*, pp. 61–255. Other omissions are less important. Weber's economic analysis in *Theory*, pp. 158–323, has been ably presented in Parsons' introduction to that volume (pp. 30–55), and the sparse references to Weber's work on the city are compensated for by the recently published translation and introduction by Don Martindale and Gertrud Neuwirth.

tribution. In conception and scope his political analysis stands on a par with his sociology of religion.

With Weber's intellectual perspective in his early studies as a starting point, I have endeavored to present the material contained in his subsequent work in keeping with his own intentions, as I understand them. Thus, while the presentation in Part One gives my interpretation of Weber's perspective, the major chapters in Parts Two and Three are expository. My own contribution in this exposition consists primarily in an effort to reorganize, to eliminate digressions and details, to omit whole parts where these detract from the main line of argument, and to put together materials when they belong to the same context, regardless of where they appeared originally.

It remains for me to note here where, in my judgment, the present study supplements the existing secondary literature. Weber's work belongs to the intellectual heritage of European liberalism, a point discussed by Carlo Antoni, Raymond Aron, H. H. Gerth and C. Wright Mills, Karl Löwith and others, but not sufficiently developed in Talcott Parsons' utilization of Weber's work in his own sociological theories. So far, no attempt has been made to bring to the fore the thematic coherence of Weber's sociological work, which arises from this liberal tradition, although Weber's debt to the tradition is, of course, well known. In the present book I have, therefore, organized the materials of Weber's sociological studies in line with what I take to be the systematic core of his posthumous work, *Wirtschaft und Gesellschaft.* It is in this sense that my book presents an intellectual portrait of Weber's sociological studies, as well as an introduction to them.

Since I believe that Weber's work has enduring value, my purpose has been to present it without burdening the reader with criticisms and digressions of my own. To avoid both confusion and the repetition of Weber's name, I wish to make clear at the outset that my own interpretation of his work will be found in the following sections: Chapter I; Chapter II, Section C; Chapter IV; Chapter VIII; Chapter IX; Chapter X, Section D; Chapter XII, Section A; Chapter XIII, Section C; Chapter XIV. And following Chapter XIV, "A Contemporary Perspective," I have added to this edition a summary restatement that seeks to place Weber's work—on the basis of the interpretation offered here—in the context of European intellectual history. In this respect, much more needs to be done than I have attempted, but it seemed appropriate to round out my presentation with a statement of this kind. Since I have entitled this new concluding chapter "Max Weber's Image of Society," which was originally the title of Chapter VIII, I have changed the title of Chapter VIII in this edition to "Max Weber's Sociology of Religion."

Everything not specifically referred to in the preceding paragraph is an exposition of Weber's own work (except for occasional explanatory comments that I have attempted to label clearly as my own).

MAX WEBER

CHAPTER I

CAREER AND PERSONAL ORIENTATION

Max Weber was born in 1864. His father, who came from a family of textile manufacturers in western Germany, was a well-to-do lawyer and National-liberal parliamentarian in the Germany of Bismarck; his mother was a woman of culture and piety whose humanitarian and religious interests were not shared by her husband.[1] Weber spent most of the first twenty-nine years of his life in his parents' house, which was a meeting place for both prominent liberal politicians and celebrated professors from the University of Berlin. After completing school in 1882, he attended the University of Heidelberg, where he was enrolled as a law student. A year later, at the age of nineteen, he went to Strasbourg to serve his year of military training, and he returned to the army for briefer periods of military exercises in 1885, 1887, and 1888. After two more years at the universities of Berlin and Göttingen, he took his examination in law in 1886, while continuing his studies at Berlin.

His independent academic work began in the fields of law and legal history. In his doctoral dissertation, entitled *A Contribution to the History of Medieval Business Organizations* (1889), he examined the various legal principles according

[1] For further biographical details, cf. the perceptive sketch in *Essays*, pp. 3–31. The major source is the biography written by Marianne Weber.

to which the cost, risk or profit of an enterprise were to be borne jointly by several individuals. After completing this dissertation Weber started the in-service training required for the German bench or bar. During this training (and also as a reserve officer on temporary duty), he became acquainted at first hand with the social and political problems of agrarian society in the provinces east of the Elbe River. At the same time he began a study of legal institutions, which was formally to qualify him as an instructor in law at the University of Berlin. This second work was his *Roman Agrarian History and its Significance for Public and Private Law* (1891). By examining the methods of land surveying in Roman society, the different terms used to designate the resulting land units, and the extant writings on agriculture by Roman authors, Weber analyzed the social, political and economic developments of Roman society.

While completing this study, he prepared himself for his duties as a *Privatdozent* in Roman, German and commercial law at the University of Berlin. He also undertook an extensive investigation of rural labor in the German provinces east of the Elbe, which led to the publication of a 900-page volume in 1892, and he investigated the stock exchange. As full-time lecturer, consultant to government agencies, and researcher he carried an enormous burden. He was no doubt referring to this period when he wrote some years later of his "need to feel crushed under the load of work." In 1893 he married Marianne Schnitger and at last left the house of his parents. In the fall of 1894 he became full professor of economics at Freiburg University, where in 1895 he delivered his inaugural lecture on "The National State and Economic Policy." In 1896 he accepted a position at the University of Heidelberg.

In the fall of 1897, when he was thirty-three, Weber fell ill and was forced to reduce and finally to suspend his regular academic work. For four years he suffered from an acute state of exhaustion and anxiety. Even small diversions proved too taxing at times, and this apparently vigorous man would sit for hours at the window, staring into space. Travel eventually proved to be one of the activities he could enjoy, and for major parts of this period he lived in Italy, especially in Rome. After almost four years he seemed to recover gradually and resumed his habit of omnivorous reading. Some of it was concerned with the history, organization and economic activities of medieval monasteries. The literature on this subject apparently provided one starting point for his subsequent studies of the relation between religious beliefs and economic activity.[2]

In the years of his recovery, from about 1901 on, Weber returned to his scholarly work despite many temporary setbacks. In 1903 he accepted a position as associate editor of the *Archiv für Sozialwissenschaft und Sozialpolitik* (Archives for Social Science and Social Welfare) and through this position renewed his contacts with the academic world. There were negotiations for a renewed offer of a professorship at Heidelberg, but in the end Weber felt unable to take the position. In 1904 he accepted an invitation to visit the United States and participate in the Congress of Arts and Sciences held in connection with the World's Fair at St. Louis. In the same year the first results of his resumed scholarly activity were published: an essay on methodology, a discussion of agrarian policies in eastern Germany, and *The Protestant Ethic and the Spirit of Capitalism*. Despite his inability to resume regular academic duties, the University of Heidelberg, in cooperation with the Ministry of Education, made a generous financial arrangement with him, but in 1907 a private inheritance enabled him to terminate this burdensome, part-time association and to live as a private scholar. For the remainder of his life he engaged in intense and wide-ranging scientific activity, which was disrupted only during World War I when he served for a time as director of the army hospitals in Heidelberg. In 1918 he became a consultant to the German Armistice Commission in Versailles and to a commission charged with the drafting of the Weimar Constitution. In the summer of that year he also taught at the University of Vienna and in 1919 he accepted an offer from the University of Munich. In June, 1920, he died of pneumonia at the age of fifty-six.

This bare outline of Weber's career is relevant to an understanding of his scholarly work if we inquire into the extraordinary tensions that characterized his life and that would have

[2] A reflection of this reading may be found in *WuG*, Vol. II, pp. 786–88.

incapacitated a lesser man. An attack of meningitis at the age of four, the stimulating environment of his family, and a predilection for books made him withdraw from his contemporaries early in life and resist the routine schooling offered by his teachers. Repelled by both the Victorian complacency of his father and the strong personal piety of his mother, he developed into a precocious student who wrote historical essays at the age of thirteen, adopted systematic study habits a year or so later, and created for himself a world of the mind in which he tested his rapidly growing intellectual strength in the assimilation and critical appraisal of historical and philosophical writings. But when he went to the University of Heidelberg at the age of eighteen, he quickly adopted the way of life of a German fraternity with its dueling, drinking bouts, and coarsely Romantic conviviality. Without neglecting his studies, he turned from a slender, withdrawn adolescent into a large, pompously virile young man—so pompous and so virile that his mother could not hide her repugnance.

This ambivalence between withdrawal and forceful participation also was apparent in Weber's deliberations concerning his future career. Toward the end of his studies he felt increasingly oppressed by his financial dependence on his father, and he prepared for an academic career primarily in the hope of gaining his independence more quickly. But other feelings were expressed in his statement:

> I am quite clear that I would never leave the life of practical experience since I know now that I could achieve something in this line, which is by no means certain in the case of an academic career. . . .

Thus, shortly before his first academic appointment, he applied for a legal position with the municipal government of Bremen because of his "extraordinary longing for a practical job." Though he had made a reputation as a scholar by the age of twenty-seven, and at twenty-nine had the definite prospect of a brilliant academic career, he wrote at that time:

> I am not really a scholar after all; scientific activity is for me primarily an occupation for the leisure hours. . . . The feeling of being active in a practical way is entirely indis-

pensable for me, and I hope that the pedagogic side of the teaching profession will satisfy this craving. . . .[3]

Weber chose an academic career but he held a regular academic position for only five years (1893–97). At thirty-three his severe psychopathological condition forced him to abandon his duties despite determined efforts to continue on a part-time basis. After his partial recovery in 1901 Weber made occasional attempts to return to academic life. But his wife's description of the psychological turmoil to which he deliberately subjected himself, when toward the end of his life he accepted a professorship at the University of Munich, is not only pathetic evidence of Weber's will-power but also a clear indication of his lifelong disability despite his impressive scholarly output.

The craving for practical activity and the inability to cope with the duties of an academic career was only one of the many paradoxes which marked Weber's life. Though he was a dedicated German nationalist, he considered for a time the possibility of emigration. In 1903, while negotiations with the University of Heidelberg were in progress, he went on six separate trips abroad. This indicates not only how difficult it was for Weber formally to terminate his academic career but also how such trips provided an escape from the country he loved. Unable to submit to academic routine, he nevertheless developed a rigorous ethic for the teaching profession and an unusual pedagogic intensity in his occasional relations with students. Committed as few others were to the exclusion of political value judgments from academic teaching, he nevertheless endowed his lectures with such passion that they bespoke a partisanship for impartiality. Though he was extraordinarily sensitive in his relations with others, his outlook on life was concerned with the pursuit of power. Unable to engage in the practical activity which he craved and unfit to serve in the German Army during World War I, he nevertheless thought of himself as a man predestined for political life and the military virtues. In his intellectual concern with the

[3] See Marianne Weber, *Max Weber* (Heidelberg: Lambert Schneider, 1950), pp. 188–92, for this and the preceding quotation from personal letters.

problem of power, Weber was detached and profoundly unconventional, yet he adhered throughout his life to many of the conventional beliefs of his class in imperial Germany. And his preoccupation with the struggle for power among nations went hand in hand with a rigorously puritanical ethic in his own personal affairs.

Many of these contradictions were reflected in Weber's style of writing. Not only long, involved sentences but qualifying phrases and digressions served him as a safeguard against the simple declarative sentence. This was not so much the mannerism of the German scholar as the necessary device of a man of tremendous learning, for whom every generalization was a precarious victory over the infinite complexity of facts. Yet this master of the qualified phrase and the dependent clause also was capable of writing or speaking in a terse and decisive manner and could say of himself that "heaven in its wrath" had endowed him with the "gift of a certain bluntness which was difficult to suppress."[4] The same contradiction appears in Weber's political participation. The positions he took in his political writings were bold and unequivocal. His essays contain, among other things, a very realistic assessment of the role of the politician. But when it came to Weber's own political participation this decisiveness did not carry over. In 1918 he had an opportunity to be nominated for election to the National Assembly, but he refused to make any effort in his own behalf and consequently lost the nomination. A year later his wife suggested to him that the nation would yet call upon him, and he answered: "Yes, I have the feeling as if life has still withheld something from me."[5] This suggestion and reply, together with Weber's actions, can mean only that he would not become active politically unless he were called upon to play the role of the great leader and statesman. In short, he continuously engaged in the simultaneous effort to be a man of science with the strenuous vigor more common in a man of action, and to be a man of action with all the ethical rigor and personal detachment more common in a man of science.

In this effort one may see a reflection of tendencies in Ger-

[4] *GAzSuS*, p. 406.

[5] See Marianne Weber, *op. cit.*, p. 723. Weber's withdrawal from political participation is described in *ibid.*, pp. 257–59, 692–94.

man society at large. If Tocqueville could say that as a born aristocrat and lover of freedom he was able to look calmly upon the decline of his class and to see clearly the danger to freedom in the rising tide of democracy, Weber might have said that as a "lone wolf" born into a liberal, middle-class family in late nineteenth-century Germany he saw both the decline of liberalism in an emerging power-state and the threat to the individual in the bureaucratization of modern society. As a witness of Bismarck's unification of Germany and the virtual elimination of the liberal, middle-class movements from positions of political influence, Weber became convinced that great goals could be achieved only by power politics. For the rest of his life he set a premium upon examining political life without illusions, looking at it as a struggle between individuals and groups with conflicting beliefs and interests, always decided in the end by the reservoir of power available to the winning side and by its greater ability to use that power effectively. Possibly this view was encouraged by the vicarious power-orientation that Bismarck had imparted to German liberalism. But it was also strongly sustained by Weber's own passionate quest for action and for proving his strength and his convictions in daily life.

German liberalism contained a strong belief in the importance of the individual. That belief had found its consummate expression in the German classical literature of the late eighteenth century, and the concern with humanistic learning and cultivation of the personality had remained a characteristic of the educated middle class. The political defeat of this class, especially in 1848 and in the Bismarck *Reich,* gave still greater importance to these cultural preoccupations. With the unification of Germany and the predominance of the bureaucracy, the army, and the *Junkers,* one also could observe a humanistic adumbration of the code of conduct among the Prussian ruling class. The duties of deference to the higher ranks, hardness to oneself, and paternal benevolence and strictness to those below were frequently idealized in terms of honor, conscience, service to the nation, and so forth. Weber's friend and colleague, Ernst Troeltsch, put it very succinctly when he wrote:

The political thought of Germany is marked by a curious dilemma. . . . Look at one of its sides, and you will see an abundance of remnants of Romanticism and lofty idealism; look at the other, and you will see a realism which goes to the verge of cynicism and of utter indifference to all ideals and all morality. But what you will see above all is an inclination to make an astonishing combination of the two elements—in a word, to brutalize romance, and to romanticize cynicism.[6]

Thus, the power-orientation of the educated blended with the humanistic orientation of the powerful, with the result that human relations were endowed with an emotional appreciation of personal values; personal choices, with the rigidity of ultimate moral decisions; and political issues, with a mixture of "brutality and romance."

Weber reflected this climate of opinion. As his wife tells it in her biography, he showed throughout his life an extraordinary appreciation for the problems other people faced and for the shades of mood and meaning that characterized their outlook on life. Men as divergent as the revolutionary poet Ernst Toller and the liberal monarchist Friedrich Naumann sought his counsel and guidance. Upon festive as well as tragic occasions, in his circle of friends and relatives Weber would express understanding and emotional warmth in his effort to discover the larger meaning in the life of each person. In his period of military training as well as on his many travels abroad, he showed a great facility in communicating with people in many walks of life, speaking in terms each could understand and spicing his conversations with a human touch and a fund of anecdotes. Yet for the greater part of his life this same man was incapacitated from active participation in his chosen career, too withdrawn to express his personal feelings to others, as he himself stated time and again, and painfully difficult through his uncompromising insistence upon rigid moral and intellectual standards, ostensibly applied to himself alone but inevitably a tacit accusation against all who did not

[6] Ernst Troeltsch, "The Ideas of Natural Law and Humanity in World Politics," in Otto Gierke, *Natural Law and the Theory of Society* (Boston: The Beacon Press, 1957), p. 214.

live up to them. There is more than a little suggestion in Weber's life that his humanity found expression primarily in personal contacts outside his professional and political preoccupations, while the application of his rigid standards in the context of academic and political life helped exclude him from the active participation he consciously sought.

Whatever its psychological significance, the duality of his humanistic values and his orientation toward power was of major significance for Weber as a sociologist and a social historian. This perspective was the common property of German liberalism. It had found perhaps its consummate expression in Theodor Mommsen's *Roman History,* which had stripped the humanistic halo from the ancient world and combined a realistic history of group conflict with a celebration of Caesar as the personal embodiment of statesmanship and reason. But whereas Mommsen did not hesitate to use the language of nineteenth-century party struggles for his interpretation of Roman history, Weber gradually developed the same perspective into an image of society and a set of sociological categories, which he used in his world-wide comparative studies of religion and political organization.

I want to add a word concerning the moral dimensions of this scholarly work. Weber was preoccupied throughout his career with the development of rationalism in Western civilization. His lifetime study of this development revealed not only the complexity of its antecedents, but the precariousness of its achievements. He left no doubt that his profound personal commitment to the cause of reason and freedom had guided his choice of subject matter; and his research left no doubt that reason and freedom in the Western world were in jeopardy. Weber was a contemporary of Freud, whose lifework consisted in safeguarding man's reason after comprehending in full measure the depth of man's irrationality. Similarly, Weber sought to safeguard the great legacy of the Enlightenment after fully exploring the historical preconditions of that legacy. This exploration created in him a tragic consciousness of peril. When asked for the purpose of his scholarly research, Weber answered: "I want to see how much I can stand."[7]

[7] Marianne Weber, *op. cit.,* p. 731. Cf. also Weber's pessimistic prophecies in *Essays,* pp. 71–72.

From this vantage point his frequently crude German nationalism may appear, not only as an acceptance of the conventional opinions of his day, but also as an acceptance of Germany's historic mission in defending Western civilization against the Russian menace.[8] Yet Weber also combined this nationalism with a fundamental commitment to the study of non-European cultures whose basic assumptions made sense and had value in their own terms.

It is appropriate to begin with a consideration of the early investigations in which Weber defined the problems which were to occupy him during a lifetime of scholarly work. These studies were steeped in the problematics of imperial Germany at the turn of the century. One of Weber's most remarkable achievements was that he identified himself fully with these issues of German society but that he transcended their limitations by seeing them as incidents in a world-wide perspective. This combination of commitment and detachment was yet another aspect of the personal and intellectual tensions that marred his life and made it creative.

[8] This at least is the conclusion Weber reached in responding to the German defeat in World War I. See Marianne Weber, *op. cit.*, pp. 625–26, 685. Since the line which presently divides West and East Germany coincides with the line that divided the Slavic from the Germanic tribes at the time of Charlemagne more than a thousand years ago, Weber's nationalist views are perhaps easier to understand today than formerly.

PART ONE

GERMAN SOCIETY
AND
THE PROTESTANT ETHIC

CHAPTER II

WEBER'S EARLY STUDIES AND THE DEFINITION OF HIS INTELLECTUAL PERSPECTIVE

During the last decades of the nineteenth century, the major agricultural interest groups as well as leading politicians and scholars became concerned with the agricultural problem of eastern Germany. From 1865 to 1879 Germany had had a free-trade policy in grain with the full support of the land-owners. By the early seventies protectionist sentiment increased as American and Russian grain exports mounted and falling prices on the world market had an adverse effect on the sale of German grain. In 1879 tariffs were imposed for the first time, and they were increased in 1885 and 1887. Along with protection came intensified cultivation and a shift to better-paying cash crops. These changes in production methods on the large estates of eastern Germany led to a decrease in German farm laborers through migration and an increase in foreign migratory workers. To German nationalists this seemed a major threat to German, if not to European, civilization. Plans of "internal colonization" were proposed, whereby the government would finance the settlement of German peasants in the threatened border areas as a barrier against the Slavic "invasion," even though such a policy was acknowledged to be unsound economically. This situation was aggravated by the landowners (*Junkers*) themselves, who were outspoken nationalists, who stood for protection and opposed "internal colonization" where it involved the subdivision of large estates, but who also caused German farm laborers to be replaced by foreign migratory workers on their own estates.

The agrarian problem was related to a controversy over the stock exchange. Prominent conservatives had expressed the view that anyone engaged in transactions on the exchange was likely to be a swindler—an accusation linked explicitly with the anti-Semitic agitation of the period. In many agrarian circles it was widely believed, moreover, that trading in grain futures facilitated the importation of foreign grains and tended to depress farm prices. In view of this controversy, the German Chancellor appointed a commission of inquiry, which in 1893 issued a report containing a series of proposals for the reform of the stock and commodity exchanges. Yet the political agitation continued, the anti-capitalist sentiment of the landowners sometimes merging with the less powerful but equally vociferous anti-capitalist orientation of the socialists. The result was that from 1896 until 1908 trading in grain futures on the commodity exchange in Berlin was prohibited.[1]

A. THE INVESTIGATION OF AGRARIAN SOCIETY AND THE STOCK EXCHANGE

(1) The problem of farm labor was made the object of a large-scale inquiry by the *Verein für Sozialpolitik*, an association of scholars, government officials and other specialists interested in investigating current social problems and promoting reforms through legislation. In 1890 the association decided to send out a lengthy questionnaire to more than three thousand landowners in southwest, western, northern and eastern Germany.[2] Weber assumed responsibility for evaluating

[1] During this twelve-year period the Berlin grain merchants organized themselves as a private association. But trading in grain futures under legal handicaps resulted in adverse economic consequences for German agriculture.

[2] Upon inquiry the names of these landowners had been supplied by the several regional employers' associations. The detailed questionnaire, dealing with all phases of the rural labor problem, was

the returns from the German provinces east of the Elbe River. To appreciate the significance of the results he derived, it will be helpful to summarize the conclusions of the entire investigation.[3]

In the west, labor relations de-emphasized the status distinctions among different classes of peasants and farm laborers to such an extent that the latter had little sense of their legal dependence. In Westphalia, for example, so-called "hirelings" rented a piece of land and a small cottage in exchange for working a certain number of days at reduced wages on the land of independent peasants with medium-sized holdings. The hirelings worked shoulder to shoulder with their employers, they ate at the same table, their children attended the same school, and in language and local custom there was no distinction between them. To be sure, intermarriage between the two groups rarely occurred, since it involved the inheritance of property. But aside from that the Westphalian hirelings did not have the consciousness of wage laborers. Their families had occupied the same position for generations. They were able to supplement their income by domestic work or seasonal farm labor in Holland, and these additional earnings made tenancy appear more advantageous than ownership. As a result, the hirelings had a status-consciousness of their own, despite the notable differences in ownership and income between themselves and their employers.

In Lower Saxony (between the Weser and Elbe rivers) on the other hand, the rural population lived in settled villages next to medium-sized estates that depended upon the village population for their seasonal labor requirements. Social dif-

---

sent out to 3,180 landowners, and 2,277 completed questionnaires were returned. Supplementary questionnaires calling for a more general assessment of labor relations in agriculture were sent out to 562 landowners; of these, 291 were returned. Spokesmen for the *Verein* readily admitted the bias of this sample, but they appear to have been justified in claiming that the results of the inquiry were valuable despite this bias.

[3] See G. F. Knapp, "Die Ländliche Arbeiterfrage," in *Verhandlungen von 1893* (Vol. LVIII of *Schriften des Vereins für Sozialpolitik* [Berlin: Duncker & Humblot, 1893]), pp. 6–23. This lecture summarized the four volumes that had been published in preparation of the convention.

ferentiation in these villages was considerable, ranging from well-to-do peasants to cottagers who had no land of their own. But even the day laborers did not constitute a rural proletariat. Each of them was a permanent resident of the village, who for all his poverty possessed certain rights (e.g., of property in his cottage, of grazing, etc.) that freed him from complete dependence upon wage labor and enabled him to participate fully in the social life of the village community.

This simplified description of labor relations west of the Elbe suggests that a labor problem did not arise where the rural labor force was derived from long-settled tenant farmers or from a stratified but settled village population. In the provinces east of the Elbe the situation was very different. In the west small and medium-sized holdings predominated, while east of the Elbe very small farms and huge estates were the prevailing pattern.[4] In the west, self-employed peasants were in the majority; in the east there was a predominance of day laborers.[5] In addition, the land in the east sustained fewer persons than in the west.

In turning his attention to the labor problem east of the Elbe, Weber noted that throughout this area—and despite many local variations—the rural work force was divided into two categories:[6] those hired by the landowner on the basis of annual contracts and those hired by the day. The former

[4] In 1882, for example, 1.3 per cent of the number of farms occupied 44 per cent of the agricultural area on estates of 100 hectares and more in the eastern provinces (1 hectare = 2.47 acres). In the western provinces, 0.2 per cent of the number of farms occupied only 11.8 per cent of the agricultural area on estates of 100 hectares and more. Also, only 15 per cent of the land was distributed among farms of 10 hectares or less in the east, whereas 33 per cent of the land was so distributed in the west. Cf. Max Sering, *Die innere Kolonisation im östlichen Deutschland* (Vol. LVI of *Schriften des Vereins für Sozialpolitik* [Berlin: Duncker & Humblot, 1893], p. 24). For comparable later figures and a contemporary evaluation of this problem, cf. Alexander Gerschenkron, *Bread and Democracy in Germany* (Berkeley: University of California Press, 1943).

[5] Cf. Sering, *op. cit.*, p. 284.

[6] The following account is based on Max Weber, *Die Verhältnisse der Landarbeiter im ostelbischen Deutschland* (Vol. LV of *Schriften des Vereins für Sozialpolitik* [Berlin: Duncker & Humblot, 1892]). Cited below as *Verhältnisse der Landarbeiter*. Titles cited without author always refer to writings of Max Weber.

reflected the mixture of serfdom and freedom that was a legacy from the past; the latter were indistinguishable from wage laborers in industry. The principal emphasis of Weber's analysis was to indicate the process by which day laborers were gradually replacing the half-servile peasantry on the large landed estates of the east. This led him step by step from the study of agrarian society to an interpretation of the social structure of imperial Germany.

Since rural labor had been placed on a contractual basis by the reforms of the early nineteenth century, the estates had come to depend for their year-round needs upon the farm laborers on annual contract, while seasonal needs were met by the day laborers. The laborers on annual contract were legally free, but they enjoyed a degree of security not usually encountered in wage contracts. There were unmarried domestic servants who lived and ate their meals in special quarters on the estate and received in addition a stipulated annual wage. Bailiffs and other managerial personnel lived in separate quarters with their families and, instead of meals, received certain allowances in kind, in addition to some land, a few head of cattle, and an annual wage. A third category of farm laborers was frequently employed under similar conditions: annual wage, grazing privileges, and a piece of land, as well as a stipulated allowance in kind. The characteristic feature of these rural laborers was their quasi-salaried status: the annual wage and the various allowances in kind were not subject to fluctuations. Among the workers on annual contract the so-called *Instleute* (here called "attached laborers") were a category apart; during the nineteenth century they represented the most characteristic type of quasi-servile labor on the estates in the east. In many ways they worked under conditions similar to those just mentioned. An annual contract was concluded with the whole family, not the individual. And like other workers on annual contract, the attached laborers were entitled to a cottage on the estate and to a payment partly in money and partly in kind. These payments were not fixed, however, and they were associated with special liabilities. All the workers in the family of an attached laborer were obliged to render services on the estate, or to hire and pay a day laborer in order to meet this obligation.[7] This was the only form of wage payment they received, and it was paid at a rate below the local average for comparable services. Since the attached laborers could not live on their wage earnings alone, they supplemented their income through allowances in kind. For most of the winter they were entitled to do the threshing, for which they received a certain portion of the yield. This portion varied greatly in the several regions of the east, and its absolute size also depended on the total yield of the estate in each year. But in many areas the worker's portion constituted a considerable part of his total earnings, which frequently left a surplus over consumption that could be sold on the market.

These conditions of farm labor on the large estates in the east reflected the legacies of serfdom and patriarchal rule. Labor under annual contract for a fixed amount recalled an earlier condition when the landlord was obligated to support his serfs throughout the year. In the case of the attached laborers, this retention of old forms was especially important. Theirs was not an ordinary *work contract*, because on the estate the employer exercised not only proprietary but also administrative authority, and during the summer he could still make unilateral and unlimited demands upon the services of the laborer and his family. On the other hand, the agreement was not a *wage contract* either, because the attached laborer was entitled to a portion of the produce and hence participated directly in the total earnings of the estate. This pattern of labor relations involved obligations as well as privileges for the landlord, and it established a certain community of interest between the worker and his employer, though it also subjected the former to the arbitrary will of the latter.

In analyzing the several provinces east of the Elbe, Weber showed in detail that these quasi-servile, quasi-contractual labor relations had been increasingly superseded by free labor. This shift resulted from the more intensive utilization of the land, together with the greater emphasis on better-paying cash

[7] This type of wage labor, especially in the summer months, had superseded the earlier obligation to work on the estate without compensation. Similarly, the cottage of the attached laborer had been freely let in partial return for his obligatory services; subsequently the cottage was rented to him instead.

crops, which made the hiring of day laborers more advantageous.[8] These workers were not subject to the administrative and police authority of the estate owners, since they were not legally resident in the estate district. Unlike the workers on annual contract, the day laborers were hired as individuals, and their interests conflicted with those of their employers. They were interested in maximum wages and low prices so as to increase their real income; they did not depend upon, and hence took no interest in, the profitability of the estates on which they worked.

The increased employment of day laborers had not occurred uniformly throughout the provinces east of the Elbe, but depended to a large extent upon the degree to which an individual estate could be adapted to a commercialized type of agriculture, which in turn depended upon the availability of capital. The end result of these changes had been that patriarchal labor relations were still dominant in the northeast, while toward the southeast they had been increasingly replaced by wage contracts with day laborers.

Weber emphasized that the capitalist transformation of labor relations in eastern Germany had tended to depress the workers' standard of living, especially in Silesia, and he pointed to the frequent employment of women, the barracks-like living quarters of day laborers and their families, and their lack of wage supplements in the form of truck gardening or a few head of cattle. This proletarization of rural laborers was aggravated because the employers resorted to the employment of Polish and Russian migrants—a preference due only in part to the foreigners' willingness to work for lower wages, since their productivity also was lower than that of German workers. Polish and Russian workers were obedient because of their precarious status. They also were strictly seasonal laborers who could be forced back across the frontier, relieving their employers of the burden of any financial or administrative obligations.

The German workers were more demanding than the migrants in regard to nutrition and conditions of work, and be-

[8] Also, mechanization militated against the workers on annual contract and the diet of the workers deteriorated. Weber's analysis of these and other factors is quite detailed.

cause of these higher demands they lost out in the competition
with Poles and Russians. As a nationalist, Weber viewed these
facts with alarm. Existing conditions were destroyed without
being replaced by something new of equal value; indeed, the
higher civilization of the Germans was being jeopardized by
these inroads from the barbarian east.[9] Weber was unequivocal in this evaluation, yet these political judgments are of less
interest here than his scholarly analysis. He attributed the
transformation of agriculture in eastern Germany to the pressure of changing conditions on the world market. The declining number of laborers on annual contract and the corresponding increase in the number of day laborers was certainly a
response to economic conditions. The take-home pay of day
laborers was frequently higher in the short run than that of
the farm workers on annual contract, since the latter were partially remunerated by allowances in kind, which depended
upon the year-to-year productivity of the estate and which
could be affected adversely by price fluctuations. Nevertheless, the number of vacancies for laborers on annual contract
was declining because day laborers were not a fixed cost for
the landowners. However, the trend away from annual contracts could not be attributed to economic considerations alone.

Weber noted especially that these different groups of farm
workers did not have the same opportunities for social mobility. Attached laborers, for example, usually started as young
servants on an estate, where they were furnished with all ne-
cessities and where their very modest wages were, therefore,
a net surplus. These servants were completely subject to the
arbitrary whims of their master. As helpers on his estate they
were secure and well nourished, and their personal subservience occurred during the transitional period of their youth.
Eventually, they would save enough to marry, buy a cow,
seeds, furniture, and set themselves up as attached laborers in

[9] Weber used a figure of 33,000 migratory workers from Russia
and Poland in four of the eastern provinces, for the year 1891. This
was 1/24 the number of day laborers employed in agriculture.
Though really comparable figures for a later year are not available,
in 1907 there were about 215,000 foreign day laborers employed
in agriculture, or approximately 1/14 of the total number of day laborers and domestic servants in agriculture. *Statistik des Deutschen
Reichs,* Vol. 211 (1913), p. 86 ff.

their own right with a relatively good income and considerable security. They also might use their savings to set themselves up as farm laborers or, if they were especially good workers, even as bailiffs, and thus be independent of market fluctuations. Weber observed that the experience of the children in a family of farm laborers on annual contract was an appropriate preparation for such a career. The household of such families constituted a small, if dependent, farmstead in itself and as such provided the young people with experience in running a farmstead and possibly also with a proprietary disposition. To be sure, this was as far as the available opportunities would carry children of farm laborers on annual contract; moreover, such opportunities were contingent upon the quality of the soil and hence on the productivity of the estates in an area. But in long-run economic terms these prospects compared quite favorably with those of the day laborers.

Being entirely dependent upon wage earnings, a day laborer would reach his maximum earnings by the time he was thirty. After that he could look forward only to a gradually decreasing income. An exception might be those day laborers (the reports on this did not allow clear-cut conclusions) who somehow managed to put away enough savings to become tenant farmers, though the small size of their holdings would make their economic position precarious. But generally, day laborers did not or could not save enough to become tenant farmers, and their subjective disposition made them in any case disinclined as well as ill-prepared to do so. For as wage laborers their economic interests favored high wages and low prices, in direct conflict with the interests of their employers. And, after having accepted this class-conscious orientation of the proletariat, the day laborers would not be likely to make tenant farming their long-term goal, even aside from the fact that their work experience would have done little to qualify them for running a farmstead of their own.

Thus the long-run opportunities, the security, and the diet of attached laborers might well be better than the corresponding opportunities of day laborers. Yet these material advantages did not change the fact that laborers on annual contract were directly subject to the arbitrary commands of the landlord at the same time that they shared some of his interests,

and everywhere the trend was away from the personal subjection:

> Domestic servants flee the household of the master. Thresh-
> ers want to sever their close tie-in with the economy of the
> estate. The laborer on annual contract relinquishes his se-
> cure position, in order to make his precarious way as a "free"
> day laborer. The peasant with very little land would rather
> starve than accept a job and work for someone else. In-
> numerable workers prefer to pay any price to a jobber for
> a piece of land and to live in abject dependence on creditors
> who charge usurious interest-rates, all this for the sake of
> the "self-dependence" which they crave, i.e. for the sake
> of independence from personal subservience to a master.[10]

Many of the best laborers on annual contract decided to emi-
grate rather than remain in their subservient position, even
when their earnings were comparatively ample.[11] Also, attached laborers turned to day labor because it meant an easier
life. As long as their livelihood depended upon the yield of
the estate and high prices for their surplus products, they had
to worry about the weather and the world market or the threat
of disease in the cattle. Paid by the day, they were free of
these worries.

Weber thought that this individualism reflected the purely
psychological fascination of freedom. Strictly economic considerations were secondary in the face of such fundamental
tendencies.

> It is pointless to argue about such elementary movements,
> which give expression to the tremendous and purely psy-
> chological magic of "freedom." In good measure this is a
> grand illusion, but after all man and so also the farm la-

---

[10] *Verhältnisse der Landarbeiter*, p. 797.

[11] Weber noted also that in the western provinces the hirelings
regarded their work on the land of a peasant-proprietor as a neighborly act for which an appropriate recompense would be forthcom-
ing. These men would think that they had sold themselves, if even
entirely regular work of this kind was to be regarded as a permanent
obligation of personal service. Psychologically, these farm laborers
worked as independent men, even if in fact they worked as employees. Cf. "Die ländliche Arbeitsverfassung," *GAzSuW*, p. 445.

borers do not live "by bread alone." The efforts and aspirations of the farm laborers make just this evident to us, that the "bread and butter question" is of secondary importance.[12]

As Weber saw it, the basic drive on the part of the farm laborers was not for a change in labor relations or for a piece of land, but for the possibility of upward social mobility. The traditional labor relations on the large estates east of the Elbe had put a ceiling on the aspirations of the workers: they could become laborers on annual contract (in one of its many forms), but that was the limit of what they could expect. From the viewpoint of the workers, therefore, the principal rural problem was how that ceiling could be lifted to enable them to obtain an independent economic existence. Among the farm laborers of eastern Germany, it was this individualism rather than the nominal collectivism of the Social Democrats that was casting its spell. And this subjective disposition led to demands for wages and working conditions that not only were incompatible with traditional labor relations but prevented German workers from competing effectively with the migratory workers from Russia and Poland. By their demands and expectations the German farm laborers were manifesting their cultural superiority, in Weber's view, yet they were clearly inferior in the economic struggle for survival. In his examination of the conditions on the estates in eastern Germany, Weber analyzed these changing labor relations as a symptom of far-reaching changes in German society as a whole. But before presenting this broader interpretation, it is appropriate to consider his analysis of the stock exchange.

(2) The stock exchange had become a symbol of the iniquity of capitalism in the political agitation of the 1890's. Weber wrote a series of technical articles dealing with its economic and legal aspects. He also wrote a tract for the times that was specifically designed to provide the layman with basic factual information on the operation of this institution, to oppose the widespread view that "the stock exchange was a sort of league among conspirators engaged in fraud and deception

[12] *Verhältnisse der Landarbeiter*, pp. 797–98.

at the expense of the honest working people and hence had best be abolished in some fashion or other."[13]

Two aspects of Weber's general treatment need to be reviewed briefly. First, stock exchanges and commodity exchanges are simply market centers for the sale and purchase of capital and commodities. On such markets trading in standardized articles is tremendously facilitated because it no longer depends upon the owner, the producer, or their sales agents to find customers for the finished product. The commodity exchanges in particular involve transactions concerning goods that are in transit or still to be produced. And these transactions typically occur between sellers who do not have the commodities on hand, but who seek to obtain them at a profit to themselves once the sale is completed, and buyers who do not want the commodities themselves, but who attempt to sell them at a profit before the date of delivery and payment.[14] The number of sellers and buyers at both ends of such deals, and hence the number of transactions involving the same quantity of goods (or stocks and bonds), can, and frequently do, pyramid rapidly. By this mechanism it is possible to handle a tremendously enlarged volume of trade (and of credit).

Second, stock and commodity exchanges represent the means by which the individual businessman can attain the legitimate ends of his enterprise with foresight and planning. Weber criticizes the popular idea that the exchanges are only places where sudden spectacular profits or losses result from lucky or unlucky guesses about price fluctuations in the future. He points out, for example, that in international trade a time bargain (*Zeitgeschäft*) serves the purpose of guaranteeing to the businessman a definite rate of exchange at which he can purchase the foreign currency he needs to consummate his transaction at a stipulated date in the future.[15] Weber recognized, of course, that gambling and wild speculation did play a role on the exchanges, but such devices as time bargains and trading in futures (*Termingeschäft*) served entirely indispensable purposes of the modern economy in the sense that

---

[13] "Die Börse," *GAzSuS*, p. 256. This essay was published in 1894.
[14] *Ibid.*, pp. 260–62.
[15] "Die Börse," *op. cit.*, p. 308.

they enlarged the volume of trade and facilitated the orderly conduct of large-scale enterprises.

The reforms debated in the 1890's were concerned with legal controls of the exchanges that would prevent the abuse of these devices without interfering with their legitimate purpose. The regulation of admissions of members to the exchanges was a major topic of this debate, and this issue makes Weber's technical discussion relevant in the present context. From markets open to all at an earlier time, some modern exchanges had developed into centers of trade monopolized by exclusive, guildlike associations of brokers. This was a natural tendency even where access to the exchange was formally open to all, because the ordinary person generally lacked the professional knowledge of the market and the credit rating of the brokers that was necessary for a successful operation. Possession of such knowledge constituted a kind of natural privilege. Weber noted that in England and America admissions to the stock exchange were handled in a different manner from the German and Austrian practice. The English exchanges especially were exclusive private associations, which were governed autonomously in accordance with their own statutes. Admissions to the exchange were similar in principle to admissions to an exclusive club, involving such rules as annual reapplication of members, high admission fees, substantial financial guarantees by members in good standing for a new applicant, and so on. The guildlike character of these associations was especially pronounced where, as in Glasgow, the sons of members were entitled to admission on payment of half the regular fee or where members were forbidden to engage in commercial activities other than transactions on the exchange. Indeed, the transactions themselves were in effect regulated by the rules of the association rather than by the civil jurisdiction of the national government, as, for example, in the London Stock Exchange. Hence, practices regarded as questionable or any violation of these rules would be subject to penalties ranging from disciplinary measures to formal exclusion from the exchange. Thus all persons admitted to the exchange were subject to an autonomous, private jurisdiction in all matters affecting transactions on the stock exchange. This procedure made the legal prohibition of certain transactions on the exchange supernumerary and, indeed, precluded the jurisdiction of the ordinary courts.[16]

In Germany the stock exchanges as well as the several commodity exchanges presented a less uniform picture. Of the many details that Weber surveyed on the basis of the official inquiry, it is sufficient for present purposes to single out one major feature. The government of the German exchanges was for the most part in the hands of chambers of commerce whose officials were elected by merchants, by members of the community, or by both, in accordance with legal regulations that favored those well provided with capital. Otherwise, conditions varied widely among the exchanges. In the old Hanseatic towns admission to and transactions on the exchanges were almost entirely free. In Hamburg regulations were confined to the maintenance of order on the exchange, and disputes were handled by arbitration at the instance of the contending parties, under the auspices of the chamber of commerce. However, certain developments along the lines of the English exchanges were in the making in the form of associations, particularly among brokers in the different commodity markets. In Prussia, the exchanges were organized according to various mutually inconsistent criteria:

> The exchanges are neither public corporations, nor exclusive (closed) associations, nor formally free markets. Instead, they are regulated assemblies of groups of persons whose composition is mixed and fluctuating in every respect. The locale of the stock exchange is not separated from that of the commodity exchange. There are no spontaneous developments of associations among brokers as in Hamburg. Admission is not free; instead the exchanges are only to be accessible to persons who are professionally engaged in dealing on the exchange. . . . However, there is no guarantee whatever with regard to the financial position of the persons admitted.[17]

Weber noted especially that a free access to the exchange was

[16] See Max Weber, "Die Ergebnisse der deutschen Börsenenquete," *Zeitschrift für das gesamte Handelsrecht,* Vol. XLIII (1895), pp. 98–105.
[17] *Ibid.,* p. 116.

believed to be a special asset. Few seemed to advance the idea of a self-regulating association that would exclude from the exchange persons of questionable financial standing and morality. Yet these were the persons whose operations were principally responsible for a disquieting effect on the market.[18] But, while free admission prevailed at the stock exchange in Berlin as much as in Hamburg, Weber found a striking difference between the two. On the Hamburg exchange trading occurred in a very orderly manner despite the large number of participants, a consequence that could be attributed at least partially to the effective traditions of the Hamburg merchant class.[19] On the other hand, the absence of such traditions in a city like Berlin had presumably contributed to the relative instability of the market, and the official inquiry concerned itself with various remedial measures.

A special court of honor for the exchange had been suggested as one such measure, but most witnesses before the commission took a negative attitude toward it. Weber felt that the reason for this was that such an institution was feasible only under certain conditions. The individuals subject to the jurisdiction of a court of honor would have to be roughly in the same social position, with similar personal and moral qualities. A social group could develop and implement a consensus on the ethics of business only if it was not also cheek by jowl with a very heterogeneous mass. In Prussia, the people admitted to the exchanges represented all groups of the population and hence were divided among themselves by tremendous differences in wealth. The respectability and trustworthiness of businessmen certainly did not increase simply in proportion to their property. But Weber thought it entirely utopian to expect that these qualities had the same meaning for the small speculator, who made his living on the basis of the tiny daily differences in the quotations, and for the independent broker, whose transactions were backed up by a well-conducted enterprise with an ample supply of capital.[20] The principal ques-

[18] *Ibid.*, pp. 124–25. That effect frequently came about because "outsiders" tended to follow the lead of the big financial institutions, thus exaggerating every fluctuation on the market.

[19] *Ibid.*, pp. 112–13.

[20] *Ibid.*, pp. 137–38.

tion, then, was whether the persons speculating on the exchanges were fair-dealing.

This question touched upon a paradox inherent in the very organization of the exchanges. The pyramiding of sales and purchases for the same amount of goods or capital was necessary to handle the huge quantities supplied and demanded in the modern world economy. The many and complex transactions involved would achieve this extension of the market most effectively, if sellers and buyers formed an exclusive association in which membership was a synonym of commercial reliability. And the guarantee of that reliability would in turn facilitate planning and foresight in the conduct of an enterprise. Yet the techniques used in these transactions virtually invited the participation of persons with little capital and little expert knowledge of the market. These more or less unqualified persons tended to undermine the ethical standards governing exchange transactions, even as their participation in them was an inevitable by-product of the market mechanism.[21] Thus the very extension of the market inadvertently worked against the maintenance of ethical standards—a tendency that was counteracted only where existing traditions of the merchant class enforced such standards effectively.

These considerations are relevant here as a supplement to, and a contrast with, Weber's analysis of the farm-labor problem in eastern Germany. In that analysis, commercialization appeared as a destructive force undermining the patriarchal way of life, which was suited to the more or less self-sufficient economy of large estates. The only positive feature of this development, in Weber's eyes, was the farm workers' opposition to personal subservience, though from an economic point of view that opposition was "irrational." In the analysis of the stock and commodity exchanges, commercialization clearly appeared in a very different light. These exchanges helped extend the capital and commodity markets and facilitated the orderly, predictable conduct of economic enterprises. Both these functions were brought about by the pyramiding of transactions and of middlemen, by means of which the volume of trade could be increased enormously and the risk of price

[21] Weber, "Börsenenquete," *op. cit.*, Vol. XLV (1896), pp. 114–16.

fluctuations could be shifted from the enterprise to the market-wise speculator. The accent of Weber's analysis is thus on the stock and commodity exchanges as an efficient means for the expansion of trade and for the predictability of economic transactions—positive results that stood in marked contrast to the negative consequences of commercialization of agriculture in eastern Germany.

It is true, of course, that the exchanges also created opportunities for merely speculative gains that accentuated existing price fluctuations without accomplishing any other, more legitimate economic end. But the distinction between such transactions and sound business practice was elusive. Weber noted that the German Supreme Court had discarded one criterion after another that distinguished between different *kinds* of transactions, even though the distinction was real enough. But it was a distinction between the economic intentions of the men engaged in the transactions, not between the transactions themselves. In the end the Supreme Court had resorted to a distinction between the professional broker with his plentiful supply of capital and his expert knowledge of the market and the "fly-by-night" speculator who lacked both capital and knowledge. Thus, purely economic transactions apparently possessed an important subjective element: the intentions and, indeed, the ethics of businessmen were essential attributes of their economic conduct, just as the individualism of the farm workers was an essential element in their economic choices.

Weber's earliest social investigations, therefore, culminated in two major themes. First, commercialization by itself could help to destroy or to create cultural values, and, indeed, it tended to do both at the same time. It had destroyed the genuine values of patriarchalism, but in so doing it had broadened some opportunities for farm workers. The stock exchange, on the other hand, had aided the expansion of trade and the calculability of business transactions, but it also had provided new opportunities for speculative abuses. Second, economic conduct was inseparable from the ideas with which men pursued their economic interests, and these ideas had to be understood in their own terms. Both these themes illuminate Weber's view of German society and, beyond that, the fundamental conceptions that guided his lifework.

B.   THE STRUCTURE OF GERMAN SOCIETY

Weber used the foregoing studies as the basis for an analysis of social and political life from 1890 to the end of his life in 1920. He viewed the emerging trends of German society with mounting despair, which he expressed publicly for the first time at the end of his oral report on the conditions of rural laborers east of the Elbe. Addressing the convention of the *Verein für Sozialpolitik* in 1893, he stated:

Gentlemen: I am at the end of my remarks. Perhaps you will have been impressed by a certain resignation in what I have said. . . . This is indeed the case. On this occasion I have the honor of addressing gentlemen who are for the most part older and more experienced than I am [Weber was 29 at the time]. This resignation is bound up with the difference between the tasks which you gentlemen of the older generation had to face, and the tasks with which we of the younger generation are confronted today. I do not know whether all my contemporaries have this same intense experience as I do at this moment: the nation is burdened with the heavy curse on those who come afterwards. The generation before us was inspired by an activism and a naïve enthusiasm, which we cannot rekindle, because we confront tasks of a different kind from those which our fathers faced. They built a mansion for us in which we were invited to make ourselves at home. . . . But the tasks we face do not make it possible for us to appeal to the collective sentiments of the whole nation, as was the case when the unity of the nation and a free constitution were at issue. . . . Tremendous illusions were necessary to create the German empire, but now that the honeymoon of unification is over these illusions are gone and we cannot re-create them artificially. . . . If today an enemy appeared at the eastern border and threatened us with military power, there is no doubt that the nation would rally to the colors to defend the frontiers of the country. But when we undertake the peaceful defense of

German nationality on the eastern border we encounter several mutually conflicting interest groups. As we look around for allies, we find that this defense will run counter to the interests of the large landed proprietors. It must be undertaken against the instincts of large portions of the population who lean towards Manchester liberalism and free trade, and who see [in governmental measures to protect the East German peasantry] a dangerous precedent that may be extended to other fields. And as we finally consider the proletariat—well, the time is still far away when we can feel free to join the urban proletariat in the effort to solve social problems. . . .[22]

This statement reveals the somberness and passionate intensity of Weber's personal outlook at the outset of his career. Yet he managed to combine this highly political orientation with a detached analysis of changes in the agrarian society of the east.

This traditional agrarian economy had been both the image and the foundation of the rigid political and military organization of the Prussian state. The peasant or farm laborer of the east took it for granted that the commands of the landlord were issued in the interest of all concerned. The earnings of both landlord and laborer depended upon the productivity of the estate as a whole. And this community of interest had legitimized a harsh patriarchal authority and the instantaneous response to commands. Officers and men were conditioned to discipline in civilian as well as in military life, and on this basis Prussia had fought her battles.

The traditional master-servant relationship also had had political implications. The large estates east of the Elbe were the economic base of the Prussian ruling class, and as such they had peculiar advantages. Until well into the nineteenth century the *Junkers* had been economically secure in many regions east of the Elbe, though this security involved the acceptance of a very modest standard of living on their estates.

[22] *GAzSuW*, pp. 467–69. Weber made substantially the same points two years later in his inaugural lecture at the University of Freiburg, which became notorious for its unabashed nationalism. See "Der Nationalstaat und die Volkswirtschaftspolitik," *GPS*, p. 32. The same theme runs through much of Weber's later political writings.

The eastern landowners had had an undeveloped acquisitive drive, and they had been below average in economic intelligence, to use Weber's phrase.[23] This disdain for the "taint of trade" had made the political domination of the eastern provinces both inexpensive and honest. The *Junkers* were dispersed over the land; each of them was absolute master within his district, and his position did not depend upon economic exploitation. Thus the estates were centers of domination that represented a tradition of peremptory commands and absolute obedience. And it was this tradition—not the western pattern of smaller holdings, with its individualism and near equality between peasant and hireling—that had buttressed the political organization by which the unity of the *Reich* had been achieved.

As a nationalist concerned with the defense of German culture and German frontiers against the Slavic peoples to the east, Weber took the position—unpopular in some of the liberal and academic circles that he addressed—of defending the *Junkers* and their erstwhile political role. As long as their estates had been organized along traditional lines, the *Junkers* had in effect maintained the living standards—especially the daily diet—and the military efficiency of the German farm laborers; they had protected the frontiers of the nation, and they had provided her with outstanding political and military leaders. Above all, the *Junkers* had really constituted an aristocracy as long as they had been sheltered from the vicissitudes of the market. But their position had been undermined. In Weber's view this ruling class of eastern Germany had had the tragic fate (the phrase recurs in many forms throughout his writings) of digging the grave of its own social organization by what it had accomplished for the nation as a whole. Indeed, many prominent men in Prussia had opposed her integration with the *Reich* because they had feared for the maintenance of the Prussian way of life. The political unification of Germany in 1870 had given a tremendous boost to her urban and industrial development. The southern and western parts of the country had become so strong economically that they could force the east to buy their industrial products at the

[23] *GAzSuW*, p. 471.

same time that they declined its agricultural products. And the population of the eastern provinces, which had furnished recruits for the military campaigns that established the political power of the nation, now furnished a significant portion of the industrial labor force in the west, thus depriving eastern agriculture of much needed manpower. These economic changes had resulted in a major transformation of the *Junkers* themselves. With the rise of a wealthy bourgeoisie in the course of German industrialization, the *Junkers* were confronted with an economically powerful class that set new standards of consumption even if it did not effectively challenge the *Junkers'* political pre-eminence. "In his standard of living the landowner must [henceforth] stand on a par with the higher urban bourgeoisie, lest he turn into a peasant."[24] But to increase the cash income from the estates became more difficult as the agricultural products of eastern Germany with their relatively high unit cost (due to poor soil, inefficient methods, high labor costs, etc.) had to compete in the world market. The increase in productivity on the estates in eastern Germany had not kept pace with the emerging needs of the landowners. Also, the majority of these estates were not large enough to support a standard of living commensurate with that of the bourgeoisie. More than a third of the estates had 500 hectares (1,235 acres) or less, and because of the poor soil this was too small, according to Weber, to support an "aristo-cratic" family under the new circumstances. As Weber saw it, Germany was no longer ruled by a landed aristocracy but by a group of "indigent farmers, of dissatisfied recipients of char-ity."[25] In the long run the social and political position of the *Junkers* was bound to decline, but in the meantime their anomalous position would have harmful repercussions from the national standpoint.

Though the political and personal influence of this ruling group had remained considerable, the decline of its economic base meant that this influence became increasingly pretentious and politically as well as morally questionable. For now, politi-

[24] *GAzSuW*, p. 472.
[25] *Ibid.*, p. 473. This statement is, of course, a polemical exag-geration that denounces the *Junkers'* use of their privileges to ob-tain governmental support for their economic position.

cal means were used to bolster a ruling class that was threatened at its economic foundation. Instead of adjusting their estates to the new conditions of the world market, the *Junkers* used their political influence to obtain protection against the importation of cheaper foreign grain and, in addition, maintained or even increased their own production of grain, which could be sold at high prices on the domestic market at the expense of the consumer. And this was not all. Weber emphasized that an interest in maximizing the production of grain on a given land area was entirely incompatible with the aims of national policy as he conceived them. Although the tariff wall limited imports of foreign grain, it did not prevent the importation of foreign laborers. Indeed, agrarian spokesmen maintained that even with tariff protection the large estates of the east could not be operated without such cheap foreign labor. And their declared aim of maximizing domestic grain production required for its realization further increases in the size of the large estates at the expense of medium-sized and small holdings. If these were the goals, certain consequences inevitably followed. Class conflicts in the eastern provinces would become more intense, and the native rural population would be weakened further. An agrarian economy that depended on cheap foreign labor would also come to depend on the Tsarist police, which could prohibit the migration of farm workers arbitrarily.[26]

Yet Weber opposed the vilification as well as the idolization of the *Junkers*. The Prussian ruling class had played a leading role in the unification of Germany. It was a ruthless and domineering class as a result of the century-long struggle for survival in a harsh environment, and these same qualities had aided the fight for national ascendance. But by the 1890's the *Junkers'* achievements were a thing of the past. Weber was convinced that their agrarian policies were a disaster for the nation. In his view, these erstwhile aristocratic landowners had

[26] These consequences of German agrarian policy are discussed in Max Weber, "Agrarstatistische und sozialpolitische Betrachtungen zur Fideikomissfrage in Preussen," *GAzSuS*, pp. 333–35, 338, 391–92. Cited below as "Fideikomissfrage." This article was published in 1904, after Weber's partial recovery. It represents an elaboration of views expressed in his writings of 1892–93.

become a class of agricultural entrepreneurs engaged in a struggle for economic survival who had developed the plebeian manners common to such groups. At the personal level they were pleasant enough, but everything became spurious in Weber's eyes when they attempted to act like an aristocracy. The *Junkers* had become dependent upon "routine managerial work of a capitalistic nature," and the cultivation of "feudal gestures and pretensions" inevitably stamped them as a group of parvenus.[27] In Weber's judgment, the assets and liabilities of the *Junkers* as a class had come to a head in the statesmanship of Bismarck, just as the individualistic tendencies of the farm laborers in eastern Germany were writ large in the public response to Bismarck. Here is how Weber summed up his analysis of the farm-labor problem in 1892:

No social or ethical bases to ēir status claims. Belief must be backed by social (ethical) cond'y. Junkers are vacuous

① Why this doesn't happen in M'Asia.

> The development which is taking place before our eyes has still another, ethical aspect. After all that has been said it is no accident that for almost a generation the ship of state has been in the hands of a powerful landlord. Essential traits of his nature are not intelligible without reference to the soil from which he sprang. The traditional art of dominating a country and its people has produced all the qualities of brilliance but also the very great drawbacks which are united in his personality. . . . The profound and honest hatred which millions of German workers and broad sections of the bourgeoisie have conceived for this one man is their response to the basic contempt of mankind which was an indelible trait of Bismarck's every act and word. This trait was also an outgrowth of the patriarchal system, and it was especially pronounced in the most outstanding and energetic members of his status-group. . . . But in these respects the nation has become more sensitive; during the last years we have seen repeatedly that a mere intimation of the patriarchal manner from the top down provoked the stormy protest [of the people].[28]

[27] Cf. *Essays*, pp. 386–87. This is a partial translation of a pamphlet published in 1917. Weber made exactly the same points in his American lecture of 1904 (*ibid.*, pp. 380–82), and in his *Verhältnisse der Landarbeiter*, p. 796, of 1892.

[28] *Verhältnisse der Landarbeiter*, p. 804.

Thus an analysis of the economic and psychological changes that had come about in the structure of agrarian society east of the Elbe culminated in a political assessment of the German ruling class. Weber noted especially that the authoritarian bearing of the Prussian reserve officer, who represented that class ideologically, had become sharply accentuated in the attempt to bring broad sections of the population into a position of vassalage to the dynasty. Also, membership in certain student corps (fraternities) was being manipulated as an avenue of recruitment for the civil service. In Weber's judgment these methods were an inadequate and dangerous *Ersatz* for the genuine values of an aristocracy. Indeed, the ruling "aristocrats" were in part responsible for the decline of these values, because they were in reality rural capitalists who used patriotism and "loyalty to the monarch" as a smoke screen behind which they could maximize their economic interests at a time when these interests ran counter to the interests of the nation.[29] Still Weber did not attribute all these negative consequences to the dominance of the landowners. He believed rather that this dominance was due in part to the social and psychological characteristics of the German bourgeoisie.

This topic brings us back to issues that he touched on in his studies of the stock exchange. In comparing the regulation of exchanges in different countries, Weber had observed that effective standards of business ethics depended upon either the existence of a favorable tradition (as in Hamburg) or the autonomous organization of the business community, which could enforce standards of conduct (as in London or Glasgow). At a time when landowners as well as socialists engaged in anticapitalist propaganda, this emphasis upon the ethics of business had important political overtones, but it also foreshadowed Weber's later comparative approach. By giving evidence for the existence of an autonomous business ethic, Weber showed that the German bourgeoisie failed, not because it was capitalist but because it was not capitalist enough. As he saw it, the German traditions of an autonomous business ethic required strengthening in order to counteract the corruption of the middle classes, which consisted of imitating aristocratic ways for the purpose of finding favor at the royal court

[29] Cf. *ibid.*, p. 796, and "Fideikomissfrage," *GAzSuS*, p. 386 ff.

and of facilitating social advancement in aristocratic circles. The contrast between a proudly self-conscious business community, such as could be found in England or the Hanseatic cities, and the politically impotent and personally subservient middle class in Germany explains the extraordinary emphasis that Weber gave to the middle-class interest in purchasing lands in eastern Germany. This interest was involved in the political agitation in favor of increasing the lands tied up in deeds of trust (*fidei-commissum*).[30] To appreciate the significance of Weber's concern with this problem, a brief description of the issues involved is necessary.

The purpose of this legal institution was to prevent the division and alienation of land holdings by legal agreements pertaining to the hereditary transfer of property. An owner of landed property under a *fidei-commissum* was free to use the land as he saw fit. But he was obliged to act as a trustee—rather than as an owner—insofar as he was *not* entitled to sell or mortgage the land, except under very restricting legal conditions.[31] Although this institution was centuries old, it had assumed major significance in Prussia east of the Elbe only since the middle of the nineteenth century. Weber pointed out that the tendency to place new land in trust had been not merely steady but increasing. By 1900 one-sixteenth of the total German land area—an area considerably larger than the province of Westphalia—was tied up in trusts. Significant variations occurred among different districts: in 33 districts land in trust covered one-fifth of the area; in six districts the proportion was as high as 40 per cent. And of 26 districts, each with 20,000 hectares (49,420 acres) in trust, seventeen were located in Silesia and only three in the province of Saxony. That is to say, the practice of placing land in trust was most widespread in the province in which the commercialization of agriculture had progressed furthest. Thus, the tendency of placing newly acquired land in trust was most pronounced in an area

[30] To simplify the terminology I shall call *fidei-commissum* "land held in trust."

[31] A *fidei-commissum* differs from a simple trust fund in that it makes such a fund the property of a family in perpetuity. In England and in other common-law countries such a legal institution never prevailed.

where trading in landed property occurred most frequently, though the effect of the institution was, of course, to reduce the possibility of further sales. In his detailed analysis Weber was especially concerned with the increase of lands in trust, since these were to be further encouraged by the proposed legislation and since the long-established families of aristocratic landowners would derive no benefit from such encouragement. The draft law in effect gave landed proprietors a monopolistic opportunity to place their land—and many other capital assets—in trust. The establishment of new trusts was to be contingent upon the personal approval of the *Kaiser*. Families who owned land in trust yielding a minimum net income of RM 10,000 would become eligible for a title of nobility conferred upon them by letters-patent, and members of such families thereby obtained access to a civil-service career.

In criticizing this legislative proposal, Weber distinguished between land held in trust for many generations and land placed in trust during the last decades of the nineteenth century. Typically, land in the first category was of poor quality while land in the second was of good quality. The difference was significant because many aristocratic families still maintained the old patriarchal way of life despite the fact that it had become uneconomical, whereas the landowners of recent origin regarded their land as a form of commercial investment that provided them with a relatively stable income.

> This is the form which "satiated" capitalists customarily choose in order to remove their sources of income from the stormy arena of the economic struggle and find a safe haven for themselves as rent-receiving gentlemen by the grace of a letters-patent.[32]

Thus the social implications of a bourgeoisie which apparently was bent upon accommodating itself to the prevailing dominance of a land-holding aristocracy concerned Weber particularly.

A case in point was that new deeds of trust were to be approved personally by the *Kaiser* rather than by the minister in charge. To present such a provision as a means of restricting

[32] "Fideikomissfrage," *GAzSuS*, p. 331.

the land held in trust was for Weber an outrageous example of official hypocrisy. The ministers would be able to hide behind the *Kaiser's* assent, however undesirable they believed a given application to be. And there had never been a monarch, according to Weber, who had not sought to buttress his own position by satisfying the vanity of the wealthy. The real purpose of this provision was to facilitate the use of this legal device and to forestall all objections by personally involving the monarch.[33] Such thinking in official circles fit in especially well with the wishes of those who sought to expand the land they already owned. In the years 1895–1900, one-fifth to one-sixth of the existing estates held in trust had been expanded. The owners of such estates wanted to be not farmers but *rentiers,* who received a regular income commensurate with their social position. Consequently they needed ever more land in order to increase their income and status. Indeed, many of the estates held in trust had become too large for economical operation, and their owners frequently lacked the knowledge and ability to manage them efficiently. On the other hand, many estates held in trust were too small to sustain families of the ruling class "in the style to which they were accustomed."[34]

Weber added to these considerations a virulent polemic against the government that had sponsored this legislative proposal and the bourgeois circles that favored it:

It is in line with the political wisdom which is now dominant in Prussia to reconcile bourgeois money-bags with the negligible political influence of the bourgeoisie by granting them a kind of "second-class right to be presented at court." In the circles which are susceptible to such appeals nothing would be more unpopular than any action which would create difficulties for the "aristocratization" of capital assets . . . by way of their transformation into landed estates. . . . And the involvement of a personal decision by the monarch is designed to titillate to the utmost the vanity of families capable of acquiring land in trust and titles. For the mere thought is bound to warm the cockles of every "royal-

[33] *Ibid.,* pp. 362–63.
[34] *Ibid.,* pp. 365–71.

ist" heart that His Most Gracious Majesty had concerned himself personally with the position and "worthiness" of one's family, had found these in order, and had, thereafter, participated by his assent in the act of establishing the head of the family [as a landed proprietor and as a legitimate aspirant to aristocratic title]. . . ."[35]

According to Weber, these were the actual reasons for the proposed legislation, although its declared purpose was to strengthen attachment to the soil, invigorate the national character, and foster aristocratic sentiments.

Weber thought it somewhat embarrassing to discuss these resounding phrases in a scientific journal. But he felt obliged to do so, since the proposed legislation was officially justified in terms of the then fashionable agrarian romanticism. These polemics are of interest here because they reveal Weber's general characterization of the *Junkers* and the bourgeoisie. To suggest that the proposed legislation would strengthen "aristocratic sentiments" was to Weber a preposterous idea since such sentiments were by no means synonymous with a reliable, businesslike conduct of affairs. The east-Elbian proprietors of land held in trust had developed their attitude toward commercial transactions in the boom years after 1870 out of their experiences with horse traders and cattlemen, whose sharp practices had helped form even Bismarck's attitude toward business. Agrarian capitalism fostered a mixture of pretensions and acquisitive drives, which frequently resulted in low business ethics.

The proposed increase of estates held in trust became, for Weber, the symbol of an amalgamation between a landed aristocracy corrupted by money-making and a capitalist middle class corrupted by aristocratic pretensions. The effect of this amalgamation on the civil service was especially noteworthy. German civil servants were being recruited predominantly among the sons and relatives of landowners whose estates were tied up in trusts. As a result these officials generally regarded the middle- and working-class sections of the population without knowledge and understanding, and with a vaguely felt antipathy arising from the conventional prejudices

[35] *Ibid.,* pp. 379–80.

of landowners. Since these agrarian groups could rely on preferred treatment and promotion in the civil service, the talent
and qualification of the average official could certainly be
expected to decline. Weber saw only a perversion of the "Prussian tradition" left among the agrarian groups. Certain aspects
of their once meaningful tradition had become mere carica-
tures. The "spit and polish" of the Prussian reserve officer, for
example, lacked all character and conviction in persons who
lacked the superior bearing and cultivated manners ideally
found in an aristocracy. Weber castigated the petty haughti-
ness of these people in their relations with subordinates, and
he despaired at the effrontery with which such conduct was
identified with "Prussian administrative practice." Large numbers of officials imitated the "Prussian manner" in order to disguise their bourgeois origin. Indeed, the abuse of official
authority in the treatment of German "subjects," the pliability
of the lackey in relation to superiors, and the unprincipled
identification of both with a merely formal patriotism and "loyalty to the monarch" were at their worst among bourgeois
circles with feudal pretensions. And these were the people who
would be encouraged by a law that would facilitate their
acquisition of lands and of titles!

C. WEBER'S INTELLECTUAL PERSPECTIVE

In 1892 Weber had summarized his findings with regard to
the farm laborers' desire to be their own masters in a way that
foreshadowed a major part of his life's work:

In the Middle Ages the household community was retained
through many generations, for example in the commercial
houses of the cities, and people endured this way of life.
Cousins, sisters-in-law, and mothers-in-law ate and lived together. Today we want a hearth of our own; our desire is to
earn our bread on alien ground away from the family table
in the home of our parents and away from the circle of our
next of kin. And the gravity of the situation is that this desired economic independence becomes more and more unat-

tainable for the individual even in his later years, in view of the way the conditions of modern life are developing.[36]

This individualism was not adequately understood if it was simply identified as an unencumbered pursuit of gain by the individual. Each man certainly pursued his economic interests independently from his extended family; but he also judged what was to his interest, and in so doing he acted as a whole man, not a money-maximizing automaton. Weber believed that ideas about economic conduct could have a power of their own in addition to, as well as in conjunction with, the unquestioned importance of economic interest.

The significance of such ideas had emerged especially in Weber's investigation of the stock exchange. The orderly management of economic enterprises was not dictated by economic conditions and self-interest alone. The man who speculated on marginal gains to make a windfall was as self-interested as the businessman who used the stock exchange in order to safeguard himself against unanticipated price fluctuations. The distinction between these two types of man was related, therefore, to their different orientation as individuals; the marginal operator tended to be a gambler interested in speculative gains, while the businessman in the best sense of the word tended to be a strategist interested in regular profits. The two types also differed in their social relations. The speculator was usually a "lone wolf" as far as his transactions on the exchange were concerned. The businessman was usually associated with others like himself to whom he was tied by a common outlook and in whose business conduct he had confidence even as he competed with them on the market. Consequently Weber became interested in the ideas of businessmen as members of a status group rather than as individuals. To affect the operation of a complex institution like the exchange, such an outlook upon the conduct of business affairs had to grow out of the traditions of a merchant class that had a common ethic. An effective regulation of conduct depended in the last instance upon the strong common purpose of the group, whether the regulation was attempted through an exclusive association, as in England, or without such an organiza-

[36] *Verhältnisse der Landarbeiter*, p. 798.

tion, as in the Hanseatic cities. An "unconscious purposiveness" was inherent in these social conditions.[37] Merchants with ample capital and a professional interest in the market had a natural tendency to exclude "outsiders" who were not professionals, had little capital and know-how, and hence tended to accentuate the uncertainties of the market.[38] Clearly, business rationality and the ethics of mutual trust involved ideas that went beyond the immediate dictates of economic interest, even though they served to advance that interest. And these ideas could have an effect on the stock exchange only if they were the attribute of a group. Thus Weber emphasized both the importance of ideas for an understanding of economic behavior and the social foundation of such ideas if they were to have an effect upon man's conduct.

This double emphasis is also apparent in his analysis of the *Junkers*. The commercialization of agriculture in eastern Germany had been inevitable in view of the changing conditions on the world market. But, instead of transforming themselves into rural capitalists, the landowners continued to espouse the patriarchal ideology and social pretensions of the erstwhile aristocracy. And as long as the *Junkers* used their established political privileges to buttress their endangered economic position, they were, in his eyes, the pretended spokesmen of the national interest. From his own nationalist standpoint Weber especially castigated their practice of urging the government to facilitate the employment of foreign farm workers on their estates while they were ostensibly outdoing everyone else with their super-patriotism.[39]

Weber attacked the *Junkers* for the same reason that he attacked industrialists who sought to disguise their middle-class origins by acquiring lands and titles. Aristocrats who had in fact become rural capitalists and now used their social prestige to gain economic advantages appeared as dishonest to him as industrialists who had become "aristocratic" landowners.

[37] This phrase occurs in *Verhältnisse der Landarbeiter*, p. 792, in a similar context.

[38] Cf. "Börsenenquete," *op. cit.*, Vol. XLIII, pp. 100–1 and *passim.*

[39] "Fideikomissfrage," *GAzSuS*, p. 392. Cf. also the letter of resignation that Weber sent to the Pan-German League (*Alldeutscher Verband*) in 1899, quoted in Marianne Weber, *op. cit.*, pp. 258–59.

The emotional tenor of these judgments is important. Weber definitely believed that the *Junkers* and the industrialists had a choice to make—that their ideas and actions were not simply the product of their economic interests as the Marxists had maintained.[40] And he believed that the choices they had made were pernicious. From this standpoint the farm laborers appeared to him more worthy of respect than either the landowners or the industrialists:

> We want to cultivate and support what appears to us as valuable in man: his personal responsibility, his basic drive toward higher things, toward the spiritual and moral values of mankind, even where this drive confronts us in its most primitive form. Insofar as it is in our power we want to create the external conditions which will help to preserve—in the face of the inevitable struggle for existence with its suffering—the best that is in men, those physical and emotional qualities which we would like to maintain for the nation.[41]

A farm worker's preference for personal independence despite the financial loss involved was evidence of this "basic drive towards higher things," but the aristocratic pretensions of the rural capitalist were not.

Yet Weber's political judgments consisted of more than an emphasis upon the autonomy of the individual and the liberal heritage of the nineteenth century. I have mentioned already that Weber spoke of the breakup of the household community since the Middle Ages in accounting for the "individualism" and the anti-authoritarian orientation of the farm workers. In the case of the *Junkers* the emphasis upon the social foundation of individual conduct was even more pronounced. Weber had concluded his report of 1892 on the labor problem east of the Elbe by emphasizing the positive political contribution of the *Junkers*. This statement gave rise to much partisan com-

[40] For a discussion of Weber's relation to Marx, cf. the editors' introduction in *Essays*, pp. 46–50. A detailed consideration of this relation is available in Karl Loewith, "Max Weber und Karl Marx," *Archiv für Sozialwissenschaft*, Vol. 67 (1932), pp. 53–99, 175–214.

[41] Quoted from Weber's speech in 1894 before the *Evangelisch-Soziale Kongress* in Marianne Weber, *op. cit.*, p. 159.

ment in the press, which prompted Weber to make this rejoinder:

> It did not occur to me to contend that we owed the large landowners a special vote of thanks. I am of the opinion that the large landowners have served the state in the past at the same time that they pursued their own interests. . . . I believe above all that this recognition, insofar as it is well founded, should not be accorded to individuals, but to the social organization of which these individuals had been a part. . . .[42]

This social organization had been the bulwark of Prussian society. The landowners had constituted a genuine aristocracy, which could depend upon the rents received from a subservient peasantry and which was therefore available for political and military activities. Peasants as well as *Junkers* benefited from the agricultural yield of the estates. A traditionally frugal style of life together with the *Junkers'* belief in the obligations of a ruling class had tended in some measure to limit exploitative practices. But Weber left no doubt that the patriarchal manners and ideals of these power-conscious men had been harsh. Political autocrats in miniature, they mixed benevolence with brutality as their whims dictated. And their subservient workers lived a life of dull resignation, albeit freed from purely economic exploitation.[43] Nevertheless, this way of life had been all of a piece. The economy of the *Junkers,* their role as a political and military aristocracy and their authoritarian ideals were consistent and mutually reinforcing. Repeatedly Weber pointed out that as a member of the middle class he had no special reason to like the East German landowners. Yet in their erstwhile historical role they had represented a way of life whose material adjustments and ideal interests were in keeping with the harsh environment of a struggle for survival on the eastern European frontiers. In that setting the *Junkers* had developed the world image of the Prussian tradition, and such images "have, like switchmen, determined the tracks along

[42] *GAzSuW*, p. 456. See also the comments in Max Weber, *Jugendbriefe* (Tübingen: J. C. B. Mohr, n.d.), pp. 364–65, where the polemical context of his remarks is explained.

[43] *GAzSuW*, p. 474.

which action has been pushed by the dynamic of interest."[44]

It is apparent from this review of Weber's earliest social and economic investigations that he asserted the importance of ideas and of the individual against the collectivism of the Marxists and the social evolutionists, but that he also emphasized the social foundations of individual action much as Marxism had done. He did not believe that ideas like the individualism of the farm workers or the patriarchalism of the *Junkers* could be fully explained by reference to the economic interest and material environment of these groups. But this relative independence of ideas could be recognized, in his judgment, without either denying or neglecting the influence of political and economic interests on the development of ideas. What he says in the *Protestant Ethic* in 1904, he could already have said in one of these earlier studies:

> It is, of course, not my aim to substitute for a one-sided materialistic an equally one-sided spiritualistic causal interpretation of culture and of history. Each is equally possible, but each, if it does not serve as the preparation, but as the conclusion of an investigation, accomplishes equally little in the interest of historical truth.[45]

Clearly, Weber wanted to see both lines of inquiry receive their due share of attention. Yet nowhere in his work is this view of the relative independence and intricate interdependence of ideas and economic interest fully stated beyond the cryptic remark that "not ideas, but material and ideal interests, directly govern men's conduct."[46] Only specific investigations can probe these interrelations, but it is important to have before us a general formulation of the perspective that guided Weber in his work. Fortunately, such a formulation is contained in the work of the German historian Otto Hintze:

> All human action arises from a common source, in political as well as in religious life. Everywhere the first impulse to social action is given as a rule by real interests, i.e., by political and economic interests. But ideal interests lend wings to these real interests, give them a spiritual meaning, and serve

[44] *Essays*, p. 280.
[45] *Protestant Ethic*, p. 183.
[46] *Essays*, p. 280.

to justify them. Man does not live by bread alone. He wants to have a good conscience as he pursues his life-interests. And in pursuing them he develops his capacities to the highest extent only if he believes that in so doing he serves a higher rather than a purely egoistic purpose. Interests without such "spiritual wings" are lame; but on the other hand, ideas can win out in history only if and insofar as they are associated with real interests. The Marxian image of substructure and superstructure does not appear to me to give adequate expression to this peculiar connection of interests and ideas. In this image "ideologies" quickly lose all reality. Moreover, the Marxian model has the flaw that it is static despite the fact that it seeks to portray a dynamic transformation [of society]. Where a substructure is transformed, the superstructure does not follow suit by transforming itself in corresponding fashion; rather the superstructure disintegrates along with the whole of society. I think a more appropriate image is that of a polar coordination of interests and ideas. In the long run, neither of the two can survive without the other, historically speaking; each requires the other as a supplementation. *Wherever interests are vigorously pursued, an ideology tends to be developed also to give meaning, re-enforcement and justification to these interests. And this ideology is as "real" as the real interests themselves, for ideology is an indispensable part of the life-process which is expressed in action. And conversely: wherever ideas are to conquer the world, they require the leverage of real interests, although frequently ideas will more or less detract these interests from their original aim. . . .*[47]

This double emphasis was the guiding consideration of Weber's work on the sociology of religion, and looking back upon his early studies one can see how his interest in *The Protestant Ethic and the Spirit of Capitalism* emerged. His disenchantment with the world in which he lived led him to a search of the past for the origin of the values he prized. As

[47] Otto Hintze, "Kalvinismus und Staatsräson in Brandenburg zu Beginn des 17ten Jahrhunderts," *Historische Zeitschrift*, Vol. 144 (1931), p. 232. My italics.

an individualist Weber sought to uncover the historical sources of the individualism that prompted the farm workers to prefer the uncertainty of seasonal labor to the security of personal subservience. As a member of the middle class he inquired into the sources of the collectivism and rationality that prompted English and Hanseatic stockbrokers to impose an ethic of trade upon themselves—a practice that stood in marked contrast to the aping of aristocratic ways among his compatriots.

CHAPTER III

ASPECTS OF ECONOMIC RATIONALITY
IN THE WEST

The Protestant Ethic and the Spirit of Capitalism is Max Weber's most famous as well as most controversial book. In it he traced the influence of religious ideas upon the conduct of men and challenged the Marxist thesis that man's consciousness is determined by his social class. It was first published in 1904 and 1905 as a series of essays and, although subsequently it came out in book form, it remained a fragment. Instead of completing his investigation of Protestantism, Weber began a comparative analysis of urban communities and of political organization as well as a study of the relation between religion and society.[1] These wide-ranging studies had the common purpose of defining and explaining the distinguishing characteristics of Western civilization. *The Protestant Ethic* was destined to serve as an introduction to this major theme of Weber's lifework, a specification of the interrelation of religious ideas and economic behavior as the focus

[1] Weber explicitly states that he abandoned the topic of Protestantism because his friend Ernst Troeltsch, who was a professional theologian, had initiated his work on *The Social Teachings of the Christian Churches and Sects.* Another reason for Weber's decision was that the essay on Protestantism had provided the perspective for a broadly comparative treatment of religion and society. See the comments in *Protestant Ethic,* p. 284, n. 119.

for further research. Weber's particular thesis—that Puritan ideas had influenced the development of capitalism—became the subject of a voluminous literature.[2] What follows is a bare outline of Weber's argument and a consideration of the intellectual perspectives that it suggested to him.

A. THE SPIRIT OF CAPITALISM

Weber's early studies focus on a tendency that appears to be typical of modern society and on an attribute of behavior that appears to be universal. First, a general resistance to personal subservience, reflecting a century-long decline of kinship solidarity, seems to prevail today. Second, economic conduct seems to possess an ethical content of its own, whether this consists of a calculated probity or of the questionable morals of horse traders. Within his family Weber was able to observe a traditional entrepreneur, who combined individualism and an ethic of economic conduct. His uncle, Karl David Weber, was the founder of an enterprise based upon the domestic industry of the countryside surrounding the village where he lived. And Weber saw that his way of life was marked by hard work, frugal living, and a benevolent but reserved manner, which appeared to reflect the period of the great entrepreneurs in

[2] Weber's essays on Protestantism gave rise to one of the great intellectual controversies of our time, in part because he had challenged the Marxist interpretation of history by this "positive critique of historical materialism." (This was the title of his lectures at the University of Vienna. See Marianne Weber, *Max Weber* [Heidelberg: Lambert Schneider, 1950], p. 652.) The paradox of this controversy is that the critics concentrate on the problem of the causal significance of the Protestant ethic for the rise of capitalism, while Weber himself stated explicitly that his purpose had *not* been to explain the origin or the expansion of capitalism. See his "Antikritisches Schlusswort zum 'Geist des Kapitalismus,'" *Archiv für Sozialwissenschaft,* Vol. XXXI (1910), p. 580 and *passim,* but also *Protestant Ethic,* pp. 91–92, 183. A concise and illuminating summary of Weber's "anticritical" arguments, as well as a survey of the whole controversy, is contained in Ephraim Fischoff, "The Protestant Ethic and the Spirit of Capitalism," *Social Research,* Vol. XI (1944), pp. 62–68 and *passim.*. .

the early phase of modern capitalism.[3] This contact with the work-ethic of a respected businessman struck a responsive chord in Weber, who as a young scholar had assumed a back-breaking work load to sublimate his headlong drive for vigorous action and who rejected all warnings with the remark that he would not deserve to be a scholar if he could not work at this pace.[4] Later on, after his illness had subsided, this work-ethic caused Weber acute anxiety. In his eyes the duties of an academic teacher allowed no letup in pace whatsoever, and his continued university association constantly reminded him of his own unpardonable inability to fulfill these duties.

This idea of hard work as a duty that carries its own intrinsic reward is a typical attribute of man in the modern industrial world as Weber conceived it. A man should work well in his gainful occupation, not merely because he had to but because he wanted to; it was a sign of his virtue and a source of personal satisfaction: "It is an obligation which the individual is supposed to feel and does feel towards the content of his occupational activity, no matter in what it consists."[5] The American vernacular touches upon this sense of obligation in the familiar phrase, "Anything that is worth doing at all is worth doing well." This maxim represents the modern "spirit of capitalism" insofar as it is devoid of all concern with a higher, transcendental purpose, but originally it had had profound religious significance and it was to this fact that Weber turned his attention.

Weber's "spirit of capitalism" was a concept he contrasted with another type of economic activity that he designated as "traditionalism." Traditionalism is present when workers prefer

[3] For details of this personal background cf. Marianne Weber, *op. cit.*, pp. 197–99, 404–5, 435–36.

[4] Cf. *Essays*, p. 11.

[5] *Protestant Ethic*, p. 54. I substitute the word "occupational" for "professional" in this quotation, but, as Parsons observes, there is no satisfactory English equivalent for the German term *Beruf*. "Profession" is too narrow, since the word refers to all occupational activities; "vocation" lacks the ethical connotation that is intended; and "calling," which retains that connotation, is only applied to the ministry in its modern usage. Yet the whole point of the earlier usage of "calling" or *Beruf* was that the sense of a higher obligation applied to every occupational activity.

less work to more pay, when during working hours they seek a maximum of comfort and a minimum of exertion, when they are unable or unwilling to adapt themselves to new methods of work. It is present also when entrepreneurs deal in goods of varied rather than standardized quality, when they work moderate hours and at a leisurely pace except for rush periods, when they are satisfied with earnings that permit a comfortable living, and when their relations with workers, customers and competitors are direct and highly personal.[6] But leisurely work habits and a "live-and-let-live" moderation of the economic calculus are only one aspect of economic traditionalism. Another is that avarice and a completely unscrupulous acquisitive drive are world-wide phenomena that also differ from the "spirit of capitalism." If anything, they are more characteristic of precapitalist than of capitalist societies. Chinese mandarins, Roman aristocrats and the east-Elbian landowners, among privileged groups, as well as porters, taxi-drivers and craftsmen among the lower classes of southern Europe or of Asia, were far more greedy and more unscrupulous than Englishmen in comparable positions. Moreover, "capitalist" acquisition as an adventure has existed throughout history. Enterprises that aim at windfalls, such as piracy, the financing of wars and governments, tax-farming, certain medieval trading companies, and many others, are characterized by an absolute disregard of ethical considerations in relations with foreigners that frequently coincides with strict morality and traditionalism within the community. Where traditionalism has declined, as in the late Middle Ages, the disregard of morality in economic affairs has been tolerated as unfortunate but unavoidable. Yet neither ruthless acquisitiveness in transactions with foreigners nor the mere tolerance of abuses within the community are compatible with the "spirit of capitalism" as Weber defined it. For neither avarice nor a lax moral code nor the adherence to "traditionalism" is compatible with the idea of hard work as a virtue and hence a moral obligation.[7]

These considerations from *The Protestant Ethic* may be supplemented by reference to a typology of gainful pursuits that Weber developed in order to define the type of economic

[6] *Ibid.*, pp. 59–67.
[7] *Ibid.*, pp. 56–58.

activity that originated in Western civilization. As he saw it, throughout history and in all civilizations men have pursued gain in a speculative manner

a. by trading in currency and by the extension of credit;
b. by going after the rich spoils that may accrue from the financing of political transactions like revolutions, wars, or party-struggles, as well as from profitable economic transactions with political bodies; and
c. by colonial or fiscal exploitation on the basis of force guaranteed by political authority, i.e., continuous earnings through compulsory payments, forced labor or monopolistic trade in colonies or through various methods of tax-farming.[8]

Such speculative pursuits are oriented for the most part toward political contingencies. As such they are distinguished from all those gainful pursuits that are based on, and that in turn encourage, rational calculation. This type of economic activity is present where men pursue gain

d. by continuous trading on a market on which exchanges are formally free (and subject only to the rule of law) or by "continuous productive enterprises which make use of capital accounting."
e. by financial operations that involve
   (1) speculative transactions in standardized commodities;
   (2) continuous administration of political bodies;
   (3) promotion of new enterprises through the sale of securities; and
   (4) speculative financing of enterprises with the goal of ensuring their long-term profitability.[9]

Modern capitalism is a great complex of interrelated institutions based on rational rather than speculative types of eco-

[8] Cf. *Theory*, p. 278 (points 2–5). The term "tax-farming" refers to the frequent practice of political authorities who, unable or unwilling to collect taxes from their political subjects directly, instead authorize an individual to undertake such collection, usually in return for a fixed percentage of the monies so obtained. Cf. Chapter XI for further discussion of this point.

[9] *Ibid.*, pp. 278–79 (points 1 and 6).

nomic pursuit. In particular this complex involves enterprises that are based on long-range capital investments, a voluntary supply of labor in the legal senses of that word, a planned division of labor within the enterprises, and an allocation of production functions among them through the operation of a market economy. Only under capitalism do we find, further-more, the legal form of the business corporation, organized exchanges for trading in commodities and securities, public credit in the form of government securities, and the organiza-tion of enterprises for the production of goods rather than merely for trade in goods.[10]

This later formulation of what distinguishes Western capi-talism is cited here to emphasize the narrow focus Weber uses in *The Protestant Ethic*. In his earliest work he already had investigated the history of two institutions—the business cor-poration and the stock exchange—that had furthered the de-velopment of capitalism and that could not be found elsewhere in the same form. In his later work Weber investigated a great many other developments of Western civilization: the urban communities of ancient and medieval times, the development of legal concepts and of the legal profession, forms of political organization, types of currency and currency regulation, and types of economic enterprise, to cite only major topics out-side his sociology of religion. Each of the institutions making up the complex phenomenon of Western capitalism had to be investigated in turn, for each had, in Weber's view, ante-cedents of its own that might or might not be connected with one another. And about each of these developments it was appropriate to ask whether and how it was related to the "spirit of capitalism"; that is, to the ideas and habits that favor a rational pursuit of economic gain.

In this connection Weber pointed out that this "spirit" was not uniquely Western and unprecedented, if one considered it as an attribute of individuals. There had always been eco-nomic "supermen" who had conducted their business on a highly systematic basis, who worked harder than any of their employees, whose personal habits were frugal, and who used

[10] *Ibid.*, pp. 279–80. A related and supplementary enumeration is found in *General Economic History*, pp. 312–14, and in *Protestant Ethic*, pp. 21–24.

their earnings for investment. Such "heroic entrepreneurs" could overcome the drawbacks of economic traditionalism for themselves, but they could not by themselves establish a new economic order. The quest after windfalls, the greed for gold with a minimum of disciplined exertion, the idea that work was a burden and a curse to be avoided wherever its rewards exceeded what men required for subsistence or modest comfort—these were universal tendencies of action in Weber's view. To counteract them successfully needed more than the efforts of a few great entrepreneurs. "In order that a manner of life well adapted to the peculiarities of capitalism . . . could come to dominate others, it had to originate somewhere, and not in isolated individuals alone, but as a way of life common to whole groups of men."[11]

B. THE PROTESTANT ETHIC

Having defined the "spirit of capitalism" as the object of his inquiry, Weber proceeded to cite a series of reasons why it was plausible to look for its origin in the religious ideas of the Reformation. First, astute observers like Petty, Montesquieu, Buckle, Keats and others had commented on the affinity between Protestantism and the development of the commercial spirit. Second, in some instances the Protestant aptitude for commerce and industry had become an article of secular policy. For example, Frederick William I, the founder of the Prussian military tradition, had permitted the Mennonites to engage in trade in East Prussia despite their steadfast refusal to do military service. Third, according to an investigation that Weber had had one of his students make of the relation between religious affiliation and educational choice in the state of Baden, Protestants appeared to be more ready than Catholics to choose high schools that fitted in with the industrial way of life.[12] Fourth, in imperial Germany the Catholics had

[11] *Protestant Ethic*, p. 55.

[12] This study has recently been subjected to a detailed critique by Kurt Samuelson, *Ekonomi och religion* (Stockholm: Kooperativa forfundets, 1957), pp. 150–53. For a summary see S. M. Lipset and Reinhard Bendix, *Social Mobility in Industrial Society* (Berkeley: University of California Press, 1959), pp. 54–55.

been subjected to oppressive legislation (the so-called *Kultur-kampf*) during the 1870's and suffered from the effects of this discrimination for decades thereafter. In Holland and in England Catholics had found themselves in a comparable minority position at various times. In this sense they were similar to the Poles in Russia, the Huguenots in France, the Nonconformists in England, and the Jews in all countries for some two thousand years. But these other minorities had compensated for their exclusion from social and political life by an intensified economic activity, while the Catholics had not. Fifth, it was well known that certain Protestant sects like the Quakers and the Baptists had been as "proverbial" for their wealth as for their piety. During the seventeenth century spokesmen for these groups had expressed jubilation over the confidence that all people placed in the righteousness of the pious, while the "sinful children of the world" distrusted one another in business.

Next Weber examined the question of whether the affinity between Protestantism and the "capitalist spirit" was merely an adaptation to changing economic conditions. One approach to this problem was to find early instances in which the Protestant ethic had prevailed in economically backward areas or in which Catholicism was dominant despite a flourishing capitalist economy. Thus, Weber pointed out that in a backward area like eighteenth-century Pennsylvania the "capitalist spirit" was prominent indeed, while areas of significant capitalist development, such as Antwerp and Florence, had remained Catholic during the Reformation.[13]

Such examples restate Weber's conclusion that ideas should not be regarded as a dependent variable only, but they do not touch on the major problem of *The Protestant Ethic*. The point is that Weber saw a major issue in what everyone else had taken for granted. It seemed plausible that during the sixteenth century the wealthiest regions and cities had turned to Protestantism if the latter had really facilitated the pursuit of economic gain. However, in Weber's view this was a great para-

[13] *Protestant Ethic*, pp. 74–75. Again, in the southern colonies like Virginia, the "capitalist spirit" was relatively absent, because these colonies had been founded as a business venture by "capitalist adventurers," as Weber called them, not by Puritan sects.

dox, because intense religiosity and intense economic activity involved mutually incompatible tendencies. According to all experience, religious devotion was usually accompanied by a rejection of mundane affairs, while men who were engrossed in economic pursuits tended toward religious indifference. Why, then, had the rising commercial classes embraced Protestantism when the medieval Church's control over daily life had been so notoriously lax that few real obstacles had been put in the way of the rising capitalist economy? In place of Catholic tolerance, the Protestants had introduced a thoroughgoing regulation of private and public life; yet the bourgeoisie had risen to the defense of this "unexampled tyranny of Puritanism."[14] Indeed, the middle classes, which have rarely been characterized by either heroism or intense religiosity, developed heroic qualities of character in their acceptance and defense of an ascetic way of life.[15] Thus in the Age of the Reformation the rising middle classes deviated significantly from the simple acquisitiveness, religious indifference and more or less outright hedonism usually characteristic of social groups engaged in the development of economic enterprises.

The purpose of *The Protestant Ethic* was to explain this paradox. Weber wanted to show how certain types of Protestantism became a fountainhead of incentives that favored the rational pursuit of economic gain. Worldly activities had been given positive spiritual and moral meaning during the Reformation, and in order to understand this phenomenon Weber believed it necessary to analyze certain theological doctrines of the Reformation:

> To discover the historical causes [of a major cultural change] it would certainly be much more convenient if we could simply deduce the emergence of particular styles of life from the abstract propositions of "psychology." However, historical reality just cannot be pushed around. . . . The people of that period [the Reformation] had after all very specific ideas of what awaited them in the life after death, of the

[14] *Ibid.*, p. 37.
[15] A comprehensive statement concerning the "unheroic" qualities and the religious indifference of the middle class in contrast to the religiosity of groups like the Parsis, the Jews and the Puritans may be found in *WuG*, Vol. I, pp. 273–75.

means by which they could improve their chances in this respect, and they adjusted their conduct in accordance with these ideas. The orientation of their conduct varied with the different ideas [that were developed] concerning the conditions which [the individual] must fulfill in order to be sure of his salvation. And these different ideas became significant for the development of culture—however difficult it may be for modern men to visualize the power and the torment of those metaphysical conceptions.[16]

Weber's object was to show how the secular ethical concepts of the Reformation period were related to its theological doctrines, and hence to verify that the new worldly orientation was indeed related to the religious ideas of the period.[17]

None of the great Reformers had any thought of promoting "the spirit of capitalism," but Weber hoped to show that their doctrines nevertheless contained implicit incentives in this direction—especially the Calvinist doctrine of predestination according to which each individual's state of grace was determined by God's inexorable choice, from the creation of the world and for all time. It was as impossible for the individual to whom it had been granted to lose God's grace as it was for the individual to whom it had been denied to attain it. Hence the state of grace was conceived as the "sole product of an absolute power," which could not "owe anything to [man's] own cooperation or . . . be connected with achievements or qualities of [man's] own faith and will."[18]

The idea of predestination had been developed by John Calvin (1509–64) in his doctrinal controversies with opponents. According to Calvin, men exist for the sake of God. To apply earthly standards of justice to His sovereign decrees is evidence of presumption and lack of faith. We can know only that some men are saved and the rest are damned. To assume otherwise is to believe a manifest contradiction, namely that

---

[16] Max Weber, "Kritische Bemerkungen zu den vorstehenden 'kritischen Beiträgen,'" *Archiv für Sozialwissenschaft*, Vol. XXV (1907), p. 248.

[17] Cf. the restatement of his procedure and his purposes in Max Weber, "Antikritisches Schlusswort zum 'Geist des Kapitalismus,'" *Archiv für Sozialwissenschaft*, Vol. XXXI (1910), pp. 581–82.

[18] *Protestant Ethic*, pp. 101–2.

mere human merit or guilt can influence God's absolutely free decrees.[19]

Weber was interested primarily in the development of Calvinist doctrine in the Puritan movements of the sixteenth and seventeenth centuries, which revealed its implicit incentives. By quoting from the text of the Westminster Confession of 1647 rather than from Calvin's original formulation, Weber characterized the terrifying austerity of this belief as it must have appeared to the Puritans of this later period.

> Man, by his fall into a state of sin, hath wholly lost all ability of will to any spiritual good accompanying salvation. So that natural man, being altogether averse from that good, and dead in sin, is not able, by his own strength, to convert himself, or to prepare himself thereunto.[20]

In spelling out the substance of this decree, the Confession speaks of God's "eternal and immutable purpose, the unsearchable counsel and good pleasure of His will," according to which He extends or withholds mercy out of His free grace and love, "without any foresight of faith or good works, or any other things in the creature as conditions," solely for the glory of His almighty power.

Weber believed that the ordinary man was bound to feel profoundly troubled by a doctrine that did not permit any outward signs of his state of grace and that imparted to the image of God such terrifying majesty that He transcended all human entreaty and comprehension. Before this God, man stood alone. The priest could not help because the elect could understand the work of God only in their own hearts. Sacraments could not help because their strict observance was not a means of attaining grace. The Church could not help because its membership included the doomed, who must be forced to obey God's commandments even though this could not help them attain salvation. And the sectarian community could not help, though it excluded all nonbelievers, because this only added the fear of social ostracism to the terror of religious uncertainty. Even God did not help, for Christ had died only

[19] *Ibid.*, p. 103.
[20] Quoted in *ibid.*, pp. 99–100.

for the elect: He could not have died to redeem those who
had been condemned to everlasting death. Finally, private confession had fallen into disuse so that the individual believer
had no opportunity to find relief from the pressing consciousness of his sins.[21]

Calvin had taught that one must find solace solely on the
basis of the true faith. Each man was duty-bound to consider
himself chosen and to reject all doubt as a temptation of the
devil, for a lack of self-confidence was interpreted as a sign of
insufficient faith. To attain that self-confidence, unceasing
work in a calling was recommended. By his unceasing activity
in the service of God, the believer strengthened his self-confidence as the active tool of the divine will. This idea implied a
tremendous tension: Calvinism had eliminated all magical
means of attaining salvation. In the absence of such means the
believer

> could not hope to atone for hours of weakness or of thought-
> lessness by increased good will at other times. . . . There
> was no place for the very human Catholic cycle of sin, re-
> pentance, atonement, release, followed by renewed sin. . . .
> The moral conduct of the average man was thus deprived
> of its planless and unsystematic character. . . . Only a life
> guided by constant thought could achieve conquest over
> the state of nature. It was this rationalization which gave
> the Reformed faith its peculiar ascetic tendency. . . .[22]

And it was this ascetic tendency that explained the affinity between Calvinism and the "spirit of capitalism."

Weber believed that these and related theological doctrines
should be considered from the viewpoint of the promises
they placed before the believer, the dangers they foretold, and
hence the lines of conduct this picture of the relation between
man and God encouraged. But in order to see whether Calvinism had in fact encouraged unremitting effort, it was necessary

[21] *Ibid.*, pp. 114–18. It may be added that critics have questioned
Weber's analysis on this point, since it inferred a psychological condition—the feeling of religious anxiety—from an analysis of doctrines
and institutions. This and other critical questions of the sociology
of religion are considered in Chapter VIII of this book.

[22] *Protestant Ethic*, pp. 117–18.

to show that in the everyday conduct of the community Calvinist doctrines had provided effective incentives for the layman, and with this question in mind Weber examined the pastoral writings of Puritan divines.[23]

These writings were filled with exhortations and warnings that frequently represented answers to questions of conscience arising among members of the congregations. Weber's analysis of these writings may be summarized as follows: Man can find repose only in the world beyond, and possessions jeopardize his soul because they tempt him to relax his efforts. St. Paul's injunction, "He who will not work shall not eat," applied to all alike. The rich like the poor must work in a calling for the greater glory of God. Only an intensely active life measures up to the Puritan idea of religious piety. "It is for action that God maintaineth us and our activities: work is the moral as well as the natural end of power. . . . It is action that God is most served and honoured by . . ." wrote Richard Baxter. And with characteristic pungency John Bunyan stated: "It will not be said: did you believe? but: were you Doers, or Talkers only?" Indeed, an active life was thought of as a form of devotion, so that a common vocabulary was applied to both.

The Puritan divines praised work as a defense against all such temptations as religious doubts, the sense of unworthiness, or sexual desires. In this negative sense the praise of work gave rise to a detailed code of conduct. To waste time is a

[23] Cf. "Antikritisches Schlusswort," *op. cit.*, p. 582 ff., where Weber distinguished sharply between the analysis of doctrines and the analysis of their practical application. He also pointed out (*ibid.*, p. 592) that except for letters and autobiographies no type of material was as suitable for an analysis of this second problem as writings that reflected the concrete pastoral experience of the minister. Consequently, Weber used certain classic seventeenth-century texts of this kind, especially Richard Baxter's writings for the Presbyterians, Spener's *Theologische Bedenken* for German Pietists, Barclay's *Apology* for the Quakers, and others. These texts were a part of an extensive literature, which has been described and analyzed by William Haller in *The Rise of Puritanism* (New York: Columbia University Press, 1938). Professor Haller states in part (p. 154): "The endeavor of the preachers was . . . to arouse men out of indifference by warning them of the wrath to come. After that they were engrossed with two supreme dangers to morale, the failure of confidence and the excess of confidence."

deadly sin, for the span of life is infinitely short and precious, and man must use his every minute to serve the greater glory of God and make sure of his own "election." To use time in idle talk, in sociability, in sleep that exceeds the requirements of health, even in religious contemplation if it be at the expense of daily work, is evil because it detracts from the active performance of God's will in a calling.[24]

But unremitting labor was not merely a negative good; it was the way of life ordained by God in which every man must prove himself. The usefulness of labor was judged by the fruits that signify its favor in the sight of God. Profit and wealth were ethically bad only insofar as they led to idleness and dissipation; they were commended insofar as they resulted from the performance of duty. Man should not refuse to accept God's gifts and to be His steward: "You may labor to be rich for God, though not for the flesh and sin."[25] As long as it involved unremitting effort and the absence of indulgence, the successful pursuit of gain was, therefore, the duty of the businessman.

The full force of Puritan piety was enlisted in the attempt to safeguard this encouragement of worldly activities against

[24] In this connection Weber contrasts Franklin's entirely utilitarian advice, "Time is money," with Baxter's comment: "Keep up a high esteem of time and be every day more careful that you lose none of your time, than you are that you lose none of your gold and silver. And if . . . temptations rob you of any of your time, accordingly heighten your watchfulness." Quoted in *Protestant Ethic*, p. 261, n. 14. In keeping with these attitudes the believer was advised to keep a diary, for the Christian must one day give a strict account to his Lord.

[25] Quoted from Baxter's *Christian Directory* in *Protestant Ethic*, p. 162. Lest Baxter's statement be read as an unequivocal endorsement of gain, it is useful to add some comments from Richard Bernard's *Ruth Recompense* (1628), which contain the pertinent qualifications: "We may not think that he which is rich, can not be religious. True it is, that it is hard for a rich man to enter the Kingdome of heaven; but it is not impossible." Cited in Haller, *op. cit.*, p. 126. Weber contrasted this approach with that of Thomas Aquinas (1225–74), who regarded labor as part of the natural order and, as such, as necessary to maintain the individual and the community. Work not needed for these ends had no meaning; the rich man need not work, and religious contemplation has greater value than any worldly activities.

the great dangers to the soul arising from concern with mundane affairs. In opposing vain ostentation, the diversions of music and the theater, and all indulgence of the senses in art and popular festivities, the Puritan preachers sought to eliminate aimless pursuits on the ground that these served to glorify the flesh rather than God. Also, there were frequent warnings against emotional indulgence in personal life. Emotional relations among men, involving as they did the danger of idolatry, were suspect. Baxter advised caution even in relations with one's closest friend.[26] Bailey recommended that one should place one's trust in no one but God, that each morning one should think of going among people as of going into a wild forest full of dangers. And Spener warned that a friend gives his advice for reasons of the flesh, not for the greater glory of God. The Puritans even rejected song and ritual at the burial ceremony to keep it free of superstition and idolatry. Any expenditure is morally suspect if it serves men's pleasure, since man is a steward who must give an accounting for all the goods God has placed at his disposal.

In his essay on the Protestant ethic, Weber did not go substantially beyond the analysis of theological doctrines and pastoral writings. He sought to show that the inherent logic of these doctrines and of the advice based upon them both directly and indirectly encouraged planning and self-denial in the pursuit of economic gain. Weber stated explicitly that he was investigating

> . . . whether and at what points certain "elective affinities" are discernible between particular types of religious belief and the ethics of work-a-day life. By virtue of such affinities the religious movements have influenced the development of material culture, and [an analysis of these affinities] will clarify as far as possible the manner and the general *direction* [of that influence]. . . .
>
> We are interested in ascertaining those psychological *impulses* which originated in religious belief and the practice

[26] He wrote of friendship that it was "an irrational act and [it is] not fit for a rational creature to love any one farther than reason will allow us. . . . It very often taketh up men's minds so as to hinder their love of God." Quoted in *Protestant Ethic*, p. 224, n. 30.

of religion, gave direction to the individual's everyday way of life and prompted him to adhere to it.[27]

In his judgment this preliminary work had to be completed before it would be possible to estimate to what *extent* certain aspects of modern culture could be attributed to these religious forces.[28] It must be kept in mind, therefore, that, by itself, Weber's essay on Protestantism does not deal with the problem of causal imputation except incidentally. This essay merely defined a problem for further investigation, and it is interesting to see the lines of inquiry that appeared promising to him.

C. IDEAS AS CAUSES AND AS CONSEQUENCES

Weber pointed out that in the areas affected by Puritanism the ideas and the conduct of the people revealed significant traces of that influence long after the Age of Reformation had passed. He saw such traces, for example, in the modern ideal of a middle-class standard of living that approves of expenditures as ethical if they are necessary and practical. The Quakers developed this idea in their campaigns against temptations of the flesh and dependence on external things. Also, Puritanism had tended to eliminate from work the satisfaction of creative experience. Work as such was decreed by God, its ultimate purpose was the world beyond, and drudgery itself was a means of attaining certainty of grace. In this way impersonal mechanical labor, low wages and exploitation were given a religious sanction in the early period of modern capitalism.

The religious ideas of the sixteenth and seventeenth centuries were also reflected in certain forms of behavior. The unremitting energy with which the Puritan believer devoted himself to the fulfillment of his task often appeared to the Lutheran as a bustling that detracted from God. Lutheran

[27] *GAzRS*, Vol. I, pp. 83, 86. The same passages are translated somewhat differently in *Protestant Ethic*, pp. 91–92, 97. The term "elective affinity" was taken from the title of a novel by Goethe. Weber used it frequently to express the dual aspect of ideas, i.e., that they were created or chosen by the individual ("elective") and that they fit in with his material interests ("affinity").

[28] *Ibid.*, pp. 92, 183.

piety, with its cultivation of a childlike simplicity and sensitivity in man's relation to a God whose grace could always be regained through penitent contrition, contrasted sharply with the Puritan emphasis upon constant self-control over every action. And Weber saw that contrast still reflected in such characteristics as the somewhat sentimental good nature (*Gemütlichkeit*) of the Germans compared to the self-controlled reserve of the English or the impersonal friendliness of the Americans. In Weber's view *Gemütlichkeit* stemmed from an emotional religiosity that had originated in the Lutheran concept of man as the vessel of God's grace, while the high esteem of unsentimental impersonality in daily conduct had originated in Calvin's belief that man was the tool of the divine will. Accordingly, Germans deprecated the English control of impulse as an inner constraint that destroyed spontaneous feeling, while Englishmen and Americans regarded the personal emotion with which the Lutheran tradition endowed every performance, even of the humblest daily task, as sentimental self-indulgence.[29]

Still more important than these legacies of different religious tradition was the secularization that Puritanism had undergone. By imparting an ethos of planning and self-control to all economic activities, Puritan teaching encouraged worldly success, which in turn undermined the ascetic way of life. At an earlier time the asceticism of the monastic orders had also led to the acquisition of possessions, which subsequently jeopardized the way of life that had produced them. Accordingly, the Methodist revival of the eighteenth century was a close Puritan analogue to the earlier movements for monastic reform. Both aimed at the revival of asceticism. In a passage quoted by Weber, John Wesley wrote of the "continual decay of pure religion. . . . I fear, wherever riches have increased, the essence of religion has decreased in the same proportion. . . . For religion must necessarily produce both industry and

29 This characterization of the Puritan and the Lutheran traditions is contained in *Protestant Ethic*, pp. 126–28 and *passim*. It gives point to Weber's cryptic assertion that "the appeal to national character is generally a mere confession of ignorance," *ibid.*, p. 88, presumably because this appeal avoids the investigation needed to show the historical antecedents of observable national differences.

frugality, and these cannot but produce riches. But as riches increase, so will pride, anger, and love of the world in all its branches."[30]

These reflections point to the massive process of secularization, in the course of which utilitarian industriousness replaced the search for the kingdom of God and created a specifically bourgeois economic ethos.[31] The consciousness of standing in the fullness of God's grace and the belief that the pursuit of gain was the fulfillment of a higher duty had been superseded by "an amazingly good conscience" concerning the acquisition of money and the unequal distribution of worldly goods. In a famous passage toward the end of his essay, Weber wrote:

> The Puritan wanted to work in a calling; we are forced to do so. For when asceticism was carried out of monastic cells into everyday life, and began to dominate worldly morality, it did its part in building the tremendous cosmos of the modern economic order. . . . Since asceticism undertook to remodel the world. . . , material goods have gained an increasing and finally an inexorable power over the lives of men as at no previous period in history. . . . Victorious capitalism, since it rests on mechanical foundations, needs its support no longer. The rosy blush of its laughing heir, the Enlightenment, seems also to be irretrievably fading, and the idea of duty in one's calling prowls about in our lives like the ghost of dead religious beliefs.[32]

Weber saw a large number of possible investigations along these lines. How had the ascetic rationalism of the Puritans affected the organization and the daily life of social groups, from the congregation all the way up to the national state? How was it related to humanistic rationalism, to scientific empiricism, to the development of modern technology and culture? But Weber did not pursue this line of inquiry further.

[30] Quoted in *Protestant Ethic,* p. 175.

[31] Benjamin Franklin's autobiography expressed this ethos in his advice to a young tradesman. Weber cited this document in his attempt to define the "spirit of capitalism," but this proved to be confusing to many readers, since Franklin's work was also evidence of a stage in the secularization of the Protestant ethic.

[32] *Ibid.,* pp. 181–82.

Instead, he turned to the question of how the doctrines of the Reformation and the moral admonitions of the Puritan divines had become a "way of life common to whole groups of men." In order to answer this question, he examined the sectarian community.[33] Protestant sects and denominations and voluntary associations in the United States served him as a reminder of the social mechanism by which the moral strictures of the Puritan divines had been inculcated in the past. Puritan sects had been a special case of voluntary association among persons who shared a common style of life and who wanted to exclude nonbelievers from the social intercourse of their group. Members of the sects developed strong feelings of solidarity on the basis of common religious beliefs, and their conviction that they were chosen by God established a spiritual aristocracy of predestined saints within the world in contrast to the spiritual aristocracy of monks, who stood apart from the world. These Puritan saints had felt separated from the rest of humanity; their consciousness of divine grace gave them an unshakable belief in their own future salvation,[34] and they looked with contempt and hatred upon the sins of others.

Admission to the congregation—especially the privilege of being admitted to the Communion—had been the vehicle of organized social control from the very beginning of the Reformation. This control of the sects over their members had "worked . . . in the direction of breeding that ascetic occupational ethic which was adequate to modern capitalism during the period of its origin."[35] The organizational basis for this thoroughgoing religious regulation of life had been initiated by the Baptists of Zurich in the early sixteenth century,

[33] Cf. "The Protestant Sects and the Spirit of Capitalism," *Essays,* pp. 302–22. Weber repeatedly emphasized the importance of this article, which he subsequently incorporated in his collected essays on the sociology of religion. The essay was based in part on observations of religious life in the United States, made during his visit in 1904.

[34] Cf. Weber's remark that "the conception of the state of grace as a sort of social estate . . . is very common." *Protestant Ethic,* p. 228, n. 46.

[35] *Essays,* p. 312. Weber uses the term "adequate" both in the colloquial sense of equal to the requirement or occasion and in the legal and causal sense of grounds that are reasonably sufficient to start a legal action.

when they restricted their congregation to "true Christians."
Other movements of ascetic Protestantism had adopted a similar principle, according to which the true believers formed a
voluntary community, segregated from the world, in which
each man was guided solely by the Scriptures in his relation
to God.[36] The "church" discipline of the Protestant sects was
in the hands of laymen. Enforcement of that discipline was
the result of social pressure on the individual who lived under
the ever watchful scrutiny of his fellows:

> The member of the sect . . . had to *prove* repeatedly that
> he was endowed with these qualities. For, like his bliss in
> the beyond, his whole social existence in the here and now
> depended upon his "proving" himself. . . . According to all
> experience there is no stronger means of breeding traits than
> through the necessity of holding one's own in the circle of
> one's associates. . . .[37]

The social organization of the sects had provided the means
by which the ethical teachings of Puritan religiosity had become inculcated in a methodical style of life.

Weber pointed out that the Protestant ethic was only one
of several phenomena that pointed in the direction of increased
rationalism in various phases of social life. Rationalism had

[36] By their emphasis upon the religious qualification of laymen,
the Puritan sects had had to cope with recurrent organizational
problems in their attempt to keep the Lord's Supper pure and to
exclude from it all persons who were not sanctified. Wherever the
principle of the "believer's church" was adopted, there arose the
questions: Who was to be admitted to the sacraments, who was to
decide this matter, and on what basis? Weber touched upon some
of these controversies that have characterized the development of
Protestantism until modern times.

[37] *Ibid.*, pp. 320–21. One reason for this collective control of the
individual was that the congregation as a whole was responsible to
the Lord for the worthiness of the brethren admitted to Communion. And since only the members of the congregation could assess
the religious qualifications of one another, it was often felt that a
proper judgment was possible only in small congregations. A case
in point is the "Amsterdam Confession" of 1611, which declared
"that the members of every church and congregation *ought to know
one another* . . . Therefore a church ought not to consist of such a
multitude as cannot have practical knowledge of one another."
Quoted in *ibid.*, p. 456, n. 20.

had a many-sided development peculiar to Western civilization and more or less directly related to the development of
capitalism. For example, knowledge and observation had been
developed in many lands, but the Greeks were the first to
relate astronomy to mathematics and to develop a rational
proof in geometry; Babylonian astronomy lacked mathematics
and Indian geometry remained without rational proof. Similarly, the experimental method was first introduced in western
Europe, although natural science based on observation alone,
without experimentation, was developed in many countries.
Again, the West took the lead in the formulation and use of
rational concepts in historical scholarship and jurisprudence.
And in government administration as well as in economic enterprise, Western civilization came to be characterized by a
rational systematization for which there was no analogue in
the Orient. Thus, the study of the Protestant ethic merely ex-
plored one phase of that emancipation from magic, that "disenchantment of the world," that Weber regarded as the distinguishing peculiarity of Western culture.[38]

Moreover, this one phase had antecedents of its own.
Though Weber steadfastly maintained that in this case religious ideas had helped change the course of events, he also
pointed out that as yet he had done nothing to assess the impact of social and economic conditions upon the religious
movements of the Reformation.[39] In this respect he devoted
special attention to the history of the city in medieval Europe.
This part of his work is of interest here because, by tracing
the prior emergence of an ethics of trade and of a socially
cohesive urban middle class, it helps explain the special impact of Puritanism.

[38] Cf. *Protestant Ethic,* pp. 13–26, 76–78, 182–83, for various
statements on the many-sided development of rationalism.

[39] And in a whimsical aside he added that once he did so, his
critics would probably accuse him of materialism, as they now ac-
cused him of idealism. "Antikritisches zum 'Geist des Kapitalismus,'" *Archiv für Sozialwissenschaft,* Vol. XXX (1910), p. 196,
n. 28.

D. ETHICS OF TRADE AND THE
MEDIEVAL CITY

In his analysis of the Puritan sects, Weber emphasized the extraordinary internal cohesion that collective control and strict exclusion of nonbelievers had produced. Such a degree of cohesion, to use one of Weber's favorite lines of argument, usually resulted in a sharp and lasting cleavage between the in-group and the out-group. In the case of the Protestant sects, the great paradox was that there was no such cleavage. Instead of adopting a double standard that enjoined brotherliness within the community but sanctioned the exploitation and deception of all those outside, some of the sects prided themselves on their reputation of trustworthiness among the "sinful children of the world." This single ethical standard Weber found of particular significance for the development of modern capitalism. Although he showed that it was an aspect of Puritanism, he also traced its antecedents in the urban development of medieval Europe, going back ultimately to the basic presuppositions of Christianity.[40]

Puritanism's ethic of trade, which applied to believers and nonbelievers alike, was related to both religious doctrine and pastoral practice. Intense religious education, together with the threat of social ostracism, provided powerful incentives and sanctions, which explained the confidence that believers had in each other when engaged in business transactions within the community. These social controls were buttressed by the Puritan devaluation of all personal ties. Unwittingly, the Puritan divines brought about a profound depersonalization of family and neighborhood life when they demanded that a man be sober in his love for his next of kin and his associates so as not to jeopardize the work of his "calling." This emotional detachment within the community also reduced the so-

[40] I should add that Weber did not treat this problem in a systematic fashion, despite the fact that he dealt with its most important elements in many different parts of his work. Since he planned to investigate the early development of Christianity but did not live to do so, it is probable that he intended to provide this "missing link" eventually.

cial distance between its members and the strangers beyond the "gate." Hatred is as dangerous to the soul as love, and where the relation to one's kindred and associates is detached the rejection of the stranger becomes less imperative.

Originally, this attitude had a profoundly ethical basis. Implicit in it was the demand that man should order *all* his relationships with detachment, so that he could be single-minded in attending to the purpose in life that transcends all mundane concerns. Yet it also presupposed a decline in kinship loyalties and a separation of business affairs from family affairs, which were in fact the legacies of the century-long tradition that favored the development of mutual trust among men as individual members of a Christian community. This factor was of great significance in the development of economic rationalism:

> Originally, two opposite attitudes toward the pursuit of gain exist in combination. Internally, there is attachment to tradition and to the pietistic relations of fellow members of tribe, clan, and house-community, with the exclusion of the unrestricted quest of gain within the circle of those bound together by religious ties; externally, there is absolutely unrestricted play of the gain spirit in economic relations, every foreigner being originally an enemy in relation to whom no ethical restrictions apply; that is, the ethics of internal and external relations are categorically distinct. The course of development involves on the one hand the bringing of calculation into the traditional brotherhood, displacing the old religious relationship. As soon as accountability is established within the family community, and economic relations are no longer strictly communistic, there is an end of the naïve piety and its repression of the economic impulse. This side of the development is especially characteristic of the West. At the same time there is a tempering of the unrestricted quest of gain with the adoption of the economic principle into the internal economy. The result is a regulated economic life with the economic impulse functioning within bounds.[41]

This world historical transformation, then, was *not* the product of Puritanism; rather, Puritanism was a late development that

[41] *General Economic History,* p. 356.

reinforced tendencies that had distinguished European society for a long time past.[42]

Weber studied these tendencies in a comparative analysis of urban institutions.[43] In all parts of the world, cities are settlements of persons who are either entirely or in part alien to the locality. Urban settlements, therefore, are the most ancient setting in which the social and legal relations among aliens or between aliens and natives can be studied.[44] This can be stated most clearly by an extreme example. In ancient China, Mesopotamia, and Egypt, military leaders often founded a city at will or removed one to another site. In such cities the residents were composed of both volunteers and conscripts. In Mesopotamia forced settlement was especially pronounced, because the new residents had to dig a canal without which urban settlement in the desert was impossible. In such cities the military and political overlord, with his entourage and officials, remained the absolute ruler, and a community organization of the residents was either prevented or very much restricted. Those who settled in the city either remained members of tribes which did not intermarry or retained other previous local and kinship associations. Weber pointed out

[42] In what follows I make use of materials contained in Weber's study of *The City*, which was published posthumously in 1921 and which was later incorporated in his *Wirtschaft und Gesellschaft*. Probably, this study was written from 1911–13, though materials relevant to it are contained in Weber's works from the 1890's on. This book-length study is a major link in Weber's work as a whole, but he did not live to make this interrelation explicit. Like his other studies, Weber's analysis of the city encompasses many different themes, and, while I emphasize its relevance for the essays on Protestantism, it is just as legitimate to treat the study as a partial history of western European democracy. In previous discussions of Weber's work the study has been unduly neglected, especially by those who have criticized the essays on Protestantism without giving any attention to Weber's other writings. Fortunately, a translation is now available; see *The City* (tr. and ed. by Don Martindale and Gertrud Neuwirth [Glencoe: The Free Press, 1958]). The reader may also wish to consult *General Economic History*, Chapter 28, which contains a partial summary of these materials.

[43] Cf. Benjamin Nelson, *The Idea of Usury* (Princeton: Princeton University Press, 1949) for a study of these tendencies that corroborates Weber's approach on the basis of different materials.

[44] Cf. *WuG*, Vol. II, p. 533. *The City*, pp. 100–4.

that in ancient times this phenomenon was world-wide, whether or not the city was the result of forced settlement. In China the town resident usually was regarded as belonging to his native rural community. In the Hellenistic Near East broad strata of the population were in the same position. It is true that the town residents who possessed rights at all frequently did so as individuals, as, for example, in ancient Greek cities. But such rights were dependent upon their actual or at least nominal membership in kinship groups, which were in turn organized as military and political units.[45] Every such association represented the organization of a religious cult, to which the individual belonged on the basis of his blood relationship and of his membership in a military and political unit.

The town residents constituted a joint settlement of associations with their *separate* rights and duties, not a group of citizens who as residents of the same community possessed the *same* rights and duties. This differential legal status was powerfully reinforced by the separate cults of the kinship groups and the religious sanctions that buttressed the individual's kinship affiliation. Such affiliation also was a mark of social status; the common people who were not related to prominent kinship groups did not possess any political rights, and consequently only they were organized on the basis of their common membership in the local community. The full citizen, on the other hand, retained his traditional affiliation with his kinship group, his military unit, and his political association, because these alone legitimated his participation in the community cult and his eligibility for public office.[46]

[45] In ancient Greece—and elsewhere—these extended kinship groups were organized in military associations (*phratries*) and on a tribal basis in political associations (*phyles*). Weber used the term "sib" where I shall use the term "kinship group" or "extended kinship group." Technical terms do not seem pertinent where the reference is in general to group action based on kinship. Weber's reasons for using the term "sib" will be found in *GAzRS*, Vol. II, 56 n. and his more detailed discussion of kinship in *WuG*, Vol. I, pp. 201–4 and *passim*. In quotations using the term "sib" I have substituted the term "kinship group."

[46] It should be added that this structure of the urban community was retained in the many cases in which aliens settled together with natives in the same locality. In such cases aliens and natives were

All this was different in the medieval cities of western Europe, especially in the newly established communities in the north. Here the burgher joined the citizenry and swore his civic oath as an individual. This personal membership in the local association of the city, not his kinship or his tribal affiliation, was the basis of his legal rights as a citizen. Frequently, the new communities included aliens, either from other localities or from other regions and countries. Acceptance of aliens as equal citizens was less pronounced in old settlements, which were reconstituted as urban communities under the leadership of the local propertied classes. But the citizenship of even foreign merchants was not prohibited in principle. Only the Jews were excluded, because they could not go to Communion.

> For the medieval city like the ancient was an association based on a common cult with its city church, its patron saint, the participation of all citizens in the Communion and in the official church festivals of the community. Christianity had deprived the kinship group of all ritual significance. Every Christian community was basically *a confessional association of individual believers, not a ritual association of kinship groups.*[47]

But despite this dependence upon a common cult, the medieval city was a secular institution. Though church membership was a prerequisite of full citizenship, the parish was in the hands of lay elders in legally binding actions of the community.

---

joined together in a religious community through a ritual act while remaining divided into separate associations, often on the basis of quite artificial criteria, for the purpose of distributing the tax burden.

[47] *WuG*, Vol. II, p. 534. My italics. (See also *The City*, pp. 102–3. This translation appeared after the completion of this book; I have added references to this translation in parentheses after each quotation of the original.) The relevance of this distinction for economic development is best seen in relation to Weber's earliest study of medieval trading associations. In that study he showed the gradual legal separation between the workshop or office and the private dwelling of the family, between the firm and the family name, between business capital and private wealth. Such a separation was obviously impeded as long as kinship solidarity prevailed over the personal and economic interests of the individual. Cf. *Protestant Ethic*, p. 276, n. 78. Cf. *General Economic History*, pp. 202–29.

The "confessional association" of the medieval city underwent a major political transformation, beginning in the eleventh century and spreading rapidly during the twelfth century.[48] Originally the citizenry had been subject to many different and partly overlapping jurisdictions, which possessed
territorial rights in the community and from which the citizens
received assorted economic and legal privileges in return for
the payment of taxes. Bishoprics with territorial and political
authority, vassals or officials of kings or bishops who resided
in the city, lower ranks of such vassals and officials, family
freeholders of various types, status groups of privileged landlords with fortified castles and a more or less considerable following of dependents, urban craft guilds—all exercised authority over the city and its residents. Subsequently this legal and
political pluralism was either abolished or modified substantially and the city became an autonomous association of local
property owners whose goals were: the amicable settlement
of disputes; an administration of justice and a monopolization
of economic opportunities that would safeguard and enhance
the interests of the town residents; a reliable allocation of the
obligations due to the local lord in lieu of arbitrary taxation;
and, finally, the institution of a military organization that
would enhance the political and economic power of the community.[49]

This development of medieval cities toward local autonomy
occurred, broadly speaking, in one of two ways. In newly established cities the autonomous civic association often was
based on contracts with, or enactments by, the founder of the
community or his successors. In addition, there were many instances in which the successive privileges that were granted
to the community eventually legitimated a condition of legal
and political autonomy. Such cases of voluntarily conceded or
gradually evolved autonomy contrasted with a line of development, especially in some of the oldest cities, in which local

[48] The broad outline of Weber's thesis that is of interest here
has not been altered by subsequent research on the emergence of
urban autonomy in medieval Europe. A brief summary and evaluation of this recent work is contained in Otto Brunner, *Neue Wege
der Sozialgeschichte* (Göttingen: Vandenhoeck & Ruprecht, 1956),
pp. 80–115.
[49] *The City*, pp. 104–5, 108–11.

autonomy resulted from usurpation of authority. In these cases the propertied residents, especially the notables among them, organized themselves as a fraternal association bound by oath to oppose the powers that exercised or claimed "legitimate" authority over the community.[50] The details varied from place to place, and as a rule legal autonomy resulted from contractual changes, authoritative enactments, and acts of usurpation without clear-cut distinction.

The social and political effects of this development were far-reaching. Wherever it ran its full course, the communities acquired a municipal court and a partially autonomous power to enact and administer laws of their own. This partial autonomy was based on a status group of property owners, whose membership in an oath-bound, fraternal association entitled them to participate in some fashion in the election of municipal officials.[51] Such elections, in place of the earlier appointments by the established authorities, represented the decisive step toward urban emancipation from feudal or patrimonial rule.[52] City officials were prohibited from becoming subservient to any other type of authority; the fortresses of all secular and clerical rulers within the city walls as well as the privileged rights of residence on the part of these rulers were abolished in one way or another. Most important, a municipal law was codified and made mandatory, trial by combat was eliminated, and legal action against citizens outside the municipal jurisdiction was prohibited.

To be sure, this over-all characterization oversimplifies even

[50] In Weber's view these cases had been more frequent than appeared from the record, in part because such acts of usurpation tended to be gradual and in part because the city officials probably stressed the legal continuity of their government even if it was based on usurpation. Once autonomy had been established in some prominent cities, it tended to spread rapidly through voluntary adoption by secular authorities, since the legal and economic privileges of such autonomous rule gave the cities in which it had been accepted an obvious competitive advantage. See *The City*, pp. 107–8, 117–19.

[51] *Ibid.*, pp. 80–81, 110–12.

[52] The meaning of these terms is discussed below in Chapter XI. It should be added that from another viewpoint the drive toward urban autonomy can be interpreted as an elaboration of feudal or patrimonial rule.

the development of the Italian cities on which it is based, and which Weber compared in considerable detail with analogous developments in other parts of Europe. But in the present context these few references may suffice to remind the reader of the historical background that can help to "correct the isolation" of Weber's essay on the Protestant ethic.[53] A single standard of ethics in all business transactions and the use of community controls to guarantee both personal probity and the reliability of legal procedure obviously had important antecedents in the drive for urban autonomy that occurred four centuries before the Protestant Reformation. The use of an oath-bound fraternal association was an important precedent for the congregational form of church government. The city as a confessional association of all believers as *individuals* was evidence of the destruction of ritually sanctioned kinship ties (as in ancestor worship, for example) that the Christian tradition had bestowed on both the medieval city *and* the Protestant Reformation.[54] That tradition encouraged not only the religious but the legal equality of all believers in the urban community and facilitated the acceptance of foreigners as citizens with equal rights, as long as they were admitted to Communion. By depriving kinship ties of their religious significance, Christianity made it possible for the citizens of a

[53] Cf. *Protestant Ethic,* p. 284, n. 119, where Weber uses this phrase in his concluding footnote.

[54] Weber clarified this point further by stating that fraternization and community of worship were possible only because early Christianity had shattered the ritual barriers dividing Jews and Gentiles. This principle of a community of all believers was established clearly when Paul reproached Peter with dissimulation for withdrawing from his meal with the Gentiles because the Jews had approached and Peter had feared their censure. Paul told Peter that as a Jew who lived "after the manner of the Gentiles" he had no right to compel the Gentiles to live after the manner of the Jews. "Man is not justified by the works of the law [such as those pertaining to foods and circumcision], but by the faith of Jesus Christ. . . . For if righteousness come by the law, then Christ is dead in vain" (Gal. 2:16, 21. See also 2:11–14). Weber called this destruction of the ghetto and its ritual barriers an event of tremendous significance in the history of Western Christianity for that destruction was the indispensable prerequisite of solidarity and collective action among men who were *not* united by kinship ties. Cf. *Religion of India,* pp. 37–38.

community to establish an association without violating the magical and religious sanctions of their kinship group. This same tradition also encouraged that separation of business affairs from family affairs which developed with the expanding need for credit and the innovations in bookkeeping methods, especially in the Italian cities, and which culminated eventually in the Puritan injunction against emotional involvement with family and friends.

Christianity was not, however, the only factor responsible for the development of the Occidental city as an autonomous association with its own municipal officials. This development had been facilitated from the very beginning by the privileged legal position of the citizen, which consisted in the recognition of his subjective rights and especially of his right to participate in the process of adjudication.[55] These privileges related in turn to major characteristics of military organization. Weber pointed out that in the Occident until the time of the Roman Empire the army was composed of self-equipped soldiers. This meant that the secular authorities depended upon the good will of the army, especially where the highest administrative officers had to be recruited from the officer ranks of that army. Military associations of self-equipped soldiers were the basis of effective opposition to the supreme ruler, and such associations were established not only among landowners but among town residents as well.[56] Indeed, full citizenship in the towns of medieval Europe involved the obligation of military service, and it was on this basis that the struggle for the city's legal and political autonomy was won. That struggle could be successful because the decline of the religious sanctions of kinship solidarity contributed to the unity of the urban communities and because the secular authorities did not have at their disposal a nation-wide military establishment and administrative apparatus. In his studies of China and India, Weber devoted his attention to an analysis of the factors that accounted for the unbroken strength of kinship ties in both countries, the establishment of a nation-wide bureaucracy in China, and the

[55] For details see *Law*, pp. 86, 90, and *passim*. Cf. the discussion of the legal developments of Western civilization in Chapter XII, B.

[56] The significance of this background for the development of European feudalism is discussed in Chapter XI.

absence of the political autonomy in cities and other institutions that is so characteristically Western. This contrast between Oriental and Occidental civilization puts *The Protestant Ethic* in proper perspective. The ideas analyzed in that essay could not have had the impact Weber attributed to them without the manifold ideological and institutional legacies that gradually formed the urban population of medieval Europe into a "ready-made" audience for the doctrines of the great Reformers:

> The origin of a rational and innerworldly ethic is associated in the Occident with the appearance of thinkers and prophets . . . who developed in a social context which was alien to the Asiatic cultures. This context consisted of the *political* problems engendered by the bourgeois status-group of the *city*, without which neither Judaism, nor Christianity, nor the development of Hellenistic thinking are conceivable.[57]

[57] *GAzRS*, Vol. II, p. 372. (*Religion of India,* pp. 337–38. This translation appeared after the completion of this book; I have added references to this translation in parentheses after each quotation of the original.)

PART TWO

SOCIETY, RELIGION, AND SECULAR ETHIC: A COMPARATIVE STUDY OF CIVILIZATIONS

CHAPTER IV

INTRODUCTION

The Protestant Ethic raises the question: What are the roots of the Western idea that man has a duty in his calling? From this specific problem Weber moved on to an inquiry of much broader scope, i.e., the relation between religion and society in different civilizations. By comparing the ethics of several religious doctrines he sought to show how some had an accelerating and others a retarding effect upon the rationality of economic life. In this context it is appropriate to remind ourselves of Weber's legal background.[1]

In history as in law, causal analysis is based on mental experiments and hypothetical constructions that relate a specific event to a potential infinity of antecedents. Such antecedents can be assessed by asking: If condition X had not occurred, would result Y have come about anyway? Or does the absence of X lead us to expect either the absence of or a substantial modification of Y? Such questions can be answered in terms of rules of experience and relevant comparative or circumstantial evidence, but the answers remain proximate. In the

[1] At the time he was working on the *Protestant Ethic* he also was writing a methodological essay in which he referred specifically to the importance of legal reasoning for the causal analysis of historical phenomena. Cf. *Methodology*, p. 166 ff.

present case Weber concluded that no one can say how the capitalist economic system would have originated without the Protestant ethic, while there is circumstantial evidence that the absence of such an ethic retarded economic developments elsewhere.[2] There also is considerable evidence of the affinity between the Protestant ethic and the "spirit of capitalism." Weber's view was that this ethic had been a causal factor of uncertain magnitude whose importance could be denied only if the origin of the "capitalist spirit" in the West were explained more convincingly on some other ground.[3] But "causal analysis" is only one of several problems that he pursued in his study of religion.

At least three such problems can be distinguished in Weber's work: (1) the effect of major religious ideas on the secular ethic and economic behavior of the average believer; (2) the effect of group formation on religious ideas; and (3) the determination of what was distinctive for the West by a comparison of the causes and consequences of religious beliefs in different civilizations. Weber contended that a causal analysis of Western cultural development would be possible only after these problems had been investigated, and he wanted to examine the influence of ideas on economic behavior and of social conditions on ideas "so far as it is necessary in order to find points of comparison with the Occidental development."[4] This emphasis on the differences between East and West does not, however, provide a clear-cut framework. Since his writings are an intricate web of related themes, it is necessary to articulate the questions he asked and the perspective that guided him in his approach.[5]

[2] For a detailed exposition of this causal analysis, cf. Talcott Parsons, *The Structure of Social Action* (Glencoe: The Free Press, 1949), p. 500 ff.

[3] He denies the possibility of quantitative precision in this field. See "Antikritisches Schlusswort zum 'Geist des Kapitalismus,'" *Archiv für Sozialwissenschaft*, Vol. XXX (1910), p. 598.

[4] Cf. *Protestant Ethic*, p. 27, for the full statement of purpose.

[5] I confine myself here to a summary characterization of this perspective. An analysis of Weber's approach is presented in Chapter VIII.

A. STATUS GROUPS AND CLASSES

In his early studies of farm labor in eastern Germany and the stock exchange, Weber used the term *Stand* (status group) in an offhand manner to refer to such groups as *Junkers*, industrialists, and German civil servants. In imperial Germany *Stand* designated the social rank of an individual and of his group. In common parlance the term occurred frequently when people spoke of a marriage as being in accord with, or beneath, the station of the bride or groom. This rank-consciousness was part of a complex phenomenon. Weber emphasized that the collective actions of *Junkers* as well as of farm workers could not be understood in economic terms alone. It also was necessary to analyze the ideas derived from the subculture of each group—in Weber's terms, its "style of life"—which entered into the evaluation of its economic interests. In this sense the farm workers were as much a *Stand* as the *Junkers*, for their resistance to personal subservience had become as ineradicable an element of their whole outlook as the patriarchal manner had become part and parcel of the *Junkers'* way of life. Though one would commonly apply the term *Stand* only to higher social ranks, Weber used it for all social groups, stressing that the distinctions of prestige had a positive as well as an invidious aspect. For example, the *Junkers'* refusal to associate on equal terms with members of the middle class was evidence not merely of personal conceit but of the desire to preserve a way of life, which at one time embodied the genuine values of Prussian civilization.

The significance of this concept of *Stand* or status group[6] becomes apparent in the contrast Weber made between it and class:

The term "class" refers to any group of people . . . [who have the same] typical chance for a supply of goods, external living conditions, and personal life experiences, insofar as this chance is determined by the . . . power . . . to

[6] I believe that "status group" is an adequate translation of *Stand*. In medieval society its original meaning was "estate." However, Weber's use of the term includes all instances of cohesive social groups with their subcultures and their exclusion of outsiders.

dispose of goods or skills for the sake of income in a given economic order. . . . "Class situation" is, in this sense, ultimately "market situation."[7]

For Weber as for Marx, the basic condition of "class" lay in the unequal distribution of economic power and hence the unequal distribution of opportunity. But for Weber this economic determination did not exhaust the conditions of group formation. A concept had to be formulated that would encompass the influence of ideas upon the formation of groups without losing sight of economic conditions.

> In contrast to the economically determined "class situation" we wish to designate as *"status situation"* every typical component of the life fate of men that is determined by a specific, positive or negative, social estimation of *honor*. . . . In content, status honor is normally expressed by the fact that a specific *style of life* can be expected from all those who wish to belong to the circle. Linked with this expectation are restrictions on "social" intercourse (that is, intercourse which is not subservient to economic . . . purposes). These restrictions may confine normal marriages within the status circle. . . .
>
> Stratification by status goes hand in hand with a monopolization of ideal and material goods or opportunities. . . . Besides the specific status honor, which always rests upon distance and exclusiveness, we find all sorts of material monopolies. Such honorific preferences may consist of the privilege of wearing special costumes, of eating special dishes taboo to others, of carrying arms. . . .
>
> The decisive role of a "style of life" in status "honor" means that status groups are the specific bearers of all "conventions."[8]

These two conditions of collective actions are antithetical. The market knows of no personal distinctions. For example, transactions on the stock exchange are reduced to a few standardized phrases or signs. The only relevant distinction among brokers is their respective credit rating. In short, economic ac-

[7] *Essays*, pp. 181, 182.
[8] *Ibid.*, pp. 186–87, 187–88, 190–91.

tions are oriented toward "a rationally motivated adjustment of interests."[9] The reverse is true of the status order, in which men are grouped by their prestige and way of life. All actions based on considerations of status are oriented to the "feeling of the actors that they belong together."[10] To safeguard status, men will oppose all suggestions that wealth as such is a valid basis of prestige. Otherwise, a rich man could claim more "honor" than one with a distinguished family lineage, and this would undermine the status order.

The distinction between class and status group is directly related to Weber's sociology of religion. On the one hand, he investigated group formation on the basis of shared religious ideas. Here ideas serve as a bulwark of group cohesion, as a means of status distinction, and as a basis for monopolizing economic opportunities. On the other hand, he examined given social groups, such as craftsmen or feudal knights, in terms of the religious propensities engendered by their class situation and status interests. Here ideas become a reflection of material interests.

B. RELIGIOUS LEADERSHIP

According to Weber the great world religions originated in religious ideas and should be studied in terms of "the content of [their] annunciation and promise."[11] This doctrinal aspect involves a "rationalization of religious life" that goes beyond prayers and sacrifices for the sake of good fortune. Also, the development of a systematic concept of man's relation to the divine is inseparable from the groups—priests, prophets, and others—engaged in such "rationalization."[12] By analyzing the

[9] *Ibid.*, p. 183.

[10] *Ibid.*, pp. 183, 192. The phrases in quotation marks define Weber's distinction between *societal* and *communal* actions.

[11] *Ibid.*, p. 270.

[12] The importance of this emphasis in Weber's approach is reflected in the subtitle of his systematic sociology of religion, which may be translated as "Types of Communal Association Based upon Religious Belief" (*Typen religiöser Vergemeinschaftung*). Cf. *WuG*, Vol. I, p. 227. This part of Weber's work is being translated by Dr. Ephraim Fischoff and is scheduled for eventual publication by The Beacon Press.

emergence of such groups, their changing position in the society, and their "material and ideal interests," the impact of ideas upon society becomes understandable.[13]

Man's relationship to the transcendental powers may be one of prayer, sacrifice, and worship, or one of magical compulsion. Accordingly, one may designate as "gods" those powers that are venerated and as "demons" those that are compelled by magic. The distinction is not hard and fast,[14] but it is a useful starting point for a distinction between "priests" and "magicians." Priests superintend the worship of the "gods," while magicians seek to compel "demons"; priests are employed functionaries in a permanent organization for influencing the deities, while magicians are free-lance professionals hired by individuals from time to time; priests possess a knowledge of formulated doctrines and hence a professional qualification, while magicians—and prophets also—prove their personal charisma through miracles and personal revelation.[15] Each of these distinctions creates difficulties that cannot be entirely resolved. Still, the decisive criterion of a priesthood is the regular organization of religious worship that is bound by definite norms and occurs at specified times and places. Although such worship can occur without a separate priesthood, the latter does not occur without the former; and although magicians often were organized in guilds and developed religious doctrines, they have nowhere been associated with a religious organization.

The distinction between priests and magicians is related to Weber's major interest in the "rationalization of religious life."

[13] See *WuG*, Vol. I, especially pp. 240–45, 249–54, 257, 260–67.

[14] This emphasis on the relative artificiality of all distinctions recurs throughout Weber's work. The complexity of his text arises in part from his effort to show the validity of the proposed distinction *after* a full discussion of the "gradual transitions" of the phenomena in question.

[15] "The term 'charisma' will be applied to a certain quality of an individual personality by virtue of which he is set apart from ordinary men and treated as endowed with supernatural, superhuman, or at least specifically exceptional powers or qualities. These are . . . not accessible to the ordinary person, but are regarded as of divine origin or as exemplary, and on the basis of them the individual concerned is treated as a leader." See *Theory*, pp. 358–59.

A systematization of man's relation to the divine and a religious ethic based on such metaphysical conceptions are absent where worship is conducted without an established priesthood or where magicians prevail and regular worship does not exist. Under these conditions religious ideas tend to make all traditional practices sacred and, therefore, unalterable.

> Every magical procedure which has been "proved" efficacious is naturally repeated strictly in the successful form. That is extended to everything which has symbolic significance. The slightest departure from the approved norm may vitiate the action. All branches of human activity get drawn into this circle of symbolic magic.[16]

The "rationalization of religious life," which contrasts with this sanctification of tradition, develops fully only where a priesthood has successfully established a status ethic and a power position. Priests are continuously preoccupied with religious worship and pastoral functions. On that basis they gradually develop an ethical concept of a deity, according to which the order of nature and society is under a god's protection and those who violate the sanctified norms will be punished.[17] This rationalization replaces magic ideas of evil with a religious ethic; misfortune results not from the failing power of one's god but from his wrath, which has been aroused by man's violation of his commandments.

At times these tendencies, which are inherent in the institution of the priesthood, have been powerfully aided by religious prophecy. A prophet is any man who "by virtue of his purely personal charisma and by virtue of his mission proclaims a religious doctrine or a Divine command."[18] In contrast to the priest, who serves a holy tradition, the prophet claims authority on the basis of a "personal" call—a major reason why prophets have rarely originated in the ranks of the priesthood. Even when the priest possesses a personal charisma, his function is legitimate only by virtue of a regular organization of

[16] *WuG*, Vol. I, p. 230.
[17] This concept contrasts with the anthropomorphism that makes gods and demons appear merely superhuman in their unrestrained passions but not omniscient, omnipotent, or even particularly moral.
[18] *Ibid.*, p. 250.

worship, while the prophet's effectiveness depends on his personal endowment and sense of mission.[19] Weber distinguished between the ethical prophecy of the Near East and exemplary prophecy, especially of India, yet both types seek to give coherent meaning to the world and orient man's conduct accordingly for the sake of his salvation. All prophecy attempts to systematize conduct into a normatively regulated way of life. If successful, prophets win permanent disciples as well as adherents who support them occasionally. A permanent religious community develops only when the prophet's personal mediation of divine grace becomes the function of a permanent institution and his personal following is organized into a congregation.[20]

Because of its appeal to the laity, all prophecy is a challenge to priestly traditions and to the magical elements surviving in religious ritual. The holiness of new revelation stands against the holiness of tradition. In this struggle the priesthood seeks to protect established doctrine or to systematize the prophetic teaching if it is victorious, to delimit orthodox from heterodox belief, and to inculcate that belief in the laity.[21] Even in the absence of a prophetic challenge, priests endeavor to systematize established beliefs in order to protect their position against attack and to combat skepticism or indifference. Eventually such systematization results in canonical writings containing revelations and holy traditions, and in

[19] Prophets are closely related to other types of religious leaders. Like magicians, they have personal charisma and use magic as a means of authentication; but they differ from magicians because their mission consists of proclaiming doctrines or commands without compensation. Again, prophets are similar to the great lawgivers in that their divinely inspired doctrine is not easily distinguished from laws that are subsequently sanctioned by invocations of divine blessings; yet prophets are entirely concerned with religious questions, even where they touch on social questions, while with the great lawgivers the emphasis is reversed. Prophets also have elements in common with teachers of ethical philosophy, like Pythagoras, who gather disciples and found schools; but such teachers lack the emotional sermon through which the prophet proclaims religious truths. See *ibid.*, pp. 250–57.

[20] Weber also discussed comparable institutional developments in the case of other types of religious leaders.

[21] For a more detailed analysis of this process, cf. *AJ*, p. 336 ff.

dogmatic expositions containing the priestly interpretations of their meanings. Gradually the orally transmitted secret knowledge of magicians and priests becomes a written tradition and, as such, the basis of education for priests and laity. The religious communities that arise provide the priesthood with an ever-recurring impetus for further systematization of its holy knowledge, which becomes a symbol of membership in the religious community and demands vigilance to safeguard the purity and efficacy of the received doctrine. Thus, an "otherworldly" orientation as the only appropriate and specifically religious attitude has been the work of religious leaders who have constituted dominant status groups in each of the great world religions.

Weber identified each of the great systems of religion with a status group of religious leaders. Confucianism was the ethic of government officials in the Chinese dynasties, men with literary education who excluded from their privileged position those who lacked the cultural prerequisites, and it influenced the entire Chinese way of life. Early Hinduism also was the product of cultured literati who, unlike the Chinese bureaucrats, did not occupy any office but functioned as a hereditary caste of expert advisers on questions of personal ethic and ritual propriety. Educated in the Veda, the Brahmins were a fully recognized religious status group that placed its stamp on the social order. Subsequently Buddhism emerged. This movement of contemplative and mendicant monks rejected the world and represented a sacramental religiosity in comparison with which the more worldly Brahmins were inferior religious laymen. Early Islam was a religion of disciplined, world-conquering warriors, the highest stratum of Arab society. During the Islamic Middle Ages, however, a new religious movement, Sufism, which emphasized contemplative and mystical practices, came to the fore and eventually took the form of fraternal associations under the leadership of lower-class specialists in orgiastic practices. Judaism since the Exile was the religion of pariah people—a group of second-class citizens specializing in occupations despised by others and separated from them by ritual and legal barriers that limited social intercourse—which during the Middle Ages came under the leadership of intellectuals trained in ritual and literature. Again, Christianity originated as a doctrine of itinerant artisans. Throughout its history it remained an urban middle-class religion. The Occidental city became its main center, beginning with the ancient religious communities and extending through the mendicant orders of the Middle Ages to the Reformation and the modern Protestant denominations.[22]

Each of these religions underwent a development toward a "book religion" while the charismatic qualifications of religious functionaries became depersonalized and literary. According to Weber, this development arose from the contact among prophets, priests, and the lay public, since the inspired message of the prophet as well as the more casuistic ethic of the priest had to relate to the conventions and imperatives of everyday life. In their endeavor to guide laymen in accordance with the divine will, priests adapt their doctrines and counsel to the traditional thoughts and feelings of the laity, especially if their priestly power and income depends upon a pastoral function. Yet the religious traditionalism of the masses frequently consists of magical beliefs and practices that tend to satisfy the hope for mundane benefits. The same applies to prophecy. Initially prophets disrupt the popular belief in magic and the tradition-bound ritualism of the priests and oppose both with their inspired ethic of a new or renewed view of man and God. But the authentication of the prophetic message before the public always presupposes that the magic power of the prophet appears superior to that of others. And although prophets regularly reject the persistent demands for new miracles, they are unable to control the process of institutionalization that entails their own deification or in which the religious traditionalism of the people reasserts itself. Neither prophets nor priests can afford to reject all compromise with the traditional beliefs of the masses.

C. THE RELIGIOSITY OF THE MASSES

Weber believed that ordinary men are influenced by religion because of their mundane expectations rather than because they have any concern with great religious ideas.

[22] See *Essays*, pp. 268–69, and *WuG*, Vol. I, especially p. 293.

Men act in obedience to religious or magical beliefs so that they "may prosper and have a long life on earth". . . . Such actions are moreover relatively rational: though not necessarily based on considerations of means and ends, they are still based on rules of experience. The "magical" gesture of the wise man induces rain from the sky, just as the twirling-stick elicits a spark from the wood. And the spark which the stick produces is just as much a "magical" product as the rain which the rainmaker has produced through his manipulation. Thus, the actions or ideas which are religiously or "magically" motivated are by no means to be separated from the round of everyday, purposeful activity, especially since the purposes of those actions and ideas are themselves predominantly economic.[23]

He therefore found it appropriate to examine the religious propensities of different social groups whose material interests might give rise to divergent religious beliefs.[24]

Weber distinguished between groups that depend upon commerce, handicrafts, or industry, and those that depend upon agriculture. Commerce and industry are steady; agriculture is seasonal. Commerce and industry require calculation; the relation between work and the end-product is by and large foreseeable. They are much less dependent than agricultural work upon natural forces and the unfathomable character of organic birth and growth. Commercial or industrial pursuits occur in the confinement of houses and hence under conditions of relative alienation from the processes of nature. But these processes become a problem and a mystery precisely where they are no longer taken for granted. Rationalistic questions arise concerning the "meaning" of existence in a beyond, and these lead to religious speculations.

During the nineteenth century it became customary in Europe to attribute a high degree of religiosity to the peasantry, but Weber pointed out that this view merely reflected the recent development of agrarian Romanticism. A comparative approach suggested rather that social strata that are dependent

[23] *WuG*, Vol. I, p. 227.
[24] The following discussion is based on *WuG*, Vol. I, pp. 267–78, and Vol. II, pp. 793–96.

upon agricultural production tend toward magic or religious indifference. Systems of religious belief have rarely been the work of peasants; as a result of their dependence upon natural events their economic interests do not lend themselves to a rational systematization. Exceptions occur primarily when peasants are threatened by enslavement or proletarization. On the other hand, a landowning military aristocracy or other ruling class based on land ownership has a general aversion to any form of emotional religiosity.

> A warrior's style of life has no affinity with the idea of a kindhearted Divine providence nor with the idea of an otherworldly God who makes systematic ethical demands. Concepts like "sin," "salvation," or "religious humility" are not only remote from the feeling of dignity which is characteristic of all politically dominant strata . . . but they are also seen as a direct insult to that dignity. A war hero or a man of high rank will regard it as plebeian and undignified to bow down before a prophet or priest and to accept a religiosity which uses such concepts.[25]

Neither lords nor peasants have a desire for "salvation" or a clear idea concerning the fate from which they should want to be saved. Their gods are powerful beings with passions much like those of human beings: cunning or courageous, friendly or full of wrath, and in addition quite amoral by ordinary standards. They are subject to bribery through sacrifices or to coercion through magical manipulations. Priesthood and the fulfillment of ritual prescriptions are seen in a utilitarian manner: they serve as a means for the magical control of natural forces, especially as a defense against demons, whose ill will brings bad weather, disease, and damage from insects or wild animals. Under these conditions there is little tendency to develop a theodicy or to engage in ethical speculations about the order of the cosmos.

Weber's interest in the development of Western capitalism led him to a special concern with the religious propensities of "bourgeois" strata. As previously mentioned, the adherence of the middle classes to the Puritan movement is unusual be-

[25] *Ibid.*, Vol. I, p. 270.

cause Puritanism involved heroic and ascetic qualities that the middle classes of other times and places generally have lacked. Weber elaborated this point by showing that this general trait is compatible with many different propensities. Great merchants and financiers everywhere have a skeptical or indifferent orientation toward religious questions. On the other hand, a rigorous religious orientation has been true not only of the Puritans but also of the Jainas in India, the Parsis in India and Persia, the Jews, and perhaps the mercantile groups in Islam as well. This religiosity of bourgeois strata seems to originate in urban life. In the city the religious experience of the individual tends to lose the character of an ecstatic trance or dream and to assume the paler forms of contemplative mysticism or of a low-keyed, everyday piety. For the craftsman, steady work with customers can suggest the development of concepts like "duty" and "recompense" as basic orientations toward life. On this basis the gods can be conceived as ethical powers that desire and reward "good" while punishing "evil." The gods themselves conform to ethical demands while men in turn develop the feeling of "sinfulness" and the longing for "salvation." And indeed certain religious developments *had* occurred in conjunction with commercial developments in the cities.

However, religious rationalization is occasioned by urban developments only in conjunction with the emergence of priestly education. Ancient Judaism probably was influenced by the great cultural centers, but compared with that in Egypt and Mesopotamia there was little commercial development in Palestine and cities did not play a prominent role in the emergence of ethical rationalism. The later development of Judaism, on the other hand, was the work of the priesthood in Jerusalem. Again in ancient Greece, the cities did not produce a religious rationalization at all in view of the influence of Homer and because of the absence of an established priesthood. These examples suggest that urban commerce by itself has no determinate effect on religion in the absence of an organized priesthood. But once a priesthood develops, it will find ready support for its own tendencies toward autonomy and religious rationalism among the urban, bourgeois strata.

In this way, according to Weber, certain general propensities do in fact arise from the material conditions and status situation of different social groups and give rise to particular styles of life to which some religious ideas give congenial expression and others do not.[26] This very general compatibility between status groups and systems of belief can be nullified by historical conditions that militate against the "typical" orientation of such groups. Moreover, ideas are more than intentional or unwitting adjustments to the exigencies of the social situation. For these reasons Weber emphasized the importance of intellectual leaders in the development of religious ideas, though their contribution is in turn affected by their social origins and their varying relations to the priesthood and the political powers.[27] Weber believed that the links between ideas and given historical conditions result from choices—but from choices that are limited by what the status groups concerned find congenial with their respective life experience.

The preceding discussion suggests that Weber's studies of Confucianism, Hinduism and Judaism may be considered in terms of a three-fold subdivision, a task undertaken in the next three chapters. The first section of each of these deals with the broad features of the social structure of China, India, and Palestine. Since the great religious innovators of China, India and the Near East all lived during the thousand years preceding the beginning of the Christian Era, Weber's studies centered upon this age of religious creativity. The second section of each of the next chapters deals with the principal tenets of the prevailing religious orthodoxy and with the implicit economic ethics of those tenets. Also, since orthodoxy has been challenged everywhere by sectarian movements and doctrines, which in the West proved to be of major importance for the "spirit of capitalism," Weber dealt in each case with these heterodox beliefs as well. Finally, the third section of the next

[26] Cf., for example, Weber's discussion of the religious propensities of craftsmen (ibid., Vol. I, p. 275 ff.) who played an important role in the development of Christianity. It should be added that Weber also reversed this approach by analyzing the varying appeal of religious conceptions to the major status groups under different historical conditions. Cf. Essays, Chapters 11 and 13. This discussion has been omitted in the present volume.

[27] Cf. WuG, Vol. I, p. 286 ff.

chapters seeks to assess the particular ordering of human life
that is encouraged by the given system of religious beliefs,
how this ordering compares with those of other religious systems, and especially how it is related to the rationality of economic conduct that characterized the Occidental development.

CHAPTER V

SOCIETY AND RELIGION IN CHINA

Weber's essay on Confucianism and Taoism[1] was his second study in the sociology of religion. In contrast to *The Protestant Ethic*, it begins with an analysis of Chinese society. Two aspects of that analysis should be explained by way of introduction. First, Weber confined himself by and large to the early period of Chinese history—the period during which China's great half-legendary teachers and religious innovators lived and in terms of which their work could best be understood.[2] The emphasis on the early period was not exclusive, however. Weber freely cited data up to the beginning of the twentieth century and in so doing ignored chronology. While this aspect of his work has often been criticized, it is sufficient for our purposes to point out that it had a rationale. Certain

[1] *The Religion of China* (Glencoe: The Free Press, 1951) is a translation of GAzRS, Vol. I, pp. 276–536. The translator, H. H. Gerth, changed the title in order to avoid the "isms" of the original.
[2] Confucius lived from approximately 551 to 479 B.C.; Lao Tzu, whose followers were called Taoists, probably lived somewhat later, in the fourth century B.C., and Mencius, a major expositor of Confucian doctrine, lived from 372 to 289 B.C. At the time Weber wrote, it was believed that Lao Tzu had lived in the sixth century, as a near-contemporary of Confucius, but this view has since been revised.

aspects of the Chinese social structure had remained relatively unchanged—at any rate up to the fall of the Manchu dynasty in 1911—and the various possibilities inherent in that structure therefore could be elucidated by reference to events from different periods. In addition, Weber made clear that he was not a specialist in this field and that he had no intention of writing a social and economic history of China.[3] He merely wanted to focus attention on those conditions of Chinese society that could be distinguished from analogous conditions in western Europe. In such comparisons and contrasts he neglected chronology for the sake of formulating concepts that could then be used in an analysis of historical events.[4]

A. CONTRASTS AND EARLY HISTORY

In order to characterize the more enduring aspects of Chinese society Weber singled out the distinctive features of Chinese cities, Chinese patrimonialism and officialdom, and Chinese religious organization.

Cities. The contrast between Chinese and western European cities was not absolute. As in the Occident, Chinese cities frequently originated as fortresses and princely residences. They were centers of trade and craft production, their separate quarters were under the control of guild organizations, and the money expended in them frequently was derived from rents as well as from trade. But in China, cities never acquired political autonomy in any of the forms familiar in the West. They had no charter that stipulated the political privileges of the community and, indeed, fewer guarantees of self-government than the villages. Rather than constituting legally independent districts, the cities consisted of several "village districts"—or blocks—so that they could not function as corporate bodies. Also, no forces like the oath-bound associations and autono-

[3] *Religion of China,* pp. 80, 252.
[4] This is what Weber means when he says that he would consider Chinese and Indian society and religion "in order to find points of comparison with the Occidental development."

mous political bodies of the Occidental cities emerged to facilitate their legal and military independence.

The absence of such urban independence in China was
partly due to the fact that "the fetters of the kinship group
were never shattered." Every new resident of a town retained
his ties with the native place of his family by maintaining all
ritually and personally important relations in the ancestral
land.[5] This preservation of family ties was related to the practice of ancestor worship, which made the kinship tie the inviolable basis of man's relation to the spirits, in contrast to
Christianity which emphasized each individual's relation to
God. By binding each town resident to the village in which
the worship of his family's ancestors took place, the ties of
kinship necessarily militated against the citizens' political solidarity. Although the Chinese guilds of merchants and craftsmen had considerable power over their members, there was
no basis for solidarity among them. Instead, the guilds, like
the kinship groups on which they were based, were mutually
competing associations for self-help, which sought to gain favors from the Emperor and his officials. Thus the residents of
Chinese cities never constituted a separate status group of citizens subject to an autonomous urban jurisdiction involving distinct privileges and obligations.[6]

Patrimonialism.[7] Another equally important reason for the

[5] *Ibid.*, p. 14.

[6] These and other peculiarities of Chinese as contrasted with
western European cities are analyzed in Weber's *The City*, p. 80 ff.
For a summary and evaluation of more recent research, cf. Wolfram
Eberhard, "Data on the Structure of the Chinese City in the Pre-
Industrial Period," *Economic Development and Cultural Change*,
Vol. IV (1956), pp. 253–68.

[7] A full discussion of this concept is contained in Chapter XI, but
since the term recurs in the intervening chapters a brief explanation
is in order. Weber used the term to refer to any type of government that is organized as a more or less direct extension of the royal
household. Officials originate as household servants and remain personal dependents of the ruler as long as patrimonialism remains intact. Weber contrasted this with feudalism, in which government is
organized on the basis of a fealty relation between the ruler and his
vassals, independent, self-equipped warriors who exercise the authority of government in more or less autonomous fashion in the
lands granted to them on a hereditary basis.

absence of urban autonomy in China was the early, albeit relative, centralization of the imperial government. Weber cited several reasons for this. In the great river valleys, the recurring danger of floods as well as the needs of agriculture led to the early construction of dikes, dams, and canals; at the same time, the defense of the country against nomadic invaders demanded the construction of frontier fortifications. The economic prosperity of the cities, the central collection of taxes, as well as the central organization of defense depended upon this regulation of rivers and canals.[8] All this required a relatively centralized, large-scale administrative staff from about the third century B.C. onward. With a bureaucracy at their disposal, the early Chinese rulers were able to organize a centrally controlled military establishment. Officers and men were equipped and maintained out of government storehouses and locally recruited soldiers usually were moved to areas far from their home district to minimize the danger to the ruling authorities.

These evidences of centralized power must be put against evidences of local power to obtain a balanced picture. In the military field, for example, recruitment was in the hands of local officials. Although cities were unable to organize "militia" of their own, prominent local families were able to do so, especially in times of emergency. The imperial government endeavored, of course, to curb tendencies toward local independence by its control over the officials and the demobilization of emergency troops, and despite many vicissitudes these efforts were successful in the long run. Weber attributed this success —and hence the absence of a self-equipped army in the hands of urban residents or of feudal lords—to the absence of autonomous, effectively organized local status groups and to the peaceful times of the early Chinese Empire. This latter factor made it possible to rule the country with a standing army of

[8] Since Weber's day this emphasis on the regulation of rivers and the construction of irrigation systems has been developed into a theory of Asiatic society by Karl A. Wittfogel, *Oriental Despotism* (New Haven: Yale University Press, 1957). It will be noted, however, that Weber's emphasis on centralization is much more qualified than Wittfogel's.

moderate size, which reduced the central authority's dependence upon its military forces.[9]

Still, the degree of patrimonial centralization was very limited and the absence of local political autonomy in the Western sense was *not* a token of local weakness. Indeed, the main point of Weber's analysis was to explain why local groups in China were very strong and yet unable to unite and oppose the central government, except in sporadic rebellions that did not change the structure of power relations permanently. The answer, he believed, was that local power was in the hands of extended kinship groups, which consisted of families residing on the ancestral lands, families of merchants and officials residing in the towns and provincial capitals, and families of officials at the imperial court. According to Weber, the strength of these kinship groups originated in the independent power of tribal chiefs or princes who were believed to possess supernatural or superhuman qualities (charisma) that entitled them to the exercise of authority. These qualities and hence the right to rule were thought to be hereditary in the male line.[10] Eventually the male descendants of earlier chiefs or princes became affiliated with the territory surrounding the residence of a victorious ruler. When such affiliations took place,

> the emperor's kinship group had precedence, but the kinship groups of princes who had submitted in good time were left in partial or full possession of their power. There was often a reluctance to deprive chieftains' families of all their lands because of the powerful ancestral spirits of charismatic kinship groups. . . . Status was not created by the feudal fief nor by receiving fief as a vassal through free

[9] Cf. *Religion of China*, p. 75 ff. and *passim*, and *The City*, pp. 119–20; also *WuG*, Vol. II, p. 710.

[10] In Weber's usage the term "hereditary charisma" refers specifically to the most prominent male descendants of chieftains who had extraordinary personal appeal to their followers, which rested on actual and imputed gifts and powers. Similar gifts and powers were attributed to, as well as claimed by, the extended families of such chieftains, so that Weber frequently refers to a family as possessing "hereditary (or familial) charisma." The concept "familial charisma" is discussed in more detail below on p. 146, and p. 308 ff. Concerning the term "sib," cf. p. 73, n. 45 above.

commendation and investiture. Rather, at least in principle, the reverse obtained. A man qualified for an office of a certain rank because he was a member of a noble family with a customary rank.[11]

The charismatic appeal of the leaders of tribal societies and the belief in ancestral spirits gave a spiritual foundation to the claims of noble families whose local power was already considerable because of the vast expanse of the Chinese mainland and the primitive conditions of transportation. Thus the Chinese emperors had to contend with a hereditary nobility that possessed great local power on the basis of kinship ties but that did not at the same time constitute a relatively united status group as it did in the West.

In China the early unification of the state and the consequent establishment of a centrally organized officialdom meant that the struggle for political power turned on the distribution of offices rather than on the distribution of land. The members of prominent hereditary landowning families vied for appointment to office and for the income of fees and taxes derived therefrom. The imperial government depended upon the administrative services of these benefice-holders, not upon the military services of self-equipped knights. As individuals the Chinese officials were freely removable, unlike the analogous benefice-holders of western Europe who were able to appropriate their positions and pass them on to their heirs. Once this structure had been established, it tended to be perpetuated by the *collective* interest of the officialdom in the existing opportunities for income and prestige. Any change in the direction of a more rational administrative organization would have destroyed these opportunities.[12]

Religious organization. A third feature by which Weber characterized Chinese civilization was the absence of religious prophecy and a powerful priesthood. The emperor was the supreme ruler *and* high priest of the realm. Although he occasionally was subject to the ritual control of official censors,

[11] *Religion of China*, p. 34. The Gerth translation has been slightly altered.

[12] *Religion of China*, p. 58 ff. The implications of this contrast for the Chinese social structure are discussed below. For an analysis of the Western development, cf. Chapter XI.

the cult of the great deities was in his hands as an affair of state. His supreme religious function never was challenged by religious prophecy like that of ancient Judaism, which opposed the official creeds with an independent ethic based on a doctrine of future salvation.[13] Thus Chinese religious cults remained in the hands of secular rulers supported by an officialdom of educated laymen who opposed the political ascendance of priests and looked upon religion as a useful instrument for the control of the masses. The imperial power was regarded as maintaining the social order by virtue of its religious consecration, which placed it above the large number of popular cults honoring heroes and magical spirits. Chinese religion, therefore, consisted of a state cult with the emperor functioning as the high priest; of the belief in, and the worship of, the ancestral spirits, which were supported by the state; and of many lesser, popular deities, which were more or less tolerated by the authorities. This unity of cult and state and the separation of state cult and popular religions contrasted with the place of religion in medieval Europe, where the Church curbed the power of secular rulers for many centuries and where the same faith was professed by rulers and people alike.[14] These contrasts between China and the Occident were the starting point of Weber's analysis.

Early history. The relations between town and village, the existence of strong local kinship groups, the early development of a weak but pervasive central government, and finally the identity between secular rule and state cult formed a pattern during the early history of China. A distinctly Chinese civilization emerged with the gradual rise of the state of Chou, which originally was located in the modern province of Shensi. In 1050 B.C. the conqueror Wu Wang founded the Chou dynasty, which began to decline about 700 B.C. and finally was overthrown in 247 B.C. Certain features of this feudal period of Chinese history may be characterized briefly.

The conquest led by Wu Wang was based on an alliance of various tribes. To retain their power, the successful conquerors built garrison towns across the land, each constituting

[13] Cf. Weber's analysis of Jewish prophecy in Chapter VII.
[14] *Religion of China,* pp. 142–44.

the center of a fief held by members of the Chou family or
by former princes and tribal chieftains. Originally, independent
princes made voluntary gifts to the emperor as a token
of their submission and, theoretically at least, the emperor was
obliged to compensate them with property rights over land.
Obligatory military contributions were prorated according to
the size of the land held in fief. In theory, the emperor was
free to determine a qualified heir upon the death of the previous
fief-holder. In practice, the emperor relinquished this
right for the most part. As a result, the Chou dynasty constituted
a loose "federation" of some 1,000 feudal territories
rather than a unified state. For a period (about 600–400 B.C.)
the ruling overlords of these territories met in princely assemblies.
Correct ritual demanded that the emperor preside over
the assemblies; but the vassals frequently used the assemblies
to curb the prerogatives of the emperor.

Nevertheless, the emperor represented a principle of cultural
unity that became of decisive importance despite his frequent
political impotence. His position was buttressed by certain
religious concepts that were an integral part of Chinese
civilization. Like the peasants who worshiped the ancestral
spirits of their families and the local deities associated with
agriculture, the founder of the Chou dynasty worshiped the
spirits associated with his imperial territory and the God of
Heaven, who was conceived of as the ancestral spirit of the
imperial family. As the "Son of Heaven" the emperor alone
was entitled to offer the sacrificial rites to Heaven.

> The Chinese monarch . . . was the old rainmaker of magical
> religion translated into ethics. . . . The Chinese emperor
> ruled in the old genuine sense of charismatic authority.
> He had to prove himself as the "Son of Heaven" and
> he was the lord approved by Heaven insofar as the people
> fared well under him. If he failed, he simply lacked charisma.
> Thus if the rivers broke the dikes, or if rain did not
> fall despite the sacrifices made, it was evidence . . . that
> the emperor did not have the charismatic qualities demanded
> by Heaven. In such cases the emperor did public
> penitence for his sins. . . . If this was of no avail the emperor
> had to expect abdication; in the past, it probably

meant self-sacrifice. Like other officials he was open to official reprimand by the censors.[15]

Thus the monarch maintains the ancient social order by his ritual acts and in this way also preserves the providential harmony of heaven and earth. Warfare against a ritually incorrect prince or emperor was considered meritorious. But a dynasty based on conquest also was considered legitimate if the conquerors adhered to the ritual in the correct manner.[16]

By doing just that the Chou emperors helped create a cultural unity despite the almost continuous struggle for power among the territorial princes. Each feudal prince sought to preserve the harmony of heaven and earth by the correct performance of ritual and was as responsible for his domain as the emperor was for the country as a whole. In their respective territories, the princes were the leaders of a warlike nobility whose code of chivalry was similar to that of the medieval knights of western Europe. But since the princes—like the emperor—were also priests and administrators, they had to employ men trained in the arts of writing and diplomacy. During the feudal period these literati did not possess great prestige. Indeed, the code of chivalry they expounded necessarily praised the military virtues, but they also functioned as court astronomers and astrologers and hence as experts in expounding and supervising the correct performance of ritual.[17] The books containing this ritualistic knowledge, as well as their authors or expounders, became objects of competition among the territorial rulers under the Chou dynasty because such knowledge was believed to be indispensable for maintaining

[15] *Ibid.*, pp. 31–32. A brief comparative account of this concept and references to the research since Weber's day may be found in Wolfram Eberhard, "The Political Function of Astronomy and Astronomers in Han China," in John K. Fairbank (ed.), *Chinese Thought and Institutions* (Chicago: University of Chicago Press, 1957), pp. 33–40 and *passim*.

[16] *Religion of China*, p. 40.

[17] The priests of the Shang dynasty (1450–1050 B.C.) became unemployed when this dynasty was overthrown by the Chou, for the Chou emperor himself was the high priest. Yet the Chou rulers also needed administrators and experts in ritual, and these were recruited among the unemployed Shang priests.

the social order and preserving the harmony of heaven and earth.

Political unity under the Chou emperors endured only during the first centuries of the dynasty. The great size of the empire, the independence of the feudal lords and the exposure of the Chou capital to nomadic attacks weakened the position of the emperor. Also, the dispersion of the ruling nobility across the country contributed to a gradual cultural amalgamation at the local level of the conquering rulers and the native population. From about the seventh century B.C. on, the central power of the emperor was nominal in the political sense, though his importance as the consecrated high priest of the realm endured. To maintain his position the emperor would align himself with various feudal rulers in accordance with the shifting power constellations among them, and for a time such rulers established a dictatorship on the basis of their military might. Yet none of these rulers was able to maintain his supremacy for long and the feudal regime of the Chou dynasty gradually disintegrated. This disintegration occurred during the seventh and sixth centuries B.C., ending finally with the period of the Warring (or Contending) States, from 481 to 256 B.C. This whole period of a dissolving feudal system was a major turning point in early Chinese history, and it was during this period that Confucius and Lao Tzu (as well as many other philosophers) lived.

Just as English feudalism was terminated by the War of the Roses and the ascendance of the Tudor monarchy (1465–85), so Chinese feudalism came to an end during the period of the Warring States. Beginning in the seventh century B.C., the "thousand" states of the Chou dynasty were reduced to fourteen, and these fourteen were eliminated one after another from the fifth century B.C. until the unification of the empire in the middle of the third century B.C. In the course of these wars many feudal princes and nobles were expropriated and large numbers of peasants died or migrated. On the land that had become unoccupied, the victorious feudal lords settled peasants who had migrated or been conscripted. As many noble families were expropriated, land began to be bought and sold. At this time metals came into more general use, both as currency and in the production of implements. Trade increased rapidly, and the rising merchants invested their money in land. As traders and landowners, the merchants also took over the collection of taxes for the remaining feudal rulers, whose states had greatly increased in size at the same time that the recurrent wars had eliminated the lesser lords who had collected the taxes from the peasants.

The decreasing number and increasing size of the "contending states" had other repercussions. By consolidating and increasing his political and military power, each of the contending rulers also faced greater administrative tasks. As the urban centers of administration grew, roads had to be built to provide the towns with food and to maintain the army. Along with the construction of roads went the construction of canals, both to facilitate communication and to increase agricultural productivity. In the northern areas it was also necessary to build frontier walls in order to protect the peasants against the sudden raids of the nomadic tribes. By these administrative changes, the contending states prepared the way for the first unification of the "Middle Realm" in 221 B.C. under the Emperor Shih Huang Ti, the founder of the Ch'in dynasty (256–207 B.C.).

Successful conquests had transformed the remaining feudal states into one imperial realm divided into provinces. The military and civilian government of the provinces was separated and placed in the hands of two officials, who in turn were supervised at first by princely officials and later by traveling inspectors. Because of the rivalries among them, none of these officials could develop his power independently, as could a feudal prince. The administrative unification of the empire under Shih Huang Ti was hampered, however, by differences of language and the diverse weights and measures that were a legacy of feudalism. The government therefore ordered that the language of the country be unified, and that measures and the style of writing be regulated. These policies had been advocated by the so-called legalists, men who recognized the decline of feudalism, favored a strong central government under the emperor and his advisors, and therefore opposed the idealization of the feudal regime by the Confucian literati. In 213 B.C. the Confucian writings were destroyed, and tradition has it that the emperor ordered 460 literati to be buried alive.

This vigorous suppression of all feudal tendencies also meant that Shih Huang Ti's regime was marked by a tremendous increase in taxes, forced labor, and military service. Centralized administration made these increases possible and the protection of the country against invasion from the north made them necessary.[18] Upon Shih Huang Ti's death, the Ch'in dynasty was overthrown in a violent reaction against autocratic rule by all parts of the population. Despite its short duration, the Ch'in dynasty abolished the feudal system—though there were occasional relapses in subsequent periods—and established a system of administration that was consolidated under the Han dynasty (206 B.C. to A.D. 220).

This very brief survey of early Chinese history has emphasized the country's development from a loose federation of feudal states to a unified empire with patrimonial rule. I turn now to Weber's analysis of government in relation to the social structure.

B.   DYNASTIC GOVERNMENT AND THE SOCIAL STRUCTURE

Weber's analysis focused upon the balance between the countervailing powers of the central bureaucracy and local self-government. In a country as large as China, administrative centralization was necessarily limited. Hence the relation between the local administration in towns and villages and the provincial governors appointed by the emperor was of special interest. Since the collection of taxes depended upon this relationship, the recurrent issues of tax policy provide a clue to the enduring features of the Chinese social structure.

The weakness of the central government was reflected in the fact that the emperor had a completely free hand only in the appointment of provincial governors; in the case of most lower officials he had to be guided by the names the provincial governors had placed in nomination. Furthermore, the

[18] A large permanent army was maintained in the north, and earlier frontier walls were rebuilt and extended, until one great system of fortification, the famous Great Wall, was completed in 214 B.C. .

number of appointed officials in each area was quite small. With reference to these agents of the central government, the emperors used the typical devices of a patrimonial regime.

> There were short office terms, formally of three years, after which the official was to be removed to a different province. Employment of an official in his home province was prohibited and likewise the employment of relatives in the same bailiwick. There was a thorough spy system in the form of so-called censors.[19]

Above all, appointment to office was based upon examinations and thus upon educational qualifications rather than upon birth and rank. After an official had been appointed in accordance with the number and rank of the examinations he had passed and the "gifts" he had distributed, he still remained under the control of the educational authorities and government censors. (The latter even passed on the ritual propriety of the emperor.) Every three years the record of each official was scrutinized. His merits and faults, his retention, promotion, or demotion, as well as the reasons for these actions, were put on record and well publicized. All these measures centralized the control over the provincial administrators and effectively prevented the officials "from becoming independently powerful in the manner of the feudal vassal."[20] This important though largely negative result was achieved by making sure that the provincial governor and a part of his administrative entourage were strangers in the province under their control—a practice that had three important consequences:

(1.) The governor would nominate relatives, friends and personal clients for appointment by the central government.

(2.) Because of their short term in office these officials would be compelled to make the most of their financial opportunities, since many of them had become indebted in order to secure the appointment and since they were both underpaid and personally responsible for the full tax quota.

(3.) Because they assumed office in a strange province

[19] *Religion of China,* p. 48.
[20] *Ibid.,* p. 49.

whose dialect, local laws and sacred traditions they did not know, they were necessarily dependent upon the services of interpreters and unofficial advisors, who were chosen from qualified candidates native to the province. The dependence of centrally appointed administrators upon unofficial, local advisors meant that the decrees of provincial governors actually were issued by unofficial subordinates who considered them ethical, albeit authoritative, proposals of the imperial authority, not orders that had to be carried out.

This administrative situation also had important effects on the payment of salaries and the collection of taxes. In theory, officials were obliged to cover the costs of administration out of the salaries they received, although these salaries were totally inadequate for this purpose. In practice, the government established tax quotas for each region, so that the official was responsible to the government for the delivery of a fixed portion of the tax yield while he met the costs of administration and enhanced his own income out of the fees and tax income of his area.[21] Thus the officials' income and their personal expenses were indistinguishable from the tax revenue collected in an area and the expenditures needed to administer it. Even in the smallest districts the appointed officials depended upon staffs of from thirty to three hundred officials, many of whom were recruited from the district itself. Superior officials derived their income from the gross income of the lowest official, who was directly at the tax source and had to transfer to his superior an amount determined by tradition. Each official act had to be paid for by "gifts," for which there was no legal schedule, and the good will of superior officials

[21] And since the quotas were assessed on the basis of the taxable land and the number of taxpayers, the officials had a strong interest in understating both so as to reduce the amount they were obliged to deliver to the government and hence increase their own take. Weber cited evidence for an underenumeration of 40 per cent for selected years of the fourteenth to seventeenth centuries (ibid., p. 47). In a personal communication Professor Wolfram Eberhard has pointed out that officials also had an interest in overestimating the population, especially when they were about to leave, for population increase was regarded as proof of good administration. The two principles together provide another illustration of the "seesaw" between the central government and the local officials. Cf. also ibid., p. 270, n. 60.

had to be secured by additional "gifts" as occasion demanded.

These practices applied as much to the relations among officials at the various ranks of the hierarchy as they did to the relations between the ultimate taxpayer and tax collector. The revenue received at each level of the hierarchy was, therefore, a small fraction of the actual amount collected at the lower levels, although the amount to be received at each level was traditionally fixed. In this way the government could be both all-pervasive and weak. Superior officials perennially demanded additional fees and "gifts" while lower officials made every effort to tap all potential sources of tax income, with the result that the pressure upon the taxpaying peasant was very great. But, if this pressure actually increased the amount of taxes collected, the additional revenue did' not necessarily strengthen the central government since, as likely as not, the increase would be dissipated in fees and "gifts" on its way up the hierarchy of officials.

This situation was reflected in the relation between government administration and the structure of rural society. All governmental policies had a direct effect upon the rural community since the peasants were the principal source of taxation and recruitment. From very early times imperial officials had defined the extended family rather than the village as the unit to which all taxes and other public charges were allocated. The head of the family was held responsible for their further allocation and collection, and during certain periods the government grouped five to ten families into compulsory associations that were held jointly liable for payment of taxes in money or in kind. Within this general framework the methods of tax assessment and collection and the attempts at land regulation varied considerably. Weber discussed some of these changes, but for present purposes it is sufficient to characterize their common denominator. The central government sought to increase its own revenue, to reduce the take of the appointed officials, and to prevent wealthy families and officials from accumulating land and gaining political independence. The appointed officials, in turn, sought to increase their own incomes by increasing the tax yield in their district and thus enlarging the spread between the total amount they collected and the quota due to the government. Finally, the kinship groups resisted all efforts to increase their tax obligations by the strategic use of "gifts" and of family connections. As Weber put it, "patrimonial rule from above clashed with the kinship group's strong counterbalance from below," especially in the villages.[22]

In this three-cornered struggle of the central government, its appointed officials, and local interest groups, kinship solidarity played a strategic role. The cohesion of the kinship group, founded upon the ancestor cult, rested on the belief in the power of the ancestral spirits and, hence, on the need to satisfy them and win their favor by sacrifices. The solidarity of the family was further ensured by the large number of social and economic functions that were regarded as familial obligations. Legally, joint liability existed only with regard to criminal cases. In practice, it extended much further, including the granting of credit, aid to the needy such as widows and aged people, and the provision of medical care, education, and burial services. Also, the kinship group as a unit owned or leased property, which could be leased in turn but which could not be owned by the heads of individual households. To perform these and many other functions, family councils were organized:

> Within the kinship group a combination of hereditary-charismatic and democratic principles prevailed. All married men had equal franchise; unmarried men had only the right to be heard in council; women were excluded from these family councils altogether as well as from the right of inheritance. . . . The executive committee consisted of the elders, each representing a separate lineage within the kinship group. . . . The functions of the elders were to collect revenues, utilize possessions and distribute income, and most important of all, attend to the ancestral sacrifices, the ancestral halls, and schools. The retiring elders nominated candidates for election according to seniority; in case the office was declined, the next eldest was presented.[23]

Such councils exercised extensive legally recognized authority

[22] *Religion of China*, p. 86.
[23] *Ibid.*, p. 89. I omit Weber's reference to the election of elders, which appears to have been the exception, not the rule.

over the members, who would not willingly sever their ties
with the extended kinship group since it was the ceremonial
unit for the semiannual ancestor festivals important to each
individual as well as the source of capital at low interest rates.
And it was the family elders who elected the young men qualified to study and paid the expenses connected with their education, examinations, and the eventual purchase of an office.

The locus of these kinship groups was in the villages, and
hence the authorities' efforts to assert their power beyond the
cities came to naught. As Weber put it: "A 'city' was the seat
of the mandarin and was not self-governing; a 'village' was a
self-governing settlement without a mandarin."[24] The villages'
self-government had grown out of the necessity to defend the
community, which the central government was unable to do.
Guard duty and police or military action had to be organized,
and provision had to be made for money loans, for the construction and maintenance of roads and canals, and for schools,
doctors, and burials. These administrative functions of the kinship groups—or, in some cases, of the village temple—were
financed and executed by the house fathers, who took their
turn according to a division of the village into districts.[25]

With this survey of the social structure before us, it is readily
apparent why a capitalist economy did not develop in China.
To begin with, the extended kinship groups functioned as protective associations in the sense that they defended the individual member against economic adversities in his relations
with landlords, moneylenders, and employers outside the
family. In this way, the payment of debts, and to some extent
work discipline, were discouraged. Moreover in many periods
the sale of land was either prohibited by the government or

[24] *Ibid.*, p. 91.
[25] Although the village was organized to protect itself against
military threats, robbers, and the central government, it was not
equally well protected against organized protests or uprisings of the
non-propertied villagers, i.e., the peasants who were the exploited
tenants of the powerful, landowning kinship groups and a ready-
made audience for Bolshevist propaganda, as Weber noted in 1913.
These village poor were occasionally protected by measures of the
central government that were designed to safeguard the productivity of the village as a tax source and to curb the power of the village
notables.

made very difficult by family regulations, even though the development of a money economy facilitated the transfer of landed property. The opposition to this was similar to the opposition to technical innovations—both land sales and inventions were thought to disturb the ancestral spirits and thus to result in magical evils.

The patrimonial organization of government also militated against a development of administration along rational lines. The income of officials and the revenue of the state were inextricably intertwined, and Chinese officials had a high stake in preserving the existing, highly profitable income opportunities from holding office. The increasing use of money in the payment of taxes only enhanced the financial opportunities of office-holding and hence reinforced the traditionalism of Chinese government and society. The incumbent officials remained obligated to their families, both because the education and money needed for appointment could not be obtained without their support and because ancestor worship and filial piety gave this financial dependence an enduring spiritual foundation. The same combination of factors hindered legal developments that would have been favorable to capitalism. The prerogatives and self-protective power of village-based kinship groups were incompatible with the concept of a natural law—as contrasted with sacred tradition—and the establishment of legal institutions like those of western Europe. There, the existing law had been systematized because, among other factors, jurists constituted a separate status group, urban business life required fixed legal procedures, and the officialdom of absolutist states had a positive interest in regularized legal procedures. In China, no comparable status group of jurists existed. The sacred ceremonies were the only unchangeable laws accepted by the educated officials, and the formal codification of laws would have been a threat to the established order. Under the Ch'in dynasty (256–207 B.C.) a minister had stated that if the people could read the sacred books they would despise their superiors.[26] Chinese judges generally discharged their business in terms of equity and propriety. They adjudicated with due regard to persons and circumstances, in keeping with

[26] Quoted in *ibid.*, p. 101.

sacred tradition and the accepted notions of family relationships—a striking contrast to the Western tradition with its
typical tension between the social world and legal rules based
upon abstract principles.[27]

Weber also listed a number of conditions that favored the
development of a capitalist economy in China. Under the
Manchu dynasty (1644–1911) the empire was at peace (after
ca. 1700), and more effective control of the rivers reduced
the number of floods. These improved conditions, together
with changed methods of cultivation, led to a tremendous
population increase, from approximately sixty million people
in the late 1500's to about twice that number by the early
eighteenth century. Very considerable private fortunes also
accumulated. Other favorable factors were increasing freedom
to acquire land and settle outside one's native community,
relative freedom of choosing an occupation, and, in the modern period, the absence of compulsory schooling and military
service. Although these factors did not favor capitalism un-
equivocally, Weber pointed out that in western Europe capitalism had developed in spite of such unfavorable conditions as
frequent wars, slow population growth, and restrictions on
migration, occupational choice, trade, and apprenticeship
training. In China, however, the factors inherently favorable
to a capitalist development did not outweigh the obstacles
created by the patrimonial structure of the state and the unbroken tradition of the extended family. These obstacles were
strongly reinforced by a particular mentality, the Chinese
"ethos," which Weber characterized as the status ethic of the
literati.

C. THE LITERATI AND CONFUCIAN
ORTHODOXY

Government officials constituted the ruling stratum in China
for more than two thousand years. Literary education was the
yardstick of their social prestige and the basic qualification for
office. But although they were proficient in ritualism, the Chi-

[27] *Ibid.*, pp. 100–4, 148–50. These points are elaborated in
Chapter XII, B.

nese literati were a status group of educated laymen, not ordained priests or ministers. They also were not a hereditary
social group like the Brahmins of India, for their position
rested in principle upon their knowledge of writing and literature, not their birth. Scholars had the same high prestige regardless of their social origins, though access to the requisite
education depended for the most part upon the wealth of the
family. Still it was not the ancient lineage of a family that
was decisive in this respect.

Compared with intellectuals in other civilizations, the Chinese literati were singular in many respects. The ritual books,
the calendar and the Annals constituted a body of ancient
scriptures possessing magical character—the same character
that in India was inherent in a man's birth as a Brahmin—and
the Chinese literati were thought to possess "magical charisma," i.e., extraordinary capacities, by virtue of their familiarity with the sacred books.[28] Yet these men were not professional magicians or sorcerers whose task it was to heal the
sick or otherwise alter the fate of private persons. While such
magicians were well known in China, the fate of the community did not depend on them; it rested, instead, in the hands
of the house father, the elders of the kinship group, the prince,
and the emperor. Each of these was "responsible" for orderly
administration in the secular sense and each also had the task
of influencing the spirits; any disorder or disaster meant that
he had failed to do so properly. Knowledge of the scriptures,
the calendar and the stars was required to discern the will of
Heaven. Hence the literati alone were considered competent
to advise the princes and the emperor in the ritually and politically correct conduct of affairs and of their personal lives.

This close relation of the Chinese literati to princely service
involved them directly in the struggle over feudalism. The lives

[28] Weber noted in this connection that in China as well as in
India charismatic qualities had been attributed to kinship. But the
Chinese system of examinations had curtailed the power of magical
beliefs upon which "familial charisma" was based by separating classical learning, which also was endowed with charisma, from the
charisma attributed to kinship. India differed from China in this
respect because learning was monopolized by the Brahmins, whose
familial charisma was, therefore, strengthened further by an identification with sacred learning.

of Confucius (551–479 B.C.) and Mencius (372–289 B.C.) coincided with the period of the Warring States (481–256 B.C.), during which the struggles among many feudal powers finally gave way to the first unification of the Chinese Empire. The oldest sections of the Confucian classics reflect this transitional period. The heroic songs of the Hymn Book (Shih Ching), like the Homeric and Indian epics, tell of kings fighting from war chariots. But these legendary Chinese kings no longer win simply because they are great heroes. They win because they are morally right before the Spirit of Heaven. Their enemies, on the other hand, are godless criminals who have lost their charisma as heroes because they have violated ancient customs and thus brought harm to their people. Weber speculated that Confucius' special contribution might have been to expurgate the classic texts by replacing simple hero-worship and gloating celebration of victory with moralizing reflections upon the spiritual "propriety" of victory and defeat.[29] The chronicle explicitly attributed to Confucius contains only a very sober account of military campaigns and punitive expeditions. Confucius rejected the glorification of heroic virtues, and Mencius already maintained that within the frontiers of the empire no war could be "just." Consequently "the princes and ministers of the classics act and speak like paradigms of rulers whose ethical conduct is rewarded by Heaven. Officialdom and the promotion of officials according to merit are topics for glorification." Moreover, the military were despised in China: "a cultivated literary man would not engage in social intercourse on an equal footing with army officers."[30] Thus the ascendance of the literati was a by-product of declining feudalism even though Confucius sought to ingratiate himself with some of the feudal rulers of his time.

The ascendance involved a process spanning centuries. During Confucius' lifetime appointments to official positions al-

[29] This speculation was confirmed some fifteen years later by the German sinologist, Otto Franke, who demonstrated that in the *Annals of Spring and Autumn* Confucius had falsified historical events in order to depict his image of the ideal ruler. Cf. Wolfram Eberhard, *A History of China* (Berkeley: University of California Press, 1950), pp. 40–41.

[30] *Religion of China*, pp. 114, 115.

ready depended to some extent upon the merit of the candidate. The principle of appointment according to merit was not
prima facie incompatible with the fact that kinship with one of
the "great families" remained of decisive importance. The belief that the official must prove his qualification for office by
preserving social tranquillity was an important ideological safeguard in this respect. Under the Han emperors (206 B.C. to
A.D. 220) a system of training candidates for government offices was instituted. The selection of candidates favored those
from well-to-do families with good connections, regardless of
their capacity, and the training was frequently at a low level.
Nevertheless, it inculcated the ethical precepts of Confucianism and established a status ethic among Chinese officials.
Under the T'ang dynasty (A.D. 618–906) the training system
was consolidated (in A.D. 690) by the establishment of col-
leges for the education of officials and by an elaborate series
of examinations.

These measures officially regulated the social position of the
literati, making them a status group of "certified claimants to
office prebends."[31] Officials were recruited exclusively from
this group, and the qualifications of candidates were judged
in terms of the number of examinations they had passed. Three
major classes of examination were offered, each augmented
by preliminary, repetitive and intermediary examinations and
the stipulation of additional prerequisites. In its fully developed form, this system was used as the basis for establishing
the social rank of individuals and families.

> The question usually put to a stranger of unknown rank
> was how many examinations he had passed. Thus, in spite
> of the ancestor cult, how many ancestors one had was not
> decisive for social rank. The very reverse held: it depended
> upon one's official rank whether one was allowed to have
> an ancestral temple (or a mere table of ancestors, which
> was the case with illiterates). How many ancestors one was
> permitted to mention was determined by official rank. Even

[31] *Ibid.*, p. 115. It should be added, however, that the schooling
of officials and the system of examinations were frequently modified
in detail as a result of struggles for power among government de-
partments and regions and among the emperors, their entourage,
and the literati.

the rank of a city god in the pantheon depended upon the rank of the city's mandarin.[32]

The examinations institutionalized an order of ranks in Chinese society that promoted the competitive struggle for offices among the candidates and so "stopped them from joining together into a feudal office nobility"—a result obviously in the interest of the emperors.[33] The system also solidified the prestige of the literati, who enjoyed special exemption from labor service and corporal punishment as well as privileged access to offices and government stipends.

These status privileges belonged to all those who had passed the examinations, although demotions led to an immediate loss of privilege. However, the availability of offices and stipends depended upon the finances of the state; hence, a quota system was used so that the number of candidates who passed corresponded to the number of vacancies. This meant that the proportion of those who failed was very high, and men with a literary education but without office became numerous. One reason for this continued oversupply was that the financial burden of education fell upon the extended family as a whole, and it always hoped that the expenses would be recovered by an eventual appointment to office with all its attendant social, political and financial advantages. Moreover, the government encouraged the competition for offices and stipends, and in many periods income from the sale of offices was an important means of raising revenue. Thus the incentive to compete for offices, and hence to acquire the requisite education, continued in force despite the relative scarcity of available positions.

The great prestige of Chinese officialdom was sustained by certain popular beliefs. Although the Chinese masses distrusted the lower officials and avoided contact with the government whenever possible, they believed that literary education bestowed extraordinary magical powers upon the officials.

By passing the examination, the graduate proved that he was to an eminent degree a holder of *shen*. High mandarins were considered magically qualified. They could always be-

[32] *Ibid.*
[33] *Ibid.*, p. 119.

come objects of a cult, after their death as well as during their lifetime, provided that their charisma was "proved." The primeval magical significance of written work and of documents lent semidivine and therapeutic significance to their seals and to their handwriting, and this could extend to the examination paraphernalia of the candidate.[34]

The best graduates of the highest degree were believed to bring honor and advantage to their native provinces. Each village accorded public recognition to those who had passed the examination successfully. All associations, like guilds or clubs, had to have a literary man as secretary. Even in family councils office-holders and examined candidates had great weight, though they still were subordinate to the authority of their elders.

The paradox is that the literary education of the officials did not correspond to the popular emphasis on magical or heroic gifts. Chinese education, according to Weber, aimed at cultivating men "for a certain internal and external deportment in life."[35] This differed from education in magic because it did not depend upon the charismatic gifts of the novice, and it differed from the specialized training of the expert official because it did not aim at the acquisition of practically useful knowledge. Instead, Chinese examinations tested whether the candidate was thoroughly familiar with the classical literature and whether he had acquired ways of thought and a code of conduct based on the classics.[36] Similarly, Chinese domestic education consisted of the inculcation of rules for the exercise of self-control and ceremonially correct behavior, especially piety and awe toward parents, superiors, and elders.

This purely literary education had certain singular characteristics. Writing and reading rather than speaking were valued artistically and considered worthy of a gentleman.

[34] *Religion of China,* p. 135.

[35] *Ibid.,* p. 120.

[36] This type of education superseded an earlier orientation during the feudal period, when the military arts and the dance were taught in addition to rites and literature. This earlier education under feudalism had much in common with the education of young noblemen in ancient Greece.

Training in the art of logical reasoning was not stressed, and geography, natural science and grammar were absent from the curriculum. Classical Chinese education, according to Weber, remained primarily oriented toward the "practical problems and the status interests of the patrimonial bureaucracy."[37] As such it was purely a lay education emphasizing conventional propriety and classical learning. Its aim was expressed in the idea that the world and man contained a basic dualism: the good and evil spirits (*shen* and *kuei*), the heavenly and earthly substance (*Yang* and *Yin*). The task of education was to aid the unfolding of the *Yang* substance in the soul of man.

> For the man in whom the *Yang* substance has completely gained the upper hand over the demonic *kuei* powers resting within him also has power over the spirits; that is, according to the ancient·notion, he has magical power. The good spirits, however, are those who protect order and beauty and harmony in the world. To perfect oneself and thus to mirror this harmony is the supreme and the only means by which one may attain such power. . . . Since the Han period at the latest, it was a firmly established belief among the literati that the spirits reward "beneficence," in the sense of social and ethical excellence. . . .
>
> The Chinese . . . official proved his status quality, that is, his charisma, through the canonical correctness of his literary forms. . . . On the other hand, the official had to prove his charisma by the "harmonious" course of his administration.[38]

Accordingly, the restless spirits of nature and man would cause no disturbance as long as the gentleman-official acted in keeping with the *Yang* substance.

On this basis Confucianism stressed some and neglected other phases of the human personality and of social life, in keeping with the status interests and ideals of the literati. Confucian doctrine consists of ethical maxims pertaining to political life and social intercourse. The order of society is part of the cosmic order in which the great spirits desire the hap-

[37] *Ibid.*, p. 127.
[38] *Religion of China*, pp. 131–32.

piness of the world and man. Each man can best serve Heaven by developing his true nature; in this way the good within him will appear. Men are not basically wicked. Rather, they have faults that result from deficient education and that therefore may be remedied by education. In the same way, disturbances of nature and society are due to the disorderly leadership of officials, while tranquillity may be restored by officials who behave properly. Accordingly, Confucianism gives special emphasis to maxims of *propriety*. The educated man participates in the old ceremonies with due respect. All his outward activities are marked by graceful poise and polite dignity. His outer "controlled ease and correct composure" reflect his inward peace with himself and with the society in which he lives. This image of man has no room either for passion and ostentation, which disturb the harmony of the soul, or for a withdrawal from the world. Detachment and the control of desire aim rather at a prudent mastery of existing opportunities. Unlike Buddhism or Catholicism, Confucianism has no concept of salvation. The orthodox Confucian performs his rites of ancestor worship for the sake of his fate in this world—for a long life, male heirs, and wealth—and not for the sake of the "hereafter." In order to ensure the tranquillity of the social order and the inner man, Confucianism enjoins one supreme virtue upon which all other virtues depend: piety (*hsiao*) toward parents and superiors. "Filial piety was held to provide the test and guarantee of adherence to unconditional discipline, the most important status obligation of bureaucracy."[39] Thus Confucianism represents a peculiar form of rationalism that seeks to maintain the order of Heaven, the tranquillity of the social order and the inner harmony of man through an ethic of human conduct. Here reason means the control of all human passions for the sake of peace and harmony. As the emperor Ch'ien Lung (1736–96) wrote: "The ways of Heaven are changeable and reason alone is our aid."[40]

This basic orientation had important implications for economic life. Confucian writings on economic matters reflect the preoccupations of officials rather than the thoughts of men

[39] *Ibid.*, p. 158.
[40] Cited in *ibid.*, p. 169.

actively engaged in economic enterprises. It is not worthwhile for the educated man to learn the management of economic affairs, for such work is unbecoming to his station and therefore morally dubious. Such a man should be concerned, however, with the propriety of consumption: both lavish expenditure and undue thrift are condemned, the one because it involves "extravagance" and the other because it indicates a vulgar frame of mind. This is not to say that wealth was deprecated. On the contrary, under a good administration the people would be ashamed of their poverty, though under a poor administration they should be ashamed of their wealth if it was acquired dishonestly, as was likely under these conditions. In this way wealth was linked to the administrative regulation of the social order. Considerable attention was devoted to such matters as supply and demand, and the profitability of money and interest on loans were accepted as a matter of course. However, according to Confucius the educated man must stay away from the pursuit of wealth, though not from wealth itself, because acquisitiveness is a source of social and personal unrest. To be sure, this would not be the case if the success of economic pursuits was guaranteed, but in the absence of such a guarantee the poise and harmony of the soul are jeopardized by the risks involved. Office-holding alone is becoming to the superior (educated) man. To perfect his personality he must be unperturbed, and Mencius argued that it is difficult to achieve this result without a permanent income.[41] The cultured man strives for the perfection of self, whereas all occupations that involve the pursuit of riches require a one-sided specialization that acts against the universality of the gentleman.

> The fundamental assertion, "a cultured man is not a tool," meant that he was an end in himself and not just a means for a specified useful purpose. . . . Confucian virtue . . . was greater than the riches to be gained by one-sided thoroughness. Not even in the most influential position could one achieve anything in the world without the virtue derived from education. And vice versa, one could achieve nothing, no matter what one's virtue, without influential position.

[41] *Ibid.*, pp. 159–60.

Hence, the "superior" man coveted such a position, not profit.[42]

In his analysis of these beliefs Weber emphasized their great political significance. Confucianism tolerated the great multitude of popular cults without making any effort to systematize them as a religious doctrine. In lieu of metaphysical speculation it taught adjustment to the world. In this way, the religion of the citizens remained in the hands of the elders and the private practitioners of magic while the management of the official cult was in the hands of the emperor and the literati. The ordinary person was concerned only with the performance of ritual acts; prayers were the function of princes and high officials on behalf of the political community. The official state cult was deliberately sober and unadorned, minimizing all ecstatic and ascetic elements that involved irrational excitement and hence jeopardized the desired tranquillity of the social order. It is indicative of this whole orientation that Confucianism rejected mystic contemplation and treated with reserve or indifference the popular Messianic hope for a model emperor in the future.

D. STATE CULT AND POPULAR RELIGIOSITY

According to Confucianism, the worship of the great deities is an affair of state, ancestor worship is required of all, and the multitude of popular cults is merely tolerated. The nature of this compromise is illustrated by the fact that on occasion the emperor would salute the Taoist and Buddhist shrines with a polite bow, reserving the formally required act of reverence—the kowtow—for the official great spirits of the state cult.[43] Although the official cult recognized popular deities, such as the masters of thunder and wind, it also relegated them to the

[42] *Religion of China,* pp. 160–61. In a personal communication Professor Peter Boodberg has pointed out that the maxim quoted by Weber also may be translated as "a cultured man does not implement" anything, he merely establishes broad principles that others apply. This translation makes the maxim more closely echo the aristocratic distaste for labor.

[43] *Ibid.,* p. 214.

crowd of supernatural spirits that did not require more than polite attention. In time, as the state cult turned into mere ritual and the great spirits of nature gradually lost all personalized significance, official religion was emptied of all emotional content and appeal. The rejection of all religious ecstasy and of the idea of a world beyond presumably satisfied the literati, but it is improbable, in Weber's judgment, that such a religion could also satisfy the typically emotional needs of the masses.[44]

For Weber the division of Confucianism and popular religion illustrated a problem that arises wherever an educated minority is confronted with religious beliefs that are vigorously alive among the masses. In ancient Greece, for example, the public authorities allowed the philosophers great freedom of metaphysical speculation and the philosophers merely tolerated the traditional religious rites. Plato expressed the desire to replace the Homeric deities and the hero-gods with his own nonmagical doctrines as the official creed of his ideal state. The Greek philosophers did not succeed in this respect, however. The state demanded that the heroic and folk deities of the Homeric epoch be worshiped in the proper manner lest misfortune befall the city. The teachings of the philosophers remained a matter of choice for the individual citizen.[45] The Chinese development took a very different course. There, the doctrines of the literati rather than popular religious beliefs were dominant and remained dominant. The rituals of the state cult were elaborated and supervised by an educated minority that regarded the worship of popular deities with disdain and suspicion. The dominance of the literati was not complete, however. Magic and popular deities continued to flourish. Eventually this popular religiosity came under the patronage of Taoist and Buddhist priests, whose doctrines and practices reflected the beliefs of the masses in a way that Confucianism did not. But, although Taoism and Buddhism occasionally gained the ascendance, the Confucian literati in the long run successfully prevented the rise of a popular religious movement. In China the ethics and social theories of the intellectuals became the dominant creed of the state, whereas

[44] *Ibid.*, p. 173.
[45] *Ibid.*, pp. 175–77.

in the West the popular doctrines of Christianity took over.[46] Since the popular movement of Puritanism helped create a rational ordering, especially of economic life, Weber thought it necessary to analyze the nature of popular religiosity in China in order to understand fully why a parallel rationalism had had little chance to develop in that country.

The Confucian world view embraced not only an emphasis upon gentlemanly conduct but also mystical experiences and metaphysical speculations. This latter tendency was first associated with the name of Lao Tzu, who lived a century or so after Confucius. The antagonism between these two half-legendary teachers and their doctrines appeared early. Both regarded the perfection of self as man's consummate quest, but they had very different ends in view. The Confucian scholars thought it proper for an official to withdraw into solitude only when a state was poorly governed. According to tradition, Confucius himself opposed such withdrawal as a sign of selfishness. He claimed that those who lived in hiding and performed miracles did so "in order to win fame among later generations." Possibly this was a polemic against an early form of Taoist mysticism that aimed at a long life and the attainment of magical powers. Both teachers lived alone and without office, but Confucius felt himself deprived of office while Lao Tzu rejected office-holding. Both taught self-control, but for Confucius the ideal was the educated and superior man who had adjusted to the world as it is while for Lao Tzu it was the educated man who was indifferent to the world in which he lived. The contrast is highlighted by the Taoist interpretation of the four cardinal virtues of Confucianism: the love of man (*shen*), the rules of living (*li*), the obligation of liberality (*I*), and the importance of knowledge (*chi*). According to the Taoist poet, Chuang Tzu (fourth century B.C.), these virtues jeopardize the self-perfection of man:

(1) The search for "intelligence" means attachment to externals;

[46] In this respect Weber emphasized that the Confucian scholars consistently refrained from systematizing popular religious beliefs, while in the West the philosophers and theologians did exactly that with the basic tenets of Christianity.

(2) the search for "reason" means attachment to words;

(3) the "love of man" means confusion in one's practice of virtue;

(4) to do one's duty means to rebel against the laws of nature (the omnipotence of *Tao*);

(5) adherence to the rules of living means attachment to externals;

(6) adherence to sanctity means affectation; and

(7) the quest for knowledge means hairsplitting.[47]

The antagonism between these two ways of thought resulted from a later elaboration of what originally had been only a difference in emphasis. Both schools were based on the same classical literature. Both shared the idea of *Tao*, which means the eternal order and orderly change of the cosmos, but the writings and deities added by Taoists were regarded as nonclassical by the Confucians. Both schools consisted of literati who took for granted that the good of man ultimately depends upon the qualities of the ruler rather than upon salvation in a world beyond. Both accepted the traditional deities and shared the belief in good and evil spirits. Both thought that the good order of government could best be preserved by keeping the demons or evil spirits at rest. Indeed, the same man could be a Confucian as an official and head of a family and a Taoist (worshiping a different deity) after he retired or when he had encountered some adversity such as dismissal from office. For Lao Tzu and those who claimed to be his followers (Taoists), it was easy, therefore, to accept the basic assumptions of Confucianism, and in so doing they helped secure its predominance. But the followers of Lao Tzu also elaborated his mysticism and withdrawal from the world, and in so doing they gradually increased the difference between Taoism and Confucianism and came closer to the magical practices and personalized deities of popular religion.

Lao Tzu placed the ideal of the mystic "saint" above the Confucian ideal of the gentleman. Though he remained within the Confucian tradition, he designated the acceptance of the world as it is and the ideal of propriety as the "little" virtue, which he contrasted with the "great" virtue of ethical perfec-

[47] *Ibid.*, pp. 189–90.

tion. Through mystic contemplation man shall perfect his goodness and humility by leading an "incognito existence in the world"; by minimizing his actions he can prove his state of grace, which is the best guarantee for the permanence of life on earth and possibly also for a permanence beyond life. The followers of Lao Tzu consequently advocated the greatest possible self-sufficiency of the individual and of small communities; there should be as little bureaucracy as possible, for man's self-perfection could not be enhanced by state interference. For Confucius this ideal of sanctity through mystic contemplation and humility was unattainable as well as egoistic, and the mystic's rejection of knowledge as a means of working for one's own or the general good was entirely unacceptable. But for Lao Tzu the cardinal point was

> the appreciation of physical life *per se,* hence of long life and the belief that death is an absolute evil. For when rightly considered death should be avoidable for a truly perfect man. The truly perfect man must be endowed with invulnerability and magical powers. . . . According to all experience the restriction of excitement and quiet living were effective to ensure a long life. The thesis seemed to be unassailable that abstention from passionate desires was the primary means to this end and the cardinal virtue. . . .[48]

Taoism opposed the intrusion of mundane affairs upon the individual, for this jeopardized his attainment of inner harmony, but it also encouraged the use of magic, which Confucianism only tolerated. In this way some of those who claimed to be followers of Lao Tzu brought about a fusion between the withdrawal of intellectuals from the world and the very mundane trade of practicing magicians.[49] Magicians usually were re-

[48] *Religion of China,* p. 191. Cf. also the following comment: "The physiologically ascertainable fact that the regulation of breathing may facilitate mental conditions of a specific sort led further afield. The 'saint' must be 'neither dead nor alive' and should behave as if not alive. 'I am a stupid man, hence I have eluded worldly wisdom,' said Lao Tzu in affirming his sanctity. Chuang Tzu did not wish to be 'harnessed' to an office but rather to exist 'like a pig in a muddy ditch.'—The aim was 'to make one's self equal to ether,' to 'throw off the body.'" *Ibid.,* p. 179.

[49] Experts differ on this affinity between the philosophical Taoism of Lao Tzu and his followers and the popular Taoism of the magi-

cruited from the people rather than from the families of well-to-do landowners like the literati. They made their living by catering to the popular demand for magical means by which to quiet the spirits or procure their favorable intervention. While Confucianism tolerated the magical beliefs and practices of popular religiosity, popular Taoism cultivated them and made them a decisive influence in Chinese life.

Weber discussed this impact of Taoism under the suggestive title: "The Systematic Rationalization of Magic." By this phrase he meant that empirical knowledge and the craftsmanship of artisans were developed in the direction of magical ideas and practices. Because of its presumed magical significance, knowledge of the calendar was first used to allocate agricultural work to the proper seasons. Subsequently it became the basis for the allocation of tasks and ritual duties to months or even days in accordance with speculative notions concerning the cosmos. This magical use of the calendar became a source of profit to the official soothsayers. Though astronomy was cultivated, astrology flourished as magicians and rainmakers used such phenomena as the visibility of Venus, earthquakes, monstrous births and many others as telltale signs on the basis of which they declared whether or not the spirits were in order.[50] Likewise Chinese medicine and pharmacology developed in a magical direction, characterized by the search for plants that prolonged life and by the belief that the human body was related to natural elements, the weather, and the seasons. It also was believed that cures could be effected through gymnastics and breathing techniques, which aimed at the "storing up" of breath as the carrier of life. Geomancy, or the practice of divination by means of figures made at random from dirt or dots, was used to determine

---

cians. The fact is that the philosophical writings of the Taoist school declined after the fourth century A.D. while the shamanistic ideas of popular Taoism continued to flourish for many centuries thereafter. In his discussion of heterodox Taoism Weber was primarily concerned with popular Taoism, though he emphasized its continuity with the ideas of Lao Tzu.

[50] Professor Wolfram Eberhard has shown (cf. p. 106, n. 15 above) that these practices had a political function, but I take it that Weber referred here to popular magic, not to magic practiced at the imperial court.

not only the time appropriate for the construction of buildings but also their form and location. This in turn led to the idea that the forms of mountains, rocks, trees, water and so on had divinatory significance.

A single piece of rock by its form could protect whole areas against the attacks of evil demons. Nothing at all could be irrelevant. Moreover the geomantically very sensitive tombs were considered seats of pestilential influence. And geomantic control became indispensable for all construction, even for such internal construction as water mains in homes. Hence every death at a neighbor's might be traced back to one's building, or might signify revenge; any new funeral place might disturb all the spirits of the tombs and cause terrible misfortune.[51]

It is true that there are Western analogues for many of these ideas and practices, but the point is that they did not become as pervasive in Europe as in China. Weber believed that by encouraging these popular beliefs, Taoism helped create an image of the world and the cosmos in which wild and unmotivated spirits were capable of any action and in which the good or bad fortune of men depended upon the efficacy of charms and countercharms. This image of a "magic garden" had special significance for economic life. As a matter of principle, Taoism was opposed to all innovations because they were apt to arouse the wrath of the spirits. Indeed, the belief in spirits led to the view that any technical artifice or any enterprise like the construction of roads, canals and bridges was dangerous and called for special magical precautions, which might lead to the modification or even the abandonment of the undertaking if this were deemed necessary.

The profusion of demons and magic proved to be a tremendous hindrance to the indigenous economic development in China, and Weber emphasized that these beliefs were an integral part of the Chinese social structure. The magicians of the Taoist tradition had an obvious economic stake in the cultivation of popular demonology. In the minds of the masses the practice of magic could bring good fortune or prevent great misfortune. Moreover, although they disdained magic

[51] *Religion of China*, p. 198.

and mysticism, the Confucians could not reject the folk deities or the belief in spirits and in magic without jeopardizing their own position of power. Confucianism attributed all natural disasters or other misfortunes to spirits that had been aroused by the ritual impropriety of some particular official; in such cases the aroused spirits could be appeased only by appropriate ritual acts. Though individual officials were blamed, the legitimacy of officialdom was never questioned; to do so would have challenged the idea that the harmony of heaven and earth is maintained by a good ruler. Besides, the belief in spirits provided the literati with a defense against the usurpation of power by the emperor. As one of them put it, "Who will hinder the emperor from doing as he pleases when he no longer believes in omens and portents?" Thus the belief in magic served the interests of many: the magicians found it profitable; for the masses it held out promises and gave emotional satisfaction; and orthodox Confucianism used it to defend the social order against both mass uprisings and dictatorship.[52]

Though this reciprocal adaptation of interests is certainly an important reason for the famous stability of the Chinese social structure, the Confucian tolerance of magic and the Taoist acceptance of Confucianism did not eliminate conflict. Under the Han dynasty Taoist leaders had formed secret societies and organized worship among the peasantry. In A.D. 184 these societies were denounced, resulting in a revolutionary movement (the "Yellow Turbans") that was eventually suppressed. Yet upon submission as a princely tributary in A.D. 215 the hereditary chief priest of this Taoist "church" was confirmed in his religious functions by the authorities. He was the first of many magical practitioners (*Tao shih*) whose claim to power over the demons assumed political significance. Any group that opposed the Confucian literati, with their rites and their emphasis on education, aligned itself with the Taoist magicians. In many instances this took the form of an alliance of eunuchs, generals and other favorites of the emperor, who would enlist the Taoist priests in their struggle against the Confucian literati. On the other hand, the Confucian mandarins, too, called upon the Taoist priests for certain services,

[52] *Ibid.*, pp. 199–201.

in line with the official if disdainful acceptance of magic. Thus
Taoism was an enduring element of the established order at
the same time that it was a constant source of potential opposition to the ruling officialdom.

The main contention between the Confucian literati and the
Taoist priests concerned the distribution of offices and spoils.
Repeatedly Taoists succeeded in gaining recognition from the
emperor. In the eleventh century, for example, they established a system of examinations alongside the orthodox examinations so that students educated in Taoism became eligible
for appointments. Since the examinations were administered
by an office of the imperial government, struggles repeatedly
occurred among the emperor's favorites, Taoist priests and
Confucian literati over the appointment to the presidency of
the Academy.[53]

The official tolerance of Taoist beliefs and popular magic
prevailed only as long as the material interests and status ethic
of the Confucian literati, as well as the basic worship of the
ancestors, remained unaffected. Tolerance gave way to the
persecution of heresy whenever the conflicting claims and
ideas of Taoism or the religious practices of Taoist and Buddhist priests appeared to become a political threat to the prevailing order.[54] From early times religious edicts of the emperor had made the persecution of heresy a duty. But in China
heresy was not a question of doctrine in the same sense that
it was in Catholic Europe. The state cult and obligatory ancestor worship rested on philosophical and ethical maxims and
rules of behavior that encompassed or at least condoned heterodox ideas and magical practices. Both Taoism and Buddhism encouraged submissive obedience by emphasizing withdrawal and the contemplative search for salvation. These ideas
and practices were regarded as heretical only when they challenged the extraordinary powers (charisma) attributed to the
offices of the bureaucracy, from the emperor downward.

Such a challenge was presented whenever Taoist and Buddhist mystics turned from the perfection of self and the per-

[53] *Religion of China,* pp. 192–95, 202–3.
[54] Mahayana Buddhism was introduced in China in the first century B.C. but became a major influence only three centuries later,
at the end of the Han dynasty (A.D. 220).

formance of magical rites to the instruction of the people in
the religious mysteries and the establishment of religious organizations. The imperial edicts reproached the heretics for
preaching to the people in terms of promised rewards and the
salvation of the soul in the beyond and for separating themselves from their parental families (removing the ancestral tab-
lets from their houses) for the sake of a monastic way of life.
Any belief in rewards and salvation in the beyond—through
the performance of special rites—implied contempt for the efficacy of the state administration and threatened the idea that
the ancestors cared for the soul of the individual. The outright
rejection of familial ties for a monastic way of life threatened
the basis of piety and, hence, the discipline and obedience
upon which the power of the emperor and his officials depended.[55] In addition, monasticism was interpreted as a form
of parasitism, involving as it did the rejection of ploughing
and weaving and the dependence upon charity, as well as a
loss of tax income to the state. Begging and preaching outside
the monasteries was repeatedly forbidden. Eventually the
number of Buddhist monasteries was drastically curtailed and
each monastery was obliged to obtain a license (A.D. 843)
because the great diffusion of Buddhism curtailed the revenue
received by the state.

The most important challenge came, however, when laymen banded together in sectarian communities under the leadership of married, secular priests. These Buddhist communities were nonlicensed associations for the practice of virtue,
and they were singled out for suppression because they appeared to threaten the whole structure of Chinese society. The
Confucian man practiced the cardinal virtues within the circle
of the patriarchal family, whereas these associations in effect
renounced the whole rank-order of society, which was based
on blood ties and literary examinations. Confucianism tolerated magic and mysticism as long as they were useful means
for controlling the masses; it denounced them as heresy and
resorted to merciless suppression whenever institutions developed that threatened the established order.

[55] *Ibid.*, pp. 215–16.

E.   CONFUCIANISM AND PURITANISM

Weber concluded his analysis of religion in China by contrasting Confucianism with Puritanism, not as the status ethic of two different groups in two of the great world civilizations but as two possible orientations toward man and God. His emphasis was still on the meaning of religious world views for man's life on earth, but considered abstractly rather than in relation to the history and social structure of a given country. Thus he made several contrasts between Confucianism and Puritanism in terms of "the degree to which [each] religion has divested itself of magic . . . [and] the degree to which it has systematically unified the relation between God and the world and therewith its own ethical relation to the world."[56]

Orthodox Confucianism merely tolerated magic, but the popular belief in magic was an important factor in maintaining the power of Confucian officialdom. On the other hand, Puritanism rejected all trust in magical manipulation. Its spokesmen forbade the use of sacraments and symbols as external signs that distracted men from the inwardly experienced fear of, and trust in, God and hence from conduct guided solely by God's commandments.

Every religion has an attitude toward the things of this world. Confucianism accepted the world and man as inherently good; Puritanism regarded them as inherently evil. The ethical demands of Confucianism created a minimum of tension with the world and Puritan ethics a maximum. By means of a classical education the Confucian man was capable of unlimited perfection; the absence of peace and prosperity were the fault of government, the result of the ritual impropriety of officials. The Puritan man was incapable of achieving perfection by his own efforts; guided by faith in God he had to be diligent in his calling and implicitly trust God's inexorable choice of the elect and the damned.

Every religion also develops an ideal image of man that projects the right path to his salvation. By adjusting to the requirements of the social order the Confucian man adjusted

[56] *Religion of China*, p. 226.

to the cosmic harmony of heaven and earth. His cardinal virtue was to fulfill the traditional obligations of family and office, to observe the proper ceremonies in all circumstances of life. To achieve these ends he had to perfect himself by "watchful and rational self-control and the repression of whatever irrational passions might cause poise to be shaken."[57] A man who acted in this way was free of "sin," though Confucianism avoided this term as lacking in dignity and preferred such phrases as "improper" or "not in good taste." Such a man had no conception of basic evil, no orientation toward a world beyond, and so he experienced no conflict between the temptations of this world and the ethical demands of the next. Evil consisted of a lack of respect for traditional authorities and breaches of ceremonial or convention; it was caused by a lack of education and so could be corrected here and now. Accordingly, the goals of a good man were health, a comfortable income, a long life, and a good name after death—clearly ends of this world, not of the next.

In all these respects Puritanism differed profoundly. The Puritan had to obey God's commandments and in so doing reject the evil ways of the world. His cardinal virtue was a way of life in which he achieved justification by faith and by works, always trying for a precarious balance between too great a preoccupation with man's sinfulness, which led to selfish withdrawal and self-mortification, and too much misguided pride and confidence that outward success was a sign of grace. To achieve such a way of life he had to act as God's steward during the short span of his life, ever aware that in the end he must give an accounting for his conduct. No man could do this without sinning; it was enough if he were ever ready and watchful, aware of the danger of pride in the most humble acts of faith and of the danger of worldliness in diligence and work itself. This meant that there was a basic evil in man that could be abated only by the true believers who served in God's invisible church and strove with every act of their busy workaday lives for salvation in the world beyond.

Attitudes toward magic, toward the things of this world and toward an ideal image of man are in turn related to the phe-

[57] *Ibid.*, p. 228.

nomenon of prophecy. Prophecy typically confronts men with demands that conflict with worldly interests and the exigencies of mundane affairs, either in the sense that God makes ethical demands upon man and thus enjoins obedience as an ethical duty or in the sense that the prophet himself calls upon men in their need for salvation to turn away from the world and follow him in his exemplary conduct. Such ethical prophecy was absent from Confucianism but was the very foundation of Christianity—a difference that is reflected also in the contrast between an impersonal Spirit of Heaven and the idea of God as a personal Father in Heaven.

Weber speculated about the relation between these religious ideas and the economies of early Chinese and Middle Eastern civilization. In both areas agriculture and the consequent prosperity of the people had depended from early times upon irrigation and, hence, upon a centralized administration. The king or emperor stood at the head of this administration. He was the "rainmaker" who "produced" the harvest, and this fact might have suggested the idea of a deity on whose will the welfare of the people depended. Yet there was also an important difference. In the Middle East, the image of the personal God-Father was related to the shifting fortunes of war and foreign relations. When the Jewish people "remained a small state in the midst of world powers to which they finally succumbed," Yahwe became the "supramundane ruler of destiny" whose wrath would chastise all who failed in their obedience to his commandments. As "political publicists" the prophets dramatized the fate of their people among the world powers by relating it to the obedience or disobedience with which the people had observed their ethical covenant with God.[58] In China, a different, more impersonal conception of the deity developed, perhaps because the country had become an internally peaceful world empire at an early time. With the decline of feudalism internal warfare became illegitimate and the defense against nomadic invasions was made a police duty of the government. Change itself implied unrest and disorder, related to unrest among the spirits. Order was preserved by the Spirit of Heaven, whose tranquillity was maintained

[58] *Religion of China*, pp. 21–24, and *WuG*, Vol. I, pp. 255–57. Cf. the detailed discussion of Jewish prophecy in Chapter VII below.

by the ritual propriety of the emperor and his officials. This image of the "deity" left no room for wrath or passion or even a personified identity, nor did it allow for the idea of a covenant containing ethical demands that man must fulfill. Also, since the tranquillity of heaven and earth and the undisturbed preservation of bureaucratic authority were regarded as mutually reinforcing, the officialdom had an obvious interest in eliminating all emotional and orgiastic elements from the state cult and in suppressing all forms of religious prophecy.[59]

The absence or presence of religious prophecy may be related in turn to the image of the world and of man that a specific religion projects. By demanding obedience to the divine commands, the Old Testament prophets created the image of a world that must be fashioned by man in accordance with ethical norms. This deliberate contrast between the world as it is and as it ought to be required that man develop himself as a tool for the attainment of goals that transcend the world. In this view, man's life and personality are unified by an ethical aspiration that gives the individual autonomy in confronting the world. In this sense the Puritan ethic "amounts to an objectification of man's duties as a creature of God," for they are duties outside the "organic relations of life."[60] Such an ethic represented an unbridgeable contrast with Confucianism, which favored adjustment to the world as it is and a style of life based upon a traditional cultivation of familial relationships.

> Completely absent in Confucian ethic was any tension between nature and deity, between ethical demand and human shortcoming, consciousness of sin and need for salvation, conduct on earth and compensation in the beyond, religious duty and socio-political reality. Hence, there was no leverage for influencing conduct through inner forces freed of tradition and convention.[61]

Instead, conduct was governed by filial piety, buttressed by ancestor worship and the belief in spirits. The Confucian man aimed at a poised adjustment to the world through the con-

[59] Cf. *Religion of China*, pp. 26–27.
[60] *Ibid.*, p. 236.
[61] *Ibid.*, pp. 235–36.

scientious observance of duties toward the people close to him, whether they were living or dead. Religious duty toward the family rather than toward a supramundane God and, hence, personal relations as an end rather than as a means were the watchwords of Confucian piety. Yet, this absence of ethical demands transcending mundane affairs also meant that Confucianism rejected the idea of a universal ethic like the Christian demand for the "love of man." As Mencius commented, such an idea would "extinguish piety and justice. . . . It is the way of animals to have neither father nor brother."[62]

The absence or presence of prophecy is therefore related to the predominance or subordination of familial and personal ties. In China, ethical considerations pertaining to economic transactions were by and large coextensive with the personal associations controlled by filial piety and founded upon the Confucian rejection of prophecy and ethical demands that conflicted with the world as it is. In Western civilization, on the other hand, familial ties became subordinated to impersonal considerations, in part at least because religious prophecy had brought about the ascendance of universal ethical principles over the obligations of kinship.

> The great achievement of ethical religions, above all of the ethical and asceticist sects of Protestantism, was to shatter the fetters of the kinship group. These religions established the superior community of faith and a common ethical way of life in opposition to the community of blood, even to a large extent in opposition to the family. From the economic viewpoint it meant basing business confidence upon the ethical qualities of the individual proven in his impersonal, vocational work.[63]

Confucianism and Puritanism also illustrate the paradox of rationality. In China, material welfare was exalted above all other goals in life and the political and economic teachings of Confucianism deliberately sought to maximize the well-being of the people. Yet in the absence of the appropriate economic mentality Chinese economic policies did not achieve this end. Puritanism, which rejected the pursuit of wealth as an end,

[62] Quoted in *ibid.*, p. 236.
[63] *Religion of China*, p. 237. Cf. Chapter III, D, above.

unintentionally helped create an economic mentality and a methodical way of life that led to an increase of wealth and jeopardized true religion, as Wesley pointed out. There is then a "strange reversion of the 'natural'" relation between what men intend by their acts and what actually comes of them—the paradox of unintended consequences.[64]

In the preceding pages several differences between Confucianism and Puritanism have been discussed. As an aid to the reader these contrasts may be summarized as follows:

Confucianism	*Puritanism*
Belief in impersonal, cosmic order; tolerance of magic	Belief in supramundane God; rejection of magic
Adjustment to the world to maintain harmony of heaven and earth; the ideal of order	Mastery over the world in unceasing quest for virtue in the eyes of God; the ideal of progressive change
Vigilant self-control for the sake of dignity and self-perfection	Vigilant self-control for the sake of controlling man's wicked nature and doing God's will
Absence of prophecy related to inviolability of tradition; man can avoid the wrath of the spirits and be "good" if he acts properly	Prophecy makes tradition and the world as it is appear wicked; man cannot attain goodness by his own efforts
Familial piety as the principle governing all human relations	Subordination of all human relations to the service of God
Kinship relations as the basis for commercial transactions, voluntary associations, law and public administration	Rational law and agreement as the basis for commercial transactions, voluntary associations, law and public administration

[64] *Ibid.*, pp. 237–38.

Confucianism	*Puritanism*
Distrust of all persons outside the extended family	Trust of all persons who are "brothers in faith"
Wealth as the basis of dignity and self-perfection	Wealth as a temptation and unintended by-product of a virtuous life

From these differences it appears that Confucianism and Puritanism represent two comprehensive but mutually exclusive types of rationalism, each attempting an internally consistent, intellectual ordering of human life based upon certain ultimate religious beliefs. Both world views encouraged sobriety and self-control and made all personal and mundane affairs matters for conscious deliberation. Both world views were compatible with the accumulation of wealth. But neither rationalism nor acquisitiveness is intelligible without an understanding of the ends men have in view. The Confucian aimed at attaining and preserving "a cultured status position," and he used as means to this end adjustment to the world, education and self-perfection, the polite gesture and the observance of proprieties, the enjoyment of wealth as opposed to acquisitiveness, esthetic refinement as opposed to specialized skills, and, above all, familial piety as the model of conduct in a bureaucratic context. For the Puritan, rationalism and acquisitiveness had a different meaning. The systematic control of one's nature and the moral bookkeeping of daily life were tools in the service of God that led to a mastery of the world. As "tools of God" the Puritans combined their ascetic conduct with an intensity of belief and an enthusiasm for action that were completely alien to the esthetic values of Confucianism. It was this difference in the prevailing mentality that contributed to an autonomous capitalist development in the West and the absence of a similar development in China.

CHAPTER VI

SOCIETY AND RELIGION IN INDIA

Hinduism and Buddhism was Weber's third study in the sociology of religion.[1] In outline it was similar to his study of China, dealing first with the social structure of Indian society, next with the orthodox doctrines of Hinduism and the heterodox doctrines of Buddhism, then with the modifications brought about under the influence of popular religiosity, and finally with the impact of religious beliefs on the secular ethic of Indian society.[2] Weber approached the first of these topics by a consideration of caste in comparative perspective.

A. THE HINDU SOCIAL SYSTEM

The Concept of Caste

In India, caste was the central fact of the social structure just as the relation between kinship group and bureaucracy

---

[1] He did not live to revise this part of his work before its publication in book form. An English translation by H. H. Gerth and Don Martindale has been published under the title *The Religion of India* (Glencoe: The Free Press, 1958); it became available after this chapter had been written.

[2] For reasons stated below, p. 189, n. 69, I omit Weber's discussion of Buddhism from this presentation of his work.

was the central fact of Chinese dynastic society. The castes of India established a direct link between religious belief and the social differentiation of society—a link that in most other societies was indirect. Weber emphasized this contrast by considering caste in relation to the sects and churches of Western civilization. Castes share with the Protestant sects the element of social exclusiveness: a person who violates the ritual of his caste may be ostracized, so that the members of the caste, including his own parents and relatives, will terminate all contact with him. This ostracism is analogous to the sectarian practice of excluding members from admission to Communion if they have been found guilty of wrongdoing. Caste differs from the religious sects in that membership does not depend upon the individual's religious qualifications but his birth. In Catholic communities, too, individuals are born into the Church but, unlike the Church, caste members are recruited only from a particular social group and they do not aim at the conversion of nonbelievers. Accordingly the castes combine religious beliefs with a rigid observance of status differences. They are exclusive communities of persons whose social status is indicated by their birth and who share the same status by virtue of their ritual practices.[3]

[3] For the orientation of the reader I add a brief note on the most general aspects of the caste system. According to the classical formula the system was divided into four groups, or *varnas* (originally meaning color): the Brahmins (priests), the Kshatriyas (warriors), the Vaisyas (merchants), and the Sudras (laborers). The first three are the so-called twice-born castes, which are entitled to wear the sacred thread. Every male child who belongs to a twice-born caste undergoes an elaborate ceremony of initiation, in the course of which the right to wear the sacred thread is conferred upon him. Sudras, on the other hand, are not entitled to wear the sacred thread and therefore are "once-born." Below the Sudras rank the untouchables, who are barred from entry into temples and who may not be served by any member of a twice-born caste. Untouchables are believed to defile others by mere touch or in some cases by their presence at a distance. The four *varnas* and the untouchables are divided into a vast number of subcastes (*jati*). Today these broad categories may perhaps be regarded as a nation-wide standard, which has a clear-cut meaning only at the top and the bottom of the hierarchy. Although disputes over rank are rife throughout the hierarchy, the classical division retains its importance, in part because the conflicting claims are made in terms of

Weber saw "caste" as a special case of status groups. In all societies such groups maintain their identity by imposing restrictions upon intermarriage and social intercourse with persons who "do not belong." Castes are hereditary status groups whose restrictive practices are unparalleled both in the degree to which they erect barriers among members of different castes and in the detail with which they regulate the life of the individual.

Intermarriage is a case in point. According to Weber, marriage between a high-caste girl and a low-caste man was prohibited originally as a violation of status honor, while the marriage between a high-caste man and a low-caste girl (hypergamy) was disapproved but tolerated. (Men in the highest castes, who could afford several wives, had an interest in having the latter type of marriage accepted.) As a result, high-caste girls are restricted to men of their own caste. In order to avoid having a girl remain single, parents see to it that her marriage is arranged before puberty. Indeed, a fear of failure in this respect drove some of the higher castes to female infanticide, a practice that is usually resorted to only by an impoverished population in response to an acute food shortage.[4] That the higher, well-to-do castes would resort to such measures indicates the extremes to which the caste principle could

that division and because presumed historical antecedents are cited in order to justify the ranking of a caste in one of the four categories. Since there is a bewildering variety of ritual practice, one can say only that among the twice-born castes rank appears to vary according to strict adherence to endogamy, child-marriage, the chastity of widows, cremation of the dead, sacrifices to ancestors, vegetarian and nonalcoholic diet, and correct conduct in relation to Sudras and untouchables. Among the lower castes rank also depends upon the rank of the Brahmins who are still, or no longer, ready to render services to the caste in question and also upon which other castes are willing or unwilling to accept water from that caste. A note on spelling: Brahmin refers to a member of the highest caste; Brahman refers to the Hindu concept of a highest, impersonal Divine Being; Brahma refers to the Creator.

[4] The reason for the arrangement of early marriages was phrased in ritual terms. At each menses a "grown" girl who was unmarried brought pollution—if not sin—on herself and her parents, i.e., among the higher castes. Such ritual considerations might be set aside, on the other hand, if no suitable marriage could be arranged, in which case families might prefer to leave their girls unmarried.

be carried. A similar extremism developed with regard to the rules that prohibited particular foods, determined who could eat at the same table,[5] and specified from whose hand a given caste could accept certain foods. These rules are only the first step in an intricate system of invidious discrimination in which the castes place every contact between their respective members under ritual control, each utilizing the fear of magical pollution in its strategy of downgrading others and upgrading itself.[6]

The castes differ among themselves in the degree to which they adhere to many of the rules. In some instances castes use strict compliance as a means of improving their relative rank in the caste hierarchy, though for the most part such endeavors are successful only in the long run. In the case of some offenses, on the other hand, the highest castes are rather lax in their compliance, since a high-caste man can redeem his transgression by ritual purification—usually through bathing and/or by dabbing himself with a solution of cow dung. Thus, although ritual practice is common to all castes, variations in compliance reflect social aspiration or status consciousness as well as religious orthodoxy. Where ritual practices are strictly observed, life tends to become a daily round of prescribed acts.[7]

[5] The technical term "commensality" is derived from the Latin *mensa*, table, so that *commensa* means "a common table" and all persons who customarily are willing to share a common table practice "commensality."

[6] Weber did not explicitly analyze the idea of pollution, except to observe that it was based on magical beliefs. Most of his illustrations referred to contacts between castes rather than to the many bodily functions, e.g., menstruation, shaving, sexual relations, bodily emissions, etc., which are regarded as polluting irrespective of their bearing on intercaste contacts. I suspect that Weber would have attempted to relate the idea that bodily functions are a source of defilement to the religious and magical significance of blood relationships. Where kinship determines man's place in this world and his chances in future incarnations, the "potency" of that kinship needs to be preserved and elaborations of this idea may be involved in the concern with ritual purity in bodily functions as well as in the more usual concern with intermarriage and the "purity of the blood."

[7] This ritualism implies, for example, that every change of occupation and work-technique can lead to social degradation. It also is used to protect established *jajmani* or clientele relationships so that

These social and ritual barriers between the castes are ultimately based on a belief in magic, which supports the idea that kinship relations are sacrosanct. In Weber's view, Indian society depended to a much larger extent than any other society upon the principle of "familial charisma" or "charisma attributed to kinship."

> By "familial charisma" we want to designate certain personal qualifications, which originally were thought to be magical, and which are in any case extraordinary and not readily accessible to other persons, insofar as these qualifications [i.e., charisma] are attributed to persons by virtue of their membership in a kinship group.[8]

In Western civilization this concept took the form of hereditary kinship "by the grace of God," but in India it spread throughout the society. Weber spoke of the "routinization of charisma" to designate the process by which the personal charisma of the heroic leader, of all persons in positions of authority, and, finally, of all persons exercising specialized skills, devolved upon their kin so that eventually charisma became attributed to kinship rather than to the individual.[9]

The Spread of the Caste System

In India the invidious distinctions that exist in all societies were given an all-embracing religious or magical significance. Weber's question was how the beliefs sustaining the caste system could have become the dominant religion of an entire subcontinent. He sought to answer this by reference to the direct and indirect consequences of conquest, the Hinduization of tribes, and the subdivision of existing castes.

---

a given caste has the hereditary and exclusive right to render services to the members of another caste in return for a remuneration that is fixed in keeping with local custom.

[8] *GAzRS,* Vol. II, p. 51. (*Religion of India,* p. 49.)

[9] *Religion of India,* pp. 49-50. Weber uses the term "gentile charisma" in the sense that charisma is regarded as an attribute of the "gens" or clan or extended family. Since this is not readily intelligible in English, I use the phrase "familial charisma" or "charisma attributed to kinship." Cf. Chapter X, B, for a discussion of this phenomenon in the context of Western political history.

1. *Consequences of conquest.*[10] India was subject to repeated conquests by alien invaders, leading to the encounter
and subsequent acculturation between peoples of markedly
different physical type. Race differences probably had an important influence upon the caste system, though in Weber's
judgment they had nothing to do with the so-called race instincts or qualities that writers bandied about in his day as
well as ours. The point is, rather, that the conquerors rejected
intermarriage with the despised natives. Such discrimination
against intermarriage with social inferiors is practiced by ruling classes all over the world. But in India this increased the
existing alienation between racially and culturally divergent
peoples, whose contact had frequently resulted from military
conquest and who were prevented from merging with one another despite the frequent occurrence of racial mixture between conquerors and native women. Magical beliefs, too,
gave special significance to the idea that an individual's rights
and duties were an attribute of his birth, and these beliefs
reinforced the restrictions on intermarriage.

Other developments of the Indian social structure also can
be understood as a result of conquest. The conquerors of India
tended to distribute the land in characteristic fashion. Noble
families settled in the native villages, where they treated the
subject population as rent-paying tenants, village laborers in
agriculture or craft production, or pariahs ("serfs") who were
obliged to engage in certain despised occupations and to reside
outside the village limits. The conquering families and the subject population confronted each other as collectivities, the one
realizing its "right to the land" by claiming a portion of the
village production, the other occupying a position of obligatory
service, not to individuals but to the ruling castes as a whole.
On this basis production and commerce led to a division of
labor and exchange among, rather than within, the villages
and therefore among, rather than within, different ethnic
groups. This occupational specialization might have been
curbed by a vigorous development of centrally located urban
markets, but this did not occur.[11] Instead, villages and royal

[10] *Religion of India,* pp. 123–33.
[11] Though some developments toward urban autonomy occurred,
the administration of the cities came into the hands of *royal* officials,

residences remained for centuries the principal outlets for the sale of village products.

Early governments favored these conditions by their system of taxation. It was convenient to deal with only one person who was responsible for the collection of taxes and to treat all landowners of the village as jointly liable. By leaving all details of administration in the hands of the ruling families, the ruler increased both their social cohesion and their social distance from the village population. Weber speculated that the conquered tribes and pariahs were held jointly liable for the payment of a lump sum, which further strengthened occupational specialization by locality and by group affiliation, and contributed in turn to the predominance of the caste system.

2. *Caste and tribe.* A second process accounting for the spread of the caste system was the conversion of tribes to

---

and later passages of the Mahabharata refer to the city as "a place where the learned priests are." The patrimonial kings, with their disciplined armies and officials, naturally resented their financial dependence upon the guilds. Although the wealth of the merchants had led to their increasing influence, the special conditions of Indian society prevented that wealth from being transmuted into an enduring position of political power. In the cities of western Europe such a development had been possible, because under the leadership of craft and merchant guilds the town residents had become an armed citizenry. But in India the rise of cities had coincided with the development of pacifist religious movements—Buddhism and Jainism—that militated against an urban autonomy on the basis of armed might. The caste system militated against the city-wide fraternization of merchants and craftsmen and hence against the solidarity necessary for effective military and political action.

Apparently the guilds were unable to enforce their own regulations; to do so they had to appeal to the king or to the several castes that had the requisite power to enforce these regulations on the guild members. Thus the king and his officials could remain dominant in the great majority of Indian cities, even though on occasion they had to come to terms with the merchant guilds in view of the wealth that the guilds had at their disposal. Cf. *Religion of India,* pp. 33–39, for Weber's contrast between guild and caste.

For these and related details concerning the early political history of India Weber relied in part on the work of E. W. Hopkins, "The Social and Military Positions of the Ruling Caste in Ancient India as represented by the Sanskrit Epic," *Journal of the American Oriental Society,* Vol. XIII (1899), p. 57 ff.

Hinduism. On the basis of several criteria, such as caste name, recruitment from a particular locality, and others,[12] the Indian census identifies a large number of castes as "tribal," although conceptually "caste" and "tribe" have little in common. Weber pointed out that castes limit the occupations acceptable to them, that they are identical with a status group of a given rank, that they are purely social groups, and that they practice endogamy. Tribes, on the other hand, encompass all occupations and ranks, are specifically political associations, and practice exogamy of kinship groups and totems. Also, tribes are confined to a territory, while many castes are not. Most tribes lack rules concerning foods and commensality, whereas all castes imposed such rules on their members.[13] Despite these differences, transitions from tribal communities to castes occurred frequently in the past, usually in one of two ways.

In the course of Indian history the established caste order came into contact with ethnically distinct tribes that occupied territories of their own. The ruling families of such a tribe might decide to become vegetarians, to oppose the slaughter of cows, to change their marriage practices and eating habits in relation to the lower social strata, to demand that widows remain chaste, to cremate rather than bury their dead, and so on. By incorporation in Hindu society the ruling groups of such communities could obtain a religious legitimation of their position as against the lower social groups in their own society. After renaming their deities in keeping with Hindu nomenclature and abolishing their native priests, such rulers might then approach a Brahmin with the request that he conduct their rites and confirm their high caste status, which had merely been "forgotten" temporarily. If successful, such efforts would inevitably result in the transformation of the tribe into a number of Hindu castes.

The transition from tribe to caste may take a second form, where the established caste order comes into contact with ethnically or occupationally distinct groups that no longer oc-

[12] A survey of castes in terms of such criteria is contained in G. S. Ghurye, *Caste and Class in India* (Bombay: Popular Book Depot, 1957), Chapter 2.
[13] *Religion of India*, pp. 30–33.

cupy territories of their own, though they may have done so in the past. For the Western reader this alternative is best illustrated by the Jews and the Gypsies. Originally both of these peoples were communities with all the attributes of a tribe, but they lost their native territories and became guest- or "pariah-people," in Weber's terms. As such, Jews and Gypsies have many caste characteristics: they have no territory of their own; they are limited in the occupations they are allowed to pursue; they have become identified as a status group that practices endogamy and imposes rules on food and social intercourse. Thus, groups that at one time were tribes which functioned as political associations in their native territory could become castes. In India the spread of the caste system was helped by such developments. There are, of course, many ways in which permanently settled tribal groups may lose their residence and come to depend entirely upon producing for, or serving, the settled population.[14] Although such pariahs have existed in many civilizations, the Hindu castes went furthest in elaborating the methods of excluding them from the community of the orthodox. In India members of the lowest castes are regarded as sources of pollution, held at arm's length and forced to observe ritual proprieties that confirm their social inferiority in every act.

3. *Subdivision of castes.* The spread of the caste system may also occur through a process of subdivision. For example, migration brings about a change to a new social environment with different ritual practices, and the individuals involved are consequently suspected of having violated their ritual duties. Permanent changes of residence lead regularly to the sub-

[14] On the basis of his comparative studies of Asiatic societies Professor Wolfram Eberhard has pointed out that the process often takes the following form. A tribal group finds itself surrounded by more advanced agrarian groups, such as high-caste Hindu landowners. As agriculture expands, the tribe finds that its means of livelihood become more and more restricted (e.g., hunting grounds). As a consequence the tribe must establish contacts with the other groups, which may like to use its services (e.g., as professional skinners of animals). In this way the economic system of the autonomous tribe breaks down and the tribe becomes a specialized caste of inferior rank. I cite this example since it clarifies what Weber had in mind.

division of a caste.[15] Other subdivisions occur when certain caste members cease to regard particular ritual duties as binding upon themselves or, conversely, when members accept new ritual duties as obligatory. There are several possible reasons for such actions:

(1) membership in a Hindu sect, which exempts from some, or imposes new, ritual duties;

(2) increasing inequality of property holdings, which prompts wealthy persons to assume the ritual duties of a higher caste in order to be accorded a higher rank. Today, property differentiation is a fairly frequent reason for severance from the caste community, which always presupposes the rejection of intermarriage and of commensality where both were practiced previously;

(3) change of occupation or even a change of work technique, because the orthodox regard such changes as incompatible with the continuation of the caste community;

(4) relaxation of ritual observances by some members, which prompts the more orthodox of the community to terminate the relationship;

(5) quarrels within the caste, whatever the occasion, insofar as these cannot be settled, although such quarrels are not readily admitted and ritual offenses of the opponents are cited to rationalize the subdivision.[16]

These considerations suggest that the spread of the caste system reflects at each stage a complex interweaving of differences that arise from economic processes, such as increasing inequalities and the division of labor, from the incorporation of tribal communities in positions of varying social and economic dependence, and, above all, from the effort of each

[15] This accounts in part for the fact that less than one-tenth of the Indian population lives outside the *district* of their birth. Weber relied on the 1911 census, whose figure of 8.7 compares with 9.8 for the 1921 census. In 1931 district figures were not published, but only 3.59 of the population lived outside their native *provinces* or *states*. Kingsley Davis has made it clear, moreover, that even these low figures probably exaggerate the extent of migration. See his discussion of migration in *The Population of India and Pakistan* (Princeton: Princeton University Press, 1951), p. 107 ff.

[16] *Religion of India*, pp. 102–8.

caste to use ritual practices as a weapon in the struggle for a higher social rank. In India such competition for social rank did not in the long run lead to the formation of interest groups that were capable of participating in the political life of their country and hence of having a permanent effect upon the distribution of power in their society. As in the case of China, Weber noted that India lacked the development of autonomous political forces within her social structure because of the magical powers attributed to kinship. In the absence of internal political unification—other than that imposed by conquest—the result was a bewildering proliferation of castes and subcastes.

The Brahmin and the Confucian Intelligentsia

Weber's consideration of the caste system was an effort to understand the setting in which the Brahmins have occupied the pre-eminent place for many centuries. As in his other studies his interest focused upon the priests and literati who have had a surpassing influence on the formation of religious thought. A study of such educated minorities in the early period revealed similarities and differences that have had significant repercussions on the development of world civilizations.

Weber pointed out, for example, that many ideas of Hinduism could be found also in ancient Greece. The ideas of the world as a transitory abode and a place of sorrow, of release from a cycle of "rebirths" and of a memory of previous births were familiar to Greek writers from Homer on.[17] Similarities could also be observed in the Brahmin and the Confucian intelligentsia. Both groups were composed of high-ranking literati whose magical charisma depended upon a knowledge of ceremony and ritual derived from a holy or classical literature written in a sacred language remote from everyday speech.

[17] There is also evidence of direct influence of Indian upon Greek thought, especially in the philosophy of Pythagoras. In referring to this problem Weber relied upon Richard Garbe, *Die Samkhya Philosophie* (Leipzig: H. Haessel Verlag, 1917), pp. 113–37. For a recent and very striking treatment of such affinities in ancient thought, cf. E. R. Dodds, *The Greeks and the Irrational* (Boston: The Beacon Press, 1957), Chapter 5.

Indian and Chinese literati possessed a pride of culture that identified this classical knowledge—as well as the mystical experiences associated with it—with man's cardinal virtue and good fortune, while ignorance was the basic vice responsible for human misfortune. Weber stated that these educated minorities of early civilization developed similar ideas because they used their learning to distinguish themselves from the popular magicians, to claim high rank, and to commend their services to the secular rulers. Yet notable as the similarities are, the contrasts between such educated minorities are even more instructive.

The Chinese intelligentsia was a status group of men who were officials or who aspired to office, while the Brahmins were a somewhat motley group of royal chaplains, family priests, theologians and jurists who functioned as spiritual advisors and administrators, teachers, consultants, and authorities in questions of ritual propriety. To be sure, only a fraction of the Confucian scholars were officials and only a fraction of the Brahmins were priests, but the strategic position and power of those who were, as well as the expectations of those who aspired to such positions, made the bureaucratic or priestly career and office a most influential as well as the ideal way of life. The mandarin considered the career of an official the only one worthy of a cultivated man, although his sinecure in any locality was in principle temporary and his income was derived from a governmental salary and various forms of blackmail. To a Brahmin such a career would appear a matter of expediency and without merit. The Brahmin depended upon fixed rents or royalties derived from the land in return for his administration and upon "gifts" in return for his priestly services. His right to such income was not subject to recall or limited to short periods; he enjoyed it for life, and his family might enjoy it for several generations. This contrast between the typical income of the mandarin and the Brahmin was related to the contrast between the early political unification of China and the lack of political unity in India.[18]

[18] That is, the salaries and short tenure of Chinese officials were an index of centralization, while the fixed benefices ceded to Brahmins for life or even for generations were an index of local autonomy, relatively speaking. The reader should bear in mind that this

The position of mandarins and Brahmins as a class of officials and landowners corresponded to their position near the center of power. In China, the literati of all schools identified themselves with the emperor, who was the high priest of the realm and, as such, the principal supporter of holy tradition. According to the Confucian interpretation, the emperor combined in one person the highest secular with the highest sacred office. Nothing comparable existed in India. No Indian king ever performed the functions of a priest, however great his power might be otherwise. In the oldest period the king required the sanction of his *purohita* or royal chaplain in all religious matters. Although kings frequently manipulated these powerful priests, the latter were always recognized as the only legitimate arbiters in questions of ritual. The contrast with China suggests that this bifurcation of authority contributed to the relative weakness of the secular rulers. Apparently the Brahmin priests encouraged political disunity in order to strengthen their own position. Under these circumstances authority could be legitimate only in the sense that the individual ruler acted with ritual correctness according to holy tradition, especially in his relations with Brahmins. Otherwise he was a barbarian.[19] This subordination of secular rulers to the religious authority of the Brahmins meant that the latter came

is a broad comparison, which does not exclude the local autonomy of Chinese communities or the temporary centralization of power in India. But the contrast is so great as to suggest that in the face of administrative centralization the local autonomy of Chinese villages fared best by a politics of withdrawal from contact with the officialdom. Analogous consideration suggests that in India centralization did not fare well because it was unable to break down the strength of local autonomy that previous political disunity had encouraged.

[19] The oldest written documents already refer to this contrast between China and India. Vedic tradition characterizes the "black" opponents of the Aryan peoples as "priestless" (*abrahmana*) in contrast to the Aryan rulers whose ritual sacrifices were supervised by a learned priest. On the other hand, the oldest Chinese tradition makes no reference to priests who were independent of the purely secular rulers. Among the nomadic tribes that conquered China and established the Chou dynasty (1050 B.C.), the warrior chief was at once the headman and priest of the leading family household and consequently the ruler as well as the chief priest of the tribe. Among the Aryan peoples conquering India, rulers and priests apparently were already separated.

to constitute an independent priestly caste that possessed complete power over the education and recruitment of novices.

These differences between the social position of the Chinese and the Indian intelligentsia are reflected in the general contrast between Indian and Chinese literature.[20] Chinese learning was bound up with the art of writing, which may be attributed to the early importance of official annals and calendar reckoning at the imperial court, even at a time when Chinese writing was quite primitive. Moreover, writing was essential for the highly developed administration of the Chinese Empire.

It was otherwise in India. For a very long time the Brahmin priests upheld the principle that the sacred teachings could be transmitted only by word of mouth. Court proceedings, too, were entirely oral. Speeches were generally regarded as the most important means for the defense of given interests as well as for the exercise of power, and magic was used to secure victory in debate. Religious disputations, practice in debate and forensic contests for prizes were important institutions in Hindu culture. The history of Indian literature is the history of men who sought to excel by their oratorial skills: first, the rhapsodic bards of the Vedic age, then the Brahmin priests who emphasized the oral tradition, then the poets and reciters who combined teaching with storytelling in the form of either myths or law texts. Only by the second century A.D. had the learned men of the Brahmin caste become a class of scribes as well. The great importance of oral tradition and recitation helped determine the character of India's sacred literature. Easy comprehension and ready reproducibility were imperative. Hence the oldest philosophical writings and the sutra literature (dealing with the ritual practices of everyday life) are written in the form of epigrams that can be learned by heart and commented upon by the teacher. For the same reason much of the nonphilosophical literature is written in verse form. Statements of an idea or prescriptions for a ritual observance are repeated endlessly, each time with the modi-

[20] In making this contrast Weber had special reference to the Brahminic literature that followed the epic writings of the Vedic period, specifically the Brahmanas, which describe and interpret sacrifice and ritual, and the Upanishads, which contain esoteric speculations on the inner meaning of life.

fication of only one word or sentence, in keeping with the
sequence of thought. Similar reasons may account for the profusion of numerical schemata and the pedantically detailed
outline of the material.

These mannerisms of Indian literature, which may have
originated in efforts to facilitate memorization, led to an endless accumulation of embellishing adjectives, comparisons, and
symbols, as well as to endeavors to simulate an impression of
the great and the godly through the use of gigantic numbers
and luxuriant fantasies. Such mannerism stands in striking contrast to the economy and clear visual imagery of Chinese writing, which combines graceful brevity with a sober quality of
expression. Weber thought it probable that the Indian pen-
chant for rhetoric and embellishment diminished the sense of
the empirical—a tendency that ultimately stemmed from a
studied indifference toward the world.

Chinese and Indian literature reflect the world views of the
two groups. We have seen that Confucianism held all magical
practices in contempt, and though asceticism flourished in
China at one time and magic continued to be practiced, the
successful establishment of a certified officialdom helped make
the Confucian opposition to magic into a state doctrine. For
the Brahmins such a position was not possible. They constituted a priestly caste, not a status group of candidates for
public office. Their high rank, and indirectly the whole caste
order as well, depended upon a belief in the efficacy of magic.
Consequently the Brahmins could not relegate the attainment of magical powers to the popular, professional magicians,
who could compete with the priests. The magical powers of
the ascetic were revered so unquestioningly in India that the
ascetic ideal appears to have outweighed even the obligations
of family piety, whereas in China asceticism was rejected in
part because it proved incompatible with the preponderance of
family ties. But the Brahmins were an educated minority like
the Confucians; and accordingly they accepted and developed
apathetic forms of asceticism that were compatible with the
pride of rank and culture characteristic of an intellectual elite.

These differences between the Chinese and Indian elites also
influenced their socio-political attitudes. The Chinese literati
and officials subscribed to the idea of a welfare state with its

strong emphasis upon material comfort in the frequently expressed belief that the masses want to have their bellies filled. In Weber's view this orientation combined proud disdain for the uneducated masses with the very mundane interest of officials in a secure and stable income as the basis of a gentlemanly life.

India's early history, unlike China's, was marked by protracted struggles between the priestly caste and the secular rulers. Though the resulting power relationship was unstable, the Brahmins were supreme in all religious matters and claimed the highest social rank. Brahmin theory elaborated the rights and duties of kings in accordance with holy writ, just as it specified the social and ritual position of all other castes. This ethical pluralism was intensified by the success with which the Brahmins asserted their claim to social and jurisdictional superiority. The result was that a large number of separate, caste-bound orientations emerged, while the world view that was universally valid for Indian society as a whole consisted of metaphysical and magical beliefs that explained and justified the castes and their separate ways of life.

Not only the caste-order of this world, but also the entire rank-order of all divine, human, and animal creatures was interpreted in terms of the doctrine of retribution for the deeds of a previous life. [In Indian society] it was no problem, therefore, that status groups were juxtaposed, whose ethical orientations not only differed, but stood in harsh opposition to one another. Prostitutes, robbers and thieves could have a *dharma* of their occupations quite as much as Brahmins and kings, at any rate in principle. . . . The conflict of man with man, the struggle of men against animals and also against the gods, the existence of downright ugliness, of stupidity, and of utter abomination: all this was unquestioned. Men were not equal in principle, as in the view of classical Confucianism. Instead, men had been of unequal birth throughout time, as unequal as were men and beasts.[21]

Brahmin theory interpreted the regulations of each caste as holy and also accepted all positive laws that supplemented the

[21] *GAzRS*, Vol. II, pp. 142–43. (*Religion of India,* p. 144.)

caste rules. In this view the rank-order of the cosmos was eternal, because every animal or god and every man—according to the caste of his birth—were souls whose positions resulted from the merits earned and the sins committed in a previous life. A "natural equality" among men cannot be conceived by a theory that attributes existing inequalities to the cumulative merits and demerits in previous incarnations, nor can men have common "rights" or "obligations" when all existing differences among them—including their different rights and duties—are interpreted as well deserved.[22]

As a consequence Hinduism accepted and promoted every specialization, in contrast to the Confucian literati, who opposed specialization as incompatible with the ideal of classical learning. In keeping with the model of a social order in which each caste has its own way of life (*dharma*), this specialization took the form of separate techniques for each occupation or sphere of activity.[23] Thus, formal logic developed as a technique of rational proof and disputation, just as political writings contained a technique for the exercise of power and erotic writings elaborated the techniques of sexual relations. By the same token Indian philosophical writings discussed the techniques by which man could obtain the ends marked out for him by the *dharma* of his caste—an ethical pluralism completely different from the universal ethic of both Confucianism and Christianity.

[22] This complete acceptance of the existing social order precluded the development of ideals that aimed at its transformation. Indian religious and social thought therefore militated against the ideas of "natural law" and "natural rights," although such ideas were not completely absent. Weber noted that intimations of the idea of a "natural law" occurred in the epic literature. Cf. *Religion of India*, p. 352, n. 8.

[23] The term "*dharma*" has many meanings. "The existing moral code is identified with *dharma*. A man who accepts the caste system and the rules of his particular subcaste is living according to *dharma*, while a man who questions them is violating *dharma*. Living according to *dharma* is rewarded, while violation of *dharma* is punished, both here and hereafter." See M. N. Srinivas, *Religion and Society among the Coorgs of South India* (Oxford: The Clarendon Press, 1952), p. 26.

B. THE EARLY SOCIAL
ORGANIZATION OF INDIAN SOCIETY

Weber attempted to deal with the early social organization of Indian society because of its bearing on the formative period of Indian religious thought. Although the existence of great city cultures in 2000 B.C. and earlier is known from excavations, the earliest documentary evidence stems from the Vedic period (1500–800 B.C.).[24] These documents contain very few references to the typical beliefs and practices of Hinduism, which probably developed during the so-called Brahminical period (800–500 B.C.). The following period, from 500 to 100 B.C., was an era of religious and philosophical innovation, culminating in the great religious synthesis of Hinduism in the Bhagavad Gita on the one hand and in the heterodox movements of Jainism and Buddhism on the other.[25] In his study Weber concerned himself especially with this last period and it will be sufficient for our purposes to consider his analysis of the Brahmins and the Kshatriyas, insofar as their relations in early Indian society illuminate the great cleavage between Hinduism and Buddhism.

Brahmins

In early Indian society the Brahmins probably did not constitute the highest rank and the caste system as it developed subsequently was very likely unknown. The earliest Indian literature, the Rigveda (1500–1000 B.C.), suggests the existence of magicians who sing the praises of the gods and compete with one another in the superlatives and mysterious images

[24] A convenient chronology of Sanskrit texts and authors is contained in K. M. Kapadia, *Marriage and Family in India* (London: Oxford University Press, 1955), pp. xxvii–xxviii, where the different estimates of various authorities are listed.

[25] The period during which the Bhagavad Gita was composed is usually given as 500–200 B.C.; i.e., evidence of ideas contained in this poem goes back to the sixth century B.C., while the version that has come down to us underwent numerous subsequent revisions. The Buddha lived approximately from 560 to 480 B.C., while Mahavira, the founder of the Jain sect, lived from 539 to 467 B.C.

of their poetic invocations. Similar conditions elsewhere suggest that these magicians were organized in guilds. Weber also assumed that a caste of hereditary priests developed from these antecedents.

The Brahmins probably became prominent because, as family priests of kings and noblemen, they gained ascendance over the priests who officiated at communal sacrifices. In that role the Brahmins could buttress their position by the elaboration of ritual practices and by magical threats. But their prominence depended upon personal service, and this fact worked against the formation of an impersonal hierarchy comparable to that of the Catholic clergy. The king could select Brahmins who were amenable to his wishes and would serve his political interests. It was the king who originally decided the disputes over rank that became an endemic feature of the caste order. Yet this did not prove to be a token of secular power over the priests; for evil magic would befall anyone who violated the traditional rites, and the Brahmins justified overthrow of a king who was guilty of such violations. The king's decisions thus remained subject to the influence of the Brahmins, who pressed home their demand that the family priest of the king or prince (*purohita*) be selected from their midst. In that position the most prominent Brahmins became the king's guides and counselors in all personal and political affairs, which explains the extraordinary social and political power of the Hindu priesthood despite the absence of a formal church hierarchy. In Weber's view the eventual strength of the caste order could be understood as an outgrowth of the power that the Brahmins had at their command by virtue of their position as family priests:

A king without a *purohita* is not a king in the full sense of the word, just as a Brahmin without a king is not a Brahmin of the highest rank. Even until the present, the position of the Brahmins depends far more on this ritual position of the confessor and on their indispensability in many family-ceremonies of high-ranking households, than in the almost non-existent, formal organization of the Brahmin caste. Accordingly, the Brahmins have imposed the regulations of the caste order (such as those pertaining to marriage and the kinship system) upon the castes which claimed high rank, but they have done so by virtue of their position as house-priests, not through decisions of any organized caste-authority. . . . Strict etiquette governed the competition among Brahmins, whose clientele-relations (*jajmani*) were protected according to the principle that without pressing need one should not change the priest, once his services had been requested. . . . These voluntary clientele-relations [between families and priests] take the place of the parish in a hierarchically organized church; in this respect the position of the Brahmins has remained similar to that of the old magician and medicine man.[26]

In accordance with their position as family priests, the classical occupation of the Brahmin caste was Vedic studies, religious teaching, and the performance of priestly functions in return for "gifts." A Brahmin did not "earn" his living by such services; he merely accepted the gifts (*dakshina*), which were a ritual duty on the part of those who requested his service. Sacrifices without gifts brought evil magic, and because of their magical power Brahmins could revenge themselves through curses or deliberate mistakes in the prescribed ritual. Though the size of the "gifts" was more or less regulated, it was legitimate for Brahmins to inquire how large a prospective "gift" might be, thus leaving ample room for extortionate practices. For a long time these gifts consisted of extensive land grants or of rents to be received in perpetuity from the agricultural or tax yield of a given area. To receive gifts of land was a Brahmin monopoly according to Brahmin theory; medieval

[26] *GAzRS*, Vol. II, pp. 62–63. (*Religion of India*, p. 61.) Despite its superior rank the Brahmin caste has been challenged both within Indian society and as a result of conquest. Weber mentioned, for example, that certain recalcitrant castes defied the Brahmins by claiming a high status on the basis of their orthodox ritual despite the fact that they employed the services of priests recruited from their own ranks. Historically speaking, the great challenges to Brahmin supremacy occurred during the Buddhist period (500–100 B.C.), in the period of Mohammedan supremacy (beginning in the thirteenth century), but probably not under British rule since the eighteenth century. None of these challenges proved successful in the long run.

inscriptions reveal that this theory was implemented in a large number of cases.

The emphasis upon "gifts" reflected the paramount concern with rank among Brahmins of the highest caste. Brahmins faced a loss of social status if they became permanent employees of a Hindu sect or of a community. Even the acceptance of a position as temple priest was regarded as very degrading under certain circumstances. In these ways Brahmins insisted upon independence from permanent ties and avoided all relations that might be interpreted as implying a servile status. Moreover, the oppression of Brahmins was prohibited (*ajucyata*), which meant among other things that in cases of litigation an arbitrator could not decide against the Brahmin. In terms of their claims at least, the status of Brahmins exceeded the status of kings and demanded a deference (*arca*) commensurate with that claim. Weber pointed out that nowhere else in the world has a priesthood ever achieved a comparable position.[27]

Kshatriyas

The classical Indian literature indicates that the Kshatriyas, or warriors, comprised all persons of authority, ranging from kings, princes and nobles down to village notables. The texts deal with the proper function (*dharma*) of kings and nobles, and, according to Weber, these moral prescriptions revealed

[27] Although the priestly function of the Brahmins was the basis of their superior rank, the number of Brahmins who performed this function at any one time was necessarily small. For example, Brahmin families inherited the large grants of land that their ancestors had been given in return for the performance of priestly services, so that many Brahmins were in fact large landowners. A large number of Brahmins also were forced to take up other occupations, although agricultural work and all productive activities were avoided. On the other hand, certain occupations, such as the cooks in high-ranking households or employment in administration, attracted Brahmins. Great differences in social rank developed among Brahmins as a result of this occupational differentiation, which represented an ever-present threat of a degradation in rank. This threat probably encouraged the elaboration of ritual, especially among high-ranking Brahmins, since the observance of ritual was both a symbol of high rank and a weapon for its protection.

rudiments of the oldest charismatic conception of kingship. That king is good whose subjects are well off and under whose reign there is no famine. His duty is to protect the population, politically and militarily. If he fails to do so, he is obliged to pay compensation to the injured population. The king who is defeated in war has sinned and is magically burdened with the sins of his subjects. This welfare conception of the patriarchal ruler played an important role in ancient India, but it was accompanied and gradually superseded by the idea that warfare rather than welfare was the proper function of the Kshatriya. The secular and religious literature of Hinduism assumes that the king always aims at conquering his neighbors, by force or by cunning. Since this literature was principally written by Brahmins and since the Brahmin position was strengthened in proportion to the weakness of the secular rulers, Weber inferred that this idealization of war as the *dharma* of the king was an important element in the struggle between Brahmins and Kshatriyas.

In India the rank-order of the castes was related to land ownership in important respects. Reference has been made to the large "gifts" of land Brahmins received in return for their priestly services. However, the ancient landowners were to be found primarily among the Kshatriyas who held political power. The history of these landowners and local administrators is at the same time the history of patrimonial administration under conditions of relative decentralization.

The principal concern of each secular ruler was to obtain the necessary recruits for his army and to collect taxes. Most efforts to realize these goals took the form of distributing benefices or sinecures in return for a lump sum or for the conscription of a given number of military recruits. In addition, landowners generally were put in charge of administrative duties like road-building, adjudication, and police surveillance, while the costs of this local administration were financed out of the penalties, license fees and assorted taxes collected from the population. Under this system of patrimonial rule the tax-leaseholder or the person who held a military benefice was free from all governmental control as long as he guaranteed the military and financial performance of the district and paid for the costs of administering it. By the same token, all peasants and agricultural laborers depended completely upon the local owners—a dependence reinforced by the fact that not one but several "intermediaries" stood between the peasant who did the work and the person who was directly responsible to the royal officials for the recruitment of soldiers and the payment of taxes. The peasant had to pay taxes to the landowners, but the latter were responsible to other middlemen who were entitled to a portion of the tax received and had other far-reaching property rights as well. In some instances still other persons intervened between the village and the officials. Where villages fell into tax arrears, for example, a wealthy man might assume responsibility for the payment of such debts and thus appropriate a portion of the total future yield. Hence the collective character of the landowning class was determined by the association of ownership with the performance of administrative functions, and the income of this class was always in part derived from the taxes, fees and other emoluments collected in the course of performing these functions.

Local administration of this type was not the only basis of landownership, however. Feudalism in the form best known to us in western Europe also existed in India. The coexistence of patrimonial and feudal elements is reflected in the organization of military forces, from the time of the ancient Indian epics down to the Moghul emperors. Armies of mercenaries, equipped and maintained out of the royal granaries and storehouses, stood side by side with individual knights who equipped and maintained themselves and who, therefore, owned the "tools of war," as the mercenaries did not. The social status of the knights was obviously higher than that of the mercenaries, and they were rewarded by land grants like feudal lords. This division between knights and mercenaries was related in turn to the coexistence of feudal and patrimonial methods of administration. Neither a warlike nobility nor a centralized administration gained permanent political ascendance, and India's history alternated between a fragmentation into petty kingdoms and a concentration of many of these into centrally governed, patrimonial empires.[28]

[28] A number of quite diverse groups came to assume the positions of secular rulers, warriors, and landlords. Kings and their extended families, knights who were retainers or vassals of a king, the tax-

Social and Religious Change in the Early Empires

Legend has it that the old Kshatriya families were wiped out in revenge for their revolt against Brahmin rule. There is probably some truth in this, since these families constituted a highly educated nobility that challenged the Brahmin monopoly on education and opposed Brahmin landowners politically. In the period of petty kingdoms preceding the Maurya dynasty (before 321 B.C.) society had been dominated by the Kshatriyas, and several passages of the Bhagavad Gita appear to reflect the ideals of that society and the subsequent controversies with the Brahmins.[29] There are speculations concerning the nature of the gods, the destiny of heroes, and the justice of wars, similar in many ways to the heroic age of the Homeric epics. Sometimes the hero's fate is seen as being in the hands of a great god who plays with men to suit his whims; at other times the good hero is believed to be immortal by the grace of a god, though it is mentioned also that without this belief the people would not remain virtuous. There are references to the great hero who does not fear the gods of the Veda and who hopes to enter the warrior heaven of Indra once he has met an honorable death on the field of battle. Occasionally it is mentioned that heroic action is better than austerity, and that action is better than inaction, for a man seeks virtue, profit, and pleasure. According to Weber, such statements reflected the ideals and speculations of a Kshatriya-dominated society, in which the ruling groups were not yet subordinate to the Brahmin priests in questions of religion.

Eventually the position of the old Kshatriya nobility was

---

leaseholders in administrative districts who were given land grants, the entrepreneurs in military recruitment who became attached to the land, the mercenaries who settled down to a peaceful occupation, and even tribal groups like the Mahratta, who established an empire by conquest in the seventeenth century—all claimed the rank of the ancient Kshatriya nobility, if need be after their actual origin had become obscure with the passage of time. Though such claims were contested, these attempts at upgrading illustrate how the ancient caste names were used as a frame of reference recognized throughout India.

[29] Cf. pp. 192–96 for a more detailed consideration of the Bhagavad Gita.

undermined not only by the Brahmin priests but also by the rise of a warrior caste in northwest India.[30] Most of the Rajputs were illiterate mercenaries in the service of a king. Their support may well account for the fact that the rulers of the Maurya dynasty (*ca.* 321–185 B.C.) destroyed the old Kshatriya monopoly on office-holding. In addition, the Mauryas undermined the pre-eminent position of the Brahmins, at least for a time, by supporting Buddhism, and the social setting of the Buddhist movement provides one of the clues for an understanding of the social change during this period.

The followers of early Buddhism came principally from the nobility and the rich merchant class. During the period of petty kingdoms preceding the Maurya dynasty these groups were a highly cultured elite, while the Brahmin caste was not yet very powerful, at least in the areas of northern India where Buddhism originated. Early Buddhism consequently reflected both the status pride of a cultured elite and the qualified opposition of that elite to the claims and pretensions of the priestly caste. Weber saw evidence of that pride in the rules that required Buddhist monks to be decently clad and that made provisions for their habit, in contrast to the ascetics who neglected their outward appearance as a symbol of their escape from the world. The rules pertaining to the forms of begging similarly adhered to conventional proprieties and reflected a feeling for dignity and good taste. The idea of release through contemplation and the bourgeois idea that the ordinary believer might earn what merit he could by supporting the monks financially appeared to reflect the orientation of high-status groups rather than the hopes of oppressed classes for a better future in this world or redemption in the next. Furthermore, the teachings of the Buddha presupposed a high level of schooling among his disciples; they were systematic, dispassionate discussions that appealed to the intellect, in contrast to the popular similes, ironic retorts and emotional preaching of Jesus or the visionary messages of Mohammed. On the other hand, a cultural elite of this kind was not likely to stand in conscious opposition to the social order. Buddhism was a re-

[30] The caste name of Rajput is reflected in the place name of Rajputana, the region in which this warrior caste presumably originated. "Rajaputra" means "king's son" or "prince."

ligious, not a social, movement, and hence unconcerned with
social issues, at any rate in any direct way. This apolitical
orientation, indifference to the world and idealization of a life
devoted to contemplation were so much in accord with established tradition that the Buddhist movement was tolerated
initially, even though its doctrines were greatly at variance
with Brahmin orthodoxy.

In his sermons the Buddha left the nature of the gods unde-
cided. He explicitly devalued the importance of Brahmin philosophy and the ritual knowledge of the priests, and he rejected the incomprehensible Sanskrit language in which the
Brahmin priests justified the minute ceremonial regulation of
life. With reference to the Brahmin caste the Buddha maintained that it was not birth but right conduct that made a
man a .true Brahmin. The monastic rule that commanded
itinerant friars to beg from rich and poor alike presumably
symbolized the Buddhist belief that the distinctions among
men in this world were of no interest to the monk who sought
salvation. By rejecting asceticism in a country in which ascetic
practices were an age-old and revered tradition, Buddhism invited not only incredulity and contempt but also the determined opposition of those who saw in these practices the high
road to salvation. Buddhism sought to diminish the religious
significance of the caste order by treating it with a kind of
studied neglect,[31] and Buddhist monasticism opposed the exclusiveness and pretensions of the Brahmin priesthood with a
group of holy men whose religious life was in dead earnest.

Weber saw early Buddhism, Jainism, and Hindu orthodoxy
as religious developments of a cultured elite that regarded the
laity as second-class citizens in all matters pertaining to religion. Early Buddhism especially made no severe demands
upon the laity and so accommodated the interests of secular
ruling groups. Under these circumstances, according to Weber,
the major religions came to compete with each other by under-

[31] During the ascendance of Buddhism the caste order was not
yet firmly established. Although the adherents of Buddhism came
primarily from families of high status, admission to the Buddhist order was granted irrespective of caste. Indeed, some early schools of
Buddhism are reported to have been founded by members of a
Sudra caste, some of whom also became officials under the Maurya
dynasty.

going a massive process of "popularization." Buddhism was transformed from an exclusive religion of a cultured elite to a great missionary movement, while Brahmin orthodoxy accommodated itself to the religious interests of ordinary believers in order to fight more effectively against the Buddhist heresy.[32]

This response to the religious interests of the laity was connected with the changing structure of Indian society that followed the establishment of a unified empire under the Maurya dynasty. The rule of the Mauryas marked the ascendance of the standing army and its officers, of the royal officialdom and its legions of scribes, and of the leaseholders who collected taxes and recruited soldiers. This meant that the laity no longer consisted only of a cultured nobility but, in addition, of the courtier, the official scribe, the merchant, and the landlord. Some evidence of the conflict between these groups and the Brahmin priests may be gleaned from the famous rock edicts of the Buddhist Emperor Asoka (*ca.* 264–226 B.C.). One of these edicts states that "the men who were, all over India, regarded as true, have been, with their gods, shown to be untrue" —presumably reflecting the Buddhist conflict with the Brahmins.[33] Another edict declares that glory and renown do not bring much profit unless the people obey the law of piety. But to do so is difficult. It requires the utmost exertion and complete renunciation, and these are extraordinarily difficult for people of high rank—clearly a pointed reminder to the nobility of the time.[34] Thus the "fruit of exertion . . . is not to be obtained by the great man only; because even the small man can by exertion win for himself much heavenly bliss." And for this purpose an edict declared, "Let small and great exert themselves."[35] Such deliberate leveling tendencies were already implicit in the religious ideas of the Buddha and were made explicit by the Emperor Asoka, indicating, according to Weber, that the secular rulers used religious appeals to satisfy the emotional needs and ensure the peacefulness of the popula-

[32] See section C. below.

[33] See Vincent A. Smith, *Asoka* (Oxford: The Clarendon Press, 1901), p. 139. Weber used this work, in which the rock edicts are reprinted.

[34] *Ibid.*, pp. 126–27.

[35] From the Minor Rock Edict No. 1 (Rupnath version) in *ibid.*, p. 141.

tion. Under the sponsorship of Asoka, Buddhism became for a time the dominant religion on the Indian subcontinent. Asoka himself became a devout Buddhist and, in keeping with the importance of written records in his regime, he saw to it that the century-old oral tradition of Buddhism was committed to writing. In the same spirit he initiated the spread of Buddhism beyond his realm.

The rise of this movement was paralleled by a decline of the Brahmin priesthood. Weber noted that during the four centuries after the reign of Asoka there was no evidence of endowments on behalf of Brahmins, probably reflecting the fact that under Buddhist rulers the Brahmins lost political influence. For a considerable time the Brahmins must have occupied a subordinate position in relation to the monastic congregations of the Buddhist order and the Jaina sect. Yet the Brahmin priests retained their great influence because the heterodox movements merely ignored or devalued, but made no attempt to attack, the existing caste order and so did not replace the Brahmins in the performance of religious rites. Thus, while Buddhism became one of the great missionary religions of the world over a large part of Asia, its influence in India proper eventually declined.

Beginning approximately in the first century B.C., schismatic tendencies came to the fore within Buddhism, followed by a gradual weakening of the movement. Compared with the Brahmins Buddhism lacked strong roots in the society; it consisted principally of monastic communities, made few demands upon the laity, and encouraged an itinerant way of life on the part of its monks. These factors made it especially vulnerable to attack by hostile rulers, while the Brahmin priests, who possessed no monastic organization that could be destroyed, remained strong as long as the caste order in the villages was intact. In the end Buddhism virtually disappeared from India proper, as a result of the Islamic conquest. Under Mohammedan rule Buddhist monks and cult-objects became special targets of destruction (A.D. 1193), and eventually even the locations of Buddhist holy places were lost to memory.[36]

[36] Weber believed that the temporary success as well as the eventual decline of the Buddhist mission in India could be explained by the characteristics of the movement in its early phase. The monks

As Buddhism gradually declined, the Brahmin priests began to reassert their position. In the long run the Brahmins
were able to restore their political influence with the aid of
secular rulers who opposed the rising power of town guilds
and of Buddhist monks. These efforts involved a struggle along
several fronts that lasted for many centuries. They consisted
of the stereotyping of caste ritualism, which is documented in
the law books of the first century A.D., and of the development of Hindu sects (beginning in the eighth and ninth centuries A.D.) that, through propaganda and the organization of
monastic movements within Hinduism, sought to defeat the
heterodox movements of Buddhism and Jainism. Weber interpreted the rise of these sects as another response to the religious interest of the social groups that had replaced the old
and highly educated Kshatriya nobility.[37]

C. HINDU ORTHODOXY AND THE
BRAHMIN RESTORATION

The second step of Weber's analysis was the study of religious beliefs. There are two principal doctrines of Hinduism:
the idea of transmigration of the soul (*samsara*) and the idea
of retribution (*karma*) in each life for the sins of the previous
life (incarnation).[38] Originally the Indian belief concerning
the fate of the soul after death was quite similar to analogous
beliefs elsewhere. The soul was not regarded as immortal, and

had a materialistic interest in increasing the number of their supporters (*upasaka*). In the period of Buddhist expansion their efforts
were aided by the absence of a strict monastic organization and by
the fact that laymen could earn merit by gifts to the monks. As long
as these conditions prevailed, the country was flooded with itinerant
missionaries. Yet these conditions also revealed the inherent weakness of early Buddhism, for the absence of organization made it
difficult in the long run to compete with the Brahmin priests and
the Jaina sect, while the relative neglect of the laity made the success of early Buddhist propaganda easy rather than durable.

[37] Cf. pp. 183–89 below, where Weber's treatment of religious
developments following the Brahmin restoration of the eighth and
ninth centuries A.D. is considered.

[38] See *Religion of India*, pp. 25–29, for Weber's qualification of
this statement.

sacrifices to the dead were designed to bring peace to the departed spirit and prevent his envy and wrath against the living. But there was also the idea that sacrifices would prevent the starvation of the departed spirit, and prayers to the gods frequently expressed a wish for their "long life." The existence of men and gods in the beyond was not regarded as eternal, and eventually Brahmin speculation developed the idea of another death that would lead the dying spirit or god into another existence. This idea of reincarnation was associated with the idea of retribution for man's good or bad deeds, and although this speculation was not unique to India it was nowhere else systematized to the same extent. By holding that man's actions have an inescapable effect upon his fate in the next life and by tying each man's social position to the caste order, the Brahmins established an account book, as it were, for the ritual and ethical merits—and offenses—of the individual. Hence the individual's fate in the next life would be exactly proportional to the positive or negative balance that he had earned for himself in his previous life.[39] These beliefs are directly related to the caste system. The individual is born in the caste that he deserves as a result of his conduct in a previous life, and his faithful adherence to the ritual of his caste is interpreted as merit earned for a higher incarnation in the next life. The orthodox Hindu rejects the fundamentally critical view that an individual's position in society results from the "accident" of his birth; the untouchable appears to him as a man who must pay the penalty for an unusually large number of sins in a previous existence.

The impact of this view does not depend upon a full awareness of the cosmic theories of transmigration and retribution. Weber maintained rather that the individual Hindu was caught up in a way of life for which these theories had very practical consequences. Like the workers who have a world to

[39] In this connection Weber referred to the popular superstition that attributes our misfortune to some magically significant mistake of our own. The Brahmin interpretation is an extension of this idea in the sense that all of man's fate in life becomes the product of his own deeds. The misfortune of good men and the good fortune of evil men are readily "explained" if man's fate in this life is the reward or punishment for the merits or offenses of "his soul" in a previous life.

win once they have lost their chains, the devout low-caste Hindu also can win "the world" and become a Kshatriya, a Brahmin, or even a god—not in this life, of course, but in his next incarnation. Eternal and unchangeable like the stars in the sky, the caste system provides incentives of appalling majesty. The risk of abysmal degradation and the promise of abrupt ascent in a future life depend upon the strict fulfillment of ritual duties appropriate to the caste into which one was born. Even the deficient adherence to one's own caste duties is praised as superior to the most devout fulfillment of the duties of another caste.[40] The neglect of one's own duties is prejudicial to one's well-being in this life and the next. As long as the idea of retribution is accepted, there is no room for a radical change of the caste order or for any idea of "progress," since the lower castes have most to gain—at least in the long run—from a strict observance of their duties.

Asceticism and the Hindu World Image

The beliefs of Hinduism and the caste system with its emphasis upon the magical significance of hereditary succession cannot be understood apart from the "material and ideal interests" of the Brahmins. "As family-priests, arbitrators in questions of ritual, confessors and advisers in all life-situations" the Brahmins developed the caste order and made it dominant.[41] They buttressed their position by an ascetic ideal that distinguished between the laity and holy men, though they also adapted that ideal in order to transcend this basic division of the religious community.

According to Weber, the practice of religious austerities originally was associated with ecstatic practices and a belief in their magical power. Like the magician, the ascetic thought of himself as possessing power over the gods, who fear him and must do as he commands. Even a god must practice aus-

[40] S. Radhakrishnan, *The Bhagavad Gita* (London: George Allen & Unwin, 1948), pp. 146–47 (Chapter III, verse 35). See also p. 368 (Chapter XVIII, verse 47). This edition is especially useful for purposes of comparing Weber's interpretation with that of a distinguished Indian philosopher. See pp. 179–83 below for Weber's discussion of the Bhagavad Gita.

[41] *GAzRS*, Vol. II, p. 130. (*Religion of India*, p. 130.)

terities if he is to accomplish an exceptional feat, and early Indian philosophy attributed the creation of the world to the powerful ascetic exertions of a Highest Being. The capacity to get into a state of ecstatic rapture and thus achieve magical powers was a highly personal attribute, not identified with any one group. Many of the early ascetics were recruited among popular magicians.

The oldest Indian classic, the Rig-Veda, contains ecstatic elements, such as the drunkenness and dance of Indra, the sword dance of Marut, and the great soma sacrifice. In Weber's view these passages reflected the influence of an earlier period when the ecstasy of the warrior before battle and sexual or alcoholic orgies were accepted forms of magic.[42] But he also noted that already in the Rig-Veda emphasis was placed on prayers and sacrifices rather than on ecstatic acts. The belief that magical power can be obtained through ecstasy gradually was superseded by the belief that it can be obtained through austerities. This apathetic form of asceticism is at the core of the Hindu ideal of life.

As a householder (*grihastha*), the Brahmin was expected to avoid vulgar occupations like trade and agriculture and to observe a vegetarian, alcohol-free diet. The dietary rules may have originated in the Brahmin opposition to the eating and drinking orgies of popular magicians. The injunctions against adultery and the general admonition to practice sexual restraint[43] also suggest an anti-orgiastic attitude. Ritual cleanliness, especially in relation to eating, was demanded because of the fear of magical pollution. As in China, rage and passion were discountenanced because all emotions were believed to be of demonic origin. Similarly, elegance of manners and the proprieties of conduct were to be observed.

While these and other austerities of everyday life improved

[42] Cf. pp. 222–24 below for an analysis of this phenomenon on the basis of the Old Testament.

[43] In a characteristic digression Weber added here a brief typology of the position of women in Indian society. Cf. *Religion of India,* pp. 151–52. The present relevance of the ascetic orientation in marriage, which Weber noted, is suggested by Gandhi's opposition to birth control on the ground that the use of contraceptives would be an incentive to sexual licentiousness.

the chances for a higher reincarnation, they did not enable man to attain salvation. The Brahmins alone claimed to be qualified for this mystical quest. Only Brahmins who had decided upon a life of religious austerities were holy men (*sramana*). The Ramayana epic tells of a Sudra ascetic possessing great magical powers who was beheaded by the hero for having dared to acquire superhuman faculties. The story not only exemplifies the Brahmin claim but suggests that orthodox doctrine recognized the capacity of a Sudra to acquire such faculties. In fact, the Brahmins could be challenged by any mystic who practiced religious austerities and consequently was revered by the people for his holiness and miraculous powers. Implicit in this idea is the assumption that the power of any man will be commensurate with his holiness. To answer such challenges the Brahmins could not fall back upon a hierarchic organization. Nor could they, in the long run, deny the relative merit of non-Brahmin mystics without questioning the foundations of their own beliefs.[44] Instead, they sought to meet these challenges by tying the encouragement of asceticism to the privileges of the Brahmin caste.

The classic ideal of the Brahmin way of life is withdrawal from worldly activities once the aging Brahmin has seen the son of his son. As a man who has returned to nature (*Vanaprastha*) he seeks the eternal silence of the hermit (*asrama*), and through austerities he may attain an internal emancipation from the world (*yati*). It is probable that from very early times such ascetics functioned as teachers (*gurus*) and magicians who attracted disciples and lay worshipers. Each *guru* accepted only five pupils of noble family, presumably an indication that the Brahmins of that early time were not interested in mass propaganda and would teach only other Brahmins or, at best, members of other twice-born castes who came from noble families. Such informal communities of hermits with their disciples or *gurus* with their pupils were the seat of Brahminic learning, which depended entirely upon the bond of piety between the teacher and his pupils. Each *guru* possessed an authority over his pupils that had precedence over

[44] In the Ramayana a Kshatriya ascetic who wants to become a Brahmin sage succeeds after a tremendous struggle.

the authority of their fathers.[45] True wisdom could be learned only from a *guru*, who was believed to possess magical powers by virtue of his correct knowledge of the Veda and who was prepared to prove that power by submitting to an ordeal by fire. By designating their successors, many famous miracle-working *gurus* became the founders of sects and philosophical schools in which their doctrines and ascetic techniques were taught for centuries. Eventually monasteries were organized, probably in response to the challenge of the Buddhist movement.

As an ideal and in educational practice the Brahmins differentiated more or less sharply between the religious life appropriate to the ordinary householder and the quest for salvation accessible only to the holy man. In regard to the latter, Brahmin theory substituted the personalized idea of a "blissful state" for the vulgar notions of popular magicians with their belief in secret magical powers. The means of attaining a condition of holiness were elaborated in a manner consistent with the status pride of a high-ranking intelligentsia, as, for example, in the doctrine and technique of Yoga.

Autohypnotic practices like the regulated retardation and temporary stoppage of breathing were known in India in very ancient times. They produce psychological conditions that are valued as a holy withdrawal of the soul, in keeping with the principle that man can hear the voice of God in his soul only when he abandons all mundane concerns and waits in silence. Various metaphysical doctrines seek to give a reasoned account of the relation between these psychological states and the salvation of the soul. One such doctrine is Yoga, which concentrates upon blissful feelings like friendship with God, a compassionate identification with all creatures, and complete indifference toward the world. The aim is to produce a consciousness emptied of anything that can be expressed in words

[45] The teacher must be worshiped in complete submission. The novice (*brahmacharin*) was required to observe a large number of ascetic rules, and it is symptomatic that the old expression for "study" was "to practice chastity." In addition to the usual abstentions the novice was forbidden to comb his hair, brush his teeth, or seek shelter from the rain. He also was required to beg for his food, to bathe regularly, to hold his breath periodically, and to attend to his devotion of the syllable "Om."

and to achieve a conscious control over various bodily functions. In this way the individual induces in himself a passive receptivity. His grasp of the Divine is an emotional experience that can be obtained only through means like breath control, which have nothing to do with intellectual understanding. The object is to acquire miraculous powers, such as the elimination of gravity, mind reading, and the creation of imagined events by the power of will. Weber emphasized, however, that the techniques used to achieve such magical powers are specifically intellectual. Yoga consists of carefully thought-out methods of self-control that induce a state of religious apathy in contrast to the naïveté of simple religious devotion.[46] Although the specifically irrational element of Yoga never was accepted by the more classical Brahmin approach, the aim of both was to get away from the world of the senses and passions and to create a state of quiescence that would bring release from the bustle of life and a union with the Divine.[47]

This quest for salvation is common to all orthodox and heterodox approaches that were developed by the intellectual strata of Indian society. Brahmin theory idealized the escape from all transitory existence, not merely from the suffering, sinfulness and imperfection of the world. In its most consistent development it conceived of the world as an eternal "wheel" uniformly rolling down the endless passage of time, in which the souls that are thought to endure throughout the recurrence of births and deaths constitute the only other stable element. Not escape from the world but escape from this eternal "wheel" of reincarnation and retribution was the Brahmin conception of salvation.

[46] Weber used the term "rational" in referring to the ascetic practices of Brahmins because he wished to refer to the systematic use of means, regardless of the ends men have in view. Any goal or value can be achieved by a systematic or haphazard use of means. In the present case, Brahmin theory endorsed religious austerities as the magical means by which men may attain salvation. The belief that asectic practices enable man to achieve this goal is an ultimate conviction to which the term "rational" cannot be applied meaningfully. But given these convictions, the term can be applied to the techniques of asceticism if these techniques are deliberately chosen and systematically practiced.

[47] *Religion of India*, p. 166.

Brahmin theory developed this image of the world only gradually. It was no more able than other religious theories to maintain such a view without a great deal of intellectual controversy. In his analysis, Weber was concerned with the spiritual and psychological problems reflected in these conflicting ideas.

Varieties and Synthesis of Orthodox Doctrine

Weber's discussion of the Hindu conception of God illustrates his exploration of the varieties within orthodoxy as well as his attempt to discern the basic social issues that were at the root of such differences. According to the earliest sources, a personal God-Father (*Prajapati*) was thought to have created the world in all its diversity. Subsequently, the concept of an impersonal Divine Being, the Brahman, developed, first in the sense of a magical prayer formula and then in the sense of a magical world potency transcending all finite things on earth and in heaven. The duality between the idea of a personal God and the concept of an impersonal Divine Being recurs throughout the history of Hinduism.

The concept of a remote, impersonal but all-powerful deity necessarily gave rise to the question of how man could best reach identity with the Brahman. In answer to this question many philosophies were developed, which Weber surveyed because questions of interpretation touch upon the vital interests of the believers, as in all great religions. Since Weber himself examined these doctrines in terms of their broad impact on the laity, I will confine myself here to this latter topic.

The idea of man's salvation through mystical identification with the Brahman contained no ethical prescription for man's conduct in this world; indeed, it devalued the whole pantheon of individual gods, the traditional content of the holy scriptures, and the ritual of caste. By its very nature, mysticism of this sort was incompatible with, or perhaps indifferent to, these specific elements of Hindu religiosity. The mystical road to salvation also raised the question of whether those who traveled it had a privileged access to union with the Brahman. The Brahmin intelligentsia appeared to endorse the view that studied apathy and the acquisition of "holy knowledge" (*gnosis*) were the principal means that enabled men to escape from the demonic entanglement of the mind. The ascetic is a man who breaks all ties with the world and aims at a condition in which all suffering through restlessness has ceased, like a flame that burns steadily when not a breath of wind is stirring. The genuinely holy man (*sramana*) experiences heavenly bliss by attaining emancipation from the inexorable chain of retribution in this life, not the next. Such a man is without sin—he is untroubled by the question of whether he does good or evil. Some Indian philosophers even drew the conclusion that a holy man was no longer bound by ritual, that he could do anything without jeopardizing his blessedness, though they assumed him to be incapable of doing evil.

To be sure, this complete contrast between the ascetic way of life and the ritual duties of everyday life was not generally accepted. But by its extraordinary idealization of asceticism Brahmin theory implicitly questioned the promise of salvation for the ordinary man. There was no institution that could intercede for the individual and enable him to attain grace, as in the Catholic Church. Although the *sramana* could aid a person through his teaching, his exemplary conduct, and his magical powers, the individual Hindu believer could attain salvation only through his own efforts. Though the believer could acquire merit by revering a holy man and presenting him with gifts, he was a man of inferior religious status and attainments compared with the ascetic. These contrasts indicate a deep-seated tension between the ascetic ideal as personified in the holiness and "knowledge" of the *sramana* and the ideal of ritual propriety for the ordinary believer.

All religions must grapple with the fact that men are differently endowed, some showing religious virtuosity in their quest for salvation and others being pedestrian in their approach. Hinduism is no exception in this respect. It is unique, however, in that only the ritual duties of the Brahmin appear to lead directly toward the meditation and religious austerities of the holy man. This does not appear to hold out any promise of salvation to the Kshatriyas, for example. As warriors and rulers, they presumably found the idea of studied apathy incompatible with their way of life and their sense of honor; yet they could hardly be inclined to accept a position of religious in-

feriority. Hence, the struggle among the castes that we observed earlier in connection with their conflicting claims over
ritual proprieties and relative social rank recurs at the level of
orthodox doctrine. Throughout the history of Hindu religion
the tendency to conceive of the Divine as a personal God-
Father rather than as an impersonal Brahman also recurs. In
Weber's opinion these tensions between a personalized and
impersonal image of the Divine Being, as well as the tensions
between the *dharma* of the warrior caste and the ascetic quest
for religious salvation, are revealed in the great epic of the
Mahabharata, and especially in the intellectual synthesis of
its most famous section, the Bhagavad Gita.[48]

The Bhagavad Gita is a dialogue between the hero Arjuna
and his charioteer Krishna, who is represented as the human
incarnation of the highest Divine Being. The dialogue takes
place before the great battle at Kurukshetra in which close
relatives are arrayed against each other. Arjuna is profoundly
troubled by the prospect of killing kinsmen in the coming battle. He describes the consequences of this horrible crime—
the breakup of families, the neglect of ritual, the mixture of
castes, the dishonor done to ancestors—and he shrinks from the
battle. The poem consists of Krishna's answers to Arjuna, starting with a refutation of his scruples against the killing of relatives and going on to a full exposition of an ethic of conduct
and the nature of God. As Weber pointed out, Krishna gives

[48] The final revision of the Mahabharata probably occurred in the
sixth century A.D. However, the original version was composed a
thousand years earlier, since only later additions of the epic reveal
the influence of Buddhist ideas that originated in the sixth century
B.C. The epic tells the story of King Bharata and his descendants;
the prefix *maha* means "great." *Bhagavad Gita* means "song (*gita*)
of the Exalted Being or God" (*Bhagavad*). In his discussion of the
Bhagavad Gita, Weber relied on the first edition of Richard Garbe,
Die Bhagavad Gita (Leipzig: H. Haessel, 1921), whose translation
is still accepted as philologically accurate, even though his interpretation of the poem has been rejected. The references below are
to chapters and verses but not to pages. For an authoritative interpretation and translation by a Western Sanskritist, cf. Franklin
Edgerton, *The Bhagavad Gita* (Vols. 38–39 of Harvard Oriental
Series; Cambridge: Harvard University Press, 1944). Direct quotations are taken from the translation by S. Radhakrishnan unless
otherwise noted.

several answers. He restates the doctrine of reincarnation: the bodies of the enemies will pass away, but the Atman is eternal and cannot die the death of the body. He tells Arjuna to rise and win glory by killing the enemies whom He (the God) has killed already; thus Arjuna is merely the instrument of an inexorable fate.[49] Also, Arjuna is a Kshatriya, and his nature will compel him to enter the battle even if, in his vanity, he resolves not to fight.[50]

The major point is that Arjuna cannot fight what does not exist. Like all human action, the battle is entangled in the material world, bound to the eternal chain of reincarnation. Only a mind that has attained true knowledge can lead man out of this entanglement, for it recognizes that man does not act but suffers himself to be acted upon by the material world of the senses. The man who has acquired such knowledge will not be reborn, however he may have lived.[51] It is true that as a Kshatriya Arjuna must obey the *dharma* of his caste, so that escaping from the battle will bring him shame. But the question is how such obedience to the *dharma* of caste can aid man in his quest for salvation since it brings entanglement with the world rather than escape from it. Weber found the originality of the Bhagavad Gita in its answer to this question. No one, says Krishna, should renounce the caste obligations of his birth, even though all actions are surrounded by imperfections as fire is surrounded by smoke.[52] The task is, therefore, to engage in action and yet to escape from involvement in the material world and hence from the chain of reincarnation. Even in the midst of the battle the enlightened man minimizes his entanglement with the material world. Sacrifices and austerity lead to salvation only if they are engaged in for their own sake.[53] A man who abandons all desire for the fruits of action is engaged in action but untainted by it; he acts as if he did not act. Without expectation, self-controlled, and abandoning all possessions, he incurs no guilt, because his action

[49] *Bhagavad Gita*, Chapter XI, 32–34. "Atman" is the term for "inner soul," though at times it is used synonymously with "Brahman."

[50] *Ibid.*, Chapter XVIII, 59.

[51] *Ibid.*, Chapter XIII, 23.

[52] *Ibid.*, Chapter XVIII, 48.

[53] *Ibid.*, Chapter XVIII, 5, 6, 11.

aims merely at maintaining the body and he is content with
what comes to him by itself.[54] By acting in "the calm of self-
surrender" men can escape the chain of reincarnation.[55]

Indifference to the world in the very midst of mundane affairs thus appears as the crowning idea of a religiosity that, in
Weber's view, reflected the ethos of the Brahmin intelligentsia.
Because of their priestly role the Brahmins could not forego
magic, but as high-ranking literati they shunned all outwardly
ecstatic forms of religious devotion and preferred magical
practices in which apathy and austerity formed the keynote.
But the ideal of the ascetic holy man did not hold out a promise of salvation to the ordinary believer; to accomplish this,
the Brahmins developed the idea of detachment in action according to each man's *dharma*. This idea accentuated the religious significance of caste distinctions. The Bhagavad Gita
teaches that all genuine religious observances lead to salvation,
but it recognizes that men differ in their capacity for religious
experience. There are those who lack true knowledge and cannot bring themselves to become indifferent to the results of
their actions; the wise man should give his approval and not
disturb the conviction and self-confidence of the unknowing,
lest they be led astray.[56] There are any number of religious
persons who wish to serve one or another appearance of the
Divine, and the god, Krishna, confirms them in their faith.
Such persons will be rewarded if they serve "their gods" faith-
fully, but their reward will be as finite as the gods to whom
they offer sacrifices.[57] Even knowledge of the Vedas and the
practice of austerities is not enough to apprehend Krishna, and
the effort to do so through identification with the impersonal
Brahman is very difficult, though possible.[58] Only those whose
minds are fixed on Krishna, who serve him with steadfast devotion and who are imbued with a consummate faith, are
judged to be true believers in the highest sense. Such men are

[54] *Ibid.*, Chapter IV, 20–22.
[55] I take this phrase from the translation by Swami Prabhavananda
and Christopher Isherwood, *The Song of God: Bhagavad Gita*
(New York: Mentor Books, 1954), p. 41.
[56] *Bhagavad Gita*, Chapter III, 26.
[57] *Ibid.*, Chapter VII, 21–23.
[58] *Ibid.*, Chapter XII, 3–5; Chapter XI, 52–53.

certain of their salvation from the "ocean of death-bound existence."[59]

This summation of Brahmin wisdom achieves an image of the world in which not only each man's daily duties but also each man's goal of salvation has become relative to his position in the caste order. Whatever they might be, each man's actions and devotions are valuable *in their own terms;* in a world that has been devalued few men can have more than relative merit.

In addition to this synthesis of the doctrine, the Bhagavad Gita gives evidence of countervailing tendencies. The old teachings of the Veda contained a strong desire for happiness and the fruits of this world, and certain ideas of this Kshatriya-dominated age are still in evidence.[60] In the Mahabharata as a whole, the Krishna figure itself is noteworthy for its unquestioned lack of virtue, a reflection presumably of the early epics in which the gods disported themselves like superhuman heroes. At issue also is the religious merit of the holy man whose escapist mysticism is compared with the innerworldly detachment of the man of action.[61] Over and above these themes is an emphasis on a religiosity of faith centering on the figure of Krishna, the personalized God. "Abandoning all duties, come to Me alone for shelter," says Krishna to Arjuna in the last song of the Bhagavad Gita.[62] Even wicked men and those who are of low birth, such as women, Vaisyas, and Sudras, will reach the highest spiritual goal if they but love God and take their refuge in him.[63]

These and many similar passages of the Bhagavad Gita combine indifference to the world in the midst of action with a sense of faith in God. In religious devotion, in unconditional and trusting obedience, man devotes his life to Krishna, who

[59] *Ibid.,* Chapter XII, 7.

[60] *Ibid.,* Chapter II, 31–38, 46.

[61] *Ibid.,* Chap. V, 2. In this passage, action rather than renunciation is said to be the superior means to salvation, a reflection presumably of the Kshatriya influence at the time the poem was composed. The reverse ranking is also found occasionally. However, the dominant theme is the equivalence of asceticism and detached action.

[62] *Ibid.,* Chapter XVIII, 66.

[63] *Ibid.,* Chapter IX, 30–32.

lets divine grace (*prasada*) shine upon him. This concept is at variance with classical Brahmin doctrine in that it presupposes a supramundane personal God. It is also at variance with the old principle that the soul is on its own as the architect of its fate. And it runs counter to the theory of retribution in the sense that man can achieve salvation from this world and hence from the eternal "wheel" of reincarnation by his devout faith in God (*bhakti*) as well as by detachment in austerity and action.[64] Weber interpreted these beliefs as a priestly concession to the laymen who wanted to put their trust in a Savior and whose sense of dependence gave rise to the quest for divine grace.

The Hindu Restoration

The Bhagavad Gita is the great intellectual synthesis of Hindu religion. Like other great documents in the history of ideas, its world view had a surpassing influence upon the minds of men, perhaps because it gave promise of release to all. But it did not abolish the contrast between those who can achieve illumination and the mass of others who fall short of the task, nor between ascetic and other, more ordinary means to attain salvation. Neither did it abolish the age-old tendencies toward magical and orgiastic practices that were the fountainhead of religious devotion to a highest personal God and a Savior who would aid men in their quest for salvation. All of these tendencies have existed throughout Indian history from the earliest times, just as the ideas incorporated in the Gita existed long before its actual composition. According to Weber, much of the later development of Hindu religion could be understood in terms of these conflicting tendencies, which mirrored in some measure the changing relationships between the beliefs of the laity and the esoteric status interests of the highest Brahmin caste.

[64] This religiosity of faith and the belief in a divine Savior flourished especially during the Buddhist period, which began in the sixth century B.C. It is regarded as improbable, however, that these ideas originated with Buddhism. A comprehensive account of studies in this field is contained in A. L. Basham, *The Wonder That Was India* (New York: Macmillan, 1955).

The divergent tendencies of thought and action expressed in the Bhagavad Gita gave rise to bitter conflicts among men who saw their very lives and souls at stake in these issues. The rise of the Jaina and Buddhist movements at the time of the composition of the Gita is evidence of this fact, and these movements may be interpreted as alternative efforts to cope with the same issues that the Bhagavad Gita attempted to resolve. Jainism chose the road of religious austerities and Buddhism that of inner detachment. Both opposed the Brahmin synthesis in the Gita, and for a time, as we have seen, Buddhism gained the upper hand. The Brahmins eventually regained their pre-eminent position as priests and religious teachers, and this restoration found its literary expression in the later versions of the epics, especially the Mahabharata, and in the Purana literature, especially the Bhagavata Purana.

Compared with the earlier Vedic writings, these sources reveal a much greater emphasis upon magic and animism. Spirits of rivers, ponds, and mountains, and magic by verbal formulas, manual gestures, and written symbols, are placed next to the veneration of old and new deities. The worship of ancestors, priests and cows is amplified by a patriarchal veneration of the king, who is envisaged as a kind of mundane god of his people and thus given pre-eminence in contrast to his more subordinate position in the Vedic literature. (This patriarchal emphasis presumably commended the Brahmin priests to the secular rulers.) An analogous amplification occurs with reference to the promise of salvation. In addition to the heroic pantheon of Indra, the universal heaven of Brahma, and the union with the impersonal Brahman, the epics contain the ancient popular belief that the souls of good men will be transformed into stars. This jumble of heterogeneous elements is still the subject of public recitation in India, and Weber addressed himself to the question of what new ideas had been added in the process of Brahmin restoration.

The popular interest in magic had persisted throughout, even though the old Brahmin doctrine of salvation rejected or at most tolerated the orgiastic and emotional elements of popular religiosity. In the effort to combat the appeals of the Buddhist and Jaina movements, such toleration or even concessions were not enough and so were replaced, at least in part, by an acceptance or transformation of orgiastic practices, the so-called *Tantra* magic. Originally these practices consisted in orgies induced by the common enjoyment of alcohol, meat, fish, sexual relations, and sacred manual pantomimes—the five *Mudra*. The aim was to achieve an ecstatic self-deification and hence magical capacities through union with the female creative power (*Sakti*). To Weber the major Hindu sects appeared as so many different—and often farfetched—sublimations of these ancient practices through which lower social groups sought salvation. This sublimation was the work of Brahmin as well as non-Brahmin mystics, and transitional forms of the amalgamation of popular cults and Brahmin orthodoxy can still be observed today.

The general acceptance of popular religious ideas and practices in the doctrines and practices of Brahmin orthodoxy affected the Hindu pantheon. The ancient female demonic spirits of fertility were elevated to become the wives of the traditional deities. For this purpose, the most suitable Vedic deities appeared to be Siva (the Vedic Rudra), the god of fertility, and Vishnu, the god of the sun and of fertility. Both gods had been minor figures in the classic writings, in keeping with the earlier anti-orgiastic orientation of the Brahmin priests. Similarly three of the old goddesses of fertility became the subordinate wives of the three major deities: Lakshmi, the wife of Vishnu; Parvati, the wife of Siva; and Sarasvati, the wife of the Brahma. Other goddesses followed suit. A great multitude of gods and goddesses that had not appeared in the classical writings became part of orthodox doctrine, although this proliferation of the Hindu pantheon was replaced in turn by a new, if rather eclectic, synthesis. In this respect a most influential contribution was made by Sankaracharya, a commentator on the Vedanta literature who lived in the ninth century A.D.[65] He restored the old idea of a single highest Divine Being (Brahma-Para-Brahma); all deities were merely incarnations of this God, who was personal and yet was with-

[65] The most distinguished Brahmin school in modern India, the so-called Smarta Brahmins (from *Smriti*, meaning "tradition"), adheres to the teachings of Sankaracharya. The centers of learning of this school are located at the Svingeri monastery in the south and at the Sankeshwar monastery in the north.

out understandable identity, the ruler of the world and yet not its basic cause. On this basis the concept of a trinity of deities, Brahma, Siva, and Vishnu, was developed, in which Brahma became a rather theoretical conception, while orthodox and sectarian views were divided on whether Siva—and to a lesser extent Vishnu—were the incarnations of this supreme deity or rather the highest and indeed the only God.

Weber saw these changes in the Hindu pantheon as the efforts of Brahmin priests to assimilate the popular cults by bringing them into line with the orthodox practices of a vegetarian diet and abstinence in drinking and sexual relations. The formal method of this assimilation was the identification of a popular demon or god with one of the Hindu gods, or, in the case of animal cults, with one of their incarnations. The ancient fertility gods, Siva and Vishnu, appeared most suitable for this purpose since they were derived from the ancient orgiastic cults. It is indicative of this origin that the Tantra literature consists in good part of dialogues between Siva and his bride. Also, the fact that the phallic symbol of the ancient demons of fertility has remained an object of religious veneration demonstrates the great strength of the popular religious traditions. However, the Brahmins succeeded in divesting this cult of its orgiastic character by transforming it into a purely ritualistic temple worship whose special attraction for the masses was the cheapness of the ceremonial requirements—water and flowers.[66] Weber believed that the priests furthered this process for materialistic reasons: the popular deities were ineradicable, and considerable income could be derived by priests who devoted themselves to their service. Another factor was the struggle against the appeal of Buddhism and Jainism, which could be countered most effectively by this accommodation to the popular religious traditions.

Weber discussed the religious ideas of the Brahmin restoration in relation to two major religious movements, Sivaism and Vaishnavism. Whereas Sivaism transformed the popular or-

[66] Brahmin theory relates the spirit that resides in the *Linga* symbol to the god Siva. (*Linga* is the Indian term for a phallic symbol that represents a combination of the male and female organs.) Weber stated that at least eighty million Hindus were *Linga* worshipers and that in the villages most houses possessed an idol.

giastic practices into the ritual of the Linga cult, Vaishnavism made them a fervent religious devotion to a Savior. For our purposes a brief consideration of the latter must suffice. Vaishnavism became the religion of a highest god (Vishnu), who came to earth in ever new incarnations, chief among which were the two gods, Krishna and Rama. Broadly speaking, Krishna is the object of pious devotion and retains survivals of orgiastic practices in a highly sublimated eroticism while Rama appears more in the role of a moralizing savior whose aid is solicited through predominantly ritualistc prayer formulas.

The major characteristic of the Krishna cult was a new quality of religious devotion, a passionate, inner abandonment to the savior and his mercy (*bhakti*), which appears in the later interpolations of the Mahabharata. The Krishna cult differs from the doctrines of the Bhagavad Gita in that it subordinates every form of worship to this enthusiastic piety as the principal means to salvation. The acquisition of holy knowledge, the fulfillment of ritual duties, ascetic practices and Yoga meditation have value only insofar as they help create religious devotion. *Bhakti* can be attained by abandoning oneself to an irresistible divine grace or by active cooperation with it, by a sacrifice of the intellect, by work that is disinterested, and so forth. This sublimated form of piety readily appeals to the educated and to those highly placed in society, but it was accompanied for a long time by forms of worship in which orgiastic elements were retained. Even where sexual orgies and religious ecstasies were abandoned as part of ceremonial practice, the psychological quality of the Krishna cult retained ecstatic elements. The attainment of *bhakti* is characterized in the Indian manner in terms of the various steps needed to acquire higher degrees of merit, and these steps culminate in a quasi-erotic fantasy of the believer in his religious experience of the savior.[67]

The Rama cult was set in motion by two religious leaders, Ramanuja in the twelfth century and Ramananda in the four-

[67] For example, the Chaitanya sects specify five stages of merit: meditation (*santi*), active divine service (*dasya*), feeling as for a personal friend (*sakhya*), feeling as for a father (*vatsalya*), feeling as of a girl for her lover (*madhurya*).

teenth century. Like Sankaracharya, these leaders concerned
themselves particularly with religious teaching and the organization of a monastic order, which in this case gained considerable stability by being made hereditary. Doctrinally Ramanuja departed from the Vedanta system of Sankara by
denying the "impersonal Brahman" and the idea of the world
as an illusion (*maya*). Instead, he maintained that the world
was a manifestation of the Divine and that immortality rather
than union with the Brahman was the promise of salvation.
By going back to the classic Vedic learning and emphasizing
the subordination of the laity to the *guru* who was educated
in the Vedas and whose position was hereditary, Ramanuja
initiated a protracted struggle against the Sivaite sects and
especially the Linga cult. Ritual meals took the place of this
cult, and in the Rama sects initiated by Ramananda prayer
formulas became prominent, leading eventually to the *mantra*
—devotional appeals to Rama, the Savior—that consisted of a
few words or even of meaningless syllables. In this fashion the
Rama cult completely replaced all orgiastic survivals with its
devotional prayers and avoidance of all erotic tendencies.

Ramananda's mission was characterized by resistance to the
caste order, not in everyday life but in the sense that members
of the lower castes were admitted to the position of *guru*.
Weber interpreted this fact as an effort to establish contact
with the masses at a time when Islamic rule had deprived the
Brahmins of most political means to buttress their pre-eminent
position.

Regardless of the differences between them, most Hindu
sects are characterized by some kind of compromise in which
orthodox beliefs and practices are combined with the religious
ideas and cults that appealed to the masses.[68] It is appropriate to speak of an adaptation of the Brahmin tradition in the
sense that orthodox beliefs and practices were modified in the
protracted competition with the Buddhist movement and in
the effort to maintain the religious autonomy of the Hindu social order under Islamic rule. Since this adaptation helped
the Brahmins regain their social superiority and religious authority, it is appropriate to speak of a "Hindu restoration."

[68] Cf. *Religion of India*, p. 237, for Weber's characterization of
mass religiosity in this context.

Weber maintained that this restoration was achieved at the price of concessions to popular religiosity. And his analysis of Buddhism indicated that the heterodox movement that exacted this price from the Brahmin elite underwent a parallel transformation from the religion of an educated minority to a religious mass-movement that adapted the tenets of Buddhism to the demands of popular religiosity (Mahayana Buddhism).[69]

The term "Hindu restoration" seems to imply that the Brahmins somehow remained unaffected by the transformation of religious beliefs sketched above. This implication is misleading. Since most of the sectarian communities that emerged in the course of the transformation enhanced the position of the *guru*, it is appropriate to conclude here with a consideration of the Brahmin teacher.

The Changing Position of the Guru

In the course of the religious development described above the Brahmins regained their function as priests and teachers. The lay believer had to acquire his mystical knowledge from his *guru* rather than from books. In some cases the layman's salvation came to depend upon unconditional surrender to his spiritual counselor. Though there was classical precedent for this absolute authority of the teacher, it had been confined originally to schools of religious learning and to the position of private chaplain and tutor in the royal household or the families of the nobility. With the rise of the Hindu sects the practice was broadened so that *gurus* included not only men who were learned in the Vedic scriptures but also a much

[69] For this reason I omit Weber's extensive discussion of Buddhism, which analyzed the differences in religious orientation between early Buddhism and Mahayana Buddhism and examined the spread of the latter across the Asian continent. Interesting as this exploration is, it has many points in common with the analogous adaptations of Brahmin orthodoxy, and it is the latter that prevail in India today. It may be added that in this respect India contrasts with China. In India both the orthodox *and* the heterodox religious systems underwent an analogous adaptation to popular religiosity, while in China Confucianism rejected the magical beliefs and practices of Taoism and Buddhism as "unclassical."

larger stratum of less educated religious counselors and mystagogues.[70] The vast majority of mendicants and *gurus* were and continued to be Brahmins, and the frequently considerable income of *gurus* who functioned in the more popular sects no doubt reduced the reluctance of orthodox Brahmins to serve in such a capacity. It was the universal authority of the *guru* rather than the novelty of the sectarian doctrines that marked the restoration of Hinduism in India.

The leading *guru* of a district takes the place of the bishop in the Occidental Church. In the company of his disciples he visits his "diocese," whose extent is fixed by tradition or formal stipulation. He can excommunicate persons who have committed grave sins, give absolution in return for penitence, levy taxes (contributions) from believers, and, above all, function as the final counseling authority. Each member of a sect has a *guru* from whom he receives religious instruction, by whom he is received into the sect—upon being told the prayer formula (*Mantra*) and being marked with the insignia of the sect— and to whom he can turn for advice under all circumstances. The degree to which the *guru* exercises effective authority in everyday life varies from sect to sect, though Weber noted that his authority tended to be especially extensive in the "plebeian" sects. For the masses the veneration of the *guru* frequently takes the place of other forms of religious observance. Instead of a transcendental cult of Krishna and Rama, the *guru* is regarded as the living Savior: the helper in times of need, the magical therapist, and the object of worship. All founders of the Hindu sects were accordingly deified, and their descendants and disciples are objects of veneration. To be a *guru* came to be regarded as the typical position of a Brah-

[70] In this context it should be mentioned that Weber discussed the Hindu restoration in terms of religious organizations as well as religious ideas. At the time the Hindu sects developed, Sankaracharya (A.D. 788–820) also introduced monastic reforms to combat the Buddhist and Jaina movements. Mendicant orders composed of educated monks were organized in monasteries and the teacher-disciple relationship was systematized to regularize the position of monks and *gurus*. To some extent these reforms are comparable to the development of the Counter-Reformation in western Europe, in which the Church restored its hold over the masses by an intensification of the confessional and by the foundation of monastic orders.

min, who thus was conceived of as a living god (*Thakur*). This development imparted an increasingly plebeian character to the position of the Brahmin teacher, aside from providing opportunities for heterodox teachers to act as *gurus* and gather disciples. But the same development also greatly strengthened the position of the Brahmins, especially during the period of religious persecution under Islamic rule (twelfth and thirteenth centuries A.D.), when everything depended upon making an effective appeal to the masses of the population. During this time of stress the *gurus* provided spiritual as well as external support to the masses, much as the Catholic bishops of Europe did following the period of the great Germanic migrations, in the sixth and seventh centuries A.D.

The effect of these developments on the position of the Brahmins can be appreciated only if their singular privileges are recalled. As the *purohita* of kings and the private chaplains of noble families, the Brahmins had been entitled to receive gifts (*dakshina*). Brahmins who were educated in the Vedas sought to monopolize such gifts. In the Middle Ages Brahmins who knew the ritual and functioned as scribes, administrators and teachers received large endowments in return for their services to secular rulers. Other Brahmins of high rank functioned as lawyers and judges, expounding sacred law, and as superiors of the great monasteries, deciding questions of ritual for the sects that acknowledged their authority. In these and similar cases the possession of holy knowledge or of literary and legal skills was the decisive criterion of high rank that enabled a Brahmin to lay claim to secular appointments. Similar criteria are still very influential in determining rank within the Brahmin caste.

This pre-eminence of the Brahmins was affected adversely by the widespread development of Vaishnavism, especially of those variants that abandoned the use of Sanskrit and in which Brahmins accepted gifts (*dakshina*) from the lower castes (e.g., the Vaishnavite sects going back to Ramananda and Chaitanya). This popular religious movement lacked the unified monastic organization that Sankaracharya established for orthodox Sivaism, especially in southern India. Instead, each recognized "dynasty" of *gurus* established its own hierocratic community that was frequently hereditary, leading to an extreme fragmentation of the sects. Moreover in the Vaishnavite sects knowledge of Vedic ritual and the esoteric knowledge of magic were replaced by an emotional religious agitation that used typically plebeian means of canvassing and solicitation, like processions, popular festivals, and so on. The opportunities for such agitation multiplied with the increasing wealth of bourgeois strata in the cities and the increasing number of lower middle-class or proletarian strata. By appealing to these groups *guru* demagogues could exploit religious agitation for additional income. Although orthodox Brahmins regarded such teachers and their agitation with the utmost contempt, many Brahmins defected to the popular Vaishnavite cults. As a result, the authority of classically educated Brahmin *gurus* suffered a decline in favor of these hierarchs or mystagogues of the masses who were comparatively uneducated in the Sanskrit literature.

According to Weber, this development intensified during the last five or six centuries, leading to a veritable hagiolatry of the *guru* as the living Savior. Not only in the Vaishnavite sects but also in those that had thoroughly eliminated idolatry and ecstatic and orgiastic elements from their cult the *guru* came to occupy a quasi-divine position. One reason for this was the absence of a Church in the Occidental sense. Although the secular rulers endowed temples for public sacrifices and for Brahminical schools, frequently other temples and monasteries were created, established by public subscription and maintained by a committee that supervised their external order and economic upkeep. The practice of founding new sectarian cults became especially prominent under Islamic rule, which destroyed the political power of the highest Hindu castes and so provided an opportunity to oppose the monopolistic claims of the Brahmin caste. Indirectly, this development led to the increased prominence of the broad middle groups of Indian society, whose religious interests and economic power provided the proliferating sects with the necessary impetus and material means for the establishment of new temples and cults. The secular rulers tolerated the increasing power of monks and charismatic or hereditary sectarian leaders insofar as that power was useful for the "domestication of the masses," as Weber liked to put it. Since the ability of these native ruling groups to hold the sects in check also was undermined by the impact of Islamic rule, the *gurus* became objects of deification with a corresponding increase of their power vis-à-vis the orthodox Brahmin priests.

This development was further intensified when British rule created new sources of wealth and opportunities for economic advancement, which in turn facilitated religious agitation among the masses. In the absence of an ecclesiastical establishment and a papal power like that of the Western world, Hindu religion had no means of legitimizing these religious orders or sects, of subordinating them to strict discipline, and hence of preventing the deification of man (i.e., of the monk or *guru*).

D. SECULAR ETHIC

Weber's study of the structure and the religious development of Indian society dealt principally with religious leadership and the religious propensities of the population in the context of the caste system. In addition he tried to answer the question: did Hinduism (and Buddhism) have any bearing upon the daily round of mundane activities, and if so, what direction did these systems of belief impart to economic conduct?

First, Weber found, most orthodox and heterodox tendencies of Hindu thought adhered to the idea of an immutable world order consisting of the eternal cycle of rebirths. Second, as in all religions of salvation, the mundane world was deprecated. In India this was expressed by the ideal of escape from the world, with mystic contemplation rather than an ascetic activism in daily life regarded as the principal means of attaining the desired indifference or escape. The prestige of this mystic quest for salvation never really diminished, however the many doctrines of Hindu religion diverged in other respects. Third, all the accepted means of attaining salvation were extraordinary and irrational. This was the case not only in all orgiastic forms of religious worship but in the various ascetic methods that are so marked a feature of Hindu religion. Weber pointed out that Indian asceticism, while methodical in its means, aimed at a state of mind that was extraordinary (in the sense of being turned away from ordinary affairs) and irrational (in the sense of involving an ecstatic experience). Even when the means of attaining salvation were compatible with worldly activities, as in the Bhagavad Gita with its emphasis upon the duties of caste, the result was still a traditional and mystically oriented way of life. Men should be in this world but not of it; they should act but remain detached in action.

> It could not have occurred to a Hindu to see the economic success he had attained through devotion to his calling as a sign of his salvation. And what is more important, it could not have occurred to a Hindu to prize the rational transformation of the world in accordance with matter-of-fact considerations and to undertake such a transformation as an act of obedience to a Divine Will.[71]

To this conclusion Weber added two qualifications designed to put his entire discussion of Hindu religion in proper perspective. It must always be remembered, he wrote, that throughout India's history only a very thin and highly educated stratum of the population was at all preoccupied with the intellectual problem of "salvation." Even the Hindu sects did not have a real contact with the masses; probably less than 5 per cent of the population had been formally admitted by all the sects taken together. This was probably always true, except perhaps for short periods. By and large the masses of ordinary Hindu believers are religious without being affiliated with *any one* type of doctrine or worship.[72] They behave much as did the ordinary people in ancient Greece when they worshiped Apollo *and* Dionysus, or in China when they worshiped alternately at Buddhist masses, Taoist magical rituals, and Confucian temples. Not only Jaina and Buddhist but also

[71] *GAzRS*, Vol. II, p. 360. (*Religion of India*, p. 326.)

[72] Some sects, like the Lingayats of southern India, are exceptions to this statement, since they represent a sizable proportion of the population and since as a sect they adhere more strictly to a definite set of religious ideas and practices. In view of the diversity encompassed by Hinduism, no general statement is likely to be entirely correct, as Weber pointed out at the beginning of his study.

Islamic and Christian saints are objects of worship in "orthodox" Hindu festivals. Weber believed that in the face of these diverse religious ideas and practices the masses were concerned, as always, with very mundane desires for a good life in this world, with the use of crude magical means by which to obtain good and avert ill fortune, and with the endeavor to improve their chances for a higher rebirth in the next life.

Weber's second point referred to the probability that the Indian masses had been influenced by certain basic religious ideas despite the mundane orientation that they shared with people elsewhere and despite the diversity of religious ideas that characterized Hinduism. This influence has to be understood in the proper sense. Weber made clear that the "other-worldliness" of Indian religion did not diminish the average Hindu's interest in this world. In his view it was the direction rather than the degree of materialistic striving that was influenced by religious ideas.

> The people of Asia are notorious all over the world for their unlimited and unequalled greed. . . . But the point is that this "acquisitive drive" is pursued by all the tricks of the trade and with the aid of that cure-all: magic. In Asia the element was lacking which was decisive for the economy of the Occident, namely the sublimation and rational utilization of this emotional drive which is endemic in the pursuit of gain. . . .[73]

These conclusions from Weber's study of India present a superficial paradox. On the one hand, he asserted that the masses of ordinary Hindus, like people elsewhere, have a mundane orientation toward religious questions and are unaffected by the doctrines of philosophers and theologians. On the other hand, he analyzed those doctrines in the belief that they had affected the direction of materialistic striving, not only of the educated minority but of the broad middle strata of Indian society. Part of the answer lies in the analysis itself. Weber showed that orthodox Hindu doctrine gradually accommodated itself to, but thereby also influenced, the propensities he attributed to the people at large. In addition, certain common denominators of Indian religion—the belief in reincarnation,

[73] *GAzRS*, Vol. II, p. 372. (*Religion of India*, p. 337.)

the idea of retribution (*karma*), and the identification of virtue with ritual observance—influenced the masses through the social pressures of the caste system.[74] Caste was the "transmission belt" between the speculative ideas of an intellectual elite and the mundane orientation of religious observance among the people at large. For that reason Weber believed that the analysis of ideas in conjunction with an analysis of caste provided important clues for an understanding of that orientation.

What, then, were the effects of this system upon economic life? In general Weber's answer was simply that by its traditionalism the caste system retards economic development and, conversely, that intercaste barriers become attenuated wherever economic activities attain an increased momentum. However, Weber also emphasized that this general answer was insufficient. Hindu religion and the caste system proved to be adaptable in the same way that all other religions of the world have come to terms with practical exigencies that run counter to basic religious tenets. One might suppose, for example, that caste ritual would have prevented large enterprises whose division of labor required craftsmen from different castes to cooperate in the same workshop. Yet, according to the law book of Baudhayana, every workshop is ritually pure—with the exception of distilleries—so that Hindu ritual as such interfered as little with the development of enterprises as the medieval prohibition of usury interfered with the accumulation of capital. A similar adaptation occurred where the high castes required the services of low-caste or untouchable craftsmen, in keeping with the principle that "In his occupation the hand of the craftsman is always pure."[75] But in Weber's view these convenient adaptations helped only to circumvent particular difficulties; they did not alter the fact that the "spirit" of the caste system militated against an *indigenous* development of capitalism.

[74] Here the analysis of caste plays the same role in Weber's analysis of India as his discussion of the sect and the urban community does in his discussion of Protestantism or the discussion of kinship groups and bureaucracy in the analysis of Confucianism.

[75] The same principle of purity applies to all publicly displayed commodities. Cf. the Baudhayana law book cited in *GAzRS*, Vol. II, p. 110. (*Religion of India*, p. 111.)

Weber's conclusion from his study of India was in one sense negative. The religious and institutional developments of India did not provide the intellectual prerequisites for "the incorporation of the acquisitive drive in an innerworldly ethic of conduct."[76] The Indian thinkers saw the world as a transient abode and an impediment to man's spiritual quest, whereas the Occidental doctrine of salvation placed a heavy emphasis on the short span of human life during which man's actions determined his "eternal" salvation or perdition. In the Hindu view man can do good or evil only in the sense that he is obedient to or violates the *dharma* of his caste. Man's virtue is, therefore, an attribute of his conduct in this world, so that Brahmin theory precludes the Christian contrast between man's relative virtue in this life with his blessed innocence in a primeval "state of nature" (Paradise). Similarly, man's sin consists only of violations against caste ritual, for which there are specific penalties in this life or in future incarnations. Hindu theory has no conception of man's fundamental sinfulness as symbolized by the fall of Adam and Eve or of a "radical evil" as found in the Christian idea of the devil. Nor does the doctrine of retribution and the belief in an eternal cycle of rebirths permit any speculation about a final state (eschatology) as in the idea of a last judgment for all mankind.[77] Instead, Hindu speculation turns on the individual's attempts to escape from the eternal recurrence of births and deaths.

As Weber saw it this internally consistent metaphysical interpretation must raise profoundly disturbing questions in any individual with an inquiring mind. What is the meaning of life when each individual is part of a cosmic order governed by an eternally valid mechanism of retribution? Each life is

[76] *GAzRS*, Vol. II, p. 372. (*Religion of India*, p. 337.)

[77] Hindu religion therefore can make no sense out of the Christian idea that the good man will be saved for an eternal existence in heaven and the evildoer will be condemned to an eternal existence in hell. To the Hindu believer it appears unethical and unjust to have finite human goodness or evil receive an everlasting reward or punishment. Nothing men do in their temporary abode here on earth can be in any way commensurate with such a judgment. The ideas of transmigration and retribution are closely related to a profound sense of ethical proportionality, however strange they may appear to Westerners on other grounds.

merely an instance in an unending sequence of lives and can
be regarded as a matter of profound indifference. Perhaps, he
reasoned, this attitude was responsible for the lack of interest
in social and political life that was reflected in the absence
of historiography from the Indian cultural tradition. At the
level of the individual this orientation could be a source of
great preoccupation, not so much because he could not enjoy
life but because the cycle of births continued forever.

> "The soul would become entangled again and ever again in
> the concerns of human existence, becoming attached to
> things and above all to loved ones with all the strings of
> his heart. And the soul would be torn away from these at-
> tachments without rhyme or reason, become entangled
> through reincarnation in new and unfamiliar relationships,
> only to face the same destiny once more."[78]

Accordingly the sermons of the Buddha and other Indian
prophets of salvation are concerned with the question of
whether man must seek release from life itself in order to be
saved from ever new deaths in his lives to come.

This world view contrasts with the innerworldly ethic which
was developed in the West by thinkers and prophets who
stood in specific relation to a politically conscious urban bourgeoisie. Such status groups did not develop in the cities of the
Orient because of the enduring power of kinship groups, the
dominance of caste differences (in India), and the centrally
organized officialdom that could gain power in the absence of
autonomous and politically effective group formations (in
China). Under these circumstances Asian intellectuals tended
to be apolitical in their orientation. This was true of the Brahmin world view, which aimed at the individual's emancipation
from worldly entanglements. It was equally true of the Confucian scholar-officials, who cultivated literary learning and
polite manners and if possible left politics and administration
to subordinates. The efforts of Brahmins, Buddhists and Taoists to comprehend and interpret the meaning of life always
culminated in some form of otherworldly mystical experience.
The effort of Confucianism to achieve the highest inner perfection by the conscious cultivation of grace and dignity in

[78] *GAzRS*, Vol. II, p. 133. (*Religion of India*, p. 133.)

the beautiful gesture culminated in the ideal of gentility. In Weber's view the intellectual culture of the Asian continent alternated between these two tendencies or sought to combine them. But the mystical as well as the esthetic aims of self-discipline can be pursued only by turning away from the mundane world; they are remote from the material interests of the masses. The social world is fundamentally divided between the educated, whose lives are oriented toward the *exemplary* conduct of a prophet or wise man, and the unlettered masses, who remain caught up in their daily rounds and their unbroken belief in magic. In Asia, no *Messianic* prophecy appeared that could have given *plan and meaning to the everyday life of educated and uneducated alike*. It was this Messianic prophecy in the countries of the Near East—as distinguished from the exemplary prophecy of the Asiatic mainland—that prevented the countries of the Occident from following the paths of development marked out by China and India. Weber's study *Ancient Judaism* was, therefore, the cornerstone of his attempt to explain the distinguishing characteristics of Western civilization.

CHAPTER VII

SOCIETY AND RELIGION IN ANCIENT PALESTINE

"Anyone who is heir to the traditions of modern European civilization will approach problems of universal history with a set of questions, which to him appear both inevitable and legitimate. These questions will turn on the combination of circumstances which has brought about the cultural phenomena that are uniquely Western and that have at the same time . . . a universal cultural significance."[1] This statement of the over-all purpose of Weber's studies in the sociology of religion, written shortly before his death, applies specifically to his work *Ancient Judaism.* In this study Weber set out to explain the "combination of circumstances" that were responsible for the initial differentiation between Occidental and Oriental religiosity. The significance of this topic is best understood if mystical contemplation—especially as it developed in India—is contrasted point by point with innerworldly asceticism as it developed in Western Christianity.[2]

[1] *GAzRS*, Vol. I, p. 1.

[2] In introducing his studies Weber stated that the qualitative contrasts in which he was interested could also be comprehended as "purely quantitative differences in the combination of single factors" but that such a presentation would inevitably miss what was of special interest for a study of typical contrasts such as he had in mind. See *Essays*, p. 292. These remarks are, of course, especially pertinent with regard to the abstract confrontation that follows.

A. TYPES OF ASCETICISM AND THE SIGNIFICANCE OF ANCIENT JUDAISM

All religions project ideal images of conduct, which vary from one religion to another in terms of the qualities that are demanded of men and the goals that are held out to them.[3] Judaism and Christianity are typified by an active religious asceticism, by the idea of positive ethical action under divine guidance. Man is merely a tool in the hands of God and he therefore should be constantly aware that his actions are among the means by which God accomplishes his designs. In this view the world is a source of temptation; all sensual satisfactions lead away from God. There also is the special danger of self-satisfied contentment with the mere fulfillment of everyday religious duties, which militates against single-minded concentration on those actions that alone can lead to salvation. In Christianity this religious dedication gave rise to an asceticism that either rejected all worldly concerns (as in medieval monasticism) or that sought to transform the world (as in the Puritan sects).

Weber was especially interested in the second type, which sought to conquer rather than to withdraw from the imperfection of the world. To the devout Puritan the world was God's creation and the only arena in which God-fearing men might reach a state of grace and become certain of salvation. There are some similarities between active and contemplative religious asceticism, but they are superficial. The contemplative ascetic is not a fighter for his God; he does not seek a consciousness of divine grace through ever new victories over ever new temptations in his constant struggle with the world and man as they are. He does not grapple with the world; he rejects it.[4] In order to do so he seeks to empty himself of every mundane trace and to attain a state of "repose" in the Divine. This emotional experience does not involve knowledge

[3] The following presentation is based on *WuG*, Vol. I, pp. 310–17.

[4] In this respect he has many points in common with the otherworldly asceticism of Catholic religious orders that also escapes from the world, though its religious orientation differs from Hindu or Buddhist asceticism.

of facts or doctrines but the comprehension of what has or does not have value in the world, and as such it is asserted to be eminently practical. The contemplative state to be achieved involves negative defenses against natural and social disturbances and, on the positive side, energetic concentration on certain "truths," though again it is not their content or the mere act of comprehension that are the religious concern of the mystic but rather an emotional experience that he identifies as practical wisdom.

From the viewpoint of "innerworldly asceticism" this type of contemplation appears a lazy and religiously sterile indulgence. A Puritan theologian would say that the mystic does not think of God but only of himself. To be consistent, the mystic would only live on what is freely available to him: alms and the berries in the forest. Such dependence on charity means that he could not live if the world did not do the work that he regards as sinful and alien to God. For example, the Buddhist monk regards agriculture as sacrilegious because it involves the destruction of life in the soil, but he lives on alms that are products of agriculture. Indeed, he makes alms-giving the highest virtue of the laity, which is forever barred from the experience of spiritual illumination.

For Hinduism and Buddhism, on the other hand, the active asceticism of the Puritan is a constant violation of the Divine. Ancient Buddhism viewed action with a purpose as a dangerous form of secularization. "He who wants to do good deeds should not become a monk," is a Buddhist saying. To be a tool of God is incompatible with being a "vessel" that is ready to receive God. Puritan asceticism leads away from God and toward impossible contradictions and compromises, for all actions in this world are rent by irreconcilable tensions between violence and kindness, objectivity and love.

The two religious orientations also may be contrasted in terms of their diverse approach to common problems. The religious ascetic who seeks to prove himself by his actions in this world suffers from a kind of happy narrow-mindedness. The Puritan is the ideal type of vocational specialist. He does not ask about the significance of his specialty for the world at large—this is God's responsibility, and he is satisfied to know that by his work he is fulfilling God's inscrutable designs. The

Puritan rejects the world because enjoyment and contentment are creature comforts and temptations that are ethically meaningless and imperil his efforts to work out his salvation. His humility is of doubtful authenticity, however, because the success of his actions is, after·all, in the hands of God and therefore at least a token of His special blessing.

The mystic is concerned with attaining a vision of cosmic "meaning." In the last analysis he cannot comprehend this "meaning" in a rational form because he sees it as a unity beyond reality. Mysticism of this kind is not always an escape from the world. The mystic may seek to achieve his contemplative vision in the midst of a world that he rejects. But for him, action as such is a temptation that imperils his state of grace. He merely acquiesces in his inevitable involvement, and his actions are meek and fragmented, for he seeks a quiet intimacy with the Divine. However, this quiet euphoria may turn into an acute experience of divine possession. Then God speaks through the mystic, He is imminent, He promises eternal salvation at once, if only men will receive Him in their hearts as the mystic has. In this case the mystic may become a mystagogue who engages in magical practices and instructs persons in the religious mysteries. Or he may become an exemplary prophet who gives to the world the divine message of a mystically renewed community of men.

Contemplative mysticism and ascetic activism indicate a fundamental contrast between Oriental and Occidental religiosity. The contrast can be illuminated by distinguishing the Christian belief in miracles from the Oriental belief in magic.[5] A miracle is seen as a divine dispensation of grace, an act of world rule that is assumed to be governed by principles. This tacit assumption has been the driving force behind the two-thousand-year-old quest for the "principles" of a God who has created a world in which it is possible for evil to triumph over good. A belief in magic, on the other hand, makes sense, if it is assumed that the whole world is brimful of powers that act in a manner beyond human comprehension. In Asia this image of the world became diffused in everyday life. The people had recourse to magic in their attempts to master the tasks

[5] *GAzRS*, Vol. II, p. 370 ff.

of daily life. Magic served them as a therapeutic tool to ensure the birth of male heirs, the successful completion of examinations, lawsuits, and economic transactions—indeed, the attainment of all possible material ends. Though the practice of magic was discountenanced or suppressed by the educated elite, daily life tended to be governed by magical considerations that militated against a systematization and ethical penetration of daily conduct.

Initially, this contrast between Oriental and Occidental religiosity developed from the idea of an omnipotent God who had created the world out of nothing and who, according to ancient Judaism, was the supramundane ruler of the changing destinies of nations. Before this God all men were lowly and guilty creatures for whom any mystical union with the Deity was a form of blasphemy amounting to self-deification. Men could work out their salvation only by actions through which they "justified" or proved themselves in His eyes. Occidental religion, however, could never resolve the paradox of an imperfect world created by a perfect God, and any determined effort to do so betrayed a lack of faith leading away from God. In contrast, Oriental religiosity remained more purely intellectual because it consistently attempted to reveal the "meaningfulness" of the empirical world and to seek the unity of "knowledge" and action through spiritual illumination.

The fundamental distinctiveness in the religious orientation of the Occident stemmed originally from ancient Jewish prophecy. Here is Weber's statement of his reasons for investigating ancient Judaism:

> Ritually correct conduct, i.e., conduct conforming to caste standards, carried for the Indian pariah castes the premium of ascent by way of rebirth in a caste-structured world thought to be eternal and unchangeable. . . .

> For the Jew the religious promise was the very opposite. The social order of the world was conceived to have been turned into the opposite of that promised for the future, but in the future it was to be overturned so that Jewry could be once again dominant. The world was conceived as neither eternal nor unchangeable, but rather as having been created. Its present structures were a product of man's ac-

tivities, above all those of the Jews, and of God's reaction
to them. Hence the world was an historical product designed to give way again to the truly God-ordained order.
The whole attitude toward life of ancient Jewry was determined by this conception of a future God-guided political
and social revolution. . . .

There existed in addition a highly rational religious ethic of
social conduct; it was free of magic and all forms of irrational quest for salvation; it was inwardly worlds apart
from the paths of salvation offered by Asiatic religions. *To
a large extent this ethic still underlies contemporary Middle
Eastern and European ethic. World-historical interest in
Jewry rests upon this fact.* . . .

Thus, in considering the conditions of Jewry's evolution, we
stand at a turning point of the whole cultural development
of the West and the Middle East.[6]

B.   HISTORY AND SOCIAL ORGANIZATION
OF ANCIENT PALESTINE

Ancient Judaism originated in the plains and mountains of
Syria and Palestine, an area exposed by turns to the influence
of the two great river-valley civilizations of Mesopotamia and
Egypt, which were the cultural and political centers of the
ancient Middle East. Prior to the eighteenth century B.C.
neither of these powers had been able to conquer this territory permanently. This condition changed when the horse
and chariot came to be employed in warfare. Beginning in the
late eighteenth century B.C., there was a period of great migrations, in the course of which the Hyksos established their rule
in Egypt (1710 B.C.) and the Cossaeans began their conquest
of Babylonia and Assyria (after 1686 B.C.).[7] It may be added

[6] *AJ*, pp. 3–5. My italics.
[7] All dates in this chapter are B.C. and will be given without this
identification hereafter. Their purpose is solely to orient the reader;
they have been taken from standard historical reference guides. I
have added some factual materials from various sources in order
to provide information that Weber took for granted. In addition to

that Abraham's migration to Palestine as well as the entrance
of Israelite tribes into Egypt probably coincided with this great
movement of peoples.[8] The overthrow of the Hyksos rulers
around 1550 was followed by an expansionist drive of Egypt
as far as the Euphrates. For some four centuries Syria and
Palestine came under Egyptian rule, though this rule apparently was more or less nominal. Under Ramses III (1175–44)
Egyptian power over this area declined altogether.

The Exodus from Egypt probably occurred about 1280,
with the gradual occupation of Palestinian territory by Jewish
tribes following later in that century.[9] Despite the decline of
Egyptian and Assyrian power, this was not a period of peace
for the developing national community. The Jewish conquest
of the Canaanite towns was followed almost immediately by
the threat of Philistine invaders from the Aegean Sea (last half
of the twelfth century). About 1050 the Philistines defeated
the Israelites, destroyed the sanctuary of Shiloh, and captured
the Ark of the Covenant. This attack from the west followed
or perhaps coincided with the terrifying invasion from the
south of the Midianites, who used the recently domesticated
camel in their long-range raids across the desert. There also
was intermittent fighting with the Canaanite city-states, with
the Moabites and Ammonites from the desert in the east, and
with Aramaean tribes from the Syrian desert in the north. Finally, there was internal strife among the Israelites themselves.[10] The foundation of the United Monarchy under Saul
(1030–10) and David (1010–971) and the highly centralized
kingdom of Solomon (971–932) were temporarily successful

---

his reliance on the Biblical scholars of his day, Weber made many
independent investigations of the Biblical text that are interspersed
throughout his book. These were arguments for the specialist that
are omitted from the following presentation. All Biblical citations
used in this chapter were given by Weber to illustrate his argument; at times I have used such citations in place of Weber's own
paraphrase of their content.

[8] See William F. Albright, *From the Stone Age to Christianity*
(2nd ed.; Garden City: Doubleday Anchor Books, 1957), pp. 236–
43, for a summary of the current state of knowledge and speculation.

[9] *Ibid.*, pp. 255–56.

[10] In a period of one hundred years (1200–1100) the town of
Bethel was destroyed four times. *Ibid.*, p. 287.

efforts to counter these massive threats by replacing the earlier, highly unstable confederacy of the Israelite tribes with a central military and administrative organization. After a century, however, the United Monarchy fell apart.

These events were related to the social organization of ancient Palestine.[11] The almost continuous strife and warfare and the short duration of political unity were partially the result of the contrasting ways of life in different sections of the country. In the central and northern regions irrigation and an annual rainfall comparable to that of Central Europe made grain cultivation and cattle-breeding possible. However, an absence of rain quickly turned a lean year into one of famine and destruction. The southern and eastern regions, periodically subject to cloudbursts, were marginal areas providing pasturage for camels and small stock and also permitting settlement with larger cattle and occasional crops in favorable years. But it was always necessary to change pastures with the seasons, either by alternating between summer and winter villages or by a permanent nomadism that allowed breeders of small stock to drive their herds over great distances in search of grazing lands. To the east and south of these marginal lands lay the desert.

The Bedouins. The desert surrounding Palestine was the habitat of the Bedouins, who scorned agriculture, permanent houses, and fortified places. Nomadic camel herders, they supplemented their subsistence diet of camel's milk and dates by income derived from convoy services, trade, and robbery along the caravan routes. As rulers over the caravan routes and as highly mobile groups, the Bedouins were the natural enemies of the more settled Israelite tribes. Israelite tradition shows no significant traces of Bedouin influence.

The cities and the gibborim. The earliest settlements in the area were probably castles of warrior chiefs and fortified places of refuge for men and cattle. Biblical tradition refers to later settlements of a more highly organized type, both small, fortified agricultural communities with a market and fully developed cities. The latter not only contained a fortress and a

[11] See *AJ*, Chapters 1–2.

market place; they were the "seat of the army, the local deity, the priests, and [of] the respective monarchical or oligarchical authorities of the body politic."[12] Many of the smaller communities were political dependencies of the chief fortified city in the area.[13]

The ruling group of larger cities consisted of an "armed patriciate," organized in extended kinship groups and dependent for its power upon landownership and the military equipment that its wealth enabled it to procure. Accordingly, the Hebrew term for warrior (*gibbor*, plural *gibborim*) refers regularly to the "sons of property" (*bne chail*), since service in war, political privilege and inherited wealth were preconditions of one another.

The herdsmen. A third group of great importance were those breeders of small stock who led a seminomadic existence. Unlike the camel-breeders of the desert, the herdsmen were breeders of sheep and goats who sought permission from the landlords to cross their lands and use them for grazing. Although violations as well as violence occurred frequently, formal agreements regulated the relations between these itinerant herders and the settled population.

The intermediate position of the herdsmen is illustrated by the sagas of the Jewish patriarchs, which may reflect the gradual settlement of the wealthier families among these seminomadic stock-breeders. Abraham has camels as well as sheep, and like the Bedouins he drinks no wine; he is an alien who wanders to and fro on the basis of contractual grazing rights, and he acquires an hereditary burial ground only at the end of his life, after long transactions (Gen. 23:3–20). Jacob is a tent-dwelling stock-breeder, but he settles in Shechem and buys land—outside the city gates.

[12] *Ibid.*, p. 14.

[13] This political relationship appears to be presupposed in such references as that to "Ekron, with her towns and her villages" in Josh. 15:20–47. Comparable city-states already existed in ancient Canaan prior to the Israelite occupation. Baron has stated that "In Israel and Judah, for the most part covering only about seven thousand square miles, there were not less than four hundred settlements classifiable as towns." See Salo W. Baron, *A Social and Religious History of the Jews* (New York: Columbia University Press, 1952), Vol. I, p. 72.

The Israelite peasant. Like other ancient sources, the Bible contains no direct reference to the free peasant. Analogies with comparable conditions make it probable that the peasants occupied a position of landowners or tenants similar to the peasants described in Hesiod, and that they had certain well-protected rights as long as they constituted the backbone of the Israelite army.[14] With changes in military technology, however, the peasant militia lost its earlier importance, and eventually the peasants lost their political rights and whatever independence they may have enjoyed at one time.

Patterns of conflict in ancient Palestine. From the time of the Israelite settlement in Palestine until the reign of Solomon, the position of the herdsmen and peasants gradually declined while urban residents, especially the patriciate, increased in numbers and in political and economic power.[15] The common interest of all Israelites in the pacification of the desert resulted from time to time in military alliances among kinship groups and tribes. The political and economic welfare of the urban merchants with their interest in the caravan routes, the breeders of small stock and the settled peasants varied with the degree to which the Bedouin tribes could be held at bay. Ascendancy over these nomads was achieved only under David (1010–971) with the conquest of Edom and the control over the caravan routes to the Red Sea.

Sharp clashes of interest and violent conflicts occurred between stock-breeders and peasants, such as the wars of Ephraim against Gideon (Judg. 8:1 ff.), against Gilead (Judg. 12:1–6), and others. In the Deborah war, in which the peasants fought against a Canaanite city-state, the stock-breeding eastern Jordanian tribes of Reuben and Gilead did not join the battle. In Weber's view such events represented peasant

[14] Such a condition appears to be assumed in the so-called Song of Deborah, which describes the war of the Israelite tribes against the Canaanite King Sisera about 1250. Scholars regard this song (Judg. 5) as the oldest preserved text in the present version of the Bible.

[15] None of these groups was sharply distinguished. The urban merchants were also landowners; the peasants were village, and sometimes city, residents; tribes of herdsmen included peasant proprietors, and if these tribes had cattle they even formed temporary alliances with the Bedouins.

invasions of mountain lands inhabited by stock-breeders and counter-attacks by herdsmen against peasant territory. Lasting antagonisms resulted from such warlike actions.[16]

These conflicts must be ascribed mainly to the economy of the herdsmen. In times of peace, when the population increased and property was accumulated, more land was brought under cultivation. As the available pasturage became limited and the exploitation of grazing lands was intensified, the herdsmen were restricted in their movements or even limited to small and fixed grazing districts. Their herds as well as their families and tribes gradually diminished in size. Under these conditions, the stock-breeders might either disperse or join larger associations under a warrior-chief in order to expand their grazing lands by military action. Such wartime unity was precarious since conflicts over grazing lands also accentuated the divisive tendencies among the herders themselves. As their grazing areas and their herds decreased under the impact of expanding settlement—as well as of wars and epidemics—the Israelite tribes were gradually transformed into a more urban society with its leading kinship groups and a more settled agriculture with its peasants, who were free but debt-ridden and subject to forced-labor drafts.[17]

Antagonism also existed between the city patriciate and the peasants. The leading urban families were merchants and absentee landowners who augmented their income from trade and land rents by squeezing the free peasants into debt slavery through usurious loans. The adoption of the chariot-fighting technique enabled these wealthy landowners to buttress their economic position because other groups were unable to finance their own military equipment. Under these conditions the "armed patriciate" became the natural antagonist of the peasants, who were consequently most exposed to the imposition of forced labor.

In the course of these conflicts the old division of society into peasant proprietors, herdsmen and artisans was replaced by a new one. The ascendancy of the "urban landlords" was opposed at every turn by the Israelite tribes in the rural areas, whose military power had rested from early times on a tribal

16 *AJ*, p. 54.
17 *AJ*, p. 42.

or intertribal summons of all able-bodied men by a charismatic war leader. The Biblical story of the United Monarchy preserves a picture of this tribal warfare but also makes it clear that political unification could not endure on this basis. In the war against the Philistine city-states David's power depended upon his own kinship group and his personal followers. Some of the latter came from other families in David's tribe of Judah, others were of non-Judaic and non-Israelite origin, and still others were debt slaves and mercenaries. The tribe of Judah as a whole backed David only later on, and the peasant tribes of the north joined this national war under the leadership of a "herdsman" only on the basis of a special treaty between David and the tribal elders. Even this treaty did not prevent repeated rebellions of northern peasant tribes against David's rule once his reign was secure after the capture of Jerusalem. For David had established a city-kingdom, and the antagonism of the peasants against city domination did not cease merely because it was now identified with national unity and legitimate monarchical rule. Indeed, the opposition of non-urban tribes against a kingship identified with urban domination remained vigorous throughout, culminating in the Division of the Monarchy after the death of Solomon and persisting in the northern kingdom of Israel until its destruction two hundred years later. Thus the history of the monarchy illustrates the continued importance of non-urban tribes despite the over-all ascendancy of the "armed patriciate."

The rise of the monarchy also increased the antagonism between the king and the urban oligarchies. Although the early kings originated as rural war leaders, they had to rely upon the support of the cities once they had established their power. On the other hand, the king might seek to counteract this dependence by winning a personal following, hiring foreign-born mercenaries for his bodyguard, and recruiting personally devoted officials from various dependent groups of the population rather than from the leading families.[18] In emergencies, and especially if he was successful, such a leader might be accepted as the legitimate "prince," entitled to his position by the hereditary charisma attributed to his kinship group. In this positive role he was viewed as a humble man, who rode

18 *Ibid.*, p. 18.

an ass, and this image merged eventually with the belief in a Messianic prince. But if such a prince relied exclusively upon his personal following, his rule became identified with that of a "king" who possessed war horses and chariots like the pharaoh and who, from his castles, held sway over the city and the dependent region.[19]

This was the situation under Solomon, who transformed the quasi-tribal military organization of Saul and David into a city-dwelling, Oriental despotism. According to Biblical tradition, Solomon's reign closely approximated the Egyptian state, with its centralized administration under an all-powerful king. His power rested on an army of knights, for which horses and chariots were imported from Egypt. Major construction projects of palaces, of fortifications, and of the Temple were undertaken by royal artisans and large numbers of forced laborers. The expanding royal domain was also worked by forced labor. Royal officials were given land grants and benefices and functioned as officers and judges. A special crown treasure was accumulated through the king's personal trade on the Red Sea, tributes exacted from foreign territories, and a regular tax in kind imposed on all subjects. Such activities required an elaborate organization, and so Palestine was divided into twelve administrative districts, each district taking a monthly turn of providing foodstuffs for the royal table.[20] At the head of this centralized administration stood a corps of officials, some of whom were priests or the sons of priests whose skill in writing favored their employment.

The reign of Solomon marked a turning point in ancient Jewish history. Because of its rise in wealth and power the small state had for the first time an opportunity to engage in world politics. Political alliances with Egypt and Phoenicia were confirmed by intermarriage with their royal houses; this in turn led to the introduction of foreign cults and the incorporation of strange gods in the indigenous religious observances. These developments coincided with changes in the social and political organization, bringing to a head the de-

[19] *Ibid.*, pp. 18–19.
[20] The stereotype of the twelve tribes of Israel may have been derived from this administrative arrangement.

militarization of the peasants and herdsmen and the rise of the "armed patriciate" in the cities.

The monarchical development was of short duration; its epitome under Solomon lasted about forty years.[21] The following period of some 400 years (922–538) witnessed a series of political and military catastrophes, culminating in the Babylonian captivity and the subsequent dispersion of the Jews. The monarchy appears as a mere "episode," dividing the period of the confederacy since the Exodus and the settlement of the Israelites in Palestine from the period of political decline following the Division of the Monarchy. This division into periods had major implications for religious history. The basic tenets of Judaism (which are discussed in section C below) were formulated during the time of the Israelite confederacy. After the fall of the United Monarchy these beliefs became the basis of the prophetic movement that left a lasting imprint on Western civilization (see section D below).[22]

[21] After the death of Solomon the rebellion of the northern tribes in 922 led to the Division of the Monarchy into the northern kingdom of Israel, with its capital in Shechem (later in Samaria), and the southern kingdom of Judah, with its capital in Jerusalem. I shall resume the review of historical events from this date on in section D of this chapter.

[22] Some prophetic figures (like Samuel) antedate both the United Monarchy and the beginning of Biblical prophecy proper, while some institutions of the confederacy (like the rural sanctuaries or the legal rights of the resident alien) existed throughout most of the period following the Division of the Monarchy. Moreover, the prophetic movement from the ninth century on tended to idealize the confederate past in contrast to the "degenerate present" of foreign cults and threatening invasions from abroad. Yet the real differences between the periods that preceded and followed the political unification under the United Monarchy are important despite these inevitable complications.

C. POLITICAL ORGANIZATION AND RELIGIOUS IDEAS IN THE TIME OF THE CONFEDERACY AND THE EARLY KINGS

The Confederacy[23]

The Israelite confederacy had no permanent political institutions. The people were organized in tribal associations of extended family groups, bound together by common worship. No common citizenship, judiciary or administration existed among the tribes. Feuds between tribes occurred more or less frequently. Unity among them occurred only in times of war against a common enemy. Even then some member tribes of the confederacy withheld their support (as in the Deborah war).

The type of legal authority that existed in times of peace reveals the political instability of the confederacy. Successful war heroes and proven prophets settled legal disputes by oracles given upon request rather than through regular adjudication. The so-called judges (*shofetim*) as well as the first kings were in all likelihood religious and military war leaders who appeared as redeemers when they made the necessary religious, military and political decisions in war emergencies. In the cities conditions were somewhat different. The Bible frequently refers to the several elders (*zekenim*) of the leading families, who functioned both as judges and as the legitimate representatives of the community.

Despite the absence of a unified legal and political organization, some degree of cohesion existed on the basis of common religious beliefs. Specifically, the great instability of many tribes of stock-breeders as political organizations contrasted with the great permanence of religious orders, i.e., organizations based on a common "cult." The Rechabites are a case in point. These people were stock-breeders who sanctified their customs and their seminomadic way of life by viewing it as the fulfillment of a heavenly command that had come down

[23] See *AJ*, pp. 75–89.

to them through their ancestors.[24] In the Bible references to this group occur from Jehu's time (in the ninth century) to Nehemiah's time (in the fifth), and there is some evidence that remnants of the Rechabites survived in the Babylonian desert until the Middle Ages or even later.[25] Such social cohesion depended upon a religious fraternization through which extended families of diverse ethnic origins were joined together in a common worship.

This principle of organization had some political effect, particularly in regard to foreigners and aliens. Such people posed a problem in this hub of the ancient Near East with its constant movement along trade routes and among grazing lands. A distinction was made between foreigners—i.e., non-Jews—and Jews from other tribes who did not possess land in their area of residence. Foreigners could obtain personal protection either as temporary guests or as permanent clients of an established family, their security depending, of course, upon the power of that family to make good such protection in cases of dispute. Landless Jews from other tribes were in a different position. They were considered of foreign stock; as resident aliens (*gerim*) they were clearly distinguished from the families of the "armed patriciate" and of the ordinary residents. The Biblical tradition does not allow us to distinguish between different kinds of alien but it does make clear that the *gerim* enjoyed the legal protection of the community and not merely the personal protection of a prominent family. Though these aliens were excluded from landownership and thus from army service, they were entitled to receive dwelling sites and pasture land outside the city gates. Also, they were ritually segregated from the established families of the community and hence were excluded from intermarriage with these families. Because of this segregation and their separate legal status the resident aliens retained their tribal identity. But their rights were recognized as religious obligations of each community and tribe, and violations of such rights could provoke a holy war of the confederacy against the offending party.[26]

The cult organization of the Rechabites and the legal posi-

[24] See Jer. 35:6–8.
[25] *AJ*, p. 79.
[26] Judg. 19:20.

tion of the *gerim* illustrate the social cohesion that existed in the confederacy despite the absence of permanent political institutions and point to the unifying effect of religious ideas and practices even in times of peace. Yet the confederacy became activated as a body politic primarily in times of war, and it was in connection with its holy wars that the basic tenets of ancient Judaism were developed. In war the confederacy was based on an "armed assembly" of all Israelites that functioned as a legislative and judicial body through acclamation of the motions put before it by the war leaders or war prophets, who claimed authority beyond the boundaries of their own tribes by virtue of a mission certified by God. This idea of a covenant with God, and of all Israel as a confederation bound by oath under this covenant (*berith* in Hebrew), was a basic tenet of ancient Judaism.[27]

Throughout antiquity political alliances and private contracts were generally confirmed by oath and thereby placed "under the protection of God as a witness and avenger of perjury."[28] The ancient Judaic concept of a *berith* on the part of Israel as a whole, a basic covenant with God Himself, differs decisively from this practice.[29] We have already encountered several instances of such covenants among Israelites with God as a partner rather than a witness to the agreements.[30] In the era of the confederacy, unity was presumably difficult to achieve except by acts of consecration that sanctified a joint military undertaking.[31] Once such religious fraternizations proved their military and economic efficiency, they contributed tremendously to the diffusion of the beliefs upon which

[27] *AJ*, p. 75.

[28] *Ibid.*, p. 78.

[29] *Ibid.*, p. 78.

[30] David becomes a legitimate king on the basis of a *berith* with the tribal elders; through a *berith* Abraham becomes a resident alien in Beersheba (Gen. 21:31); relations between tribes were sanctified by *berith* as in the case of the Gibeonites, who became a tributary community of Israel (Josh. 9:14–21).

[31] Nothing certain is known about the nature of such early fraternizations, but it appears probable that they consisted of certain rites at places of Yahwe worship and that they enjoined special taboos against the use of war booty (it must be consecrated to God), against the murder of compatriots, and against the violation of "guest rights" (the rights of the *gerim*). See *AJ*, pp. 93, 126.

they were founded. But the beliefs themselves could not be explained, in Weber's view, as a mere by-product of social organization. They emerged, rather, within specific historical circumstances, in which a prophet like Jonadab ben Rechab or Moses expressed his highly personal religious experiences and intentions.[32] I turn now to Weber's discussion of the basic beliefs of ancient Judaism that were formulated in the course of the Exodus from Egypt and the settlement of the Jews in Palestine.

Israel and Yahwe[33]

The Israelite tradition traced its basic religious orientation to the ancient covenant that Yahwe had made with the "children of Israel" through Moses, His servant and prophet. The liberation from bondage had been accomplished by a miraculous destruction of the Egyptian army—a sign of God's power and the dependability of His promises and also of Israel's lasting debt of gratitude. To be sure, this concept had much in common with other religions. The god of the tribe or the king is seen everywhere as an ally against the enemies. Many peoples have worshiped a god like Yahwe, a god of war and of catastrophe who was believed to aid "the people" and to punish their enemies. The idea of God as a guardian of the social order is a nearly universal concept, as is the idea of God's rewarding the faithful with a promise of riches, many children, long life, and a good name.

But the specific beliefs of Judaism rested on the unique assumption that Yahwe had explicitly pledged Himself to His people. He had given His vow to favor Israel before all other peoples solely on the condition that He would be Israel's God and would be worshiped as such.

Ye have seen what I did unto the Egyptians, and how I bare you on eagles' wings, and brought you unto myself. Now therefore, if ye will obey my voice indeed, and keep my covenant, then ye shall be a peculiar treasure unto me

[32] *Ibid.*, p. 80.
[33] See *ibid.*, Chapter 5.

above all people: for all the earth is mine: And ye shall be unto me a kingdom of priests, and an holy nation.[34]

In turn, the people of Israel had pledged themselves to be His people:

Thou hast avouched the Lord this day to be thy God, and to walk in his ways, and to keep his statutes, and his commandments, and his judgments, and to hearken unto his voice: And the Lord hath avouched thee this day to be his peculiar people, as he hath promised thee, and that thou shouldest keep all his commandments.[35]

Yahwe was the "contractual partner to the ritualistic and social order of the confederacy," and other peoples were inferior to Israel because they did not know God's commandments.[36]

It is decisive that the covenant involved a bilateral agreement. The people of Israel had chosen Yahwe as their God and concluded a covenant with Him at the same time that they had established unity among themselves through a treaty of confederation, much as later they installed a king on the basis of a covenant. Thus, whoever did not obey the summons of the confederacy, thereby refused the summons of the Lord. Yahwe in turn had freely chosen Israel, He had made promises to her as to no other people, and He had accepted Israel's pledges in return.[37]

Who was this God who was a contractual partner to all laws established under a covenant with Him? Originally, Yahwe was the heavenly war lord of His people, a "god from afar," essentially unapproachable and separate; the sight of Him was deadly, and only Moses was said to have seen His back. Like the Indian god Indra, Yahwe thirsts for the blood of enemies and the disobedient. In the boundless might of His passion He devours them with fire and throws them into the sea (like the chariots of the Egyptians). In keeping with this warlike image Yahwe also was a god of natural catastrophes.

[34] Exod. 19:4–6.
[35] Deut. 26:17–19. See also the description of the sacrifices and the cultic meal by which the covenant with Yahwe was sanctified (Exod. 24:4–11).
[36] AJ, p. 120.
[37] Ibid., pp. 130–31.

His appearances were accompanied by earthquakes, volcanic eruptions, fires, desert winds, and storms; He punished the enemies of His people with locusts, He sent snakes to punish His own people and pestilence to the Egyptians.

Yet this frightful and demonic image had another side. Yahwe behaved like a king given to wrath when the obligations due Him remained unfulfilled, and like a king He had a changeable heart. One could provoke His wrath through some unwitting oversight, or one could be threatened with sudden destruction by a divine command as a token of God's unlimited power. But under the covenant Yahwe also acknowledged the pledges He had given His people and He was reminded of them. Thus, when Yahwe speaks to Jeremiah He "pleads" with His people: "What iniquity have your fathers found in me, that they are gone far from me, and have walked after vanity, and are become vain?" Jeremiah follows his admission of sins on behalf of the people with the plea: "Do not abhor us, for thy name's sake, do not disgrace the throne of thy glory: remember, break not thy covenant with us."[38]

Both the frightful majesty and the benign features of this God were from the beginning part of His covenant with Israel. Although Yahwe protected the customs and laws of the confederacy in this fashion, He did not sanctify an immutable order in the manner of the Indian deities. Since the law of Israel had been established by covenant, new revelation and a new covenant could change it. Yahwe's ordinances were permanent only if He chose to be bound by them; any other idea would have been incompatible with His unsurpassed majesty.[39] Moreover, under the covenant with Israel His wrath as well as His mercy were the reward that the people

[38] Jer. 2:5; 14:19–21. See also Mic. 7:18 ff. The Bible contains other positive images of Yahwe. He personally intervenes to assist His friends, He repents His boundless wrath, He is the master of rainfall and tells His people that in Israel rain is the work of God's free grace, not the result of irrigation and bureaucracy as in Egypt. This image of the rain god Yahwe was merged later with the idea of God as a benign governor of the universe.

[39] When Job requested God to answer for the injustice of man's condition, Yahwe does not refer to the wisdom of His order but to His sovereign might over the events of the cosmos. See *AJ*, pp. 132–33, and Job, Chapters 38–40.

had brought upon themselves through their conduct. God's omnipotence was specifically related to the events that befell His chosen people: He had promised escape from Egypt, not from a world out of joint; He had promised dominion over a land of "milk and honey," not bliss in another world. God proved His incomparable power not by the existence of a wise order but by directing the events of history in accordance with His inscrutable designs.[40]

Foreign Cults and Native Demons

In the ancient Middle East the idea of a special covenant with God had no precedent. When the Israelite tribes occupied Palestine, they necessarily came into contact with peoples whose beliefs and forms of worship differed from their own and had many points in common with the neighboring culture areas of Egypt and Babylonia.

The worship of Baal and the death cult.[41] Baal was a deity of the Canaanites. Actually the name referred to many deities who ruled over specific objects or processes of nature in the same way in which a man "ruled" over the animal or piece of land he owned. This very widespread concept was either *functional,* in that the deity was a god of dreams or of war, or it was *local,* in that he was a god of the land. The latter concept implied that the god was entitled to all first products of the soil and of the cattle and men living on that soil. Thus human as well as animal sacrifice was widespread. Like other agricultural cults, Baal worship involved ritualistic cohabitation on the field as a fertility charm and alcoholic and dance orgies with sexual promiscuity, as in the "dance around the golden calf." In Canaanite territory the local Baals were the outstanding competitors of Yahwe. They were the divine "proprietors" of each city and each local area, in the political and economic as well as in the religious sense, and they retained possession of these local shrines even after the Israelite occupation. As the Baals continued to be lords of the local

[40] Cf. Josh. 23:14–16 and Deut. 7:8–10, among many similar passages.
[41] See *AJ,* p. 139 ff.

cults, Yahwe was somehow joined with them in worship. At times both deities stood side by side, and heroes of Israel like Jerub-Baal and the sons of King Saul were given Baal-names. Until some time after the exile it was still possible for a Jewish community to worship Yahwe together with strange gods in the same temple. Such syncretism was at its height during times of peace, when the protagonists of a pure Yahwe worship met with much opposition.

That the struggle over foreign gods and foreign idols was closely linked to Israel's political and military relations with her neighbors becomes apparent in the cult of the dead. Nothing is known concerning this cult prior to the Israelite occupation of Palestine, though the present version of the Bible rejects such cults so emphatically that their existence in some form may be presumed. At any rate, the worship of Yahwe bypassed folk beliefs about the soul after death. Yahwe was never a god of the dead; this realm is absent from His creation. Emphasis was placed entirely on the good name that would and should live on after a man had died. The name of a blessed man would be a blessing to his descendants, and numerous progeny were desired lest the treasured name be extinguished in Israel. In this respect death sacrifices and mourning customs certainly existed,[42] but the sacrifices were not believed to be of special importance for the fate of either the dead or the living. There were a number of reasons for this rejection. The oracles associated with the death cult were dangerous competition for the oracles of the Yahwe priests. Moreover, this cult was prevalent in Egypt and therefore was excoriated by the Israelites as a religious abomination. Similarly, later religious leaders rose as inspired opponents to kings like Solomon, who made alliances with Egypt and introduced Egyptian and other deities and cults among Yahwe's own people, making Israel into an Egyptian "house of bondage." Finally, the death cult and ancestor worship would have strengthened the cultic significance of the family, and the Yahwe believers feared the power of ruling families as much as they feared the competition of other cults.[43]

These brief references to Baal worship and the death cult

[42] Cf. Deut. 26:14.
[43] *AJ*, p. 145.

must suffice as examples of the many forms of worship existing in ancient Palestine.[44] The struggle of the Yahwe believers against these "alien" beliefs and practices was very protracted, in part because of certain tendencies within Judaism itself. The religious practices of the confederacy provided a ready basis for the reception of alien worship and survived in one form or another until long after the Division of the Monarchy in the tenth century, especially in the northern kingdom of Israel. In an area where all other peoples accepted idol worship and orgiastic practices and where the amalgamation of native and foreign cults was an accepted consequence of foreign rule, it is not surprising that the ancient Israelites did so as well. One can appreciate the unique contribution of Judaism only after one has considered the magnitude of the task confronting these religious leaders, who sought to expurgate every alien vestige from the worship of Yahwe. One can understand these leaders themselves only if one sees them in relation and contrast to their antecedents among the religious ecstatics of the confederate period.

Types of religious ecstasy.[45] The name "Israel" referred to "the people of the fighting god"; it designated a league with a common cult and was not the name of a tribe.[46] This concept had important ritualistic and political consequences. The army leader was chosen and the aims of war were decided upon by the armed assembly, guided in turn by the inspirations and oracles sent by Yahwe as the supreme warlord. A confederate war was, therefore, a holy war, and the assembled army consisted not only of sworn confederates but of "men of God" who were sworn to follow the leadership of Yahwe.[47]

For the warriors themselves, uncut hair, fasting and sexual abstinence were prescribed as acts of purification. Quite probably the rite of circumcision originally was related to this asceticism. The story of Samson illustrates the connection between ascetic practices and the ecstasy and prowess of the

[44] For a vivid description of their variety, cf. II Kings 23:1–25.
[45] See *AJ*, Chapter 4.
[46] *Ibid.*, p. 81.
[47] *Ibid.*, p. 91. Cf. Judg. 5:11, 20.

warrior. When the spirit of Yahwe seized him, Samson engaged in an orgy of destruction. As long as his hair was uncut, he retained his strength; he lost it when he violated the sexual taboo of the warrior.

Warrior ecstasy was of special significance for the war leader in consecrating military or political decisions through prophetic inspirations. Thus, at the news of Jabesh's negotiation to capitulate, King Saul was seized by holy fury, cut up the oxen, and, with a religious curse against the tardy, summoned all Israel to the battle of liberation.[48] Again, in his struggle with David, Saul is depicted as an ecstatic:

> . . . And the Spirit of God was upon him also, and he went on, and prophesied, until he came to Naioth in Ramah. And he stripped off his clothes also, and prophesied before Samuel in like manner, and lay down naked all that day and all that night.[49]

While these stories show the relationship between ecstasy, prophecy, and leadership in war, the story of David shows the king as the ecstatic leader in a religious ceremony. When the Ark of the Covenant was returned,

> David danced before the Lord with all his might; and David was girded with a linen ephod. So David and all the house of Israel brought up the ark of the Lord with shouting, and with the sound of the trumpet.[50]

Specialists in attaining magical powers through ecstatic transports were another phenomenon of the confederacy. Professionally trained ecstatics (*nabi*, plural *nebiim*) were not

[48] I Sam. 11.

[49] I Sam. 19:23–24.

[50] II Sam. 6:14–15. In addition to these ecstatic practices of individual war leaders, there also are some examples of collective ecstasy, although the later priestly revisions of the tradition tended to identify such orgiastic practices with Baal worship and other alien cults. Weber cited I Sam. 14:32, which describes the consumption of raw flesh and blood after a victory, in violation of a religious taboo. Though there are few similar references to collective ecstasy, Weber thought it probable that such practices had been widely accepted among the Israelite tribes at the time of the confederacy. See *AJ*, pp. 94–95.

peculiar to ancient Israel; they also were found in ancient
Greece, in Phoenicia, and in India. As elsewhere, these magicians were organized in schools or guilds and were distinguished from ordinary men by special tattoo and costume.[51]
By music and dance, self-punishment, and other methods,[52]
they would produce an ecstatic trance in order to acquire
magical powers. The miracles of Elisha give a picture of such
professional sorcery.[53] However, these Yahwe magicians functioned not only as medicine men and rainmakers but also as
war prophets. This involved the incitement to a crusade—as in
the case of the prophetess Deborah, the "Mother of Israel"—
and the use of magic to ensure victory. The story of Saul shows
that the prophetic ecstasy of such dervish bands was at times
related to the ecstasy of a leader in war and peace. Samuel,
who anoints Saul, tells him:

> . . . when thou art come thither to the city, that thou shalt
> meet a company of prophets coming down from the high
> place with a psaltery, and a tabret, and a pipe, and a harp,
> before them; and they shall prophesy: And the Spirit of
> the Lord will come upon thee, and thou shalt prophesy with
> them, and shalt be turned into another man.[54]

The relation between the ecstasy of the magician and the
act of prophecy was close, and political and military leaders
were not always clearly distinguished from magicians and
prophets.[55]

Still another religious figure appears in the role of the "seer"
or oracle-giver (*roeh*). In the Bible the first reference to this

[51] I Kings 20:41.
[52] II Kings 3:15; I Kings 20:35 ff.
[53] II Kings, Chapters 4, 6, 8.
[54] I Sam. 10:5–6.
[55] This blending of different roles may be seen in various combinations of leadership and prophecy. The charismatic war leaders of
the Israelite tribes personally asked the god for an omen to which
they related their decision. Before beginning the attack on the
Midianites, for example, Gideon asked the angel to authenticate
God's message by a miracle. Again, David is represented as having
received the oracle from God, and as an inspired ecstatic on the
throne he is shown to be his own prophet of good fortune (II Sam.
23:1 ff.). Another part of the tradition puts a comparable prophecy
into the mouth of the prophet Nathan (II Sam. 7:8 ff.).

type of prophet occurs when Saul requests an oracle-giver to bless his army and curse the enemy. The kings of the ancient Middle East wanted dynastic continuity, and unambiguous oracles of good fortune by a recognized prophet were believed to have magical effect. The royal prophets gave oracles by interpreting their own dreams or those of others, or by announcing visions that had come to them in solitude. Other oracle-givers were sought out for everyday questions, and their oracles were paid for with gifts. Such "seers" were distinguished from the *nebiim* by the absence of orgiastic frenzy or mass ecstasy, and from the Biblical prophets by the methods and content of their oracles.

Toward the end of the confederate period a new type of prophecy appeared, especially among the cattle-breeding tribes in the south. These men shunned the mass ecstasy of the *nebiim* as much as the dream-visions of the *roeh*. Instead, they claimed to have heard the voice of God, and in the name of the Lord they transmitted His decisions to the political authorities. The term *nabi* came to be used with reference to these auditory prophets, whose direct intercourse with a deity (epiphany) was believed to authenticate the oracle. Here again there were various transitions. These "men of God" at times announced the will of Yahwe upon request, but eventually they did so without being asked. Increasingly they were distinguished from the royal prophets of good fortune because their oracles of doom displeased the authorities. This opposition to those in power was reflected in the later interpretation, according to which men who held no office might be seized by the spirit of Yahwe, as well as in the fact that the first of the great prophets, Elijah, addressed his oracles to the public at large and not only to the authorities.[56]

The Biblical tradition contains some references to the use

[56] These characteristics of the Biblical prophets appeared only after the Division of the Monarchy; hence the full discussion of prophecy is reserved for section D below. The Biblical tradition does not make these distinctions between the *nebiim*, the *roeh*, the royal prophets, the warrior ecstatic, the Nazarite, and the Biblical prophets. It is quite possible that the same man functioned in more than one capacity. Here as elsewhere Weber's own discussion preserved to the full the gradual transitions between these types as well as the ambiguity and inconsistency of the Biblical tradition.

of idols in ancient Judaism. Domestic shrines and cult objects (*teraphim*) are mentioned. Above all, the *Ark of Yahwe* or the *Ark of the Covenant* was an important cult implement in the worship of Yahwe. The Ark was a portable field shrine that was brought into the army camp; there God was ritually requested to rise and lead the army, and after the battle He was requested to resume His seat. The snake staff—an ancient cult implement—was traced back to Moses. These examples suggest that in its original form the worship of Yahwe was not free of idols or implements, and in the fusion between the Yahwe cult and the worship of Baal new images, like the representation of Yahwe as a bull, were readily added. Even such vigorous opponents of the Baal cult as the prophets Elijah and Elisha did not object to the use of these images. Weber concluded that the settled Israelites possessed other gods besides Yahwe and that these other cults were not only legitimate but so important that later priestly revisions did not efface their memory.[57]

The struggle of the priests against ecstasy and idol worship.[58] The history of ancient Judaism is a history of protracted struggles between priests who stood for a pure Yahwe cult and others who retained the ecstatic practices and religious syncretism that were a widespread phenomenon of ancient civilization. In order to understand these struggles we must consider the position of the priests at the time of the confederacy and the United Monarchy. In times of war the military and religious leaders of the confederacy offered sacrifices on behalf of the assembled tribes. In times of peace the deity had to receive his share of offerings at every meal. Princes and heads of families would either perform the rites themselves or employ ritually trained priests at shrines that were their private property. The Biblical tradition represents the king (e.g., David) rather than the priest as the person who was qualified to offer sacrifices on behalf of the body politic and who was entitled to call the people together to renew their pledges under the covenant with God. Under

[57] *AJ*, p. 138.
[58] See *ibid.*, Chapter 7.

these conditions the priests could not play an independent political role.[59]

In addition, sanctuaries existed from early times, which were visited by people from afar and in which solemn ceremonies were conducted by resident priests for rulers and private notables, e.g., the sanctuary at Shiloh that was destroyed by the Philistines in 1050. Weber interpreted the competition among the various shrines, the existence of private shrines and the political dependence of the priests as evidence that no collective organization of sacrificial priests existed.[60]

In the Bible identifications of priests as "Levites" alternate with references to a non-priestly military "tribe of Levi." According to Weber, one can assume either that a tribe of Levi was dispersed while its former members became priests, or that an occupational status group of trained priests became hereditary while members of these priestly families were dispersed and lost their priestly qualification. In any case, there is evidence that in confederate times the Levites constituted a status group of resident aliens who specialized in oracle-giving and the performance of religious services for a fee. This position was compatible with the Levites' work for private patrons, their service in the households or private sanctuaries of notables, and their service in tribal or communal sanctuaries as well. In all these cases the Levites were apparently sought after because their training in law and ritual enabled them to advise their clients as to the reasons for Yahwe's wrath and the steps needed to win His favor.[61] The prestige of the Levites de-

[59] See II Sam. 8:16 ff., 20:23 ff., where the cult priests of the royal temple are enumerated as officials of the king who accompanied him to war.

[60] Weber's emphasis on the conflicts among different groups of religious leaders appears compatible with the idea, suggested by Albright, that whatever organization of the priests may have existed waxed and waned with the changing fortunes of the confederacy itself. See Albright, op. cit., pp. 281–83. The question is important because its resolution would affect our understanding of the cohesion achieved by the confederacy on the basis of religious beliefs as well as on the basis of war emergencies.

[61] Biblical tradition still preserves some references to this early Levitical instruction of patrons. Judg. 17 tells of the landlord Micah who conferred upon a Levite the functions of a priest and "father confessor" of his house in return for a stipulated reward. Mic. 3:11

pended upon a knowledge of law and ritual, not upon ecstasies and dreams.

These common characteristics of the Levites were compatible, however, with a considerable differentiation among them and with a wide variety of religious beliefs and practices. Some priests claimed recognition by virtue of their vocational qualifications and personal charisma, while others claimed priestly status in terms of their birth and the hereditary charisma of their families. The absence of a recognized priesthood probably intensified the tension between these rival claimants. Also, as long as war ecstasy, war prophecy and the consultation of "seers" were practiced, the hereditary priests had to concede that the gift of prophecy could exist outside their circle. Though the priests denounced the "sorcerer" as a heretic practicing the worship of idols and of foreign cults, "heresy" was not confined to "sorcerers." Many Levites apparently conformed without scruple to the idol cult of the north, and they became degraded for being idolatrous only after the ascendancy of the Levites from the south had tipped the scales in favor of pure Yahwe worship.

It is probable that the priestly spokesmen for religious orthodoxy originated among the herdsmen of the southern steppes. From the outset the war god of the covenant was their only important deity; other, functional deities did not become prominent in this seminomadic culture. In contrast to the more elaborate ritual and religious syncretism of other areas, the Levites of the rural sanctuaries insisted on a Yahwe worship in accordance with the oldest law books, which prescribed a simple altar made of earth and unhewn stone. Only the priests possessed an intertribal authority in contrast and competition with the purely personal prestige of the tribal sheik. Such authority was important for the acts of religious consecration by which the tribes organized for military campaigns to protect their grazing lands or to conquer new ones.[62]

---

refers to instruction given for hire. Lev. 4:20, 31 and 5:10 state that by the sacrifices the priest "makes expiation" for his patrons and they shall be forgiven.

[62] *AJ*, pp. 138, 187–89, 192–93, 216–18. A few of Weber's details may be added to illustrate the contrast between north and south. In the struggle between Saul and David, the first was of peasant

Under the monarchy the tensions among different groups of priests were further intensified. The royal priests and prophets sought to monopolize the ritual of Yahwe worship and all related activities. The religious and military ecstatics who had led the armies of the confederacy were replaced by schooled priests and by a king who stood at the head of an army of chariot-fighting knights. The demilitarization of the herdsmen and peasants coincided, therefore, with the "demilitarization" of the warrior ecstatic and the *nabi*.[63] The warrior hero became a Nazarite (in the legend Samson is already called a Nazarite) who led a ritually exemplary life, and asceticism for war turned into an asceticism of contrition. The Biblical tradition that related the first kings to manifestations of religious ecstasy intimates that this religiosity of the old peasant army—and hence of the *nebiim* as the religious leaders of that army—was on its way out. As the story is told of Saul prophesying among the dervishes, the tradition adds derisively: "What is this that is come unto the son of Kish? Is Saul also among the prophets?"[64] And after David dances before the Ark, he is met by Saul's daughter Michal with the words: "How glorious was the king of Israel today, who uncovered himself today in the eyes of the handmaids of his servants, as one of

origin and stood for a combined Baal-Yahwe worship, while the second was a "shepherd" who eventually brought the Ark to the sanctuary in Jerusalem and by this act identified this old symbol of the confederate war god with the pure Yahwe cult. Ritual differences paralleled this legendary division between north and south. In the north, at the sanctuary in Shechem, the covenant between the Israelite community and Yahwe was concluded in the form of a communal meal, and this ritual was attributed also to the original Sinai covenant, in which seventy elders were guests who, together with Yahwe, shared in the sacrificial meal. In Judah, on the other hand, the sacrificial animal was cut up, and those who solemnly bound themselves in the covenant filed through the pieces. In this latter ritual—and in the related practice of sprinkling the altar with sacrificial blood—Weber saw evidence of the Yahwistic opposition to the orgiastic tendencies of cultic meals, which were primarily associated with agriculture. He hypothesized that herdsmen naturally were opposed to such practices, and he noted that a number of prominent religious leaders who opposed foreign gods and ecstatic practices were men from the herdsmen tribes of the south.

[63] *Ibid.*, pp. 100–2.
[64] I Sam. 10:11–12.

the vain fellows shamelessly uncovereth himself!"[65] Thus, practices were derided that had been held in high honor when the peasant army of the confederacy had been at war with the chariot-fighting knights of the Canaanites and the Philistines.

The manifest weakness and disunity of the Levitical priests and other religious leaders make clear that ancient Judaism was not the deliberate product of a group that rejected all foreign cults and eradicated all "alien" tendencies merely by its intellectual power and single-minded religious devotion. Indeed, the preceding discussion with its emphasis on the many conditions that favored the reception of foreign cults raises the question of how in the end pure Yahwe worship could triumph as it did. Weber attempted to formulate an answer by a political interpretation of the functions of the Levites. In general, Baal worship tended to become more important in times of peace whereas pure Yahwe worship and the idea of the covenant between God and Israel gained ascendance during periods of war and foreign invasion. Mounting political adversity led to a renaissance of religious orthodoxy, since all hope for the future rested on the people's obedience to God's commandments. Weber believed that under these conditions purely technical peculiarities of oracle-giving were in part responsible for the rise of the Levites. The various irrational methods practiced in Babylonia—the inspection of entrails, the observation of bird flight, etc.—had never been prominent in Israel. Instead, oracle-giving by throwing lots was used, and, although this was a primitive way of answering questions with "yea" or "nay," it militated against esoteric mysticism from the beginning. With the worsening of political conditions, these simple oracles with their cryptic answers no longer sufficed and increasingly rational or intellectualized methods of ascertaining God's will came into use.

The idea of obedience to Yahwe's commandments distinguished ancient Judaism from the religions of neighboring cultures in which a god's power to grant favors was thought to depend upon the offering of sacrifices. Since the confederacy did not possess priestly authorities who could offer sacrifices in its behalf, this means of winning God's favor did not ac-

[65] II Sam. 6:20.

quire the significance it had elsewhere, though the Israelites were required to appear before the Lord three times a year with appropriate gifts. Because of Israel's covenant with Yahwe the people owed their God the avoidance of things "unheard of in Israel," and under the covenant all members of the confederacy had a joint religious liability for the offenses of each individual.[66] This emphasis upon the observance of the law imparted to Judaism an ethical orientation that was retained even when, during periods of great catastrophe, sacrifices as a means of expiation increased in importance. For these sacrifices to be effective, it was imperative to decipher God's will and to know the actions that had given offense to Him. To do "what was right in the eyes of the Lord" was more important than sacrifices. This concern with the people's duties under the covenant with God increased the demand for priests who were believed to have a knowledge of Yahwe and His commandments.[67]

It must be remembered that ancient Palestine was subject to foreign rule through much of her history, that conquerors demanded the worship of their own gods as a sign of subservience on the part of the subject population, and that other peoples of the ancient Middle East more or less readily accepted such demands as an inevitable consequence of military defeat. It is true that within Judaism an ethical orientation prevailed over ecstatic or idolatrous practices, especially in periods of national misfortune. But ancient Judaism originated despite and not because of the political and military disasters that befell the Jewish people. In Weber's view the exponents of Yahwe worship re-fashioned the basic tenets of the confederate period into a religious creed that enabled the Jews to retain their identity for 2,500 years after the Babylonian captivity. This was the major intellectual achievement of the

[66] The Babylonian hymns mention the liability of the individual for the sins of his ancestors and relatives, but the joint liability of the people as a whole for the actions of each individual is an idea peculiar to ancient Judaism. Weber pointed out that this distinction parallels the difference in political organization, since joint liability for the obligations under the covenant made sense in a confederacy but not in a bureaucratic state.

[67] AJ, pp. 167, 179.

great Biblical prophets and of the Yahwist party among the Levitical priests.[68]

This achievement is related to the fact that ancient Palestine was at the crossroads of the great civilizations of the Middle East. Alphabetical writing went back to the second millennium. The earliest documents of Biblical literature, like the Song of Deborah, were the work of professional poets and storytellers, and at the time of the United Monarchy there is evidence of administration based on archives and historical writing. In contrast to the despotic regimes in the surrounding states, the seminomadic tribes and the "armed patriciate" of the cities preserved their independence even under the monarchy and supported the professional teachers of Yahwe worship and the critics of kingship. The same circumstances furthered the reception of religious ideas among the common people, who, as Weber remarked, become "dumb" only when they face the bureaucratic machine of a great state. Under the impact of social change during the period of the United Monarchy, Yahwism developed through the interaction of a public composed of demilitarized and socially declassed strata with a stratum of inspired intellectuals.[69] This creative interaction was related in turn to a condition that ancient Palestine shared with the other areas of religious innovation. Weber observed that new religious concepts never have originated in the great centers of civilization but rather in areas adjacent to these centers and subject to their influence.

> The reason for this is always the same: prerequisite to new religious conceptions is that man must not yet have unlearned how to face the course of the world with questions of his own. Precisely the man distant from the great culture centers has cause to do so when their influence begins to affect or threaten his central interests. Man living in the midst of the culturally satiated areas and enmeshed in their

[68] Weber went to some length to demonstrate that in the long run Judaism rejected the religious ideas and practices of Egypt and Babylonia, notwithstanding the evidence of religious syncretism among the Jews. This rejection was aided by the fact that Egyptian culture militated against religious proselytism. For details see *ibid.*, Chapters VI, VIII, and *passim*.

[69] *AJ*, p. 206.

technique addresses such questions just as little to the environment as, for instance, the child used to daily tramway rides would chance to ask how the tramway actually manages to start moving.

The possibility of questioning the meaning of the world presupposes the capacity to be astonished about the course of events.[70]

D. POLITICAL DECLINE,
RELIGIOUS CONFLICT, AND
BIBLICAL PROPHECY

We now can return to the political condition of ancient Palestine at the time of the United Monarchy under Solomon. The establishment of a despotic regime after the Egyptian model provoked a rebellion of the northern tribes and a Division of the Monarchy into the states of Israel and Judah. A brief review of the events that followed will reveal the close relation between political history and the rise of the prophetic movement, which, for Weber, marked the turning point of Western civilization.

Political Decline

In the northern kingdom of Israel a syncretism of religious beliefs and practices developed. The revolt against the Solomonic reign was in part a protest against the construction of the Temple in Jerusalem and the concomitant predominance of the Jerusalem priesthood. The first king of Israel, Jeroboam I (after 922), established the worship of golden bulls in the old sanctuaries at Dan and Bethel, presumably as a religious and political protest against the cult monopoly at Jerusalem.[71]

Under the influence of Phoenicia, pagan cults flourished, especially during the reign of Ahab (871–852) and his wife Jezebel, who patronized Baal worship. Eventually the supporters of a pure Yahwe worship rose in protest under the

[70] *Ibid.*, p. 207.
[71] See I Kings 12:26–31.

leadership of the prophet Elijah (d. 850), and the Omri dynasty was overthrown by Jehu (845–818). The non-Israelite cults were suppressed, but Jehu became a vassal king of the Assyrians. During the first half of the eighth century peace returned because of lessening pressure from abroad, and with it the worship of foreign cults resumed. The renewal of prophecy under the great scriptural prophets, Amos, Hosea, and Isaiah (d. after 700), falls in this period. The second half of the century was marked by the rapid expansion of the Assyrian Empire—especially under Tiglath-Pileser III (746–727)—which eventually led to the destruction of Israel's capital, Samaria (722–721), the forced removal of many Israelites to Mesopotamia, and the forced settlement of Babylonian and Syrian peoples in the former territory of Israel. The northern kingdom disappeared, and a mixed population again combined the worship of Yahwe with various other cults and deities.

For about two centuries after the Division of the Monarchy in 922, the southern kingdom of Judah was less subject to invasions than the north. Though an attempt was made to destroy the Davidian dynasty—Solomon's son Rehoboam (932–917) had been the first king of Judah—and to establish Baal worship in Jerusalem, the south preserved the purity of its religious tradition. After the fall of the northern kingdom, however, Judah's period of peace came to an end. Tribute had to be paid to the Assyrians during the reign of Hezekiah (725–697), who instituted religious reforms and opposed the Assyrian overlord, partly under the guidance of the prophet Isaiah.[72] Under Hezekiah's successor Manasseh (696–642), political subordination to Assyria became complete, pagan cults that Hezekiah had suppressed were reintroduced and children were killed as sacrificial offerings; the occurrence of systematic murders also is mentioned, possibly referring to a suppression of the prophetic movement. These practices elicited a reaction: Manasseh's son was murdered, though the conspirators were slain in turn. His grandson, Josiah (639–609), was elected king of Judah at the age of eight, presumably due to the influence of the Yahwists. Both the work of the prophet Jeremiah (d. after 585) and the so-called Deu-

[72] II Kings 18:4 ff.

teronomic reform fall in this period. The Deuteronomic reform was initiated by the discovery of a law book in the Temple in Jerusalem.[73] In 621 King Josiah made this book the basis of a thorough religious reform by binding the people in solemn covenant to the observance of its commandments. Specifically, he destroyed and defiled the ancient sanctuaries outside Jerusalem, killed or subordinated their priests, and celebrated the Passover in accordance with the new law.[74] In addition, Josiah sought to restore the Davidian state by taking advantage of the decline of the Assyrian Empire during this period, but he was killed in the battle of Megiddo in 609.

The Deuteronomic demand that the Temple in Jerusalem be the only legitimate place of sacrifice raised the question of what was to become of the Levites who officiated at other sanctuaries. On the one hand, Deuteronomy admonished all Israelites not to leave the "Levites within their gates" without sustenance; on the other hand, the law book required the priests to move to Jerusalem where they could participate in the cult. These contradictory admonitions reflect the great difficulty of the question. The demand for a cult monopoly in Jerusalem sought to eliminate the ancient Yahwe worship in the old sanctuaries; hence it provoked the opposition of landlords, peasants and priests who had a religious and material interest in such rural sanctuaries. But the authors of the Deuteronomic reform combined their demand for a cult monopoly with other, more popular appeals. They protested against the Solomonic type of despotism and demanded that the king be like the ancient Israelite leader—without chariots, harem, forced labor, taxes, aspirations of world leadership, and firmly

[73] The present version of this book (*Deuteronomy* means "second law," so called in relation to the first law of the covenant), was probably written during the seventh century. Its demand for a cult monopoly under the Jerusalemite priesthood constituted a major break with the decentralized religious practices of the confederacy, which had survived in some measure until this time. Cf. the discussion below. For speculations concerning the discovery of this book cf. E. Kautzsch, *An Outline of the Literature of the Old Testament* (London: Williams and Norgate, 1898), pp. 64–65 (a source that Weber used), and the recent appraisal in Albright, *op. cit.*, pp. 319–21.

[74] II Kings 23:4–25.

bound to obey the Mosaic law of Deuteronomy. This idealization of an ancient, popular kingship led to extensive revisions
of the ancient traditions, so that Saul was anointed by the
prophet Samuel, David was turned into a shepherd boy fighting Goliath, and each king was rated in terms of his record of
orthodoxy or idol worship. These demands and ideas were fully
articulated for the first time under the reign of Josiah, but
when the king fell in battle only thirteen years after the discovery of the Deuteronomic law book the position of the
Levitical Yahwe priests was jeopardized once again.

In the years that followed Josiah's defeat at Meggido Judah
became a vassal state, first of Egypt, then of Chaldea, and
finally of Babylonia. After two unsuccessful uprisings against
Babylonian rule Jerusalem was destroyed by Nebuchadnezzar in 587 and large parts of the population were carried off
into captivity. The prophecies of Ezekiel (d. after 570) and
the second Isaiah (or Deutero-Isaiah, d. after 535) fall into
this period. The abduction of the priests into captivity finally
made it necessary to settle the relations among them. Apparently a solution was reached after large numbers of Jews were
permitted to return to Palestine (538) following the conquest
of Babylonia by the Persian king, Cyrus. Under the leadership
of the priest Ezra, all Jerusalemite priests were regarded as
qualified to officiate at sacrifices in Jerusalem, which was to
be the sole sanctuary. All other recognized Levites were
made into inferior cult officials who were to take turns in con-
ducting the service. Still others became liturgical servants, such
as singers or doorkeepers. This tripartite division was made
acceptable through tax regulations that ensured the livelihood
of the low-ranking priests.

The final establishment of a cult monopoly in Jerusalem
irrevocably destroyed the sacred significance of tribal and kinship ties, which had for so long prevented the ascendancy of a
centrally organized Levitical priesthood. Domestic slaughter-
ing and meat dinners now were secularized, since "sacrifices" or
"sacrificial feasts" could be proffered only in Jerusalem and no
longer in the family household or at local sanctuaries. Membership in the Jewish community now depended on religious
confession rather than on familial or tribal affiliation. Hence-
forth, the segregation of resident aliens was abolished, with

the explicit stipulation that one law applied in all things to Israelite and alien alike.[75]

The Temple of Jerusalem was restored between 520 and 515, and in Judah, now a vassal state of the Persian Empire, the Jerusalemite priesthood re-established the Jewish community on a religious foundation. The great religious movements of the preceding centuries had come to a head in the Babylonian captivity, which marked the end of the independent Jewish state and the beginning of the Diaspora (literally, "scattering") of the Jews among the Gentiles. The Exile was also the great turning point of Western civilization. For by the end of the sixth century the great prophetic movement that began in the time of Samuel in the eleventh century had given form to that religious ethic of social conduct which, in Weber's view, helped create the distinctiveness of the "whole cultural development of the West." His analysis of this movement is the subject of the remainder of this chapter.

Social Aspects of Biblical Prophecy[76]

Beginning with the prophet Elijah in the ninth century, the great Biblical prophets appeared during the political crises of the Divided Monarchy. Prior to these events, the period of the confederacy had been terminated by the great wars of liberation against the Philistines and by the rise of urban culture and of kingship. The grandeur of this development was never forgotten, and in retrospect it found its reflection in the image of Yahwe as an overwhelming god of war. But within a hundred years the monarchy had been turned into a despotic state, internal revolt had divided the country, and the political structure of Israel and Judah was threatened from abroad. Political independence had been permitted merely by the lull in the expansionist policies of the great states. Mesopotamia and then Egypt resumed their conquests, and Syria became a theater of war.

[75] Num. 9:14; 15:15. And, as the ritual segregation of the *gerim* was abolished, the meaning of the term changed from "resident alien" to "proselyte."

[76] See *AJ*, Chapter XI.

Never before had the world experienced warfare of such frightfulness and magnitude as that practiced by the Assyrian kings. . . . The oracles of classical prophecy express the mad terror caused by these merciless conquerors. As impending gloom beclouded the political horizon, classical prophecy acquired its characteristic form.[77]

Social orientation of the prophets. All the prophets extoll the glories of the confederacy, with pacifist and military images of God and His social order standing side by side. The patriarchal legends depict the brotherliness and plain manner of the confederates during the early period, and they idealize the ancient social rights that protected the debtor and the resident alien. Hence the patriarchs appear as thorough-going pacifists. They are fathers of extended families who as resident aliens secure grazing rights from the settled population, and divide the land peacefully among themselves when the need arises, and whose actions generally reveal a complete lack of personal heroism. But, the prophets also emphasize the crusading legends of the tradition. As the demilitarized successors of the more warlike *nebiim*, they engage in utopian fantasies that are saturated with the bloody images of Yahwe's heroic feats. In the patriarchal legends some tribes of stock-breeders, such as those of Reuben, Simeon, Levi, and Judah, are masters over the land, renowned for their violence and with the cities dependent upon them. Indeed, patriarchs like Abraham and Isaac combine a pronounced pacifism with very military virtues.[78]

Against this populist and military idealization of the confederacy is set the foreboding image of the future, when a king would rule over Israel.

This will be the manner of the king that shall reign over you: He will take your sons, and appoint them for himself, for his chariots, and to be his horsemen; and some shall run before his chariots. And he will appoint him captains over thousands, and captains over fifties; and will set them to ear his ground, and to reap his harvest, and to make his instruments of war, and instruments of his chariots. And he will

[77] *Ibid.*, p. 267.
[78] *AJ*, pp. 49–52, 285–86.

take your daughters to be confectionaries, and to be cooks, and to be bakers. And he will take your fields, and your vineyards, and your oliveyards . . . and give them to his servants. And he will take the tenth of your seed, and of your vineyards. . . . He will take the tenth of your sheep: and ye shall be his servants. And ye shall cry out in that day because of your king which ye shall have chosen you; and the Lord will not hear you in that day.[79]

This prophecy clearly attacks the innovations that kingship had brought about but it is also aimed at the power of the "armed patriciate," the *gibborim* who constituted a mainstay of the monarchy despite frequent clashes of interest. In addition, the prophets echo the complaints of the people, which were widespread in antiquity: justice was corrupted by gifts; innocent blood was shed; and the godless were favored over the righteous.[80]

The first appearance of these oracles coincided with the great transformation of society under David and Solomon. The prophets address themselves to such questions as the construction of the Temple, the royal succession, the private sins of the monarchs, social injustice, forms of worship, and so on. Their basic ideal is the time-honored "law" of the ancient Israelite confederacy; the basic evil is the transformation of this good society of the past into an Egyptian "house of bondage."[81] However, this is not an opposition to the monarchy as such, since during the wars of liberation the monarchy had enormous prestige.[82] The prophets do not deny the legitimacy of the Davidian dynasty, and there were kings like David, Jehu and Isaiah who did "what was right in the eyes of the Lord." But prophetic opposition to the political alliances, idolatry and despotic methods of the kings from Solomon on down left little room for a recognition of kingship as a positive force, and in times of increasing external threats this opposi-

[79] I Sam. 8:11 ff.
[80] See *AJ*, p. 116, for appropriate citations.
[81] *Ibid.*, p. 111.
[82] Some parts of the Biblical tradition emphasize that in the times preceding the monarchy disorder and arbitrariness had prevailed. "In those days there was no king in Israel, but every man did that which was right in his own eyes." (Judg. 17:6.)

tion grew in intensity. The king was implored to do away with the paraphernalia of the "sultan" and become again the wise leader and judge of the common people. Then the God of the old covenant would put their enemies into the hands of His people, regardless of how overwhelming these enemies appeared to be.

Demagogues and pamphleteers. The prophets represented a distinctive type of religious leadership.[83] Unlike the royal prophets, they were independent of the existing political regime, and frequently they stood in uncompromising opposition to it. Also, unlike all other oracles, their prophecies of doom could not be exploited for profit, since no one would buy an evil omen. Prophecies of doom could not be taught professionally, in contrast to the oracles of good fortune. Consequently the scriptural prophets thunder against those "lying" prophets who base their predictions of good or ill fortune upon the payment they receive.[84] These harbingers of bad tidings conceive their ideas in isolation and in opposition to all prevailing opinion.

In Weber's view the prophets before the Exile were demagogues in the specific sense that they addressed their audiences in public. Such men could not have arisen in the great powers or, for that matter, in the short periods of strong kingship within Palestine. The rulers of the day treated oracle-giving as an affair of court and prohibited public prophecy when it appeared. Accordingly, royal prophecy gained in prestige at the expense of the confederate war prophets and war leaders as long as the monarchy was strong. But under the rising threat of danger from abroad free prophecy became important again. Though some prophets answered queries brought to them, for the most part they addressed the public at large in the streets or through open letters, always prompted by a spontaneous inspiration. Their predominant concern was the destiny of the state and the people, and they usually expressed this concern by emotional invectives against the overlords. As a result, the appearance of the prophets had all the aspects of frantic passion that usually were associated with party struggles in antiquity. Curses, threats, personal invective, desperation, wrath

[83] *AJ*, pp. 110–17, 279–81.
[84] Mic. 3:5, 11.

and thirst for revenge were part of the prophetic addresses and oracles. Conversely, the prophets were personally attacked and pilloried by the public in the open streets, and, of course, the political authorities proceeded against them by attempting to win them over, by studied indifference, or by suppression, as the situation demanded.[85]

Despite all this the prophets were not political demagogues in the usual sense, and the analogy with the struggle of political parties is no more than an analogy. Unrestrained by convention or self-control, these "titans of the holy curse," as Weber called them, appear to have been moved solely by a glowing passion for the cause of the wrathful God. Though they were agitators who promoted definite foreign policies, they were apparently not moved by either private motives or political considerations. For them all political relations were what they were by virtue of Yahwe's will; only Yahwe could change them. Accordingly the prophets adopted a utopian view toward political events. In the midst of disaster they voiced the old popular hope of world dominion that would come about by another divine miracle. All political alliances were anathema to the prophets, for such actions manifested a trust in human help and hence a godless disbelief in Yahwe's unsurpassed power and His special covenant with Israel. All world events were interpreted as the direct result of Yahwe's will. In the pre-exilic interpretation of Jeremiah the Babylonian king, Nebuchadnezzar, appears as "God's servant"; his conquest of Judah and his destruction of the Temple could only mean, according to Jeremiah, that Yahwe had ordained this punishment of His people.[86]

This religious orientation toward political events necessarily resulted in a complete disregard of political realities. Jeremiah incessantly preached submission to Nebuchadnezzar in a manner that appears as high treason; later he issued a prophetic curse against Babylon when the conqueror sent him

[85] See *AJ*, p. 273, for Weber's statement of the analogy between Biblical prophecy and party struggles.

[86] Jer. 43:10. In keeping with this view the post-exilic interpretation went so far as to make Nebuchadnezzar a convert to Judaism. Cf. Dan. 4:33–37.

gifts and an invitation to come to that city. When the Assyrian king, Sennacherib, stood before Jerusalem after devastating Judah, the prophet Isaiah—who had welcomed these attacks earlier as deserved punishment—prophesied that Jerusalem would be saved, though every sign pointed to its speedy destruction. These men were moved by passionate religious inspirations that made them interpret *all* events as an outgrowth of Yahwe's will and that enabled them to stand against the stream of events.[87] The unsurpassed prestige of the prophets rested on predictions of political disaster in the midst of prosperity, or of good fortune in the midst of disaster. Amos prophesied disaster when the northern kingdom was apparently strong; Hosea predicted the downfall of Samaria; Isaiah's prophecy was fulfilled (Sennacherib's army withdrew from Jerusalem because of an outbreak of pestilence); and the oracles of disaster for Jerusalem also came true. To be sure, many oracles were not fulfilled, and some of these are even included in the scriptures. But the people remembered the prophetic words that had been confirmed by events,[88] and their belief in Yahwe's intentions and promises appeared to be strengthened when the disasters that had been predicted actually came to pass.

The prestige of the Biblical prophets also depended upon their social prominence and their independence from political involvement. Isaiah came from a family of notables, had close contact with distinguished priests, and acted as the king's counselor and physician. Zephaniah was the great-grandson of King Hezekiah. Ezekiel was an eminent priest in Jerusalem. Jeremiah came from a long line of rural priests. Only Amos came from a family of shepherds, though he was well educated. None of this, however, throws much light on the social orientation of the prophets. They cursed the outrages of the great regardless of their own social origins, and they denounced with equal vehemence the rule of the uneducated

[87] Weber did not exclude the possibility that the prophets made conscious assessments of the political situation, but he stressed that merely political assessments could not explain the prophetic message.

[88] Jer. 26:18 refers to a prophecy during the reign of Hezekiah that was remembered a century later.

plebeians. Until the Exile none of the prophets proclaimed a social or political program; their entire message presupposed—rather than discussed—the ethical and ritual demands of the Levitical priests.[89] This independence from conventional politics in the very midst of the political struggle had a social foundation only in the support of some Jerusalemite notables, especially among the elders, who considered themselves guardians of the pious tradition. Among the other social strata the prophets found no support at all. The peasants did not support them because the prophets denounced the fertility cults of the rural sanctuaries. The kings did not support them for the reasons already indicated. And the priests merely tolerated them for want of a better alternative.

The last point is of special significance. The very existence of free prophecy from the earliest times was a symptom of weakness in the position of the priesthood. In confederate times the absence of a central organization made the suppression of the prophets impossible. Under the monarchy the royal prophets gained prestige, but since free prophets were backed by powerful families the priests had to tolerate them. In some instances, as with Isaiah and Ezekiel, the relationship of priests and prophets was quite close. But the prophets also clashed with the priests in the sharpest possible way. Amos denounced the cult practices at Bethel and Gilgal.[90] Jeremiah clashed with the priests of Jerusalem because he prophesied the destruction of the Temple, and in the trial against him, which was instigated by the priests, his acquittal was secured only by the intervention of the elders.[91] This antagonism did not extend to the teachings of the Levitical priests or, for that matter, to the rules of prudent living advocated by these teachers of wisdom. In addition to their own oracles the prophets recognized all the authoritative sources of morality.[92]

[89] The exception is the prophet Ezekiel, who, during the exilic period, projected a theological construction of an ideal state.

[90] Amos 4:4; 5:5.

[91] Jer. 26.

[92] "They neither announced a new conception of God, nor new means of grace, nor even new commandments." *AJ*, p. 300. See also *ibid.*, p. 304. This conservatism of the prophets contrasts with the emphatic statement of Jesus: "It is written, but I say unto you. . . ."

But in contrast to the ritualism of the priests the prophets were spokesmen of an ethical righteousness; they pointedly denounced the people whose religion was a "mere tradition learned by rote."[93] There is no more dramatic expression of this view than Jeremiah's prophecy of the day when God will punish "all them which are circumcised with the uncircumcised. . . ."[94] This consistent downgrading of ritual naturally increased the antagonism between priests and prophets. In the eyes of the latter, the charisma of divine inspiration had a higher value than the priestly claim to recognition on the basis of the written word and formal ecclesiastical authority.[95]

Ecstasy and politics. The prophets were lonely men who pitted the frightfulness of their impassioned vision against all the mundane interests of their day and thereby gave ethical meaning and religious significance to calamities in which ordinary men presumably saw undeserved cruelty and the mutability of fortune. The inspirations of the prophets were preceded by a wide variety of pathological states. Ezekiel beat his loins and stamped the ground; after one of his visions he was paralyzed for seven days; he felt himself floating through the air; he was inspired to consume filth. Jeremiah was like a drunken man with his bones shaking; he carried a yoke around his neck. In his case the Biblical description points to schizophrenic phenomena: he did not wish to speak but felt compelled to utter words not coming from himself; unless he spoke he suffered terrible pains and burning heat; and he experienced speaking as an act of relieving himself from an unbearably heavy pressure. Occasionally the Biblical tradition refers to physical symptoms, as in the case of Isaiah who described himself as writhing in anguish as a woman in labor, affected in vision and hearing, with his heart pounding.[96] Many prophets had visual and auditory hallucinations; they also fell into autohypnotic states and engaged in compulsive speech.[97]

The relation of ecstasy to Biblical prophecy had certain unique characteristics. At times the prophets were carried

[93] Isa. 28:13.
[94] Jer. 9:25.
[95] Cf. Jer. 7:8.
[96] Isa. 21.
[97] See *AJ*, pp. 286–88.

away and spoke out in a state of ecstasy, while at other times they merely described their ecstatic experience. In the rare cases in which they were asked to prophesy—rather than doing so on their own—they would ponder long in prayer until they received the "word" in an ecstatic state and only then would they speak out. In all of these forms prophetic ecstasy retained a distinctive character, because it was not connected with the traditional means of attaining ecstasy. There is no report of guilds or schools of prophets, which had been known earlier. The prophets despised alcohol; we hear nothing of fasting or mass ecstasy. Miracles had as little to do with the prophets' self-legitimation as did their ecstatic states. Rather, both tended to support their consciousness of being tools in the hands of an almighty God. This consciousness distinguished the prophets in their own eyes from the "lying prophets" who substituted "dreams" for Yahwe's word:

> I have heard what the prophets said, that prophecy lies in my name, saying, I have dreamed, I have dreamed. How long shall this be in the heart of the prophets that prophecy lies? yea, they are prophets of the deceit of their own heart; Which think to cause my people to forget my name by their dreams which they tell every man to his neighbour, as their fathers have forgotten my name for Baal. The prophet that hath a dream, let him tell a dream; and he that hath my word, let him speak my word faithfully. What is the chaff to the wheat? saith the Lord.[98]

With this consciousness of being tools of Yahwe's will went an awareness of infinite, if borrowed, strength. As Amos says, "Surely the Lord God will do nothing, but he revealeth his secret unto his servants the prophets."[99] This sense of self-assurance was not a consciousness of virtue, however. The prophets never claim to be free of suffering and sin, and the ethic of the prophets does not differ in any respect from that of ordinary men. Though the prophets demand unconditional faith in their communication of the divine imperatives, they clearly separate their mission from their own personal behavior.

[98] Jer. 23:25–28. See also Ezek. 13.
[99] Amos 3:7.

Consequently the prophets have little in common with the
ecstatics of the confederacy, even though psychopathological
states are an attribute of all types of prophecy. The prophetic
mission is bestowed upon them as a free gift of divine grace.
The prophets receive the divine message in complete solitude.[100] Their call is a sudden, unmotivated occurrence:
Yahwe called Amos away from his flocks; He laid a glowing
coal on Isaiah's mouth. The prophets then fulfill their mission
by appearing with their frightful messages in public. They feel
themselves standing before people who have done evil in the
sight of the Lord and who soon will suffer terrible misfortunes
at His hands. Inevitably these dire oracles were met with disbelief and hostility. Where prophecies of doom stood against
prophecies of good fortune, who could claim to possess
Yahwe's truth?

Weber sought the answer to this question in certain positive
traits of Biblical prophecy that distinguish it from the general
view that psychopathic states are a validation of divine inspiration. For the prophets themselves, visions, dreams, voices
and so on were *not* significant experiences in themselves, in
contrast, for example, to the Indian mystic.[101] For them the
hearing of Yahwe's voice was the sign that they must speak in
Yahwe's name. His ability to hear the divine voice was the
prophet's self-legitimation, a uniquely personal experience of
a burdensome mission.[102] Hence there were *no* external signs
assuring the audience that the prophet had heard the voice of
Yahwe. For the public at large, oracles of the prophets were
authenticated politically. Unless compelled by a higher power,
no man in his right mind would willingly incur the hostility of
kings, great families, the established priesthood and the public
by prophecies of doom that frequently identified the speaker
with the merciless conqueror from abroad. Men who spoke out

[100] *AJ*, pp. 289–92.

[101] It must be kept in mind that the great prophets appeared after
the Division of the Monarchy in the ninth century and hence after
the apogee of the warrior ecstatics and the war prophets had passed.
Also, the royal prophets opposed free prophecy, the Biblical prophets
in turn opposed the "lying" prophets, and, as competing prophets
appealed to ecstatic states as a sign of legitimation, the value of this
sign presumably diminished.

[102] *AJ*, p. 291.

as these men did were believed to have heard the voice of Yahwe.

The prophets were religious leaders of extraordinary qualities. Despite their concern with foreign affairs they were not prompted by political considerations. Despite the vehemence of their messages they were spokesmen of the traditional Judaic morality. The prophet's mission lay basically in his moral exhortation of the people and in his thundering oracles of doom for all those who did evil. His accent was on retribution in the here and now, not on salvation in the beyond, for Israel had a special duty to adhere unswervingly to the binding law of its God. The great contribution of the Biblical prophets was to make the *morally correct actions of everyday life into a special duty of a people chosen by the mightiest God.* This contribution may be contrasted briefly with other forms of prophecy.

In ancient times prophecy was political in the sense that it involved oracles concerning future political and military events. We saw that in great bureaucratic kingdoms like Egypt or the Roman Empire emotional prophecy of the Biblical type did not appear because the religious police suppressed such dangerous demagogues. In Israel, on the other hand, prophecy had a long tradition because it was supported by families of pious notables and the monarchy was too weak to suppress it permanently.[103] In ancient Greece an intermediate solution was found: prophecy was permitted in the famous oracle at Delphi, but the ecstatic states of Pythia were treated as portents to be interpreted and controlled by the priesthood. Outside such recognized cult places, psychopathological states were regarded as indications of sickness and a lack of dignity. The contrast between the Hellenic and the Israelite types of prophecy is reflected in the language used in the oracles. In Greece that language was tempered and in "perfect" form; in Israel it was an impassioned outpouring of striking images. At Delphi the well-turned verses were answers to questions that the citizenry had addressed to the official oracles; in Israel the prophets were religious demagogues who spoke out as private citizens, for the most part without being asked. In Greece the oracles were given by the established religious authorities; in

[103] Cf. Jer. 26:20–23, for an example of such suppression.

Israel they were brought to the political authorities who reluctantly paid attention to them because such good or evil
omens had an effect upon the masses.[104]

These primarily political distinctions between Hellenic and
Israelite prophecy differ from the religious distinctions between
the *ethical* prophecy of Judaism and the *exemplary* prophecy
of India. The Biblical prophets experienced their mission either
as a fortunate possession, giving them proud assurance, or as a
special burden, giving them the sense of being overpowered by
Yahwe's might. However, none of the prophets experienced

> . . . the tranquil, blissful euphoria of the god-possessed,
> rarely the expression of a devotional communion with God,
> and nowhere the merciful pitying sentiment of brotherhood
> with all creatures typical of the mystic. The god of the
> prophets lived, ruled, spoke, acted in a pitiless world of
> war and the prophets knew themselves placed in the midst
> of a tragic age.[105]

But neither the prophets nor, so far as one can tell, their
audience ever doubted that the world is meaningful. For them
Yahwe was a ruler whose motives were not concealed from
human comprehension, a ruler from whom one desired to
know how to obtain His grace. Yahwe's world government
was plain; in Isaiah (28:23–29) it is represented in the form
of a simple parable taken from farm life. The task of the
prophet was to understand Yahwe's commands. Since Yahwe's
commands were binding, any question concerning the meaning of the world was precluded. God's incomparable majesty
also precluded all thought of a mystic communion with the
divine, or of a permanent inner peace for the believer. Hence
the Israelites rejected the mystic euphoria of the Indian
prophet in favor of an active service in obedience to a supernatural but understandable deity, an obedience that militated
against metaphysical speculations.[106]

[104] Cf. *AJ*, pp. 319–20, for a discussion of parallels rather than
contrasts. Remarks on the similarities and differences between Hellenic and Jewish prophecy are also found in *ibid.*, pp. 270–71, 281,
287–88, 290–92, 295.
[105] *Ibid.*, pp. 312–13.
[106] See *ibid.*, pp. 314–15.

These concepts rested on the *a priori* assumption that the events of the world were not determined by magic or blind chance but by Yahwe's will. To believe otherwise would be a token of disbelief in the overpowering majesty of the world ruler. Thus Biblical prophecy represents a view of man and of God that is diametrically opposed to the Indian quest for holy knowledge. Since the Biblical prophets initiated this divergence, the analysis of their ideas was the capstone of Weber's sociology of religion.

Ethic and Theodicy of the Prophets[107]

We have seen that the central problems of prophecy were posed by the political events of the day. Panic, rage, thirst for vengeance, fear of war, of death, of devastation, the issue of foreign alliances—all these came to a head in the question of the reasons for God's wrath and of the means to win His favor. The prophets answered that misfortune was the result of God's will. This answer was by no means self-evident. It would have been psychologically easier and also more in accord with popular opinion to assume either that foreign deities were for the time stronger than Yahwe or that Yahwe did not care to help His people. But the prophets rejected such interpretations. If calamities occurred, God had willed them because He made all things: ". . . shall there be evil in a city, and the Lord hath not done it?"[108] But Yahwe was also the God who had made a special covenant with Israel: "You only have I known of all the families of the earth: therefore I will punish you for all your iniquities."[109] The misdeeds referred to were predominantly violations of confederate institutions that stood under Yahwe's protection: oppression of the poor, idol worship, disregard of ritual, perversion or suppression of prophecy. The demands for charity and religious purity were not unique in Israel. But in Israel these demands were enjoined upon the people as a whole, not merely upon the rulers, because under

[107] See *AJ*, Chapters 12, 14, 16.
[108] Amos 3:6.
[109] Amos 3:2.

the covenant the people were jointly responsible for one another.[110]

In using these ancient Judaic ideas in their oracles of doom, all of the pre-exilic prophets confronted the same basic issue. How could the people retain or regain unshakable faith in the promise of Yahwe when misfortune befell them at every turn and when each was responsible for all? By the time of the prophets this question had already disturbed the minds of religious leaders for a long time. The image of God is a case in point. The most primitive view was that God was guided by His selfish interests and passions; the old sagas had Yahwe "regret" His resolutions and change His decisions. These views had raised the rationalistic question of whether this image was compatible with the majesty of a great God. Repeatedly it is stated: God is not a man that He should repent or change his mind.[111] Yet this· thoroughly consistent image was incompatible with the Levitical interest in the cure of souls: if God's decisions were unalterably fixed, prayer and expiation would be useless. This interest helped to keep alive the belief in the changeability of Yahwe's decisions.

The same considerations apply to Israel's covenant with God. Yahwe's promise to stand by His chosen people was apparently contradicted by the political disasters that befell them at every turn. At times this contradiction was resolved by the belief that man continually did evil, yet this belief made all confessional practice useless and failed to explain the special misfortunes of Yahwe's own people. Eventually the dilemma was resolved by a transformation of Yahwe's ancient and unconditional pledges into resolutions and promises that depended upon man's conduct,[112] though the same prophet might express more than one view on this decisive question. Since the oracles were responses to the state of sin among the people and to the world political situation, Biblical prophecy underwent many adjustments in addition to the revisions and

[110] Weber noted that this insistence on the "joint liability" of the people was more conservative than Deut. 7:10, which had replaced this idea with the principle of personal responsibility for sin. See *AJ*, pp. 244–45, 315–17.

[111] Num. 23:19; I Sam. 15:29.

[112] *AJ*, pp. 213–15.

interpolations of the priestly editors. Yet throughout there emerges the simple idea that the "Day of Yahwe" is at hand, that it will be a day of horror and doom as a punishment of sins but that it will also be a day of good fortune for the "pious remnant" of those who amend their ways and avoid evil.[113] The faith in the promise of Yahwe under the covenant precluded a prophecy of doom without hope and an image of Yahwe as a God of wrath and revenge without grace and compassion.

The God of the prophets assumed a majesty that was incomparably greater than that envisaged in the old God of the confederacy or in the teachings of Deuteronomy. In the prophetic image God instantly changed nature and history to achieve His designs; He moved kings and empires at will to punish His sinning people. All the old images of Yahwe were merged in a conception of a ruler of universal majesty who governed earth and heaven. The similes used by the prophets were those of the great royal courts in the surrounding empires. God no longer was the ancient warlord surrounded by his following, but the sovereign Lord of a heavenly court with a host of heavenly spirits at His service. As such He retained a changeable character. Occasionally benevolent, He was for the most part a fearsome god, capable of passion and deceit, even hardening His people in order to destroy them, often, it appears, for the glorification of His majestic power over all creatures. Weber concluded: "His total image remained uncertain. One and the same prophet saw Him now in superhuman holy purity and again as the ancient warrior god with a changeable heart.[114]

This uncertainty extended also to the abode of Yahwe. The same prophet (Amos) would see the deity as the Creator of heaven and earth and as the God "roaring from Zion." When the rural sanctuaries were destroyed and the cult monopoly in Jerusalem was established, the fate of the Temple became a major concern. At times Isaiah was convinced that the seat of Yahwe in Jerusalem could never fall; others, like Micah and Jeremiah, believed that the downfall of Jerusalem was a God-

[113] See *ibid.*, pp. 321–24, for Weber's summary and interpretation of the evidence.
[114] *AJ*, p. 310.

ordained fate. In the end, when the Temple was destroyed, Yahwe's glory seemed to be enhanced, not diminished. The prophets maintained that this catastrophe could not be the work of foreign deities who were besmirched by such abominations as idol worship and temple harlotry. There existed no gods or demons beside or opposed to Yahwe: one God brought good or ill fortune to all creatures, and thus to Israel. Yahwe had been the god of a political association, a god of action, not of eternal order; in the image of prophecy He retained this character, but, through the unheard-of calamities that were His work He had attained a cosmic and historical universalism. In this way, the prophets developed a *theodicy of misfortune* through which Yahwe ascended to the rank of the one God deciding the course of the world.

This theodicy of the prophets became the central religious mentality of ancient Judaism. Though Yahwe is the majestic ruler of the cosmos, His ancient promises to Israel remain entirely concrete. The people will prosper in the here and now, if they obey His commandments. Conduct in keeping with these commandments is what alone concerns man. All questions about the beyond, about life after death and about the meaning of the world are excluded. Yet the observance of particular rules is not the decisive religious demand; other religions demand much the same workaday ethic as does Judaism. What matters is that the people have faith in the messages inspired by God. This means "unconditional trust in Yahwe's omnipotence and in the sincerity of His word" out of the conviction that the divine word will be fulfilled "despite all external probabilities to the contrary."[115] Hence obedience and humility are the prime virtues of man, and this view is directly applicable to the here and now. Yahwe has ordained the course of events; He has ordered the great kings and their armies to destroy the people because of their sins. This prophetic accusation and threat is not in the nature of a moral exhortation such as is found in the Deuteronomic law book, nor is the hope that the prophets held out distant, at least for the "remnant" of those who practice virtue. The expected good or evil can come to pass at any time.

[115] *Ibid.*, p. 318.

Here again, Judaism differs from other religions, not so much in the content as in the quality of its religious mentality. Other religions have entertained hopes for the future and have interpreted disasters as God-ordained punishment for sins. Other religions also have extolled obedience and humility out of the ancient fear of arousing divine jealousy by excessive good fortune and self-confidence. But in prophetic Judaism these expectations of good and ill fortune and this demand for virtue concern the immediate future. In the context of impending disaster from abroad and passionate prophesying at home, the whole populace became agitated by this direct relationship between the course of events and their own way of life, by the conviction that calamity or good fortune was immediately at hand. In the absence of all hope in a beyond, in the absence also of any attempt to represent and justify the world as an order that God has established for all time, the prophetic message makes clear that misfortune is deserved and just retribution is at hand for those who have cause to fear it, while the righteous can dare to hope for the "Day of Yahwe" during their lifetime. By their unparalleled religious passion the prophets lived in a mood of constant expectation. Immediately after the outbreak of disaster they expected good fortune: when the fall of Jerusalem was imminent, Jeremiah bought land because the hope for new times would soon be realized.[116]

Thus the belief of the people was confirmed rather than undermined by the political and military destruction that befell them. Near the end of his study Weber wrote:

> It is a stupendous paradox, that a god does not only fail to protect his chosen people against its enemies but allows them to fall, or pushes them himself, into ignominy and enslavement, yet is worshiped only the more ardently. This is unexampled in history and is only to be explained by the powerful prestige of the prophetic message. This prestige rested . . . on the construction of certain events as the fulfillment of prophecies.[117]

The prestige of prophetic religiosity reached its consumma-

[116] *AJ*, pp. 326–27.
[117] *Ibid.*, p. 364.

tion during the Babylonian captivity, when all the oracles of doom had come to pass. The Exile came to be viewed as the place of all hope and future welfare in contrast to the "loathsome and detestable impieties" of the people who did not keep the ordinances of the Lord.[118] This idea was elaborated in the prophecies of the second Isaiah (so-called Deutero-Isaiah) in such a way that the ignominious fate of Israel became the most important means for the realization of Yahwe's hidden designs. And, as Yahwe is the God of the universe, His world rule encompasses all the people: ". . . mine house shall be called an house of prayer for all people."[119]

In these exilic and post-exilic interpretations emphasis shifted from misfortune as a punishment of sins to a positive meaning of suffering for the salvation of all people. People who know righteousness are admonished not to fear the abuse and taunts of the world.[120] The prophet says of himself that he let them lash his back and pluck his beard out, yet he never hid his face from shame and spitting.[121] This image of the suffering prophet merges with that of the "Servant of God," who suffered without protest, who bore the sins of others, and who made his life an offering for these sins.[122] Such redemption through the suffering of the "Servant of God" fulfills the promise of Yahwe, who declares:

[118] Ezek. 11:16–21. Under the influence of the priests who had been carried off into captivity, the prophetic image of a better future was merged with ritualistic practices in the reconstitution of the Jewish community on an exclusively religious rather than a political basis. Weber's analysis of this development is omitted.

[119] Isa. 56:7. This passage and others in which the world mission of Israel's fate are elaborated were added by later compilers to the book of Isaiah. Chapters 56–66 are thought to have originated in the writings of an anonymous post-exilic author (about 500) who is sometimes referred to as Trito-Isaiah. The passages of Deutero-Isaiah (Isa., Chapters 40–55) were composed some forty years earlier, while the activity of the prophet Isaiah occurred before and during the reign of Hezekiah (727–699). For details see Kautzsch, *op. cit.*, pp. 53 ff., 96 ff.

[120] Isa. 51:7.

[121] Isa. 50:6–8: ". . . I set my face like a flint, and I know that I shall not be ashamed. He is near that justifieth me; who will contend with me?"

[122] Isa. 53:3–10.

> In a little wrath I hid my face from thee for a moment; but
> with everlasting kindness will I have mercy on thee. . . .
> For the mountains shall depart, and the hills be removed;
> but my kindness shall not depart from thee, neither shall
> the covenant of my peace be removed. . . .[123]

So Yahwe restores His people whom He had punished inex-
orably. Just as once He made faithful promises to David, so
now He promises to Israel majesty and honor "because of the
Lord thy God."[124] Here the theodicy of misfortune finds its
final culmination. Israel in exile now appears as the champion,
the object of salvation, glorifying the endurance and suffering
of the people before God by giving their fate the meaning of
a world historical mission.

With these concepts the prophets of the exilic and post-
exilic periods prepared the ground for the emerging belief in
Christ, the Savior. From demagogues prophesying doom and
oriented toward contemporary religious politics, the prophets
had become teachers consecrated by the Lord, who "hath
anointed me to preach good tidings unto the meek; He hath
sent me to bind up the brokenhearted."[125] With this change
in character the great age of prophecy drew to a close; in the
Jewish congregations, now reconstituted as confessional communities, the priesthood gained the ascendance until all those
who claimed to prophesy were ridiculed in the name of the
Lord.[126]

This decline did not undo the unique contribution of Biblical
prophecy which in its later elaboration attained at once a
religious universalism and a childlike simplicity. Though any
child can understand the Homeric heroes or the heroic figures
of the Mahabharata, the ethical content of Greek mythology,
the Bhagavad Gita or the teachings of Buddha are not immediately comprehensible.

[123] Isa. 54:8, 10.
[124] Isa. 55:3–5, 10–11.
[125] Isa. 61:1.
[126] Cf. Zech. 13 where the prophets are identified with the "un-
clean spirit." Whoever still prophesies will be stabbed to death by
his parents. And every prophet is said to be ashamed of his visions
and to admit that he is a peasant whose scars on his hands were
caused by the fingernails of harlots.

Against this, the Jewish Scriptures represent a "rationalism," moralistic as well as pragmatic-cosmological, which is immediately popular and in its most decisive parts addressed to childlike understanding. . . .

"The paradigm of the one super-worldly god constructs him in part as a father, in part as a now gracious, now ungracious king controlling the vicissitudes of the world. To be sure, he loves his people, yet when it disobeys he punishes it sternly, but can be won again through prayer, humility, and moral conduct."[127]

Free of magic and esoteric speculations, devoted to the study of the law, vigilant in the effort to do "what was right in the eyes of the Lord" in the hope of a better future, the prophets established a religion of faith that subjected man's daily life to the imperatives of a divinely ordained moral law. In this way ancient Judaism helped create the moral rationalism of Western civilization.

[127] *AJ*, pp. 397–98.

CHAPTER VIII

MAX WEBER'S SOCIOLOGY OF RELIGION

A. THEORETICAL PERSPECTIVES

The preceding chapters have presented Weber's sociology of religion in terms of *his* intentions as I understand them; the following comments are my own. Weber called his "essays" on the ancient Chinese, Indian and Jewish religions "The Economic Ethic of the World Religions."[1] This title suggests a continuation of his initial interest in the influence of the Protestant ethic on economic activities, but actually Weber reverted to this common theme of his studies only from time to time. A shift away from the emphasis of this title in its literal sense became necessary, because some religious beliefs are indifferent to economic activities or discourage them. Nevertheless, all religions endeavor to give ethical guidance to the worldly activities of their followers, whether or not that guidance includes an explicit "economic ethic." In this broad sense Weber dealt with the secular ethic that is a part of every world religion and that may be called its special "armory of spiritual incentives for the lay believer." Even this broader statement of purpose is not adequate, however, because Weber also analyzed the reciprocal effects of society and religion "so far as it is necessary in order to find points of com-

---

[1] *GAzRS*, Vol. I, p. 237.

parison with the Occidental development." As stated earlier,[2] his three main themes were to examine the effect of religious ideas on economic activities, to analyze the relation between social stratification and religious ideas, and to ascertain and explain the distinguishing characteristics of Western civilization. The preceding presentation has shown how he combined these diverse objectives, and it is now appropriate to make explicit the underlying unity of his perspective.

Weber's analysis centered on the relations between religious beliefs and the status and power structure of the groups composing a society. He used an analogous approach in his earlier studies: the changing position of farm laborers and the problem of stock-exchange regulations in relation to the typical orientation of the participants revealed major aspects of the German social structure. Next he focused attention on the religious leaders of ancient China, India, and Palestine, who had formulated and propagated the central tenets of several world religions. The ethical impulse of these tenets can be understood in part as a response to the material and ideal interests of identifiable social groups, and in part as the independent and socially formative influences of religious inspiration and charismatic personalities. As his studies progressed, Weber's interests gradually shifted from the detailed analysis of these reciprocal influences to a comparative study of social structures, for which the mundane ethical implications of different world religions provided a convenient focus. The world view of the great religions was the work of clearly identifiable social groups: the Puritan divines, the Confucian scholars, the Hindu Brahmins, and the Jewish Levites and prophets. Each of these status groups possessed a "style of life," and each developed certain religious beliefs. Weber's specific objective was to analyze the social conditions under which the charismatic inspirations of the few became first the "style of life" of a distinct status group and eventually the dominant orientation of a

---

[2] Cf. p. 84 above. This diversity of objectives created difficulties, even when Weber explicitly stated the purpose of an inquiry as in *Ancient Judaism*. The retention of many different topics in each of his studies suggests that any synoptic presentation such as the foregoing is only one of several that could be derived from Weber's work.

whole civilization. This common theme provided him with a basic set of questions that he could address to each of the great civilizations at the time when its distinctive religious beliefs originated.

Weber's work does not contain a full discussion of what this common theme implies for his view of society. This somewhat implicit view may be formulated rather broadly as follows. Each society is a composite of positively or negatively privileged status groups that are engaged in efforts to preserve or enhance their present "style of life" by means of social distance and exclusiveness and by the monopolization of economic opportunities. In order to understand the stability and dynamics of a society we should attempt to understand these efforts in relation to the ideas and values that are prevalent in the society; or, conversely, for every given idea or value that we observe we should seek out the status group whose material and ideal way of life it tends to enhance. Thus, Weber approached the study of religious ideas in terms of their relevance for collective actions, and specifically in terms of the social processes whereby the inspirations of a few become the convictions of the many. He also considered every social group as "idea-prone" in a given direction by virtue of its way of life: peasants incline toward nature worship and magic, Christian piety is a typically urban bourgeois phenomenon, military aristocracies and other politically dominant groups possess a feeling of dignity that makes them reject the religious idealization of humility, and so on.[3] Both lines of inquiry have in common the assumption that society is a composite of status groups whose partial divergence of ideas and interests is a response to divergent status situations and whose partial convergence of ideas and interests requires inquiry into past conflicts and the reasons for their eventual resolution into a pattern of dominance and compliance.

This approach to the study of "social organization" is, I believe, characteristic of Weber's scholarly work as a whole. It will be useful, therefore, to state its salient points in the form of propositions.

(1) Every society is divided into several social strata that

[3] Cf. the reference to this material in Chapter IV, pp. 92–96, above.

are characterized by the esteem in which they are held, by their monopolistic practices in social and economic life, by a specific style of life, and by a distinctive, more or less articulated world view.

(2) Collective actions—including economic actions—that are based on ideal and material considerations of status run counter to all collective actions that are based entirely on the cash-nexus.[4]

(3) As members of a status group, individuals are the product of a social organization. The actions and ideas of individuals may be studied, therefore, as attributes of that social organization.

(4) Status groups may be—and frequently are—the fountainhead of moral ideas that shape the conduct and world view of the individuals belonging to them, and that may affect the self-interested actions of large numbers of others. On the other hand, the ideas of a few may provide also the basis for the formation of a status group.

(5) Such ideas are in the first instance responses to the challenges of the material environment, as, for example, in the case of the *Junkers,* who had idealized the military way of life in response to the exigencies of eastern European frontier society. However, the world view of a status group is never solely a response to material conditions or a product of economic interest. It is also the product of ideas that are the result of human inspiration in response to a spiritual challenge, as, for example, in the case of an exemplary prophet like the Buddha.

Weber's approach to the relation between status groups and ideas has important implications for the study of culture. Contemporary social science tends to use the term "culture" to refer to the total way of life of a people, their artifacts and patterns of conduct as well as their ideas and ideals. For this general phenomenon Weber used the word "ethos" in order to emphasize that each man's participation in his society involves a personal commitment both to the behavior patterns and to the material and ideal interests of a particular status group. Such *styles of life* frequently spread beyond the groups in

[4] Cf. Chapter IV, pp. 85–87, above.

which they originate. For example, many aspects of German society were influenced by the domineering and patriarchal manner of the *Junkers*. Similarly, certain beliefs of early Protestantism, such as the idea of duty in one's calling, gained widespread influence beyond the particular religious groups that developed them. Thus, Weber attempted in each case to trace a style of life to the particular social group or groups from which a characteristic pattern of conduct and ideas had spread. In this way the culture of a nation can be construed as an outgrowth of group power and group conflict in its historical development.

This image of society has many ramifications in Weber's work, of which I shall mention two in the present context. It is related, on one hand, to his view of political action, which seeks to encompass both the very great limitations that every social situation imposes upon the individual and the great opportunities for action that are inherent in the instability of social structures. As Talcott Parsons has pointed out, Weber combined these two perspectives by conceiving historical situations as:

> . . . a relatively delicate balance between the forces working in radically opposed directions, so that the *difference* made by a war, a political movement, or even the influence of a single man may be of very far-reaching consequences. . . . It is not that such a factor "creates" the result. It is rather that, in addition to the other forces working in that direction, it is sufficient to throw the total balance in favor of the one possible outcome rather than the other.[5]

The view of society as a balance between opposing forces is the reason why Weber quite explicitly rejected the attempt to interpret social structures as wholes, at least in the context of sociological investigations.[6] For him, sociology was a study of

[5] Talcott Parsons, "Max Weber and the Contemporary Political Crisis," *The Review of Politics*, Vol. IV (1942), pp. 168–69. Cf. the author's similar comments in *Theory*, pp. 31–32.

[6] *Theory*, pp. 101–7. Cf. also Johannes Winckelmann, "Max Weber's Opus Posthumum," *Zeitschrift für die gesamte Staatswissenschaft*, Vol. CX (1949), pp. 378–79, for further documentation of this point. It may be added that this image of society is compatible

the understandable behavior of individuals in society, and collectivities like a state or a nation or a family do not "act" or "maintain themselves" or "function." To be sure, there is an important nexus among individuals that may contribute to the stability of a society; each man's actions are oriented toward the actions of others, and all men attribute specific values to the collectivities in which they participate. It is appropriate to relate such subjective orientations and values to the conditions of social existence in which they originated. But in Weber's view it was not appropriate to attribute both these conditions of existence and the subjective responses to them to some collectivity like "society" or "state" or "nation" as if these observable phenomena were somehow manifestations of such "higher entities."[7]

Weber's approach conceived of society as an arena of competing status groups, each with its own economic interests, status honor, and orientation toward the world and man. He used this perspective in his analysis of the landed aristocracy, the rising bourgeoisie, the bureaucracy, and the working class in imperial Germany. He used the same perspective in his comparative sociology of religion. The eventual success of each

---

with the deterministic position of Weber as stated in his *Methodology*, p. 187.

[7] It was not Weber's intention, therefore, to raise "the question of how far the several different variables involved . . . in fact *necessarily* vary together," as Parsons has done (cf. *Theory*, p. 75). In Weber's view this question posed an empirical, not a definitional and theoretical problem in contradistinction to the "organological" orientation both of German Romanticism and of the French sociological tradition (as in the later Comte and in Durkheim). Cf. the following quotation: "Unless one gives a detailed explanation of this concept, one may say that everything or nothing is functionally related (*angepasst*) in historical life. Mormonism is as 'adapted' to the economic conditions of Utah as are the [various] forms of life in other mountain states; the state of the Jesuits in Paraguay was as adapted to the jungle as the life of the Indians who preceded and followed that state. . . . Indeed, I could specify the theme of my investigations [in the sociology of religion] by declaring that they seek to ascertain in what sense one can perhaps speak of an 'adaptation' among various cultural elements in the several contexts." See "Bemerkungen zu der vorstehenden Replik," *Archiv für Sozialwissenschaft*, Vol. XXVI (1908), p. 276 n. Quotation marks in the original.

of the great religions was the end result of protracted struggles. Each of the leading status groups encountered opposition
from one or several others that were likewise pursuing material
and ideal interests for the sake of maintaining or enhancing
the exclusiveness and material privileges of their distinctive
"styles of life." The Confucian literati had to contend with
magicians, Taoist mystics, and Buddhist monks; the Hindu
Brahmins with the pretensions of the Kshatriyas, the competing appeals of Buddhism and Jainism, and various heterodox
tendencies among the Brahmins themselves; and the Jewish
prophets with the long list of royal prophets, oracle-givers,
ecstatics, and various groups of Levites. This emphasis upon
the struggle among different social groups was at the core of
Max Weber's personal and intellectual outlook on life. It was
his reasoned conviction that some conflicts among men are
due to an opposition of ultimate values that no amount of argument or clarification can undo. His studies in the sociology of
religion are an empirical demonstration of this view. The poise
and refined gestures of the Confucian gentleman-scholar, the
contemplative asceticism of the Brahmin holy man and the
ethical rationalism of the Jewish prophet are ultimately irreconcilable orientations toward life. A man cannot consistently
adhere to more than one of these systems of belief and action.[8]

To say that irreconcilable conflicts are an endemic feature
of society is not to assert that society is characterized by per-

[8] This approach poses ethical problems that I do *not* go into in
this book. Weber himself sought to safeguard his position against
relativism or nihilism by the ethical demand that each person fully
articulate his own value position in terms of its internal consistency
and in full awareness of its ultimate implications. This position has
been criticized by pragmatists who contend that all "ultimate" values
turn out on examination to be means to still other ends. Cf. John
Dewey, *Theory of Valuation* (International Encyclopedia of Unified
Science [Chicago: University of Chicago Press, 1939]). Weber has
also been criticized by ethical absolutists who contend that in the
study of society judgments of facts are inseparable from evaluation
and that the superiority of one over all other ethical positions is rationally demonstrable. Cf. Leo Strauss, *Natural Right and History*
(Chicago: University of Chicago Press, 1953), Chapter 2. Weber
would have regarded such contentions among ethical theorists as
evidence for his own recognition of several, ultimately irreconcilable
value positions.

petual instability. In his studies of China and India Weber showed rather that status groups like the Confucian literati or the Brahmin priests eventually became the dominant "carriers of culture." He used the term *Träger* to indicate that such groups set the tone of social relations by their ideas and style of life and thus may give great stability to a society.[9] Weber left no doubt that this approach involved a great simplification. In the case of China he tried to offset this by juxtaposing the leading stratum of literati with a more or less opposing stratum—the Taoists and popular magicians. He then attempted to show that Confucianism became dominant because of its affinity to the structure of Chinese society, while the heterodox beliefs helped satisfy the people's mundane interest in religion and reconcile them to the prevailing system of domination.[10] In Weber's view the religious orientation of such groups becomes the conventional ideal that the people at large eventually take for granted as a result of domination. Once the dominance of such conventional beliefs is established, it can be readily explained in terms of the "expression of approval and disapproval" that induces men to conform.[11]

The very inertia of convention raises the question of "how anything new can ever arise in the world," for ideas have "to originate somewhere, and not in individuals alone, but as a way of life common to whole groups of men."[12] Though applicable to all spheres of culture, this question was pursued by Weber only in his *Ancient Judaism* and in his sociology of law. Whereas his analysis of China and India focused primarily on the long-term domination by the Confucian literati and

[9] The term *Träger* is not mentioned in Weber's compendium of definitions, but this omission may be due to the fact that his discussion of "status groups and classes" remained a fragment, like Marx's discussion of class at the end of *Das Kapital*. Cf. *Theory*, pp. 424–29.

[10] We have seen, that in the case of India orthodox *and* heterodox beliefs were adapted under the influence of popular religiosity.

[11] Weber defined convention as conduct induced "without any direct reaction other than the expression of approval or disapproval on the part of those persons who constitute the environment of the actor." He added that "in countless situations the individual depends on his environment for a spontaneous response, not guaranteed by any earthly or transcendental authority." See *Law*, pp. 20–21.

[12] See *ibid.*, p. 22, and *Protestant Ethic*, pp. 54–55.

the Brahmin priests and on the conventional ideas and behavior patterns resulting from that domination, *Ancient Judaism* is a study in the sociology of innovation.[13] This should not be understood in the simple sense that the Old Testament prophets broke with established custom merely by virtue of their unparalleled gifts.[14] However decisive these founders of a great religion were, their work could not have endured if their basic religious orientation had not become the way of life of whole groups. In the case of Bismarck, Weber showed that a great man could be endowed with charisma yet lack the ability to make his work endure and, indeed, leave a legacy of political mediocrity through his unwillingness to accept men of stature.[15] Weber's *Ancient Judaism,* therefore, combines an emphasis upon religious innovators with an analysis of the process by which their unique inspiration became the dominant orientation of the rabbis of post-exilic Judaism, of the Jewish people at large, and, in modified forms, of Western civilization. In this way one of the great world religions is shown to emerge through the contentions of conflicting groups before it became the dominant orientation of a whole society.

The intellectual impulse behind this approach was similar to that behind Jacob Burckhardt's statement at the beginning of his world historical reflections: "We shall start out from the one point accessible to us, the one eternal centre of all things —man, suffering, striving, doing, as he is and was and ever shall be."[16] Weber was not content to see any accepted belief

[13] In principle, it would have been possible for Weber to concentrate as much on Confucius, Buddha and the early Brahmin priests as he did on the Jewish prophets. He did not choose to do this, however, because the studies of China and India served him as vantage points for the analysis of the Western development.

[14] Cf. Chapter X, D, for a further discussion of this point.

[15] See pp. 35–36 above and pp. 443–44 below.

[16] Jacob Burckhardt, *Force and Freedom* (New York: Pantheon Books, 1943), pp. 81–82. In the introduction to his history of Greek culture Burckhardt amplified this statement: "[Culture history] goes to the heart of past mankind; it declares what mankind *was, wanted, thought, perceived and was able to do.* In this way culture history deals with what is constant, and in the end this 'constant' appears greater and more important than the momentary, a quality appears to be greater and more instructive than an action. For actions are only the individual expressions of a certain inner capacity,

or convention or institution as something given; he sought to demonstrate that the dominant beliefs and institutions of today are the relics of past struggles among "suffering, striving, doing" men. Perhaps this explains why a man who was passionately involved in the events of his day nevertheless spent a major portion of his scholarly career on an investigation of social changes that had occurred some twenty-five hundred years ago. Moreover, Weber was not content to accept the idea that past struggles established beliefs and conventions that are eventually imposed upon men as their "immemorial" heritage. If the idea of duty in one's calling is today a "ghost of dead religious beliefs," he nevertheless asked what meaning people attach to their work, even if this consists of no more than the acceptance of custom. The perpetuation of established beliefs and institutions cannot be understood without attention to the meaning that people associate with these beliefs and institutions. In this respect Weber thought of the most routine actions of men in society as comparable to the religious innovations of charismatic leaders. Both are examples of "the fact that we are *cultural beings,* endowed with the capacity and the will to take a deliberate attitude toward the world and to lend it *significance.*"[17]

Weber did not ignore the fact that a great deal of human behavior is inconsistent or unreflective. He was fully aware that men seldom articulate their principles with the kind of "last-ditch" consistency that he expected of himself and that he thought necessary for conceptual clarity. He also knew that in ordinary life men do not examine the usages in which they persist by "unreflective imitation."[18] But he wanted to emphasize that his sociology would deal with men as "cultural beings," and that much of what men in a society take for granted even in their most routine behavior actually involves

which is always able to re-create these same actions. Goals and presuppositions are, therefore, as important as events." See Jacob Burckhardt, *Griechische Kulturgeschichte* (Stuttgart: Alfred Kroener, 1952), Vol. I, p. 6. (Originally published 1898–1902.)

[17] *Methodology,* p. 81. This, it seems to me, is the proper context for a consideration of Weber's definition of sociology as the study of "all human behavior when and insofar as the acting individual attaches a subjective meaning to it." Cf. *Theory,* p. 88.

[18] Cf. *Law,* p. 20 ff., for a definition and discussion of usage.

basic beliefs and assumptions without which they cannot function.[19] In his sociology of religion he set himself the task of formulating clearly these underlying principles and assumptions.

This program necessarily posed certain problems for the
empirical study of society. An emphasis on principles and on
the inescapable opposition among ultimate values tends to
minimize the internal divergences that characterize every
great system of belief.[20] This emphasis can be applied in varying degree, and Weber did not apply it to the same degree in
all of his studies. For example, his study of China presents
Confucianism as a unified doctrine in contrast to Taoism,
while his study of India reveals a much greater differentiation
within orthodox Hinduism. In the case of ancient Judaism he
went still further in showing the great variety of orthodox and
heterodox doctrines from which the central tenets of Judaism
only gradually emerged. In part, such differences of emphasis
were fortuitous; Weber's knowledge of Judaism, for example,

[19] This emphasis upon the cultural manifestations of subjective experience is related to the work of Wilhelm Dilthey as well as to
that of Burckhardt. Cf. Johannes Winckelmann, *Legitimität und
Legalität in Max Webers Herrschaftssoziologie*, (Tübingen: J. C. B.
Mohr, 1952), pp. 8–24. But, as Professor Paul Lazarsfeld has pointed
out, Weber's conceptual analysis, especially of "action," as well as
his causal analysis, as we saw earlier, was strongly influenced
by the German legal tradition. See Paul Lazarsfeld, "Some Historical
Notes on the Study of Action," (unpublished), p. 46 ff., Depart-
ment of Sociology, Columbia University. At the time Weber wrote
he relied in part on a summary of the literature by Gustav Radbruch,
Der Handlungsbegriff in seiner Bedeutung für das Strafrechtssystem
(Berlin: J. Guttentag Verlagsbuchhandlung, 1903), though this author dealt with a special logical problem—involving the proper treatment of criminal negligence—that was not of concern to Weber. The
basic relevance of criminal law consists in the fact that all crime is
action—or negligence—that is attributable to an individual, and since
criminal law concerns itself with the logic of "attribution" Weber
found it apparently suggestive as an analogue to his own effort to
develop a logic of "attribution" in terms of the cultural meaning
that men associate with their actions in society. Cf. Edmund Mezger,
Strafrecht (Berlin: Duncker & Humblot, 1949), pp. 89–109, for a
recent summary of this literature. See also Hans Welzel, *Das Neue
Bild des Strafrechtssystems* (Göttingen: Otto Schwartz, 1957), pp.
3–13.

[20] Weber's justification of this procedure will be considered
presently.

was more detailed than his knowledge of Confucianism. In part, his stress on the "typical" orientation of the different world religions was a by-product of the effort to contrast several civilizations. But there are also more substantive differences among these studies that can now be presented in a schematic manner.

SCOPE OF WEBER'S STUDIES IN THE SOCIOLOGY OF RELIGION

Title	Social Structure	Status group	Ideas	Secular Ethic
I. Protestant Ethic and the Spirit of Capitalism			Religious ideas	Ideas concerning economic behavior
II. Confucianism and Taoism	Position of dominant status group in the social structure		Religious ideas	Secular ethic
III. Hinduism and Buddhism	Social structure	Contending status groups	Contending religious ideas	Secular ethic
IV. Ancient Judaism	Changing social structure	Changes in the contending status groups	Changes in contending religious ideas	Emergence of ethical rationalism

Though the studies overlap more than this chart can indicate, it is still true that Weber gradually enlarged their internal complexity and that Numbers II and III are preliminary investigations for the full-scale analysis contained in *Ancient Judaism*. In his studies of China and India his aim was to delineate religious orientations that contrasted sharply with those of the West, because only then could he specify the features that were peculiar to Occidental religiosity and hence called for an explanation.

The whole enterprise involved at least five different levels of analysis: (1) the interpretation of inductive generalizations; (2) the interpretive explication of religious doctrines; (3) a method of conceptualizing historical materials; (4) the use of this method on a comparative basis in order to bring out the distinctive features of each historical phenomenon; and (5) a causal analysis in order to account for the rationalism of Western civilization. Each of these levels merits comment.

B. METHODS OF ANALYSIS

(1) Weber's generalizations have often been called "illuminating" yet little attempt has been made to indicate in what way this description is appropriate. His observation that religious innovation occurs in areas adjacent to the great world empires is a case in point. On the basis of comparative evidence Weber concluded that the great religious leaders had been active in urban areas but not in the great culture centers of the world. He linked this generalization to the idea that men in these culture centers believed or assumed they knew the answers and were no longer able to ask questions of profound religious significance because they had become enmeshed in the techniques of civilization. Only men who were not so enmeshed but whose central interests were affected by the culture centers retained the capacity to be astonished by events and to question their meaning. This idea illuminates the inductive generalization, because it generalizes about the relationship between conditions of existence and types of religious experience.[21]

This example illustrates a method of interpretation to which Weber frequently resorted. In the studies I have reviewed he commented on the "affinity" between the concept of God and certain very striking characteristics of the political community. The "Spirit of Heaven" thus "corresponds" to the early pacification of the Chinese Empire; the ideas associated with Yahwe "reflect" the political and military history of the early

[21] Weber's insight consisted specifically of the idea that religious innovation is impossible without the capacity to be astonished, and that this capacity will be maximized where men are affected by great events without becoming preoccupied with the techniques of civilization. This is a good example of what he meant by the importance of interpretive understanding (*Verstehen*) for sociological inquiry. Such a thesis can be tested, but it cannot be formulated, with the use of modern research techniques. It may be added that Weber's own writings on methodology and the voluminous secondary literature on this topic do not shed much light on these generalizations. In his substantive writings Weber usually referred to them with such phrases as "according to all experience" or "as is well known."

Jews; the Near Eastern origin of ethical monotheism may be "related to" the ideas suggested by the role of omnipotent kings and their bureaucratic regimes.[22] Weber interpreted the terms put in quotation marks by showing that under given political conditions specific status groups develop material and ideal interests that can be maximized by these concepts of the deity. He employed a similar method when he asked what religious ideas were congenial—or uncongenial—to different status groups, such as peasants, warriors, and craftsmen, given the tendencies intrinsic to their occupational experience. He used the same method once again when he suggested that ecstatic prophecy of political events was incompatible with great bureaucratic kingdoms, that it was controlled by the religious and political authorities in ancient Greece, but that it was in effect uncontrolled in ancient Palestine because the monarchy was weak and the centripetal forces of tribes and kinship groups were strong.

These examples of Weber's interpretive method have in common a kind of "existential psychology" that involves generalizations concerning probable responses to certain conditions of human experience:

(1) Involvement with the techniques of civilization militates against religious innovation; lack of such involvement in areas affected by world politics encourages such innovation.

(2) The groups providing religious leadership in a civilization will tend to formulate the prevailing concept of the deity in a manner that "fits in" with their basic political experience.

(3) Because of the dominant values of their occupational experience, social groups tend to vary in their religious propensities, though contrary tendencies may prevent these propensities from finding expression.

(4) All ruling groups will seek to control religious prophecy

[22] For the last point, cf. *WuG*, Vol. I, pp. 255–56, where Weber wrote that the Near Eastern king's control through his bureaucracy of the central irrigation system and hence his ability to "create a world out of nothing" suggested the idea of an omnipotent divine ruler. The Egyptian and Babylonian priest opposed the monotheistic challenge to the established deities; the existence of the priesthood was identified with their worship. However, the Jewish conception of the deity in part reflected the imagery of a great king.

of coming events, but their ability to do so varies with the political structure and hence the varying position of prophecy in different societies is a key to that structure and to related aspects of the culture.

Some of these are judgments (Number 3) based on common-sense experience, which makes them appear obvious, perhaps deceptively so. For example, warriors usually develop a strong identification with military strength; hence they will tend to reject the idea of religious humility, but they also will become fighters for the faith and adhere to religious ideas that are consonant with the military virtues. The other statements (1, 2, and 4) are hypotheses concerning causal relationships, dealing as they do with the reasons why the capacity for astonishment, the concept of the deity and the position of prophecy vary from one society to another. Such causal explanations are functional, in that they make assertions about what types of response go with what conditions of human existence. They also are structural, in that they relate these responses to the social and political environment of large numbers of men rather than impute them to their attitudes or motivations. Finally, these explanations involve comparisons in that they examine the same type of human experience—e.g., religious innovation or prophecy—in divergent historical settings and hence lead to systematic contrasts of the relations between these settings and the responses men have made to them.[23] Many of these judgments involve an intuitive grasp of what

[23] As far as I am aware, Weber did not discuss all phases of this procedure explicitly; he merely stated that the analogy of a "system" did not apply to society. (Cf. references cited above p. 261, n. 6). In practice he seems to have said in each case: if I find that X (e.g., monotheism) goes with Y (e.g., centrally organized regulation of rivers and of irrigation in an absolute monarchy, as in Egypt), can I find an instance, where X does *not* go with Y, but with Z (e.g., monotheism under conditions of constant exposure to foreign attack, as in ancient Judaism)? The intellectual impulse behind this procedure is the conviction that X does not have to go with Y, since there is considerable evidence to the contrary, and that it is therefore necessary to explain the correlation between X and Y where it does occur. In this way the comparative approach accentuates the specificity of causal relationships in society, which Weber then analyzed in terms of the degree of affinity between social structure and ideas.

certain conditions of existence imply, and Weber's special distinction lay in his ability to combine such judgments with a comparative historical check on their validity.

(2) The attribute "illuminating" has also been applied to Weber's interpretive explications of religious doctrines. For example, in the case of Puritanism he noted certain explicit demands and values: the negative attitude toward art, sexuality, and friendship; the rejection of all magic and symbolism, of the confessional, and of burial ceremonies; the contemptuous attitude toward poverty and the poor; the distrust of human relations but the reliance on impersonal probity. Weber interpreted the presumptive meaning of these values when he observed that men who adhere to them experience a deep inner isolation, that in a mood of pessimism and without illusion they have only themselves and their work to rely on, that they reject all sensual pleasures and worldly enjoyment, that they do not practice the neighborly love of the Christian who is conscious of his own weakness but rather pursue the sinner with hate and contempt as an enemy of God who wears the sign of his own eternal damnation. All these "observations" interpret what the Calvinist doctrine "meant" to the devout believer who was intensely concerned about his salvation before an absolutely transcendent God. Since the attitude of the individuals concerned can only be inferred, Weber characterized the "atmosphere" that Calvinist doctrine tended to create.[24] As he stated pointedly at the beginning of his essay, he was interested in "ascertaining those psychological *impulses* which originated in religious belief and the practice of religion, gave

[24] The distinction between explicit demands and values, their presumptive meaning to the individuals and their relation to Calvinist doctrine has been suggested by Alexander von Schelting, *Max Webers Wissenschaftslehre* (Tübingen: J. C. B. Mohr, 1934), pp. 396–99. I am indebted to Paul Lazarsfeld for the observation that the English translation of Weber's *Protestant Ethic* contains the term "attitude" about forty times but that in the original Weber used instead a large variety of nouns, such as "mood" (*Stimmung*), "conduct and view of life" (*Lebensführung und Lebensanschauung*), "ethical attitude" (*ethische Haltung*), "religious situation" (*religiöse Gesamtlage*), "peculiar atmosphere" (*eigentümliche Luft*), and others. See Paul Lazarsfeld, *op. cit.*, p. 63.

direction to the individual's everyday way of life and prompted him to adhere to it."[25]

Weber's analysis of such "incentives" says little about their effectiveness except to state generally that in these earlier ages people were deeply affected by their religious beliefs.[26] It focuses attention on the hypothetical question of what a religious person would do and feel if he were prompted by the incentives implicit in his religious creed, and I believe that it succeeds in characterizing the climate of human relations that Calvinism, Confucianism, Hinduism and Judaism tended to foster. Such a "climate" is the unwitting by-product of formulated doctrines and pastoral exhortations, of conventions and reciprocal expectations in the congregation, and of personal beliefs and psychological dispositions in the individual believer. Weber did not analyze these separate aspects. His attention was centered on the incentives and deterrents of different creeds and on the image of man that these creeds project. He analyzed a common denominator of rhetoric and action that people have to take into account even when they defy it or when they are indifferent to it.

[25] See the full quotation, pp. 63–64 above. Weber attributed importance to the term *Antrieb*, which means "impulse," not "sanction." (Cf. *Protestant Ethic*, p. 97.) It is instructive, however, that Weber did *not* use the term *Anreiz*, or "incentive," which would have been more accurate, since the problem turned, after all, on the extent to which the orientation of Calvinist doctrine and pastoral practice had become internalized, i.e., had become impulses of the believers. Even in his answers to critics of his first essay Weber continued to use a variety of terms, which seems to reveal some uncertainty concerning the proper level of abstraction in this case. At one point he spoke of the "existence of this 'driving force'" (*Vorhandensein dieser "Triebkraft"*); another time he stated that his essay is concerned with the question "whether a certain type of religiosity had created in its adherents the psychological disposition (*Vehikel*) . . . which was well adapted to create a typical line of conduct"; in a third place he referred to the question whether a religious doctrine has placed "psychological rewards" (*psychische Prämien*) on conformity with its precepts. (Cf. "Antikritisches zum 'Geist' des Kapitalismus," *Archiv für Sozialwissenschaft*, Vol. XXX [1910], p. 191, and "Antikritisches Schlusswort . . . ," *ibid.*, Vol. XXXI [1910], pp. 582–83.) Many other such synonyms could be cited, and, while they all have their rationale, their very number suggests that Weber had not resolved this issue.

[26] Cf. pp. 57–58, above.

(3) Weber maintained that this type of analysis—as well as the analysis of social groups and institutions—required the use of general concepts derived from historical material, and in his methodological writings he was much concerned with the rationale of this conceptualization. Accordingly, he emphasized that his work was

. . . "unhistorical" in the sense that the ethics of individual religions are presented systematically and essentially in greater unity than has ever been the case in the flux of their actual development. . . . If it were done arbitrarily, this simplification would be a historical "falsification." This, however, is not the case, at least not intentionally. The author has always underscored those features in the total picture of a religion which have been decisive for the fashioning of the *practical* way of life, as well as those which distinguish one religion from another.[27]

Weber was convinced that all historians implicitly operate with such "unhistorical" concepts and that it was necessary to make them explicit. In his own case this "typological simplification" meant that for each world religion he constructed a "model" based on the ideas of many writers but not found in any one of them in this integrated form and with such a clear statement of implications. These models are artifacts of the researcher based on historical materials; Weber felt that such artifacts were justified as long as the special purpose of such constructions was clearly stated.[28]

[27] *Essays*, p. 294. Weber used this typological method in several different ways and his practice of labeling all of them "ideal typical" is merely confusing. In the passage cited he referred to the conceptualization of religious ideas; elsewhere he used similar "exaggerations and simplifications" from a specified viewpoint with regard to social groups like the Chinese literati or institutions like the Indian castes. In all these cases his concepts are derived from specific historical configurations as distinguished from concepts like charisma or exemplary prophecy, which are derived from a comparative study of many divergent historical configurations. These last concepts are, again, different from models such as the economist's "free competitive market." For an elaboration of these and other distinctions, cf. Schelting, *op. cit.*, pp. 329–35, 353 ff.

[28] These "as if" constructions avoid the imputation of such attributes as consistency, integration and others to society as a whole or to any aspect of society.

This procedure had, in my judgment, one major consequence for Weber's substantive work. By eliminating ambiguity and inconsistency from the religious orientations of status groups in different civilizations, Weber inadvertently obscured the impact of these orientations on the practical way of life of these social groups. Though the elucidation of this impact was one of Weber's explicit objectives, he neglected the modifications by which practical men as well as intellectuals develop even their most sacred beliefs in relation to the exigencies of circumstance and of historical change. Thus, Weber never quite came to grips with the question of how to assess the influence of religious ideas on the mundane activities, and especially on the economic behavior, of the believers.[29]

This point may be illustrated with reference to Weber's assertion that Puritan believers felt deep anxiety because the absolute uncertainty of their salvation had become an article of faith, and as a result they sought to relieve their anxiety by intense and self-disciplined activity. Weber based this inference on the general assertion that in the Age of the Reformation such metaphysical conceptions swayed the minds of men to an extent that is no longer fully appreciated. No doubt this is true, but is it reasonable to assume that a majority of believers faced up to this anxiety rather than evaded its consequences? Evidence from the seventeenth century suggests that the expectations of the congregations could give to the doctrine of predestination a positive as well as a negative emphasis.

Argue though they might that many were damned from all eternity, the preachers were to find it practically inadvisable as well as theoretically impossible to name the many who might not be saved. . . . They spoke and acted, therefore, as though there were no conscience which could not be awakened, as though every common sinner might be converted into a saint. The inferences from all this . . . were

[29] Cf. the similar judgment by Schelting, *op. cit.*, p. 282, and by Ephraim Fischoff, "The Protestant Ethic and the Spirit of Capitalism —The History of a Controversy," *Social Research*, Vol. XI (1944), p. 73 ff.

obviously that grace was vouchsafed to all who did not voluntarily reject it.[30]

Weber did not allow for such accommodations. He probably came closer to a study of the impact of religious ideas on actions when he emphasized the importance of social controls within the sectarian community. It is possible, therefore, that he overestimated the importance of religious ideas whenever he moved more or less unwittingly from analyzing the direction of religious influence to assertions concerning the degree to which religious ideas became internalized. But it is not necessary to take this problematic step; an analysis of the secular ethic of the world religions is valid at the level of "goals and presuppositions" (Burckhardt's term) that characterize cultures and have an important if indeterminate impact on conduct. Though Weber's approach may not fully elucidate the uncertain relation between culture and conduct, this drawback is unavoidable, given his larger objective of comparing the great world religions systematically, of relating these religions to complex social structures and their dominant climate of opinion, and finally of explaining the rationalism of Western civilization. These larger objectives are well served by the "unhistorical" method of exaggerating and simplifying historical phenomena.

(4) In each of his substantive studies Weber tacitly chose one central problem and, by considering as many of its ramifications as possible, analyzed the structure of the society under consideration. This was already evident in his analysis of eastern German farm labor, which led him step by step to an examination of the structure of German society. It is equally true of his work on ancient civilization, in which he used the relations between military organization and agricultural production as his focal point.[31] It is evident in his sociology of

[30] William Haller, *The Rise of Puritanism* (New York: Columbia University Press, 1938), p. 169. For an analysis of this central problem from the viewpoint of psychoanalysis, see the distinguished work of Oskar Pfister, *Christianity and Fear* (London: G. Allen & Unwin, 1948).

[31] This part of Weber's work has had to be omitted from the present volume. See "Agrarverhältnisse im Altertum," *GAzSuW*, pp. 1–288.

religion, in which the examination of the secular ethic of the great world religions leads to an analysis of the principal status groups in relation to the climate of opinion characteristic of Chinese, Indian and Western civilization. This procedure has at least three different applications.

First, it provides a manageable device for analyzing the structure of societies. Though Weber rejected an organic approach, he was interested in the structural coherence of societies. He approached this by selecting a problem that had ramifications throughout the society. A study of these ramifications could then reveal the interrelations of major aspects of the society.

The second contribution of this procedure is its suitability for purposes of comparative analysis. The comparisons of the Brahmin and Confucian intelligentsia, of prophecy in ancient Greek and Judaic civilization, of the secular ethic in Puritanism, Confucianism, and Hinduism, of the religious propensities of aristocracies, middle classes, and other groups in different times and places, of the political position of cities in oriental and Occidental civilization—all are among the examples of this procedure that have been reviewed above. Different societies face similar problems, as, for example, the threat to secular authorities that is implicit in religious prophecy. Once such a problem has been defined, it becomes fruitful to examine how the same problem has been approached in different societies, and the different approaches thus revealed may then be related to other aspects of the respective societies.

Third, Weber's choice of a central problem is frequently linked with "paired concepts" that provide artificial bench marks for the analysis of empirical evidence. A case in point is the problematic relation between ideas and "material conditions" that Weber related to the contrast between classes and status groups. This contrast served as the basis for a theory of social change according to which periods of stability favor stratification by status whereas periods of rapid change militate against status distinctions by pushing the cash-nexus into the foreground.[32] Thus, as trade declined in the late Roman

[32] *Essays,* pp. 193–94. Many of Weber's formulations have a similar character, especially in his political sociology with its contrasts

Empire free peasants were turned into serfs; hence status distinctions grew at the expense of relations based on market transactions. Conversely, the commercialization of eastern German agriculture undermined the patriarchal relations between classes and threatened the prevailing status relations. In order to understand the direction of such changes, Weber looked upon each tendency in terms of what would happen if it prevailed completely. If economic change slows down enough, the conventions of the prestige hierarchy will destroy the impersonality of market transactions; if economic change is rapid enough, the impersonal relations on a market will destroy existing status distinctions. Neither of these *logical* possibilities is probable, however, because the economic and social orders influence one another at every point. Actions based on economic interests frequently aim at the preservation or acquisition of "honor," as in the organization of exclusive associations among stockbrokers or in the quest after lands and titles among German industrialists. Also, status groups frequently seek to monopolize their economic opportunities as the *Junkers* did when they used the political privileges of their social status to further their economic interests as landowners. Weber believed that such combinations between the economic and the social order can be analyzed only after the two tendencies of action have been formulated in terms of hypothetical extremes.

(5) These methodological considerations have a bearing on Weber's effort to account for the rationalism of Western civilization.[33] His sociology of religion culminates in the attempt to

---

between personal and institutional charisma, between patrimonialism and feudalism, and between formal and substantive rationality. Some theoretical implications of this approach are discussed in Reinhard Bendix and Bennett Berger, "Images of Society and Problems of Concept-Formation in Sociology," in Llewellyn Gross, ed., *Symposium on Sociological Theory* (Evanston: Row, Peterson & Co., 1959), pp. 92–118.

[33] Rationality had at least three distinct meanings for Weber. As an object of study, rationality was important as the manifestation of individual freedom, which was most appropriate in an era of capitalism and also most congenial to him personally. Second, rationality was for Weber a synonym of clarity; social science is possible only on the basis of conceptual distinctions that have no exact counterpart in social reality. The phrase that all nominally distinct phenomena

explain the initial differentiation between mystic contemplation and ascetic activism. In one sense the study was complete
once he had explained the origin of ethical rationalism by the
contribution of ancient Jewish prophecy. Yet in another sense
all of Weber's essays in the sociology of religion are a mere
preface to what he had not yet explained for the West. Although the studies of China and India account for the development of a dominant value orientation to the extent that he proposed to do this, his essay on Judaism is only the starting point
of an explanation that occupied him for the rest of his life. His
studies of ancient civilization, his sociology of law and of the
types of domination, his essay on the city and his lectures on
general economic history—all are continuations of the sociology
of religion. While the study of religion explains the initial differentiation (*Ancient Judaism*) of ethical rationalism in the
West, as well as analyzes one of its late developments in *The
Protestant Ethic,* these continuations are addressed in large
part to the question of how the basic assumptions of that rationalism had become the dominant value orientation of the
Western world.

A major part of Weber's answer is contained in his political
sociology, which I examine in Part III of this book.[34] These

in fact shade off into each other is a constant refrain in his writings.
Third, there are Weber's findings concerning the process of rationalization. In this sense the term has a number of substantive meanings, depending on the sphere of life in which that process is examined. For example, Weber identified the systematization of belief
as an aspect of religious rationalization, but then he distinguished
between different systematizations like those involved in ethical as
against exemplary prophecy. Or, again, he identified the reduction
—to principles—of the reasons relevant in the decision of individual
cases as an aspect of legal rationalization, but then analyzed the different "reductionist" procedures developed by English as against Roman jurists. The value of Weber's studies lies in the analysis of the
many different meanings of "rationalization" in the various spheres
of human activity. Though Weber often referred to these different
meanings as manifestations of one over-all process, his constant
analysis of the historical foundations of "rationalization" and of its
possible irrational consequences should guard against the idea
that for him this process was either inevitable, unequivocal, or irreversible.

[34] See *WuG*, Vol. I, pp. 245, 316–19, for summaries of the factors
accounting for the rationalism of Western civilization. By concen-

studies supplement the initial essay on the Protestant ethic by showing that this religious development of the Reformation was one late element in the century-long emergence of certain unique features of Western civilization. It is therefore legitimate to ask whether *in part* the impact of Puritanism is to be explained by the forward-looking (eschatological) orientation of Christianity, even if the religious developments of the Reformation added a last, all-important synthesis of this orientation with the mundane interests of the believers. The fascinating aspect of Weber's original essay is that it explains how theological ideas and religious fervor could unwittingly promote secular striving and success. But this thesis loses some of its intriguing paradox when one realizes that this effect was made possible by the whole history of Western civilization.[35] Even though it diminishes the paradox of Weber's initial essay, this realization also serves to buttress the major thesis he advanced. *The Protestant Ethic* does not contain a direct approach to the problem of causal imputation; it deals only with the affinity between religious precepts and the self-discipline of mundane conduct. The effect of religious "goals and presuppositions" on conduct is surely enhanced if it is shown to depend not only on the devoutness of the believers and the social controls

---

trating on the political sociology, certain other contributions of Weber's are necessarily neglected, especially his study of ancient civilization and his economic analysis in *Theory*, Part II, and in *General Economic History*.

[35] I have in mind such factors as the declining religious significance of kinship, the religious equality of believers, the partial decline of magic, and above all the general assumption that man must prove his virtue before God by his actions in this world for the sake of his eternal salvation in the beyond. These elements of the Christian heritage were in turn buttressed by other, especially political developments. This qualification concerning the thesis contained in *The Protestant Ethic* is a by-product of Weber's own later work, though he nowhere mentioned this explicitly. For suggestions along these lines I am indebted to the illuminating essay by Carlo Antoni, *Vom Historismus zur Soziologie* (Stuttgart: K. F. Koehler, n.d.), p. 161 ff., esp. pp. 215–16, 222, as well as to the earlier criticism by R. H. Tawney in his introduction to *The Protestant Ethic*. Neither of these critics makes clear that Weber's later work appears to support their own strictures.

of the community but also on the century-old cultural legacy of Occidental civilization. Part III of this book is devoted to Weber's studies of this legacy insofar as these come under the general heading of political sociology.

PART THREE

DOMINATION, ORGANIZATION, AND LEGITIMACY: MAX WEBER'S POLITICAL SOCIOLOGY

CHAPTER IX

BASIC CONCEPTS OF
POLITICAL SOCIOLOGY

Weber's earliest work as a social scientist was devoted to the study of status groups and the influence of ideas on behavior. These interests set the stage for his three-volume work on the sociology of religion, which dealt among other things with the *power* of individual religious leaders or of status groups like priests in their relations with the masses. In his later studies this subordinate interest in the phenomenon of power became the dominant theme, and one may ask what Weber conceived to be the relation between these two major parts of his work. Unfortunately he died before he could integrate his various substantive studies in an explicit manner.[1] It is possible, however, to find clues for such an integration in his work, especially in the framework of definitions that he wrote toward the end of his life.[2]

[1] When Max Weber died in 1920 at the age of fifty-six he left behind him a series of incomplete studies, many of which (including his *Wirtschaft und Gesellschaft*) had to be edited and published posthumously. He had intended further studies in the sociology of religion, especially of early Christianity and of Islam, and he had projected a comprehensive sociology of the modern state and of art, to mention only the most important topics on which he was working at the time of his death.
[2] Cf. the first part of *Wirtschaft und Gesellschaft*, which Talcott Parsons has translated under the title *The Theory of Social and Economic Organization*, especially pp. 87–157. As Max Rheinstein

A.   INTERESTS AND AUTHORITY

Weber's definitions of sociological concepts (in *Theory*) were an effort to "decompose" three overlapping dimensions of social life—authority, material interest, and value orientation—into their separate parts.[3] We will understand these highly abstract considerations better if we approach them on already familiar ground. We saw that Weber analyzed the influence of religious ideas on economic behavior as well as the influence that the interest in material gains and social honor can have upon the development of religious ideas. One aspect of this program of research was the analysis of authority relations among religious leaders, their disciples, and the laity. Considered in the abstract, these lines of inquiry suggested that men in society act with and against each other on the basis of their material and ideal interest and that they stand in a relation of authority and obedience on the basis of shared understandings.

Weber's compendium of definitions starts with the observation that sociology in his sense deals with social action only insofar as it has some subjective meaning for the persons involved.[4] "Usage" or customary activity in which men persist by "unreflective imitation" is, therefore, marginal to the discipline. But while much religious worship borders on "usage" in this sense, Weber believed that most church attendance—and also failure to attend—has some meaning for the persons in-

has stated, Weber's principal purpose was "to let us know what *he* means when *he* uses these terms so that we know clearly what he is talking about." Cf. Rheinstein in *Law*, p. xxxix. Professor Rheinstein's introduction makes clear the importance of Weber's legal background for this part of his work. Weber occasionally referred to these definitions of basic concepts as "casuistry" in analogy to the analytic casuistry in legal thought. Cf. *ibid.*, pp. 61–64. Many of these definitions were written after they had been tried out on a large body of historical evidence.

[3] In what follows I go into Weber's sociological terminology only insofar as this seems necessary for a consideration of his political sociology; and for the sake of easy comprehension I use examples of religious behavior in addition to abstract formulations.

[4] *Theory*, p. 88.

volved, though much of it is admittedly inarticulate. Whether persons go to church or only think about it or do not go or do not think about it at all, their actions and thoughts—as well as their inaction and lack of thought—are usually oriented toward what other people in their environment do or think about churchgoing. They may conform or act contrary to what others do, but in either case, they orient themselves toward these others and in so doing they attach some meaning to their own behavior. In the case of mere conventionality, that meaning consists of some awareness of the value of convention, and the failure to attend church involves some sense of convenience or secularism or irreverence. The orientation toward others should not be identified with mere conventionality, however. Many persons go to church because of a deep belief in the mundane and transcendental norms that their religion upholds, though conformity also plays a part in their behavior. However important conformity may be, it should not be permitted to obscure the belief in religious values. An act like churchgoing or, for that matter, any behavior, always has two related attributes: men in society are oriented toward each other (even when they are alone), *and* they are oriented toward norms (even when these are inarticulate).[5]

According to Weber, these two attributes of all behavior can be examined in terms of why and how men act in concert, and in terms of why and how they believe in the existence of a moral order that imposes obligations upon them. They also parallel his emphasis on *types of religious group formation*, like the Chinese literati or the Indian Brahmins, and on *types of leadership*, like prophets and disciples or priests and their congregations; and they reappear in his systematic work, which is divided into sections dealing with *constellations of interests*[6] among men and others dealing with the *types of domination*. This recurrent subdivision was hardly accidental. Though Weber nowhere discussed its significance for his work, it may

[5] Several dimensions of "meaning" are discussed in *Theory*, pp. 93–98 and *passim*. See pp. 265–67 above for a discussion of the significance of this starting point for Weber's image of society.

[6] Weber used the phrase *Interessenkonstellation* (*Law*, p. 324), but he did not discuss this term. The context makes clear that he was referring to group formation on the basis of material and ideal interests that a number of individuals have in common.

be suggested that for him the conditions of solidarity on the basis of ideas or interests and the moral order of authority on the basis of a belief in legitimacy were the two perspectives through which a comprehensive view of society could be obtained.

Weber's definitions of these two perspectives also apply to religious behavior. Let us see what "constellation of interests" means when we formulate it in terms of "church attendance."

(1) The members of a community attend church regularly, and thus act in a predictable way, because they share a *feeling of solidarity that finds expression* in the common worship.[7]

(2) The members of a community attend church regularly, because they share an *interest in the values that will be realized* by the common worship.[8]

That is, when people attend church they are responding to each other in terms of certain beliefs that they cherish, whether these consist of an emotional identification with each other as members of the same friendly neighborhood or of a traditional respect for religion or of a regard for either the holiness of the sacrament or the social usefulness of church attendance.

All these communal and associative ties affect the authority relationship between the minister and his congregation. The minister occupies a position of authority by virtue of the rights and duties conferred upon him by his Church; he is an official of a corporate group as well as a member of the community. And on behalf of the values of its religious mission the Church claims that the minister exercises his authority legitimately. This claim is explicitly recognized only by some members of the congregation; others take it for granted. Like all organized institutions the Church invokes certain norms or maxims that together comprise the idea of the Church as a legitimate order.

[7] This is an example of a *communal social relationship* (*Vergemeinschaftung*), which is called "affective" when it is based solely on sentiment and "traditional" when it is based on an identification with tradition.

[8] This is an example of an *associative social relationship* (*Vergesellschaftung*), which is called "value-rational" when it is based on a belief in a supreme value (say, the sanctity of religious observance) and "instrumental" (Weber said *zweckrational*, or "purposive-rational") when it is based on a belief that the common worship will implement some other end (such as community stability).

The conduct of church officials and laity alike is oriented toward this idea in varying degrees, and this orientation differs in kind from the feelings of solidarity and the common interests that govern the members' communal and associative relationships.[9]

Such distinctions introduce arbitrary "bench marks" that can prove their utility only through application. In his use of such distinctions Weber moved back and forth between them in order to analyze actual relationships. In the preceding chapter I called his *Ancient Judaism* a study in the "sociology of innovation," because he centered his attention on the innovations of religious leaders. However, although he stressed the charismatic authority of such leaders over their followers, he also referred time and again to the constellations of interests that provide the setting for such leadership. The Old Testament prophets, for example, can be understood only against the background of the competing ecstatics, oracle-givers, priests and others who preceded them. Moreover, their charismatic appeals were related to the social structure of ancient Palestine, which tended to create differences in awareness and hence a varying receptivity for these appeals. The same consideration applies throughout. When Weber turned his atten-

[9] The contrast between voluntary agreement and authoritative imposition is clearly stated (e.g., *Theory,* p. 148; *Law,* p. 324), and indeed Weber's economic sociology (*Theory,* pp. 158–323) primarily analyzed constellations of interest while his political sociology (*ibid.,* pp. 324–423) primarily analyzed types of authority. Note also Weber's distinction between the church into which one is born (authority) and the sect that one joins like a voluntary association (constellation of interests). It is true that Weber discussed constellations of ideas and interests in the context of authority relationships, and vice versa, but this was not to say that the distinction between the two, which governs the whole of *WuG,* is merely a device of exposition. It is more accurate, I think, to speak of the contrast as a continuum involving the purely associative and instrumental relations of the marketplace (emphasizing voluntarism and formal equality) at one extreme, and the purely authoritarian superordination of the personal despot (emphasizing subjection and inequality) at the other. The division of *WuG,* Part II, into "Typen der Vergemeinschaftung und Vergesellschaftung" (types of communal and associative social relations) and "Typen der Herrschaft" (types of domination) may, therefore, be seen as an analysis that begins first from one end of this continuum and then from the other.

tion to the established authority of the priesthood, he at once showed that this authority can also be seen as a constellation of interests among the priests in relation to the interests of the laity. When he turned his attention to status groups such as magicians in terms of their communal and associative relationships, he demonstrated how such relationships can eventuate in corporate organizations—guilds in this case—involving relationships of authority.[10] Repeatedly in his empirical work Weber turned from one level of abstraction to the other, though his sociology of religion on the whole gave greater weight to constellations of ideas and interests than to the theme of authority. In his political sociology that emphasis was naturally reversed.

B. DOMINATION, ORGANIZATION, AND LEGITIMACY

Weber defined power as "the possibility of imposing one's will upon the behavior of other persons,"[11] and he pointed out that in this general sense power is an aspect of most, if not of all, social relationships. Men can exercise power in the market, on the lecture platform, at a dinner party, in sports or scientific discussions, in erotic or charitable relationships. Used in this way the term has no scientific utility. However, Weber noted that among the many sources of power two contrasting types are of special interest to the social scientist: power derived from a *constellation of interests* that develops on a formally free market, and power derived from *established authority* that allocates the right to command and the duty to obey.

[10] Cf. the earlier discussion of ideas and interests in Chapter IV, A, which dealt with Weber's analysis of classes and status groups *apart* from a consideration of authority relationships.

[11] *Law*, p. 323. Chapter XII of the Rheinstein-Shils translation is the introductory section to Part III of *Wirtschaft und Gesellschaft*, which is entitled "Types of Domination." Though relevant to the "sociology of law," the chapter sets forth the major purpose of Weber's analysis of domination, which is separate from his study of law. Cf. also the more detailed definition of power in *Theory*, p. 152, and the comment on this definition, p. 153. It may be noted in passing that Weber's definition of power is very similar to Clausewitz's definition of war.

Weber used the example of a large central bank that dominates potential debtors by virtue of its monopolistic position in the credit market. Though such a bank can impose conditions for the granting of credit, it does not exercise authority and the debtors submit to it in their own interest. If the bank controls credit institutions by virtue of its central position, however, it may attempt currency management or the control of the business cycle through regulations and special agencies that approximate the formal authority of government. This example illustrates that the constellation of interests between a central bank and its debtors may shade off into an authority relationship between that bank and the "member banks" of a national banking system.[12] Accordingly Weber proposed to use the term "domination" (*Herrschaft*) only in the narrow sense, excluding from its scope all those situations in which power is derived from constellations of interest. For Weber "domination" was identical with the "authoritarian power of command."[13]

Weber concluded these preliminary considerations with the following definition:

The manifested will (*command*) of the ruler or rulers is meant to influence the conduct of one or more others (*the ruled*) and actually does influence it in such a way that their conduct to a socially relevant degree occurs as if the ruled had made the content of the command the maxim of their conduct for its very own sake.[14]

[12] *Law*, p. 325. Weber's example is well illustrated by the Federal Reserve System, in which the "open-market operation" exemplifies reliance on the constellation of interests on the stock market, while the requirement that member banks maintain a stipulated reserve ratio of liquid assets exemplifies the authority relations of government.

[13] *Law*, pp. 327–28. This arbitrary terminological decision did not imply a neglect of power that arises from "a formally free interplay of interested parties." The studies discussed in Chapters II, VI, VII and VIII illustrate that power in this sense was for Weber an all-pervasive phenomenon. It may be added that this terminological decision does not reappear in *Theory*, pp. 152–53, although it justifies the arrangement of the whole work, another indication that the compendium of definitions contained in *Theory* should not be considered in isolation.

[14] *Law*, p. 328.

To understand this complex statement it is helpful to separate its analytical components. For domination to be present there must be: (1) an individual who rules, or a group of rulers; (2) an individual who is ruled, or a group that is ruled; (3) the will of the rulers to influence the conduct of the ruled and an expression of that will (or a command); (4) evidence of the influence of the rulers in terms of the objective degree of compliance with the command; (5) direct or indirect evidence of that influence in terms of the subjective acceptance with which the ruled obey the command.

Domination involves a reciprocal relationship between rulers and ruled, in which the actual frequency of compliance is only one aspect of the fact that the power of command exists.[15] Equally important is the meaning that rulers and ruled attach to the authority relationship. In addition to the fact that they issue commands, the rulers claim that they have legitimate authority to do so, and hence they expect their commands to be obeyed. In the same way, the obedience of the ruled is guided to some extent by the idea that the rulers and their commands constitute a legitimate order of authority.[16]

Domination requires an administrative staff to execute commands, and, conversely, all administration requires domination in that the power of command over the staff must be vested in an individual or a group of individuals. These imperatives of domination and administration are at a minimum only where the organization is local and limited in size, administra-

[15] The contrast between the frequency of compliance and the legal question of normative validity aside from questions of actual behavior is discussed in *ibid.*, pp. 11–16.

[16] Weber did not use "authority" as a separate technical term but appeared to think of it as a synonym for "domination." Cf. *WuG*, Vol. I, p. 122, and *Law*, p. 328. Since he distinguished domination by virtue of market interests from domination by virtue of authority (cf. *WuG*, Vol. II, p. 604 ff. and *Law*, p. 324 ff.) and since he used "domination" only in the latter sense, he probably did not feel free to use the term "authority" subsequently. But, since he specifically identified "authority" as the power to command and the duty to obey, I shall use the term as a synonym for "domination" whenever this is in the interest of fluency. My use of terms differs from that of Talcott Parsons, who translates *Herrschaft* not as "domination" but as "imperative coordination." Cf. his editorial comments in *Theory*, p. 152, n. 83.

tive functions are relatively simple, and the members are by and large equals and possess a minimum of skill for the administrative tasks to which each might be called in turn. But these conditions of direct democratic administration are highly unstable. Wherever the group increases beyond a certain size, or the members become differentiated from one another, or the administrative functions become too difficult to be performed by everyone who might be designated through rotation or election, domination and administration tend to develop into more enduring structures. The result is the technical superiority of the officials who have had training and experience, and the likelihood that they will continue in office because of this superiority. In this way an administrative structure arises to serve the purposes of the rulers, and "all administration means domination."[17]

In "mass structures," a given system of domination can endure more or less permanently. All ruling minorities possess the advantage of small numbers.[18] And all administrative organizations consist of persons who: (1) are accustomed to obey commands; (2) are personally interested in seeing the existing domination continue because they derive benefits therefrom; (3) participate in that domination in the sense that the exercise of functions is divided among them; and (4) hold themselves in readiness for the exercise of these functions.[19]

Since the advantage of small numbers is an attribute of all rulers, structures of domination vary in the ways in which the powers of command are distributed between the ruling minority and the "apparatus." They also vary in the general princi-

[17] *Law*, p. 334. In this connection Weber stated that "as soon as mass administration is involved, the meaning of democracy changes so radically that it no longer makes sense for the sociologist to ascribe to the term the same meaning as in the case [of direct democratic rule]."

[18] Any ruling minority has the opportunity to communicate rapidly, to organize its defense, and hence to defeat any mass challenge, as long as the opponents do not organize in a comparable fashion. Such ruling minorities also have the advantage of being able to keep their knowledge, intentions and decisions secret: increasing secrecy always indicates an effort to buttress the existing system of domination. See *ibid.*

[19] *Ibid.*, p. 335. I have again "decomposed" Weber's definition into its several parts.

ples of legitimacy on the basis of which the "officials" obey the ruling minority and the people at large obey both. Thus Weber emphasized both the organization that implements and the beliefs that sustain a given system. This corresponds to his double emphasis on status groups and ideal interests in his analysis of religion. His study of domination, too, stresses the importance of group formation *and* of beliefs.

In Weber's view beliefs in the legitimacy of a system of domination are not merely philosophical matters. They can contribute to the stability of an authority relationship, and they indicate very real differences between systems of domination. Like all others who enjoy advantages over their fellows, men in power want to see their position as "legitimate" and their advantages as "deserved," and to interpret the subordination of the many as the "just fate" of those upon whom it falls. All rulers therefore develop some myth of their natural superiority, which usually is accepted by the people under stable conditions but may become the object of passionate hatred when some crisis makes the established order appear questionable. Weber saw only three principles of legitimation—each related to a corresponding type of "apparatus"—that have been used to justify the power of command:

(1) *Legal domination* exists where a system of rules that is applied judicially and administratively in accordance with ascertainable principles is valid for all members of the corporate group. The persons who exercise the power of command are typically *superiors* who are appointed or elected by legally sanctioned procedures and are themselves oriented toward the maintenance of the legal order. The persons subject to the commands are *legal equals* who obey "the law" rather than the persons implementing it.[20] These principles apply also to the "apparatus" that implements the system of legal domination. This organization is continuous; its officials are subject to rules that delimit their authority, institute controls over its exercise, separate the private person from the performance of official functions, and require that all transactions be in writing in order to be valid.

(2) *Traditional domination* is based on the belief in the

[20] *Theory,* p. 328.

legitimacy of an authority that "has always existed." The persons exercising the power of command generally are *masters* who enjoy personal authority by virtue of their inherited status. Their commands are legitimate in the sense that they are in accord with custom, but they also possess the prerogative of free personal decision, so that conformity with custom and personal arbitrariness are both characteristic of such rule. The persons subject to the commands of the master are *followers* or *subjects* in the literal sense—they obey out of personal loyalty to the master or a pious regard for his time-honored status. The "apparatus" appropriate to this system consists either of personal retainers—household officials, relatives, personal favorites—in a typically patrimonial regime, or of personally loyal allies—vassals, tributary lords—in a feudal society. In their official capacity personal retainers are subject to the customary or arbitrary commands of their master, so that their sphere of activity and power of command is a mirror-image of that master at a lower level. By contrast, in a feudal society, officials are not personal dependents but socially prominent allies who have given an oath of fealty and who have independent jurisdiction by virtue of grant or contract. The distinction between feudal and patrimonial rule and the juxtaposition of customary and arbitrary commands under both systems pervades all forms of traditional domination.

(3) *Charismatic domination.* Personal authority also may have its source in the very opposite of tradition. The power of command may be exercised by a *leader*—whether he is a prophet, hero, or demogogue—who can prove that he possesses *charisma* by virtue of magical powers, revelations, heroism, or other extraordinary gifts. The persons who obey such a leader are *disciples* or *followers* who believe in his extraordinary qualities rather than in stipulated rules or in the dignity of a position sanctified by tradition. Under a charismatic leader officials are selected in terms of their own charisma and personal devotion, rather than in terms of their special qualifications, status, or personal dependence. These "disciple-officials" hardly constitute an organization, and their sphere of activity and power of command depends upon revelation, exemplary conduct, and decision from case to case, none of which is

bound either by rules or tradition but solely by the judgment
of the leader.

In history these "pure types" of domination are *always* found
in combinations, but Weber insisted that clear concepts are
needed to analyze such combinations in terms of their legal,
traditional or charismatic elements.[21] The first step is to show
how these more or less heterogeneous elements are combined
in different historical configurations such as feudalism or the
modern state. On this basis Weber believed it was possible to
show that certain incompatibilities in a system of domination
are related to modifications of the institutional structure and
to changed beliefs in legitimacy. For example, a fully consistent charismatic leadership is inimical to rules and tradition,
but the disciples always wish to see the leader's extraordinary
capacities preserved for everyday life. As the disciples have
their way, rules and traditions develop that de-nature the charisma they consciously mean to serve. In this way one may
analyze the tendencies by which one system of domination can
change in the direction of another.[22]

Yet change is not necessarily a change from one type of
domination to another. Each system of domination possesses
certain built-in safeguards of its own identity, which result
from the belief in the legitimacy of the relation between rulers
and ruled.[23] It follows that every system of domination will

[21] The material available in English (*Theory*, p. 324 ff.) contains
primarily Weber's definitions rather than examples of the use to
which he put them. Cf. the bibliographical note at the beginning of
this book.

[22] Weber had a special interest in such developments from the
viewpoint of "rationalization," but too much emphasis on this theme
gives the false impression that he advanced a unilinear theory of
social change. He sought to avoid this impression by stating that he
examined other systems insofar as they deviated from the ideal type
of legal domination but this statement is lost in his wealth of details.
I shall, therefore, emphasize the mutability of each system of domination, which is, I believe, an accurate indication of Weber's purpose. Cf. also Chapter X, D, below.

[23] "To a considerable extent a modern 'state' exists as a complex
of specific interactions among men. This is so because there are
specific persons who act in the belief that this state exists or should
exist in this way." And such beliefs are the sociological reasons for
the validity of the legal order. See *WuG*, Vol. I, p. 7, and *Theory*,

change its character when its rulers fail to live up to the standards by which they justify their domination and thereby jeopardize the beliefs in those standards among the public at large. Under legal domination the "superior" is himself subject to law, and he can undermine the beliefs sustaining the legal order if he uses formal compliance to extend his domination indefinitely. Under traditional domination the "master" can undermine belief in sacred tradition if he uses his arbitrary powers of command to put himself above the tradition that confers these powers upon him. Similarly, the charismatic leader forfeits his authority when he fails to prove himself in the eyes of his disciples.[24]

In Weber's view every historical relation between rulers and ruled contains heterogeneous elements that can be analyzed on the basis of his three "pure types." The predominance of one or another of these elements in the organization of rule and in the beliefs in legitimacy is related to certain more or less enduring historical configurations. But rulers are constantly tempted to transgress the built-in limitations of their power, and so under every system of domination men tend to change the system in the course of pursuing their material and ideal interests.

---

p. 102. I have modified the translation to bring out the point more clearly. See also *WuG*, Vol. I, p. 13.

[24] Cf. Winckelmann, *Legitimität und Legalität,* pp. 39–43. Weber did not treat this aspect of authority as a separate theme but only in the context of analyzing each type of domination. But, since each of these types depends upon certain beliefs, each also can change its character when the form of domination is retained but the belief in its validity has disappeared. Thus a legal order can decline into a bureaucratic absolutism, a patrimonial rule can change into sultanism, a feudal balance between king and estates may lead to a disintegration of kingship or of the estates, and so forth. In each of these cases the system loses its character by persistently violating the limitation that is based on the reciprocity of expectations between rulers and ruled.

CHAPTER X

CHARISMATIC LEADERSHIP
AND DOMINATION [1]

Weber's analysis of charismatic domination is easier to understand if domination as a result of charismatic leadership is distinguished from domination as a result of charismatic authority, even though he did not make this distinction explicit in his work.[2]

[1] I discuss Weber's three types of domination in reverse order, although he attached some importance to analyzing legal domination first and then treating the other types in contrast to it. However, the point gets lost in his own analysis, and the present reworking of his materials makes it superfluous. Unless otherwise noted, the discussion in this chapter is based on *WuG*, Vol. II, Chapters 9–10, which are entitled "Charisma" and "Transformation of Charisma" respectively. See *Essays*, pp. 245–52, for a translation of the first of these chapters.

[2] The distinction between leadership and authority has been emphasized by Robert Bierstedt. "A leader can only request, an authority can require. . . . Leadership depends upon the personal qualities of the leader in the situation in which he leads. In the case of authority, however, the relationship ceases to be personal and, if the legitimacy of the authority is recognized, the subordinate must obey the command even when he is unacquainted with the person who issues it. In a leadership relation the person is basic; in an authority relation the person is merely a symbol." See "The Problem of Authority," in Morroe Berger, Theodore Abel and Charles Page, eds., *Freedom and Control in Modern Society* (New

Weber always used the term "charisma" in the sense of an "extraordinary quality," possessed by persons or objects, that is thought to give these persons or objects a unique, magical power.[3] In his analysis of domination the term designated one of his three major types. The man who possesses genuine charisma exercises domination, but this power of command differs from legal and traditional domination in that it is extraordinary. Since the distinction between extraordinary and everyday types of domination is as basic as the distinction between the "constellation of interests" and the "order of authority," it clarifies Weber's intentions to think of "charismatic leadership" as a separate level of analysis. In this way we get a threefold division of the phenomenon of power: (1) power on the basis of constellations of interest, e.g., on the market or in status-groups; (2) power on the basis of established authority; i.e., legal, traditional, or charismatic domination; (3) power on the basis of leadership (the extraordinary qualities of a person and the identification of followers with that person).

A. CHARISMATIC LEADERSHIP

Aspects of its legitimacy and organization. Weber saw legal and traditional domination as *permanent* structures that provide for the everyday needs of the community. Such structures are not well adapted to the satisfaction of needs that are out of the ordinary. Hence, in times of trouble the "natural" leader is neither the official nor the master whose authority is based on the sanctity of tradition, but the man who is believed to possess extraordinary gifts of body and mind. The troubles that make men call for such a leader and the leaders who respond to such a call can be of many kinds. The leaders may be prophets and heroes, magicians and demagogues, doctors and quacks, leaders of mobs or orchestras or robber bands; if they dominate by virtue of their charisma, their relationship to their followers is of the same type from a sociological point

York: D. Van Nostrand, Inc., 1954), pp. 71–72. I am indebted to Professor Bierstedt for this distinction, which is also embedded in Weber's analysis but is not clear from his terminology.

[3] Cf. the definition of "charisma" quoted above on p. 88, n. 15.

of view. According to Weber, the possibility of sociology, as of any social science, depends on our ability to use specifically defined concepts in this value-neutral sense, though this does not imply a disregard of values. Leaders of robber bands still are criminals, and leaders of religious movements like St. Francis still are saintly men. But Weber put questions of good and evil on a different level from questions of fact, and the fact is that both very evil and very good men have exercised domination through their extraordinary gifts of mind and body. For better or worse, charismatic leadership is especially in demand in times of trouble, though it recurs also in the permanent systems of domination.

Since charismatic leadership occurs most frequently in emergencies, it is associated with a collective excitement through which masses of people respond to some extraordinary experience and by virtue of which they surrender themselves to a heroic leader. Therefore charismatic leadership approximates its "pure type" only at the time of its origin, in contrast with the other two more enduring structures. The charismatic leader is always a radical who challenges established practice by going to "the root of the matter." He dominates men by virtue of qualities inaccessible to others and incompatible with the rules of thought and action that govern everyday life. People surrender themselves to such a leader because they are carried away by a belief in the manifestations that authenticate him. They turn away from established rules and submit to the unprecedented order that the leader proclaims. In this way charismatic leadership effects an "internal" revolution of experience, in contrast to the "external" revolution that occurs when, for example, people adapt themselves to a major change in legal rules without at the same time internalizing the ideas behind it. In its "pure form" charismatic leadership involves a degree of commitment on the part of the disciples that has no parallel in the other types of domination.

Both charismatic leadership and traditional domination differ from a legal order in that they involve personal rather than impersonal rule. But the difference between charisma and tradition is more important than the similarity. The patriarchal master possesses authority because he represents the inviolable sanctity of tradition, whereas the charismatic leader dominates others because through his person a mission has become manifest, which very often revolutionizes the established order. Traditional rule is characteristically permanent, however temporary may be the power of an individual patriarchal master. Charismatic leadership, on the other hand, is the product of crisis and enthusiasm.

The contrast between the emergency character of charismatic leadership and the everyday routine of legal and traditional domination also has implications for the problem of succession. Charismatic leadership is a uniquely personal response to a crisis in human experience; those who succeed the charismatic leader therefore face the problem of preserving a personal charisma after the leader and the crisis have passed away and everyday demands have again come to the fore. Legal and traditional domination must meet the opposite dilemma; they are adapted to everyday demands and are prepared for the crisis of succession, but leadership under these routine conditions is at a premium. By speaking of charismatic *leadership* rather than authority, I follow Weber's own emphasis on the major distinctions between charisma and the more enduring types of domination.

The charismatic leader is a man who demands obedience on the basis of the mission he feels called upon to perform. His claim is valid if those whom he seeks to lead recognize his mission; and he remains their master as long as he proves himself and his mission in their eyes. Legitimacy in this case has nothing to do with choice. The leader is called by a higher power and cannot refuse, and the followers are duty-bound to obey the leader who possesses the charismatic qualification. This relationship of ruler and ruled is typically unstable, because the leader may lose his charisma—he may feel that his god has forsaken him or that his power has left him. In that case his mission may be at an end, and his followers may leave him. For the charismatic leader derives his authority solely from the demonstration of his power and from his disciples' faith in that power, whatever that power is conceived to be.

Although extraordinary and unstable by definition, charismatic leadership has an economic structure. To be sure, some charismatic leaders reject all possessions and regular income, but it is the rejection of any concern with regular sources of income, not the rejection of worldly goods as such, that is the decisive criterion. The leader who seeks to acquire possessions receives them in the form of donations, endowments or contributions when his mission is peaceful, or in the form of booty or loot when it is not. This rejection of orderly economic life is related to the rejection of worldly entanglements generally. The leader and his disciples do not have a regular occupation, and they reject their everyday familial duties. The rules of religious orders are an example: the statutes of the Jesuits prohibit the acceptance of clerical offices as well as material possessions by members of the order, and similarly St. Francis forbade his order to possess material goods. The rule of celibacy for the Roman Catholic clergy and the practical celibacy of many charismatic prophets have much the same significance. No more radical break with the world of everyday affairs is possible than this renunciation of family life, as in the admonition of Jesus: "If any man come to me and hates not his father, and mother, and wife, and children, and brethren, and sisters, yea, and his own life also, he cannot be my disciple."[4]

This rejection of everyday concerns can nevertheless give rise to a definite type of organization that is peculiarly adapted to the mission of the charismatic leader. This organization is composed of disciples, chosen for their qualifications, who constitute a charismatic aristocracy within the wider group of followers. The disciples are bound together by their common allegiance to the charismatic leader and his mission. Their material sustenance and social position do not depend upon benefices, salaries, or other kinds of compensation, or on titles or a rank hierarchy. Instead, the disciples live in a community in which they share in the use of the goods that have been donated to or appropriated by the leader, who distributes these goods without being accountable. As members of such a community the disciples may take their meals together with the leader; they may expect to be clothed or to receive gifts; and they may share in the social, political or religious esteem in which the leader himself is held. This authoritarian community originates in the charismatic appeal that stands opposed to all

[4] Luke 14:26.

regular economic activity and familial ties and thus constitutes one of the main sources of communism. Its appeal may be based on the common danger that threatens the military camp, or on the love through which world-alien disciples are drawn together. Accordingly Weber spoke of the booty communism typical of the military camp and the communism of love characteristic of the cloister.[5] But this appeal loses its force and the organization of disciples or camp followers quickly disintegrates as soon as permission is given to found families and engage in economic pursuits, i.e., as soon as charisma is exposed to everyday demands.

Everyday demands and the problem of succession. Charismatic leadership gives rise to generic problems that lead time and again to a "transformation of charisma," though it should be remembered that genuine charisma also recurs in combination with other types of domination. As a historical configuration, charismatic leadership has prevailed wherever the belief in magic is dominant. In Weber's view the tribal chieftain of early times combined all the functions of charismatic leadership: he was the patriarchal head of a household and of an extended family; he was the leader on hunting or war expeditions; he was the chief magician, rain-maker, and medicine man; and he was the judge. Three developments have occurred very frequently: the leadership functions become divided among different individuals; the power of these individuals waxes and wanes, depending upon the occurrence of emergencies that make the individual leader and his charismatic magic appear important in the eyes of the people; and every regularization of a leadership function tends to produce both institutional permanence and a decline of charisma. The last point refers to the "transformation of charisma" and the reasons for this transformation vary. External circumstances like continued war emergencies may require a standing army and the permanent kingship of the war leader. Or efforts to influence the gods may give rise to a permanent cult that transforms the charismatic prophets and magicians into, or replaces them by, an established priesthood. Changes of this

[5] He elaborated the analysis of the latter with regard to the historic role of monastic organizations, but this belongs to the discussion of "institutional charisma" in the next section of this chapter.

kind signify that the relationship among a charismatic leader, his disciples and the people is losing its "emergency character" and is assuming the character of a permanent institution.

The transformation has one very general reason generic to charismatic leadership itself. "Charisma" means magic power as a unique and hence transient attribute of an individual. The leader's disciples and the people at large want to see that power preserved for themselves and their descendants, as long as they believe in its legitimacy.[6] This interest in the "benefit and use of life," as Bacon called it, is in Weber's view the inevitable turning point of charismatic leadership. The leader's camp followers and disciples become his privileged companions and, subsequently, fief-holders, priests, state officials, officers, secretaries, editors, publishers, and others who want to live off the charismatically inspired institution or movement. The people in turn become tax- or dues-paying "subjects," whether they are members of a church or party, disciplined soldiers who are obligated to serve, or citizens who abide by the law. The charismatic message becomes variously a dogma, theory, legal regulation, or the content of an oral or written tradition. The relation between the leader and his followers—or between the successors to that relationship—loses the belief in an extraordinary power and mission and becomes founded instead upon a belief in authority sanctified by tradition.

In this process a special affinity emerges between charisma and tradition. Though in its pure form the revolutionary implications of charisma are quite incompatible with tradition, both types of domination depend upon a belief in concrete persons whose authority is regarded as sacred and to whom followers or subjects feel bound in religious reverence and duty. As tradition gains, the appeal to charisma is used no longer to oppose everyday routine with an extraordinary mes-

[6] Weber did not consider the alternative possibility, namely that the disciples and the community do *not* wish to preserve the charisma of the leader and indeed reject him as a "false prophet." Such an eventuality would be evidence in Weber's terms that the leader has lost his charisma; the people reject him because he has failed to "prove" himself, or because he has proved himself "false."

sage and power but rather as a legitimation of "acquired rights" in the possession of wealth or social position.

Such a transformation from charismatic leadership to traditional domination occurs most frequently when the *problem of succession* must be solved. In a strict sense that problem is insoluble, for charisma is an inimitable quality that some higher power is believed to have bestowed upon one person. Consequently a successor cannot be chosen at all. Instead, the followers wait in the hope that another leader will appear who will manifest his own charismatic qualification, though such a new incarnation of charisma may be ruled out by dogmatic considerations, as in the case of Christ or in the original conception of the Buddha. Where it does exist, such passive hope for a new epiphany often fails to satisfy the interest in preserving the power of charisma for the long-run benefit of all. As a result, methods are developed to find successors so that the community will be assured of the beneficent power of charisma. Weber distinguished three such methods:

(1) A new charismatic leader is designated on the basis of criteria that are thought to ensure the requisite charismatic qualities of the chosen one. (The Dalai Lama is chosen in this manner.)

(2) The original charismatic leader designates his own successor or representative, and the followers recognize this designation through acclamation. (In this way Roman magistrates designated their successors in the position of command, and the assembled army responded by acclamation.) However, if the leader does not designate his own successor and if there are no external criteria that are believed to be authentic, then:

(3) The disciples and followers of the charismatic leader are believed to be best suited to designate a qualified successor. Here again recognition by acclamation is originally required, if the people's belief in the charisma of the successor is to be preserved. This third method is not an election in the modern sense of the term, although the recognition of the ruler by the ruled shows some resemblance to it. Because the charisma of leadership is thought to exist in the person, his designation and acclamation as the successor are regarded as his rightful claim, and his "election" as the duty of the ruled. Only one man is believed to be the "right successor," and all those who

fail to designate and acclaim him—whether they are in the majority or not—thereby commit a magical offense.[7]

All three methods, of course, lead away from "charismatic leadership" in the sense of a uniquely personal mission. To select a successor in terms of criteria or rules objectifies what was originally personal. Personal designation of a successor means that the leader himself has become the source of legitimate authority, in place of the "higher power" that legitimated his own mission. Designation by the disciples transforms the meaning of "charisma" still further. But all three methods retain the one element that distinguishes "charismatic leadership" from other types of domination: the exercise of authority is bound up entirely with a concrete person and his distinctive qualities.

This relationship between rulers and ruled occurs in combination with all forms of domination. Weber repeatedly drew attention to the importance of charisma in economic life. Colonial exploitation, risky financial transactions, private financing of military ventures, and slave trade or piracy are all forms of "booty capitalism," in which the stakes are enormous and success frequently depends upon the spellbinding leadership of some individual. Such economic activities are worlds apart from the methodical management of a large-scale corporation, in which success depends upon professional competence and an everyday steadiness in the conduct of affairs that is incompatible with the indispensability of any individual and the sporadic character of very risky transactions. Again, charismatic leadership occurs in patrimonial or feudal regimes, in which authority is in the hands of an individual master to whom subjects are bound by personal loyalty and respect for tradition. Whether a war leader under these conditions commands the respect of his followers merely on account of tradition or whether, in addition, he inspires them with the peculiar magnetism of his charisma is not immediately obvious but can be ascertained only by examining the "spirit" of the relationship.

Weber placed special emphasis on the role of charismatic leadership in representative government. The choice of a suc-

[7] *Theory*, pp. 364–66, and *WuG*, Vol. II, pp. 763–65.

cessor on the basis of designation by the most powerful retainers and the confirmation of that choice through public acclamation were the beginnings of a representative system in western Europe. Once communities adopt the practice of choosing a leader rather than depending on charismatic leadership in its original sense, that choice becomes bound up with electoral rules that are legitimated by a social tradition or by legal principles. Historically, such rules have been of two kinds. As the powerful vassals or court officials or clerics assumed or were given the right of prior designation, their choice of a successor gradually became an oligarchic privilege, while the acceptance of that choice by popular acclamation receded into the background. Such oligarchic privileges developed in the Catholic Church, in the Holy Roman Empire, and in a very large number of cities in which the ruling families chose the leading officials through co-optation while reducing the status of the mayor or local potentate to that of *primus inter pares* (first among equals) and excluding community participation altogether. The other type of election has been a gradual elaboration of the principle that the highest ruler must be confirmed by public acclamation. Frequently this principle has evolved from the acclamation of a charismatic leader to the election of a new ruler by the community of the ruled. But a fully developed representative system has occurred only in Western civilization, and then only very gradually.[8]

So far I have discussed charismatic leadership as a pure or ideal type in contrast to permanent institutional structures, in terms of the reasons for its transformation, and as a recurrent element in permanent institutional structures. In all these instances the exercise of power is bound up with a concrete person and his distinctive qualities. However, in history charisma also has existed as a "depersonalized" quality, and I now turn to Weber's discussion of this aspect of the problem.

[8] See Chapter XIII, C, for a more detailed discussion of charismatic leadership under a system of legal domination.

B. FAMILIAL AND INSTITUTIONAL CHARISMA AS ASPECTS OF DOMINATION ON THE BASIS OF AUTHORITY[9]

Domination on the basis of charismatic leadership alone is highly unstable because the desire to preserve the original charisma can be "satisfied" only by its transformation. However, this amorphous wish of the charismatically led community is only one reason for transformation and not the most important one. Much more important, according to Weber, are the interests of the disciples and retainers, who wish to appropriate the leader's powers of control, determine the rules of succession and recruitment, and monopolize the economic opportunities that the leader's influence has made available.[10] The pursuit of these interests is in jeopardy as long as charisma is bound up with a concrete person, i.e., as long as it is incompatible with any type of regularization. The pursuit of these interests becomes easier, on the other hand, when the idea of charisma has been transformed into a "depersonalized" quality. In this sense, charisma may be transmitted to the members of a family or become the attribute of an office or institution regardless of the persons involved. In Weber's view one is justified in speaking of charisma in this impersonal sense, as long as

> . . . the characteristics of an extraordinary quality are preserved, which is not accessible to everyone and which in principle possesses pre-eminence as over against the endowment of those who are subject to charismatic rule. Precisely and only because [families or institutions are believed to possess extraordinary powers] can the members of such

[9] Charisma in an impersonal sense may be combined with "domination on the basis of authority," in its traditional or legal form, or with "domination on the basis of constellation of interest." In this section I discuss Weber's definitions of familial and institutional charisma and his use of these concepts in the analysis of church and state. The latter materials are taken from *WuG*, Vol. II, Chapter 11, which is entitled "State and Hierocracy" and which has not been translated.

[10] Cf. *Theory*, pp. 367–73.

families or the incumbents of offices exercise the social function of charismatic domination.[11]

Impersonal Charisma and its Implications

An impersonal charisma has been attributed to families in the belief that this extraordinary quality has been transmitted through blood ties. Thus the household community of a kinship group is regarded as immortal and magically blessed from time immemorial. Because of this magical blessing the "house" is believed to possess certain unattainable qualities that elevate it above all others, and only persons born in this community are believed to be endowed with charisma. It is in this sense that we speak of a princely house or a royal dynasty as a sequence of rulers from the same family or stock. The same idea applies to an aristocracy that derives historically from the disciples of a charismatic leader or the followers of a royal house.

As a principle of domination, familial charisma has generic problems of its own, especially in regard to succession. The belief in the charisma of a family does not make the choice of a successor unequivocal. Familial charisma may lead to wild palace intrigues and revolutions, particularly where polygamy is practiced and the wives' struggle for the future of their children is added to the ruler's interest in eliminating rival contenders. In such cases the only alternatives are to divide the realm among the descendants like any other property or to select a successor among them according to some regular procedure, such as combat among the sons or priestly oracles or public acclamation. All these methods are fraught with uncertainty, and royal power has become stabilized only where the principles of monogamy and primogeniture (inheritance by the first-born) prevailed, though even in such a case the rule of succession is jeopardized when a royal house dies out

[11] *WuG*, Vol. II, pp. 771–72. See also *Religion of India*, pp. 49–50. The last sentence is a translation of the meaning rather than the wording of Weber's text. "Depersonalized" or "impersonal" charisma is my translation of *Versachlichung des Charisma*. Depersonalization is the precondition of "routinization" or *Veralltäglichung*. This differentiation between personal and "depersonalized" charisma parallels to some extent Weber's distinction between "constellations of interests" and "orders of authority."

—like the Carolingian kings—or when the properly chosen successor proves himself too inept to rule. In any case, the whole meaning of charisma is changed in the process. From a quality that authenticates and ennobles a person through his own actions, charisma becomes an attribute of the forefathers through whose deeds a man's authority and privileges become legitimate. Thus the Roman nobility came to consist of men whose ancestors had occupied offices regarded as ennobling, and these men sought to monopolize office-holding within their own group. In the United States the reverse was true: the Puritan tradition glorified the charisma of the self-made man, while the "heir" counted for little. On the basis of his observations before World War I, however, Weber concluded that this evaluation was gradually being reversed, so that descent from the families of the founding fathers or membership in families of "old" wealth were ranked more highly in America than individual success and "new" wealth. Such attempts to increase prestige by creating a monopoly of privilege for the select few are similar to tests of ancestry or to the rejection of the newly rich as socially inferior. In this way familial charisma serves to monopolize political and economic as well as social opportunities.

The "depersonalization" of charisma also may occur through institutionalization. In this sense charisma is thought to be transmitted through a magical ceremony rather than through blood ties. The Catholic idea of "apostolic succession" is an example: the priest acquires the indelible charismatic qualification through the bishop's ceremony of consecration. By this symbolic act charisma is transmitted to the new priest, not as a person but as the new incumbent in an established office. Such institutionalization of charisma is necessarily a gradual process. Originally, the pre-eminent position of the Bishop of Rome in the Catholic Church was based on the belief that God would not permit the church of the world capital to err; hence the Roman church possessed authority despite the intellectual superiority of the Hellenistic Orient, where most of the great church fathers originated. Rome as a fountainhead of doctrine with universal jurisdiction over all local churches is a later development, and the full bureaucratization of the church is a modern phenomenon. But from the beginning it was the church as an institution that possessed charisma, not the Roman bishop as a person.

Although the idea of institutional charisma is not confined to the church, Catholic theory represents the most complete separation between the charisma of office and the worthiness of the incumbent. Through a magical act the priest acquires charismatic qualification as a functionary of the hierarchy. This depersonalization of charisma was the means whereby the organization of the church was grafted upon a world in which the belief in magic prevailed. The church as an institution could be removed from all the accidents of the personal only if the charismatic qualification of the cleric remained unquestioned, however depraved the priest himself might be.

In this way charisma loses the sense of an extraordinary personal gift that can be tested and proved, and becomes instead an impersonal capacity that in principle can be taught and learned. This, too, is the product of a long development, for originally heroic and magical capacities were regarded as inborn, and charismatic education consisted only of the appropriate selection and training of the qualified. Children who were believed to possess such qualifications were separated from their native environment and were perfected and tested through ascetic practices until, through a graduated and ceremonious reception, they were admitted to the circle of those who had proved their charisma. In all this, emphasis was placed on the evocation of qualities that the pupil was believed to possess already, not on the inculcation of specific skills, and important elements of this charismatic education remain, especially in the case of priests and soldiers. But, with the bureaucratization of the army and the church, ever increasing emphasis has been given to specialized knowledge on the assumption that such knowledge must be taught and that no one is born with it.[12]

Weber drew several contrasts between familial and institutional charisma. Familial charisma depends on kinship ties and institutional charisma on a separation from these. In the former the individual qualifies for the exercise of authority on the basis of blood relationship and in the latter on the basis

[12] Cf. pp. 138–41 above for a discussion of charismatic versus specialized education in the context of Chinese culture.

of education and investiture. For a ruling family the great problem of continuity is succession; the personal qualification of the ruler is by comparison secondary. For a ruling institution the process is reversed: the great problem of continuity is the personal qualification of its functionaries, and the problem of succession is by comparison secondary. This is related to the fact that familial charisma refers primarily to the identity of the rulers and their descendants and has little bearing on the functioning of an organization; institutional charisma, on the other hand, refers primarily to the organization and depends little on the personal identity of the ruler. In familial charisma the typical problem of deterioration is the drift of aristocratic privilege toward social snobbery and the monopolization of advantages without commensurate performance. In institutional charisma the typical problem of deterioration is the drift of functionaries and their education toward specialized performance at the expense of personal inspiration or substantive rationality. These implications of Weber's concepts suggest that each type of "impersonal charisma" possesses what the other lacks, and this complementary quality may be one reason why historically neither of these authority structures has gained full ascendancy, at least in the long run. Where the two principles have been embodied in kingship (familial charisma) and the church (institutional charisma), as in western Europe, they have almost always arrived at some compromise between their more or less conflicting claims.[13]

[13] Kingship and the church are not the only embodiments of familial and institutional charisma. Familial charisma is present in some form in all aristocracies and finds its most intensive development in the Indian caste system. Institutional charisma, on the other hand, is present to some extent in all government. The belief in the sanctity either of tradition or of the legal order has usually some affinity with religious concepts and loses this affinity only under very special conditions. Weber pointed out in this connection that the German tradition tends to endow all offices with a special halo, partly because of the very widespread view that the authority of government was ordained by God and that hence it was each man's duty to accept his place in the established order. Lutheranism has given special force to this view in Germany, whereas in the countries affected by the Puritan tradition the tendency prevails to regard all official business as in no way different from any other business. To the Puritans the ruler and his officials are sinners like every-

Weber's analysis of these compromises illustrates the use he made of his concepts, but to clarify this a recapitulation is in order. He defined charismatic domination as a relation between a leader and his followers characterized by a belief in the leader's extraordinary powers and a loose organizational structure. In their desire to preserve the benefits of charisma the disciples introduce a gradual "depersonalization." As a result charisma comes to be seen as either an attribute of blood and hence of heredity or an attribute of an institution that is transmitted through education, consecration, and appointment. Since familial charisma refers only to the succession of rulers rather than to a correlative administrative organization, Weber did not discuss it apart from the legal or traditional systems of domination.[14] Institutional charisma, on the other hand, represents a strong and enduring system of domination wherever priestly rule has developed into the organization of a church. Because this institution is believed to be endowed with

---

one else and no smarter than anyone else. Through God's inscrutable will they have been given the power to execute laws, and although anyone who is evidently damned must be removed from church office the same principle does not apply to government. One accepts the power of rulers and officials as long as they do nothing to violate conscience and the honor of God; any change of personnel would merely replace these sinners with others who are just as foolish. All this leads to the view that rulers and officials are merely cogs in a government that is necessary for certain purposes, and these holders of offices possess no charisma whatever since the institution of government itself possesses none. Thus, Puritanism typically discouraged respect for office since it vigorously opposed all idolization of mundane affairs. This opposition to the institutional charisma of government also was bound up with very specific ideas and historical conditions. The Calvinist principle that only Christ rules the church, the principle of the believer's church according to which no authority must intervene between man and God, or such expressions of asceticism as the Quaker's refusal to kneel or bow before secular authority because veneration belongs to God alone—such traditions are still reflected in the relative immunity of England against dictatorial tendencies, as well as in the American's lack of deference to formal authority. See *WuG*, Vol. II, pp. 775–76. I go into this point because it is an important link between Weber's sociology of politics and of religion. Cf. pp. 64–65 above.

[14] Because of the affinity of familial charisma to the organization of rule under traditional domination, the two are discussed together in the following chapter.

extraordinary powers it has had a lasting effect, both as a guarantor of and as a check upon the exercise of secular authority. Let us first consider Weber's analysis of church organization and then examine its relation to, and its compromises with, the exercise of secular authority.

Priests, Monks, and Kings in Western Europe

Aspects of church organization. The material interests of priests and the belief in the charisma of their vocation have often led to an organized priesthood. Wherever priests achieve autonomy, they attempt to set up an independent hierarchy with its own system of taxation and legal order, which they use to acquire and protect their collectively owned property. Priestly rule of this kind becomes a church insofar as

(1) A priesthood develops, with salaries, promotions, professional duties, and a regulated, otherworldly way of life.

(2) Its claims to domination are "universalistic," at least in the sense that household, kinship and tribal ties are destroyed, and ultimately all ethnic and national barriers as well.

(3) Religious doctrine and worship become rationalized as holy scriptures with commentaries that become the subject of a systematic education.

(4) All these elements are combined in an institutional structure.

In this process charisma becomes the attribute of an institution. The church regards itself as the trustee that has sole power over the administration of eternal blessings. In principle these blessings are offered to everyone, because the church is the sole embodiment and administrator of a charisma that resides in its own institutional structure rather than a community of persons who possess the requisite charismatic qualifications.[15] Churches in this sense have existed only in the

[15] This distinction between church and sect was first stated in Weber's essay on the Protestant sects (*Essays*, pp. 319–22) and was subsequently elaborated by Ernst Troeltsch in his *The Social Teachings of the Christian Churches* (London: George Allen & Unwin, 1931), Vol. I, p. 331 ff. This typology has since become the subject of critical appraisals and empirical investigations. See Milton Yinger, *Religion, Society and the Individual* (New York: Macmillan & Co., 1957), *passim.*

West, in Islam, in Lamaist Buddhism, in Judaism, and perhaps at one time in ancient Egypt.

This kind of priestly rule has always been a bulwark of tradition. Since the church itself embodies charisma, it is unalterably opposed to all personal religious experience that promotes man's direct relationship to God. Whoever possesses charisma and works miracles but is not properly "institutionalized" is suspect as a heretic or magician; for example, one of the four deadly sins of the Buddhist monastic order is the claim to supernatural powers. The church, on the other hand, incorporates miracles in its own ceremonies—e.g., the miracle of the sacraments—and "depersonalizes" charismatic qualifications, as in the ordination of the priest.[16] As the position of charismatic prophets and teachers declines, the church's administrative apparatus and economic substructure become adapted to the conditions of everyday operation. A hierarchy of offices with delimited authority, a regular appeals procedure, a schedule of fees for official acts, prebends,[17] disciplinary regulations, professionalization of the clergy and rationalization of doctrine all are aspects of this adaptation. Such bureaucratization is more or less inevitable once charisma is institutionalized and the "unworthiness" of the incumbent is separated from the "sacredness" of the office. But the "bureaucratized" church is then confronted with the same problem in a new form; within its organization it must incorporate the monks who reject compromises with mundane concerns and adhere strictly to the demands of the original, charismatic prophet or saint.[18]

Monasticism. Monastic orders were of special interest to Weber, because they were both a challenge and an opportunity for the church and had played an important role in its struggles with secular authority. In its genuinely charismatic phase

[16] In this connection Weber cited the Donatist controversy, in which this sect of the fourth to fifth century A.D. declared all official acts of the church invalid if they were performed by unworthy priests.

[17] That is, stipends allotted from the revenues of a cathedral or a collegiate church to a canon or member of the chapter.

[18] Not all churches have developed monastic orders, however. In Judaism the supreme virtue consists in faithful observance of the law and ascetic practices are rejected.

monasticism is typically otherworldly, as in the case of early Buddhism, with its discouragement of permanent residence and its complete rejection of all mundane ties. Monks in this sense are quite like the original charismatic disciples. However, in the course of their development the monastic orders generally undergo a process of "depersonalization" that transforms their asceticism from a means of escape into a means of extraordinary achievements. For example, through their discipline the Mormons created in the forbidding environment of Utah settlements that far exceeded what might have been accomplished by more ordinary methods. In the mountainous wastes of Tibet Lamaist monks produced economic and architectural results that in magnitude and quality equal the most famous achievements of man. The artistic creativity of Buddhist monks had far-reaching consequences for the whole Far East. Similarly, during early medieval times the cloisters of as remote an island as Ireland preserved the cultural traditions of antiquity and through their missionaries decisively influenced the whole development of the Occidental church. Many characteristic features of Western music and science were first developed by members of the Benedictine, Franciscan and Dominican orders.[19] In the economic sphere, these and other monastic communities were the first to develop rationally planned estates and commercial establishments. All these achievements were for Weber aspects of "depersonalization": as the ecstatic or contemplative union with God becomes an object of achievement for many—rather than the charismatic gift of a few—it becomes a state of grace that may be acquired through ascetic means, and these means in turn become an object of education. Though the practice of asceticism differs in the various religions, its common denominator is the achievement of complete self-control. And self-control for the greater glory of God or the attainment of union with the divine aims at the control or eradication of all drives and actions that do not serve these ends and hence to a further and further rationalization of conduct. As a community of ascetics, monks constitute

[19] Cf. Max Weber, *The Rational and Social Foundations of Music*, tr. and ed. by Don Martindale and Johannes Riedel (Carbondale: The Southern Illinois Press, 1958), for an elaboration of this point.

an elite formation of religious virtuosi in the midst of ordinary believers, and their work and organization have regularly reached their greatest effectiveness in missionary activity.

In the case of Christianity, monastic orders have been incorporated into the church in one of two ways. Since strict adherence to the Christian ideal cannot be expected of everyone, monastic asceticism is considered an accomplishment on behalf of the church by a select few who in this way accumulate a repository of blessings for the laity. Along with this interpretation goes another that regards asceticism from the viewpoint of the monk's training for missionary work on behalf of the church. This means that the monk leaves his cloister and works in the world at large, sharing in the institutionalized work of the church. Friction between monastic orders and the established priesthood is likely to occur in both of these functions, at least wherever the monks take an uncompromising stand and seek to find their way to God solely on the basis of their own charisma. The institution of lay brethren who free the monks for spiritual duties aids such efforts and further enhances the monk's distance from the ordinary priest.[20]

The church persistently endeavors to eliminate every remnant of charisma based on an individual search for salvation as well as all irrational forms of asceticism, which jeopardize the institutional charisma of regular church functionaries. Only those disciplinary and ascetic means are acceptable that serve the ends envisaged by the church.[21] Accordingly the church insists on central control over the religious orders. By prohibiting property ownership and requiring itinerant preaching, pastoral counseling, and charitable labors, the church turns monks into a "task force" by means of which it can integrate its own organizational structure and spread monastic ideals among the lay public. But by thus controlling the monastic movement,

[20] So, too, does the organization of lay members (so-called "tertiaries" living in community or in the world), who are affiliated with the monastic orders and spread the monastic ideals among the laity.

[21] This is the original meaning of the Jesuit principle that "the end justifies the means," although this principle is by no means confined to the Jesuits. In its secular application the principle is equally compatible with opportunism and idealism, but in either case it loses its original meaning, which had reference to the "means of self-control," i.e., ascetic practices.

the church itself is profoundly affected. For example, the principle of celibacy for the priesthood was adopted under monastic influence to ensure the "institutional charisma" of the church. Monasticism also affected the ideals of conduct that the church espoused.

The monk became the model of the religious person, and, as such, the first "professional" of Western civilization: his time is scheduled; he practices self-control and rejects all spontaneous enjoyment; he excludes all merely personal preoccupations that do not serve the purposes of his vocation. This orientation predestined him to serve as the principal tool of bureaucratic centralization of the church at the same time that it also provoked a century-long struggle. As confessors and teachers without local ties, the itinerant monks were frequently more popular and cheaper than the local church authorities, who often opposed the monks in an effort to retain local control against the bureaucratic centralization of the church. In the long run the church prevailed, largely by using its vanguard of organized ascetics—above all, the Jesuits—to safeguard and extend its power, especially in relation to the secular authorities.

C. THE STRUGGLE FOR POWER UNDER CHARISMATIC DOMINATION

Church and state. To safeguard and enhance the special dignity of the priest the church early demanded his immunity from secular jurisdiction and his freedom from taxation and the other public duties of the average citizen. It also demanded severe punishment of all who showed lack of respect toward him. This, added to a clerical education and a strictly regulated admissions policy, created a distinct way of life for the clergy, which in turn acquired a dominant influence upon lay education and also upon successive generations of government officials. To achieve these ends the church had impressive powers at its disposal. Believers were subject to the social and religious ostracism of excommunication and they were forbidden to deal with those whom the church had punished, which imposed an economic boycott as well.

To justify these demands and powers the church attempted to enhance its own charisma by degrading the political order ideologically. All secular power was represented as the work of Satan because it claimed a charisma of its own that was in competition with the charisma of priestly rule. Or, secular power was considered an inevitable concession to the sinfulness of the world, with which one should have as little to do as possible. On the other hand, secular power also was seen as God's tool for the control of all forces that opposed the church; hence, governments had to hold themselves in readiness to serve the ends of the church. But as a practical matter, the church needed the explicit or tacit consent of the secular authorities in order to achieve its ends, and this consent could be obtained either by subordinating these authorities or by compromising with them.

The church's endeavor to subordinate secular power was aided by one major factor. Priests had the power of legitimation, and secular rulers, whose authority depended upon familial charisma, usually desired this legitimation. In the case of royal succession any question concerning the identity or qualifications of the ruler undermined the monarchical system. Such questions arose whenever a ruler lacked personal charisma or the absence of unequivocal rules concerning the succession put his familial charisma in doubt. Hence rulers typically sought to legitimate their authority by an act of priestly consecration. The charisma of the king was then authenticated by God, i.e., by the priest who was the professional expert in all things divine. In ancient Judaism, for example, the priesthood consulted the oracle in reference to the king; the priesthood of ancient Egypt at times actually decided the royal succession; and the confirmation of Charlemagne by the Pope set a precedent for the relation between royalty and the church through many centuries of medieval history. In all these cases the church accepted the principle that legitimacy could not be denied to the person who, in accordance with sound judgment, possessed the requisite charismatic qualification. Yet the act of consecration was regarded as indispensable in making the charisma of the ruler fully effective. In some extreme cases this dependence of royal power on priestly sanction led to such an amalgamation of priesthood and kingship that the head priest personally ruled in secular affairs as well. But such theocratic solutions were relatively rare because priestly rule would not readily press its opposition to the secular authorities to the point where they were effectively undermined. All priestly rule tends to be a bulwark of tradition; hence it supports both faith in its own sacred calling and compliance with the established secular authorities.

In their relations with these authorities the priests serve a second function that favors compromises between the two powers. All secular rulers are interested in the obedience of the ruled, and priests tend to aid them in this "domestication" of the masses. Thus priests often have been used by conquerors to control the subject population. The Buddhist monks of Tibet pacified the Mongols, thereby ending their periodic invasions of the surrounding areas, which had gone on for some fifteen hundred years. Again, the Persian Empire promoted the rabbinical domination of the Jews. What was true in relation to conquered peoples was equally true of the relations between rulers and ruled within a nation. Under the rule of the Roman senate all forms of ecstasy were suppressed, partly because they were regarded as politically dangerous. Similarly, many military and mercantile notables in the ancient and medieval world sought to "cleanse" religious practices of all charismatic attributes because they feared the political consequences of a religiosity that had mass appeal. Much the same is still true of the modern world: Weber mentioned, for example, that the most radical Italian parliamentarian who opposed the church on every point still did not want to do without convent education because this aided the "domestication" of women! While such examples indicate that in the interest of their own power priests frequently help the secular authority to stamp out "dangerous" charismatic tendencies, they also suggest that governments utilize the priesthood for secular ends.

Every secular power has strong interests of its own in keeping the priesthood in a subordinate position. Since the priests have the power of legitimation, secular rulers are obviously concerned with seeing to it that this power is exercised in keeping with their own interests. Since the church demands freedom from secular jurisdiction for its functionaries and complete autonomy in its own affairs, rulers naturally want to make sure that such freedom and autonomy are not abused and so they usually demand to be given some influence in the appointment of certain church officials. Moreover, every church depends on the secular rulers for aid in the collection of church dues, for the punishment of religious dissenters, and in other ways. Such dependence has led at times to the more or less successful subordination of the priesthood by secular rulers. This may mean that the king is also the priest in the charismatic sense, or that he performs both priestly and royal functions by virtue of his office, or that as a secular ruler he also possesses the highest authority in all matters relating to the church.

In the last and most extreme of these alternatives the secular ruler exercises authority over state and church at the same time—a type of government that differs from theocracy or secular rule by a high priest. Such complete supremacy of secular over priestly power occurred in fairly typical form in ancient Greece and Rome, in the Byzantine Empire, in China and Russia, and in the "enlightened" despotism of western Europe. In all such cases church affairs are handled as a branch of government administration. Gods and saints are deities of the state whose worship is a state affair, and new gods or doctrines are accepted or rejected at the discretion of the political authorities. The priesthood is entirely subject to these authorities; it is paid by the government and hence lacks economic autonomy. The apparatus of functionaries on which it depends also is furnished by the government, and its ceremonial and other official acts are regulated by the state. There is no clerical way of life, no specific education for the priesthood, no theology properly so called, and consequently no way in which the priests can give direction to the conduct of the laity independently. All these tendencies are further accentuated if the ruling aristocracy transforms the prominent positions of the priesthood into a hereditary property of individual families that can be used as a source of prestige and power. In that case the minor priestly positions become benefices after the manner of positions at the royal court, endowments turn monasteries into institutions for the proper maintenance of unmarried daughters and younger sons, and the performance of the traditional religious ritual becomes the conventional ceremony of a status group. Under these conditions the spirit of a religion becomes a mere technique for ritually influencing the higher powers.

Conditions of compromise between priestly and secular rule. Weber noted that frequent attempts have been made to establish the pre-eminence of either state or church but that they rarely have been completely successful. Every political order retains some remnant of a magical derivation; even rulers who subordinate the priesthood in all other respects usually will not interfere with doctrine or ritual. On the other hand, the priesthood also depends upon the support of these authorities. Weber therefore concluded that, despite their inherent antagonism, the two forces have usually arrived at some kind of compromise, either tacitly or through a written concordat. Indeed, many age-old ties between secular and priestly power originated in the coincidence between local cults and the extent of a political territory. The god or saint of a city was the indispensable patron of any local political organization. Hence the development of great states was accompanied by the juxtaposition of gods and saints from affiliated or conquered cities. Sacred relics were transported from the cathedrals of provincial towns to Moscow at the time when the Muscovite state was established. The "tolerance" of the old Roman state had a similar character—the religious cults of all affiliated states were accepted, although under the Empire every religious creed except Judaism had in turn to accept the cult of the emperor. The triumph of a country's god gives final confirmation to the triumph of its ruler and also is the token of a people's political subordination. The subjects of the ruler, on the other hand, constitute a ready-made field of missionary activity for an independent priesthood.

Though compromises between secular and priestly power are the rule rather than the exception, they are rarely equitable. Usually one or the other power prevails, in part because of the position that different creeds take regarding the relation between church and state. Some religions—Lutheranism and Islam, for example—reject or neglect a separate church organization. In Luther's case his personal religiosity led to a complete indifference toward the organization of the church, if only the purity of the Biblical message was ensured. Hence the Lutheran Church has been an easy victim of dictatorial rule. A somewhat similar subordination occurred in Islam, which was tied from the beginning to the expansionist drive of the Arabs and consequently espoused the idea of forceful subjugation of infidels. This initial constellation so increased the secular power of the caliph that the Mohammedan priests could not seriously attempt to subordinate his rule.[22] On the other hand, Catholicism and Calvinism clearly favor a separate church organization. The Catholic Church possesses an independent organization buttressed by the Roman tradition and divinely ordained in the eyes of the believers. Though compromises have been inevitable from time to time, the Church has been successful in resisting secular dictatorial tendencies in the long run. Calvinism bases its church constitution on the presbyterian principle—rule by elders—but it has been able to preserve its independence from the secular power only in some local areas, such as Geneva, New England, and the Netherlands.

Another important determinant of the struggle between secular and priestly rule, according to Weber, is the power constellation among competing status groups. In his view, general statements are possible only with reference to the relations between priesthood and "bourgeoisie" on the one hand and priesthood and the feudal powers on the other. Even then the statement is complex. Evidence for the affinity between the bourgeoisie and the priesthood is fairly ample. In medieval Italy the bourgeois strata of the Guelphs provided the troops that protected the church against encroachments by feudal powers. Comparable conditions are mentioned in the earliest Mesopotamian inscriptions. In ancient Greece, bourgeois strata supported the religion of Dionysus while the aristocratic strata rejected it. The early Christian Church was a typically urban institution. Middle-class groups are prominent in Thomas Aquinas' conception of the Church, with its degrading classification of the peasants. Also, the Puritan priesthood as well as almost all earlier medieval and ancient sectarian movements were based in urban areas, as were the most violent advocates of papal rule. The aristocracy, on the other hand,

[22] Even the Shiite sect does not seriously challenge the preeminent position of the shah, although it originated in the rejection of the legitimacy of the caliph.

tended to oppose religion. Weber cited the case of the ancient Greek aristocracy whose quite derogatory treatment of the gods—as reflected in the Homeric epics—strongly influenced the development of Hellenic religion. The feudal aristocracy of the early Middle Ages and the Cavaliers who supported King Charles I against the Puritans showed a comparable disregard, not so much for religion as such but for the intense piety characteristic of middle-class groups. Even the Crusades do not disprove this point, in Weber's judgment, since they were in good part an undertaking of the French aristocracy, which sought to provide benefices for its descendants—a desire to which Pope Urban II appealed quite explicitly.

Weber saw the affinity between priesthood and bourgeoisie as the result of specific historical constellations. In the initial, enthusiastic phase religious movements appeal to all strata of the population, including the aristocracy. As they become routinized a differentiation of allegiance sets in, and the similar orientation of the bourgeoisie and the priesthood comes to the fore. Within Western civilization Weber attributed this tendency to the inherent rationalism of commercial and industrial as contrasted with agricultural pursuits, so that merchants and craftsmen responded more readily than peasants and feudal lords to the ethical rationalism of the church.[23] This affinity did not preclude conflicts, of course, but it meant that the church found support among urban strata in its endeavor to retain and enhance its autonomy against royal and feudal encroachments. On the other hand, the landed aristocracy of medieval Europe sought to curb church autonomy by turning bishops into feudal lords through grants of land and political rights and by ceding benefices to priests so as to make them into patrimonial officials. Under these conditions the church could maintain its independence only on the basis of the monasteries, which also depended on land but were organized through an ascetic renunciation of property and family and therefore constituted a highly disciplined protective guard. Thus organizations based on a belief in charisma exerted a major influence on the development of civilization, but that influence depended upon the ascetic exclusion of everyday

[23] Cf. the earlier discussion of bourgeois and aristocratic strata in terms of their contrasting life orientations on pp. 92–96.

life. In the strict sense even an impersonal, institutionalized charisma remained extraordinary, but as such it provided a strong bulwark for the maintenance of traditional domination. I shall turn to a consideration of this second type after a brief consideration of some implications of the foregoing analysis.

D. THEORETICAL IMPLICATIONS

Before concluding this presentation of Weber's analysis of charismatic domination it is useful to consider the sequence of his discussion. It begins by focusing attention on a basic relationship between ruler and ruled: the charismatic prophet or war leader and his disciples or followers. In a major portion of his lifework Weber was concerned with various historical manifestations of charisma. His sociology of religion is devoted to the age of religious creativity in the first millennium before Christ, especially to the different types of charismatic prophecy in ancient Judaism. His sociology of law examines the role of charismatic oracle-givers and law prophets. Weber did not discuss charismatic leadership in war to the same extent, but he apparently envisaged this as another important field of study. The formulation of the concept of "charisma" as an archetype in his political sociology is thus based on extensive comparative investigations.[24]

In his analysis of domination Weber put this comparative evidence to one side and began instead with the concept of "charisma." I emphasize this point because this procedure, which starts with an ahistorical concept and then discusses the depersonalization of charisma, tends to give the impression of a unilinear devolution or deterioration. This impression results from an artifact of exposition. It would be strange if a

[24] Weber repeatedly referred to the analysis of charismatic leadership and organization in the early Christian Church by Rudolph Sohm, *Kirchenrecht* (Part VIII of "Bindings Systematisches Handbuch der Deutschen Rechtswissenschaft" [Munich: Duncker & Humblot, 1923]), Vol. I, pp. 26–28, and Vol. II, pp. 178–82, 226–41. Sohm's analysis of a specific historical configuration, together with his own comparative analysis of religious leadership, provided the basis on which the generic concept of "charisma" was formulated.

scholar who subjected the idea of progress to a sophisticated critique forgot his own strictures by adopting the view that history consists of the routinization of genuine charisma, for that view only reverses the theory of progress he has rejected.[25]

It is certainly more to the point to suggest that in Weber's view history alternates between the charisma of the great man and the routinization of bureaucracy.[26] Weber clearly believed that the "decline of charisma" is a major historical tendency.

> It is the fate of charisma, whenever it comes into the permanent institutions of a community, to give way to powers of tradition and of rational socialization. This waning of charisma generally indicates the diminishing importance of individual action . . .[27]

and, it may be added, the increasing importance of status and office. On the other hand, Weber made it clear that charisma has been a recurrent phenomenon because persons endowed with this gift of grace—for better or worse—have asserted their leadership under all historical conditions. We have, therefore, two apparently paradoxical assertions, namely, that charismatic leadership gives way to routinization and that it represents an ever recurrent phenomenon. It may be plausible to resolve this paradox by imputing to Weber a "pendulum" theory of history such as that suggested above, but I doubt that this is in accord with his intention or does justice to the subtlety of his approach.

The point is that Weber was not interested in developmental theories but used this double perspective as a guide to empirical research. For example, he assessed the "decline of charisma" very differently, depending upon the specific case. In the case of the early Christian communities he was convinced that their later institutionalization in the Church impaired major cultural values. He applied much the same judgment to the transition from Jewish prophecy to the rabbinically controlled Jewish communities in ancient Palestine. Yet he made

[25] Cf. *Methodology*, p. 28 ff.
[26] This is an interpretation suggested by H. H. Gerth and C. Wright Mills in their introduction to *Essays*, pp. 51–55.
[27] *Essays*, p. 253.

it clear that in the field of government the prevalence of charismatic leadership is an attribute of chieftainship in primitive tribes, which as such is bound to decline with the development of permanent institutional structures.[28] This "decline of charisma" is less the statement of a trend than the explication of a term. Charisma as a dominant pattern is incompatible with permanent institutions by definition, but this did not prevent Weber from analyzing the charismatic leadership of kings or party leaders in the context of permanent institutions. It is therefore mistaken to assume that charisma and bureaucracy are mutually incompatible—that the charismatic prophet, for example, is the religious innovator who opposes magic and priestly routinization while the priests are responsible for the institutionalization and the spiritual decline of the prophetic message. This view neglects the fact that, according to Weber, no prophet can completely extricate himself from the involvement with magical acts by which he "proves" his mission, while the priests for their part cannot permit institutionalization to undermine their charismatic mission without losing their authority over the laity. These examples suggest that for Weber charisma and its routinization were omnipresent possibilities in all phases of history and had to be examined anew in each case.

The test of this interpretation is contained in Weber's sociology of law. In that study he showed in detail, albeit by implication, that he did not identify all positive and dynamic historical forces with "charisma" and all negative and retrogressive forces with "routinization."[29] Specifically, he discussed decision-making through charismatic revelation in the earliest forms of legal procedure, and he showed how these charismatic practices were gradually superseded by other forms, indicating a "decline of charisma." Yet this decline was concomitant with the creation of *new* legal norms, so that in this case innovating activity was associated with the process of routinization rather than with charismatic leadership. Indeed, Weber regarded the development of legal rationality as a major factor in the emerging distinctiveness of Western civi-

[28] Cf. *WuG*, Vol. II, pp. 770–71.
[29] See Chapter XII, B, for a more detailed consideration of the sociology of law.

lization. Accordingly, he did not subscribe to a theory of history that sees history's dynamic element in the charismatic "break-throughs" of great men and its stable element in the "decline of charisma" through routinization.[30]

[30] Thus I do not agree with the interpretation of Gerth and Mills, *op. cit.*, where Weber's approach is related to the "great man theory of history," following such earlier writers as Carlyle, Lecky, and others.

CHAPTER XI

TRADITIONAL DOMINATION

All forms of domination occurring in history constitute, according to Weber, "combinations, mixtures, adaptations, or modifications" of the charismatic, the traditional, and the legal type.[1] In each case his analysis begins with the "pure" type. For example, charismatic leadership is a basic relationship between ruler and ruled which is formulated in so abstract a manner that examples of it may be found in *all* historical contexts. In each case the type is considered on three levels: the beliefs in legitimacy that sustain the system of domination, the organization that enables it to function, and the recurrent issues that characterize the struggle for power. On the third level the typological perspective is combined with the historical. Thus, in contrast with charismatic leadership in its pristine form, familial and institutional charisma *cannot* occur under all historical conditions. To illustrate: familial charisma plays a role in kingship and in the Indian caste system, but it may be absent from legal domination; institutional charisma is a

[1] See *Law*, pp. 336–37, and the posthumously published essay "Die drei reinen Typen der legitimen Herrschaft," reprinted in *Staatssoziologie*, pp. 99–110. This essay contains a summary of Weber's three ideal types. An English translation by H. H. Gerth has been published in *Berkeley Publications in Society and Institutions* (1958).

significant element in all church organizations, but it is absent from any priesthood that fails to develop a church organization. In other words, these concepts are less general than charismatic leadership but more general than any one historical configuration. They also represent mixtures of the "pure" types: familial charisma is a mixture of charismatic and traditional elements, and institutional charisma is a mixture of charismatic and legal elements. In Weber's view it is still another task to analyze the mixture of these elements in a given instance.

I turn now to Weber's analysis of traditional domination.

A. PATRIARCHS AND THEIR HOUSEHOLDS

Weber used the term "patriarchalism"—generically the authority of a master over his household—to designate the pure type of traditional domination.[2] The solidarity of the household arises from the fact that its members share lodging, food, and the use of tools, and that they live together in close personal proximity and mutual dependence. The personal authority of the master rests on the physical and mental dependence of women, the helplessness of young children, the habituation and education of adult children, and the servant's acceptance of patriarchal power from childhood on as well as his need for protection. Filial respect for the head of the family clearly differs from the contractual obligations of a subordinate in a legally constituted enterprise or the faith of a disciple in the personal mission of a prophet.

Within the household authority is the private prerogative of the master, who has been designated in accordance with definite rules of inheritance. He has no administrative staff and no machinery to enforce his will but depends on the willingness

[2] This "pure" type is discussed in *Theory*, p. 346; *WuG*, Vol. II, pp. 680–81; and *Staatssoziologie*, pp. 101–2. Weber's concept of patriarchalism was based on a prior consideration of the household in its relation to the neighborhood and the wider community, and of the structure of kinship in its relations to the economic and military organization of the community. These materials are discussed in *WuG*, Vol. I, pp. 194–215, but have been omitted from the present volume. No translation is available.

of the group members to respect his authority, which he exercises on behalf of the group as a whole. The members of the household stand in an entirely personal relation to him. They obey him and he commands them in the belief that his right and their duty are part of an inviolable order that has the sanctity of immemorial tradition. Originally the efficacy of this belief depended on the fear of magical evils that would befall the innovator and the community that condoned a breach of custom. This was gradually superseded by the idea that the deities had originated the traditional norms and acted as their guardians. Even under conditions of secularization such beliefs are still implicit in the unwitting acceptance of usage. In this way filial piety for the person of the master is combined with reverence for the sanctity of tradition, and while the first element greatly enhances the power of the master, the second tends to keep it within bounds.[3]

This double emphasis on the arbitrary power of the master and the limitation of that power by sacred tradition is a basic characteristic of traditional domination in all its forms.

The content of commands is bound up with, and limited by, tradition. A master who violated tradition without let or hindrance would thereby endanger the legitimacy of his own authority which is based entirely on the sanctity of that tradition. As a matter of principle it is out of the question to create new laws which deviate from the traditional norms. However, new rights are created in fact, but only by way of "recognizing" them as having been valid "from time immemorial." Outside the norms of tradition the will of the master is limited only by considerations of equity in the individual case, and this is a highly elastic limitation. Thus his

[3] Within the patriarchal household there are gradations among the personal dependents, though in principle these result from the master's arbitrary will. Paternal power and filial piety do not necessarily depend upon kinship; rather, the master treats the members of his household as a species of property, and he may deal with them in terms of his regard for their value. This is reflected in the patriarchal view that all children of female members of the household belong to the master, regardless of paternity, much as the young of his domestic animals are his property. Accordingly, the master may elevate or reduce the position of any dependent and the resulting status differences may be very great.

domination is divided into a sphere which is strictly bound by tradition and another in which his arbitrary will prevails. . . .[4]

This legitimation of traditional domination occurs wherever the "authorities" claim obedience on the basis of established usage, and some authorities do this at least some of the time in every historical constellation. In contrast to charismatic leadership, traditional domination is as routine as the father's authority over his household, after which it is modeled.[5]

Problems of organization come to the fore as soon as a patriarchal master enlarges his property and thus increases the task of managing it. Under these conditions the master usually sets up his personal dependents and their families on individual holdings, in their own lodgings, and with their own animals and utensils, though in principle all these possessions remain his personal property. Personal subjection and filial piety remain intact, the master's will prevails, and custom obliges the dependents to aid him with all the means at their disposal. In extraordinary cases this duty becomes unlimited, as when ransom must be paid to free the master from debts or imprisonment, or when a dowry must be provided for his daughters, or in time of war. Even where the ordinary services and fees of the dependents are limited by tradition, the master is entitled to make arbitrary and unilateral demands whenever it suits his whims or interests, because the traditional limits upon such demands are ill defined. The master obviously has a major interest in keeping these limits vague, even where he seeks to observe them, for once he adopts a formal regulation he may be forced to observe his own rules, especially when circumstances increase his dependence on the good will of his subordinates.[6]

[4] *Staatssoziologie,* p. 101.

[5] Hence it need not undergo a complete transformation in order to become compatible with specific and stable historical patterns. To repeat: for charisma to become compatible with everyday affairs it must undergo a process of depersonalization. In the case of traditional authority the patriarchal principle of legitimation need merely be extended beyond the household.

[6] The mere existence of such official regulations—like the medieval court ordinances or the statutes regulating the royal domains

The formal stipulation of traditional obligations is only one of many factors that can weaken the integrity of patriarchal authority. However powerful a master is, he must nevertheless see to it that his dependents' ability to render services, as well as their willingness to do so, is preserved. In this sense he "owes" something to his dependents, namely, humane treatment and a limit upon exploitation. This curtailment of his power is compatible with his interests wherever there prevails a subsistence economy, in which the master's way of life differs from that of his dependents only in degree. Moreover, the master requires his dependents' help in times of need so that the security of his position as well as the bounty of his yields always rest in some measure upon the good will of those who are personally subordinate to him. That good will is ensured as long as the master keeps his demands for services, fees, gifts and so on within the limits established by tradition. Even though these "limits" do not preclude personal arbitrariness, the master must consider the religious and social dangers that arise when too frequent and unmotivated an interference with established rights and duties jeopardizes the feeling of obligation among his dependents. Finally, the master is likely to have in mind that his absolute power over the individual dependent stands side by side with his impotence against his dependents as a collectivity. Accordingly, his absolute power may be countered by his dependents' demands for a reciprocity of obligations and the result may be a distribution of rights and duties, even though tradition fully endorses the master's arbitrary use of his power.

The problems of an extended patriarchal household are naturally multiplied at the level of government over large territories. Here the exercise of traditional domination requires an administrative staff that will show the same combination of traditionalism and personal arbitrariness as the ruler himself.

---

under the Emperor Hadrian—tends to transform a master's personal dependents, who to some extent share his interests, into his contractual partners, who can develop an awareness of their own interests and hence an inclination to advance these interests collectively against the master. It may be recalled that Weber analyzed this process in his study of agricultural labor on the *Junker* estates of eastern Germany.

Weber discussed the problems of extended patriarchal rule under the heading "patrimonialism."

B.   PATRIMONIALISM[7]

Government as the Ruler's Private Domain

Patriarchal authority has been adapted to the imperatives of large political communities in the great despotic regimes of Asia and in many ancient and medieval regimes of the West. A principal purpose of this adaptation has been to provide for the needs of the ruler's personal household, though that "household" might grow to gargantuan proportions.[8] The food, clothing and armaments needed by the ruler are apportioned among the districts of the realm, while the court is maintained by the subjects of the district in which the ruler resides for the time being. To ensure the regularity of these provisions, patrimonial rulers often seek to control their political subjects as much as they control their personal dependents, that is, the rulers exercise authority as an aspect of their personal property, similar in all respects to their patriarchal control over their household.

Patrimonialism means, first of all, that the governmental offices originate in the household administration of the ruler. All political transactions that do not involve the household directly are nevertheless amalgamated with the corresponding function of the court. For example, the supervision of cavalry is put in the hands of the "marshal," who supervises the stables of the royal court.[9] Hence, government administrators are

[7] The remainder of this chapter will reproduce the salient points of two chapters called "Patrimonialism" and "Effects of Patriarchalism and of Feudalism." Cf. *WuG*, Vol. II, pp. 679–752. These chapters have not been translated. Weber's later conceptual summary of these materials is available in English in *Theory*, pp. 341–58, 373–81.

[8] This tie between the royal household and government administration is vividly portrayed in the diatribes of the Old Testament prophets against the court of King Solomon. See pp. 238–39 above.

[9] Weber listed several such offices by their German names, which reveal the early identity of governmental and court administration.

originally personal servants and personal representatives of the ruler. As such they are recruited among the dependents—slaves, serfs, and others—on whose obedience the ruler can rely. Patrimonial servants of this kind are maintained as members of the household; once they have attained some rank, they eat at the table of the ruler—an important symbol of prestige that patrimonial officials retained long after the privilege had ceased to have any economic significance. In principle, the ruler is in a position to withdraw such privileges at will, in the same way that the patriarchal master might penalize a member of his household.

A second extension of patriarchal authority lies in the economic sphere. In Weber's view, patrimonialism is compatible with many different economic structures, but the development of strongly centralized patrimonial rule is often dependent upon trade, in which the ruler engages as his personal prerogative. He also utilizes the trading of others through the imposition of duties, fees for safe conduct, market concessions, grants of monopoly, foundation of cities, and related devices.[10] Thus the ruler maintains his extended household and his military personnel on the proceeds from his own trade and from his exploitation of others' trade. His special position with regard to landownership is often the result rather than the cause of the political domination whereby he can exploit available economic opportunities.

But patrimonial government on the basis of a ruler's personal resources and household management usually cannot cope with the problems that arise when large extrapatrimonial territories become subject to his rule. In that case it becomes imperative to organize an administrative staff and a military force that ensure the performance of public duties on which the regime depends. This task is complicated by the fact that the political subjects of a patrimonial ruler are free within

The same topic has since been treated in the work of Thomas F. Tout, *Chapters in the Administrative History of Medieval England* (London: Longmans, Green & Co., 1920–33), 6 vols.

[10] Cf. *WuG*, Vol. II, pp. 739–40. Weber added that patrimonial regimes that show little development of trade are relatively rare and often are the result of conquests in which tribes invade territories with a highly developed money economy and exploit the riches of these territories to the detriment of trade.

limits to dispose of their personal property, including land. They have the right to inheritance and to marriage without the consent of the ruler, and in cases of dispute their rights and duties may be determined by independent courts, not by officials of the royal household. Political subjects may have the right to own and bear arms, and their public duties are subject to traditional restrictions, unlike the duties of the patrimonial dependents.[11]

Again, the distinction is not hard and fast. With the extension and decentralization of a patrimonial regime, the duties of the personal dependents may become attenuated as their actual independence from the master's control increases. And, conversely, in the case of political subjects their rights diminish and their duties increase as their physical and political dependence upon the ruler is enhanced by circumstances or as the ruler increases his reliance on force and diminishes his adherence to tradition. Though it may be difficult in a given case to distinguish between the personal obedience of a dependent and the public duties of a political subject, it is clear that the extension of patrimonial rule tends to remove the dependent *and* the political subject from the direct control of the ruler. The extension of that rule, which leads to such a decentralization of authority, frequently goes together with an increased need for revenue in money and in kind. Also, an undeveloped transportation technology and a relative scarcity of administrative personnel further complicate the exercise of authority. It follows that in large patrimonial states administrative regula-

11 Thus, in England the duty to aid in the building of fortresses, roads and bridges and the obligation to render military service were imposed on the property of the free subject, not on him personally as in the case of patrimonial dependents invested with land. In southern and western Germany until the eighteenth century a legal distinction was made between the public duties of a political subject, which were under the jurisdiction of the courts, and the service obligations that arose from a condition of servitude. Weber added that patrimonial regimes tend to make their assessments of public duties on property, especially real estate, shops, and trading establishments, rather than in the form of a personal liability. This is the case, at any rate, where the assessed property can be bought and sold. It is in this sense that freedom of the market is a major prerequisite of civic freedom.

tion from the center is only intermittently effective and is a last resort rather than the routine basis of government.

In order to counteract this tendency toward decentralization, patrimonial rulers frequently resort to the organization of associations that are held collectively responsible for the performance of public duties. This method is closely related to the ancient responsibility of the kinship group for the crimes or obedience of its individual members. In Anglo-Saxon England, for example, kinship groups were held responsible by the ruler for the obedience of their members. In addition, all village residents were collectively liable for the political and economic obligations of each. The peasant's residence in his village was compulsory and hereditary, and from this followed both the right of the individual peasant to a share of the land and his duty to help produce a yield that could maintain the village and enable it to meet its obligations to the ruler.

Patrimonial rulers have used the same method of a hereditary subjection on a much broader basis. For example, guilds and other occupational associations are held jointly responsible for the services or contributions of their members. As a rule such impositions are accompanied by granting the members the exclusive right to engage in their branch of production and by making membership in the association obligatory for the individual and his heirs. In this way the ruler grants privileges in exchange for the duties he imposes. Such compulsory associations for meeting the economic needs of government are a frequent correlate of patrimonialism, though they are not confined to this type of domination.

"Liturgical"[12] methods of public finance are compatible with quite divergent historical conditions, though they are aided by the view that political subjects exist for the sake of the ruler and the satisfaction of his needs. Thus, in the Orient,

[12] Weber distinguished between states whose needs are met through taxation and states whose needs are met by payments in kind—whether these consist of services or products. He called the latter method "liturgical," after the liturgies of the ancient city-states in which "certain groups of the population were charged with the burden of providing and maintaining naval vessels or of providing for the public performances of the theatre." Cf. editor's footnote in *Law*, p. 163. A more complete classification of methods of public finance is contained in *Theory*, pp. 310–15.

in ancient Egypt, in the late Roman and the Byzantine empires, and elsewhere, political subjects were in fact personal dependents of the patrimonial ruler, hereditarily bound to the soil or the occupation, as well as liable for the required services or assessments to a compulsory association and, through it, to the ruler. Consequently they were exposed to the arbitrary demands of the ruler, which were limited only by his interest in preserving the productive capacity of his subjects.

Ancient Egypt was probably the most consistent example of patrimonialism. The mass of the Egyptian population was entirely dependent upon the coordinated control of the waterways in a country geographically dominated by one main river. This dependence and the ease of travel on the waterways facilitated the central political control of the people. Moreover, the lengthy period during which men were free from work in the fields meant that the population could be extensively employed in forced-labor projects. Those political subjects who were not recruited as forced laborers, as well as all landed property and all craft enterprises, were liable to tax payments that were exacted by all manner of coercion. Although the individual appears to have possessed certain rights, such as the right to choose his occupation, these rights were very precarious. As soon as the royal household required it, the individual had to be present in the locality to which he belonged and in which he had to perform his public duties. Thus the whole country and its government were constituted as one vast patriarchal household of the pharaoh, especially after foreign conquests had destroyed the previously existing private landholdings of families of notables.[13]

The power of the pharaoh and the functioning of his "household" depended entirely upon the army and the officialdom, which were centrally controlled. In times of war the army was equipped and maintained out of the royal storehouses; mercenary soldiers were remunerated from the royal treasury. In times of peace soldiers were rewarded with land grants and probably also performed police functions. Such benefices as well as allowances in kind also were the reward for administra-

[13] Weber referred in this context to the parallel effect of Mongol rule in Russia, which also led to the subordination of the landed nobility under the Muscovite rulers.

tive services. Originally Egyptian officialdom appears to have been recruited from the personal dependents of the king, though later on officials also were recruited among the scribes. In return for their services some officials—and also priests as functionaries of a temple—were granted enormous landed properties, but even this did not lead to a decentralization of patrimonial rule. Weber concluded that

> the chances for advancement and the dependence upon the royal storehouses were apparently sufficient to prevent the extensive appropriation of benefices by the officials, which is technically easier in any case where the benefices involve fees or land, rather than allowances in kind (as they did predominantly in Egypt). The numerous grants of immunity show by their wording (repeated promises of the inviolability of these grants and repeated threats of punishment against officials who will violate them) that on the basis of his patrimonial power the ruler could treat these privileges as precarious, so that the beginnings of a state based on estates are entirely lacking and patriarchalism remained intact. The extensive use of allowances in kind, together with the marked decline in the New Empire of families of notables who possessed private lands, had the effect of maintaining a patrimonial officialdom.[14]

Though the Egyptian case is a striking example of despotism, Weber pointed out that comparable methods of government have been applied in western Europe. The collective liability of associations for the performance of public duties by the individual existed in England, for example. Similar also was the English frankpledge, a compulsory and collective responsibility of neighbors for the proper moral and political conduct of each of them, just as in Japan and China neighbors were organized and registered in groups of five or ten for the same purpose. After the Norman Conquest of England, the principle of compulsory liturgical associations was very widely applied. But in this case such associations were the starting point of developments that resulted in a high degree of local self-government. The distribution of obligations among the members of the association became a matter of autonomous,

[14] *WuG*, Vol. II, p. 707.

internal regulation. Certain public duties that could be performed only by the propertied and influential members of such associations developed into acknowledged rights that were the monopoly of a status group of notables. The liturgical method of public finance resulted in a system of traditionally limited assessments against property and a local administration of notables who were largely independent of the ruler.

The method of imposing a collective responsibility for the performance of public duties is, therefore, a response to the administrative problems of a regime that does not possess a coercive apparatus extensive enough to enforce the personal liability of the political subjects but instead assigns the power of enforcement to compulsory liturgical associations. Such associations are part of the mixture of traditionalism and arbitrariness that characterizes patrimonial regimes. The degree to which one or the other tendency prevails under patrimonialism depends on the military forces and the administrative apparatus at the disposal of the ruler.

> By the use of these instruments of force the ruler tends to broaden the range of his arbitrary power which is free of traditional restrictions and to put himself in a position to grant grace and favours at the expense of the traditional limitations typical of patriarchal structures. Where authority is primarily oriented to tradition but in its exercise makes the claim of full personal powers, it will be called "patrimonial" authority. Where patrimonial authority lays primary stress on the sphere of arbitrary will free of traditional limitations, it will be called "Sultanism." . . . Both are distinguished from primary patriarchalism by the presence of a personal administrative staff.[15]

These alternatives of a more traditional or a more despotic variant of patrimonialism depend largely upon whether the soldiers and the officials of the ruler are completely dependent upon his bounty and his will or are in a position to oppose arbitrary authority in their own interest.

[15] *Theory,* p. 347.

The Instruments of Patrimonial Rule

The personal entourage of a patrimonial ruler obeys him out of a regard for his traditional status. This belief can be used by a ruler to extend his power over territories and people outside his immediate domain, even though these people may not believe in his legitimacy. In this way patrimonial authority over military forces and an administrative corps that are personally loyal to the ruler may be used to create a sultanistic regime.

Military forces. Weber analyzed this transformation of traditional domination with special attention to the social organization of the military force that enables a patrimonial ruler to extend his power "free of traditional restraint." He distinguished between five types of military organization that may be characterized briefly:

a. A military force may consist of slaves, peons, serfs, *coloni,* and other personal subordinates, to whom the ruler has assigned land and utensils in return for services or payments in kind. Thus the pharaohs of Egypt, the Mesopotamian kings and the great patrimonial landlords of ancient and medieval times, used their *coloni* as a personally owned bodyguard or military force. In the Orient much the same practice occurred with the serfs, who were branded like cattle to identify them as the property of their master. But where these dependents were settled on the land, they became unsuitable as recruits for a permanent military force at the instant disposal of the master because their agricultural work made them unavailable and their loyalty was more easily jeopardized. Consequently patrimonial rulers sought to organize a military force whose interest was identical with their own.

b. Such a force could be composed of slaves who were entirely divorced from agriculture. The Islamic empires under the caliphate illustrate two organizational patterns that may arise on this basis. Under the Abbasside dynasty, which ruled at Baghdad until the middle of the thirteenth century, Turkish slaves were purchased and given military training. As aliens and slaves they were entirely dependent upon the

Abbasside rulers and constituted a disciplined force at their disposal. From the thirteenth to the sixteenth centuries a very different development occurred in the case of the Mamelukes, a military class originally composed of Turkish and Egyptian slaves. Although the members of these troops remained slaves, especially in Egypt, they gradually increased their independence, partly because membership in the troop became hereditary and partly because they were given land in lieu of military pay, first as security and later as property. Eventually the officers of the Mamelukes succeeded in dominating the nominal rulers, while the leaders of the slaves-turned-landowners controlled the civil administration.[16] The point of these examples is that a military force composed of slaves requires considerable liquid assets on the part of the ruler, since in the long run the good will of such a force depends upon adequate subsistence and regular pay. On the other hand, this type of patrimonial regime develops in the direction of feudalism once the pay of the troops becomes based on the taxes derived from the land and finally on the income that the soldiers obtain as landlords. In the latter case the troops are in a position to exploit the population, whose resources and taxpaying capacity are under direct military control.[17]

[16] The influence of this class was finally destroyed in 1811 through a slaughter instigated by Mohammed Ali.

[17] This development of independence on the part of a patrimonial military force provoked countermeasures wherever the ruler found himself in a favorable position. The purpose of these measures was generally to limit the independence of the troops on the one hand but to reward them sufficiently, on the other, so that their loyalty was ensured. In this respect Weber cited the case of the Ottoman dynasty, which organized the professional army of the Janizaries after the middle of the fourteenth century. These forces made possible the great military conquests in Europe, and their case is of special interest because of the manner in which they were organized. The Ottoman rulers decreed the conscription of boys, aged ten to fifteen, among such subject peoples as the Bulgars, Bedouins, and Greeks. These boys from alien tribes were drilled and instructed in Islam, though without forced conversion, and after five years they were enrolled in the army. The original rules stipulated that they remain single and live an ascetic life under the supervision of a religious order; they were housed in barracks and forbidden to engage in trade. However, the incentives were commensurate with

c. A third and widespread practice of patrimonial rule is the recruitment of mercenaries. It is usually adopted when the ruler has a regular income from trade, production, or the imposition of taxes. This presupposes the development of a monetary economy, which tends to increase the chances of military despots who base their power on mercenary armies. Such armies are especially dependable when they are composed of aliens who have no real contacts with the subject population. From the time of King David, who employed Philistines and Cretans, to the Swiss troops of the Bourbon kings, patrimonial rulers have used aliens as recruits for their bodyguards.

d. A patrimonial ruler may also base his domination on troops composed of persons to whom he has granted land solely in return for their military service. Again, such persons are most reliable if they are aliens and hence entirely dependent upon the domination of the ruler. (This variant is, of course, closely related to feudalism; it remains distinctive only as long as these personal troops are of low social origin.) But the alien derivation of such recruits is not an indispensable condition of their reliability.

e. A patrimonial ruler may also recruit his personal military force among his own subjects. In that case he will usually adopt certain measures to protect his interests. He will exempt the privileged strata from recruitment in the standing army, or he will allow their members to purchase their release from this obligation. He will recruit his force, therefore, among the nonprivileged, especially the rural popula-

these restrictions. Subject only to the jurisdiction of their own officers, these troops were highly privileged; promotion to officer rank was based on seniority, and in old age they were entitled to a pension. In military campaigns they received daily pay if they furnished their own weapons, although in peacetime they depended upon resources that were administered collectively. These privileges increased the demand for admission to the army, but the Janizaries were successful in monopolizing these desired positions for their own relatives and eventually also for their children. But the ruthless violence of this army became dangerous for the sultans themselves. Military training and service were reintroduced for Mohammedan believers, who were organized into a new army, and in 1825 that army destroyed the Janizaries, who had risen in revolt.

tion, in order to disarm his potential competitors.[18] Certain developments favor this practice: the intensification of commerce and agriculture often makes privileged groups economically indispensable, and this, together with the development of military technique, the necessity of military training, and the ruler's need for a standing army, make military service a full-time profession. In such an army officer rank is usually reserved for members of the privileged strata, because in that position they are no longer dangerous competitors of the patrimonial ruler.

In all these cases the military forces remain the personal instrument of the sultanistic ruler, insofar as equipment and maintenance are supplied from his own storehouses and revenue. Where land grants are given in return for military services and the costs of equipment and maintenance are imposed on the soldiers themselves, the forces tend to lose this character, and the ruler's control over them may be seriously weakened.

Important as a military force is, fear of that force cannot be the exclusive basis of patrimonial authority. This becomes evident in the paradox of sultanism, Weber's term for the extreme form of personal despotism. The more reliance a ruler places on his military force in order to hold down the subject population, the more dependent he becomes on the support of that force in order to maintain himself in power. Yet in case of his death, in military defeat, or in other adversities, the soldiers may run away or go on strike, or they may overthrow old and establish new dynasties. Even if they remain loyal to the ruling house, that loyalty must be won ever anew by donations or promises of high reward. The sudden collapse of such patrimonial regimes as well as their equally sudden reestablishment manifest the fundamental instability of traditional domination that places reliance on force alone.

Patrimonial administration. Although initially a ruler recruits his officials among his personal dependents, this hardly ever suffices for the government of large territories. As the

[18] This differs from armies based upon the recruitment of notables, which regularly make the duty to bear arms—and the ideas of honor associated with this duty—a privilege of every member of such a dominant stratum. Cf. section C of this chapter.

ruler's personal staff increases, it becomes difficult to maintain as part of his household. Consequently central offices are created, often under the supervision of a highest official. This official and his subordinates are powerful favorites as long as they possess the confidence of the patrimonial ruler. For entirely personal reasons they may rise or fall with equal suddenness. In time the highest court official, such as the guardian of the ruler's harem or the supervisor of some other entirely personal matter, may become the highest political official as well.

The character of this highest official varies. In some Negro empires the executioner is the regular companion of the king who administers the royal power over life and death. In military regimes the principal war leader performs similar functions. In the Orient the grand vizier is a regular institution even outside the Islamic states in which this term originated. In all these cases patrimonial rulers face a recurrent dilemma. The absence of a supreme official can bring about the disintegration of the regime, but the existence of such an official can endanger the ruler's supreme authority, especially if the official succeeds in enlisting the loyalty of the ruler's personal dependents and political subjects.

Under patrimonialism the ruler treats all political administration as his personal affair, in the same way in which he exploits his possession of political power as a useful adjunct of his private property. He empowers his officials from case to case, selecting them and assigning them specific tasks on the basis of his personal confidence in them and without establishing any consistent division of labor among them. Even in large states organized in this manner, it is impossible to discover any system in the deluge of official titles, which have a constantly changing meaning.

The officials in turn treat their administrative work for the ruler as a personal service based on their duty of obedience and respect. Their "rights" are in fact privileges, freely granted or withdrawn by the ruler, and a delimitation of their functions can result only inadvertently from the economic and personal competition among them. In their relations with the subject population they can act as arbitrarily as the ruler acts toward them, provided that they do not violate tradition and the interest of the ruler in maintaining the obedience and productive capacity of his subjects. In other words, patrimonial administration is administration and adjudication from case to case, combining the discretionary exercise of personal authority with due regard for sacred tradition or certain fixed rights of individuals. As a result the patrimonial official faces a dilemma whenever the absolute commands of the ruler conflict with tradition.

This pervasive combination of traditionalism and arbitrariness is compatible with many different organizational structures. In the later summary of his discussion Weber pointed out that the patrimonial retainer or official

> may receive his support in any of the following ways: (a) by maintenance at the table and in the household of the ruler; (b) by allowances from the movable property and the treasure of his ruler, predominantly allowances in kind; (c) from the use of land which has been granted as a right in return for services; (d) from property-income, fees, or taxes which the retainer has appropriated [with the consent of the ruler]; (e) from a fief.[19]

Each of these methods has institutional ramifications, which may be mentioned briefly. In the case of *allowances in kind* the patrimonial retainer remains dependent for life upon the wealth and physical assets of the ruler; however, his right to such allowances could become salable. In the case of *land grants in return for services* the retainer receives his support in a manner that quickly increases his personal and economic independence from the ruler; usually such a grant is given for life, with the ruler seeking to retain the right to dispose of it anew at the death of the incumbent, and the latter seeking to make it hereditary.

Similar tendencies occur in the case of *income from rents, fees, or taxes;* our consideration here will be confined to fees. A patrimonial ruler and his officials are not obliged to perform official functions unless sacred tradition demands it of them. For the most part they are free to use their discretion, and

[19] *Theory,* p. 351. The translation has been slightly altered. The discussion of "(e) fief" belongs in the section on feudalism. Cf. pp. 360–63 below.

they will perform official acts only in return for a fee, which is determined from case to case or in accordance with a schedule. The authority to perform official acts for which fees must be paid has very frequently become a patrimonial property that could be sold, leased or inherited like any other property. Thus a patrimonial official may purchase or rent that authority from the ruler and then lease or sell it to some person in return for a rent or purchase price; in this way he relinquishes his right to the fees that are received, though he still retains the right to designate to the ruler the name of the incumbent. Initially the ruler resists the lifelong appropriation, as well as the right to the inheritance of such positions, but once circumstances compel him to relinquish his control he will seek to obtain a share of the profits accruing from these transactions. Where the appropriation of offices has developed, patrimonial officials can be dismissed only if the ruler repays the purchase price of the office.[20]

We have now considered the instruments of patrimonial rule that can be used "to broaden the range of arbitrary power which is free of traditional restrictions." The analysis points up two persistent problems of this system of traditional domination. The ruler has maximum control over his military forces and administrative staff when these are composed of personal dependents and maintained from his own resources. Such maximum control militates against an effective government over a large territory, because the cost involved readily exceeds the personal resources of even powerful rulers. Moreover, exclusive reliance upon his personal "instruments of force" can jeopardize the ruler's authority because it exposes him to the possibility of united action against himself on the part of his "dependents." Conversely, if a patrimonial ruler extends his domination, he is bound to delegate his authority sooner or later by granting benefices in return for services rendered to him or in his behalf. Thus the extension of patrimonial domination necessitates a decentralization of the ruler's personal authority. All patrimonial states of the past have involved a

[20] Weber used the term "prebend" to refer to *all* nonhereditary forms of support for patrimonial officials, other than their maintenance in the household (i.e., *c–d* in the quotation above). Following Talcott Parsons, I shall use the term "benefice."

pattern of decentralization that has been determined by the struggle for power between the ruler and his retainers and officials. Weber analyzed this struggle on a comparative basis by considering the principal methods that patrimonial rulers used to centralize the exercise of authority and that officials used to increase their independence.

The Struggle for Power under Patrimonial Rule

Rulers and officials. Patrimonial officials and retainers who obtain an office through a grant from the ruler or through payment of a purchase price to him try to protect their right to that benefice for themselves and, if possible, their descendants. Where their efforts succeed, a traditionally stereotyped separation of powers between the ruler and these officials results. Such a structure tends to frustrate all efforts to introduce more efficient methods of administration, because these will jeopardize the existing opportunities of fiscal exploitation in which the incumbents have a vested interest. When these office-holders become local dignitaries who constitute themselves as a status group of notables, they may be able to prevail over the ruler and his personal dependents.[21]

[21] The term "notable" recurs in the following discussion and calls for an explanation. In *Staatssoziologie,* p. 102, Weber referred to "independent people who are socially prominent by virtue of their position" in the community and who on that basis serve their ruler as functionaries. The distinguishing characteristic is the specific status honor of the group. (See also *WuG,* Vol. II, p. 681.) Elsewhere Weber spoke of *honoratiores* as persons whose economic situation is such that they can occupy positions of leadership or authority without remuneration and whose prestige is such that they enjoy the confidence of their fellows (*Theory,* p. 413). But, as noted by the editors in *Law,* p. 52, n. 25, Weber also referred to *legal honoratiores,* where neither expertise nor remuneration are excluded as in the preceding definition, although in this case economic dispensability and social prestige are also relevant. As far as I can see, Weber designated by the category "honoratiores" all persons who *can afford* to perform official functions without remuneration, whether they do so or not, and who on some basis possess a common style of life that has prestige in the society, and this *occasionally* includes the prestige of knowledge, as in the case of lawyers. Through various applications the term becomes in fact a synonym of "status group with wealth and prestige," and I have adopted the term "nota-

The development of France is a famous case in point. Trading and inheritance of benefices was practiced by all ranks of French officialdom. An official who resigned would sell his benefice to his successor. The heirs of a deceased official claimed the right to his office as part of his property. After many attempts to terminate these practices the king's treasury began to participate in them (in 1567) by demanding the payment of a fixed sum from the successor. In 1604 a new regulation recognized the right of inheritance, reduced the take of the treasury, but required the official to pay the crown 1⅔ per cent of the purchase price annually. The collection of this tax was in turn leased by the crown on an annual basis. For centuries the French parliaments, which were composed of benefice-holders, protected this system. There was, to be sure, the patrimonial principle that an official could not resist or contradict his ruler. When the king appeared personally in the assembly or sent written directives, he could command the legalization of any decree he desired. But immediately afterward the parliament frequently called into question the validity of a decree that ran counter to tradition and endangered the appropriated rights to office. In a good many instances the parliament prevailed and was therefore effectively in power. In 1771 Louis XV attempted a *coup d'état* by accepting the mass resignation of the benefice-holders—who sought thereby to force their will upon the king—but refusing to repay the purchase price of their offices. The officials were placed under arrest, parliament was dissolved, substitute offices were created, and the appropriation of offices was prohibited. But this attempt of the king to establish a dependable patrimonial officialdom did not succeed. Louis XVI withdrew these decrees (in 1774) in view of the overwhelming protest against them, and the old struggles flared up again. Finally, in 1789, the French Revolution eliminated not only the monarchy but also the system of office-purchase and hence the whole group of benefice-holders.

The appropriation and trading of benefices developed nowhere else to the extent that it did in sixteenth- to eighteenth-

---

able" to convey this meaning. Different adjectives, such as "legal," "landed," "bourgeois," and others, can then specify the meaning intended in a given context.

century France, where every step in the direction of such appropriation led to a further fragmentation of patrimonial authority. The rights to the exercise of authority were based on special privileges and, although their extent varied, the ruler could not touch them because that provoked the resistance of the office-holders. Such an administrative organization is peculiarly inflexible, incapable of handling new tasks, impervious to any systematic regulation, and a striking contrast to the purposive organization of a bureaucracy, which will be considered in the next chapter.

However, the widespread appropriation of benefices need not result in the development of an independently powerful officialdom, as it did in France. When the officials are celibate clergymen who hold benefices as grants from higher authorities, they may become pawns in the struggle for power among these authorities. The relations between church and state are a case in point and also help to round out the discussion in the preceding chapter. Originally the Catholic clergy was maintained out of the means provided by the community. These means were in the hands of the bishop, and the church as a whole had a definitely urban character. Subsequently this urban concentration declined and the churches became dependent to a considerable extent on the peasant community or the landlord; if the latter was the case the clergy was often in a position of subservience. Such dependence also increased when secular rulers or wealthy persons endowed a local church and then claimed the right to appoint or dismiss members of the clergy. The issue of secular control over church benefices and the clergy was central to the struggle between patrimonial rulers and the church from the time of the Gregorian reforms in the eleventh century until the fourteenth and fifteenth centuries. It need concern us here only insofar as it illustrates that for the church, for the emperor and for baronial landlords control over church benefices was important, not only as a source of income but as a means of administration and a weapon in the struggle for power.

A celibate clergyman is cheaper than an official who has to maintain a family. He is not in a position to appropriate the benefice, and he can be attracted and made subservient by the prospect of a pension. These are some of the reasons why each of the major contending powers became involved in the struggle over church benefices. In their endeavor to regain control of the church, the Popes saw to it that the clergy and the local landlords had many personal and familial ties with one another; as a consequence they made ready allies of the Popes in their opposition to the German emperor. Another development of major significance was the papal grants of church benefices to universities and—among personal favorites of Rome —to scholars who were specifically exempted from the performance of clerical duties. In this way the Popes sought to create a dependent intelligentsia, though by ignoring national differences in the distribution of these benefices they also helped provoke the later nationalist opposition to Rome. The German emperor, on the other hand, was successful for a time in creating a political status group of clerical notables who were not recruited or involved locally and whose administrative and political powers remained at his disposal. In England secular control over church benefices eventually prevailed, though only after the development had seesawed between an alliance of king and Parliament against the Pope in the interest of creating a monopoly of church benefices for Englishmen and an alliance of king and Pope against these native groups in the interest of maximizing the revenues of state and church.

So far we have considered the struggle for power in terms of conditions that lead to a decline of central authority, either because officials appropriate benefices or because their inability to do so turns them into pawns in the struggle of competing authorities. The decline of central authority is also furthered by the officials' physical distance from the center of authority. Unless a realm is compact, transportation good, and the dependence of the people on the central authority crucial (as in ancient Egypt), officials become more independent as their distance from the center increases. Governors of provinces will pay either a fixed tribute to the ruler or only what surplus is left over after local needs are met. They will utilize the local resources independently,[22] and difficulties of communication

[22] Weber noted particularly that such governors have a special interest in controlling both taxes and military conscription in their district, whereas the ruler endeavors to assign the authority over these two functions to separate officials.

plus the need for quick decisions may increase their autonomy still further. Dependence on the ruler may become so nominal that tributes or taxes can be exacted only at the price of periodic campaigns of blackmail.

Patrimonial rulers, however, do not accept such fragmentation of their authority without resistance. Even where authority must be decentralized, opportunities for the ruler to make his will prevail remain. When new administrative problems arise that are outside the jurisdiction and power of the established benefice-holders, the ruler may assign these to his personal favorites and dependents. After the death of an incumbent, the patrimonial ruler may also be in a position to revoke his grants of land and privileges. The heir of a benefice-holder in most cases had to present the benefice to the ruler to obtain his confirmation. Where confirmation is automatic, the principle of revocability has been superseded by the permanent appropriation of "well-deserved privileges." But where confirmation is not automatic, a ruler may use special occasions like his accession to the throne to cancel these privileges and regain the initiative. In the West this method was repeatedly applied in the process of transition from patrimonial to bureaucratic administration.

At this higher level patrimonial administration is characteristically unstable, even after the appropriation of benefices has developed to a considerable extent. Much depends on the personal forcefulness of the ruler, who has three typical means at his disposal to prevent or at least curtail the further fragmentation of his authority:

(1) He can personally visit the different parts of his realm on a regular basis. In the absence of adequate transportation this is a method of distributing the maintenance of the royal household among the different domains of the king. More important, the repeated presence of the ruler reinforces his authority over his subjects.

(2) He can supplement or replace such personal supervision by appointing officials who travel in a circuit—e.g., the *missi dominici* of Charlemagne or the circuit-court judges of England—and conduct legal and administrative affairs on a periodic basis.

(3) He can obtain all manner of personal guarantees—like hostages or regular visits to court—from officials who are appointed to positions that cannot readily be controlled. In Japan, for example, the daimyos were forced to leave their families at the court of the shogun and were personally required to reside at the court every other year. Other methods include requiring that the sons of officials enter the court service; that important positions be filled by relatives (a dubious measure, Weber added); that the tenure of office be brief; that officials be excluded from districts in which they own land or have relatives; that only celibates be appointed to certain positions; that the appointed officials be supervised by spies or official overseers recruited from the personal dependents of the ruler; and that officials with competing jurisdictions be appointed in the same district so that they can supervise each other. All of these methods of ensuring the reliability of officials can be made more effective if recruitment is confined to persons—including foreigners—who do not possess any power or prestige of their own but owe their elevation to the ruler.

Weber cited evidence for these different methods from Japan, medieval Europe, Islam, the Roman Empire, and elsewhere. But since China has already been discussed,[23] it will be simplest to exemplify this arsenal of patrimonial controls by summarizing Weber's conclusions with regard to China. The tendencies of officials toward an appropriation of benefices and hence an increasingly independent status in relation to the imperial center of authority certainly existed in China. The size of the empire, the relatively small number of officials, the entrenched traditionalism and power of local families, the preference of officials to use the wealth they acquired in office to buy land, the Chinese idealization of filial relations between a candidate for office and his teachers and superiors, the importance of familial relationships—all these tended to create "hereditary office-domains with an entourage of steady customers."[24] The patrimonial emperors of China opposed these ever threatening developments by short-tenure appointments, the exclusion of

[23] See pp. 109–13 above.
[24] *WuG*, Vol. II, p. 708.

officials from areas in which they had relatives, the supervision of officials through spies, and, above all, official examinations and certificates of conduct. These methods did not eliminate the purchase of benefices and personal patronage, but they institutionalized both competition and distrust among the officials and a positive social evaluation of the educational certification acquired through examinations. This institutionalization forestalled a return to feudalism and the appropriation of benefices to a sufficient degree to permit the growth of bureaucratic status conventions with their combination of utilitarianism, classical training, dignity, and poise, and their dependence on the central authority for chances of advancement.[25]

In the struggle for power between the Chinese emperors and officials, authority was centralized to the extent that the officials became a group whose distinct way of life set it apart from the rest of society and made it dependent upon the will of the ruler. Such an outcome of the struggle between rulers and officials depends upon the absence within the society of groups that can actively oppose the patrimonial authority on the basis of their independent wealth and power. In Chinese society the local powers confined their opposition to withdrawal, subterfuge, bribery, and other indirect forms of resistance. The controversy over church benefices in medieval Europe, on the other hand, illustrates how groups capable of direct action have a decentralizing effect on the struggle for power under patrimonial rule. And the destruction of independent landowners by foreign conquest in ancient Egypt and in Russia under the Mongols points to the specific circumstances under which the relation of rulers and officials may be considered by itself without undue distortion.

More often than not, however, patrimonial rulers find themselves confronted by a status group of landed notables who by their position within their home districts possess prestige and an independent source of power. Where this is the case, the rulers can suppress such groups only if they possess an efficient and reliable military and administrative organization that can hold the notables in check *and* exercise all administrative, judicial and police functions at the local level. The Em-

[25] *Ibid.*, pp. 708–9, for Weber's cautious formulation of this conclusion.

peror Nero actually tried this policy in Africa, but such attempts have been rare because the resources and administrative apparatus needed for their implementation are usually not available. The coexistence of central authority and local notables with independent sources of power has usually led to compromises involving some delegation of authority to those local groups. Even where such compromises have been effective, they have not ended the underlying conflict of interests in which patrimonial rulers have used their more or less dependent officials as a weapon in the struggle with the independent landlords.

Rulers and notables. Landlords typically demand that the patrimonial ruler guarantee, or at any rate not infringe upon, their own patrimonial authority over their tenants. Hence the landlord is the person of last resort, the indispensable intermediary whenever the ruler seeks to get in touch with the tenants. If the latter become liable to legal prosecution, the authorities should turn to the landlord, who is also responsible for furnishing the required number of conscripts and apportioning and collecting the tenants' taxes. In this process the landlord naturally exploits the tenants' productive capacity in his own interest so that their services and tax payments to the patrimonial ruler are reduced, or at least fixed.

To achieve these demands landlords regularly try to obtain immunity against the interference of patrimonial officials. Where this is fully realized, landlords are exempted from the duties that patrimonial rulers regularly impose upon communities, much as the personal possessions of the monarch are exempted. This means that the landlords as well as the bailiffs of the royal domain exercise not only the rights of the patriarchal master but also those of the political authorities. A regular feature of such rights is the insistence that the ruler's local official be a propertied resident in his own administrative district and hence a member of the local status group of landed notables. In Prussia such groups had the right to nominate candidates for local office until the nineteenth century, and during the Middle Ages powerful barons were able on this basis to get into their hands the office patronage of entire territories. Wherever patrimonial rulers are confronted with independent status groups of landed notables, the latter tend to claim sole and hereditary possession of the political offices that "mediate" between the ruler and the subject population.

The rulers' struggle against these pretensions of local notables has assumed many forms. Above all, rulers are concerned with protecting their military and fiscal interests. They want to make sure that their subjects' productive capacity does not suffer through the exploitation of the landlords. They also want to retain the power of direct taxation and conscription, contrary to the medieval principle *"nulle terre sans seigneur"* (no land without its sovereign) by which the landlords sought to prevent the patrimonial administration from treating village communities of peasants as possessing any rights of their own.

Usually, neither rulers nor landlords are able to realize their demands fully. The ruler ordinarily lacks the private resources to maintain all administrative, judicial and police functions at the local level, and the landlords are too disunited among themselves and too dependent upon the ruler to press for complete independence. As a result, there are compromises between these opposing forces that give the local notables complete authority over their tenants *insofar as* this is compatible with the fiscal and military interests of the ruler. Local administration and the lower jurisdiction over the tenants are entirely in the hands of the landlords, who therefore "represent" their tenants before the ruler and his officials; however, higher administrative and judicial powers remain at the disposal of the latter. Such compromises usually include a series of privileges for the landed notables, among them privileged access to the officer corps and high administrative positions; exemption from taxes on persons and property; prerogatives with regard to the courts competent to adjudicate and with regard to the types of penalty and evidence admissible in disputes involving notables; and, frequently, the exclusive right to own patrimonial estates and exercise patrimonial authority at the local level. The scope of these privileges depends in any given case on the relative unity of the local powers and the antecedent conditions that limit or facilitate the ruler's strategies in dealing with them.

In this respect Weber analyzed the case of Russia, which strikingly exemplifies how a status group of landowning notables can become completely dependent upon a patrimonial ruler. Although social rank depended at one time on land-ownership, this foundation of local prestige and power was destroyed under the Mongols. After the establishment of the Muscovite state rank came to depend increasingly—and finally altogether—on the dignity of the office that the Tsar as the owner of all land had bestowed upon a person. The lands granted in return for service to the Tsar as well as the elevation in rank acquired in office eventually became hereditary, so that the rank-order of aristocratic families (*mestnichestvo*) was regulated on a permanent and cumulative basis. The young aristocrat entered Tsarist service at a level determined by the highest rank achieved by his forebears and the number of generations intervening between that achievement and his own entry. No aristocrat would accept an office in which he would be subordinate to a person of lower rank than himself, nor would he sit at table below an official whose family ranked lower than his own, even if that official occupied the highest office, and if this refusal involved considerable personal risk. This system severely curtailed the Tsar's power of appointment. At the same time it induced the aristocracy to enter the service of the Tsarist courts in order to preserve their social position and the opportunities for gain involved in the race for offices. The higher the inherited rank, the greater the drive, so that the Russian aristocracy became a court aristocracy with no power of its own.

This was the situation that Peter the Great (1689–1725) abolished by having the official list of ranks burned, revoking established hereditary privileges, and making social rank entirely dependent upon the performance of military or administrative services. Peter also stipulated that members of the aristocracy forfeit their privileges if they failed to meet their service obligations for two generations.[26]

Although this second regulation was revoked in 1762, the system of social rank based on service remained in force and at least a temporary performance of government service re-

[26] The competition of candidates for office is reminiscent of Chinese conditions. But in Russia these conditions were associated with the exclusive privilege of the aristocracy to own land settled by serfs and with family-lineage rather than examinations as the condition of office-holding.

mained a status convention of the aristocracy. This obligation was combined with a monopolistic hold on local administration and the exclusive right to own serfs.[27] Social prestige and, above all, the chances for economic gain through political manipulations, depended upon office-holding and the proper connections at the Tsarist court. This gave the Tsar a position of power that had few analogues elsewhere, in part because the leading office-holders in civilian and military administrations were completely dependent upon him and in part because the aristocracy lacked all solidarity of interests.

Kinship solidarity and the sense of family honor were apparently strong throughout the history of the Russian aristocracy. Ordinarily these factors enhance the cohesion of a social group, but in Russia this did not prove to be the case because of the early dependence of rank upon the favors of the Tsar. By competing for offices and court favors, aristocratic families prevented both the cohesion of their own status group and the appointment by the ruler of persons of his own choosing. The Petrine reforms presumably aimed at eliminating this curtailment of the Tsar's power without provoking the emergence of a common aristocratic front against the ruler. This aim was achieved because the aristocracy remained internally divided through its competition for office and social rank and through the deep antagonism between landowning aristocrats and Tsarist officials. Thus the Russian aristocracy did not become a status group cohesive and independent enough to oppose the patrimonial ruler and his officials.[28]

In Weber's view social cohesion based on a sense of status honor distinguishes a feudal nobility from the landed notables under patrimonialism, and he took England as a borderline case in which patrimonial and feudal elements were inextricably mixed. Unlike the Russian Tsars, the English kings were faced with thoroughly entrenched groups of landed notables, al-

[27] Exceptions from this exclusive privilege were made for the royal domains, monastic holdings, and survivals of earlier conditions such as military benefices of Cossacks. For a time the right to own serfs was also extended to nonaristocratic persons, but this extension was subsequently revoked.

[28] The failure of landowning notables to develop such characteristics occurred repeatedly, for example, in the late Roman and the Byzantine empires, in ancient Babylonia, and in Islam.

though the Norman Conquest had favored a centralized patrimonial regime. To prevent the complete appropriation of local authority by the baronial landlords, the kings placed that authority in the hands of a middle stratum of landed and urban notables, whose numbers and power were sufficient to hold their own against the barons. The kings also reminded these notables of their duty to equip themselves with arms. This strategy was initiated at the time of the Norman Conquest and developed during the Hundred Years' War against France (1339–1453), in which English yeomen played a considerable role as combatants. By the fourteenth and fifteenth centuries the dissolution of serfdom and the development of commerce had made it difficult for the baronial aristocracy to cope with increased administrative and judicial tasks. Supported by the "Commons," the Crown had a strong interest in pushing the entrenched power of the barons aside, and it succeeded in doing so by appointing "justices of the peace" from the landholding gentry. Since this gentry developed a strong status honor of its own, and since it later came to play a major role in curtailing the power of the Crown, a consideration of this case properly belongs in the discussion of feudalism. However, Weber cited it in the present context because it exemplified the elevation of one group of landed notables by rulers who thereby sought to break the independent power of another group.[29] This strategy was successful in England, albeit at the price of increasing the power of a landholding gentry that eventually challenged royal supremacy. As strategy this example belongs to the analysis of patrimonialism, but in terms

[29] From the perspective of patrimonialism the English case illustrates the difficulties of centralization by means of a militia. In the English revolution of the seventeenth century, the citizen-recruits supported the protest against the taxes demanded by the Stuarts and the negotiations between Charles I and the eventually victorious Parliament turned on the question of control over the militia. The great importance of the right to bear arms in the development of a politically autonomous urban bourgeoisie was discussed in Chapter IV. Weber planned to develop a typology of military status groups, but he did not complete this part of his work. Cf. *WuG*, Vol. II, pp. 640–41. His repeated analysis of the "right to bear arms" recalls that during the nineteenth century German liberals agitated against the exclusive military prerogatives of the *Kaiser* and the Prussian aristocracy.

of the conditions under which a status group develops its power position and a distinct style of life it belongs to the analysis of feudalism.

C. FEUDALISM

Weber treated patrimonialism and feudalism as the two major variants of traditional domination. Though the history of this distinction does not concern us here, it is worth noting that Machiavelli referred to it as a more or less familiar idea:

> Kingdoms known to history have been governed in two ways: either by a prince and his servants, who, as ministers by his grace and permission, assist in governing the realm; or by a prince and by barons, who hold their positions not by favour of the ruler but by antiquity of blood.[30]

Patrimonial government is an extension of the ruler's household in which the relation between the ruler and his officials remain on the basis of paternal authority and filial dependence. Feudal government replaces the paternal relationship by a contractually fixed fealty on the basis of knightly militarism.

This distinction is clear only so long as it is formulated in abstract terms. As we have seen, patrimonial officials can acquire personal independence on the basis of hereditary land grants, and landed notables who possess this independence may lose it. Thus political structures that arise from the enlargement and transformation of the patriarchal household merge imperceptibly with political structures that arise from the partial centralization of independent status groups under stress of war, conquest, or other contingencies. Only where the personal position of patrimonial officials and landed notables is traced historically does the distinction between an early condition of dependence or independence emerge more clearly. Yet this inevitable blurring should not be permitted to obscure the analytic difference "between the patriarchal structure and the estate-structure of traditional domination that is of fundamental importance for the entire sociology of the state in the

[30] Niccolo Machiavelli, *The Prince* (New York: The Modern Library, 1940), p. 15.

pre-bureaucratic epoch."[31] Weber emphasized this distinction despite his own analysis of many transitional phenomena because he was interested in the contrast between the Orient, where estates as distinct from status groups did not develop, and the Occident, where such estates helped shape the development of the modern state.

Feudalism and Patrimonialism

According to Weber, the institutions of feudalism originally served the purpose of creating a cavalry composed of warriors who were similarly equipped and constantly in training. For example, the feudalism of the Franks originated in resistance to Arab cavalry, and estates of the church were appropriated to reward knights for their military service. In Turkey during its period of great expansion, a vassal forfeited his land (fief) if he failed to do military service for seven years. Several external conditions favored the development of feudal military forces in these and similar cases. During prolonged periods of peace, the mass of landowners failed to engage in military training both because they lacked the inclination and because their productive labor could not be spared for distant military campaigns. Under these circumstances men whose labor was not needed and who could afford to equip themselves with arms became prominent as warriors. Such warriors flourished especially where the ruler did not have the resources to equip an army and where the differentiation of property among his subjects destroyed the economic capacity of many to equip themselves with arms.

Feudalism always involves a contract between free men. Vassalage does not diminish the honor or status of a man; rather, it can enhance them. If a knight enters the service of a ruler, he remains a free man; he does not become a personal dependent like the patrimonial retainer. In Japan, where the feudal ideology of personal fealty was more elaborate than elsewhere, the samurai could change his feudal lord at will. A full fief of the European type always involved a complex of

[31] *Staatssoziologie*, p. 103. I use the term "estate" here since in the present context Weber referred to "medieval estates" rather than more broadly to status groups.

rights that could and should provide a standard of living appropriate to a lord who was the master of an estate as well as a local ruler over men. The property rights of a landlord thus were joined with territorial rights as a local ruler. As a consequence, the taxes and fees accruing to the lord in his official capacity, as well as the costs of his administration, were in no way distinguished from his personal domain, either legally or economically. The costs of office had to be paid for like all other household expenses of a feudatory, usually by the work of his own patrimonial tenants and political subjects. The fief was the property of the vassal for the duration of the feudal relationship. It was a personal, inalienable, indivisible possession, which the ruler wanted to see conserved as such in the interest of maintaining the productive capacity of the tenants. Furthermore, the fief was or became hereditary, so that by the later Middle Ages a nonhereditary fief was regarded as second-rate.[32] All this contrasts sharply with the benefices of a patrimonial government, at least in legal theory. Benefices involve a lifelong remuneration of the incumbent in exchange for his real or presumed services. The income accruing from the benefice is an attribute of the office, not of the incumbent as a person; the latter utilizes the proceeds but does not own them outright. The benefice-holder is either relieved of payments for the costs of administration or a certain portion of the fees accruing to the benefice is set aside for this purpose.

The social distinction between the two institutions remains, even where the legal distinctions disappear. Though benefice-holders could divest themselves of all traces of patrimonial dependence (as in France), they were still only *rentiers* with certain official duties, more comparable in some respects to a bureaucratic official than to a feudal vassal. The latter is not merely free of all patrimonial subordination but is obliged to adhere to an ambitious code of duties and of honor. In their highest development feudal relationships combine two quite contradictory elements: a highly articulate cult of personal fealty to the ruler, and a contractual stipulation of rights and duties with its specifically materialistic and impersonal relation to certain sources of income. This combination is evident in the

[32] In the early Middle Ages the fief reverted to the ruling house upon the death of the reigning monarch.

complex process involving the inheritance of a fief, at least as this process was formalized originally. In order to make a valid claim to the fief of his father, an heir had to prove that he was personally qualified to perform the services incumbent upon a vassal and to make a personal declaration of fealty to the ruler. In return, the ruler was obliged to accept this declaration of fealty, if the heir was qualified. Yet fealty involved a contractual relationship despite these personalized conventions. The vassal could terminate it at any time upon relinquishing the fief, and the ruler could not impose duties on the vassal arbitrarily. The vassal's duties consisted only of fixed obligations patterned after a code of honor that was binding upon both parties in terms of personal loyalty and brotherly affection.

Weber was principally interested in the status group of feudal vassals, because their solidarity and power was of major significance for the political institutions of the West. Feudalism's distinctive element is its combined appeal to the duty of filial obedience and the sense of high social rank that provided the vassals with their ideals of conduct and style of life. These men tended to identify their own honor with the honor of their ruler, in part, according to Weber, because the ruler's fortunes affected their chance of providing fiefs for their descendants. The only legitimate basis for a vassal's fief was his unreserved support of the personal authority of the ruler. Thus western European feudalism depended upon men of rank and wealth who were capable of equipping themselves with weapons and made professional competence in the arts of war a major purpose of their lives. Their combination of personal loyalty and pride of status was due to the fact that in the West a fully developed feudal system originated in a cavalry, while elsewhere analogous systems originated in grants of fiefs to infantrymen from the middle or lower strata of the population.

Weber found feudal relations unusual because the sentiments of loyal obedience and pride of status occur most frequently apart from each other. An army of slaves, the personal dependents of a patrimonial ruler or the tenants of a landowner may be loyal, but such loyalty is "plebeian." On the other hand, there are many instances in which the sense of honor has occurred by itself. In ancient Sparta the feeling of status dignity was based on a code of martial honor and etiquette that required, among other things, that anyone who had violated the code of battle fight a "duel of purification." This case and its ancient Greek analogues have in common with Western and Japanese feudalism the fact that the sentiment of honor was the object of education for all members of the status group. But ancient Greek practice differed from feudalism proper in that it lacked the element of personal loyalty. In western Europe and Japan the specifically feudal combination of loyalty and status honor was made the basic outlook on life that affected all social relationships, from obedience to the master and veneration of the Savior to adoration of the beloved.

In feudal ideology the most important relations in life are pervaded by personalized ties, in contrast to all factual and impersonal relationships, which are regarded as plebeian and specifically devoid of dignity. This contrast has several aspects. Originating in an army of warriors for whom the battle between individuals was decisive, feudalism made skillful handling of weapons the object of its military education; it had little use for mass discipline to perfect a collectively organized military effort. As a result the feudal style of life incorporated the *game* as an important means of training that inculcated useful abilities and qualities of character. The game was not a "pastime" but the natural medium in which the physical and psychological capacities of the human organism came alive and became supple. In this form of "training" the spontaneous drives of man found their outlet, irrespective of any division between "body" and "soul" and regardless of how conventionalized the games often became. The knightly strata of medieval Europe and Japan regarded the game as a serious and important aspect of life that had a special affinity with spontaneous artistic interests and helped bar the way to all forms of utilitarian rationality. The aristocratic sentiment of these feudal strata found its expression in pomp and circumstance, in utensils and equipment that displayed the splendor of the household. From this standpoint luxury is not a superfluous frill but a means of self-assertion and a weapon in the struggle for power. This antiutilitarian attitude toward consumption was of a piece with the equally antiutilitarian orientation toward one's life. Aristocratic strata specifically rejected any idea of a "mission in life," any suggestion that a man should have a purpose or seek to realize an ideal; the value of aristocratic existence was self-contained.[33] Thus feudal ideology was contemptuous of a businesslike approach to economic affairs, which it saw as sordid greed. Aristocrats deliberately cultivated a nonchalance that stemmed from the conventions of chivalry, a pride of status, and a sense of honor. Their orientation was more worldly than the idealization of the charismatic warrior, more heroic and belligerent than a literary education, and more playful and artistic than professional training.

The ideology of patrimonialism differs from that of feudalism in all these respects. Feudalism is domination by the few who are skilled in war; patrimonialism is domination by one who requires officials for the exercise of his authority. A patrimonial ruler is in some measure dependent upon the good will of his subjects (unless his domination is based on military occupation); feudalism can dispense with such good will. Patrimonialism appeals to the masses against the privileged status groups; not the warrior-hero but the "good king," the "father of his people," are its prevailing ideal. That the patrimonial ruler sees to the welfare of his subjects is the basis on which he legitimates his rule in his own and their eyes. The "welfare state" is the legend of patrimonialism, in contrast to the feudal image of a free camaraderie of warriors pledged in loyalty to their leader.

Education under patrimonial rule is a preparation for administrative service and can be of at least three types. The Chinese literati were an officialdom based on literary learning. In a second type, education remains in the hands of priests who serve as the officials of a patrimonial administration on the basis of their skills in writing and reckoning; this was the pattern in the countries of the ancient Near East and in medieval Europe. The third type consists of a secular legal education as in the universities of medieval Europe; this education is also literary, but through a process of rationalization it may

[33] Weber added that the Islamic fighters for the true faith are an exception to this generalization but that in this case the artistic elaboration of the game also declined.

become the basis of the modern, professionalized bureaucracy. All three types are incompatible with the most characteristic features of education under feudalism: its emphasis on the game as a serious pursuit, its affinity with individual artistry, its idealization of heroic virtues, its heroic sense of honor, and its studied opposition to the matter-of-fact attitude and to business routine. All these feudal virtues seem to the patrimonial official dissipation and a lack of fitness.

It is consonant with these contrasting ideologies that patrimonial regimes tend to be principally concerned with administrative functions while feudalism becomes concerned with the welfare of tenants only when it is imperative for economic survival. Under patrimonialism every new administrative function provides additional benefices for the officials, and this may add to the power position and symbolic significance of the ruler. But the ruler has no interest in a fixed distribution of property. In a money economy patrimonial rule is likewise compatible with the free transferability of land; indeed, new property owners are favored so long as they do not give rise to new social groups capable of acquiring an authority independent of the arbitrary will of the ruler. It is therefore a peculiar characteristic of patrimonialism that it occasionally permits the precipitous rise of a slave or servant to the precarious omnipotence of a royal favorite.

Patrimonial rulers must oppose with all the weapons at their disposal both the economic and the social independence of a feudal aristocracy. Every evidence of personal pride and self-assertion on the part of the "subjects" is suspect as a symptom of opposition to authority. Devotion to the "father of his people," not the loyalty of self-conscious vassals to a ruler, is inculcated.[34] In all these respects patrimonialism stands opposed to the typical efforts of a landed aristocracy under feudalism to prevent the transfer and fragmentation of landed property and to bar the social and economic ascent of individuals or groups outside the privileged status groups.

These differences between feudalism and patrimonialism are also reflected in the field of law. Under patrimonialism a ruler does not willingly issue any rules that would be binding upon

[34] Concerning this subservience to the authoritarian ruler cf. pp. 351–53 above.

him or his officials. He either may give commands from case to case and thus preclude any conception of "law" or of "right," or he may issue general directives to his officials that are binding upon their actions until they receive further directives.[35] Logically, at least, this system transforms all problems of law and adjudication into problems of administration:

> The prince's administrative officials are at the same time judges, and the prince himself, intervening at will into the administration of justice in the form of "cabinet justice," decides according to his free discretion in the light of considerations of equity, expediency, or politics. He treats the grant of legal remedies to a large extent as a free gift of grace or a privilege to be accorded from case to case, determines its conditions and forms, and eliminates the irrational forms and means of proof [like oracles or ordeals] in favor of a free official search for the truth. . . .
>
> The boundaries between law and ethics are then torn down just as those between legal coercion and paternal monition, and between legislative motives, ends, and techniques.[36]

Under feudalism political power is also regarded as the legitimate right of the ruler. But the ruler may voluntarily relinquish a portion of his power by granting to some official or notable a special right or privilege that must then be respected in the administration of affairs or the adjudication of disputes. This system tends to transform the "entire legal order . . . into a mere bundle of assorted privileges."[37] Lawmaking and adjudication involve negotiation, bargaining and contracting about claims and privileges, the content of which is fixed thereby and rigorously formulated. If consistently developed,

[35] Weber added that if consistently carried out this system transposes the pattern of the patriarchal family into the body politic. The father issues commands according to his discretion, and if he complies with some wishes of his child or servant he does not thereby bind himself to a precedent or principle that might limit his discretion in the future.

[36] *Law*, pp. 264, 266; also pp. 43–44. Weber referred to the edicts of the Buddhist King Asoka as a striking example of this patriarchal approach. Cf. pp. 168–69 above.

[37] *Law*, p. 262.

this system transforms all problems of administration into problems of law and adjudication, a tendency symbolized by the administrative proceedings of the medieval English Parliament and the Royal Council, which were administrative and judicial bodies at one and the same time.[38]

The contrast between patrimonialism and feudalism is most clear-cut at the ideological level. Weber made clear that for the sake of simplicity he analyzed the two structures as if the exercise of authority was either in the hands of a patrimonial ruler and his personally dependent officials or in the hands of feudal vassals,[39] but he emphasized that at the institutional level the contrast is not nearly so simple. Patrimonial governments have a "feudal" aspect wherever territorial rights are granted by the ruler—or appropriated by a landed aristocracy —on a hereditary basis; and feudal regimes have a "patrimonial" aspect wherever the fief system described above is combined with some degree of central administration.

Some amalgamation of the two systems is frequent in history. For example, the military forces of Turkey were divided into the Janizaries, who represented the personal troops of the ruler, and the cavalry, who were benefice-holders of a quasi-feudal type. In northwest India the rule of the Rajputs involved grants of territorial rights to members of the leading clan by the clan elder in return for military services and other duties, and under threat of forfeiture if these duties were not met; in this case patriarchal and feudal elements were combined directly. Yet another amalgamation occurred in western Europe. The recruitment of officials among the servants of European rulers entailed mounting tensions when these officials acquired much prestige and economic advantage. The political subjects became restive when men of low origin acquired more power and rank than they. But the prominence of patrimonial officials also prompted free men to enter the service of a ruler voluntarily, even when he insisted that they become his personal dependents. The free man who entered the service of a ruler in medieval Europe surrendered his lands to him and received them back from him, suitably enlarged,

38 *Ibid.*, p. 263.
39 *WuG*, Vol. II, p. 737.

as a fief in return for services.[40] These ministerial officials and other types of patrimonial retainer were bondsmen of the ruler but usually retained the characteristic prestige of their former status even after they entered the ruler's personal service. Only services in keeping with their prestige and status conventions were demanded of them, so that they remained distinct from the ruler's personal dependents. In this way feudal elements became an integral part of patrimonial administration.

It might be tempting to argue that no distinction between patrimonialism and feudalism need be made since both types have in common rulers who grant rights in return for military and administrative services. But the intellectual task Weber set himself was to make analytically useful distinctions between facts whose contrasting attributes were obscured by imperceptible gradations. In the present case the ruler's grants of authority could entail either liturgical obligations of political subjects and the personal dependence of patrimonial officials, or the elements of contractual freedom, personal fealty and social and economic prominence on the part of the vassals. Weber believed this distinction was crucial for his purposes. In Western civilization the tendency toward a decentralized traditionalism through the appropriation of benefices and contractual relations between rulers and their vassals prevailed. In the Orient the usurpation of patrimonial authority by ever new conquerors frequently helped prevent this decentralizing tendency and favored sultanistic regimes based on centrally controlled military and administrative organizations. The difference between the estate structure and the patriarchal structure of traditional authority was closely related, in Weber's view, to the question of "whether estates and what estates have been the principal carriers of ideas and ideals."[41] Estates were an integral part of Western feudalism, which Weber analyzed in terms of different admixtures of patrimonial and feudal elements in several concrete cases.

[40] In Germany such officials were called *Ministeriale,* which may be translated as "ministerial officials."

[41] *Staatssoziologie,* p. 104.

Historical Approximations of Feudalism

In Weber's view there are several kinds of feudalism. At one point he enumerated three major types with a total of seven subtypes, but in a later formulation he reduced the latter number to two.[42] These more or less tentative classifications became definite and useful for Weber's work whenever he combined them with a specific research objective. In the present case his attention focused on feudalism in Western society, with its peculiar combination of personal fealty and status honor on the part of a landholding aristocracy. This particular combination has often been absent even where other elements of feudalism can be found.

For example, feudalism in Japan was not feudalism in the Western sense. The Japanese daimyo did not possess a fief; he was an official of the emperor who had the definite obligations of furnishing military units and paying a fixed tribute. Within his district the daimyo exercised authority in his own name in all administrative, judicial and military matters, in the manner of a territorial ruler. But he could be penalized by removal to another district in cases of misdemeanor. In the terminology used above he was a patrimonial governor rather than a feudal vassal.[43] The great cleavage in Japanese feudalism was the difference between these territorial rulers and their vassals, the samurai, who were personally free soldiers of varying ranks. The samurai were entitled to carry weapons and to receive hereditary fiefs or, more often, a fixed allowance in rice, but they were subject to penalties of degradation in rank or forfeiture in cases of felony or administrative abuses. The Japanese fief was more or less analogous to a military benefice in that all fiefs were registered in terms of the amount of rice due from

[42] Cf. *WuG*, Vol. II, pp. 725–26, and *Theory*, pp. 373–81.
[43] The relative independence of the daimyo becomes clear by contrast with the patrimonial retainers or officials (fudai), personal dependents of the shogun who were sometimes granted daimyo districts but who could be removed at will even in the absence of any misdemeanor. These benefice-holders were subject to extensive disabilities, including such obvious measures as the prohibition of alliances and of fortresses, and the requirement of periodic residence in the capital. However, the daimyo also was required to reside in the capital periodically.

them and this determined the number of soldiers that had to be furnished from the fief as well as the social rank of its owner. The samurai who were maintained on the basis of allowances in kind—rice—and the small number of those who had been granted a fief proper developed an intense and personal fealty to their masters, the daimyos. Thus Japanese feudalism shows a highly developed feudal ideology on the part of samurai who were for the most part benefice-holders rather than landowning aristocrats, while the daimyos, who constituted the highest rank, exercised territorial rights, and also adhered to this ideology, were not owners of fiefs but high officials. Japanese feudalism is a case of personal fealty and military honor in the absence of a more or less autonomous landed aristocracy to whom territorial rights had been granted.[44]

Islamic feudalism is a case of territorial rights in the hands of landlords who lack a feudal ideology. The special character of Islamic feudalism is related to its origin in an army of mercenaries and in the institution of tax-farming. Patrimonial rulers without the necessary resources found themselves obliged to remunerate their mercenaries by assigning to them the tax payments of the political subjects. Although military officials (*emir*) were originally separate from the salaried tax officials (*amil*), impecunious rulers eventually transferred the authority for the collection of taxes to the military officials. Three distinct forms of remuneration existed: (1) tax collection in a village or district was leased to a tax-farmer (*mukthah*); (2) deserving or indispensable retainers were granted land as fiefs; (3) arrears in pay were covered by tax payments of the population that were either appropriated as security by military officials and mercenaries or assigned to them by the ruler. All three forms eventually merged in the concept of benefice (*iktàh*). A benefice-holder was obliged to render military service and to surrender that portion of the incoming taxes that was in excess of his own military pay. In practice this system led to the arbitrary exploitation of the subject population by the soldiers, who rarely passed on any of the tax surplus

[44] Weber's discussion of Japan was not extensive. The preceding characterization is based on *WuG*, Vol. II, p. 728, and *Religion of India*, pp. 270–82.

they received. Finally the rulers decided to relinquish their claim to the tax surplus and make outright grants of land to officials and soldiers in return for military service. As a result, the soldiers who had been tax-farmers and mortgagees became landlords with an interest of their own in improved cultivation by the subjects, so that the friction between the military officials and the fiscal interests of the ruler disappeared. The state was organized on the basis of an army of mercenaries who were gradually turned into a group of landlords and tax collectors but who retained the obligation to render military service in return for their privileges.

Because of its origin in a tax system developed to finance a mercenary army, this system of landed benefices shows no traces of the personal fealty between rulers and notables that existed in medieval Europe, where the territorial rights of a landholding aristocracy and feudal ideology appeared in combination.[45] But even in medieval Europe, where Weber's deliberately restricted definition of feudalism applies, the combination was compatible with more than one social structure. Weber used his tremendous historical learning to formulate usable concepts, but he thought of the resulting definitions as only the first step of analysis. In this respect it is instructive to examine his discussion of English feudalism as an example of the admixture between patrimonial and feudal elements in a specific case.

English feudalism illustrates how a ruler can prevent the appropriation of local authority by an elite of territorial barons, even in the absence of sufficient resources. As we saw, the English kings accomplished this by placing local authority in the hands of a middle stratum of notables at a time when increased commerce made the reduction of personal insecurity appear imperative. The Crown recruited the justices of the peace of a given district among the landlords who qualified as local notables in terms of a minimum income from their land and in terms of their style of life. Their position as keepers of the peace with a rapidly increasing proliferation of judicial

---

[45] Weber's comments on Islamic feudalism were based on the work of C. H. Becker. Cf. *WuG*, Vol. II, pp. 728–29. A more extended consideration of Islamic jurisprudence is contained in *Law, passim.*

and police functions was originally subject to recall but quickly became an appointment for life and a specific privilege of the "gentry." The power of supervision was in the hands of the court; a justice of the peace, the lord lieutenant, was commander in chief over the militia. Appeals against the decisions of a justice of the peace were not possible, except in special cases before the king's "star chamber," and this exception was destroyed by the gentry during the revolution of the seventeenth century. However, it remained possible to obtain the right to appeal to the central courts by special writ (*certiorari*). The power of appointing the justices remained in the hands of the king and his advisers, despite repeated attempts to base their appointment on election by the local notables. As a result, patrimonial officials, above all the chancellor, controlled patronage and frequently exploited it financially. Yet these powers of the Crown did not prevent the gentry's control over all positions of justice of the peace; under Elizabeth I complaints were frequent that the recommendation of incumbent justices decided the new appointments. In the long run the king could not govern effectively in opposition to the justices of the peace.

Originally, the justices of the peace received fees for their official acts as well as per diem allowances, like other royal officials. But the income from these sources was so low that it became an honorific convention to refuse such payments. Ownership of property became a required as well as a necessary condition of appointment. Moreover, the English gentry increasingly adopted the practice of leasing their estates so that they had time for the conduct of official business. In so doing they excluded all economically active members of the urban bourgeoisie whose economic indispensability did not allow them to perform honorific functions. Still, the urban bourgeoisie also comprised well-to-do people in retirement and entrepreneurs whose acquired wealth enabled them to live as *rentiers,* and such men were likewise appointed as justices of the peace. This monopolistic hold of the landed gentry and the middle-class *rentiers* on the office of "justice of the peace" strongly furthered the cultural fusion of the two groups.

It became the status convention of both groups to have

their young men appointed justices of the peace after the completion of their humanistic education. Though the duties of this office became obligatory for all qualified persons, only a portion of the justices performed their duties for more than a short time. But since the office was a source of social prestige and power, it continued to be sought after despite the considerable amount of work it involved. Even the century-long competition of professional lawyers for appointment to these positions was of no avail, since the gentry succeeded in excluding them, in part through its refusal to accept payment. The individual justice of the peace relied on the advice of his personal lawyer and handled all official business with the aid of clerks who were available for this purpose. In practice, these gentry officials administered and adjudicated in keeping with their honorific concept of duty. As Weber noted, this is one of the rare cases in which professionals were unable to displace an officialdom of notables despite the increasing volume of administrative tasks.

In England local administration through justices of the peace tended to make all other administrative agencies unimportant, at any rate outside the cities. Official business was transacted in keeping with the characteristics of traditional domination. The justices of the peace acted in their official capacity in cases of major violations or upon the appeal of the injured party rather than on a regular basis. Their exercise of authority was pervasive, nevertheless, involving everything from the control of taverns, card-playing and the proper costume to the price of corn, the level of wages, and the problems of vagrancy and religious heresy. But whether or when the justices of the peace would act and what means they would use or how thoroughly they would interfere was largely a matter of personal discretion. The justices were incapable as well as unwilling to adopt and execute an internally consistent welfare policy for the country as a whole.

There is a superficial resemblance between this operation and that of Chinese administration. In both cases government is pervasive *and* intermittent, acting in an abrupt and momentarily effective manner in specific cases while issuing general directives that are in fact advisory. In both cases the patrimonial officials of the ruler can operate only if they come to terms with the local powers. Yet the difference is fundamental. In China educated officials had to deal with family elders and occupational associations. In England the patrimonial officials of the king were confronted by the educated notables of the landowning gentry. The notables of China were benefice-holders or applicants for benefices, whose classical and literary education had prepared them for an official career; they stood on the side of patrimonial authority. In England the notables made up the core of the gentry, a free status group of land-owners who had much experience in the exercise of local authority over tenants and workers, though its members also came to acquire a humanistic education. Such a socially cohesive group of free landowners was lacking in China, and as a result China represents the case of a patrimonial bureaucracy that is not confronted with an estate of landowning notables who possess independent power.

English administration, through the justices of the peace, combined patrimonialism with the exercise of authority by independent notables; after the fourteenth and fifteenth centuries the latter group definitely predominated. The efforts of the Crown to defeat the territorial barons by elevating the gentry and its subsequent efforts to control the latter by royal prerogatives in judicial and administrative affairs are clear examples of patrimonialism. The territorial barons, on the other hand, as well as the landed gentry, with their social cohesion on the basis of a common style of life and their drive for local autonomy, are examples of feudalism. Yet the English gentry did not constitute a feudal estate in the sense of an elite of landed warriors, despite the fact that its strong conventionality, its pride of status, its serious interest in sport, its loyalty to the king and its possession of territorial rights in conjunction with landholding clearly reflected feudal antecedents. The reason is that the gentry was affected by the influx of the urban bourgeoisie. Although a hiatus long existed between the semi-feudal traditions of the landed gentry and the moralistic, utilitarian orientation of the bourgeoisie, the English gentry gradually combined these heterogeneous elements, largely through the institution of "justice of the peace," which amalgamated feudal ideology and bourgeois virtues in the ideal of the gentleman. This ideal eventually affected the concept of honor and good manners as well as the administrative practices that are characteristic of English culture today.[46]

In this consideration of Japanese, Islamic and English feudalism, Weber was concerned in each case with the estate that proved to be the "principal carrier of ideas and ideals" in the three civilizations. This significance of the Japanese samurai, the Islamic landlords and the English gentry was the result of protracted struggles, which can be better understood if we consider the "problematics" and the secular tendencies of feudalism as a system of traditional domination.

The Struggle for Power under Feudal Rule

Under feudalism the power of the ruler over his vassals is more or less precarious. On the basis of the relation between a war leader and his following of independent warriors, the latter claim legitimacy for their holdings and their exercise of authority by virtue of their unreserved support of the personal authority of the ruler. But the obligations of the vassals are flexible and subject to interpretation, so that actions of the ruler in defense of his own position can easily appear "arbitrary" and jeopardize his relations with his vassals.

In the Occident this disadvantage was institutionalized so that disputes could be brought before feudal courts composed of judges who were feudal vassals in their own right. Even where this was not the case, rulers could proceed safely against an individual vassal only if they were sure of at least passive support by the other vassals. The ruler's authority was weak also because he frequently lacked direct disciplinary powers over his vassals' tenants. Such tenants owed personal loyalty to their master, whose breach of faith with the ruler did not necessarily mean that they could or would leave him. Even when the ruler ordered tenants to obey him rather than their master, the tenants might well be troubled by conflicts

---

[46] The preceding discussion of England is based on *WuG*, Vol. II, pp. 715–19. Cf. also the related analysis of English cities in *ibid.*, pp. 549–52, and of the English jury system and legal education in *Law*, pp. 78 ff., 198 ff.

of conscience, and their double obligation might lead them to examine the merits of the conflicting claims.[47]

In response to such difficulties rulers under feudalism regularly attempt to consolidate their own position by reappropriating fiefs where possible and limiting the extent of subinfeudation. Such efforts often lead to a "feudalization of office-holding." The rulers of Japan, for example, tried to emancipate themselves from the entrenched power of kinship groups (based on familial charisma) by using the concept of personal fealty to ensure the unreserved support of all office-holders. In the Frankish Empire the Merovingian dynasty was highly unstable as long as the ruler attempted to buttress his power by short-term appointments of officials and periodic inspection of the empire by major officials. This instability was reduced when the Carolingian kings made their principal patrimonial officials into vassals whose personal loyalty served (for a time) as a weapon in the struggle against the feudal nobility. The personal dependence of such officials is greater than that of the landed nobility, and they may therefore aid the ruler in curbing the political pretensions of the latter.[48] But the long-run efficacy of this method is doubtful, because the new vassals will endeavor to increase their own independence from the ruler and may in time join forces with the landed nobility. The feudalization of office-holding, other devices like the fragmentation of the vassals' authority, the appeal to familial charisma and the various means of patrimonial centralization help account for the relative power of rulers even in feudal regimes in which the opposing power of the vassals developed strongly.

But in western Europe, where not only the landed nobility but also the urban bourgeoisie and the church developed estates of great strength, the central authority of the ruler was typically precarious. Weber saw only one over-all exception: English feudalism was characterized by centralized authority at an early time as a result of the Norman Conquest. Under

[47] Cf. the earlier discussion of the relation between rulers, vassals, and tenants, on pp. 355–57.

[48] This feudalization of office-holding is the reverse of the Chinese case, where the system of fiefs was destroyed and replaced by a patrimonial bureaucracy in order to centralize the power of the emperor.

William the Conqueror all tenants of feudal barons and all subordinate feudatories were required to swear an oath of loyalty directly to the king. In legal disputes with their own masters they had the privilege of appeal directly to the king's bench, in contrast to France, for example, where they were obliged to appeal from lower to higher courts in keeping with the rank hierarchy of feudalism. In Normandy and in England, as in Turkey, feudalism became centralized because a close relation between the ruler and the mass of tenants emerged from the social and organizational cohesion of a ruling group in a conquered territory.[49] But aside from such cases of military conquest, the ruler's authority under feudalism varies with the degree to which his vassals unite in their efforts to limit his authority and enhance their own independence.[50]

In western Europe the decentralization of authority under feudalism was the result of the emergence of different estates. The exercise of authority was a privilege vouchsafed to the vassals and benefice-holders of the ruler, and from time to time people from these privileged status groups joined one another in a common action. When such casual associations develop into a more permanent order an estate society arises, in which vassals or other notables join in legal associations on the basis of their common rights. Compacts between these estates became a characteristic feature of medieval society and were eventually embodied in written regulations.[51] In west-

[49] Weber added that this was comparable to the experience of churches, whose most tightly hierarchic organizations are to be found in areas of missionary activity.

[50] Cf. the earlier discussion of these efforts on pp. 362–63.

[51] Weber spoke of *Ständestaat*, which might be translated as a "polity of estates," but "estate society" is less clumsy. Elsewhere he defined the meaning of *Ständestaat* in the following terms: "A characteristic feature was the appropriation of political rights by individuals and corporations after the manner of private property in merchandise. Another prevalent characteristic was that these owners of privileges would hold conventions in order to settle political affairs through compromises. The ownership of castles and of all kinds of military, political or financial jurisdictions were at that time hereditary privileges in the hands of individuals in exactly the same way in which today only the king still 'possesses' his crown. . . . A 'state' in the modern sense did not exist. Every political action was dependent rather upon an agreement among these independent

ern Europe the development of these estates was a response to new or unusual administrative tasks in a society in which the distribution of fiefs and benefices had become stereotyped and inelastic. Such new tasks generally arose when administrative and military costs mounted under conditions of an expanding money economy. The large sums of money then required could not be obtained by the normal methods of feudal or of patrimonial administration, in part because the ruler and his vassals were obliged to pay only the costs of their own administration and thus could not or would not meet these special financial needs. If it was imperative to do so, special agreements had to be reached from case to case, and for this purpose legal associations became inevitable.

The struggle between rulers and vassals in European feudalism generally resulted in the tax exemption of landed nobles and the gradual diminution of their military-service obligations. Where the estates succeeded in obtaining tax exemption for tenants, the rulers could count upon only the tax payments of their own tenants and dependents. Again in the legal sphere, the limitations placed on the rights of rulers became more extensive as feudalism developed. Feudal estates became especially powerful wherever vassals participated in the adjudication of disputes involving the inheritance, forfeiture and renewal of fiefs. The right of reversion, according to which a fief was returned to the ruler upon the death of a vassal, fell into disuse. On the other hand, the right of inheritance was extended from next of kin to more distant relatives. The alienation of fiefs became more frequent, and, although the consent of the ruler was required to establish a feudal relationship with the new owner, this consent could be bought in turn. The income from such purchases of consent finally became a very substantial source of revenue for the ruler.

The over-all consequence of these changes was that personal fealty to the ruler became a stereotype that had predominantly economic significance and that lost much of its utility as an instrument of power. The later conception of feudalism accepted the fact that, as a free man, a vassal could become the

owners of prerogatives, and it was the purpose of the estate-conventions to accomplish this end." See *"Wahlrecht und Demokratie,"* in *GPS*, p. 295.

feudatory of several rulers. Consequently, in cases of conflict the vassal's support was an uncertain factor for all the rulers. In France, for example, feudal law distinguished between an oath of fealty (*homagium simplex*), which included a silent reservation with regard to the vassal's other obligations, and an unconditional oath of fealty (*homagium ligium*), which took precedence over all other duties. Although the French monarchy succeeded in imposing the second type of oath upon the great territorial vassals, the possibility of multiple loyalties obviously devalued the significance of feudal duties themselves, so that eventually it became almost impossible to base a functioning administration upon the performance of these duties.

The changing relationship between a ruler and his feudatories was also affected by changes in the personal qualifications required of those who could make a valid claim as prospective vassals. Originally the vassal was a free warrior. In western Europe vassals of the same ruler possessed the right to feud among themselves. Even though these private wars could do great damage to the interests of the ruler, he could stipulate only that private feuds cease during military campaigns.[52] These freedoms were an attribute of the vassal's specific "professional" qualifications as a soldier, although military proficiency alone was not enough. Under European feudalism the landed aristocracy also insisted upon a code of status honor as the basis of the fealty relationship. A lordly or knightly style of life was expected of all those who wished to belong. But where the influence of status conventions became pervasive while opportunities to provide for descendants became restricted, the demands made of members of the estate grew more exacting. They not only had to adhere to a "knightly" style of life but had to avoid activities that might detract from the practice of military skills. Not only nobility of birth, but first two, then four, and, in the later Middle Ages, sixteen noble ancestors were demanded. The urban patriciate was excluded from the nobility on the ground that its members shared their

[52] In thirteenth-century France, for example, the monarchy suppressed feuds among the royal vassals for the duration of a foreign war conducted by the king. The institution of the "king's peace" is a later development.

authority with the guilds and associated officially with crafts-men.

Every new demand obviously increased the rigidity of social stratification and aided efforts to monopolize fiefs and offices. As a consequence, the exercise of authority was distributed between the ruler and his vassals in accordance with increasingly inflexible rights and obligations, though at one time the reciprocal obligations of feudal contracts had been the result of free agreement. Unlike Montesquieu's famous formula, this feudal separation of powers did not involve a qualitative division and a planned allocation of governmental functions. As a local ruler, the individual vassal was his own master, whose power was circumscribed only by the exemptions, immunities or traditional privileges of the ruled and by the conflicting jurisdiction of other vassals. Western European feudalism resulted, therefore, in the hereditary appropriation of territorial rights by notables at the local level, while at the level of central administration it often failed to provide for a continuously functioning officialdom.

D. CHARACTERISTICS OF THE MODERN STATE

The foregoing analysis is typological, not developmental. Weber wanted to analyze the power relationships that emerge from the extension of the ruler's household and from the patterns of interdependence between a war leader and his more or less independent, military followers. The test of such an analysis can lie only in the utility for further research of the concepts and problems that have been formulated on the basis of comparative evidence. For this reason, neither a criticism of historical details nor a demand for definite conclusions is strictly relevant to Weber's analysis, whatever their legitimacy on other grounds.[53]

[53] A continuation of Weber's work as he may have intended it, namely a further application and development of his concepts through comparative analysis, is contained in the work of Otto Hintze. See especially the essays collected in his *Staat und Verfassung* (Leipzig: Koehler and Amelang, 1941).

This is not to argue that Weber's analysis is immune to criticism on its own ground. It is clear, for example, that patriarchal household government is basic to the patrimonial but not to the feudal type of traditional domination and therefore may not be suitable as the basic model of both. It is clear, too, that patrimonial rule tends to be personal while feudal rule tends to be impersonal and legalistic, even though the fealty relationship is adumbrated with a personalized ideology. These and related considerations suggest that it might have been appropriate for Weber to think of traditional domination in terms of the two basic patterns of patriarchal household government and oligarchic rule under a headman, rather than to attempt to derive feudalism as well as patrimonialism from the patriarchal model. No doubt other modifications might be suggested as Weber's scheme of analysis is extended to other civilizations, but this need not concern us here.

The value of Weber's approach lies in its problem-orientation and conceptual clarification of historical materials. This emphasis explains why he moved abruptly from one type of domination to another, and in particular why at the end of his analysis of traditional domination he did *not* show how the mixture of patrimonial and feudal elements characteristic of the West resulted in the modern state. For Weber this problem was outside the competence of comparative sociological research; it was a task for historians who would utilize the concepts provided by that research. This division of tasks was necessary, in his judgment, because all historical changes are concrete sequences of events (rather than general tendencies), and the comparative and typological procedure of the sociologist can only delineate the distinctive aspects of historical change that call for a causal analysis.[54]

But while the concrete emergence of the modern state fell outside the scope of his research, the institutional prerequisites of that state did not. Weber was very much concerned with the distinctively rational characteristics of the state, which emerged from the patrimonial and feudal struggle for power and which can be found only in Western civilization. The

[54] This methodological position is discussed in my article "Max Weber's Interpretation of Conduct and History," *American Journal of Sociology,* Vol. LI (May, 1946), pp. 518–26.

following chapter on legal domination takes up Weber's analysis of these characteristics, but it is convenient to anticipate here the preconditions upon which the modern Western state is based. These preconditions are: (1) monopolization of the means of domination and administration based on: (a) the creation of a centrally directed and permanent system of taxation; (b) the creation of a centrally directed and permanent military force in the hands of a central, governmental authority; (2) monopolization of legal enactments and the legitimate use of force by the central authority; and (3) the organization of a rationally oriented officialdom, whose exercise of administrative functions is dependent upon the central authority. Though some of these attributes have existed elsewhere, their more or less simultaneous emergence is a distinctly Occidental phenomenon. Since the obstacles to centralization in China and India have been discussed earlier and the conditions of legal rationality will be discussed later, it is sufficient to specify here the conditions that favored the emergence of a modern officialdom in western Europe.[55]

First, the development of a money economy determined the characteristics of government administration. Bureaucratic organizations developed in many different civilizations: in ancient Egypt, in China after the decline of feudalism, in the Roman and Byzantine empires, and elsewhere. But as long as such organizations compensated their officials in kind rather than in money, the officials sought to appropriate the sources of revenue as their private property and to use them accordingly. This tendency, which has been reviewed earlier, leads to the decentralization of authority and away from a bureaucratic organization of government. Conversely, bureaucratization presupposes the existence of a steady income for the maintenance of the administrative apparatus, which at the level of government means the existence of a stable system of taxation.

Second, the development of a rationally oriented and dependable officialdom is encouraged by the quantitative and qualitative expansion of administrative tasks. These tasks have been of many kinds. In ancient Egypt the need to regulate

[55] Cf. the more detailed discussion in *Essays*, p. 204 ff., and Chapter XIII, A, below. See also *General Economic History*, pp. 338–51.

waterways collectively had this effect; a more frequent cause has been the creation of a standing army and the related development of public finance. Under modern conditions bureaucratization has resulted from heightened cultural expectations, like the demand for internal pacification and various social services, or from technical innovations, especially in the fields of transportation and communications.

Third, bureaucratic administration is technically superior to all alternative methods of administration. This encourages the expansion of an officialdom and its tasks wherever the "means of administration" are concentrated in the hands of the central authority. This concentration is in turn related to the leveling of social and economic differences insofar as these have a bearing on government administration. These distinctive aspects of bureaucracy are best discussed in relation to Weber's analysis of legal domination.

CHAPTER XII

LEGAL DOMINATION: THE EMERGENCE OF LEGAL RATIONALITY

In his study of domination as in his sociology of religion, Weber attempted to explain the distinguishing characteristics of
Western civilization. Charismatic and traditional domination
served him as foils for an understanding of the legal domination of the modern Western state, just as his studies of Chinese
and Indian society and religion provided him with contrast-
conceptions for the study of ancient Judaism. To be sure, each
of these preparatory studies has an intrinsic interest as well.
But Weber gave special emphasis to his analyses of ancient
Judaism and legal domination, which were to him the first
differentiation and the crowning achievement of Western
civilization.

A. INTRODUCTORY CONSIDERATIONS

Weber's analyses of charismatic and traditional domination
involved three related steps: first, a comparative study of relevant materials; second, formulation of the concept; and third,
a study of the processes by which major changes of legitimation and organization occurred.[1] In his analysis of legal domi-

[1] Cf. pp. 325, 329–30 for a summary of these steps.

nation these steps are not so easily discerned, because the discussion is more extensive and because it appears in different parts of Weber's writings. His sociology of law contains a comparative study of legal institutions on the basis of which he formulated his concept of legal domination;[2] he discussed the organizational implementation of legal domination in the chapter on bureaucracy,[3] and analyzed the processes of change under legal domination in his political writings.

Up to the formulation of the concepts "legal domination" and "bureaucracy" the analysis is more extensive than in the case of charisma and tradition. But there is no explicit treatment of the transformation of legal domination that corresponds to the discussion of familial and institutional charisma or of the struggle for power under traditional domination. The reason is that Weber did not complete his political sociology, which he was working on at the time of his death.[4] Yet a careful reading of his analysis together with his political writings makes it possible, I believe, to suggest an outline of his thinking in this field that may help us round out our understanding of his work as a whole.[5]

We saw earlier that in his sociology of religion Weber gave increased attention to the developmental aspects of his materials as he approached the religious orientation of Western civilization.[6] Much the same is true of his political sociology. Traditional authority appears as the ever present attribute of the household community, which can become attenuated

[2] This detailed investigation should be compared with the corresponding analysis of charisma that is contained primarily in Weber's discussion of prophecy in *Ancient Judaism* and his reference to the work of Sohm on the charismatic communities of early Christianity. It should also be compared with Weber's analysis of the household community in *WuG*, Vol. I, pp. 194–215, on which he based his concept of patriarchalism.

[3] The chapter in question has been translated in *Essays*, pp. 196–244.

[4] For an attempt to collate the relevant fragments into a sociology of the modern state cf. *Staatssoziologie*. Johannes Winckelmann's introduction to this volume contains a discussion of Weber's unfinished plans at the time of his death.

[5] An interpretation of Weber's unfinished work on the sociology of legal domination is contained in Chapter XIII, C.

[6] Cf. pp. 267–68 above.

through the conflict of generations and the struggle for power but which does not develop. Charismatic authority appears to "erupt" and then become transformed through "depersonalization." Thus, within the context of his political sociology, both types are taken as given, and Weber's attention focused on their transformation or re-emergence in the course of history.

Only legal domination is shown to be the result of a gradual development. The rule of law is neither bound up with the hero in history nor with sacred tradition; it cannot "erupt" like the first nor endure like the second. It is the specific product of human deliberation, whose gradual development in the history of Western civilization Weber analyzed in detail. At this point his work reflects the influence of ideas from which he sought to emancipate himself. His treatment of history as a causal succession of unique events, his emphasis on ideas in relation to action, his typological procedure, and, finally, his treatment of China and India, of charisma and tradition, as contrast-conceptions for the development of ethical rationalism and legal domination in western Europe all reveal traces of Hegel's philosophy of history. Like Hegel, Weber insisted that nature consists of cyclical and repetitive events, whereas history is made up of nonrepetitive acts. Not what people do but what they think about their actions is the proper subject of analysis. Every man is always both rational and passionate, never only one or the other; we must search out man's passions behind his reasoning and man's reasoning behind his passions. This is another way of rendering Weber's statement that "not ideas, but material and ideal interests, directly govern men's conduct."[7] Men's actions in history are mere events related in time and space as long as they are considered only as such; the task of the analyst is to look at these actions "from the inside." Hegel maintained that this procedure would result in the formulation of logically related concepts, and we may think in this connection of Weber's device of the ideal type, by which he formulated in logical purity the rationale that lies behind man's actions. Hegel maintained that history ends in the present, not in the future, which is unknown to man; that the future is not an object of knowledge but of hopes and

[7] Cf. the earlier discussion of this theme on pp. 46–47, 257–67 above.

fears, much as Jacob Burckhardt maintained that the "future known in advance is an absurdity," because it would confuse a man's desire and endeavor to know beforehand the day of his death. Weber's work also ended with the present, and we shall see that he envisaged the future in terms of an ever recurring struggle between political leadership and bureaucratization. Hegel saw the history of Occidental civilization as a cumulative manifestation of the idea of freedom, and this view appears to be reflected in Weber's analysis of religious, legal and organizational rationality in western Europe.[8]

Weber accepted this intellectual tradition but was keenly conscious of its liabilities. He was especially concerned with the possibility that his study of legal domination and of ethical rationalism would be mistaken for a partisan defense in favor of rationality and Western civilization. Time and again he emphasized that the object of his studies was arbitrary, like the objects of all studies. Time and again he made clear that he proposed to study other civilizations with their prevalence of charisma and tradition *only insofar as* this was needed to ascertain the distinctive elements of Western civilization. Where this procedure by itself led to an emphasis on the developmental character and the freedom of Western civilization in contrast with the static character and the coercion of Oriental society, it was to be discounted as a methodological artifact. To be sure, Weber saw genuine differences between Orient and Occident, and his studies were designed to elucidate these differences. But this was to be the result of empirical investigations, not the inadvertent consequence of preconceptions, of the problem chosen for study, or of the concepts employed.

[8] The foregoing synopsis of *certain elements* in Hegel's philosophy of history is based on R. G. Collingwood, *The Idea of History* (New York: Oxford University Press, 1956), pp. 114–20. Many more specific influences on Weber's work could be cited, but the relation to Hegel appears important to me, both because it has not been emphasized and because it shows at a glance how much Weber stood within the main stream of German and European intellectual history. A brief sketch of Weber's intellectual background is contained in Talcott Parsons, *The Structure of Social Action* (Glencoe: The Free Press, 1949), pp. 473–87. The quotation from Burckhardt is taken from his *Force and Freedom* (New York: Pantheon Books Inc., 1943), p. 90.

Therefore he never tired of analyzing the types of rationality developed in China and India as well as the enduring and recurrent significance of charisma and tradition in Western civilization. It is important to have these intentions and cautions clearly in mind as we turn to his analysis of legal domination.

Weber's three concepts of domination refer to archetypes of human experience. All of us have felt or witnessed the pervasive influence of an overpowering personality (charisma) or of a commanding father (tradition), and examples of such influences can be found in all historical situations. Legal authority also refers to an archetype of human experience, since it is an outgrowth of the usages and conventions found in all societies.[9]

Weber defined "usage" as a collective way of acting that the individual perpetuates without being required to do so by anyone. A case in point is the practice of eating three meals a day. On the other hand, an individual usually perpetuates a "convention" because his failure to do so would provoke the disapproval of "those persons who constitute [his] environment."[10] Usages and conventions may become so habitual that there is little conscious orientation toward the norms they imply. On the other hand, conventions may give rise to a sense of duty or obligation, and the point at which one begins to speak of a legal obligation is quite arbitrary. The unbroken continuity of convention and law is exemplified by legal norms that provide sanctions for the fulfillment of conventional obligations. Thus the German Civil Code stipulates that "a transaction which is contrary to good morals is void,"[11] and Weber stated generally that "there is no socially important moral commandment

[9] It may be added that Weber's tripartite division of charisma, tradition, and legality—or of faith, tradition, and statute, as he put it at one point—recalls Pascal's and Goethe's distinctions among inspiration (faith), custom and reason as the three sources of belief. Cf. Johannes Winckelmann, *Legitimität und Legalität in Max Webers Herrschaftssoziologie* (Tübingen: J. C. B. Mohr, 1952), p. 31, n. 23. These distinctions have other antecedents, but the point to note is rather that such classifications lack the European ethnocentrism of the Hegelian and Christian conceptions of history.

[10] *Law*, p. 20. Cf. also pp. 264, n. 11, 286–87 above.

[11] *Law*, p. 24.

which has not been a legal command somewhere at one time or another."[12] Both the conventional and the legal order involve the possibility of psychological and physical coercion, though both are sustained for the most part by habituation, personal interest, and the anticipation of sanctions in cases of noncompliance. However, the two orders differ in regard to the sociological structure of coercion. The legal order possesses a "specialized personnel for the implementation of coercive power (enforcement machinery: priests, judges, police, the military, etc.)," and the conventional order does not.[13]

A legal order in this sense has existed under many systems of authority, and it is not identical with legal domination. As long as the basic functions of government are appropriated by various individuals or corporations, a modern state does not exist. Under these conditions every group or locality is an independent community whose interests are made compatible with those of other communities, either by compromises or by imposition from above, where secular or ecclesiastical authorities possess preponderant power for the time being.[14]

In the preceding chapter, we considered the setting of patrimonial and feudal rule from which absolute monarchy and representative institutions more or less concurrently developed in western Europe. This process resulted in the government's monopolization of coercion and was accompanied by a development of legal rationality that culminated in the modern concept of a legitimate legal order.[15] In Weber's terms a system of legal domination exists only where the rules of a legal order are implemented and obeyed in the belief that they are legitimate because they conform with the statutes of a government that monopolizes their enactment and the legitimate use of physical force.[16]

[12] *Ibid.*, p. 27. The relation of law and convention is discussed further on pp. 407–8 below.
[13] *Law*, p. 27. Cf. also the definition of this distinction in *Theory*, p. 127.
[14] *Law*, p. 141.
[15] See *ibid.*, p. 347, for Weber's statement of these major themes of his political sociology and his sociology of law.
[16] In one of his formulations Weber stated that "today the most usual basis of legitimacy is the belief in legality, the readiness to conform with rules which are formally correct and have been im-

B. THE EMERGENCE OF LEGAL RATIONALITY[17]

Weber's sociology of law is devoted to a study of the increasing rationality of legal concepts and practices as they developed in Western civilization. He also analyzed the social groups and institutions that promoted or hindered this development. In this discussion I am concerned with legal procedures and with the status groups that helped shape the development of the law. Weber's own summary of the process of "rationalization" gives us a bird's-eye view of the problem:

> From a theoretical point of view, the general development of law and procedure may be viewed as passing through the following stages: first, charismatic legal revelation through "law prophets"; second, empirical creation and finding of law by legal notables . . . ; third, imposition of law by secular or theocratic powers; fourth and finally, systematic elaboration of law and professionalized administration of justice by persons who have received their legal training in a learned and formally logical manner.[18]

Weber pointed out at the start that these "stages" are a theoretical construction. Actually, the rationality of the law increased in many different sequences, not only in this one. Not all of these "stages" have occurred—regardless of sequence —even where the process has gone furthest, as in the Occident. Also, elements from each of these "stages" can be found in

---

posed by accepted procedure." See *Theory*, p. 131. The implication of this and related formulations as well as Weber's definition of the modern state are considered in Chapter XIII, A, below.

[17] The following discussion is based on Weber's sociology of law and on the critical and bibliographical commentary that the editor and translator, Professor Max Rheinstein, has added to the English edition of *Law, passim*. The outline of the argument presented below may serve as a guide not only to the sociology of law but to its place in Weber's analysis of domination.

[18] *Law*, p. 303. For the reasons stated above (p. 348, n. 21) I use the term "notable" in lieu of "honoratiores." The term "rationalization" in the sense of "increasing rationality" is perhaps still subject to misunderstanding, and I have therefore either avoided the term or put it in quotation marks as above.

ancient as well as in modern legal practice, as Weber showed by a profusion of illustrations. Still, his summary refers to major types of law creation and hence to the major forces that have been at work in effecting or resisting increased legal rationality and the development of legal domination. By using lawmaking through legislation as a model with which other methods of lawmaking may be compared, one comes to see not only the diversity of types that have played a role historically, but the legal practices that had to be abandoned and the conditions under which they were abandoned before the modern system of legal domination could emerge.[19]

Charismatic Legal Revelation

Charismatic legal revelation through law prophets represents the greatest possible contrast to modern lawmaking and its adherence to enacted rules. At one time, legal prophecy was the universal practice. Its fundamental principle was that law could only be revealed.[20] Legal disputes were decided by resorting to an oracle or an ordeal—or both—wherever the still more primitive method of blood feuds and vengeance had been abandoned. Priests and other law prophets increased their

[19] Weber's four categories of legal revelation, empirical creation of law, imposition of law, and systematization may be reduced to three: law prophets, imposition of law by authority, and lawmaking by legal notables. This reduction is indicated because Weber's summary appears to vacillate between types of lawmaking and types of lawmaker. Some ambiguity may be unavoidable here, but the three-fold distinction used in the subsequent discussion seeks to minimize it by placing the emphasis upon the different lawmakers—law prophets, established authority, and legal notables. This typology is in line with Weber's own orientation, since four out of eight chapters in his sociology of law (V, VII, VIII, IX) are directly and two more chapters (X, XI) indirectly related to it. (There are fourteen chapters in the English edition, but five of these are taken from other parts of Weber's work, and one of his original chapters in the *Rechtssoziologie* was subdivided.) There are two other chapters (III, VI) in which he dealt with legal concepts rather than with types of lawmaker, and the present synopsis is, therefore, not only a summary, but also an interpretation in line with the perspective stated in Chapter II above.

[20] *Law*, pp. 88, 89. This discussion of legal prophecy is based on *ibid.*, pp. 75–82, 86–91.

power by being called upon to dispense oracles and supervise trials by ordeal.

Evidence for this type of lawmaking or lawfinding[21] in early times is very widespread. Weber cited examples from ancient Egypt, Babylonia, and Greece, from Ireland, Gaul, Russia, and other northern European countries, and from various countries in Africa. A few features of legal revelation may be presented to make clear at what points elements of rationality emerge, even in this type of law and procedure.

In several countries of northern Europe the lord of the court originally did not participate in the decision of a case; instead, he presided over the proceedings and kept order in the court. According to the charismatic conception his office did not confer legal wisdom upon him; rather, his task was to bring the parties to the point where they preferred a settlement in court to vengeance by self-help. The decision itself was in the hands of charismatic "declarers" of the law, experts in the art of putting the question to the deity in the correct and hence the magically most effective way. Such law prophecy involved an elaborate ritual and adherence to certain formal procedures. Lawfinding was separate from law enforcement, since coercive power was in the hands of political officials, not the law prophets. Thus both the formalization of legal procedure and the separation of adjudication from enforcement have their rudimentary beginnings in these ancient institutions.[22]

Weber's emphasis on status groups as the carriers of ideas in historical change applies here, too. The charismatic law prophets were sages or priests chosen for their magical qualifications. Later they were legal notables who were acknowledged as such (like the *lag saga* or alderman among the North

[21] Weber used the term "lawfinding" (*Rechtsfindung*) to express the idea that the law that is declared is believed to exist—for example, as part of the divine order. Hence law and justice are "found" rather than "made" or "enacted."

[22] These as well as all other examples taken from Weber's comprehensive study are merely illustrative. The foregoing reference to the separation of lawfinding and law enforcement pertains to Germanic institutions, and this is only one of several types. The Roman system of concurrent powers, for instance, entitled several magistrates to "intercede" against each other—clearly another separation of powers in the administration of justice.

Germans) and who eventually became functionaries legitimated by periodic elections or by appointment (royal patent). These notables usually were descendants of eminent families, and their office often became hereditary where the families were regarded as charismatically endowed. From prophets or sages called upon to find the law from case to case, these notables developed into permanent officials responsible for stating annually before the assembled community the rules in accordance with which they would declare or "find" the law. The purpose was to make these rules known to the community and to keep their memory alive in the law prophet himself, which again shows a rudimentary beginning of the duty of public disclosure and of the adjudication by rules that developed later.[23] However the notable was not bound by the rules or decisions of his predecessor or by the suggestions or resolutions of the popular assembly. He could take these into account, but they were not law until he did so, and by virtue of his charisma he could ignore them and "create" new law.

These examples of legal revelation show the absence of "law" in the sense of rules of conduct that are intentionally created as such and are guaranteed by "legal coercion." In theory, tradition was immutable and the intentional creation of new norms inconceivable. Norms were valid in the sense of sacred usage, and disputes were decided as individual cases by elders, priests, or magicians, who were believed to possess a special knowledge of magical forces and tradition. In this way the law prophets did, of course, develop rules or norms that were binding for the resolution of disputes, and adaptations of tradition as well as new norms could emerge through interpretation or a new charismatic revelation. But as long as law was based on revelation or custom and the consent of the com-

[23] This approach to lawmaking became formalized after the reliance on oracles and ordeals declined. Such an "intermediate" condition is represented by the English customals or the German *Weistümer*—annual inquiries into the legal customs of a particular locality, which were recited publicly and later reduced to writing. These collections lacked legal systematization, however, since their stipulations fluctuated from case to case between laws and rights, statutes and judicial decisions, administrative decrees and normative rules. Cf. *ibid.*, pp. 73, 84–85.

munity, it was typically irrational in the sense that it was not oriented toward rules or bound by them.[24]

On the other hand, rudimentary beginnings of legal rationality existed even at the stage of legal revelation. Where tradition is sacred and magical dangers abound, legal proceedings are rigorously formal. Each legal problem requires its own magical technique, and once that has been determined the slightest error of procedure will result in the loss of the remedy or even of the entire case. Since, among other things, the magically effective formula stipulated the one and only correct manner in which questions had to be asked, an element of rationality was present even in the absence of any orientation toward legal norms.

The oblivious attitude toward rules or principles and the practice of considering each case in the light of tradition and a sense of justice are by no means characteristic merely of early legal institutions. The refusal to be bound by rules where the vital emotions and interests of people are concerned recurs time and again, both in the layman's attitude toward the law and in the development of the law itself. But this attitude and practice have become subject to normative limitations, both tacitly and explicitly.

Imposition of Law

The imposition of law by secular and theocratic powers represents a second type of lawfinding and legal innovation, though for a long time this type is hardly distinguishable from legal revelation. That is to say, laws may be "enacted implicitly," although there is no conscious departure from tradition and legal revelation. For example, heads of kinship groups or the assembled notables may impute an especially high authority to a particular interpretation of sacred tradition and so, in effect, "enact" a law. Or a magician may proclaim a new principle on the basis of revelation, and the assembly of able-bodied men may adopt it and propagate it accordingly. Or the creation of law may become secularized, as among certain Australian tribes where revelation is used only as an ex

[24] Cf. *ibid.*, p. 73, where Weber referred to the changeability of the will of Yahwe and of the prophet Mohammed.

post facto ratification of the decision. In these and other ways lawfinding through revelation may be gradually superseded by lawmaking through initiative and consensus, although there is no explicit abandonment of tradition or enactment of new laws. Where the distinction between finding and making law is absent, the creation of new laws will necessarily occur through various intermediate forms, as, for example, in England, where "the resolutions of Parliament have always retained, even until today, the character of mere amendments to the existing law."[25]

According to Weber, the secularization and systematization of legal thought were very frequently promoted by laws imposed as a result of wars and their uprooting effects. In time of war the powers of a leader are much greater than those of a "judge" or law prophet or priest in times of peace. A conquering war leader can readily increase his authority at the expense of tradition, because war disrupts the existing social order and so proves that tradition is not in fact inviolable. Also, new problems arise for which traditional practices do not provide a solution; prisoners, booty and especially conquered land must be disposed of, and breaches of discipline and domestic disorder must be prevented. To order all these disturbed conditions new norms are created, and old as well as new laws may be systematized, with the result that in the settlement of disputes the prestige of age and, to some extent, of magic, declines.[26]

Great as the power of a conquering war leader is, there are many circumstances under which he cannot or will not exercise it without the free consent of the army. This form of leadership, in which the decision proposed by the leader becomes valid through the public acclamation of the assembly, was in a number of instances the basis on which the concept of an enacted statute first developed. In Roman law this concept was related specifically to the military imperium of the magistrate. Where the magistrate had asked for and obtained the assent of the popular assembly, consisting of the citizens in arms, his decree was elevated to the rank of law and made

25 *Law*, p. 85.
26 *Ibid.*, pp. 91–92.

binding for all citizens as well as for his successor in office.[27]

Other early enactments of laws, however, were not directly related to a condition of war. Among these are the royal acts (*capitula*) through which the Frankish kings amended the popular laws that had been officially compiled;[28] the inquisitorial procedure of the Catholic Church, in which the ascertainment of the facts is the task of the judge; and the procedural innovations of the English kings, such as the establishment of trial by jury.[29] In these and similar cases the secular and theocratic powers intervened in the older forms of law and procedure to eliminate, where possible, the influence of independent law prophets and the popular assembly. Legal revelation could threaten secular authority as well as the institutional charisma of the church. Moreover, both powers had reason to fear that public participation in trials would promote the political autonomy of estates and hence challenge established authority.

In opposing legal revelation and its derivatives, the secular and theocratic powers responded to administrative and political exigencies while seeking to realize certain ethical goals. Although they may be said to have promoted the rationalization of law through legal enactment, this "promotion" was largely inadvertent. It did not imply an interest in the specialized treatment of legal questions or in the separation of law

[27] *Ibid.*, p. 85. This enactment of laws based on public acclamation was also the starting point of feudal society, with its decentralization of authority. For example, ancient German law required that the members of the community participate in a trial by publicly concurring in, and thus ratifying, the verdict of the law prophet. This right to participate in legal as well as in political decisions was dependent on property ownership and the performance of military service. Thus the Germanic *thing* was an assembly of landowners who were able to bear arms, and the Roman *populus* consisted of property holders, assembled in their military units, who had both the duty of military service and the right to vote in the popular assembly (until they were sixty years of age and no longer permitted to do either). Institutions of this type provided the basis of a decentralized estate society, with its formal contracts between a ruler and his vassals, as well as of centralized authority. And they may be viewed as a factor in the gradual rationalization of the law.

[28] *Ibid.*, p. 89.

[29] *Ibid.*, pp. 224–25. On the last point cf. pp. 403–4 below.

and ethics. This halfway step in the development of legal rationality is generally favored by patriarchal and theocratic authorities because any fixation of formal legal procedures diminishes the individual's dependence upon their good will. Indeed, wielders of power in all types of domination tend to oppose inviolable rules in the administration of justice and all other public affairs, wherever such rules curtail their power and conflict with their desire to realize substantive goals. However, secular and theocratic powers do favor a systematization of the law where it serves their political interests, as we shall see presently. The character of such systematization reflects, in Weber's judgment, the persistent preference of established authorities for a type of law and administration that allows them the greatest possible leeway for decision-making on all substantive legal and political issues.[30]

These tendencies of established authorities point to the distinction between formal and substantive rationality that is basic to Weber's entire analysis. Ancient legal practice was irrational from his point of view because it involved means like oracles or ordeals, which cannot be controlled by the intellect. But even in lawmaking that can be controlled by the intellect, it is necessary to distinguish different types. Patriarchal and theocratic powers are primarily interested in substantive rationality. They approach all legal questions from the viewpoint of political expediency or substantive justice and hence disregard any limitations on their actions that might arise from requirements of formal procedure or logical consistency.[31] Weber distinguished between this substantive approach and the procedural and logical rationality of law, which he called "formal":

> Law . . . is "formal" to the extent that, in both substantive and procedural matters, only unambiguous general characteristics of the facts of the case are taken into account. This formalism can, again, be of two different kinds. It is possible that the legally relevant characteristics are of a tangible nature, i.e., that they are perceptible as sense data.

[30] This point is elaborated below in the separate consideration of the influence of church and state on legal rationality.

[31] Cf. the earlier statement on the administration of justice under a patrimonial regime, on p. 367.

This *adherence to external characteristics* of the facts, for instance the utterance of certain words, the execution of a signature, or the performance of a certain symbolic act with a fixed meaning, represents the most rigorous type of legal formalism. The other type of formalistic law is found where the legally relevant characteristics of the facts are disclosed through the *logical analysis of meaning* and where, accordingly, definitely fixed legal concepts in the form of highly abstract rules are formulated and applied.[32]

A simple example may clarify this major distinction. Where juridical formalism prevails, the procedure of a lawsuit becomes a peaceful contest bound to fixed "rules of the game." One of these rules stipulates that under the principle of adversary procedure the judge must wait for the motions of the parties. The promotion of the suit is their concern, and it must occur in strict compliance with the forms of procedure that have been worked out by legal specialists. Whatever facts remain undisclosed in the course of this procedure do not exist so far as the judge is concerned. As Weber stated, the judge "aims at establishing only that relative truth which is attainable within the limits set by the procedural acts of the parties."[33] Thus, the formal rationality of the law guarantees only the formal rights of the interested parties. If, for example, an individual fails to remember an important fact or cannot afford the expense required to document it, he may be forced to forego the enjoyment of rights that are legally his. Thus fortuitous circumstances may produce substantive injustice under a formally rational system of law. Purely ethical considerations would demand that the administration of justice not be affected by the unequal distribution of income, but these considerations are at odds with a rationality of law that consists of the predictability of its formal procedures.

This distinction between formal and substantive rationality has special significance in the present context. Weber contended that the formal rationality of legal procedure had increased in importance in the history of Western civilization, in part as a result of laws imposed by secular and theocratic

[32] *Law*, p. 63. My italics.
[33] *Ibid.*, p. 227.

powers. Yet these powers are continually "confronted by the inevitable conflict between an abstract formalism of legal certainty and their desire to realize substantive goals."[34] We must therefore consider the particular conditions under which both church and state helped promote a system of legal domination in western Europe.

Church and legal rationality. The influence of the church on the development of legal domination may be considered first in terms of the relation between sacred and secular law.[35] In most Asiatic civilizations, religious and ritualistic prescriptions were never clearly differentiated from secular rules. Moral exhortations and legal commands were intertwined, and a nonformal type of jurisprudence prevailed.[36] In Western civilization, sacred law became separated from temporal law. Under the Roman Republic this occurred at least in part because the secular nobility of the Republic established an absolute dominion, and the priesthood was not permitted to intrude in matters of secular jurisdiction despite the great importance of ritual obligations in Roman life.[37] In addition, the early Christian Church rejected for centuries all involvement in matters of state and of law, so that its jurisdiction under canon law was clearly distinguished from secular jurisdiction.

[34] *Law*, p. 226.

[35] Weber considered this relation with special reference to private law. That is, sacred lawmaking has been concerned everywhere with the law of the family, pertaining not only to birth and marriage but above all to inheritance. Such lawmaking has also been concerned with objects or places that are consecrated, and with contracts, which involve a religious form of promise such as an oath.

[36] Weber used the term "khadi-justice" to refer to this type of jurisprudence. The *khadi* was a Mohammedan judge, but Weber used "khadi-justice" quite generally "to describe the administration of justice which is oriented not toward fixed rules of a formally rational law but toward the ethical, religious, political, or otherwise expediential postulates of a substantively rational law." See Professor Max Rheinstein's comment in *Law*, p. 213, n. 48, and the cross-references cited there. Weber surveyed the combinations of temporal and sacred law that had prevailed in India, China, and Persia, in Islam, and in Judaism, to buttress his assertion that the relative separation of these two elements in the Western church was in fact one of its distinguishing characteristics. See *ibid.*, pp. 234–50.

[37] Cf. *ibid.*, pp. 225–26, 233–34, and Professor Max Rheinstein's comments on these passages.

In this way the early church facilitated the secularization of the law, which is a fundamental prerequisite of legal rationality.

Second, canon law had a direct and positive effect on the *formal* rationality of law despite the preoccupation of the church with substantive religious and ethical considerations. Canon law itself possessed more formal rationality than other systems of sacred law, for several reasons:

a. Insofar as it had to regulate its relations with the secular authorities, the church sought to do so in terms of the Stoic conceptions of natural law, i.e., in terms of a logically articulated body of normative ideas concerning justice.

b. Canon law inherited both the professional legal techniques of Roman law and the rigorous logic of ancient philosophy.

c. In the early Middle Ages the church created a first systematic body of law in its handbooks of penances (penitentials), which were modeled after certain formal components of Germanic law.

d. The structure of the university in medieval Europe further facilitated the rationalization of canon law by separating the teaching of sacred law from the teaching of theology and of secular law. In this way the universities strengthened the separation of sacred and secular law that had been initiated by the early Christian Church.

e. The jurists of the church were not concerned with rendering opinions in individual cases and hence with developing a body of rules on the basis of precedents and logical articulation. Because of the hierarchic structure of the church, they were interested rather in developing a body of laws on the basis of official decrees and conciliar resolutions, and eventually they even "created" such authoritative documents by deliberate forgery in order to resolve certain crucial issues. Consequently, the church lawyers furthered the separation of lawmaking and lawfinding and promoted the idea that adjudication consists of the application of enacted laws.

f. The character of ecclesiastical lawmaking finally was influenced by the fact that the functionaries of the church constituted an autonomous bureaucratic hierarchy (especially after the reforms of Pope Gregory VII, 1073–85) and as such had a positive interest in the development of a formally rational legal system.[38]

All of these conditions and tendencies did not prevent canon law from containing that admixture of legal formalism and a substantive ethical orientation which is characteristic of all theocratic law. But on the whole the development of formal legal techniques prevailed. The New Testament's concept of withdrawal from the world involved a minimum of binding norms of a ritual or legal character, so that the way was left open for the deliberate enactment of decrees and laws. And in the hierarchic organization of the church everything was under the supervision of the Holy See. By its authoritative decrees, binding ethical norms were constantly elaborated, in striking contrast to Islamic and Jewish law, which developed through the activities of responding jurists. Canon law also contributed a number of important concepts to the development of secular law, among them the recognition of informal contracts, freedom of testation in the interest of facilitating pious endowments, and the idea of the corporation. It also influenced legal procedure. No organized religion can leave the discovery of truth or the expiation of a wrong to the layman. A theocratic administration of justice like that of the Catholic Church necessarily establishes ex officio an inquisitorial procedure that maximizes the possibility of establishing the facts of a case instead of leaving this important matter to the contentions of the litigants. This inquisitorial procedure of the Church was subsequently taken over by the secular administration of justice in criminal cases.[39]

Important as these influences are, they failed to establish the all-embracing regulation of life that was the theoretical aim of canon law as of all other systems of theocratic law. With regard to that aim, canon law had relatively little significance for secular law, especially private and commercial law. The reason was that in Western civilization the church encountered vigorous and successful opposition by the urban bourgeoisie,

[38] *Ibid.*, pp. 250–51.
[39] *Law*, pp. 168, 225, 253–54.

estate assemblies and organized guilds of lawyers when it sought to extend its ecclesiastical jurisdiction at the expense of secular law. This opposition was helped by the existence of the Roman law, to which the church itself was indebted and which proved to be a highly effective secular competitor of canon law.[40]

On balance the influence of theocratic authority was strong enough to help cast off the practice of legal revelation and related older forms of justice. The hierarchic organization of the church and its inquisitorial procedure increased the tendencies toward a substantive rationalization of the law. But what was crucial for the development of Western civilization was that the church and its sacred law were clearly differentiated from secular jurisdiction. This left the way free for the imposition of laws by secular authorities and the consequent growth of legal formalism in the development of the modern state.

State and legal rationality. The influence of secular authorities may be considered in terms of the gradual extension of the ruler's legal domination in the fields of criminal and private law. One of the earliest manifestations of this was the ruler's power to protect the peace. While military considerations and the interest in "law and order" were major reasons for this extension of the ruler's authority, the fear of an arbitrary exercise of it was as acute as the desire for peace. It is plausible, therefore, to assume that the early medieval tariffs of fines, which covered every conceivable crime, constituted a compromise solution, allowing as they did the establishment of a national penal law *and* the curtailment of an arbitrary exercise of power. The ruler and his officials could still preserve the peace but were bound to observe the tariffs, while their subjects could calculate in advance whether a crime or the instigation of a lawsuit would "pay."[41]

In the field of private law the intervention of secular authorities occurred much later than in the field of criminal justice. Eventually new laws were created through the "magisterial power" of the official charged with the administration of justice, which extended the jurisdiction of the royal courts as

[40] *Ibid.,* pp. 253–54.
[41] *Ibid.,* pp. 258–59.

against the popular and feudal courts. The common element in these legal innovations was the adoption of more rational procedures in lieu of the older forms of legal revelation and folk justice. Under Louis IX (1226–70), for example, trial by ordeal was abolished and the jurisdiction of feudal lords was subjected to the royal courts (*parlements*), which dispensed with many of the ancient procedural formalities.

Although such actions did away with the irrational practices of ancient law, they frequently took only a half-step toward the development of legal rationality. This is well illustrated by the origin of the English jury. In ancient legal procedure proof did not concern allegations of fact; witnesses did not swear to the truth of a statement but asserted the rightness of their side by exposing themselves to divine wrath. The issue was "which party should be allowed or required to address to the magical powers the question of whether he was right and in which of several ways this might or ought to be done."[42] A major step away from this reliance on legal revelation was introduced when Henry II (1154–89) issued royal writs that granted the petitioning party the right to interrogate twelve neighbors sworn to tell what they knew of the disputed possession. "The 'jury' emerged when the parties voluntarily, or shortly afterwards under pressure of compulsion, agreed in all types of litigation to accept the verdict of twelve jurors rather than to derive the finding of guilt from the old irrational modes of trial."[43] The jury thus promoted the "rationalization" of the law by substituting the deliberation of laymen for the verdict of an oracle, but it still retained the old concern with substantive justice. Indeed, the jury resembles the oracle in that it does not indicate rational grounds for its decisions.[44]

Public decrees were issued by the secular authorities in one of two ways: unilaterally, by virtue of the patriarchal power of the ruler, or with the assent of some representative body. Such lawmaking was necessarily related to the struggle for power among conflicting status groups discussed in the previous chapter. That discussion emphasized the conflict of interest

[42] *Law*, p. 78. See also pp. 227–28.
[43] *Ibid.*, p. 79.
[44] *Ibid.* Related examples from English legal history are cited in *ibid.*, pp. 260–61.

between rulers who sought to preserve and enhance their authority, and the feudal estates, patrimonial officials, urban bourgeoisie, church, and other groups that strove for local autonomy. The "khadi-justice" of the patrimonial ruler and the fixation of privileges on the part of autonomous groups both reflected the combination of arbitrariness and time-honored convention characteristic of traditional domination. But the fact is that in western Europe patrimonial power eventually promoted the formal rationality of law and administration, and this conflicts with the tendency of patrimonial rulers to promote substantive justice and personal favoritism.

Weber explained this paradox as the result of several more or less independent lines of development. The unification and systematization of the law were to some extent the consequence of administrative stabilization under powerful patrimonial rulers. In the process of curbing the power pretensions of vassals and benefice-holders, such rulers would buttress their authority with a centrally controlled officialdom, and this administrative apparatus set in motion tendencies favoring the development of procedural rationality. The power of the monarch depended upon the efficiency of his fiscal administration, which was enhanced wherever the earlier methods of tax-farming were superseded by a centrally organized system of internal revenue.[45] The ruler's interest in unity and order coincided with the personal interests of his officials. Once a bureaucracy is centrally organized, it requires permanent officials to run it, and these officials have a strong interest in the career opportunities it offers. Such opportunities are improved if legal uniformity prevails throughout an entire realm, for then officials no longer are restricted by their ignorance of local laws but may be employed wherever a vacancy occurs.

These developments toward increased centralization and greater legal uniformity tended to limit the possibility of patriarchal arbitrariness, but they did not thereby establish and guarantee any individual "rights." Indeed, these develop-

[45] The same consideration applies to the organization of the military forces and to other branches of administration. For a concise analysis of this process on a comparative basis, cf. Ernest Barker, *The Development of Public Services in Western Europe* (London: Oxford University Press, 1944), *passim*.

ments depended to some extent on the violation of "well-established rights," such as the appropriated rights of benefice-holders, the traditional privileges of feudal vassals, and the monopolies of craft guilds. In the struggle against the entrenched position of the estates, patrimonial rulers were frequently supported by the rising bourgeoisie. The monopolistic interests of the early capitalists in governmentally protected enterprises induced them to "pay for their privileged business opportunities by the precariousness of their legal position vis-à-vis the prince."[46] But the preponderance of patrimonial rulers in the struggle against "estatist privileges and the estatist character of the legal and administrative system" and the resulting lack of a guaranteed legal order did not prevail in the long run.[47] If the early capitalists were dependent upon the ruler for their business opportunities and for the power necessary to defeat existing privileges, the ruler was equally dependent upon the financial and political support of these economic interest groups. And these groups demanded

> an unambiguous and clear legal system, that would be free of irrational administrative arbitrariness as well as of irrational disturbance by concrete privileges, that would also offer firm guaranties of the legally binding character of contracts, and that, in consequence of all these factors, would function in a calculable way. The alliance of monarchical and bourgeois interests was, therefore, one of the major factors which led toward formal legal rationalization, [though] not . . . in the sense . . . that a direct "cooperation" of these two powers would always have been necessary. . . .

> The needs of those interested in formal legal equality and objective formal norms, coincide with the power interests of the prince as against the holders of privilege. Both interests are served simultaneously by the substitution of "reglementation" for "privilege."[48]

[46] *Ibid.*, p. 268.
[47] *Ibid.*, p. 266.
[48] *Law*, pp. 266, 267.

However, this particular, frequently tacit concurrence of interests was not the only constellation through which a codification of the law occurred. Weber pointed out that groups other than the bourgeoisie had an interest in such unambiguous fixation of the law and that powers other than monarchs undertook to promote it.[49] In these cases political interest in the unification of the legal system predominated, whatever the impact of economic and religious interests and however much such politically motivated codification was aided by a more or less dependent literary activity involving the creation of "books of law." This codification consisted of compilations that sought to bring into order the existing body of laws but did not undertake a systematic revision of their substantive content. Proper systematization was the work of university-trained judges in the patrimonial regimes of Continental Europe, who were instrumental in resuscitating Roman law. It was this work that gave a special impetus to the formal rationality of the law, which was favored by the concurrent interests of patrimonial rulers, their officials, and economic interest groups. But before we consider this particular development we must examine a third type of lawmaking.

Lawmaking by Legal Notables

The work of legal professionals emerges as imperceptibly out of ancient legal practices and conventional behavior as does the imposition of laws by established authorities. Although the whole process of lawmaking and lawfinding depends on the traditions of the community, Weber emphasized that a theory of legal development as merely an outgrowth of tradition

[49] Cf. *ibid.*, pp. 268–74, 279–83, where Weber surveyed examples of legal codification like those of ancient Rome and Israel, of the Frankish Empire and the Germanic kingdoms established on Roman soil, of the Mongol Empire under Genghis Khan, of China, medieval Spain, and others. In many of these cases the interest in a unified legal system came to prevail where a new political community was to be established, whether this occurred through the foundation of colonies or of confederations or through a new regime following a conquest or a revolution. In other instances codification resulted from the monarchical interest in unity and order.

would lead nowhere scientifically.[50] The accepted traditions
of a society as well as new practices can become law only
through interaction among interested parties and through the
work of legal notables.

Although it may be impossible to identify the individuals
involved in this process, it is possible to see the significance of
interested parties. For centuries the arrangements among them
may exist on the basis of shared understandings, without any
thought of explicit formulation or recourse to established
authority. But wherever the belief in magic and the practice
of legal revelation decline, judicial decisions become the concern of lay judges (as distinguished from law prophets) and a
subject for discussion, and the interested parties begin to estimate the probability that the judiciary will consider a given
contract or association legally valid and enforceable. This age-
old interaction between the public and the legal notables has
a bearing on the formulation and development of legal norms.

From the standpoint of the judge this formulation is easier
"wherever there is a weakening of the purely oracular character of the decision,"[51] although Weber added that the
abandonment of legal prophecy is *not* an unequivocal step in
the direction of legal rationality. In the primitive law of evidence, the precise formulation of the questions constituted a
formal element that was lost when lay judges began to consider the concrete particulars of the individual case. Nevertheless, judge-made law resulted in the formulation of legal
norms, and this was inevitable for several reasons. First, a degree of stabilization emerged where the decline of magic made
it possible for the verdict to be discussed, since discussion
usually involves some search for the grounds on which the
verdict can be based. Second, the judge would not ignore established custom or explicit agreements under normal circumstances, though political contingencies or formal considerations
might well entail exceptions to this. But even where the judge
appears to do no more than place his stamp of approval upon
norms that are already binding in terms of custom or agreement, he does in fact do more. His "decision of individual cases
always produces consequences which, acting beyond the scope

[50] *Ibid.*, p. 67.
[51] *Ibid.*, p. 74.

of the case, influence the selection of those rules which are to survive as law."[52] This consideration blends with a third factor. Judges who wish to avoid the charge of bias will seek to render consistent decisions and hence to formulate the maxims of their decision-making as an aid to their own judgment. The same holds true for their successors, so that in time norms acquire an enduring validity.[53]

From the standpoint of the interested parties and their professional counselors, the formulation of legal norms is facilitated because they seek to adapt themselves to the "expected reaction of the judiciary." In this connection Weber especially emphasized the importance of *cautelary jurists* for the standardization of agreements between the parties themselves. The term refers to "those lawyers who, like the English conveyancer or the modern American corporation lawyer, are using their skill in drafting instruments and especially in inventing new clauses for the purpose of safeguarding their clients' interests and of preventing future litigation."[54] Though these examples are contemporary, they refer to a type of activity that goes back to Roman antiquity and that, in Weber's view, led to the formulation of legal concepts in relation to everyday life. This empirical orientation toward the law increased the deliberation with which individuals entered into formal agreements. In this way cautelary jurists helped demarcate spheres of interest and impart to the law a degree of empirical dependability even in the absence of an explicit orientation toward norms.

These social aspects of the judicial process point to the importance of lawmaking by legal notables. Consequently Weber was concerned with the ways in which the legal profession became emancipated from magic and sacred tradition and promoted the development of legal rationality. However, he did not construe this emancipation and "rationalization" in a simple fashion. The most ancient and the most modern types

[52] *Law,* p. 73.

[53] The subjective desire to apply norms that are already valid applies to the law prophets as well as to all other forms of adjudication. It is the orientation toward norms and their content that varies from type to type.

[54] Cf. Professor Max Rheinstein's editorial comment in *Law,* p. 72, n. 18.

of law and legal procedure contain different combinations of the perennial elements of legal thought; i.e., every such type involves an effort at formalization and an effort to achieve substantive justice. It is probable, for example, that even in the irrational system of ancient law the law prophets and the assembly of lay notables used their sense of equity in rendering a verdict, at least insofar as ritual formalism and the fear of magical dangers permitted them to do so. Weber emphasized at the same time that the highest development of formal procedure in modern law is based ultimately on certain substantive ideas of natural law. Every type, therefore, represents an effort to reconcile tendencies of thought and action that would be irreconcilable if each tendency were elaborated fully and with complete logical consistency.[55]

Every combination of formal and substantive justice has been decisively influenced by the lawmaking of legal notables. Since the various directions in which the formal qualities of the law can be developed are "conditioned directly by . . . the particular character of the individuals who are in a position to influence [the law] 'professionally,'" Weber devoted his attention to the systems of legal training through which this professionalization occurred.[56] Law can be taught as a craft by the practitioners themselves, or in special schools as legal theory or science. These two types of legal training are represented by the English and the Continental development respectively.

Empirical training in the law. Specialists of the law can be traced back to the early times of the law prophets, who were priests like the Druids among the Gauls or special legal nota-

[55] This construction of logical irreconcilability is a technique Weber used time and again. Classes and status groups, contemplative mysticism and ascetic activism, charismatic leadership and the enduring types of traditional and legal domination all are "irreconcilable" with each other. He used such pure types to sort out the constituent elements in each empirical constellation and to pinpoint the areas of possible tension, e.g., where charisma intrudes in a system of traditional domination or where substantive ethical considerations disrupt or modify the formal rationality of the law. Cf. pp. 274–78 for a discussion of this method and pp. 398–99 for a formulation of the contrast between formal and substantive rationality.

[56] *Law*, p. 97.

bles like the Germanic aldermen (*lag saga*). The trial procedure of medieval France illustrates an early type of such legal
specialization. Trials were conducted before a popular assembly, and their progress depended upon certain words being
spoken by or for the litigant. Upon request the judge would
appoint an *advocate* from the lay notables acting in a legal
capacity as judgment-finders or declarers of the law. This advocate would speak for the litigant, who thus was freed from
speaking for himself and who could therefore correct his advocate if necessary. But as one of the judgment-finders the
advocate would also participate in the rendition of the verdict.
As yet no distinction was made between an advocate and a
judge. In trials of this kind the evidence was obtained through
oracles, and the case was "prepared" through assertions by
which the litigant exposed himself to magical dangers. This
procedure had no place for an *attorney,* who would assume
the task of obtaining the evidence and preparing the case. An
attorney who performed these functions and who acted as the
procedural "representative" of the party did not become possible until the patrimonial rulers of England and France developed the institutions of royal law, and originally such "representatives" were recruited among the clergy, i.e., among
persons who could write. A conciliar prohibition of the church
in 1215 and the expansion of training among the upper classes
resulted eventually in the organization of English lay lawyers
in the Inns of Court.

The very early distinction between an advocate and an attorney was reflected in subsequent developments.[57] There
were "attorneys" or solicitors who prepared the "brief" and
acted as intermediaries between the litigants and the "advocate" or barrister who presented the case before the court. The
latter had nothing to do with the technical services required
and eventually lost all contact with the client. Unlike solicitors,
all barristers were organized in a guild from whose members
all judges were chosen. In the Middle Ages, admission to the
guild was regulated with ever increasing autonomy, aided,

[57] *Ibid.,* pp. 199–200. The differentiation of functions among
legal professionals in England occurred in the course of a very long
and complex development, which has not been fully clarified. Cf.
the editorial notes in *loc. cit.*

perhaps, by the fact that the members came largely from the nobility. In the guild school candidates had to undergo a four-year novitiate terminating in the call to the bar, which conferred the right to plead cases in court. The guild further insisted on a strict professional etiquette, with regard to both the minimum fees to be charged and the stipulation that payment be voluntary and was not properly a subject of legal action.

The legal training of the guild was entirely practical. Lecture courses were introduced at the Inns of Court only in the course of competitive struggles with the universities, and they were eventually discontinued.[58] The character of this education reflected its direct dependence upon practitioners who had monopolized the practice of law and who handled cases in terms of precedents and of analogies drawn from precedents. Their legal practice aimed

> . . . at a practically useful scheme of contracts and actions, oriented toward the interests of clients in typically recurrent situations. . . . From such practices and attitudes no rational system of law [in the sense of formal procedure] could emerge, nor even a [logical] "rationalization" of the law as such, because the concepts thus formed are constructed in relation to the material . . . events of everyday life, are distinguished from each other by external criteria, and extended in their scope, as new needs arise.[59]

Weber stated that this type of legal reasoning "always moves from the particular to the particular but never tries to move from the particular to general propositions in order to be able subsequently to deduce from them the norms for new particular cases."[60]

Several factors helped perpetuate this approach. As practic-

[58] The Inns of Court concentrated on the teaching of "English" law as developed in the royal courts, whereas Oxford and Cambridge taught only civil and canon law. Cf. *ibid.*, p. 201, n. 12.

[59] *Ibid.*, p. 201. The comments in brackets have been supplied in order to make clear that English law, in Weber's view, lacked formal but not substantive rationality. Quotation marks around "rationalization" have also been added.

[60] *Law*, p. 202.

ing lawyers, the guild members had a pecuniary interest in stabilizing the prevailing empirical method of lawmaking and preventing its systematization through logical analysis and legislation. For example, they had an economic interest in the fees received for the examination of title, which had to be made in every transaction because of the uncertainty of all land titles, and therefore they had little interest in a system of registration that would eliminate such uncertainty. Thus English lawyers opposed systematic lawmaking and legal education in universities, partly because of their economic interests, partly because of the pronounced traditionalism of their profession, and partly because a system of legal training and reasoning possesses a momentum of its own once its basic pattern is developed. In addition, Weber noted that this opposition was compatible with the interests of the rising commercial classes. Legal training was in the hands of lawyers who worked in the service of property owners and derived their income from this social group. Consequently, the legal profession tended generally to share the conservative outlook of its clients. Also, the administration of justice was concentrated in the London courts, and this, together with the costliness of the legal process, amounted to a denial of justice to those with inadequate means.[61] In view of these circumstances and of the general ambivalence toward legal formalism among laymen, the common law tradition served the desire of interest groups for a dependable legal system.

Legal education in the universities. On the Continent a second type of legal training emerged. In contrast to England, guild organizations of lawyers did not acquire much power even where they existed. The status of the lawyers was determined by governmental regulation rather than by an autonomous profession. Eventually only law-school graduates were admitted to legal practice, with the result that the universities monopolized legal education. And the universities were the agencies through which Roman law was revived and became dominant in medieval Europe.

Weber exemplified the emergence of this second type by referring to the Italian notaries, who were especially important

[61] *Ibid.*, p. 318.

in the development of commercial law.[62] In the rapidly growing cities of medieval Italy, notaries constituted a status group of legal notables who were organized in guilds and who formed an important segment of the dominant urban bourgeoisie. In the expanding trade within and among these cities, documentary evidence was preferred to the irrational means of evidence in use before the popular courts, and the notaries decisively influenced the legal practices of documentation. In so doing they made use of Roman law, partly because of their own traditions, partly because Roman law was well adapted to meet the requirements of commerce, and partly because this was the law taught at the great Italian universities. The teaching of Roman law at the universities had been sponsored originally by the emperor, but the practice continued after the sponsorship had lost its significance.[63] Thus the Italian notaries, together with the universities, were instrumental in initiating the reception of Roman law, which eventually spread throughout Continental Europe and beyond.

Weber concluded that the advance of trained jurists—in lieu of the lay notables of the old folk justice—was caused to some extent by the growing need for their special skills in the administration of justice. These skills consisted above all in "the capacity to state clearly and unambiguously the legal issues involved in a complicated situation,"[64] and that capacity resulted from special professional training at a university. The new stratum of professional legal scholars brought to the fore the formal qualities of Roman law. In the Roman Empire, un-

[62] On the Continent notaries are specialists in legal drafting, like the cautelary jurists referred to above, not merely legal functionaries who authenticate signatures, like the American notary public.

[63] In view of the political fragmentation of the country, the Italian notaries could not form a nation-wide guild organization like their English colleagues. They were therefore unable to develop a guild system of legal education that could compete with the universities. On the other hand, university graduates who had been trained in Roman law had a major impact upon the urban bourgeoisie. The magistrates (*podesta*) of the Italian cities were frequently chosen from their midst, and the aristocratic city councils (*signoria*) based themselves upon political doctrines developed at the universities. Cf. *ibid.*, pp. 210–11, as well as *WuG*, Vol. II, pp. 545 ff., 563 ff., for Weber's discussion of Italian cities and their social structure.

[64] *Law*, p. 275.

der the influence of philosophical training Roman law had already become an object of a purely literary activity and, in the absence of binding sacred laws or substantive ethical concerns, purely logical elements of legal thinking had begun to play some role. These incipient tendencies were strengthened tremendously when Roman law was revived in medieval Europe. To make this revival possible, all Roman legal institutions had to be cleansed of their historical context and made over into a body of abstract principles that was declared to be an embodiment of right reason. Divorced from concrete cases, these principles were formulated in terms of systematic categories, which had been absent from ancient jurisprudence but which were now used as axioms from which deductive arguments were derived.

> . . . The task of "construing" the situation in a logically impeccable way became almost the exclusive task. In this way that conception of law . . . which sees in law a logically consistent and gapless complex of "norms" waiting to be "applied" became the decisive conception of legal thought.[65]

Indisputably this approach to legal thought resulted from the revival of Roman law in the hands of an increasingly important status group of professionally trained legal notables. Whether and how far this development was promoted by either patrimonial rulers or economic interest groups is uncertain. In Weber's view these influences were important but not decisive. Because of its abstract character, formal justice was

[65] *Law*, p. 277. Elsewhere Weber defined the postulates of legal science as developed by the civil law of the Pandectists as follows: "first, that every concrete legal action decision be the 'application' of an abstract legal proposition to a concrete 'fact situation'; second, that it must be possible in every concrete case to derive the decision from abstract legal propositions by means of legal logic; third, that the law must actually or virtually constitute a 'gapless' system of legal propositions, or must, at least, be treated as if it were such a gapless system; fourth, that whatever cannot be 'construed' legally in rational terms is also legally irrelevant; and fifth, that every social action of human beings must always be visualized as either an 'application' or 'execution' of legal propositions, or as an 'infringement' thereof." See *ibid.*, p. 64.

generally favored by all those political and economic interest groups "to whom the stability and predictability of legal procedure was of very great importance," as well as by "those who on ideological grounds attempt to break down authoritarian controls." From these viewpoints "non-formal justice represents the likelihood of absolute arbitrariness."[66] But the absolute monarchs and the rising bourgeoisie could also satisfy their demonstrable interest in a dependable legal system in other ways. Indeed, Weber showed that the purely logical construction of legal issues could have practical consequences that were not only unanticipated but adverse from the standpoint of the political and economic interests involved. It is therefore probable that "this logical systematization of the law has been the consequence of the intrinsic intellectual needs of the legal theorists and their disciples, the doctors, i.e., of a typical aristocracy of legal literati."[67] In a larger sense this conclusion applies not only to the Continent, where university-trained legal notables rose to prominence, but also to England, where a nation-wide legal profession already existed. Although the development of the law in the two cases was strongly influenced by law specialists of different types, both legal systems were compatible with the increasing political and economic interest in a dependable legal system. Accordingly, Weber concluded that "capitalism has not been a decisive factor in the promotion of that form of 'rationalization' of the law which has been peculiar to the Continental West ever since the rise of Romanist studies in the medieval universities."[68]

Whatever the major status groups that promoted in various ways the emergence of legal rationality, the end-product of this development is the system of legal domination.

[66] *Ibid.*, p. 229.
[67] *Ibid.*, p. 278.
[68] *Ibid.*, p. 318.

CHAPTER XIII

LEGAL DOMINATION (continued): THE MODERN STATE AND THE STRUGGLE FOR POWER

The preceding survey of Weber's political sociology contains references to many factors that promoted the development of the modern state. In western Europe familial charisma and patrimonial government furthered the centralization of authority. Institutional charisma and feudalism, on the other hand, tended to limit that centralization and to promote the autonomy of the church and the estates. Weber's comparative sociology of religion, furthermore, emphasized the all-important destruction of the extended family by the Christian communities, in which every baptized person was the religious equal of every other. This religious institutionalization of equality was the foundation upon which an autonomous bourgeoisie developed in the cities of western Europe. Weber's sociology of law added to the general background a discussion of the specific preconditions of legal rationality. The modern state that emerged from these preconditions is the prototype of Weber's concept of legal domination.

A. THE MODERN STATE AND ITS LEGITIMACY

According to Weber a modern state exists where a political community possesses the following characteristics: (1) an ad-

ministrative and legal order that is subject to change by legislation; (2) an administrative apparatus that conducts official
business in accordance with legislative regulation; (3) binding authority over all persons—who usually obtain their citizenship by birth—and over most actions taking place in the area
of its jurisdiction; (4) the legitimation to use force within this
area if coercion is either permitted or prescribed by the legally
constituted government, i.e., if it is in accordance with enacted statute.[1] Legal order, bureaucracy, compulsory jurisdiction over a territory and monopolization of the legitimate use
of force are the essential characteristics of the modern state.
This type of political community is a relatively rare phenomenon.[2] In Western civilization the several aspects of the modern state emerged only gradually, as legitimacy came to be
attributed to the body of rules that governed the exercise of
authority. "This system of rules constitutes the 'legal order,'
and the political community is regarded as its sole normal
creator."[3]

Like the other types of authority, legal domination rests
upon the belief in its legitimacy, and every such belief is in
a sense question-begging. For example, charismatic authority
depends upon a belief in the sanctity or exemplary character
of an individual person, but this person loses his authority as
soon as those subject to it no longer believe in his extraordinary powers. Charismatic authority exists only as long as it
"proves" itself, and such "proof" is either believed by the followers or rejected. The belief in the legitimacy of a legal order
has a similarly circular quality. "Legal domination [exists] by

[1] *Theory*, pp. 154, 156. In order to bring out the elements of
Weber's definition I have not quoted verbatim.

[2] It does not exist where the "forcible maintenance of orderly
dominion over a territory and its inhabitants" is in many hands, or
where centralized authority is not subject to a legal order. See *Law*,
p. 338.

[3] *Ibid.*, p. 341. In insisting that in modern times the government
"normally usurped the monopoly of power to compel by physical
coercion respect for those rules," (*ibid.*) Weber emphasized, of
course, that domination depends upon the readiness to resort to, and
the anticipation of, coercion rather than upon the extensive use of
physical force. Nevertheless the availability of that force and the
orientation toward this fact are essential characteristics of the modern political community. Cf. *Theory*, pp. 154–55; *Law*, pp. 37–38.

virtue of statute. . . . The basic conception is: that any legal norm can be created or changed by a procedurally correct enactment."[4] In other words, laws are legitimate if they have been enacted; and the enactment is legitimate if it has occurred in conformity with the laws prescribing the procedures to be followed. This circularity is intentional. Weber explicitly rejected definitions of the modern state and its legal order that focus on either the "purpose" of this political community or some specific value judgments that inspire the belief in its legitimacy. He pointed out that political communities have pursued all conceivable ends at one time or another and that they can do so without thereby losing the character of a modern state, just as charismatic leadership can be present whether the leader is a holy man or a tyrant. Similarly, the belief in the legitimacy of the legal order can be based on expediency (e.g., the usefulness of law for the protection of property) or on some ultimate value (e.g., law as an emanation of God's will) or on some combination of the two.[5] In excluding the purposes pursued by the state and the specific beliefs on which it rested from his *definition*, Weber was speaking not as a legal theorist but as a sociologist. He was concerned with "what *actually* happens in a community owing to the probability that persons . . . consider certain norms as valid and act according to them,"[6] not with the ideals of the political community or the norms of the legal order that he personally endorsed.

A consideration of the ideals that have *actually* affected the development of the modern state is an essential part of this perspective.

Conceptions of the "rightness of the law" are sociologically relevant within a rational positive legal order only insofar as the particular answers to the problem give rise to practical

[4] *Staatssoziologie*, p. 99. This is Weber's summary formulation from his posthumous essay.

[5] Cf. *Theory*, pp. 155–56, where he rejected the use of "purpose" in the definition of the state, and *ibid.*, p. 329, where he pointed out that under legal authority any legal norm may be established "on grounds of expediency or rational values or both."

[6] *Law*, p. 11. Cf. *ibid.*, pp. 11–16, for a discussion of the distinction between the legal and the sociological conception of the law.

consequences for the behavior of lawmakers, legal practitioners, and social groups interested in the law. . . . Such
a situation has repeatedly existed in the course of history,
but quite particularly at the beginning of modern times and
during the Revolutionary period and in part it still exists.
. . . The substantive content of such maxims is usually
designated as "Natural Law."

. . . Natural law is the sum total of all those norms which
are valid independently of, and superior to, any positive law
and which owe their dignity not to arbitrary enactment but,
on the contrary, provide the very legitimation for the binding force of positive law. Natural law has thus been the collective term for those norms which owe their legitimacy not
to their origin from a legitimate lawgiver, but to their im-
manent and teleological qualities.[7]

In modern times the legitimation of the legal order by reference to natural law is the only remaining alternative after beliefs in religious revelation and sacredness of tradition have
declined.

Modern concepts of natural law depend on certain formal
assumptions. Enacted laws are regarded as legitimate if their
enactment either is derived from an actual contract of free
individuals or conforms to the ideal concept of a reasonable
order based upon agreement. The basic principle of this contractual theory is the individual's freedom to acquire or dispose
of property. Thus it eliminates the system of privileges under
patrimonial and feudal rule, which was buttressed by special
laws and by the ancient maxim that special law prevails over
general law. Freedom of contract is limited only in the sense
that contracts must not infringe upon inalienable freedoms,
especially upon the freedom of contract itself.[8] Laws that do

[7] *Ibid.*, pp. 287–88. In this passage Weber restricted the continued importance of ideas of natural law to America, but I have
omitted this reference from the quotation because elsewhere he referred to natural-law tendencies among German lawyers.

[8] "Nobody may validly surrender himself into political or private
slavery. For the rest, no enactment *can* validly limit the free disposition of the individual over his property and his working power."
Ibid., p. 290. As an example Weber referred to the prolonged op-

not violate the basic freedoms are legitimate because reason reveals that they are in harmony with the "nature of things," which cannot be changed by man or God. Though it goes back to Stoic and Christian ideas, this approach was stripped of its theological underpinnings during the eighteenth and early nineteenth centuries when it emerged in the utilitarian doctrine that the "nature of things" demands laws that are reasonable or "practically appropriate."[9]

The formal doctrine of natural law has definite class implications. The legitimation of property based on the freedom of contract furthers the interests of groups engaged in market transactions; by giving legal security to the property they acquire. Thus the codifications of the French Revolution era, i.e., the Declaration of the Rights of Man and the Napoleonic Code, guaranteed the rights of the individual against the political authority in conformity with the interests of the bourgeoisie. But in the course of the nineteenth century these ideas came under attack from many sides—not only from socialist theories, but from Romanticism, the positivism of modern science, the rationalism of the lawyers, and the general increase of intellectual skepticism in the Western world.[10] As a result, the axioms of natural law became deeply discredited and "lost all capacity to provide the fundamental bases of a legal system." In Weber's view, legal positivism had advanced irresistibly, at least for the time being.[11]

Weber's concept of legal authority should be understood in the light of these intellectual trends. His definition was meant to reflect what actually happens in a community as a result of the values or norms in which people believe. In the modern

position of the U. S. Supreme Court to social welfare legislation that prohibited certain contents of free labor contracts on the ground that this was incompatible with the due process clause of the Fourteenth Amendment. In Weber's terms that clause embodies an aspect of the formal conception of natural right.

[9] *Law*, pp. 291–92.

[10] The effect of these several intellectual trends upon changing beliefs in legitimacy is discussed below on pp. 431–38.

[11] *Ibid.*, p. 298. It should be remembered here that Weber had the Continent in mind and that he emphasized the continued importance of natural-law doctrines in England and in the United States, although legal positivism had made inroads there as well.

state, people in general and legal practitioners in particular attribute legitimacy to a legal order insofar as its laws have been enacted. Weber expressed the implications of this in terms of several interrelated ideas:

(1) *Any* norm may be enacted as law with the claim and expectation that it will be obeyed by all those who are subject to the authority of the political community.

(2) The law as a whole constitutes a system of abstract rules, which are usually the result of enactment, and the administration of justice consists of the application of these rules to particular cases. Governmental administration is likewise bound by rules of law and conducted in accordance with generally formulated principles that are approved or at least accepted.

(3) The people who occupy positions of authority are not personal rulers, but superiors who temporarily hold an office by virtue of which they possess limited authority.

(4) The people who obey the legally constituted authority do so as citizens, not subjects, and obey the "law" rather than the official who enforces it.[12]

Legal domination in this sense is the end-product of the century-long development toward legal rationality.

Weber's concept of legal domination was formulated from the standpoint of the Continental legal profession, according to which

> the state is not allowed to interfere with life, liberty, or property without the consent of the people or their duly elected representatives. Hence any law in the substantive sense must . . . have its basis in an act of the legislature. . . .[13]

This denies the legitimacy of any law based on precedent rather than statute, an orientation that emerged from the struggle against monarchical absolutism in the Continental countries. The "rule of law" was identified with control of the government by the people's representatives and hence with democracy, whereas judicial and administrative decisions

[12] *Theory*, pp. 329–30. I have again paraphrased and simplified on the basis of the English and the German text.

[13] Cf. Max Rheinstein's editorial comment in *Law*, p. 47, n. 14.

based on precedent were identified with government by the judiciary and the dangers of arbitrary rule. Here again Weber used a particular constellation as the basis for his definition of legal domination as a pure type. This procedure can prove its utility only by application in specific inquiries. In the present context the most important example of such application is Weber's analysis of bureaucracy.

B. BUREAUCRACY

Weber's discussions of bureaucracy[14] distinguish among several levels of analysis: (1) the historical and technical (administrative) reasons for the process of bureaucratization, especially in Western civilization; (2) the impact of the rule of law upon the functioning of bureaucratic organizations; (3) the occupational position and typical personal orientation of bureaucratic officials as a status group; (4) the most important attributes and consequences of bureaucracy in the modern world, especially of governmental bureaucracy.[15] These topics are not strictly separate, and this accounts for the partial redundancy and discrepancy in Weber's several enumerations. Some of the reasons for the development of bureaucracy necessarily refer to attributes that have consequences in the modern world, and the rule of law necessarily affects both the functioning of bureaucratic organizations and the occupational position of the incumbents. The brief account that follows separates these overlapping perspectives.[16]

[14] The analysis published in *Essays*, pp. 196–244, was written first (1911–13); the related discussion in *Theory*, pp. 329–41, contains Weber's subsequent effort at systematization. His political analysis of bureaucracy is not available in English.

[15] These several topics are considered in the following passages: (1) *Essays*, pp. 204–24, 235–39; (2) *Theory*, pp. 329–33, *Essays*, pp. 196–98, 216–21, *Law*, Chapters 8–10; (3) *Essays*, pp. 198–204, *Theory*, pp. 333–36; (4) *Essays*, pp. 224–35, 240–44, *Theory*, pp. 337–41. This division can be only suggestive, for the reasons indicated in the text. There are many other passages in Weber's work where he dealt with the problem of bureaucratization. Cf. also pp. 438–57 for a further discussion of the fourth topic on the basis of Weber's political writings.

[16] The historical reasons for the process of bureaucratization were

Where the rule of law prevails, a bureaucratic organization is governed by the following principles:

(1) Official business is conducted on a continuous basis.

(2) It is conducted in accordance with stipulated rules in an administrative agency characterized by three interrelated attributes: (*a*) the duty of each official to do certain types of work is delimited in terms of impersonal criteria; (*b*) the official is given the authority necessary to carry out his assigned functions; (*c*) the means of compulsion at his disposal are strictly limited, and the conditions under which their employment is legitimate are clearly defined.

(3) Every official's responsibilities and authority are part of a hierarchy of authority. Higher offices are assigned the duty of supervision, lower offices, the right of appeal. However, the extent of supervision and the conditions of legitimate appeal may vary.

(4) Officials and other administrative employees do not own the resources necessary for the performance of their assigned functions but they are accountable for their use of these resources. Official business and private affairs, official revenue and private income are strictly separated.

(5) Offices cannot be appropriated by their incumbents in the sense of private property that can be sold and inherited. (This does not preclude various rights such as pension claims, regulated conditions of discipline and dismissal, etc., but such rights serve, in principle at least, as incentives for the better performance of duties. They are not property rights.)

(6) Official business is conducted on the basis of written documents.[17]

Without (1) the continuity of official business; (2) the delimitation of authority through stipulated rules; (3) the supervision of its exercise; (4) and (5) the separation of office and incumbent; and (6) the documentary basis of official business, there cannot be a system of legal domination in which the exercise of authority consists in the implementation of enacted norms.

This specification of the "apparatus" under legal domination

---

summarized at the end of Chapter XI; this topic is therefore omitted from the present discussion.

[17] *Theory*, pp. 330–32.

can be contrasted to the system of administration under patrimonial rule. First, whether or not the patrimonial ruler and his officials conduct administrative business is usually a matter of discretion; normally they do so only when they are paid for their troubles. Second, a patrimonial ruler resists the delimitation of his authority by the stipulation of rules. He may observe traditional or customary limitations, but these are unwritten; indeed, tradition endorses the principled arbitrariness of the ruler. Third, this combination of tradition and arbitrariness is reflected in the delegation and supervision of authority. Within the limits of sacred tradition the ruler decides whether or not to delegate authority, and his entirely personal recruitment of "officials" makes the supervision of their work a matter of personal preference and loyalty. Fourth and fifth, all administrative "offices" under patrimonial rule are a part of the ruler's personal household and private property; his "officials" are personal servants, and the costs of administration are met out of his treasury. Sixth, official business is transacted in personal encounter and by oral communication, not on the basis of impersonal documents.[18]

Under legal domination the occupational position and personal orientation of officials is bound to be affected by the contrasting administrative organization. Where the implementation of enacted rules is emphasized, the employment of the official is also governed by rules, and once hired, the official obeys impersonal rules, not the will of his lord and master. Obedience to rules and the conduct of official business by means of written documents require technical qualifications that are more or less absent from administrative work done as a personal service or an avocation. Under legal domination the implementation of rules must be regular as well as regulated, or else the rule of law would be applied only intermittently; also, to be continuous, administrative work must be a full-time occupation. Finally, where each office involves regulated duties and authorizations, these must be independent from the person of the incumbent. Consequently his compen-

[18] These conditions apply also under feudalism in a modified form, but there is no need to specify these modifications. See p. 361 ff. above, for the contrast between patrimonialism and feudalism.

sation cannot be derived from the revenue of the office, nor can he be permitted to appropriate either the perquisites of office or the office itself. The typical bureaucratic alternative is to reward the official by monthly allowances in money or in kind, and to ensure the quality and continuity of his service by offering him the opportunity of a lifetime career, usually with pension provisions upon retirement.[19]

Under legal domination, therefore, the bureaucratic official's position is characterized by the following attributes:

(1) He is personally free and appointed to his position on the basis of contract.

(2) He exercises the authority delegated to him in accordance with impersonal rules, and his loyalty is enlisted on behalf of the faithful execution of his official duties.

(3) His appointment and job placement are dependent upon his technical qualifications.

(4) His administrative work is his full-time occupation.

(5) His work is rewarded by a regular salary and by prospects of regular advancement in a lifetime career.

With these characteristics of administrative organization under legal domination before us, we may now turn to the most important attributes and consequences of bureaucracy in the modern world.

According to Weber, such an organization is technically superior to all other forms of administration, much as machine production is superior to nonmechanical methods. In precision, speed, lack of equivocation, knowledge of the documentary record, continuity, sense of discretion, uniformity of operation, system of subordination, and reduction of frictions, bureaucracy surpasses honorific and avocational forms of administration.[20] This is a long list of advantages, but they are relative.

[19] Weber repeatedly discussed the differences between bureaucratic and patrimonial administration, which have been restated briefly in the preceding two paragraphs. However, he did not distinguish the administrative consequences that result from the type of supreme authority and the characteristics of the officialdom that emerge from these consequences. Cf. *Theory*, pp. 342–45, and *WuG*, Vol. II, pp. 679, 737–38, 752.

[20] The translation of this passage in *Essays*, p. 214, makes Weber's statement more absolute than it is. Cf. *Law*, p. 349, for a more accurate translation.

Weber emphasized that bureaucracy also produces obstacles when a decision must be adapted to an individual case. This reservation is noteworthy as a concomitant of the attribute that is central to his conception of bureaucracy: the idea of calculability. This is a logical consequence of the rule of law. In an administration governed by rules, decisions must be predictable if the rules are known. Weber expressed this notion by the exaggerated simile of the "modern judge [who] is a vending machine into which the pleadings are inserted together with the fee and which then disgorges the judgment together with its reasons mechanically derived from the Code."[21]

> [The calculability of decision-making] and with it its appropriateness for capitalism . . . [is] the more fully realized the more bureaucracy "depersonalizes" itself, i.e., the more completely it succeeds in achieving the exclusion of love, hatred, and every purely personal, especially irrational and incalculable, feeling from the execution of official tasks. In the place of the old-type ruler who is moved by sympathy, favor, grace, and gratitude, modern culture requires for its sustaining external apparatus the emotionally detached, and hence rigorously "professional," expert.[22]

Thus, contrary to many interpretations, Weber did not maintain that bureaucratic organizations operate as efficiently as "slot machines." He said rather that such organizations operate more efficiently than alternative systems of administration and that they increase their efficiency to the extent that they "depersonalize" the execution of official tasks.

In this connection it is interesting to consider Weber's answer to critics of Prussian bureaucracy who questioned the ideal of administrative impersonality. These critics pointed out that the rules governing administrative practice merely provide outside boundaries for the "creative" activity of the official. Therefore, rules have primarily a negative effect; they do not directly and positively determine the official's action. Weber suspected this approach of being a romantic smoke screen for the harsh realities of Prussian government. To him

[21] *Ibid.*, p. 354.
[22] *Law*, p. 351.

the discretionary activity of the modern bureaucratic official differed from the discretion and personally motivated favors characteristic of prebureaucratic forms of administration. "Behind every act of purely bureaucratic administration there stands a system of rationally discussable 'grounds,' i.e., either a subsumption under norms or calculation of means and ends."[23] In a modern bureaucracy even discretionary acts imply the supremacy of impersonal ends; personal favors and arbitrariness cannot be openly avowed. To be sure, this "canonization of the abstractly impersonal" is fused with the endeavor of individual officials to preserve and enhance their power. But in modern bureaucracy this universal endeavor requires an appeal to impersonal ends.[24] The technical superiority of bureaucratic administration therefore depends on its orientation toward impersonal rules that enhance the uniform reliability and hence the calculability of its operation.

A second attribute of modern bureaucracy is its "concentration of the means of administration." By using the same terminology as Marx, Weber wanted to emphasize that this process of concentration had occurred not only in the economy but also in government, the army, political parties, universities, and indeed in most large-scale organizations. As the size of such organizations increases, the resources necessary to run them are taken out of the hands of autonomous individuals and groups and placed under the control of a ruling minority, in part because such resources exceed the financial capacity of individuals.[25] Thus the craftsman was expropriated as merchant enterprises came to own the tools of production; the feudal vassal was expropriated as a public official when governments came to monopolize the administration of public affairs; the private scholar was expropriated as the universities

[23] *Ibid.*, p. 355.

[24] The passage referred to in this paragraph may be found in different translations in *Essays*, pp. 219–20, and *Law*, pp. 354–55.

[25] This is, of course, related to the increasing complexity of functions performed by governments and other organizations as their size increases. Cf. the earlier reference to this process in Chapter XI, pp. 380–81. Weber's emphasis on the parallelism of this process in all types of large-scale organization is contained in his lecture on socialism. Cf. *GAzSuS*, pp. 498–99. See also *Essays*, pp. 221–24, and *GPS*, p. 140.

built up their own laboratories and libraries upon which the scholar came to depend. The means of production, of administration and of scholarship all were integral parts of the individual household at one time, but became separated as the process of concentration advanced. As a result, modern bureaucratic administration is distinguished by the separation of business from the family household, of public office from its incumbent, and of research facilities from the individual scholar.

A third attribute of modern bureaucracy is its leveling effect on social and economic differences. This effect is seen most easily if bureaucratic and nonbureaucratic methods of administration are contrasted:

> Every non-bureaucratic administration of a large social structure [such as patrimonial government] depends upon the fact that those who outrank others in social, economic, or honorific terms are associated in one way or another with the performance of administrative functions. This usually means that the incumbent is rewarded for his assumption of administrative duties by the economic exploitation of his position, which he may also use for purposes of social prestige.[26]

The development of bureaucracy does away with such plutocratic privileges, replacing unpaid, avocational administration by notables with paid, full-time administration by professionals, regardless of their social and economic position. Also, it rejects the "decision-making from case to case" that is typical of nonbureaucratic forms of administration. Authority is exercised in accordance with rules, and everyone subject to that authority is legally equal.[27] Connected with these leveling tendencies is a major change in the system of education. Administration by notables usually is administration by amateurs; bureaucracy usually is administration by experts. Equal eligi-

[26] *WuG*, Vol. II, p. 666. This same passage is translated more literally in *Essays*, p. 224.

[27] Weber noted that this leveling effect of bureaucratization has many equivocal results, but I defer consideration of this point to pp. 436–37 below and to Chapter XIV.

bility for administrative appointments means in fact equal eligibility of all who meet the stipulated educational requirements. Educational diplomas have replaced privilege as the basis of administrative recruitment, just as scientific education and technical expertise have replaced the cultivation of the mind through classical literature and the cultivation of manners through competitive games among social equals. The expert, not the cultivated man, is the educational ideal of a bureaucratic age.[28]

Fourth and finally, a fully developed bureaucracy implements a system of authority relationships that is practically indestructible. Whereas the notable does administrative work on an avocational and honorific basis, the bureaucrat's economic sustenance and entire social existence are identified with the "apparatus." He shares the interests of his administrative colleagues in the continued functioning of the machine in which they are so many specialized cogs. The population ruled by a bureaucracy cannot, on the other hand, dispense with it or replace it with something else. Short of chaos, public affairs depend today upon the expert training, functional specialization and coordination of a bureaucratic administration with its uninterrupted performance of the manifold tasks that are regularly assigned to the modern state. Weber emphasized that the bureaucratic form of administration is both permanent and indispensable, contrary to the arguments of anarchists and socialists who believe that administration can be done away with in an ideal society or that it can be used to implement a freer and more equitable social order. In Weber's view bureaucracy is here to stay, and any future social order promises only to be more oppressive than the capitalist society of today. But with these judgments we approach his work in the field of political analysis, presented in the following section.

[28] *Essays*, pp. 240–43. Note especially Weber's statement that the struggle between the ideal of the expert and the older ideal of the educated or cultivated man is at the basis of all present discussions of the educational system. This is as true in the age of man-made earth satellites as it was before World War I when Weber wrote. Cf. also the earlier discussion of feudal and patrimonial education, pp. 364–65, and the contrast between an autonomous and a university-trained legal profession, pp. 410–16.

C. THE STRUGGLE FOR POWER UNDER
LEGAL DOMINATION

The system of legal domination is as subject to transformation as are the systems of charismatic and traditional authority, and Weber utilized his analysis of legal rationality and of bureaucracy to identify the "problematics" of legal domination. Any system of domination undergoes change when the beliefs in its legitimacy and the practices of its administrative organization are modified. Such changes of belief occur in and through the struggle for power, which in the modern state may lead to changes of control over the bureaucratic apparatus but not to its destruction.

Changing Beliefs in Legitimacy

In his sociology of law Weber observed that the concept of natural law has become "deeply discredited" as the result of social and ideological conflicts. These conflicts originated in the very idea of natural law, which was compatible with divergent political objectives. Classes in revolt against the existing order appealed to natural law, as in the French, American and Russian revolutions. But natural law also served as the legitimation of established authorities: for example, the historical school of jurisprudence held that rules of custom are preeminent and that the legislator is unable either to restrict their validity or to prevent the derogation of enacted law by custom.[29] The historical school as well as Romanticism thus undermined the belief in reason on which the revolutionary theory of natural law depended.

During the nineteenth century natural law also came under attack because the rights that were acquired by contractual transactions were increasingly identified with vested economic

[29] The historical school is related to the Romantic belief in the spirit of the people (*Volksgeist*) or "national culture," as we would say today. According to this view law is legitimate and hence "genuine" only if it grows naturally ("organically") out of a people's sense of justice, whereas enacted laws are "artificial" or "spurious." Cf. *Law*, p. 288.

interests. Under the influence of socialist theories this opposition advanced a *substantive* theory of natural law, according to which acquisition of wealth is legitimate only if it is the product of one's own labor. This theory denies the legitimacy not only of all unearned income but of rights acquired solely on the basis of contract. Labor, not contract, becomes the basis of legitimacy, and this leads to the postulation of a "right to work" or a "right to a minimum standard of living" or a combination of the two in a "right to the full product of one's labor." This basic idea of a "right to work" and the demand for a "living wage" have helped undermine the legitimation of the legal order on the basis of contract.

Weber pointed out that this effect of socialist theories was enhanced by intellectual trends within the dominant bourgeois culture. The doctrine of natural law was attacked for its transcendental idealism by both the positivism of modern science and the increasingly Machiavellian orientation (*Realpolitik*) of modern politics. Such ideas as the "social contract" or the "natural harmony of interests" were subjected to severe criticism on historical and philosophical grounds. This rising tide of intellectual skepticism was furthered in turn by the positivism of the legal profession, which espoused in belief in the legal order solely on the basis of its instrumental value.

These intellectual tendencies have more in common than their opposition to the contractual (and hence formal) theory of natural law. Weber pointed out that it is hardly possible to eradicate the axioms of natural law completely,[30] and that many of the attacks upon these axioms are in fact associated with a substantive theory. Although it is not stated in so many words, Weber's thesis apparently was that the modern legal order is sustained by both a formal and substantive theory of natural law and hence by a more or less incompatible set of beliefs concerning its legitimacy.[31] This incompatibility is reflected in the ambiguity of even the formal qualities of modern law. For example, in theory all persons are equal before the law, yet special laws have been enacted to apply to particular occupational groups. Such interlocking of privilege and law

[30] *Law*, p. 297.
[31] The following discussion is based on *Law*, Chapters X and XI.

through special jurisdiction is an ancient legal principle, according to which a person's right is valid only by virtue of his membership in a group that has obtained legal recognition for its monopolistic claims. Historically special courts and procedures often accompanied such legalized privileges, and in theory such institutions have disappeared. But in practice something like them has been revived wherever special laws have been enacted, as in the case of labor law with its separate hierarchy of labor courts, or in the case of special tribunals dealing with claims arising under social security, war pensions, taxes, and so forth. In Weber's view two reasons are primarily responsible for these developments. With increasing occupational differentiation, various economic groups have organized themselves into pressure groups and sought to obtain special legal guarantees that their affairs will be handled by experts. In doing so such groups seek to eliminate the formalities of normal legal procedure in the interest of achieving methods of settlement that are more expeditious and better adapted to the individual case.[32] Yet these developments *bring to the fore considerations of a substantive character at the expense of legal formalism.*

In the conclusion to his sociology of law Weber noted several manifestations of this trend. On the Continent legal formalism was diluted when the Roman system of formal proof was abolished by the procedural reforms of the nineteenth century. Through these reforms the judge was emancipated from various formal restrictions on the rules of evidence, and he was authorized to make his evaluation in the light of experience and reason. In the sphere of private law this change entailed evaluations by the judge in terms of "good faith and fair dealing," so that ethical categories came to the fore in lieu of formal criteria. A similar dilution of formalism occurred as Continental legal practice shifted its emphasis from the external to the logical aspects of legal transactions. Weber attributed this shift at least in part to the importance of reciprocal trust or confidence in commodity exchanges and to the need to find legal guarantees for trustworthy conduct. Since it is impossible to define formal tests of certainty for such

[32] *Law,* p. 303.

relations of trust, the courts increasingly resorted to interpretations that construed the relations between parties from the viewpoint of their "attitudes," such as good faith or malice. Again in criminal law, the earlier emphasis on a "mechanistic remedy of vengeance" was replaced by ethical or utilitarian considerations of the "ends of punishment."

These tendencies in judicial interpretation are promoted not only by the social demands of democracy and the ideology of the welfare state, but also by legal ideologists who place ethical postulates in opposition to the dominance of legal formalism. Their arguments are designed to show that the ideal of an exhaustive and logically consistent body of enacted rules is either unattainable or pernicious or both. The idea that judicial decisions apply only the relevant statute to a given case is countered by the assertion that statutes do not encompass the multifarious facts of life, so that judicial interpretation is in fact inevitable. Such interpretation is further held to be desirable because "interpretive" decisions may be made in the light of substantive evaluations rather than "merely" in accordance with formal norms. Similarly, it is pointed out that gaps in the legal order are inevitable, that the idea of a systematic coherence of the law is a fiction, that "legal propositions" are secondary compared to the judicial decisions themselves, and finally that the latter are of less value than the vast number of conventional rules that govern everyday life regardless of their reaffirmation in the law.[33] In Weber's view these and other antiformalistic demands for substantive justice were prompted by the demand of the underprivileged for "social laws," by the layman's opposition to legal formalism, and by

[33] Weber noted that this trend of legal ideology led in a number of cases to a complete devaluation of legislative enactments in favor of the elaborations and applications by legal scholars or practitioners. This elevation of case law over statute law can be subverted in turn by the argument that no precedent is binding beyond the concrete facts of the case, so that the way is left open "to the free balancing of values in each individual case" (Law, p. 313). He noted further that this "value-irrationalism" brought about various ideological reactions, such as the Catholic revival of natural law, neo-Kantian doctrines concerning the use of an ethical system as a standard for rational legislation and judicial decision-making, and empirical doctrines basing ultimate standards on the expectations and conceptions that exist in the community. Cf. ibid., pp. 313–14.

the interests of the legal profession, since the increased importance of case law tends "to heighten [the lawyers'] feeling of self-importance and to increase their sense of power."[34] This opposition to legal formalism is also evidence of an intellectual disillusionment that leads to attacks upon rationalism at the same time that it is a product of rationalism.

Despite these intellectual tendencies, Weber was convinced that law as a formal procedure for "pacifying conflicts of interest" cannot be eradicated. Although the decline of natural law and the increase in legal positivism threaten the judges' belief "in the sacredness of the purely objective formalism," jurists "have always . . . regarded themselves to be but the mouthpiece of norms already existing . . . and to be their interpreters or appliers rather than their creators."[35] Only law prophets have consciously created new laws, and it was doubtful that either English or Continental judges could really be turned into law prophets.[36]

This is as far as Weber's discussion of changing beliefs in the legitimacy of legal domination goes. Since his illustrations are confined to discussions that were in the forefront of interest in Europe some forty years ago, it may be helpful to discuss a contemporary experience that points up the central importance of the conflict between formal and substantive justice. Over the last twenty years American collective bargaining agreements have become highly formal and elaborate. A fairly standard provision in labor-management contracts is the requirement that overtime work on Sundays be paid for a minimum number of hours, say four. Among the reasons for this provision on the side of union negotiators is usually the idea that management should not make frivolous demands on the leisure

[34] *Ibid.*, p. 315.

[35] *Ibid.*, p. 320. Cf. pp. 286–88 above for the reasons why Weber believed this orientation toward norms to be universal.

[36] Weber observed that this "peculiar antinomy" of formal and substantive elements is in fact endemic in the business interests that promote the formal development of the law. "Rigorously formalistic and dependent on what is tangibly perceivable as far as it is required for security to do business, the law has at the same time become informal for the sake of business loyalty, insofar as required by the logical interpretation of the intention of the parties or by the 'good usage' of business transactions" (*Law*, pp. 320–21).

time of the workers merely to suit its own convenience and that it should pay if it must have workers on hand for emergencies on a stand-by basis. Thus the union may consider this provision as an incentive for management to plan ahead so as to avoid overpayments for Sunday labor. Yet, eminently plausible as these reasons are, they have little or no bearing on the *exact number* of minimum hours that must be paid in the case of Sunday overtime work. This number is in all likelihood determined by such factors as bargaining skill, the relative strength of the bargaining partners, a competitive situation, and so forth. As far as the substantive reasons for the union demand are concerned, these factors are extraneous, as evidenced by the fact that the minimum number of paid overtime hours finally agreed upon may exceed the actual hours spent on Sunday overtime by any of the workers. Let us call the union's reasons for its demand a concern with substantive justice and call the stipulated minimum of paid work on Sundays a concern with formal justice. However plausible the substantive reasons are, they will appear unjustified to management if for technical reasons workers on Sunday overtime are employed for less than the stipulated minimum. In fact, they may also appear unjustified to the workers, who may feel uncomfortable about receiving, say, four hours' pay for one hour's work. For workers to accept such "excessive" pay with a good conscience, they must develop considerable sophistication with regard to the imperatives under which the union works. For the union really has no choice: it must insist on the letter of the contract if it is to justify its own functions, even if the minimum amount of overtime pay on Sundays happens to be excessive from the viewpoint of substantive equity. In Weber's terminology, the union must insist on adherence to the stipulations of the contract (formal rationality) even where this leads to results that make no sense in terms of the substantive reasons for its demands.[37]

At the level of the social structure Weber analyzed this basic

[37] I have heard of cases where unions encounter difficulties in organizing new plants, because workers who know little about the imperatives of modern collective bargaining cannot see that formal stipulations that fly in the face of their sense of substantive justice are much of an argument in favor of unionization.

antinomy of legal domination by examining bureaucracy in relation to democratic values. Bureaucracy developed with the support of democratic movements that demanded equality before the law and legal guarantees against arbitrariness in judicial and administrative decisions. As an opposition to the existing system of privilege and arbitrary powers, these demands clearly favored an impersonal exercise of authority governed by rules and a recruitment of officials from all social strata solely on the basis of technical qualification. In meeting these demands bureaucratic organizations had a leveling effect; the people subject to the law and the officials who exercised authority under the law became formally equal. But this gain in formal equality had equivocal results from the standpoint of democratic values. Where recruitment of officials is based on educational qualifications, officials can become a privileged caste on the basis of tests and diplomas rather than on the basis of social privileges. And where appointments to positions involve a lifetime career, officials may use these positions to expand their authority even if they do not abuse it. The very measures that ensure a bureaucracy against the abuse of authority and the encroachment of privilege—the certified qualification of appointees, regular promotions, pension provisions, and regulated supervision and appeals procedures—can give rise to new status privileges buttressed by monopolistic practices. It is in response to this danger that short-tenure appointments and a general access to official positions regardless of qualifications have been demanded. Such demands manifest the public desire for formal guarantees against bureaucratic arbitrariness even to the extent of undermining some of the bureaucratic guarantees against arbitrariness already existing. On the other hand, this public desire conflicts with the popular feeling that each case or person should be considered on "its merits," i.e., in terms of equitable justice oriented toward the particulars of each situation. Thus the formal guarantees that are demanded on rational grounds tend to be rejected emotionally, and often by the same people.

In the last century and a half ideas about the legitimacy of legal domination have changed, broadly speaking, from a religious or rational belief in "the laws of nature and of nature's God" to a positivistic belief in the utility of the law's formal

properties, and halfway back again to a mounting concern
with the moral and political objectives that may be achieved
by legislation. In Weber's view the conflict between formal
and substantive justice has no ultimate solution. No degree of
formalization can entirely eradicate beliefs in the legitimacy
of the legal order that transcend the actual law and its instrumental values, and no concern with substantive justice can
entirely subvert the orientation of the legal profession toward
the formal properties of the law. The instability arising from
the conflict between these values does not by itself undermine the system of legal domination; any combination of
formal and substantive justice is compatible with the belief
"that any legal norm can be created or changed by a procedurally correct enactment."[38] However, there is a tension between the interest in formal procedure and the demand for
substantive justice which parallels the tension between sacred
norms and patriarchal arbitrariness under traditional domination and between unconditional faith and the demand for
miracles under charismatic leadership. In characterizing these
basic conflicts of values, Weber was formulating the frame of
reference for analyzing the struggle for power that occurs under each system of domination.

Bureaucratization and Political Leadership[39]

Each type of domination faces problems of its own that may
be resolved through the struggle for power. Whatever indi-

[38] *Staatssoziologie,* p. 99.

[39] In what follows I characterize Weber's conception of the struggle for power under legal domination, though I shall not attempt
to complete what Weber left unfinished. Despite their polemical
note, his occasional political writings contain important general considerations, especially with regard to the problem of leadership and
bureaucracy, which give an insight into his political analysis of legal
domination. The following discussion is based on the general analysis contained in two major essays, entitled respectively, "Parlament
und Regierung im neugeordneten Deutschland" ("Parliament and
Government in a Reconstituted Germany") and "Wahlrecht und
Demokratie in Deutschland" ("Electoral Law and Democracy in
Germany"), published in 1917 and 1918 and subsequently reissued
in *GPS.* Of the writings available in English, Weber's lecture on
"Politics as a Vocation" (*Essays,* pp. 77–128) is the most relevant

vidual or group wins that struggle faces the further problem of directing and controlling the "apparatus" of disciples, retainers, patrimonial officials, vassals and bureaucrats who must carry out decisions on a day-to-day basis. In these respects there is a major distinction between charismatic and traditional domination on the one hand and legal domination on the other.

Under charismatic authority the leader contends with the "forces" of depersonalization. He must assert his personal "magic" in the midst of kinship struggles over "family interests" or of bureaucratic infighting over corporate, institutional interests. Something like this is true also of traditional authority, where the ruler contends with the "forces" of decentralization, i.e., with the tendency of patrimonial officials and feudal vassals to usurp his privileges in their own name. In either case, victory in these struggles leads to great *personal* authority, whether by virtue of charisma or by virtue of the sanctity of tradition, and the successful leader or ruler can command direct personal obedience.

Under legal domination the struggle for power and the problem of leadership are of a different order. Because authority is embodied in the rule of law, success in the struggle for power becomes manifest in decisive influence upon the enactment of binding rules. To exercise such decisive influence a politician must contend with others like himself in the competition for votes, in political organizations, and in the legislative process of enacting laws and supervising their execution. Thus politicians contend for leadership not only in elections and in legislation but with the bureaucracy. This last problem loomed largest in Weber's eyes because under legal domination the day-to-day exercise of authority is in the hands of the bureaucracy. Even success in the struggle for votes, in parliamentary debate and in legislative decision-making can come to naught

---

in the present context. It should be noted that the following presentation is limited to Weber's analytical approach and does not consider his political evaluations in their contemporary setting. The latter theme is the subject of Wolfgang Mommsen, *Max Weber und die deutsche Politik 1890–1920* (Tübingen: J. C. B. Mohr, 1959), which appeared too late to be considered for its relevance to the present study.

unless it is followed up by effective control over administrative implementation. Failure to achieve such control means that the bureaucracy usurps the process of political decision-making in keeping with its "fundamental tendency . . . to turn all problems of politics into problems of administration."[40]

Conditions of political leadership in modern society. Weber distinguished between the leaders who have the power to command and the officials who stand ready to execute the orders they receive.[41] Under legal domination this distinction has special significance. Leaders must prove themselves in the electoral and legislative process, while officials must prove themselves in the performance of administrative work. The ideal official possesses impartiality, devotion to duty, the ability to act decisively within the framework of rules provided for him, and trained competence in the handling of his assigned tasks. If he receives orders with which he disagrees, he is obliged to make his views known to his superior, but if the latter insists upon their execution the official must regard himself as honor-bound to comply to the best of his ability. He must put his sense of duty above his personal opinion, and his ability to do this well is ideally a part of his professional ethic. Under the rule of law these corollaries follow logically. They do not, in Weber's judgment, preclude qualities of leadership, which consist of personal competence and character, the ability to form independent judgments and to express them where appropriate, and the capacity to set personal opinion aside where authoritative rulings go against it.

These qualities of bureaucratic leadership differ from those of political leadership. The political leader, like the entrepreneur or the military commander, is engaged in the struggle for power. If a politician had all the capacities of the most superior bureaucrat, he would still be only a very good party official, but not a political leader. The reason is *a difference in responsibility*, even between men of comparable stature. An official must exercise his judgment and his skills, but his duty is to place these at the service of higher authority; ultimately he is

[40] Karl Mannheim, *Ideology and Utopia* (New York: Harcourt, Brace & Co., 1949), p. 105. Mannheim's apt formulation expresses a fundamental idea of Weber's.

[41] *Law*, p. 335. Cf. also pp. 300–1 above.

responsible only for the execution of assigned tasks. A politician, on the other hand, must demonstrate his capacity for independent action, for which he alone is responsible. In his personal struggle for power, in which he seeks to enlist followers and allies, he will certainly make compromises where necessary, but as a leader he will hew to a line of policy upon which he stakes his case and for which he assumes personal responsibility, in both his electoral and his parliamentary battles and ultimately as the head of government. Partisanship, not impartiality, is essential to his thought and action, and personal responsibility for the basic decisions rests upon him—it cannot be "passed on" to higher authority. Where the bureaucrat must sacrifice his personal judgment if it runs counter to his official duties, the political leader must reject the responsibility for public actions that conflict with his basic policy. If need be, he must resign his office to give public effect to his position and to live up to his responsibilities of leadership.[42]

This logical construction of the contrast between the "typical" bureaucrat and the "typical" political leader provided Weber with a framework for an analysis of political leadership in modern society. Two attributes are essential to such leadership: independent judgment and skill in the struggle for power. To these should be added "economic availability," since bureaucratic government under the rule of law has made the work of the politician a full-time occupation. One can ask, therefore, under what social conditions and in what social groups these three attributes occur most frequently.

A professional politician can be a man who lives "off" politics in the sense that he earns his livelihood by engaging in political activities as a journalist, a party official, or a salaried worker, on the basis of fees or bribes. This is the position of all men

[42] Cf. *GPS*, pp. 154–55, 166, 170, 195–96; *Essays*, p. 95. It may be noted in passing that Weber's distinction between the bureaucrat and the politician is similar to the distinction between war and politics made by the German Field Marshal von Moltke. According to Moltke the conduct of war by military officials is guided by purely technical considerations, once the political ends to be achieved are given, while the political leader has the function to determine political goals before and after the war, but to stay out of the conduct of the war itself. Cf. Gerhard Ritter, *Staatskunst und Kriegshandwerk* (München: R. Oldenbourg, 1954), pp. 247–48.

who engage in politics in the absence of a regular income. On the other hand, there are professional politicians who are able to live "for" politics because they have an assured income that requires only their intermittent attention. This distinction is not invidious: many of those who must live "off" politics are capable of great idealism, and many of those who live "for" politics use political opportunities for economic gain. But on the whole it is easier for the man of independent means to be a man who possesses "political character," i.e., who makes a claim to leadership by taking a stand publicly and independently. By contrast, an official could have great strength of personal character but be completely without "political character." In Weber's view a generous sprinkling of politicians who could afford to live "for" politics was one of the factors that favored political leadership and vitalized a system of legal domination.[43]

Men who live "for" politics are notables in Weber's sense, whether they do so on a full-time basis or as an avocation. In the past such men represented an aristocracy or a patriciate, i.e., social strata that were political elites because they enjoyed a sheltered economic existence. In modern political life the number of such people is insufficient, partly because economic security does not necessarily lead to availability for politics. Regular income as such no longer frees a man for political activities as it did when social and economic preeminence was synonymous with exemption from work. Industrialists, for example, have the necessary income to live "for" politics, but not the time. They are not "economically dispensable" like the commercial patriciate of the medieval cities, which consisted of men who were *rentiers* first and entrepreneurs only on occasion. Moreover, the modern industrialist is so inextricably bound up with economic pursuits that he tends to lack the personal detachment needed for successful political leadership. Industrialists therefore are rather underrepresented in modern political life.

In this respect lawyers represent the opposite extreme among all those whose livelihood depends on a regular occupation. For Weber, lawyers are the prototype of the modern professional politician. They are available for political activities in

[43] *GPS*, pp. 182–83, 207–8, 306–7; *Essays*, pp. 85–86.

economic terms. Through arrangements with their associates they can free their time for politics and continue to receive an income or at least can expect to return to a secure and profitable profession when their political activity has come to an end. And in another sense as well they are highly suited for political activities. As lawyers they have a trained office staff at their disposal, which can become a major asset in elections and parliamentary debates. Their legal training is excellent preparation for legislative deliberations, their skill in writing and argument an important factor in campaigns, and their experience in the peaceful contest of the trial a proving ground for the struggle for power.[44]

These observations provided Weber with a standard of political judgment. He noted that in some countries, adequate or even superb leadership is provided by an aristocracy that is imitated by the lower strata and that possesses a style of life and a public bearing favoring personal dignity, political detachment, and a capacity for silent and effective action, as well as a sense of culture and refinement.[45] In the Germany of his day, however, he saw only evidence of political ineptitude, which he attributed to the predominance of the "parvenu," whose aristocratic pretensions, ostentatious monarchical loyalty and loudmouthed patriotism were a smoke screen for the absence of gentility, for civic cowardice, and for a complete lack of "political character."[46] Thus the qualities of "political character" not only are a product of individual capacity but also depend on a favorable historical setting. Such a setting was absent in Germany as a consequence of the Bismarck regime. Weber bitterly denied that there had been a lack of leadership potential in the German *Reichstag*, contending that the available political leaders were frustrated in their efforts because Bismarck was incapable of tolerating politicians who possessed independent power and responsibility. Germany lacked political leadership because Bismarck had de-

[44] *GPS*, pp. 208–9, 303–5; *Essays*, pp. 94–95.

[45] Cf. the earlier discussion of England, pp. 372–76.

[46] I mention these points without elaboration, since we encountered this interpretation in Weber's early writings (1892) and find it repeated without modification in his political writings during World War I. Cf., for example, *GPS*, pp. 303–17.

liberately prevented a genuine parliamentary regime; one man's creative leadership had left a destructive legacy for a whole nation. As a result, the country "was totally lacking in political will . . . and accustomed to accept in a fatalistic spirit whatever had been decided for its sake at the top, all this under the slogan of 'monarchical government.'"[47] In Weber's view it was a perversion of the facts to attribute the impotence of the German parliament to this low level of political sophistication, because a parliament is bound to be at a low level as long as it represents a reluctantly tolerated rubber stamp for the ruling bureaucracy. A high level of political maturity can be attained only if great problems are not merely debated but decided at the legislative level. To consider the conditions that favor political leadership, I turn next to Weber's discussion of parties and of parliament in a functioning democracy.

Parties, leadership, and elections. Weber defined parties as associations within a political community, in which membership rests on formally free recruitment. He contrasted their "formally voluntary solicitation and adherence" with "all organized groups which are prescribed and controlled by the central corporate body" of the government.[48] This emphasis parallels the previously noted contrast between "interests" and "authority" and between political leaders and public officials.

> The party leader depends upon a formally free agitation for allegiance, and this is the decisive contrast as over against the regulated promotion of the bureaucrat. Similarly, leaders of economic interest-groups must organize their followers; this is their characteristic function which depends upon the structure of the modern economy. There exists an irreconcilable contrast between such [political and economic] organizations and any grouping which is the product of governmental initiative backed up by the threat of force.[49]

[47] *Ibid.*, p. 139.
[48] *Theory*, p. 409. This definition excludes all totalitarian "parties" which, if successful, eliminate all other parties and exercise authority over the government apparatus.
[49] *GPS*, p. 294. It is in keeping with this basic contrast that few modern constitutions acknowledge the existence of political parties. See *ibid.*, p. 143.

For Weber organizations under the control of government always meant responsibility for the performance of assigned tasks and consequent disqualification for political action.

However, political parties have undergone a process of bureaucratization comparable to the bureaucratization of governments, communities, and economic organizations. The scale of modern political life requires mass organizations administered by a permanent officialdom whose discipline and experience is a prerequisite of success at the polls. In Weber's opinion, parties based on local organizations of notables, as in France, or on city machines and the system of party bosses, as in the United States, could not survive unless they organized themselves on this bureaucratic basis. In retrospect one can say that this was too simple an extrapolation of prevailing tendencies. Weber's own emphasis on the importance of men who live "for" politics, such as *rentiers* and lawyers, might have suggested to him that in a country of great wealth like the United States it would be possible to organize even mass parties on an intermittent basis around a small core of permanent employees, a larger group of permanently involved political notables, and a periodically organized and disbanded mass of volunteer workers. But even where he overestimated the degree of bureaucratization, he certainly pointed to the essential fact: the scope and cost of party activities has increased rapidly and as a result, decision-making has become centralized while the party professional has steadily increased in importance, whether he is a permanently employed official in Weber's sense or a permanently involved notable. Clearly the ad hoc organization of parties with fluctuating members and leaders and the restriction of political life to an elite of notables has been on the decline.[50]

Some corollaries of modern party organizations may be briefly noted. Frequently parties make an effort to organize youth groups and other types of enterprise—cooperatives, train-

[50] Weber's discussion of the bureaucratization of parties is in *GPS*, pp. 147–49, 202–5, and in *Essays* (see Index under "parties"). Incidentally, Weber's underestimation of the power potential of notables under conditions of bureaucratization may have to do with the several senses in which he used the term "notable." Cf. p. 348, n. 21.

ing institutes, publishing houses, and so on—that more or less directly serve the aims of the parties and provide salaried employment for their functionaries. To finance such enterprises as well as the ever increasing costs of agitation and electoral campaigns, parties rely on income from membership fees and from a great variety of fund-raising drives. Though the activities and sources of income vary with the social setting and organizational structure of the parties, they all exhibit a general tendency toward bureaucratization. The number of campaign speeches, the candidate's need to travel and to visit even small localities and the use of mass media increase, because under conditions of universal suffrage the political struggle necessarily assumes mass dimensions. These conditions pose the problematic relationship between bureaucratization and political leadership in a new form. For Weber the question was how political leadership in and through the parties was possible when party organizations became more bureaucratic and electoral campaigns more democratic.[51]

> Do the parties permit the rise of men with leadership qualities in a fully developed mass-democracy? Are they at all capable of accepting new ideas? After all, they are subject to bureaucratization just as much as the government. To create new parties is almost out of the question, since their organization would require an extraordinary outlay of work and money in the face of the entrenched power-position of the press. Yet the established parties are stereotyped. Their positions are the "sinecures" of the incumbents. Their store of ideas is largely fixed in the party-press and its propaganda pamphlets. The publishers and authors of this literature oppose the evaluation of its content which would result from a change of ideas. And the professional politician who lives off the party does not wish to be deprived of the ideas and slogans which constitute his "intellectual stock in trade."[52]

This comment reflects the ambivalent affinity between bureaucratization and democracy. Under a system of universal suffrage the size of party organizations increases while the

[51] *GPS*, p. 209.
[52] *Ibid.*, pp. 219–20.

role of political notables declines. Party officials and other regulars either aspire to public office themselves or have a decisive influence on the nomination of candidates. Weber
acknowledged that bureaucracy is less inimical to leadership
in political parties than in government, as long as party organizations keep in "fighting trim" for electoral campaigns. But
he also noted that the party regulars and influential employees
of interest organizations tend to distrust politicians whose
power rests on their personal appeal to the voter.[53] Under
universal suffrage, tension between charismatic leadership and
the imperatives of modern party organizations is a generic attribute of elections.

A candidate's charisma as an orator can play an all-important role in a campaign even though his nomination is
primarily in the hands of party regulars who control the large
financial resources that are required. In modern electoral campaigns the quantity of oratory is ever on the increase, and it
tends to lose in content what it gains in mass appeal. The
aim of campaign speeches is to have an emotional impact, to
give the people an image of the party's power and confidence
in victory, and to convey a sense of the candidate's charismatic
qualifications for leadership. Where the campaign brings to
the fore the personal charisma of the leader, he can make himself independent of the party organization and may come into
conflict with it. However bureaucratic party organizations become, with their professional functionaries and their dependence on membership fees and party enterprises (as in Europe)
or on financial donors, personal contacts, and control over
patronage (as in the United States), the charismatic leader can
disrupt these vested interests by virtue of his vote-getting
power. The charismatic element is in this sense an integral
aspect of a party system, because the choice of representatives
depends upon the vote of the ruled, notwithstanding the great
influence of party organizations on the electoral process.

The possibility of political leadership is likewise inherent in
certain technical aspects of representative government, despite
the fact that bureaucratization militates against leadership. An
elected representative cannot easily function as a mere "serv-

53 GPS, pp. 182–83, 207–8.

ant" of his constituency, i.e., as a delegate in the literal sense of the word. Various methods have been tried to increase the accuracy with which representatives reflect the wishes of their voters, but such methods as the recall of representatives, the control of parliamentary decisions through referenda or the increased frequency of elections do not achieve their purpose, in Weber's judgment. If the representative is made more dependent on the people, the power of the party organization over him increases, since the mobilization of the voters is in the hands of that organization. Referenda decrease the elasticity of the parliamentary body, and frequent elections are costly. As a result, systems of representative elections for the most part treat the representative as the chosen leader rather than the servant of the voters. Many constitutions express this idea by stating that the representative—like the monarch—is not responsible for his votes in parliament, that he "represents the interests of the people as a whole." The actual power of representatives varies greatly, of course, because of historical and technical differences among electoral systems.[54] Such variations are less important, however, than Weber's over-all conclusion about the role of leadership in a democracy.

A system of equal suffrage necessitates appeals to the entire population, and wherever the whole population chooses the highest ruler through direct election in a plebiscite the party organization is transformed into a modern-day group of disciples and retainers and the election becomes not a vote but a confession of faith and a confirmation of the ruler by "acclamation."[55] Dictatorial tendencies are set afoot wherever any leader's "position of political power depends on the fact

[54] Weber's discussion of party organization and elections in relation to political leadership is found in *WuG*, Vol. II, pp. 766–70.

[55] Weber had reference here to the "democracy by plebiscite" of Napoleon III. A more modern example is, of course, the Nazi movement, which so transformed the methods of party organization and of electoral campaigns that the voters were called upon to affirm their allegiance to the leader. Established totalitarian regimes like Communist or Fascist dictatorships also use this plebiscitary device in the sense that they call for and obtain an overwhelming affirmative vote with no choice permitted. But, while this practice may retain charismatic elements, it is not strictly comparable with plebiscites under a multiparty system.

that he has the confidence of the masses";[56] and Weber saw demagogic mass appeals and the possibility of dictatorial rule as integral parts of even the most viable democratic system. But he argued that these acknowledged dangers have to be assessed comparatively, not allowed to serve as an excuse for opposition to democracy as they did in Germany during his lifetime.

Again, Weber used the contrast between bureaucracy and political leadership to arrive at a political assessment of the electoral process. The recruitment of officials and the election of politicians are alternative methods of selecting leaders. Every bureaucratic selection of personnel is made away from the limelight of publicity. At best, officials commend themselves to their superiors by their competence; at worst, by their compliance; and in neither case are their qualities those of political leaders. The party leader or politician, on the other hand, is constantly exposed to public criticism by his enemies and competitors, and he can be certain that all the motives and methods of his rise to power will be fully examined. Demogogic appeals are a part of the struggle in which he has to prove his mettle. The successful political leader is clearly a man who has been tested.

Weber readily conceded that the means used in the electoral struggle can give rise to the most glaring abuses. Orators who lack all political character and ability can rise to power; financial resources at the disposal of a nonentity can tip the balance; above all, demagogic appeals to sentiment and to the most shortsighted interests can bring to power the worst rather than the best leaders. But these and other unquestioned evils are entirely independent of the form of government; they are as likely under monarchical absolutism as under democratic institutions.[57]

Weber's positive evaluation of the electoral process was therefore qualified in two ways. The selection of rulers under

[56] *GPS*, p. 212.

[57] A government by notables can foster a caste system behind a smoke screen of self-serving pretensions. A monarchical regime can give rise to court intrigues and time-serving sycophants. Along these lines the only conclusion is, according to Weber, that every system is easily corrupted.

universal suffrage is better than under the appointment procedures of a bureaucracy, but the dangers implicit in equal
suffrage and demagogic mass appeals must be reckoned with;
they cannot be eliminated entirely, just as analogous dangers
cannot be eliminated from any alternative system of government. There is, however, one great danger of mass democracy
that merits special consideration: the predominance of emotional over rational elements in the process of political decision-
making.[58] Although this danger necessarily differs with the
cultural traditions and institutional safeguards of each country, its general aspects can be characterized in terms of the
tension between bureaucratic administration and political
leadership.

Bureaucratic absolutism and parliamentary leadership. Weber referred to the "politics of the street" and a "syndicalism
of immaturity" as the ultimate extremes of mass democracy.
In his judgment, the threat of mob rule was greatest where
parliamentary rule is impotent or discredited, where political
parties are not strongly organized, where the appeal to fear
can be successful because of failure of nerve among the rulers
and cowardice of the bourgeoisie, and finally, where in the
large cities idlers and coffeehouse intellectuals are permitted
to engage in political agitation in the absence of an organized
working-class.[59]

The importance of these several factors varies. In regard
to Germany, Weber's evaluation differed from that of most of
his contemporaries. He believed that the Social Democratic
Party and the trade unions were major stabilizing factors. An
idle intelligentsia did not exist in Germany as it did in France
or Italy. For Weber the crux of the German problem was
that the parliament had no positive political functions. The
strengthening of the parliament and hence of political parties
had been successfully subverted by playing on the "fear of
democracy" that was rife in monarchical circles, in the bureaucracy, and in the ranks of the middle classes. Weber's
object, therefore, was to demonstrate that this fear was unwar-
ranted, that an effective parliamentary regime could be a bulwark against mob rule as well as a safeguard against the abuses

[58] *GPS*, pp. 209–11.
[59] *Ibid.*, pp. 221–24, 317–18.

of monarchical and bureaucratic absolutism.[60] In his discussion of this problem we can ignore the necessarily dated political arguments and concentrate instead on his general considerations.

Under a system of legal domination the day-to-day exercise of authority is in the hands of the governmental bureaucracy and is subject to the rule of law only where the enactment of laws and the supervision of their implementation is controlled by political leaders. The job of analysis therefore is to specify the conditions that develop when the bureaucracy encroaches upon the political process—what might be called the "pathology" of legal domination. In addition Weber analyzed the conditions favorable to political decision-making under a parliamentary regime, i.e., conditions that favor a political control of the bureaucracy.

An ideally functioning bureaucracy is the most efficient method of solving large-scale organizational tasks. But the very conditions of efficiency that Weber specified also can be the conditions that lead to a subversion of the rule of law and the transformation of bureaucracy from a policy-implementing to a decision-making body. In this respect the official's knowledge is important. This knowledge is technical, since appointments depend upon certified qualifications, and consists of organizational know-how acquired through day-to-day experience with the minutiae of administration. Under modern conditions, the only alternative to administration by officials who possess such knowledge is administration by dilettantes.

[60] As Weber saw it, the system of legal domination was in danger where the monarch and his leading officials used the whole arsenal of demagogic appeals to subvert the parliament and the political parties, while assuming the functions of political leadership for which neither could qualify. Weber, of course, exempted Bismarck from this wholesale indictment, but he pointed out that a statesman of such stature was a rare event indeed, and we have seen that he attributed to Bismarck major responsibility for the political dilemma of Germany. In this connection he cited with approval the position of the National Liberal leaders in the 1870's and '80's, who regarded it as their political task to preserve viable parties and a viable parliament during Bismarck's reign so that these institutions would function effectively at a later time, when the political life of the country would have to operate on an even keel with politicians of more ordinary abilities. See *ibid.*, p. 134.

This alternative is ruled out wherever the expert performance of functions is believed to be indispensable for the maintenance and promotion of order and welfare. Thus the official's technical and organizational knowledge is a sign of his indispensability and hence of his power, unless he is controlled by people who possess not only the authority to supervise him but the knowledge to do so effectively. The latter condition is especially important, in Weber's view, because officials buttress their superiority as technical and organizational experts by treating official business as confidential, thus securing their work against outside inspection and control. This tendency toward secrecy has a rationale wherever the power interests of an organization are at stake in its contest with hostile organizations. Private enterprises, political parties, military establishments and foreign offices all practice concealment as a means of improving their chances of success. But this secretive tendency exists even in the absence of plausible justifications. Every bureaucracy will conceal its knowledge and operation unless it is forced to disclose them, and it will, if need be, simulate the existence of hostile interests to justify such concealment. Clearly, such practices subvert the rule of law, because an administration that cannot be inspected and controlled tends to become a law unto itself.[61]

These considerations follow from Weber's definition of bureaucracy as an administration in the hands of officials who possess the requisite technical knowledge. By definition these officials are more knowledgeable and so more powerful than their superiors, unless special provision is made for effective supervision. A bureaucracy that uses its knowledge and capacity for concealment to escape inspection and control jeopardizes legal domination by usurping the rule-making or decision-making powers that ideally should result from the political and legislative process.

Bureaucratic absolutism is the consequence of such usurpation, as in imperial Germany. Through Bismarck's maneuvers the parliament was excluded from participation in the political leadership of the country. The result was a species of "negative politics" that reduced the parliament's power to the rejec-

[61] These points are discussed in *Theory*, p. 339; *Essays*, pp. 232–35; and *GPS*, p. 171.

tion of budgetary authorizations and legislative proposals originating in the administration. Under such circumstances the parliament and the bureaucracy became hostile powers. Officials would give the legislature only the barest minimum of information, because they regarded it as an assembly of impotent grumblers full of learned conceit and a drag on efficient operations. In turn, members of the legislature as well as the people at large regarded the bureaucracy as a caste of careerists and policemen who treated the people as a mere object of their onerous and in part superfluous functions. In this atmosphere political leadership went by the board; appointments, promotions and patronage were handled by the bureaucracy, which had no responsibility to outside authority, while the highest positions of government were filled on the basis of personal connections by capable officials who possessed no trace of political ability. Such men remained in office until some intrigue led to their replacement by men just like themselves. Weber maintained that under bureaucratic absolutism the evils of personal influence and the personal struggle for power that exist under all systems of domination occur in exaggerated form because they are perpetuated behind closed doors and without any possibility of control.[62]

The conduct of parliamentary business depends on its significance for political decision-making; otherwise its speeches and committee meetings remain academic exercises in elocution. When a representative speaks in parliament, he does not express his personal beliefs or try to persuade his parliamentary opponent. Instead, he gives an official declaration of policy on behalf of his party (where political parties act under party discipline) or on behalf of himself and his political associates within his party (where parties are congeries of political groupings, as in the United States). Such speeches are for the most part the end product of prior caucusing, in which either the party as a whole has decided on a policy line or in which the attainable compromises among factions have been reached. Influence within parliament depends in good measure upon the amount of work a representative does behind the

[62] Weber appended to this a detailed critique of monarchical rule, which I omit because it has primarily historical interest. See *GPS*, pp. 156–61.

scenes and in committee, and that work depends in turn upon his personal staff. In imperial Germany this whole machinery came to naught because neither parliamentary activity nor party leadership led to responsible participation in the conduct of government. In Weber's view it was fatal, for example, that legal provisions forced the party leaders to resign their position as parliamentary representatives of their party when they were appointed to high administrative posts. In this way the leadership of the political parties was "decapitated," while the government obtained executive officials who were neither politicians (since they were forced to sever their party ties) nor trained administrators (since their party activities precluded the experience of a bureaucratic career). Moreover, parliamentarians who became ministers also had to renounce their previously expressed political convictions to become acceptable to the ruling circles in the government and at the court. In this fashion the German parliament became a convenient springboard for talented ministerial officials, not an arena for candidates for political leadership, because the latter were not, after all, interested in offices with salary and rank but in power with responsibility. Thus it became "undignified" for a statesman to be a party leader.[63]

What, by contrast, are the conditions under which a parliament has positive political functions? A modern parliament is, first of all, a body of delegates who represent a population subject to rule by bureaucratic means. By their actions the delegates express the minimum of consent that sustains the system of legal domination. The decisive power in their hands is the power of the purse. On this basis they may also possess other rights, such as that the principal executive officials of the government remain in office only so long as they command the confidence of a parliamentary majority, or that these officials are answerable to parliamentary committees. Accord-

[63] According to Weber, the impotence of parliament and the required subservience of men who would become government ministers had led to the voluntary withdrawal of the most capable leaders from political life, with the result that the bulk of potential leaders were to be found in business, where they had more room for their talents (*ibid.*, pp. 164–65). The comparable American experience suggests, on the other hand, that there may be more than one reason for this characteristic preference.

ingly the administration of legislative acts is subject to parliamentary control.

Where these functions are performed, parliament participates in the decision-making of the body politic, and this participation depends on the struggle for power. The political parties vie with one another to have their leaders appointed to the highest political positions where they assume responsibility for the policies of government. In such political contests differences of belief and judgment are inextricably mixed with a strong drive for personal power. Men who possess genuine political capacity are also eager to engage in the political struggle; they look forward to participating in, and to bearing the responsibility for, the exercise of authority. In Weber's view, it is decisive that men of such qualities are party leaders who can be elected or appointed to leading executive positions, whether this is done in the British manner, where the Cabinet is composed of the leaders of the victorious party, or in the American manner, where the party leader is elected to the highest executive position. Like all human institutions this process has defects of its own. The number of genuine political leaders is bound to remain small, even in a functioning parliament. The men likely to win out are, on the whole, not the most outstanding personalities but those who have mass appeal and a modicum of political acumen, so the voters are confronted with a choice among lesser evils. Also, the great majority of representatives in parliament are of necessity small men who subordinate themselves to the elected party leader only if their own or their party's success depends upon it. These aspects of a parliamentary regime are related to the potentially dictatorial element of mass appeal that is an ineradicable aspect of democracy. But Weber believed that these drawbacks were nothing compared to the defects of impotent parties, nominal parliaments, and autocratic bureaucracies. Despite its flaws, democracy has a very great advantage: it leads to a clear allocation of responsibility for political decisions.

Once the political leaders are chosen, that responsibility has been allocated and the leaders can fulfill their share of it only through their activities in parliament. In a system of legal domination politicians are the indispensable counterweight to a bureaucratic government. If the rule of law is to be effective, politicians must establish legislative control over the bureaucracy despite the tendency of officials to conceal their conduct of affairs and despite the fact that by comparison with the expertise and organizational know-how of the officials the politicians are ignorant dilettantes. Parliamentary control of the administration can be made effective only where the right of parliamentary inquiry and the possibility of cross-examination before commissions of inquiry exist. Weber believed that no more than occasional use need be made of such powers in order to make officials accountable. He pointed out that in Great Britain the judicious handling of such parliamentary inquiries, the publicity given to them and the public interest in them had in good part been responsible for the integrity of officials and the high level of general political education. The degree of political maturity in a nation does not depend upon the more spectacular aspects of parliamentary government but upon the fact that the nation is kept informed of the manner in which public affairs are conducted.[64] Only then is it possible for the public to develop an understanding of government administration and cease to regard it with that lack of comprehension that invariably results in sterile invectives against "bureaucracy."

Effective commissions of inquiry also provide an indispensable basis for the parliamentary recruitment of political leaders. Under modern conditions leadership can develop only through the medium of the spoken and written word. The issue is, therefore, whether or not the speeches and written documents of politicians display a strong will and a seasoned experience. Ignorance, demagogic appeals and mere routine will prevail in a parliament that can only criticize without being able to acquire a knowledge of the facts, or in which party leaders are never placed in the position of having to prove

[64] In this connection Weber's other definition of political maturity in terms of a people's response to acts of sabotage and comparable political uprisings may be cited also. Such maturity is a question of "maintaining calm nerves . . . , of meeting force with force to be sure, but then attempting in a matter-of-fact way to solve the tensions that provoked these outbreaks, and above all of re-establishing immediately the guarantees of a free social order so that in this way political decisions remain entirely unaffected by such upheavals." See *GPS*, p. 223.

themselves politically. But in a parliament with positive political functions, a politician acquires a knowledge of governmental administration through his intensive work on parliamentary committees. Such committees are the proving ground not of demagogues but of professional politicians. The contact with administrators they provide has the twofold function of controlling the bureaucracy through public disclosure and of providing both leaders and followers with the necessary political training and education.

Weber's ideal of a responsible political leader contained sharply divergent qualities. The leader must have charismatic appeal in order to win elections under conditions of universal suffrage. This "caesarist" aspect of democracy has two advantages. Individual leaders frequently make the great political decisions, and because of their authority over the masses they can counteract the consequences of bureaucratization in political parties and in government administration. But these appeals to mass emotions are also dangerous, and only a functioning parliament can keep them within bounds. Such a parliament is needed to secure a steady administration, to maintain the rule of law against a plebiscitary leader, and to provide a peaceful means of revoking his mandate if he loses the confidence of the masses. In addition, parliament provides an orderly means by which politicians, who compete for the confidence of the voters, can prove their political qualifications. The skills required of the professional politician can be acquired only in parliamentary committees, for without leadership in this second sense a victory at the polls cannot be translated into effective legislation and parliamentary supervision of the bureaucracy. Thus the plebiscitary and the parliamentary bases of leadership are both indispensable: in the absence of universal suffrage *and* of parliament, cliques of political notables and government officials will control the rule of law rather than be subject to it. Hence the tension between mass appeals and parliamentary procedures is a concomitant of legal domination.

CHAPTER XIV

A CONTEMPORARY PERSPECTIVE

Weber was working on his sociology of the modern state at the time of his death in 1920. It is appropriate now to assess this analysis in contemporary terms. Weber's speculations on the future of modern society are instructive for us because they are based on a large-scale comparative study of systems of domination, and they can be examined today in the light of events since Weber's time.

In Weber's view a system of bureaucratic rule is inescapable. There is no known example of a bureaucracy being destroyed except in the course of a general cultural decline. Also, compared with the patrimonial regimes of the past, modern bureaucracy is more efficient because of specialization and training. The more organizations come to depend on a division of labor and the work of specially trained officials, the more bureaucratic and inescapable they become. Ever new demands are made for government services, and the most elementary needs of the community come to depend upon bureaucratic operations.[1] To those who expect a socialist so-

[1] Weber's account of the reasons for the advance of bureaucratization has been discussed above on p. 381 ff. in terms of the factors associated with the origin of the modern state, and on p. 417 ff. in relation to the intrinsic attributes of bureaucratic organizations.

ciety of the future to create a major social transformation, Weber pointed out that in a centrally planned society bureaucratic tendencies would mount still higher. The division of labor and the use of special skills in administration would increase, and a "dictatorship of the bureaucrats" rather than a "dictatorship of the proletariat" would result.[2]

Universal bureaucratization was for Weber the symbol of a cultural transformation that would affect all phases of modern society. If this development ran its full course it would result in a new despotism more rigid even than the ancient Egyptian dynasties because it would have a technically efficient administration at its disposal. This new serfdom could be discerned, Weber thought, on the basis of historical parallels and by thinking observable tendencies through to their "logical" conclusion.

One of these tendencies is the growth of the welfare institutions and pension provisions that have become a regular feature of public employment. In Weber's day some welfare measures were introduced by private employers in an effort to tie the individual worker more firmly to the enterprise. Is it not possible that in a society of the future the legally free individual will be "bound" to an enterprise for life in order not to lose the material benefits that are his only on the basis of continuous employment? At the time of the first world war Weber's speculations turned in this direction. He noted a decline of the "capitalist mentality" as in the case of successful German industrialists who used their wealth to purchase lands in trust for the sake of titles and of a military or civil-service career for their children. The war and its aftermath would lead to a vast increase of pensioners exclusively dependent upon state funds and hence to a net loss from the viewpoint of productive work and economic growth. In France these pensioners had become so powerful already that they undermined the economy and jeopardized the stability of government. To Weber these straws in the wind meant that the quest for order and a secure rent was threatening to replace risk-taking and

[2] This phrase occurs in Weber's lecture on socialism. Cf. *GAzSuS*, p. 508. A more detailed discussion of centralized planning under socialism is contained in *Theory*, p. 212 ff. and *passim*. See also the editor's comments in *ibid.*, pp. 38–40.

profit. Was it not possible that in the future this whole outlook would become dominant, and the demand for a modest
but secure income from state funds would lead to a thorough
bureaucratization of the economy?[3] As Weber saw it, this
prospect meant a state economy in which economic transactions through political manipulation would replace the relative
rationality and individualism inherent in a capitalist economy.
The issue is still very much alive. One need only think of the
growth of interest organizations with their monopolistic devices for regulating admission to a profession or occupation
or industry and securing for members the advantages of special jurisdiction.[4]

Weber also speculated about the future in terms of two historical analogies. In the past the costs of government were
financed on a "liturgical" basis by making private associations
liable for the performance of public services. Is it not possible
that with the ever increasing scope of governmental functions
the same device will be used again? Weber's concern here was
all too accurate, even though no exact counterpart to the historical analogy exists today. One may think, for example, of
the use of forced labor under both fascist and Communist dictatorships, in which politically designated categories of persons were compelled to perform public works. This device is
also used as a test of political loyalty.[5] The comparative per-

[3] Here Weber also projected the experience of the war and its
aftermath, which made the centralized rationing of resources indispensable. He pointed out that, while such measures can be used to
create a better organization of the economy, they can also be used
to increase the number of pensioners and the bureaucratic regulation
of the economy. His reference to jurisdictional disputes between
Austrian upholsterers and carpenters that were arbitrated by governmental authority makes clear that he had a neo-mercantilist
economy in mind. This is also apparent from his repeated reference
to municipalities in which radical working-class groups had been
elected to office and had adopted mercantilist policies in the interest of their members.

[4] Cf. the reference to special laws as a modification of legal domination on pp. 431–35 above.

[5] These regimes resort to special campaigns, for example, in which
the younger age groups are forced to demonstrate their loyalty by
laboring for peasants at harvest time or by "volunteering" their services as pioneers in remote areas. The absence of such devices from

spective suggested to Weber that developments in the direction of democracy, with its leveling of social differences, had been replaced time and again by a rebirth of "aristocracy." Under universal bureaucratization social differentiation on the basis of property and economic function declines, but a new differentiation on the basis of education increases.

> The development of the diploma from universities, and business and engineering colleges, and the universal clamor for the creation of educational certificates in all fields make for the formation of a privileged stratum in bureaus and in offices. Such certificates support their holders' claims for intermarriages with notable families . . . , claims for a "respectable" remuneration rather than remuneration for work done, claims for assured advancement and old-age insurance, and, above all, claims to monopolize socially and economically advantageous positions.[6]

At the end of this road Weber envisaged a society in which social status depends on educational qualifications and governmental office, much like the classic Chinese model except that the education would be technical rather than humanistic.

These and related speculations are summed up in his observation that bureaucracy had turned from an ally into an enemy of capitalism.[7] At the time of the absolute monarchies the bureaucratization of government made possible a "wider range of capitalist activity." But today one can expect "as an *effect* of bureaucratization a policy that meets the petty bourgeois interest in a secure traditional 'subsistence,' or even a state socialist party that strangles opportunities for private profit."[8] Along these lines Weber anticipated some kind of reversion to patrimonialism. The dictatorial potential implicit in mass appeals added to the desire for a secure subsistence would result in a centralized bureaucracy under a dictator, a vast army of

---

the democracies of the Western world continues to be one of their important distinguishing characteristics.

[6] *Essays*, p. 241.

[7] For an elaboration of this view see Joseph Schumpeter, *Capitalism, Socialism and Democracy* (New York: Harper & Brothers, 1950).

[8] *Essays*, p. 231.

state pensioners, and an array of monopolistic privileges. This image makes sense as a modern replica of the economically stagnant patrimonial regimes of the past, with their combination of personal arbitrariness and traditionally sanctioned appropriation of privileges by special interest groups.[9]

These speculations about the future of modern society have much in common with the views of men like Alexis de Tocqueville and Jacob Burckhardt, to name two of that small number of nineteenth-century scholars whose insight into the totalitarian potential of democracy astonishes us today. In his great work on America, De Tocqueville wrote that, as the number of public officials increases, "they form a nation within each nation." He observed that governments more and more frequently acted "as if they thought themselves responsible for the actions and private condition of their subjects . . . [while] private individuals grow more and more apt to look upon the supreme power in the same light." The power of the state would become absolute, "till each nation is reduced to nothing better than a flock of timid and industrious animals, of which government is the shepherd."[10] Jacob Burckhardt envisaged much the same outcome in terms of the dictatorial tendencies of mass democracy. He wrote of the *"terribles simplificateurs"* who would usher in a society of military commandos under the guise of republicanism. He combined this idea with an image of the proletarian masses in a future state "in which a certain supervised measure of misery would be combined with promotions and uniforms, and in which every day would begin and end with a rolling of the drums."[11] These apprehensive images fit in with Weber's own speculation

[9] This summary of Weber's views is based on several scattered passages. See in addition to the sources cited *GPS*, pp. 149–52, 279–89, and "Zur Lage der bürgerlichen Demokratie in Russland," *Archiv für Sozialwissenschaft*, Vol. XXII (1906), p. 346 ff. Part of this last passage has been translated in the introduction to *Essays*, pp. 71–72.

[10] Alexis de Tocqueville, *Democracy in America* (New York: Vintage Books, 1954), Vol. II, pp. 323–24, 336–37.

[11] Quoted in Theodor Schieder, "Die historischen Krisen im Geschichtsdenken Jacob Burckhardts," in Walter Hubatsch (ed.), *Schicksalswege der deutschen Vergangenheit* (Düsseldorf: Droste Verlag, 1950), pp. 449–50.

of the universal bureaucratization that would result as much from the quest for order and economic security among the people as from the power drive of the officials. From his comparative legal perspective Weber added the idea of a society in which "private law" would be completely absent in wide areas of social life.

> This occurs where there exist no norms having the character of right-granting laws. In such a situation, the entire body of norms consists exclusively of "regulations." . . . All private interests enjoy protection . . . only as the obverse aspect of the effectiveness of these regulations. . . . All forms of law become absorbed within "administration" and become part and parcel of "government."[12]

None of these ideas was perhaps as original in the nineteenth century as it appears to a later generation, which does not remember these apprehensions and is intellectually unprepared for the development of modern totalitarianism. For De Tocqueville this foreboding image of the future arose out of the contrast between the medieval estates, which were a bulwark against the centralization of power, and the leveling tendencies of democracy, which left every individual not only defenseless against government encroachment but even desirous of it. De Tocqueville's great distinction is not his adoption of this idea, which was the common property of nineteenth-century conservatives, but his use of it for a comparative analysis of America and France and his insistence that it must be combined in some positive way with the irreversible equalitarianism of the modern age. Again, Jacob Burckhardt followed current opinion in his emphasis on the dictatorial dangers endemic in mass democracy and the popular quest for "promotions and uniforms."[13]

[12] *Law,* p. 44.
[13] Late nineteenth-century observers had before them the example of Napoleon III, and in the atmosphere of imperial Germany it was fashionable to use this example as an argument against democracy. Cf. H. Gollwitzer, "Der Caesarismus Napoleons III. im Widerhall der öffentlichen Meinung Deutschlands," *Historische Zeitschrift,* Vol. CLXXIII (1952), p. 23 ff. The denunciation of the bureaucratic and militaristic spirit of the people was equally prominent among laissez-faire liberals for economic and political reasons

No doubt these ideas influenced Weber, but for him the medieval estates were only one of many conditions that had brought about the development of modern freedom. While the great Swiss historian sought to defend the European cultural tradition, Weber was preoccupied with the problem of individual autonomy in a world that was increasingly subjected to the inexorable machinery of bureaucratic administration.

> . . . It is horrible to think that the world could one day be filled with nothing but those little cogs, little men clinging to little jobs and striving towards bigger ones—a state of affairs which is to be seen once more, as in the Egyptian records, playing an ever-increasing part in the spirit of our present administrative system, and especially of its offspring, the students. This passion for bureaucracy . . . is enough to drive one to despair. It is as if in politics . . . we were deliberately to become men who need "order" and nothing but order, who become nervous and cowardly if for one moment this order wavers, and helpless if they are torn away from their total incorporation in it. That the world should know no men but these: it is in such an evolution that we are already caught up, and the great question is therefore not how we can promote and hasten it, but what can we oppose to this machinery in order to keep a portion of mankind free from this parcelling-out of the soul, from this supreme mastery of the bureaucratic way of life.[14]

Weber's perspective for the future was a direct product of his personal position as a liberal critic of bureaucratic absolutism in imperial Germany, and today we sympathize readily with this early formulation of George Orwell's *1984*. But an intellectual test of Weber's approach cannot depend upon these political judgments and forecasts. The question for us is rather whether Weber's comparative study of bureaucracy

---

and among cultural critics for aesthetic reasons. The great polemics of Friedrich Nietzsche are relevant here.

[14] Quoted in J. P. Mayer, *Max Weber and German Politics* (London: Faber & Faber, 1943), pp. 127–28. These remarks were made in the course of a debate at the convention of the *Verein für Sozialpolitik* in 1909. A full translation of Weber's comments on this occasion appears in *ibid.*, pp. 125–31.

yields analytically useful categories that can aid our understanding of the totalitarian regimes that have developed since his time. To answer this question we must distinguish between Weber's concept of "bureaucracy under legal domination" and his political analysis of bureaucratization.

Weber pointed out that the indispensability of a technically expert administration is not by itself a token of power. In the ideal case, qualified officials would serve every legitimate ruler equally well, because they were bound to execute efficiently every legally enacted law. But bureaucratic administration can operate regularly and efficiently only if the validly enacted laws are a consistent and hence *relatively stable* system of norms.

In Weber's view several factors can militate against such a system. The belief in the legitimacy of legal domination has undergone major changes. The axioms of "natural law," which at one time gave a higher justification to the legal order, were challenged by various theories of substantive justice. The growth of special jurisdictions pointed in the direction of a neo-patrimonialism and undermined the uniform and centrally administered body of laws that is the foundation of legal domination. The government officials themselves did not always believe unquestioningly in the legitimacy of the rules they were called upon to administer, as, for example, in imperial Germany, where the highest government officials subverted the legislative process because they believed in the legitimacy of autocratic rule. Thus Weber's political analysis was concerned with the operation of a bureaucracy *in the absence* of a system of legal domination.

Bureaucratization becomes compatible with a system of legal domination only if the officials are prevented from usurping the political and legislative process. Weber believed, therefore, that bureaucratization would advance, but that it was an open question whether it would be bureaucratization under the rule of law.

At the time of the first world war Weber's analysis and forecast did not go beyond this point. His comparative perspective suggested to him a development of the future in which the "spirit" of bureaucracy with its love of routine and encouragement of a "subsistence mentality" would gain the upper hand. Many of his speculations in this respect were accurate as far as

they went. His analysis of the German political structure discerned many of the factors that eventually facilitated Hitler's
rise to power. His analysis of bureaucratization emphasized
psychological and institutional tendencies that have come to
the fore since his day in the welfare states of western Europe
and America—though he may have overestimated the incompatibility between bureaucracy and economic growth. But
Weber did not at all foresee the development of totalitarian
government. Although he mentioned that those subject to bureaucratic controls could escape their influence "only by
creating an organization of their own," he admitted that he
could not envisage a society in which communist axioms of
natural law would be the ruling principles of government.[15]

Nonetheless it is possible to use Weber's analysis to account
for the characteristics of totalitarian government.[16] To do this
we need consider only two aspects of his concept of bureaucracy: the rule of law and the tendency of officials to conceal
their conduct of affairs. In regard to the first, totalitarianism
establishes the arbitrariness of the highest authority as a principle of government. In the interest of their substantive objectives, the will of the highest party authorities is absolute. They
may disregard not only all formal procedures by which laws are
validated but also their own previous rulings. Where norms
may be changed at a moment's notice, the rule of law is destroyed. Totalitarianism also does away with the principle of
a single line of authority, which is basic to Weber's concept
of bureaucracy. Instead of relying on an enactment of laws
and the supervision of their execution at the top, totalitarian
regimes use the hierarchy of the *party* to expedite and control
the execution of orders through the *regular administrative*

[15] Cf. *Theory*, p. 338, and Max Weber, "Russlands Übergang
zum Scheinkonstitutionalismus," *Archiv für Sozialwissenschaft*, Vol.
XXIII (1906), p. 314.

[16] The following account is merely suggestive. A more detailed
analysis of totalitarianism along these lines will be found in my
Work and Authority in Industry (New York: John Wiley & Sons,
1956), Chapter VI, and in my essay "The Cultural and Political
Setting of Economic Rationality in Western and Eastern Europe,"
in Gregory Grossman (ed.), *Economic Calculation and Organization in Eastern Europe* (Berkeley: University of California Press,
1960).

channels. This is the major device by which totalitarian regimes seek to prevent officials from escaping inspection while compelling them to use their expertise to implement the orders of the regime. A totalitarian government therefore is based on two interlocking hierarchies of authority. The work of every factory, every government office, every unit of the army or the secret police, as well as every cultural or social organization, is programmed, coordinated and supervised by some government agency. It is also propagandized, expedited, criticized, spied upon and incorporated in special campaigns by an agency of the totalitarian party that is responsible to the higher party authorities.

The rationale of this principle of a double government can be stated in the framework of Weber's analysis. An ideally functioning bureaucracy in his sense is the most efficient method of solving large-scale organizational tasks. But this is true only *if* these tasks involve more or less stable norms and hence the effort to maintain the rule of law and achieve an equitable administration of affairs. These conditions are absent where the tasks are assigned by an omnipotent and revolutionary authority. Under the simulated combat conditions of a totalitarian regime the norms governing conduct do not stay put for any length of time. And in the face of an unremitting drive for prodigies of achievement officials will tend to use their devices of concealment for a systematic if tacit "withdrawal of efficiency" (*Veblen*). They will do so not only for reasons of convenience but because the demands made upon them by the regime are "irrational" from the viewpoint of expert knowledge and systematic procedure. The party, on the other hand, must prevent the types of concealment that make such collective inaction possible while putting all executive officials under maximum pressure to utilize their expertise to the fullest extent. This, I take it, is the rationale of a double hierarchy of government that places a party functionary at the side of every major official in order to prevent concealment and apply pressure. Indeed, the two hierarchies would be required even if all key positions in government and industry were filled with party functionaries. For a functionary turned executive official would still be responsible for "overfulfilling" the plan, while the new party functionary who took his place would still be charged with keeping the official under pressure and surveillance.

It is true that Weber did not anticipate the political development that has made this application of his analysis appropriate. That such an application is possible and fruitful is a striking testimony to his genius.

CHAPTER XV

MAX WEBER'S IMAGE OF SOCIETY

Max Weber died only forty years ago. But in the present era of scientific specialization he appears already like a man of the Renaissance, who took all humanity for his province. Consider the range of his interests and skills: He studied law and economics; he became a specialist in the interpretation of religious doctrines and he was a notable Biblical scholar; he had a thoroughly technical grasp of ancient Roman land-surveying methods, medieval trading companies, and the modern stock exchange; he became a specialist in the comparative history of urban institutions; he examined in detail the farm-labor problems of East German agriculture; he developed a systematic framework for an interpretation of ancient Mediterranean civilization and of the political development of Western Europe; he made a special study of the medieval origins of Western music; and he analyzed in detail the social and psychological conditions of productivity in a West German textile mill. In all this, he had the advantages of a German classical education; he was at home in seven or eight languages, to which he added Russian at the time of the Russian Revolution of 1905. And throughout his career he was as much immersed in the methodological controversies of the social sciences as in the political controversies of his time and country.

A. INTELLECTUAL AFFINITIES

Weber belonged to the generation of scholars that shaped the world image of our day. Born in 1864, he was a contemporary of Sigmund Freud (1856), Emile Durkheim (1858), John Dewey (1859), and such other figures among our intellectual forebears as Franz Boas, Henri Bergson, and Gaetano Mosca. He was also a contemporary of the American sociologists and social psychologists W. I. Thomas, George H. Mead, Robert Park, and Charles Cooley. These men differed in many ways, but all of them stood in opposition to the crude scientific materialism of their age, which tended to treat social and psychological facts as complex aggregates of physical particles. All of them believed that individual and social life demands a scientific analysis in its own terms. In this respect, Sigmund Freud was representative of his generation; here was a scientist who discovered the unconscious in man, here was a materialist who analyzed dreams, here was a doctor who studied sex in the heyday of the Victorian age. And here were Weber and Durkheim, who devoted a major part of their work to a scientific study of religion—at a time when many people felt that the theory of evolution had challenged the foundations of the Christian faith.[1]

However, unlike many of these other men, Weber is not famous for his elaboration of a key idea. Marx's theory that the organization of production is the fundamental determinant of world history, Durkheim's emphasis upon group membership as the source of individual morality and social health, and Freud's view that each man incurs emotional scars in his not so innocent childhood have all entered popular parlance. The same cannot be said of Weber's work, because it cannot be summarized or vulgarized so easily.

[1] For a perceptive analysis of this generation of intellectuals, cf. H. Stuart Hughes, *Consciousness and Society*, cited earlier. Now that this background picture is available, a comparable study, focusing on this generation in terms of its systems of ideas, can be written more easily. An approach to this is contained in Carlo Antoni, *From History to Sociology* (Detroit: Wayne State University Press, 1959).

In this comparison, two other ideas, which became most popular or were developed initially on this side of the Atlantic, should be included. Various theorists of social evolution, like Herbert Spencer or W. G. Sumner, attempted to reduce individual destinies to some larger sequence by which society moves from a lower to a higher stage. These theorists were challenged by a pragmatic philosophy, as developed by William James and John Dewey, which combined the same faith in progress with a more generous estimate of man's capacity to explore new frontiers and alter the course of events. In such a comparison, Max Weber obviously belongs with those who take a skeptical view of the human condition, in contrast to the New World, which in its abundance could give an optimistic slant to the determinism of social evolution. Yet even here he stood between the camps! Although Weber was profoundly pessimistic in comparison with so affirmative a philosophy as John Dewey's, he nevertheless shared with pragmatism the ultimate conviction that intellectually the frontiers of innovative effort can and must be kept open.

This conviction has a moral dimension on which I commented at the beginning of this study. Although Weber was preoccupied throughout his career with the development of rationalism in Western civilization, his research left no doubt, as we have seen, that in the modern world reason and freedom are in jeopardy. Yet Weber's personal commitment to the cause of reason and freedom remained unwavering, in contrast to the many writers who during his lifetime and since then embraced an irrationalist doctrine in one form or another. Like Freud's work, Weber's commitment involved an attempt to safeguard man's reason *after* having come to terms intellectually with man's irrationality—as he did in his analyses of charisma and the non-rational foundations and consequences of rational action.[2] In Weber's case, this commitment was

[2] Recent German writers like Wolfgang Mommsen, Christian von Ferber, and others have tended to decry Weber's intellectual stature by linking not only his political opinions but some of his analytical contributions with the rise of Fascism in Germany. While such a tendency is intelligible enough psychologically, it can only detract from our understanding and utilization of Weber's intellectual contributions. After all, we would not assess Freud's theoretical contributions, either, if we denigrated them because they helped to

marked by a pessimism that is reminiscent of Alexis de Tocqueville. "If I had children," De Tocqueville wrote to a friend in 1848, "I should tell them that in this age one ought to be fit for everything, and prepared for everything, for no one can count on the future. And I should add that men should rely on nothing that can be taken away; but try to acquire those things which one can never lose till one ceases to exist: fortitude, energy, knowledge, and prudence." Weber did not express himself to this effect. But he had no children, and he possessed a kind of perverse pride in facing up to the grave threats that jeopardized all he cherished, much like the psychiatric patient who has learned to live with his past in full consciousness of his guilt, his fantasies of guilt, and his weakness.

Despite this historically and morally exposed position, Weber refused to simplify the world in order to make it comprehensible and, in this sense, safe. He attempted to live up to this moral exposure by encompassing the major themes of historical materialism, moral integration, social evolution, power politics, and the ideal of free, creative activity. As I survey the intellectual armory of the nineteenth century, only a psychological theory is missing from Weber's work, and this omission is justified, I believe, by his objective of a comparative approach to the study of society.[3]

To conclude this book with a brief, over-all view of Weber's interpretation of society, I shall comment on three works that reveal his lifelong concern with the values of Western civilization: his unfinished posthumous work on economy and society, his study of ancient Judaism, and his analysis of legal domination. In these comments, I shall emphasize the principles of his

---

foster the "failure of nerve" that characterizes the modern climate of opinion. Elementary logic demands, rather, that we separate our analysis of ideas from a study of the real or alleged social consequences of a writer's scholarly work.

[3] Psychological considerations recur in Weber's studies, especially in his sociology of religion and "types of domination," but these are in the form of "truisms," as Weber pointed out. For some reasons why psychological "truisms" are appropriate, at least for certain levels of sociological analysis, cf. Reinhard Bendix, "Compliant Behavior and Individual Personality," *American Journal of Sociology*, LVIII (November, 1952), pp. 292–303.

approach, and then turn to the place of these principles in the larger context of European intellectual history.

B. SOCIETY AND POLITY

When Max Weber died, in 1920, he was working on the completion of his most systematic work, *Wirtschaft und Gesellschaft*. His wife and editor, Marianne Weber, declared that, together with her collaborator, Melchior Palyi, she had had to decide on the sequence of the chapters, since the original outline for the work had been superseded. (In addition, she apparently inserted subheadings, such as those dividing the work into a second and a third part, entitled "Types of Communal and Societal Tendencies of Action" ["Typen der Vergemeinschaftung und Vergesellschaftung"] and "Types of Domination" ["Typen der Herrschaft"], respectively.) More recently, Johannes Winckelmann has re-edited the work on the basis of the entire available record, in an attempt to give the book the form the author had intended. While this fourth edition, of 1956, is definitive, the fact remains that the original work was left unfinished. Max Weber completed the revision of only the first part (translated as *Theory of Social and Economic Organization*), and we do not know what he might have done had he had the time to reorganize the remainder of the work (pp. 181–876!), which contained the comparative historical materials on which the completed systematic part was based. The book was entitled *Economy and Society* (*Wirtschaft und Gesellschaft*), in keeping with the topic for which Weber had assumed responsibility in connection with an encyclopedic series (*Grundriss der Sozialökonomik*), but this title does not convey the content accurately enough.[4] Under these circumstances, it is necessary and worthwhile to state the over-all conception of this posthumous work on the basis of the pervasive themes in Weber's studies as a whole.

Like other social theorists of his generation, Max Weber sought to advance the scientific study of society as a phenomenon *sui generis*. But in so doing he took a position at

[4] The circumstances of Weber's participation in this series are described in Marianne Weber, *op. cit.*, pp. 462–63.

variance with both the eighteenth-century belief in rational
moral action, in opposition to history, class interest, or custom,
and the nineteenth-century tendency to reduce the individual
and his values to some social or biological process. Against the
eighteenth-century idea, Weber maintained that moral principles exist within a social and historical context, that this is
true even of a morality that claims to be universal, and that
some of the greatest moral ideas have been conceived and
advanced against custom and vested interests in typically non-
rational ways. Yet against the Marxist or Social Darwinist tendency to search for social or biological determinants, Weber
maintained that ideas and individual behavior also possess an
irreducible dimension that must be understood in its own right.
This complex, intermediate position between rationalism and
reductionism is reflected in the initial definitions, which emphasize the importance of meaning (*Sinn*) for our understanding of man's behavior in society. Such meaning originates
in the individual as well as in his interaction with others, and
Weber's definition of the subject matter of sociology emphasizes both aspects:

> In "action" is included all human behavior when and inso-
> far as the acting individual attaches a subjective meaning
> to it. . . .

On the other hand:

> Action is social insofar as, by virtue of the subjective mean-
> ing attached to it by the acting individual (or individuals),
> it takes account of the behavior of others and is thereby
> oriented in its course.[5]

In this way, Weber emphasized that action in society is individual as well as social. Like Durkheim and Simmel, he
recognized the importance of "other-directed" and "reference-
group" behavior, to use current terms, but, unlike these and

[5] *Theory*, p. 88. Weber recognized that much behavior is meaningful and yet not the result of conscious deliberation. The conventional behavior that men in a society take for granted is very often
meaningful; it makes sense to them. "Making sense" is actually a
better translation of the German *Sinn* than the term "meaning,"
which tends to have a poetic or philosophical connotation, such as
the German word *Bedeutung*.

many other sociological writers, he recognized that action in society also has an individual dimension, that it can make sense to the individual irrespective of his interactions with others.

> The inner psychological orientation towards such regularities [of convention and usage] contains in itself very tangible inhibitions against "innovations," a fact which can be observed even today by everyone in his daily experiences, and it constitutes a strong support for the belief in "oughtness." *In view of such observation we must ask how anything new can ever arise in this world, oriented as it is toward the regular and the empirically valid.*[6]

Weber answered this question by assembling evidence from ethnological literature and from comparative studies of legal and religious history to support his contention that specific innovations by individuals had indeed affected the course of human affairs. In addition, it should be remembered that the most isolated innovators (like the ancient prophets) were still oriented towards their society and that the most conventional behavior can still make sense to the individual irrespective of his interactions with others. Accordingly, Weber conceived of "meaningful action" in terms of a continuum, ranging from innovation which has, nevertheless, a social setting, to conformity which still possesses an individual dimension. His basic definitions incorporated both the individual dimension of all action, even where it is determined primarily by the social expectations of others, and the social dimension of action, even where it is determined primarily by individual inspiration.[7] These two aspects of human behavior are linked empirically, but are separable analytically.

[6] *Law*, p. 22. My italics.
[7] This interpretation of the definitions contained in *Theory* depends upon a reading of this finished first part in the light of the empirical evidence discussed in the remainder of *Wirtschaft und Gesellschaft*. Since Weber's compendium of definitions was written after the comparative historical analysis had been composed, in 1911–13, it is logical to look to the historical materials from which they were derived for clarification of these definitions. It is, therefore, awkward that the definitional materials are usually considered in isolation, even though a good many of the empirical studies are now available in translation.

One corollary of this starting point was Weber's tendency to treat all concepts of collectivities or larger social aggregates as convenient labels for tendencies of action. Wherever possible, he avoided nouns, and hence the "fallacy of misplaced concreteness" (Whitehead), by using verbs or "active nouns," though there is no English equivalent for the latter. This approach even applied to the two terms used in the title, *Wirtschaft* and *Gesellschaft*. Instead of using the term "economy," Weber entitled a major part of his book *Basic Sociological Categories of Economizing Activities* (*Soziologische Grundkategorien des Wirtschaftens*). And instead of "society," the text speaks of "societal tendencies of action" (*Vergesellschaftung*).[8]

Having defined the subject matter of sociology in terms of "meaningful action," Weber had to formulate types of meaning that distinguished the collective aggregates to which all sociological analysis refers. And here it becomes apparent that the two terms used in the title, economy and society, refer only to actions based on considerations of material advantage or utility, irrespective of personal or social obligations (*Vergesellschaftung*). This type of behavior is contrasted with all actions that are prompted by a sense of solidarity with others—like kinship relations, the feeling of affinity among professional colleagues, or the code of conduct observed by members of an aristocracy (*Vergemeinschaftung*). The constant interweaving of economic utility and social affinity—in the sense, say, that businessmen develop codes of ethics in their business or devoted parents look to the social and economic advantages in the marriage of their daughter—represents *one* ever-recurring theme in his work. Indeed, this conceptualization was also a method of analysis, in that Weber would inquire into the ideas and affinities associated with the apparently most single-minded pursuit of gain, and into the economic interests associated with the apparently most otherworldly pursuit of reli-

[8] Though Weber adopted Ferdinand Tönnies's familiar distinction between *Gemeinschaft* and *Gesellschaft*, he clearly opposed the reefication implicit in this usage. By using the terms *Vergemeinschaftung* and *Vergesellschaftung*, he characterized these different types as collectivities that emerged from given tendencies of action rather than existing with a fixed set of attributes.

gious salvation. Even then, the approach was limited to social relationships based on a "coalescence of interests," arising from actions that were construed as a reasoning, emotional, or conventional pursuit of "ideal and material interests."[9]

All men are engaged in the pursuit of "ideal and material interests." In this pursuit they may be guided not only by considerations of utility and affinity but also by a belief in the existence of a legitimate order of authority. In this way, Weber wished to distinguish between social relationships (like the supply-and-demand relations in a market) that are maintained by the reciprocity of expectations and those that are maintained through the exercise of authority. The latter typically involve a belief in the existence of a legitimate order and identifiable persons who maintain that order through the exercise of authority.

> Action, and especially social actions which involve social relationships, may be governed in the eyes of the participants by the *conception* that a *legitimate order* exists.[10]

And this order endures unaltered as long as the conception of its legitimacy is shared by those who exercise authority and those who are subject to it. In addition, a legitimate order depends upon an organizational structure maintained by the persons who exercise authority and claim legitimacy for this exercise.

> A social relationship will be called a formal organization, where the admission of outsiders is governed by limiting or exclusive rules and where compliance with the regulations [of that organization] is guaranteed by the actions of a chief and, usually, an administrative staff, who are specifically oriented towards the enforcement of these regulations. . . .[11]

[9] To indicate the main outline of Weber's framework, I am omitting all lesser distinctions, such as the subdivision of reasoning or calculating actions into instrumental and value-oriented behavior, and substituting common-sense words for Weber's complex terminology.

[10] *WuG*, I, p. 16. For a somewhat different translation, cf. *Theory*, p. 124.

[11] *WuG*, I, p. 27. For a somewhat different translation, cf. *Theory*, pp. 145–46. Since this translation was published, in 1947, the term

Thus the shared conception of a legitimate order, and the persons in formal organizations who help to maintain that order through the exercise of authority, constitute a network of social relationships that differs qualitatively from the social relationships arising out of a "coalescence of interests." In this way, actions may arise from the "legitimate order" and affect the pursuit of interests in society, just as the latter has multiple effects upon the exercise of legitimate authority.

As he did throughout his work, Weber insisted that this interdependence of social conditions had to be recognized by the scholar, who at the same time had to make such inevitably arbitrary distinctions as that between a "coalescence of interests" and a "legitimate order" of authority. The simultaneous recognition of both imperatives probably accounts for the special difficulties of Weber's writings. In the present context, it remains for me to summarize the preceding discussion in terms of the distinction between *society* and *polity* as the fundamental theme of Weber's work as a whole.[12] To do this, I shall refer once again to his *Ancient Judaism* and his analysis of legal domination before concluding with a brief attempt to place this theme in the larger context of a history of social thought.

"formal organization" has become so familiar in sociological literature, and is so accurate a rendition of Weber's term *Verband,* that I prefer to use it rather than "corporate group."

[12] As much as possible, Weber avoided nouns like *society* or *polity,* since he sought to view all collective aggregates from the standpoint of the individual actions and social relationships which sustained such aggregates. Still, the distinction between actions that sustain "types of solidary social relationships" (*Vergemeinschaftung* and *Vergesellschaftung*) and those that sustain types of domination (*Herrschaft*) occurs time and again throughout *Wirtschaft und Gesellschaft.* But while Weber's insistence on a nominalist terminology must be respected, and while his continuous interweaving of the two themes of society and polity makes a clear subdivision of his text difficult, it is also important to emphasize this distinction as a fundamental one in his theoretical work and his empirical studies. Cf. Johannes Winckelmann, *Gesellschaft und Staat in der verstehenden Soziologie Max Webers* (Berlin: Duncker & Humblot, 1957) and the discussion in Section E, below.

C. ANCIENT JUDAISM

For Weber, the events and ideas recorded in the Old Testament initiated the uniqueness of Western civilization. Against the ancient worship of many gods who must be placated each in his own domain, ancient Judaism developed over many centuries the worship of one infinitely powerful God, who had created the world. Judaism also transformed the ancient idea of divine rewards and punishments into the belief that every act in the here and now accounts for man's fate in this world and that the practice of virtue would redeem the "chosen remnant" of the people in the historical future. Against the Oriental and Greek image of the world as an ever-recurring cycle of events, Judaism conceived of a radical contrast between the world as it is and as it will be.

These familiar beliefs were the creation of the Old Testament prophets, and Weber's singular contribution was his sociological analysis of this fact. Since the Bible refers to oracle-giving in many different ways, Weber sought to develop a typology in order to isolate the distinctive traits of the men who had formulated the beliefs of ancient Judaism. Among ascetic warriors, ecstatic war leaders and kings, professional magicians, and royal oracle-givers, there had emerged after the eleventh century B.C., under the reigns of Saul, David, and Solomon, a new group of prophets. These men were prophets of doom—from the early figure of Elijah to Isaiah and Ezekiel. They were distinguished from all others of their kind in materialistic terms, because they did not accept gifts and practical men will not pay for oracles that consistently predict disaster. The prophets spoke to the public at large when the spirit moved them, whether or not their counsel had been solicited and whether or not it suited the authorities. In Weber's view, they were the first demagogues and pamphleteers, who glorified the tribal confederacy of the past in pointed contrast to the abominations perpetrated under the United Monarchy. Yet the prophets were exclusively religious men, who were so otherworldly in their attitude toward politics that some of their prophecies were treason by secular standards. This independence from political considerations greatly enhanced their prestige when their frightful visions proved correct: what ordinary man would disregard all expediency and defy the whole world? In their own eyes and in those of the public, these men were not ordinary. They dared incur the wrath of men only because they feared the infinitely greater wrath of God, and this alone was their authentication. Still, in the midst of forebodings and disasters, the prophets continued to believe in the good fortune of God's chosen people. When the fall of Jerusalem was imminent, the prophet Jeremiah bought land, because the hope for new times would soon be realized.

Consider the implications of this approach. It might seem that, through a personal identification, Weber saw these men simply as heroic figures whose extraordinary endowments set them apart from all other men and enabled them to change the course of history. But this impression is deceiving. Weber noted that most prophets were not men from the masses; many were members of patrician families. Hence they enjoyed social prestige within the community and, in some instances, actual support from its leading families. But however much the prophets were a part of their community, linked to the traditions of the confederacy, involved in the party struggles of the time, they were above all lonely men whose frightful mission set them apart from family and friends. Weber saw social cohesion at work even in this singular loneliness of the prophets who wanted to make the people believe in their message as the authentic commands of the powerful God. Hence, Weber analyzed the psychopathological conditions that appeared to authenticate these prophecies, and he related such conditions to the contempt and exaltation with which these men distinguished themselves from all "false prophets."

In this and similar studies of group formation, Weber succeeded in linking seemingly contradictory themes, which other scholars have often seen separately: social prestige and mass appeal, the power of high social rank together with the risk of and opportunity for social isolation, the drive to reform the world immediately and the mandate to remain faithful to a higher principle, the combination of a lofty ethic with uncontrolled passions, the rejection of all magic and the almost unwitting adoption of quasi-magical signs of authentication. Most important of all, perhaps, was his demonstration that the Old

Testament prophets came to constitute an "interest group" of their own, because their opposition to the secular authorities, the credulous masses, and the vested interests of other holy men forced them to distinguish genuine from false prophecy and mark themselves off as a group with ideas, and hence with interests, of its own. In the end, it was the "powerful prestige of the prophetic message" that made the tenets of ancient Judaism prevail over all competing creeds and that was given institutional permanence in the rabbinical organization of Jewish communities following the Babylonian captivity.

In this way, Weber transformed the great insight of Marx by showing that material interests are linked to man's inveterate quest for meaning and idealization, and that neither can be understood apart from the other. In his study of the Old Testament, he emphasized the ideas of mundane interest groups like the urban patriciate and the royal oracle-givers as well as the intensely secular involvement of the prophets despite their outright rejection of all mundane concerns. The struggles among social groups and religious leaders in ancient Palestine gave rise to some of the most violent civic conflicts recorded in history, and from this vantage point Weber certainly followed Marx in seeing history as a history of class struggles. But Weber gave to human ideas and ideals as much weight as he did to economic interests, so that for him the drive for power or material success was always the starting point for an analysis of ideas. Still, this balanced attention to interests *and* ideas represents only one side of Weber's approach; the other side concerns his analysis of authority or domination.

D.   LEGAL DOMINATION[13]

Weber's analysis of domination will be considered here insofar as it is concerned with modern government. From ma-

[13] It is difficult to find an English equivalent for the German term *Herrschaft,* which emphasizes equally the ruler's exercise of power and the follower's acceptance of that exercise as legitimate, a meaning which goes back to the relations between lord and vassal under feudalism. The English terms "domination" and "authority" are not equally apt, because the first emphasizes the power of command

terials of three thousand years ago we turn to the immediate present; from the prophetic innovations that initiated our civilization we turn to the rule of law, routine administration, and political leadership as further characteristics of that civilization.

Weber's study of governmental institutions can be appreciated by contrasting it with two familiar approaches. One of these, the sociological perspective, holds that the formal institutions of a society, like the courts, the legislature, the executive, and others, are best understood in terms of the interactions among socially conditioned individuals. Accordingly, modern sociologists have concentrated on political or legal problems that can be seen as an interaction process, like voting behavior or jury deliberation. Formal political institutions, on the other hand, tend to remain a thing apart, not integrated readily with a study of social interaction. The second approach, that of political science, holds that the formal institutions of government provide the framework that is indispensable for the functioning, and hence the understanding, of every complex society. From this perspective, it appears that no analysis of interaction among individuals can explain how the endless ambiguities of life can be contained within an enduring and recognizable framework. In the textbooks of political science, expositions of governmental institutions alternate with treatises on the psychology and sociology of politics, while the intellectual connection between these two parts is not always apparent. In grappling with these dilemmas, Weber proposed that the study of domination could forgo neither the emphasis on organization nor the emphasis on interaction. Every type of domination depends upon an administrative apparatus under a chief or ruling body and upon a shared belief in the legitimacy of rules or decisions.

Weber's analysis of modern government in Western societies

whether or not consent is present, while the second emphasizes the right of command and hence implies the follower's acceptance almost to the exclusion of the ruler's very real power. Weber wished to emphasize that both power and consent are problematic, but as a realist in the analysis of power he would have been critical of any translation that tended to obscure the "threat of force" present in all relations between superiors and subordinates. For these reasons, I prefer the term "domination."

dealt with these two aspects. There is, first, Weber's concept of "bureaucracy," the administrative apparatus that is the hallmark of government today. The term is used in a neutral sense, as we have seen, referring to the presence of such attributes as written regulation of rights and duties, appointments based on contracts, and others. Weber formulated this concept by his continuous contrast of bureaucratic with patrimonial forms of administration. He maintained that these characteristics of modern government will be present insofar as bureaucracy excludes "love, hatred, and every purely personal . . . feeling from the execution of official tasks."[14] Thus, we can say that all modern administration in Western societies is impersonal, if we consider it in contrast, say, to earlier, medieval forms of government. But by itself modern administration varies greatly, depending upon the degree to which groups within society push it more in one direction or the other.[15]

These conditional formulations are basic to Weber's interpretation of government under the rule of law. The tendencies toward a personal or impersonal administration of rules arise from the basic beliefs that legitimize the system of legal domination. Under this system, laws are regarded as legitimate, according to Weber, if they have been enacted by the proper authorities on the basis of procedures that have the sanction of law—clearly a totally impersonal as well as circular assumption.[16] This approach has been criticized severely, because it

[14] Cf. p. 424 for the details of Weber's definition.

[15] Cf. the full citation on p. 427 above. That is to say, major groups in modern society, such as legislators, lawyers, judges, efficiency experts, and others, are directly concerned with working out the laws and procedures that are to govern the recurrent transactions among individuals and groups. These "rule-makers" are affected, but on the whole not determined, by those subject to the rules, whereas the public at large and specially organized interest groups try to modify either the detailed application of rules or the rules themselves, in order to make them conform more closely than they otherwise would to particular interests. Ordinarily, the procedure of rule-making itself is not called into question, although all conflicts of interest verge on this possibility to a greater or lesser extent. An application of this perspective to the analysis of formal organization will be found in my book *Work and Authority in Industry*, pp. 244–48.

[16] See p. 419 above.

seems to endorse the idea that the formally correct enactment of even the most pernicious laws would be compatible with a legitimate system of legal domination.[17] There is little resemblance, however, between this interpretation and Weber's own analysis. In his sociology of law, Weber describes not only the historical conditions under which legal professionals had promoted this type of formal legality; he also shows how advance in this respect has been, and continues to be, circumscribed at every point by the concern of interested parties as well as professionals with substantive principles of justice. Repeatedly he refers to the insoluble conflict between the formal and substantive rationality of the law; indeed, in his view the system of legal domination is characterized by some balance between these two principles.[18]

At the time Weber wrote his sociology of law, this balance was at stake, in his opinion. He noted that the principle of formal legality had been in the ascendancy during the nineteenth century, while the "axioms of natural law have been deeply discredited." But he observes also that it would hardly seem possible to eradicate these axioms from legal practice altogether, and accordingly he describes how "legal realism"

[17] For a recent exposition of this view and some references to the pertinent literature, cf. Wolfgang Mommsen, *Max Weber und die Deutsche Politik 1890–1920*, pp. 414–19.

[18] As mentioned above, on p. 297, similarly antagonistic principles underlie Weber's concepts of traditional and charismatic domination. Under the first, the ruler is bound by immemorial custom, but custom itself endorses his right to an arbitrary exercise of his will. Under the second, the ruler's exercise of authority is sustained by his disciples' belief in his magical powers, but time and again his followers demand a miracle that will prove this power. In the same way, legal domination is sustained by a belief in formal legality, but ideas of equity or substantive justice intrude time and again to modify that formalism, just as formal considerations modify equity. All three concepts provide a framework for the analysis of social change; each of them allows the possibility that "too much" arbitrariness, "too many" demands for the proof of charisma, and "too much" concern for justice at the expense of formal legality will alter the respective type of domination. The opposite extremes would be equally disruptive, and while this approach clearly operates with some equilibrium assumption, Weber puts little stock in elaborating this aspect of his typology, presumably because it would tend toward a reefication of concepts.

has tended to discredit the formal attributes of the law.[19] In his view, the extreme development of one principle at the expense of the other would gradually transform the legitimacy of legal domination. Rather than endorse or reject these principles, Weber analyzes the assumptions and consequences of both. The impersonal administration of justice provides an indispensable buttress of regularity, detachment, calculability, and all the other positive attributes of order, but these gains are inextricably linked with a studied disregard of person and circumstance, and hence of considerations of equity. Yet to the extent that these latter aspects of the law are taken into account, the formal structure of the law is necessarily modified, if not impaired. In this way, Weber interprets a major historical process in modern society, and hence conceptualizes for our time the basic anguishing dilemma of form and substance in the law, which can be alleviated but not resolved, for the system of legal domination can endure only as long as that dilemma is perpetuated.

It appears, then, that Weber sees governments as *sui generis*, not, like Marx, as executive committees of the ruling class. In fact, compared with Marx, Weber sees the problem of domination exactly in reverse. The officials of a government are appointed by a ruling authority; to some extent their interests are identical with those of government and, in theory, they are honor-bound to obey its commands. But administrators frequently develop interests of their own, and in practice they often attempt to modify the policies they are supposed to execute. This fundamental tendency of bureaucratic thought is greatly enhanced by the over-all drift toward legal formalism that characterizes modern Western societies. In Weber's view, the rule of law would be undermined unless this tendency was curbed by effective political leadership.

We have seen that Weber distinguished leaders who have the power to command from officials who stand ready to execute the orders they receive, because these functions involve a fundamental difference in responsibility. This *logical* construction of political leadership and administrative implementation illustrates how Weber conceived the problematic interplay be-

[19] *Law*, pp. 297–98 and *passim*.

tween commands and obedience under the rule of law. Given his telling insights into the bureaucratic manipulations characteristic of Imperial Germany, he clearly did not maintain that politicians and administrators behaved in this way. He contended, rather, that the abdication of leadership-responsibility by politicians and the usurpation of policy-functions by administrators are ever-present hazards of government under the rule of law. And this contrast between political leaders and government officials illustrates once more the fundamental distinction in Weber's work between the pursuit of interests (in the broadest sense) and the exercise of authority. For leaders clearly are engaged in gathering a following by appealing to the interests and ideals of the people at large, while government officials have their position defined for them by their appointment, and this in turn affects their ideas and interests.

E.   INTELLECTUAL PERSPECTIVES

In his analysis of leadership and administration under the rule of law, of the Old Testament prophets and the United Monarchy under Saul and David, and in other contexts, Weber operated with a fundamental distinction between society and government. In pursuing their interests, individuals in society form groups that affect the distribution of power, but an analysis of this process cannot fully account for the enduring structure of government. On the other hand, governmental authority rests on an administrative organization and a belief in its legitimacy, which affect many social relationships, but an analysis of this process cannot fully account for the coalescence or divergence of interests within society. The ramifications of this approach in Weber's sociological studies have been examined in the preceding discussion. In conclusion, I wish to comment on this interpretation as a blend of at least three closely interrelated intellectual traditions.

One of these is the view that society is an object of government. This idea goes back to the medieval literature dealing with "advice to princes" and with an education of character designed for the sons of rulers. In his famous treatise *The*

Prince, Machiavelli transformed this literary tradition into an instrument of statecraft. In the eighteenth century, Montesquieu drew upon the literature inspired by Machiavelli when he analyzed the social and physical conditions that would facilitate or hinder the exercise of authority under different systems of rule. And at the beginning of the nineteenth century, Hegel reinterpreted elements of this approach when he outlined the relations of the Crown and its officials to the civil society. However varied in other respects, this intellectual tradition is characterized by a common belief in the capacity for autonomous action by government. In this perspective, the ruler and his officials preside over and direct the relations among men in society, though they will do so with due regard to prevailing sentiments and circumstances if they are wise. Weber's emphasis upon "domination" as a complex of ideas and social relationships based on a legitimate "threat of force" is derived from this tradition.[20]

Second, there is the view that politics and government are a product of society. Originating during the seventeenth and eighteenth centuries, this idea can be traced to many sources —to the ideas associated with the congregational form of church government, to Locke's and Rousseau's construction of government as dependent upon social arrangements, to the attacks of the Enlightenment philosophers upon the established privileges of church and aristocracy, but also to the conservative defense of these privileges on the ground that they reflected the cumulative wisdom of past social arrangements.[21]

[20] On the relation between Machiavelli and Montesquieu, cf. Friedrich Meinecke, *Die Entstehung des Historismus* (München: R. Oldenbourg, 1946), Chapter 3. See also the same author's *Die Idee der Staatsräson* (München: R. Oldenbourg, 1925), in which the history of this intellectual tradition is traced in detail. (The work is available in an English translation under the title *Machiavellism.*) With regard to the comparison between Hegel and Weber, cf. above, pp. 387–88, and the discussion below.

[21] Cf. the brilliant analysis of the rise of this intellectual tradition, especially with reference to liberalism and the Saint-Simonian tradition, in Sheldon S. Wolin, *Politics and Vision* (Boston: Little, Brown & Co., 1960), Chapters 9–10. I am especially indebted to Professor Wolin for his insight that the conception of "society" as the independent variable, and the consequent denigration of politics and government, are common themes in liberalism, classical economics,

Consider, for example, the interpretation of politics as the by-product of established prerogatives, which was developed into a principle of historical interpretation. By evaluating past events in terms of the eighteenth-century belief in reason, Voltaire made history appear a contest among vested interests, in which the better side had come out ahead eventually. Compared with the chroniclers of the past, he politicized history; compared with the traditional political theorists, he sociologized politics. If in this view you replace institutionalized prerogatives with the economic class struggle and add to it the vision of a society in which the chaos of that struggle has been replaced by an over-all organization directed by a scientific élite, you have the basic idea of the Saint-Simonian school. If, on the other hand, you add to the idea of the economic class struggle a materialistic theory of human drives, you readily get Marx's theory of history, in which all political institutions are ultimately determined by that struggle until after the revolution, when economic classes *and* politics will be superseded by a planned society. Such radical approaches see politics and government as by-products of society, and in this they resemble conservatism; they also see government as an obstacle to human progress, and in this they resemble liberalism. However different Marxism, liberalism, and conservatism are in other respects, they share the belief that analysis of the economic and social substructure will enable us eventually to understand and control government, since all three consider political institutions as the dependent variable. In our own day, many sociologists and economists look upon formal legal and political institutions as the outward shell inside of which the "real" social, economic, and psychological forces demand their primary attention. In this view, they are beholden to an intellectual tradition that analyzes social and economic life in terms of a set of elementary units, in the belief that in this way they will learn how the society hangs together.

Max Weber's work is indebted to this tradition in the sense that it attempted to build the analysis of society upon the conception of an "elementary unit," much as classical economics did with its idea of "self-interest," or as Emile Durkheim did

Marxism, conservatism, Saint-Simonianism—and much of modern sociology.

with his concept of group affiliation as the source of morality. But this debt was rather strictly limited, and the difference between Weber's work and this tradition of psychological or sociological reductionism probably deserves more emphasis. For by focusing his attention upon the interpretive understanding of "meaningful action," Weber was indebted above all to German legal theory and German cultural history.[22] Legal theorists had concerned themselves with the logical problem of attributing an action such as a criminal act to an individual to determine his culpability, and Weber adapted this approach to his own needs when he developed his theory in terms of the meaning (*Sinn*) that men associate with their actions in society. Again, he may have derived inspiration from German cultural history, and especially from the work of Jacob Burckhardt, who analyzed works of art along with documentary evidence concerning the lives of ordinary men as clues to the ideas that these men of bygone ages had taken for granted. These were anti-reductionist approaches to the study of human conduct because they focused special attention on what sense it made to the individual to be engaged in any line of action, and Weber adopted this perspective when he made meaning, or *Sinn*, a basic component of his definition of action. We have seen earlier that in his analysis of "meaning" he distinguished between social relationships arising from a coalescence of interests in the broadest sense and relationships based in addition on a shared belief in a "legitimate order" and upon a formal organization. With this distinction, he gave a behavioral foundation to an analysis that does not treat government as an epiphenomenon but, rather, considers society and polity as partly interdependent and partly autonomous spheres of thought and action. This, then, is the third approach, whose place in the social and intellectual history of Europe may be characterized briefly.

In most parts of the world today, government and society are more intertwined than they have been in several Western societies in the recent past. Beginning roughly in the seventeenth century and culminating at various times from about the middle of the nineteenth century onward, the exercise of

[22] Cf. the references cited above on p. 265, n. 16 and p. 267, n. 19.

governmental authority became emancipated very gradually
from obligations of kinship, rights of property, and special
privileges associated with inherited titles.[23] This gradual dis-
engagement of governmental administration was accompanied
first by the growth of a centralized national government and
eventually by the formal equality of all adult citizens as voters
and in their legal capacity.[24]

Efforts to cope with these developments intellectually often
anticipated, or extrapolated from, the actual separation between society and government as feudalism gave way to the
absolutist regimes of the early modern period. The idea of a
basic moral or conceptual distinction between society and government can be traced again to many sources, but it emerges
most clearly in the writings of the Utilitarians and in the philosophy of Hegel. According to the classical economists, man's
"propensity to truck, barter and exchange one thing for another" tended to reveal a "natural identity of interests," which
spontaneously enhanced the general welfare of society. At the
same time, the economists regarded the quantity of subsistence
as insufficient to allow men to live in abundance, and this insufficiency was aggravated by the failure of the people voluntarily to limit their numbers through such positive checks as
postponement of marriage or moral restraint. Hence, as Elie
Halévy has shown, it followed that the government must protect the property of the rich against the poor, as well as edu-
cate the latter so that they would exercise foresight and restraint, and accordingly curtail their natural increase. In this
way, government would act to insure the "artificial identification of interests."[25] In a modified form, this contrast reap-
pears in Hegel's philosophy of right.

Hegel certainly accepted the economists' image and positive
evaluation of the market:

[23] Cf. the reference to a study by Ernest Barker on p. 405 above.
[24] A discussion of these and related developments is contained in
my essay "Social Stratification and the Political Community," *Archives Européennes de Sociologie*, I (1960), No. 2, pp. 181–210.
[25] See Elie Halévy, *The Growth of Philosophical Radicalism*
(London: Faber & Faber, 1928), pp. 90–91, 118–20, 489–91 and
passim.

The most remarkable thing here is this mutual interlocking of particulars, which is what one would least expect because at first sight everything seems to be given over to the arbitrariness of the individual. . . . . But this medley of arbitrariness generates universal characteristics by its own working; and this apparently scattered and thoughtless sphere is upheld by a necessity which automatically enters it. To discover this necessary element here is the object of political economy, a science which is a credit to thought because it finds laws for a mass of accidents.[26]

But Hegel also saw a problem that the classical economists had neglected. The lack of abundance and the tendency of the population to increase beyond the available means of subsistence were conditions that merely made the intervention of government desirable. The "medley of arbitrariness" that gave rise to the laws of the economy could not on the same basis explain the capacity of government to act. Accordingly, Hegel sought to make the existence of organized government, as well as the self-regulating market, dependent upon subjective disposition. In civil society, men act as self-interested individuals, as the economists had described, but this is not enough. "Individuals," writes Hegel, "do not live as private persons for their own ends alone, but in the very act of willing these they will the universal [ends of government as well]."[27] But, if self-interested men have yet a sense of duty as citizens, what accounts for the fact that government not only permits but encourages the fullest development of personal individuality and particular interests? In answering this question, Hegel points to the civil servants as that class in which "the consciousness of right and the developed intelligence of the mass of the people is [sic] found," though not without adding that the "sovereign working on [this] class at the top, and Corporation-rights working on it at the bottom are the institutions which prevent it . . . from using its education and skill as means to an arbitrary tyranny."[28] In this image of civil society and the state, Hegel blended Rousseau's attempt to free the

[26] Knox, ed., Hegel's Philosophy of Right, p. 268.
[27] Ibid., p. 161.
[28] Ibid., p. 193.

individual from *personal* dependence with the ideals of enlightened absolutism, and Kant's idea of an internalized sense
of duty as the foundation of ethical conduct with the economists' emphasis upon subjective striving as the foundation of
society:

> The essence of the modern state is that the universal be
> bound up with the complete freedom of its particular mem-
> bers and with private well-being, that thus the interests of
> family and civil society must concentrate themselves on the
> state, although the universal end cannot be advanced with-
> out the personal knowledge and will of its particular mem-
> bers, whose rights must be maintained. Thus the universal
> must be furthered, but subjectivity on the other hand must
> attain its full and living development. It is only when both
> these moments subsist in their strength that the state can
> be regarded as articulated and genuinely organized.[29]

This idealistic image of mutual support between full individual freedom and supreme authority represented a theoretical synthesis that had a major influence primarily in Germany. Elsewhere, more attention was devoted to the conflict
between the rights of man and his duties as a citizen, and
hence to the need to safeguard these rights lest they become
subordinated to government. In the New World especially,
much attention was also devoted to a system of checks and
balances that would prevent the abuse of authority and hence
guarantee freedom even at the risk of limiting the government's capacity to act.[30] It remained for the German tradition to retain Hegel's double emphasis and elaborate on this
conception of the reciprocal support that the individual in his
freedom and the state in its strength would give to each other.
There is no evidence of such idealization in Weber's juxtaposition of society and government. Instead, he gave a behavioral
foundation to both concepts, and thus blended the empiricism

[29] *Ibid.*, p. 280.
[30] The theoretical reformulations of the duality between man and
citizen have been traced by Karl Löwith, *Von Hegel zu Nietzsche*
(Zürich: Europa Verlag, 1944), pp. 255–83. For an analysis of
American constitutionalism as a model derived from basic ideas of
classical economics, cf. Wolin, *op. cit.*, pp. 388–93.

of the Utilitarian tradition with Hegel's emphasis upon the distinction and reciprocal relation between "civil society and the state."[31]

In his view of social relationships in economy and society, Weber modified the utilitarian position by analyzing the ideals involved in the pursuit of gain. If this emphasis suggests that he approached that position from the standpoint of German idealism, it must be said also that he approached the idealization of social solidarity—so prominent in conservative thought throughout the nineteenth century—from the standpoint of Utilitarianism. For by his analysis of the economic interests involved in every relationship based on honor or spiritual ideals, Weber implicitly criticized writers from Rousseau and De Maistre to Durkheim and Tönnies for their praise of the community and social integration.[32] For Weber, social solidarity within society arises from the pursuit of honor and economic advantage, though this pursuit has divisive as well as integrative consequences. At the same time, Weber recognized the importance of the problem of integration, and he sought to solve it in his own way, through an adaptation of Hegel's theoretical synthesis. Though cultural norms and conventions, as well as the coalescence of "material and ideal interests," may produce a degree of social cohesion, often through the domi-

[31] These Hegelian terms were replaced subsequently by the terms "association" (*Genossenschaft*) and "domination" (*Herrschaft*) in Otto Gierke's *Das Deutsche Genossenschaftsrecht* (Berlin: Weidmannsche Buchhandlung, 1868), I, p. 13. Gierke treated association and domination as alternative types of collective behavior, and Weber's treatment of feudalism and patrimonialism, as well as his distinction between "solidary relationship" and a legitimate order with its administrative apparatus, resembles Gierke's adaptation of Hegel, though Weber was very critical of Gierke's "corporatism."

[32] Most of these writers were anathema to Weber, one imagines, since they persistently mixed the approaches of science and ethics, which Weber sought to separate as clearly as possible. Though unfortunately, few references to this literature are to be found in Weber's writings; still, it is difficult to see how he could have known Durkheim's work without taking direct issue with it. Thus, a comparison of the discussion of law, for example, in Durkheim's *Division of Labor* and Weber's *Sociology of Law* shows readily that a proper understanding of these men is hindered by an attempt to construct a theoretical synthesis based on their writings, whatever justification such an attempt might have on other grounds.

nant influence of a status group, social stability usually depends in addition upon government and the exercise of authority. By emphasizing the belief in legitimacy that is shared in some degree by rulers and ruled, Weber retained Hegel's idea that society and government stand in a reciprocal relation to each other. And Weber also retained Hegel's distinction between "civil society and the state" by his emphasis on two points—that the belief in a legitimate order differs in kind from the "coalescence of material and ideal interests" in society, and that the exercise of legitimate authority depends upon an administrative organization with imperatives of its own.

Weber's preoccupation with the reciprocal effects of society and polity has not received the attention it deserves. It came to grips with the fact that in the modern rational state, citizenship and privacy, national unity and parochial interests, a nationwide legal system and special jurisdictions exist side by side. The significance of this perspective has become clear in our own day, when totalitarian regimes have obliterated these unresolved tensions of a system of "legal domination" by their coercive identification of all human concerns with the duties of citizenship. In this way, they destroy the rule of law, subject the entire rule-making process to the goals of a one-party government, and turn the conflict among rule-makers, administrators, and various interest groups into a tangle of bureaucratic maneuvers in the absence of public accountability. Seen in this context, Weber's lifework appears, as he conceived it, as an analysis and a defense of Western civilization.

INDEX °

°Entries in the Index refer to the text by Bendix but not to the Introduction by Roth.